Lecture Notes in Computer Science   14344

Founding Editors

Gerhard Goos
Juris Hartmanis

Editorial Board Members

The series Lecture Notes in Computer Science (LNCS), including its subseries Lecture Notes in Artificial Intelligence (LNAI) and Lecture Notes in Bioinformatics (LNBI), has established itself as a medium for the publication of new developments in computer science and information technology research, teaching, and education.

LNCS enjoys close cooperation with the computer science R & D community, the series counts many renowned academics among its volume editors and paper authors, and collaborates with prestigious societies. Its mission is to serve this international community by providing an invaluable service, mainly focused on the publication of conference and workshop proceedings and postproceedings. LNCS commenced publication in 1973.

Gene Tsudik · Mauro Conti · Kaitai Liang ·
Georgios Smaragdakis

Editors

Computer Security –
ESORICS 2023

28th European Symposium
on Research in Computer Security
The Hague, The Netherlands, September 25–29, 2023
Proceedings, Part I

Editors
Gene Tsudik
University of California
Irvine, CA, USA

Mauro Conti (iD)
University of Padua
Padua, Italy

Kaitai Liang (iD)
Delft University of Technology
Delft, The Netherlands

Georgios Smaragdakis
Delft University of Technology
Delft, The Netherlands

ISSN 0302-9743   ISSN 1611-3349 (electronic)
Lecture Notes in Computer Science
ISBN 978-3-031-50593-5   ISBN 978-3-031-50594-2 (eBook)
https://doi.org/10.1007/978-3-031-50594-2

This Springer imprint is published by the registered company Springer Nature Switzerland AG
The registered company address is: Gewerbestrasse 11, 6330 Cham, Switzerland

Paper in this product is recyclable.

Preface

We are honoured and pleased to have served as PC Co-Chairs of ESORICS 2023. As one of the longest-running reputable conferences focused on security research, ESORICS 2023 attracted numerous high-quality submissions from all over the world, with authors affiliated with diverse academic, non-profit, governmental, and industrial entities.

After two rounds of submissions, each followed by an extensive reviewing period, we wound up with an excellent program, covering a broad range of timely and interesting topics. A total of 478 submissions were received: 150 in the first round and 328 in the second. 3–4 reviewers per submission in a single blind review driven by selfless and dedicated PC members (and external reviewers) who collectively did an amazing job providing thorough and insightful reviews. Some PC members even "went the extra mile" by reviewing more than their share. The end-result was 93 accepted submissions: 28 and 65, in the first and second rounds, respectively.

The 18-session ESORICS 2023 technical program included: (1) 93 talks corresponding to accepted papers, (2) a poster session, and (3) 3 impressive keynote talks by internationally prominent and active researchers: Virgil Gligor, Carmela Troncoso, and Mathias Payer. The program testifies to the level of excellence and stature of ESORICS.

We offer our deepest gratitude to:

- **Authors** of all submissions, whether accepted or not. We thank them for supporting ESORICS and for their trust in us and the PC to fairly evaluate their research results.
- **General Chairs:** Kaitai Liang and Georgios Smaragdakis, who dealt with (and addressed) numerous logistical and organisational issues. We very much appreciate it!
- **Submission Chairs:** Gabriele Costa and Letterio Galletta, for their super-human efforts and invaluable support during the submission and reviewing processes. We could not have done it without them!
- **Publication Chairs:** Florian Hahn and Giovanni Apruzzese, for handling the proceedings. We are especially grateful to them for handling numerous requests from the authors.
- **Web Chair:** Yury Zhauniarovich for creating and maintaining the conference website.
- **Poster Chair:** Bala Chandrasekaran, for taking care of the poster track.
- **All PC members** and their delegated reviewers, who were the main engine of success of ESORICS 2023 and whose hard work yielded an excellent program.

  – Special thanks to the recipients of the *Outstanding Reviewer Award*: Ferdinand Brasser and Brendan Saltaformaggio, for their exceptional reviewing quality.

In closing, though clearly biased, we believe that ESOIRCS 2023 was an overall success and we hope that all attendees enjoyed the conference.

September 2023   Mauro Conti
                                                                 Gene Tsudik

Organization

General Chairs

Kaitai Liang   Delft University of Technology, The Netherlands
Georgios Smaragdakis   Delft University of Technology, The Netherlands

Program Committee Chairs

Mauro Conti   University of Padua, Italy & Delft University of
                               Technology, The Netherlands
Gene Tsudik   University of California, Irvine, USA

Submission Chairs

Gabriele Costa   IMT School for Advanced Studies Lucca, Italy
Letterio Galletta   IMT School for Advanced Studies Lucca, Italy

Workshops Chairs

Jérémie Decouchant   Delft University of Technology, The Netherlands
Stjepan Picek   Radboud University & Delft University of
                               Technology, The Netherlands

Posters Chair

Bala Chandrasekaran   Vrije Universiteit Amsterdam, The Netherlands

Publication Chairs

Florian Hahn   University of Twente, The Netherlands
Giovanni Apruzzese   University of Liechtenstein, Liechtenstein

Publicity Chair

Savvas Zannettou   Delft University of Technology, The Netherlands

Sponsorship Chair

Giovane Moura   SIDN/Delft University of Technology,
                                    The Netherlands

Web Chair

Yury Zhauniarovich   Delft University of Technology, The Netherlands

Programme Committee

Gergely Acs   Budapest University of Technology and
                                    Economics, Hungary
Massimiliano Albanese   George Mason University, USA
Cristina Alcaraz (only Round 2)   University of Malaga, Spain
Alejandro Cabrera Aldaya   Tampere University of Technology, Finland
Mark Allman   International Computer Science Institute, USA
Elli Androulaki   IBM Zurich, Switzerland
Giovanni Apruzzese   University of Liechtenstein, Liechtenstein
Mikael Asplund   Linköping University, Sweden
Ahmad Atamli   Nvidia, UK
Vijay Atluri   Rutgers University, USA
Kiran Balagani   New York Institute of Technology, USA
Giampaolo Bella (only Round 2)   University of Catania, Italy
Antonio Bianchi   Purdue University, USA
Giuseppe Bianchi   Università di Roma Tor Vergata, Italy
Jorge Blasco   Royal Holloway, University of London, UK
Ferdinand Brasser   SANCTUARY Systems GmbH, Germany
Alessandro Brighente   University of Padua, Italy
Ileana Buhan   Radboud University, The Netherlands
Alvaro Cardenas   University of California Santa Cruz, USA
Xavier Carpent   University of Nottingham, UK
Anrin Chakraborti   Stony Brook University, USA
Sze Yiu Chau   Chinese University of Hong Kong, China
Liqun Chen   University of Surrey, UK

Scott Coull	Mandiant, USA
Bruno Crispo	University of Trento, Italy
Michel Cukier (only Round 1)	University of Maryland, USA
Sanchari Das	University of Denver, USA
Lucas Davi	University of Duisburg-Essen, Germany
Fabio De Gaspari	Sapienza University of Rome, Italy
Ivan De Oliveira Nunes	Rochester Institute of Technology, USA
Roberto Di Pietro	Hamad Bin Khalifa University, Qatar
Xuhua Ding	Singapore Management University, Singapore
Shlomi Dolev	Ben-Gurion University of the Negev, Israel
Anna Lisa Ferrara	University of Molise, Italy
Barbara Fila	INSA Rennes, IRISA, France
Simone Fischer-Hübner	Karlstad University, Sweden
Olga Gadyatskaya	University of Leiden, The Netherlands
Ankit Gangwal	International Institute of Information Technology, Hyderabad, India
Siddharth Garg	NYU Tandon, USA
Giorgio Giacinto	University of Cagliari, Italy
Alberto Giaretta	Örebro University, Sweden
Devashish Gosain	KU Leuven, Belgium
Matteo Große-Kampmann (only Round 2)	Ruhr-Universität Bochum, Germany
Berk Gulmezoglu	Iowa State University, USA
Thomas Haines	Norwegian University of Science and Technology, Norway
Hugo Jonker	Open University of the Netherlands, The Netherlands
Sokratis Katsikas	Norwegian University of Science and Technology, Norway
Stefan Katzenbeisser	University of Passau, Germany
Jihye Kim	Kookmin University, South Korea
Hyoungshick Kim	Sungkyunkwan University, South Korea
Hyungsub Kim	Purdue University, USA
Marina Krotofil	European Commission, Switzerland
Juliane Krämer	University of Regensburg, Germany
Alptekin Küpçü	Koç University, Turkey
Katsiaryna Labunets (only Round 2)	Utrecht University, The Netherlands
Peeter Laud	Cybernetica AS, Estonia
Adam Lee	University of Pittsburgh, USA
Kyu Hyung Lee	University of Georgia, USA
Valeria Loscrì	Inria, France

Eleonora Losiouk	University of Padua, Italy
Wenjing Lou	Virginia Tech, USA
Aravind Machiry	Purdue University, USA
Mark Manulis	Bundeswehr University Munich, Germany
Eduard Marin-Fabregas	Telefonica Research, Spain
Ivan Martinovic	Oxford University, UK
Roberto Metere (only Round 2)	University of York, UK
Markus Miettinen	TU Darmstadt, Germany
Chris Mitchell	Royal Holloway, University of London, UK
Yoshimichi Nakatsuka	ETH Zurich, Switzerland
Hai Nguyen (only Round 2)	Purdue University, USA
Antonino Nocera (only Round 2)	University of Pavia, Italy
Martín Ochoa	ETH Zurich, Switzerland
Gabriele Oligeri	Hamad Bin Khalifa University, Qatar
Cristina Onete (only Round 2)	University of Limoges, France
Panos Papadimitratos	KTH, Sweden
Stefano Paraboschi	Università di Bergamo, Italy
Federica Pascucci	Università degli studi Roma Tre, Italy
Marinella Petrocchi (only Round 1)	IIT-CNR, Italy
Stjepan Picek	Radboud University, The Netherlands
Elizabeth Quaglia (only Round 1)	Royal Holloway, University of London, UK
Kasper Rasmussen	Oxford University, UK
Laura Ricci	University of Pisa, Italy
Rodrigo Roman (only Round 2)	University of Malaga, Spain
Sushmita Ruj	University of New South Wales, Australia
Peter Y. A. Ryan	University of Luxembourg, Luxembourg
Amin Sakzad (only Round 1)	Monash University, Australia
Brendan D. Saltaformaggio	Georgia Institute of Technology, USA
Dominique Schröder	University of Erlangen-Nürnberg, Germany
Michael Schwarz	CISPA, Germany
Jörg Schwenk	Ruhr-Universität Bochum, Germany
Savio Sciancalepore	Eindhoven University of Technology, The Netherlands
Siamak F. Shahandashti	University of York, UK
Michael Sirivianos	Cyprus University of Technology, Cyprus
Juraj Somorovsky (only Round 1)	Ruhr-Universität Bochum, Germany
Claudio Soriente	NEC Laboratories Europe, Germany
Alessandro Sorniotti	IBM Zurich, Switzerland
Angelo Spognardi	Sapienza Università di Roma, Italy
Riccardo Spolaor	Shandong University, China
Thorsten Strufe	Karlsruhe Institute of Technology, Germany

Contents – Part I

Crypto

A Practical TFHE-Based Multi-Key Homomorphic Encryption with Linear Complexity and Low Noise Growth

Yavuz Akın[1], Jakub Klemsa[1,2(✉)], and Melek Önen[1]

[1] EURECOM Sophia-Antipolis, Biot, France
{yavuz.akin,jakub.klemsa,melek.onen}@eurecom.fr
[2] Czech Technical University in Prague, Prague, Czech Republic

Abstract. Fully Homomorphic Encryption enables arbitrary computations over encrypted data and it has a multitude of applications, e.g., secure cloud computing in healthcare or finance. Multi-Key Homomorphic Encryption (MKHE) further allows to process encrypted data from multiple sources: the data can be encrypted with keys owned by different parties. In this paper, we propose a new variant of MKHE instantiated with the TFHE scheme. Compared to previous attempts by Chen et al. and by Kwak et al., our scheme achieves computation runtime that is linear in the number of involved parties and it outperforms the faster scheme by a factor of 4.5–6.9×, at the cost of a slightly extended pre-computation. In addition, for our scheme, we propose and practically evaluate parameters for up to 128 parties, which enjoy the same estimated security as parameters suggested for the previous schemes (100 bits). It is also worth noting that our scheme—unlike the previous schemes—did not experience *any* error in any of our seven setups, each running 1 000 trials.

Keywords: Multi-key homomorphic encryption · TFHE scheme · Secure cloud computing

1 Introduction

Fully Homomorphic Encryption (FHE) refers to a cryptosystem that allows for an evaluation of an arbitrary computable function over encrypted data (first-ever scheme in [14], find a survey in [1]). With FHE, a secure cloud-aided computation, between a user (**U**) and a semi-trusted cloud (**C**), may proceed as follows:

- **U** generates secret keys sk, and evaluation keys ek, which she sends to **C**;
- **U** encrypts her sensitive data d with sk, and sends the encrypted data to **C**;
- **C** employs ek to evaluate function f, homomorphically, over the encrypted data, yielding an encryption of $f(d)$, which it sends back to **U**;

This work was supported by the MESRI-BMBF French-German joint project UPCARE (ANR-20-CYAL-0003-01). Find the full version at https://ia.cr/2023/065.

– **U** decrypts the message from **C** with sk, obtaining the result: $f(d)$ in plain.

In such a setup, there is one party that holds all the secret keying material. In case the data originate from multiple sources, *Multi-Key (Fully) Homomorphic Encryption* (MKHE) comes into play. First proposed by López-Alt et al. [20], MKHE is a primitive that enables the homomorphic evaluation over data encrypted with multiple different, unrelated keys. This allows to relax the intrinsic restriction of a standard FHE, which demands a single data owner.

Previous Work. Following the seminal work of López-Alt et al. [20], different approaches to design an MKHE scheme have emerged: first attempts require a fixed list of parties at the beginning of the protocol [12,25], others allow parties to join dynamically [5,27], Chen et al. [8] extend the plaintext space from a single bit to a ring. Later, Chen et al. [6] propose an MKHE scheme based on the **TFHE** scheme [11], and they claim to be the first to practically implement an MKHE scheme; in this paper, we refer to their scheme as CCS. The evaluation complexity of their scheme is quadratic in the number of parties and authors only run experiments with up to 8 parties. The CCS scheme is improved in recent work by Kwak et al. [19], who achieve quasi-linear complexity (actually quadratic, but with a very low coefficient at the quadratic term); in this paper, we refer to their scheme as KMS. Parallel to CCS and KMS, which are both based on **TFHE**, there exist other promising schemes: e.g., [7], defined for BFV [4,13] and CKKS [10], improved in [16] to achieve linear complexity, or [23], implemented in the Lattigo Library [24], which requires to first construct a common public key; also referred to as the *Multi-Party HE* (MPHE). The capabilities/use-cases of **TFHE** and other schemes are fairly different, therefore we solely focus on the comparison of **TFHE**-based MKHE.

Our Contributions. We propose a new **TFHE**-based MKHE scheme with a linear evaluation complexity and with a sufficiently low error rate, which allows for a practical instantiation with an order of hundreds of parties while achieving evaluation times proportional to those of plain **TFHE**. More concretely, our scheme builds upon the following technical ideas (k is the number of parties):

Summation of RLWE **keys:** Instead of *concatenation* of RLWE keys (in certain sense proposed in both CCS and KMS), our scheme works with RLWE encryptions under the *sum* of individual RLWE keys. As a result, this particular improvement decreases the evaluation complexity from quadratic to linear.

Ternary distribution for RLWE **keys:** Widely adopted by existing FHE implementations [15,22,24,29], zero-centered ternary distribution $\zeta\colon (-1,0,1) \to (p, 1-2p, p)$ works well as a distribution of the coefficients of RLWE keys; we suggest $p \approx 0.1135$. It helps reduce the growth of a certain noise term by a factor of k, which in turn helps find more efficient **TFHE** parameters.

Avoid FFT in pre-computations: In our experiments, we notice an unexpected error growth for higher numbers of parties and we verify that the source of these errors is Fast Fourier Transform (FFT), which is used for fast polynomial multiplication. To keep the evaluation times low and to decrease the number of errors at the same time, we suggest replacing FFT with an exact method just in the pre-computation phase. We also show that FFT causes a considerable amount of errors in KMS, however, replacing FFT in its pre-computations is unfortunately not sufficient.

We provide two variants of our scheme:

Static variant: the list of parties is fixed – the evaluation cost is independent of the number of participating parties, and the result is encrypted with all keys;
Dynamic variant: the computation cost is proportional to the number of participating parties, and the result is only encrypted with their keys (i.e., any subset of parties can go offline).

The variants only differ in pre-computation algorithms – performance-wise, given a fixed number of parties, the variants are equivalent (it only depends on the parameters of TFHE) and the evaluation complexity is linear in the number of involved parties. The construction of our scheme remains similar to that of plain TFHE, making it possible to adopt prospective advances of TFHE (or its implementation) to our scheme. In addition to the design of a new MKHE scheme:

- We support our scheme by a theoretical noise-growth & security analysis. Thanks to the low noise growth, we instantiate our scheme with as many as 128 parties. We show that our scheme is secure in the semi-honest model;
- We design and evaluate a deep experimental study, which may help evaluate future schemes. In particular, we suggest simulating the NAND gate to measure errors more realistically. Compared to KMS, we achieve $4.5\text{-}6.9\times$ better bootstrapping times, while using the same implementation of TFHE and parameters with the same estimated security (100 bits). The bootstrapping times are around 140 ms per party (experimental implementation);
- We extend previous work by providing an experimental evaluation of the probability of errors. For our scheme, the measured noises fall within the expected bounds, which are designed to satisfy the rule of 4σ (1 in 15 787); we indeed do not encounter *any* error in any of our 9 000 trials in total.

Paper Outline. We briefly recall the TFHE scheme in Sect. 2 and we present our scheme in Sect. 3. We analyze the security, correctness & noise growth, and performance of our scheme in Sect. 4, which is followed by a thorough experimental evaluation in Sect. 5. We conclude our paper in Sect. 6.

2 Preliminaries

In this section, we briefly recall the original TFHE scheme [11]. First, let us provide a list of symbols & notation that we use throughout the paper:

- $\mathbb{B}$: the set of binary coefficients $\{0,1\} \subset \mathbb{Z}$,
- $\mathbb{T}$: the additive group $\mathbb{R}/\mathbb{Z}$ referred to as the *torus* (i.e., real numbers mod 1),

- $\mathbb{Z}_n$: the quotient ring $\mathbb{Z}/n\mathbb{Z}$ (or its additive group),
- $M^{(N)}[X]$: the set of polynomials mod $X^N + 1$, with coefficients from M,
- \$: the uniform distribution,
- $a \overset{\alpha}{\leftarrow} M$: the draw of random variable a from M with distribution α (for $\alpha \in \mathbb{R}$, we consider the /discrete/ normal distribution $N(0, \alpha)$),
- $\mathrm{E}[X]$, $\mathsf{Var}[X]$: the expectation and the variance of random variable X.

2.1   TFHE Scheme

The TFHE scheme is based on the *Learning With Errors* (LWE) encryption scheme introduced by Regev [28]. TFHE employs two variants, originally referred to as T(R)LWE, which stands for *(Ring)* LWE *over the Torus*. The ring variant (shortly RLWE ; introduced in [21]) is defined by polynomial degree $N = 2^\nu$ (with $\nu \in \mathbb{N}$), dimension $n \in \mathbb{N}$, noise distribution ξ over the torus, and key distribution ζ over the integers (generalized to respective polynomials mod X^N+1). Informally, to encrypt torus polynomial $m \in \mathbb{T}^{(N)}[X]$, RLWE outputs the pair $(b = m - \langle \mathbf{z}, \mathbf{a} \rangle + e, \mathbf{a})$, referred to as the RLWE *sample*, where $\mathbf{z} \overset{\zeta}{\leftarrow} (\mathbb{Z}^{(N)}[X])^n$ is a secret key, $e \overset{\xi}{\leftarrow} \mathbb{T}^{(N)}[X]$ is an error term (aka. *noise*), and $\mathbf{a} \overset{\$}{\leftarrow} (\mathbb{T}^{(N)}[X])^n$ is a random mask. To decrypt, evaluate $\varphi_{\mathbf{z}}(b, \mathbf{a}) = b + \langle \mathbf{z}, \mathbf{a} \rangle = m + e$, also referred to as the *phase*. Internally, RLWE samples are further used to build so-called RGSW *samples*, which encrypt integer polynomials, and which allow for homomorphic multiplication of integer-torus polynomials. It is widely believed that RLWE sample $(b, \mathbf{a})$ is computationally indistinguishable from a random element of $(\mathbb{T}^{(N)}[X])^{1+n}$ (shortly random-like), provided that adequate parameters are chosen. If $\mathbf{a} = \mathbf{0}$ and $e = 0$, we talk about a *trivial sample*. The plain variant (shortly LWE) operates with plain torus elements instead of polynomials.

Bootstrapping. By its construction, (R)LWE is additively homomorphic: the sum of samples encrypts the sum of plaintexts. However, the error terms also add up, i.e., the average noise of the result grows. To deal with this issue, TFHE (as well as other fully homomorphic schemes) defines a routine referred to as *bootstrapping*. In addition to refreshing the noise of a noisy sample, TFHE bootstrapping is capable of evaluating a custom *Look-Up Table* (LUT), which makes TFHE fully homomorphic. Find an illustration of the operation flow in Fig. 1. For a comprehensive technical description of TFHE, we refer to Appendix A.

In this paper, we focus on the basic variant of TFHE with a Boolean message space: true and false are encoded into $\mathbb{T} \sim [-1/2, 1/2)$ as $-1/8$ and $1/8$, respectively. To homomorphically evaluate the NAND gate over input samples $\mathbf{c}_{1,2}$, the sum $(1/8, \mathbf{0}) - \mathbf{c}_1 - \mathbf{c}_2$ is bootstrapped with a LUT, which holds $1/8$ and $-1/8$ for the positive and for the negative half of $\mathbb{T}$, respectively.

$$\underbrace{\{m_i\}}_{\substack{\text{input} \\ \text{message(s)}}} \xrightarrow[\text{encr.}]{\text{LWE}} \underbrace{\{(b_i, \mathbf{a}_i)\}}_{\substack{\text{fresh/} \\ \text{bootstrapped} \\ \text{sample(s)}}} \xrightarrow[\text{addition}]{\text{hom.}} \underbrace{\sum(b_i, \mathbf{a}_i)}_{\substack{\text{to be boot-} \\ \text{strapped} \\ \text{(high noise)}}} \xrightarrow{\text{round}} \overbrace{(\tilde{b}, \tilde{\mathbf{a}}) \xrightarrow[\text{KeySwitch}]{\text{BlindRotate,}} \underbrace{(b', \mathbf{a}')}_{\substack{\text{freshly} \\ \text{bootstrapped} \\ \text{(low noise)}}}}^{\substack{\text{bootstrapping} \\ \text{(hom. LUT evaluation)}}}$$

Fig. 1. The flow of **TFHE**: homomorphic addition and bootstrapping, which is composed of other operations. The output sample $(b', \mathbf{a}')$ may proceed to another homomorphic addition, or to the output and decryption.

3 The AKÖ Scheme

In this section, we recall the notion of Multi-Key Homomorphic Encryption (MKHE) and we propose two variants of MKHE. We outline changes that lead from the basic **TFHE** [11] towards our proposal of MKHE – we outline the format of multi-key bootstrapping keys, and we comment on a distribution for RLWE keys. We provide a technical description of our scheme, which we denote AKÖ.

3.1 Towards the AKÖ Scheme

In addition to the capabilities of a standard FHE scheme, an MKHE scheme:

(i) runs a homomorphic evaluation over ciphertexts encrypted with unrelated keys of multiple parties (accompanied by corresponding evaluation keys);
(ii) requires the collaboration of all involved parties, holding the individual keys, to decrypt the result.

Note that there exist multiple approaches to reveal the result: e.g., one outlined in [6], referred to as *Distributed Decryption*, or one described in [23], referred to as *Collective Public-Key Switching*.

   We propose our scheme in two variants:

Static variant: the list of parties is fixed at the beginning, then evaluation keys are jointly calculated – no matter how many parties join a computation, the evaluation time is also fixed and the result is encrypted with all the keys;

Dynamic variant: after a "global" list of parties is fixed, evaluation keys are jointly calculated, however, only a subset of parties may join a computation – the evaluation cost is proportional to the size of the subset and the result is only encrypted with respective keys (i.e., the remaining parties can go offline). If a party joins later, a part of the joint pre-calculation of evaluation keys needs to be executed in addition, as opposed to CCS [6] and KMS [19].

Note that in many practical use cases—in particular, if we require semi-honest parties—the (global) list of parties is fixed, e.g., hospitals may constitute the parties. In addition, the pre-calculation protocol is indeed lightweight.

   As already outlined, our scheme is based on the three following ideas:

(i) create RLWE samples encrypted under the sum of individual RLWE keys,
(ii) use a ternary (zero-centered) distribution for individual RLWE keys, and
(iii) avoid Fast Fourier Transform (FFT) in pre-computations.

Below, we discuss (i) and (ii), leaving (iii) for the experimental part (Sect. 5). Note that the following lines might require an in-depth knowledge of TFHE.

(R)LWE Keys & Bootstrapping Keys. First, let us emphasize that secret keys of individual parties are *never* revealed to any other party, however, the description of AKÖ involves all of them. The underlying (and never reconstructed) LWE key is the *concatenation* of individual keys, i.e., $\mathbf{s} := \left(\mathbf{s}^{(1)}, \mathbf{s}^{(2)}, \ldots, \mathbf{s}^{(k)}\right) \in \mathbb{B}^{kn}$, where $\mathbf{s}^{(p)} \in \mathbb{B}^n$ are secret LWE keys of individual parties. We refer to $\mathbf{s}$ as the *common* LWE key. For RLWE keys, we consider their *summation*, i.e., $Z := \sum_p z^{(p)}$, which we refer to as the *common* RLWE *key*. This particular improvement decreases the computational complexity from $O(k^2)$ to $O(k)$.

For bootstrapping keys, we follow the original construction of TFHE, where we use the common (R)LWE keys. For *blind-rotate keys*, we generate an RGSW sample of each bit of the common LWE key $\mathbf{s} = \left(\mathbf{s}^{(1)}, \ldots, \mathbf{s}^{(k)}\right)$, under the common RLWE key $Z = \sum_p z^{(p)}$. In addition, any party shall neither leak its own secrets nor require the secrets of others. Hence, we employ RLWE public key encryption [21]. Let us outline the desired form of a blind-rotate key for bit s:

$$\mathsf{BK}_s = \begin{pmatrix} \mathbf{b}^{\Delta} + s \cdot \mathbf{g} & \mathbf{a}^{\Delta} \\ \mathbf{b}^{\square} & \mathbf{a}^{\square} + s \cdot \mathbf{g} \end{pmatrix}, \quad \mathsf{BK}_s \in \left(\mathbb{T}^{(N)}[X]\right)^{2d \times 2}, \tag{1}$$

where $(\mathbf{b}^{\Delta}, \mathbf{a}^{\Delta})$ and $(\mathbf{b}^{\square}, \mathbf{a}^{\square})$ hold $d + d$ RLWE encryptions of zero under the key Z; cf. TFHE.RgswEncr. For *key-switching keys*, we need to generate an LWE sample of the sum of j-th coefficients of individual RLWE secret keys $z^{(p)}$, under the common LWE key $\mathbf{s}$, for $j \in [0, N-1]$. Here a simple concatenation of masks (values $\mathbf{a}$) and a summation of masked values (values b) do the job. With such keys, bootstrapping itself is identical to that of the original TFHE.

Ternary Distribution for RLWE Keys. For individual RLWE keys, we suggest to use zero-centered ternary distribution $\zeta_p \colon (-1, 0, 1) \rightarrow (p, 1 - 2p, p)$, parameterized by $p \in (0, 1/2)$, which is widely adopted by the main FHE libraries like HElib [15], Lattigo [24], SEAL [22], or HEAAN [29]. Although not adopted in CCS nor in KMS, in our scheme, a zero-centered distribution for RLWE keys is particularly useful, since we sum the keys into a common key, which is then also zero-centered. This helps reduce the blind-rotate noise from $O(k^3)$ to $O(k^2)$, which in turn helps find more efficient TFHE parameters.

It is worth noting that for "small" values of p, such keys are also referred to as *sparse keys* (in particular with a fixed/limited Hamming weight), and there exist specially tailored attacks [9,31]. At this point, we motivate the choice of p solely by keeping the information entropy of ζ_p equal to 1 bit, however, there is no intuition—let alone a proof—that the estimated security would be at least similar (more in Sect. 5.1). For the information entropy of ζ_p, we have

$$H(\zeta_p) = -2p\log(p) - (1 - 2p)\log(1 - 2p) \overset{!}{=} 1, \tag{2}$$

which gives $p \approx 0.1135$. For $z_i \sim \zeta_p$, we have $\mathsf{Var}[z_i] = 2p \approx 0.227$.

3.2   Technical Description of AKÖ

Algorithms with index q are executed locally at the respective party, encryption algorithms naturally generalize to vector inputs.

Static Variant of AKÖ. Below, we provide algorithms for the static variant:
○ AKÖ.Setup$(1^\lambda, k)$: Given security parameter λ and the number of parties k, generate & distribute parameters for:

- LWE encryption: dimension n, standard deviation $\alpha > 0$ (of the noise);
- LWE decomposition: base B', depth d';
- set up LWE gadget vector: $\mathbf{g}' \leftarrow (1/B', 1/B'^2, \dots, 1/B'^{d'})$;
- RLWE encryption: polynomial degree N (a power of two), std-dev $\beta > 0$;
- RLWE decomposition: base B, depth d;
- set up RLWE gadget vector: $\mathbf{g} \leftarrow (1/B, 1/B^2, \dots, 1/B^d)$;
- generate a *common random polynomial* (CRP) $\underline{a} \overset{\$}{\leftarrow} \mathbb{T}^{(N)}[X]$.

○ AKÖ.SecKeyGen$_q()$: Generate secret keys $\mathbf{s}^{(q)} \overset{\$}{\leftarrow} \mathbb{B}^n$ and $z^{(q)} \in \mathbb{Z}^{(N)}[X]$, s.t. $z_i^{(q)} \overset{\zeta_p}{\leftarrow} \{-1, 0, 1\}$.
○ AKÖ...: Algorithms for (R)LWE en/decryption and bootstrapping (including BlindRotate, KeySwitch, etc.) are the same as in TFHE; cf. Appendix A.
○ AKÖ.RLwePubEncr$\big(m, (b, a)\big)$: Given message $m \in \mathbb{T}^{(N)}[X]$ and public key $(b, a) \in \mathbb{T}^{(N)}[X]^2$ (an RLWE sample of $0 \in \mathbb{T}^{(N)}[X]$ under key $z \in \mathbb{Z}^{(N)}[X]$), generate temporary RLWE key $r^{(q)}$, s.t. $r_i^{(q)} \overset{\zeta}{\leftarrow} \{-1, 0, 1\}$. Evaluate $b' \leftarrow$ RLwe-SymEncr$_q(m, b, r^{(q)})$ and $a' \leftarrow$ RLweSymEncr$_q(0, a, r^{(q)})$. Output (b', a'), which is an RLWE sample of m under the key z.
○ AKÖ.RLweRevPubEncr$\big(m, (b, a)\big)$: Proceed as RLwePubEncr, with a difference in the evaluation of $b' \leftarrow$ RLweSymEncr$_q(0, b, r^{(q)})$ and $a' \leftarrow$ RLweSymEncr$_q(m, a, r^{(q)})$, where only m and 0 are swapped, i.e., m is added to the right-hand side instead of the left-hand side.
○ AKÖ.BlindRotKeyGen$_q()$: Calculate and broadcast public key $b^{(q)} \leftarrow$ RLwe-SymEncr$_q(0, \underline{a})$, using the CRP $\underline{a}$ as the mask. Evaluate $B = \sum_{p=1}^k b^{(p)}$ (n.b., $(B, \underline{a}) = $ RLWE $_Z(0)$, hence it may serve as a common public key). Finally, for $j \in [1, n]$, output the *blind-rotate key* (related to $s_j^{(q)}$ and Z):

$$\mathsf{BK}_j^{(q)} \leftarrow \begin{pmatrix} \texttt{RLwePubEncr}_q\big(\mathbf{s}_j^{(q)} \cdot \mathbf{g}, (B, \underline{a})\big) \\ \texttt{RLweRevPubEncr}_q\big(\mathbf{s}_j^{(q)} \cdot \mathbf{g}, (B, \underline{a})\big) \end{pmatrix}, \tag{3}$$

which is an RGSW sample of the j-th bit of $\mathbf{s}^{(q)}$, under the common RLWE key Z.

○ $\overline{\texttt{AKÖ.KeySwitchKeyGen}_q()}$: For $i \in [1, N]$, broadcast $[\mathbf{b}_i^{(q)} | \mathbf{A}_i^{(q)}] \leftarrow$ LweSym-Encr$_q(\mathbf{z}_i^{(q)*} \cdot \mathbf{g}')$, where $\mathbf{z}^{(q)*} \leftarrow$ KeyExtract$(z^{(q)})$. Aggregate and for $i \in [1, N]$, output the *key-switching key* (for $Z_i = \sum_p z_i^{(p)}$ and $\mathbf{s} = (\mathbf{s}^{(1)}, \ldots, \mathbf{s}^{(k)})$):

$$\mathsf{KS}_i = \Big[\underbrace{\sum_{p=1}^{k} \mathbf{b}_i^{(p)}}_{\mathbf{b}_i} \,\Big|\, \underbrace{\mathbf{A}_i^{(1)}, \mathbf{A}_i^{(2)}, \ldots, \mathbf{A}_i^{(k)}}_{\mathbf{A}_i} \Big], \qquad (4)$$

which is a d'-tuple of LWE samples of $\mathbf{g}'$-respective fractions of $\mathbf{Z}_i^*$ under the common LWE key $\mathbf{s}$, where $\mathbf{Z}_i^*$ is the i-th element of the extraction of the common RLWE key $Z = \sum_p z^{(p)}$.

Changes to AKÖ towards the Dynamic Variant. For the dynamic variant, we provide modified versions of BlindRotKeyGen and KeySwitchKeyGen; other algorithms are the same as in the static variant. Note that, in case we allow a party to join later, all temporary keys need to be stored permanently and both algorithms need to be (partially) repeated. This causes a slight pre-computation overhead over CCS and KMS.

○ $\overline{\texttt{AKÖ.BlindRotKeyGen\_dyn}_q()}$: Calculate and broadcast public key $b^{(q)}$ as described in the AKÖ.BlindRotKeyGen$_q()$ algorithm. Then, for $j \in [1, n]$:

1: generate two vectors of d temporary RLWE keys $\mathbf{r}_j^{(q)}$ and $\mathbf{r}_j'^{(q)}$
2: for $p \in [1, k]$, $p \neq q$, output $\mathbf{b}_{q,j}^{\triangle(p)} \leftarrow$ RLweSymEncr$_q(0, b^{(p)}, \mathbf{r}_j^{(q)})$
3: output $\mathbf{b}_{q,j}^{\triangle(q)} \leftarrow$ RLweSymEncr$_q(\mathbf{s}_j^{(q)} \cdot \mathbf{g}, b^{(q)}, \mathbf{r}_j^{(q)})$
4: output $\mathbf{a}_{q,j}^{\triangle} \leftarrow$ RLweSymEncr$_q(0, \underline{a}, \mathbf{r}_j^{(q)})$
5: for $p \in [1, k]$, output $\mathbf{b}_{q,j}^{\square(p)} \leftarrow$ RLweSymEncr$_q(0, b^{(p)}, \mathbf{r}_j'^{(q)})$
6: output $\mathbf{a}_{q,j}^{\square} \leftarrow$ RLweSymEncr$_q(\mathbf{s}_j^{(q)} \cdot \mathbf{g}, \underline{a}, \mathbf{r}_j'^{(q)})$

To construct the j-th blind-rotate key of party q, related to subset of parties $\mathcal{S} \ni q$, evaluate

$$\mathsf{BK}_{j,\mathcal{S}}^{(q)} \leftarrow \begin{pmatrix} \sum_{p \in \mathcal{S}} \mathbf{b}_{q,j}^{\triangle(p)} & \mathbf{a}_{q,j}^{\triangle} \\ \sum_{p \in \mathcal{S}} \mathbf{b}_{q,j}^{\square(p)} & \mathbf{a}_{q,j}^{\square} \end{pmatrix}, \qquad (5)$$

which is an RGSW sample of $\mathbf{s}_j^{(q)}$ under the subset RLWE key $Z_{\mathcal{S}} = \sum_{p \in \mathcal{S}} z^{(p)}$. N.b., $\mathsf{BK}_{j,\mathcal{S}}^{(q)}$ is only calculated at runtime, once $\mathcal{S}$ is known.

○ $\overline{\texttt{AKÖ.KeySwitchKeyGen\_dyn}_q()}$: Proceed as AKÖ.KeySwitchKeyGen$_q()$, while instead of outputting aggregated KS_i's, aggregate relevant parts once $\mathcal{S}$ is known:

$$\mathsf{KS}_{i,\mathcal{S}} = \Big[\sum_{p \in \mathcal{S}} \mathbf{b}_i^{(p)} \,\Big|\, (\mathbf{A}_i^{(p)})_{p \in \mathcal{S}} \Big]. \qquad (6)$$

Possible Improvements. In [6], authors suggest an improvement that decreases the noise growth of key-switching, which can also be applied in our scheme; we provide more details in the full version of this paper [18].

4   Theoretical Analysis of AKÖ

In this section, we provide a theoretical analysis of our AKÖ scheme with respect to *security*, *correctness* (noise growth), and *performance*. For a detailed technical description of some of the involved algorithms, we refer to Appendix A – in particular, for those shared by AKÖ and TFHE; cf. AKÖ... in Sect. 3.2.

4.1   Security

We assume that all parties follow the protocol *honestly-but-curiously* (aka. the *semi-honest model*). First, let us recall what *is* secure and what *is not* in LWE (selected methods; also holds for RLWE):

✓ re-use secret key s with fresh mask a and fresh noise e;
✓ re-use common random mask $\underline{a}$ with multiple distinct secret keys $s^{(p)}$ and fresh noises $e^{(p)}$;
✗ publish $\langle s, a \rangle$ in any form (e.g., release the phase φ or the noise e);
✗ re-use the pair (s, a) with fresh noises e_i.

Below, we show that if all parties act semi-honestly, our scheme is secure in both of its variants. Note that rather than formal proofs, we provide informal sketches.

Public Key Encryption. In AKÖ, there are two algorithms for public key encryption: RLwe(Rev)PubEncr$(m, (b, a))$. They re-use a common random mask (the public key pair (b, a)) with fresh temporary key $r^{(q)}$. Provided that b and a are indistinguishable from random (random-like), it does not play a role to which part the message m is added/encrypted, i.e., both variants are secure.

Blind-Rotate Key Generation (static variant). Provided that CRP $\underline{a}$ is random-like, which is trivial to achieve in the random oracle model, we can assume that (our) $b^{(q)}$ is random-like. Assuming that other parties act honestly, also their $b^{(p)}$'s are random-like, hence the sum B is random-like, too. With $(B, \underline{a})$ random-like, public key encryption algorithms are secure, hence AKÖ.BlindRot-KeyGen$_q$ is secure, too.

Blind-Rotate Key Generation (dynamic variant). In this variant, party q re-uses temporary secret key $r^{(q)}$ for encryption of zeros using public keys $b^{(p)}$ of other parties, and for encryption of own secret key $s^{(q)}$. This is secure provided that $b^{(p)}$'s are random-like, which is true if generated honestly.

Key-Switching Key Generation (both variants). The AKÖ.KeySwitch KeyGen(_dyn)$_q$ algorithms employ the standard LWE encryption, hence they are both secure.

4.2   Correctness and Noise Growth

The most challenging part of all LWE-based schemes is to estimate the noise growth across various operations. First, we provide estimates of the noise growth of blind-rotate and key-switching, next, we combine them into an estimate of the noise of a freshly bootstrapped sample. Finally, we identify the maximum of error, which may cause incorrect bootstrapping. We evaluate all noises for the static variant, while for the dynamic variant, we provide more comments below respective theorems. All proofs can be found in the full version of this paper [18].

Theorem 1 (Noise Growth of Blind-Rotate). *The* AKÖ.BlindRotate *algorithm returns a sample with noise variance given by*

$$\mathsf{Var}[\langle \bar{\mathbf{Z}}, \mathsf{ACC}\rangle] \approx \underbrace{knNdV_B\beta^2(3+6pkN)}_{\text{BK error}} + \underbrace{{}^1\!/_2 \cdot kn\varepsilon^2(1+2pkN)}_{\text{decomp. error}} + \underbrace{\mathsf{Var}[tv]}_{\text{usually } 0} . \quad (7)$$

For the dynamic variant, we have $(3 + k \cdot 6pN) \to \big(1 + k(2 + 6pN)\big)$ in the BK error term, which we consider practically negligible as $6pN \approx 700$.

Theorem 2 (Noise Growth of Key-Switching). *The* AKÖ.KeySwitch *algorithm returns a sample that encrypts the same message as the input sample, while changing the key from* $\mathbf{Z}^*$ *to* $\mathbf{s}$, *with additional noise* e_{KS}, *given by* $\langle \bar{\mathbf{s}}, \bar{\mathbf{c}}''\rangle = \langle \bar{\mathbf{Z}}^*, \bar{\mathbf{c}}'\rangle + e_{\mathsf{KS}}$, *for which*

$$\mathsf{Var}[e_{\mathsf{KS}}] \approx \underbrace{Nkd'V_{B'}\beta'^2}_{\text{KS error}} + \underbrace{2pkN\varepsilon'^2}_{\text{decomp. error}} . \quad (8)$$

For the dynamic variant, key-switching keys are structurally equivalent, hence this estimate holds in the same form.

Corollary 1 (Noise of a Freshly Bootstrapped Sample). *The* AKÖ.Boot-strap *algorithm returns a sample with noise variance given by*

$$V_0 \approx \underbrace{3knNdV_B\beta^2(1+2pkN)}_{\text{BK error}} + \underbrace{{}^1\!/_2kn\varepsilon^2(1+2pkN)}_{\text{b.-r. decomp.}} + \underbrace{Nkd'V_{B'}\beta'^2}_{\text{KS error}} + \underbrace{2pkN\varepsilon'^2}_{\text{k.-s. decomp.}} .$$

$$(9)$$

For the dynamic variant, the BK *error term is changed according to Theorem 1.*

Maximum of Error. During homomorphic evaluations, freshly bootstrapped samples get homomorphically added/subtracted, before being possibly bootstrapped again; cf. Fig. 1. Before a noisy sample gets blindly rotated, it gets scaled and rounded to Z_{2N}, which induces an additional rounding error.

Lemma 1 (Rounding Error). *The rounding step before* BlindRotate *induces an additional error with variance (in the torus scale) given by*

$$\mathsf{Var}\big[\langle \bar{\mathbf{s}}, {}^1\!/_{2N} \cdot (\tilde{b}, \tilde{\mathbf{a}}) - (b, \mathbf{a})\rangle\big] = \frac{1 + kn/2}{48N^2} =: V_{round}(N, n, k). \quad (10)$$

After rounding, the noise gets refreshed inside the `BlindRotate` algorithm, which "blindly-rotates" a torus polynomial, referred to as the *test vector*, which encodes a LUT. I.e., the rounding step is where the maximum of errors across the whole computation appears. We focus on this error in the experimental part, since it may cause incorrect blind-rotation, in turn, incorrect LUT evaluation. In the following corollary, we evaluate the variance of the maximal error and we define quantity κ, which is a scaling factor of normal distribution $N(0,1)$.

Corollary 2 (Maximum of Error). *The maximum average error throughout homomorphic computation is achieved inside* `AKÖ.Bootstrap` *by the rounded sample* $1/2N \cdot (\tilde{b}, \tilde{a})$ *with variance*

$$V_{\max} \approx \max\left\{\sum k_i^2\right\} \cdot V_0 + V_{round}, \tag{11}$$

where k_i are coefficients of linear combinations of independent, freshly bootstrapped samples, which are evaluated during homomorphic calculations, before being bootstrapped (e.g., $\sum k_i^2 = 2$ for the NAND gate evaluation). We denote

$$\kappa := \frac{\delta/2}{\sqrt{V_{\max}}} = \frac{\delta}{2\sigma_{\max}}, \tag{12}$$

where δ is the distance of encodings that are to be distinguished (e.g., $1/4$ for encoding of bools).

We use κ to estimate the probability of *correct blind rotation* (CBRot). E.g., for $\kappa = 3$, we have $\Pr[\text{CBRot}] \approx 99.73\% \approx 1/370$ (aka. rule of 3σ), however, we rather lean to $\kappa = 4$ with $\Pr[\text{CBRot}] \approx 1/15\,787$. Since the maximum of error is achieved within blind-rotate, it dominates the overall probability of *correct bootstrapping* (CBStrap), i.e., we assume $\Pr[\text{CBStrap}] \approx \Pr[\text{CBRot}]$.

4.3   Performance

Since the structure of all components in both variants of `AKÖ` is equivalent to that of plain `TFHE` with only $n \to kn$ (due to `LWE` key concatenation), we evaluate the performance characteristics very briefly: `AKÖ.BlindRotate` is dominated by $4d \cdot kn$ degree-N polynomial multiplications, whereas `AKÖ.KeySwitch` is dominated by $Nd' \cdot (1 + kn)$ torus multiplications, followed by $1 + kn$ summations of Nd' elements. Using FFT for polynomial multiplication, for bootstrapping, we have the complexity of $O(N \log N \cdot 4dkn) + O(Nd' \cdot (1 + kn))$.

For key sizes, we have $|\text{BK}| = 4dNkn \cdot |\mathbb{T}_{\text{RLWE}}|$ and $|\text{KS}| = d'N(1+kn) \cdot |\mathbb{T}_{\text{LWE}}|$, where $|\mathbb{T}_{(\text{R})\text{LWE}}|$ denotes the size of respective torus representation.

5   Experimental Evaluation

For a fair comparison, we implement our `AKÖ` scheme[1] side by side with previous schemes CCS [6] and KMS [19]. These are implemented in a fork [30] of

---

[1] Available at https://gitlab.eurecom.fr/fakub/3-gen-mk-tfhe as **3gen**.

a library[2] [26] that implements TFHE in Julia. For the sake of simplicity, we implement only the static variant on AKÖ – recall that performance-wise, the two variants are equivalent, for noise growth, the differences are negligible.

In this section, we first comment on errors induced by existing TFHE implementations. Then, we introduce type-1 and type-2 decryption errors that one may encounter during TFHE-based homomorphic evaluations. Finally, we provide three kinds of results of our experiments:

1. for all the three schemes (CCS, KMS, and AKÖ) and selected parameter sets, we measure the *performance*, the *noise variances*, and the *amount of decryption errors* of the two types,
2. we demonstrate the *effect of FFT* during the pre-computation phase of AKÖ,
3. we compare the performance of all the three schemes with a *fixed parameter set* tailored for 16 parties, with different numbers of actually participating parties (i.e., the setup of the dynamic variant).

We run our experiments on a machine with an Intel Core i7-7800X processor and 128 GB of RAM.

Implementation Errors. The major source of errors that stem from a particular implementation of the TFHE scheme is Fast Fourier Transform (FFT), which is used for fast modular polynomial multiplication in RLWE ; find a study on FFT errors in [17]. Also, the finite representation of the torus (e.g., 64-bit integers) changes the errors slightly, however, we neglect this contribution as long as the precision (e.g., 2^{-64}) is smaller than the standard deviation of the (R)LWE noise. Note that these kinds of errors are not taken into account in Sect. 4.2, which solely focuses on the theoretical noise growth of the scheme itself.

Due to the excessive noise that we observe for higher numbers of parties with our scheme, we suggest replacing FFT in pre-computations (i.e., in blind-rotate key generation) with an exact method. This leads to an increase of the pre-computation costs (n.b., it has no effect on the bootstrapping time), however, in Sect. 5.2, we show that the benefit is worth it.

Types of Decryption Errors. The ultimate goal of noise analysis is to keep the probability of obtaining an incorrect result reasonably low. Below, we describe two types of decryption errors, which originate from bootstrapping, and which we measure in our experiments. N.b., the principle of BlindRotate is the same across the three schemes, hence it is well-defined for all of them.

Note 1. For the notion of *correct decryption*, we always assume symmetric intervals around encodings. E.g., for the Boolean variant of TFHE, which encodes true and false as $\pm 1/8$, we only consider the "correct" interval for true as $(0, 1/4)$, although $(0, 1/2)$ would work, too. Hence in the Boolean variant, actual incorrect decryption & decoding would be half less likely than what we actually measure.

---

[2] As noted by the authors, the code serves solely as a proof-of-concept.

Fresh Bootstrap Error. We bootstrap noiseless sample **c** of μ, i.e., `BlindRotate` rotates the test vector "correctly", meaning that $\tilde{\varphi}/2N = \mu$ selects the correct position from the encoded LUT. Then, we evaluate the probability of the resulting phase φ' falling outside the correct interval. We refer to this error as the *type-1 error*, denoted Err_1. This probability relates to the noise of a correctly blind-rotated, freshly bootstrapped sample. It can be estimated from V_0; see (9).

Blind Rotate Error. Let us consider a homomorphic sum of two independent, freshly bootstrapped samples (cf. Fig. 1). We evaluate the probability that the sum, after the rounding step inside bootstrapping, selects a value at an *incorrect* position from the test vector, which encodes the LUT (as discussed in Sect. 4.2). We refer to this error as the *type-2 error*, denoted Err_2. It can be estimated from $V_{\max}$; see (11). We evaluate Err_2 by simulating the NAND gate:

$$\left. \begin{array}{l} \text{fresh } \mathbf{c}_1 \xrightarrow{\text{Bootstr.}} \mathbf{c}_1' \\ \text{fresh } \mathbf{c}_2 \xrightarrow{\text{Bootstr.}} \mathbf{c}_2' \end{array} \right\} \ (1/8 - \mathbf{c}_1' - \mathbf{c}_2') \to \text{get rounded } \tilde{\varphi} \to \text{check } \tilde{\varphi}/2N \overset{?}{\in} (0, 1/4).$$

$$(13)$$

5.1   Experiment #1: Comparison of Performance and Errors

For the three schemes—CCS, KMS and AKÖ—we measure the main quantities: the bootstrapping time (median), the variance V_0 of a freshly bootstrapped sample (defined in (9)), the scaling factor κ (defined in (12)), and the number of errors of both types. We extend the previous work – there is no experimental evaluation of noises/errors in CCS nor in KMS. In all experiments, we replace FFT in pre-computations with an exact method. For CCS and KMS, we employ the parameters suggested by the original authors, and we estimate their security with the `lattice-estimator` by Albrecht et al. [2,3]. We obtain an estimate of about 100 bits, therefore for our scheme, we also suggest parameters with estimated 100-bit security. We provide more details on concrete security estimates of the parameters of CCS, KMS and AKÖ in the full version of this paper [18]. The results for CCS, KMS and AKÖ can be found in Table 1, 2 and 3, respectively.

In the results for CCS, we may notice that for 2 to 8 parties, the measured value of κ, denoted $\kappa^{(m)}$, agrees with the calculated value $\kappa^{(c)}$, whereas for 16 parties (n.b., parameters added in KMS [19]), the measured value $\kappa^{(m)}$ drops significantly, which indicates an unexpected error growth.

In the results for KMS, we may notice a similar drop of κ – here it occurs for all numbers of parties – we suppose that this is caused by FFT in bootstrapping (more on FFT later in Sect. 5.2). For both experiments, we further use $\kappa^{(m)}$ and Z-values of the normal distribution to evaluate the expected rate of Err_2, which is in perfect accordance with the measured one.

For our AKÖ scheme, the results do not show *any* error of any type. Regarding the values of κ (also V_0), we measure lower noise than expected – this we suppose to be caused by a certain statistical dependency of variables – indeed, our estimates of noise variances are based on an assumption that variables are independent, which is not always fully satisfied. We are able to run AKÖ with up to 128 parties, while the only limitation for 256 parties appears to be the size of RAM. We believe that with more RAM ($> 128\,$GB) or with a more optimized implementation, it would be possible to practically instantiate the scheme with even more parties.

Table 1. Key sizes (taken from [19]), bootstrapping times (t_B; median), noises and errors of the CCS scheme [6], with original parameters and *without* FFT in pre-computations (i.e., using precise calculations). *Parameters for $k = 16$ added by [19]. Labels (c) and (m) refer to calculated and measured values, respectively. Running 1 000 trials, i.e., evaluating 2 000 bootstraps; cf. (13). N.b., the actual error rate of a NAND gate would be approximately half of Err_2; cf. Note 1.

k	|keys| [MB]	t_B [s]	$V_0^{(c)}$ $[10^{-4}]$	$V_0^{(m)}$ $[10^{-4}]$	$\kappa^{(c)}$	$\kappa^{(m)}$	$\mathsf{Err}_{1,2}$ [‰]	Exp. Err_2
2	95	.58	16.2	14.6	2.19	2.30	1 24	21
4	108	2.4	19.1	18.6	2.01	2.04	3 41	41
8	121	10	6.36	6.27	3.39	3.41	0 0	.65
*16	214	86	2.15	34.5	5.07	1.49	29 128	136

Table 2. Key sizes (taken from [19]), bootstrapping times (t_B; median), noises and errors of the KMS scheme [19], with original parameters and without FFT in pre-computations. Running 1 000 trials.

k	|keys| [MB]	t_B [s]	$V_0^{(c)}$ $[10^{-4}]$	$V_0^{(m)}$ $[10^{-4}]$	$\kappa^{(c)}$	$\kappa^{(m)}$	$\mathsf{Err}_{1,2}$ [‰]	Exp. Err_2
2	215	.61	.458	11.5	12.7	2.60	1.5 12	9.3
4	286	2.1	.915	15.3	8.97	2.26	4 29	24
8	251	5.4	1.83	17.1	6.34	2.13	3 35	33
16	286	15	3.66	32.0	4.49	1.56	22.5 122	119
32	322	35	7.32	30.1	3.17	1.60	23 109	110

5.2 Experiment #2: The Effect of FFT in Pre-Computations

As outlined, polynomial multiplication in RLWE , when implemented using FFT, introduces additional error, on top of the standard RLWE noise. In this experiment, we compare noises of freshly bootstrapped samples: once *with* FFT in blind-rotate key generation (induces additional errors), once *without* FFT (we use an exact method instead). We choose our AKÖ scheme with 32 parties.

Table 3. Parameters, key sizes (calculated), bootstrapping times (t_B; median), noises, and errors of the static variant of AKÖ, without FFT in pre-computations. Running 1 000 trials, no errors of type Err_2 (let alone Err_1) experienced.

k	LWE				RLWE				$|keys|$ [GB]	t_B [s]	$V_0^{(c)}$ [10^{-4}]	$V_0^{(m)}$ [10^{-4}]	$\kappa^{(c)}$	$\kappa^{(m)}$
	n	$\log_2(\alpha)$	B'	d'	N	$\log_2(\beta)$	B	d						
2	520	-13.52	2^3	3	1 024	-30.70	2^7	2	.08	.19	4.69	4.18	4.04	4.27
4	510	-13.26	2^2	5			2^6	3	.24	.56	3.96	2.02	4.33	5.93
8	540	-14.04	2^2	5			2^4	4	.66	1.2	4.43	4.20	4.01	4.11
16	590	-15.34	2^3	4	2 048	-62.00	2^{26}	1	.93	1.8	4.56	1.02	4.04	7.90
32	620	-16.12	2^3	4			2^{26}	1	2.0	4.3	3.58	1.21	4.38	6.78
64	650	-16.90	2^3	4			2^{25}	1	4.1	8.6	3.41	1.80	4.20	5.25
128	670	-17.42	2^3	5			2^{24}	1	9.1	18	2.40	.486	4.15	5.47

We observe a tremendous growth of the noise of a freshly bootstrapped sample in case FFT is employed for blind-rotate key generation: in almost 4% of such cases, even a freshly bootstrapped sample gets decrypted incorrectly (i.e., $Err_1 \approx 4\%$). On the other hand, such a growth does not occur for lower numbers of parties, hence we suggest verifying whether in the particular case, the effect of FFT is remarkable, or negligible, and then decide accordingly. Recall that pre-computations with FFT are much faster (e.g., for 64 parties, we have 33 s vs. 212 s of the total pre-computation time).

Unexpected Error Growth in KMS. For the KMS scheme, we observe an unexpected error growth (cf. Table 2), which we suppose to be caused by FFT in bootstrapping. We replace *all* FFTs in the entire computation of KMS— including bootstrapping—with an exact method, and we re-run Experiment #1 with the KMS scheme with (only) 2 parties – due to a $\sim 40\times$ slower evaluation.

We obtain $V_0^{(m)} \approx 5.58 \cdot 10^{-4}$, which is still much more than the expected value $V_0^{(c)} \approx 0.458 \cdot 10^{-4}$, but the value of $\kappa^{(m)}$ increases from 2.60 to 3.73 and it results in no type-2 errors. At least partially, this confirms our hypothesis that the unexpected error growth in KMS is caused by FFT in evaluation.

Supporting evidence can be found in the design of KMS: in its blind-rotate, we observe that there are (up to) 4 nested FFTs: one in the circled $\star$ product, followed by three inside ExtProd: one in the $\odot$ product and two in NewHbProd. Compared with AKÖ, where there is just one level of FFT inside blind-rotate in Prod, this is likely the most significant practical improvement over KMS.

5.3 Experiment #3: Performance Comparison

We extend the performance comparison of CCS and KMS, presented in Fig. 2 of KMS [19] (which we re-run on our machine), by the performances of our AKÖ scheme. Note that the setup of that experiment corresponds to the dynamic variant – recall that performance-wise, the dynamic variant is equivalent to the static variant, which is implemented in our experimental library. For each scheme, we employ its own parameter set tailored for 16 parties, while we instantiate it with different numbers of actually participating parties; find the results in Fig. 2.

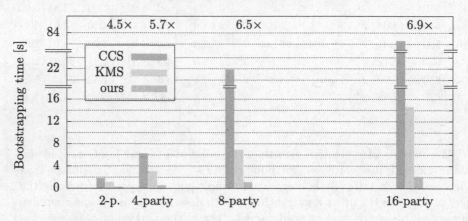

Fig. 2. Comparison of median bootstrapping times of the CCS scheme [6], the KMS scheme [19], and our AKÖ scheme. 100 runs with respective parameters for 16 parties were executed. N.b., FFT in pre-computations does not affect performance.

5.4   Discussion

The goal of our experiments is to show the practical usability of our AKÖ scheme: we compare its performance as well as the probability of errors with previous schemes – CCS [6] and KMS [19].

In terms of bootstrapping time, AKÖ runs faster than both previous attempts (cf. Fig. 2). Also, the theoretical complexity of AKÖ is linear in the number of parties (cf. Sect. 4.3), as opposed to quadratic and quasi-linear for CCS and KMS, respectively.

To evaluate the number of errors that may occur during bootstrapping, we propose a new method that simulates the rounding step of BlindRotate (cf. (13)), which is the same across all the three schemes. Our experiments show that both CCS and KMS suffer from a considerably high error rate (cf. Table 1 and 2, respectively): for CCS, the original parameters are rather poor; for KMS, it seems that there are too many nested FFT's in bootstrapping – we show that FFT in evaluation—at least partially—causes the unexpected error growth.

To sum up, AKÖ significantly outperforms both CCS & KMS in terms of bootstrapping time and/or error rate. The major practical limitation of the CCS scheme is the quadratic growth of the bootstrapping time, whereas the KMS scheme suffers from the additional error growth in implementation. A disadvantage of AKÖ is that it requires (a small amount of) additional pre-computations if a new party decides to join the computation in the dynamic variant. Also AKÖ does not enable parallelization, as opposed to KMS.

6 Conclusion

We propose a new TFHE-based MKHE scheme named AKÖ in two variants, depending on whether only a subset of parties is desired to take part in a homomorphic computation. We implement AKÖ side-by-side with other similar schemes CCS and KMS, and we show its practical usability in thorough experimentation, where we also suggest secure & reliable parameters. Thanks to its low noise growth, AKÖ can be instantiated with hundreds of parties; namely, we tested up to 128 parties. Compared to previous schemes, AKÖ achieves much faster bootstrapping times, however, a slight overhead of pre-computations is induced. For KMS, we show that FFT errors are prohibitive for its practical deployment – unfortunately, replacing FFT in pre-computations is not enough.

Besides benchmarking, we suggest emulating (a part of) the NAND gate to achieve a more realistic error analysis: the measured amount of errors shows to be in perfect accordance with the expected amount. This method may help future schemes to evaluate their practical reliability.

Future Work. We plan to extend the threat model to assume malicious parties.

A Technical Description of TFHE

We provide a technical description of the TFHE scheme in a form of self-descriptive algorithms. Parameters and secret keys are considered implicit inputs.

○ TFHE.Setup(1^λ): Given security parameter λ, generate parameters for:

 LWE encryption: dimension n, standard deviation $\alpha > 0$ (of the noise);
- LWE decomposition: base B', depth d';
- set up LWE gadget vector: $\mathbf{g}' \leftarrow (1/B', 1/B'^2, \ldots, 1/B'^{d'})$;
- RLWE encryption: polynomial degree N (a power of two), standard deviation $\beta > 0$;
- RLWE decomposition: base B, depth d;
- set up RLWE gadget vector: $\mathbf{g} \leftarrow (1/B, 1/B^2, \ldots, 1/B^d)$.

Other input parameters of the Setup algorithm may include the maximal allowed probability of error, or the plaintext space size (for other than Boolean circuits).

○ TFHE.SecKeyGen(): Generate secret keys for:

- LWE encryption: $\mathbf{s} \xleftarrow{\$} \mathbb{B}^n$;
- RLWE encryption: $z \xleftarrow{\$} \mathbb{B}^{(N)}[X]$, (alternatively $z_i \xleftarrow{\zeta} \{-1, 0, 1\}$ for some distribution ζ).

For LWE key $s \in \mathbb{B}^n$, we denote $\bar{s} := (1, s) \in \mathbb{B}^{1+n}$ the extended secret key, similarly for an RLWE key $z \in \mathbb{Z}^{(N)}[X]$, we denote $\bar{z} := (1, z) \in \mathbb{Z}^{(N)}[X]^2$.

○ TFHE.LweSymEncr(μ): Given message $\mu \in \mathbb{T}$, sample fresh mask $a \xleftarrow{\$} \mathbb{T}^n$ and noise $e \xleftarrow{\alpha} \mathbb{T}$. Evaluate $b \leftarrow -\langle s, a \rangle + \mu + e$ and output $\bar{c} = (b, a) \in \mathbb{T}^{1+n}$, an LWE encryption of μ. This algorithm is used as the main encryption algorithm of the scheme. We generalize this as well as subsequent algorithms to input vectors and proceed element-by-element.

○ TFHE.RLweSymEncr($m, a = \emptyset, z_{in} = z$): Given message $m \in \mathbb{T}^{(N)}[X]$, sample fresh mask $a \xleftarrow{\$} \mathbb{T}^{(N)}[X]$, unless explicitly given. If the pair (a, z_{in}) has been used before, output $\bot$. Otherwise, sample fresh noise $e \in \mathbb{T}^{(N)}[X]$, $e_i \xleftarrow{\beta} \mathbb{T}$, and evaluate $b \leftarrow -z_{in} \cdot a + m + e$. Output $\bar{c} = (b, a) \in \mathbb{T}^{(N)}[X]^2$, an RLWE encryption of m. In case a is given, we may limit the output to only b.

○ TFHE.(R)LwePhase($\bar{c}$): Given (R)LWE sample $\bar{c}$, evaluate and output $\varphi \leftarrow \langle \bar{s}, \bar{c} \rangle$, where $\bar{s}$ is respective (R)LWE extended secret key.

○ TFHE.EncrBool(b): Set $\mu = \pm 1/8$ for b true or false, respectively. Output LweSymEncr(μ).

○ TFHE.DecrBool($\bar{c}$): Output LwePhase($\bar{c}$) > 0, assuming $\mathbb{T} \sim [-1/2, 1/2)$.

○ TFHE.RgswEncr(m): Given $m \in \mathbb{Z}^{(N)}[X]$, evaluate $\mathbf{Z} \leftarrow$ RLweSymEncr($\mathbf{0}$), where $\mathbf{0}$ is a vector of $2d$ zero polynomials (i.e., $\mathbf{Z} \in (\mathbb{T}^{(N)}[X])^{2d \times 2}$). Output $\mathbf{Z} + m \cdot \mathbf{G}$, an RGSW sample of m.

○ TFHE.Prod$\big(\mathsf{BK}, (b, a)\big)$: Given RGSW sample BK of $s \in \mathbb{Z}^{(N)}[X]$, and RLWE sample (b, a) of $m \in \mathbb{T}^{(N)}[X]$, evaluate and output:

$$(b', a') \leftarrow \begin{pmatrix} \mathbf{g}^{-1}(b) \\ \mathbf{g}^{-1}(a) \end{pmatrix}^T \cdot \mathsf{BK} =: \mathsf{BK} \,\square\, (b, a), \qquad (14)$$

which is an RLWE sample of $s \cdot m \in \mathbb{T}^{(N)}[X]$; in TFHE also referred to as the *external product*.

○ TFHE.BlindRotate$\big(\bar{c}, \{\mathsf{BK}_i\}_{i=1}^n, tv\big)$: Given $\bar{c} = (b, a_1, \ldots, a_n) \in \mathbb{T}^{1+n}$, an LWE sample of $\mu \in \mathbb{T}$ under key $s \in \mathbb{B}^n$; $(\mathsf{BK}_i)_{i=1}^n$, RGSW samples of s_i under RLWE key z (aka. *blind-rotate keys*); and RLWE $_z(tv) \in \mathbb{T}^{(N)}[X]^2$, (usually trivial) RLWE sample of $tv \in \mathbb{T}^{(N)}[X]$ (aka. *test vector*), evaluate:

1: $\tilde{b} \leftarrow \lfloor 2Nb \rceil$, $\quad \tilde{a}_i \leftarrow \lfloor 2Na_i \rceil$ for $1 \leq i \leq n$
2: ACC $\leftarrow X^{\tilde{b}} \cdot$ RLWE (tv)
3: **for** $i = 1, \ldots, n$ **do**
4:   ACC $\leftarrow$ ACC + Prod$\big(\mathsf{BK}_i, X^{\tilde{a}_i} \cdot$ ACC $-$ ACC$\big)$ ▷ ACC or $X^{\tilde{a}_i} \cdot$ ACC if $s_i = 0$ or $s_i = 1$, resp.

Output ACC = RLWE $_z(X^{\tilde{\varphi}} \cdot tv)$, an RLWE encryption of test vector "rotated" by $\tilde{\varphi}$, where $\tilde{\varphi} = \lfloor 2Nb \rceil + s_1 \lfloor 2Na_1 \rceil + \ldots + s_n \lfloor 2Na_n \rceil \approx 2N(\bar{s} \cdot \bar{c}) \approx 2N\mu$.

○ TFHE.KeyExtract(z): Given RLWE key $z \in \mathbb{Z}^{(N)}[X]$, output $\mathbf{z}^* \leftarrow (z_0, -z_{N-1}, \ldots, -z_1)$.

○ TFHE.SampleExtract(b, a): Given RLWE sample $(b, a) \in \mathbb{T}^{(N)}[X]^2$ of $m \in \mathbb{T}^{(N)}[X]$ under RLWE key $z \in \mathbb{Z}^{(N)}[X]$, output LWE sample $(b', \mathbf{a}') \leftarrow (b_0, a_0, \ldots,$

$a_{N-1}) \in \mathbb{T}^{1+N}$ of $m_0 \in \mathbb{T}$ (the constant term of m) under the extracted LWE key $\mathbf{z}^* = \texttt{KeyExtract}(z)$.

∘ $\texttt{TFHE.KeySwitchKeyGen}()$: For $j \in [1, N]$, evaluate and output a key-switching key for z_j and $\mathbf{s}$: $\mathsf{KS}_j \leftarrow \texttt{LweSymEncr}(\mathbf{z}_j^* \cdot \mathbf{g}')$, where $\mathbf{z}^* \leftarrow \texttt{KeyExtract}(z)$. KS_j is a d'-tuple of LWE samples of $\mathbf{g}'$-respective fractions of $\mathbf{z}_j^*$ under the key $\mathbf{s}$.

∘ $\texttt{TFHE.KeySwitch}(\bar{c}', \{\mathsf{KS}_j\}_{j=1}^N)$: Given LWE sample $\bar{c}' = (b', a'_1, \ldots, a'_N) \in \mathbb{T}^{1+N}$ (extraction of an RLWE sample), which encrypts $\mu \in \mathbb{T}$ under the extraction of an RLWE key $\mathbf{z}^* = \texttt{KeyExtract}(z)$, and a set of key-switching keys for z and $\mathbf{s}$, evaluate and output

$$\bar{c}'' \leftarrow (b', \mathbf{0}) + \sum_{j=1}^N \mathbf{g}'^{-1}(a'_j)^T \cdot \mathsf{KS}_j, \tag{15}$$

which is an LWE sample of the same $\mu \in \mathbb{T}$ under the LWE key $\mathbf{s}$.

∘ $\texttt{TFHE.Bootstrap}(\bar{c}, tv, \{\mathsf{BK}_i\}_{i=1}^n, \{\mathsf{KS}_j\}_{j=1}^N)$: Given LWE sample $\bar{c}$ of $\mu \in \mathbb{T}$ under LWE key $\mathbf{s}$, test vector $tv \in \mathbb{T}^{(N)}[X]$ that encodes a LUT, and two sets of keys for blind-rotate and for key-switching (aka. *bootstrapping keys* – the evaluation keys of TFHE), evaluate:

1: $\bar{c}' \leftarrow \texttt{BlindRotate}(\bar{c}, \{\mathsf{BK}_i\}_{i=1}^n, tv)$;
2: $\bar{c}'' \leftarrow \texttt{KeySwitch}(\texttt{SampleExtract}(\bar{c}'), \{\mathsf{KS}_j\}_{j=1}^N)$.

Output $\bar{c}''$, which is an LWE sample of—vaguely speaking—"evaluation of the LUT at μ", under the key $\mathbf{s}$, with a refreshed noise. Details on the encoding of the LUT are out of the scope of this paper.

∘ $\texttt{TFHE.Add}(\bar{c}_1, \bar{c}_2)$: Output $\bar{c}_1 + \bar{c}_2$, which encrypts the sum of input plaintexts. Using just "+".

∘ $\texttt{TFHE.NAND}(\bar{c}_1, \bar{c}_2, \{\mathsf{BK}_i\}_{i=1}^n, \{\mathsf{KS}_j\}_{j=1}^N)$: Given encryptions of bools b_1 and b_2 under LWE key $\mathbf{s}$, and bootstrapping keys for $\mathbf{s}$ and z, set the test vector as $tv \leftarrow 1/8 \cdot (1 + X + X^2 + \ldots + X^{N-1})$. Output $\bar{c}'' \leftarrow \texttt{Bootstrap}(1/8 - \bar{c}_1 - \bar{c}_2, tv, \{\mathsf{BK}_i\}_{i=1}^n, \{\mathsf{KS}_j\}_{j=1}^N)$, which is an encryption of $\neg(b_1 \wedge b_2)$ under the key $\mathbf{s}$.

References

1. Acar, A., Aksu, H., Uluagac, A.S., Conti, M.: A survey on homomorphic encryption schemes: Theory and implementation. ACM Comput. Surv. (Csur) **51**(4), 1–35 (2018)
2. Albrecht, M.R.: Contributors: Security Estimates for Lattice Problems. https://github.com/malb/lattice-estimator (2022)
3. Albrecht, M.R., Player, R., Scott, S.: On the concrete hardness of learning with errors. J. Math. Cryptol. **9**(3), 169–203 (2015)
4. Brakerski, Z.: Fully homomorphic encryption without modulus switching from classical GapSVP. In: Safavi-Naini, R., Canetti, R. (eds.) Advances in Cryptology – CRYPTO 2012, pp. 868–886. Springer Berlin Heidelberg, Berlin, Heidelberg (2012). https://doi.org/10.1007/978-3-642-32009-5_50

5. Brakerski, Z., Perlman, R.: Lattice-based fully dynamic multi-key fhe with short ciphertexts. In: Robshaw, M., Katz, J. (eds.) Advances in Cryptology – CRYPTO 2016: 36th Annual International Cryptology Conference, Santa Barbara, CA, USA, August 14-18, 2016, Proceedings, Part I, pp. 190–213. Springer Berlin Heidelberg, Berlin, Heidelberg (2016). https://doi.org/10.1007/978-3-662-53018-4_8

6. Chen, H., Chillotti, I., Song, Y.: Multi-key homomorphic encryption from TFHE. In: Galbraith, S.D., Moriai, S. (eds.) Advances in Cryptology – ASIACRYPT 2019: 25th International Conference on the Theory and Application of Cryptology and Information Security, Kobe, Japan, December 8–12, 2019, Proceedings, Part II, pp. 446–472. Springer International Publishing, Cham (2019). https://doi.org/10.1007/978-3-030-34621-8_16

7. Chen, H., Dai, W., Kim, M., Song, Y.: Efficient multi-key homomorphic encryption with packed ciphertexts with application to oblivious neural network inference. In: Proceedings of the 2019 ACM SIGSAC Conference on Computer and Communications Security, pp. 395–412 (2019)

8. Chen, L., Zhang, Z., Wang, X.: Batched Multi-hop Multi-key FHE from Ring-LWE with compact ciphertext extension. In: Kalai, Y., Reyzin, L. (eds.) Theory of Cryptography: 15th International Conference, TCC 2017, Baltimore, MD, USA, November 12-15, 2017, Proceedings, Part II, pp. 597–627. Springer International Publishing, Cham (2017). https://doi.org/10.1007/978-3-319-70503-3_20

9. Cheon, J.H., Hhan, M., Hong, S., Son, Y.: A hybrid of dual and meet-in-the-middle attack on sparse and ternary secret lwe. IEEE Access 7, 89497–89506 (2019)

10. Cheon, J.H., Kim, A., Kim, M., Song, Y.: Homomorphic encryption for arithmetic of approximate numbers. In: Takagi, T., Peyrin, T. (eds.) Advances in Cryptology – ASIACRYPT 2017: 23rd International Conference on the Theory and Applications of Cryptology and Information Security, Hong Kong, China, December 3-7, 2017, Proceedings, Part I, pp. 409–437. Springer International Publishing, Cham (2017). https://doi.org/10.1007/978-3-319-70694-8_15

11. Chillotti, I., Gama, N., Georgieva, M., Izabachène, M.: TFHE: fast fully homomorphic encryption over the torus. J. Cryptol. 33(1), 34–91 (2020)

12. Clear, M., McGoldrick, C.: Multi-identity and Multi-key Leveled FHE from learning with errors. In: Gennaro, R., Robshaw, M. (eds.) Advances in Cryptology – CRYPTO 2015: 35th Annual Cryptology Conference, Santa Barbara, CA, USA, August 16-20, 2015, Proceedings, Part II, pp. 630–656. Springer Berlin Heidelberg, Berlin, Heidelberg (2015). https://doi.org/10.1007/978-3-662-48000-7_31

13. Fan, J., Vercauteren, F.: Somewhat Practical Fully Homomorphic Encryption. Cryptology ePrint Archive, Paper 2012/144 (2012). https://ia.cr/2012/144

14. Gentry, C.: Fully homomorphic encryption using ideal lattices. In: Proceedings of the forty-first annual ACM symposium on Theory of computing, pp. 169–178 (2009)

15. Halevi, S., Shoup, V.: Design and implementation of a homomorphic-encryption library. IBM Res. (Manuscript) 6(12–15), 8–36 (2013)

16. Kim, T., Kwak, H., Lee, D., Seo, J., Song, Y.: Asymptotically faster multi-key homomorphic encryption from homomorphic gadget decomposition. Cryptology ePrint Archive, Paper 2022/347 (2022). https://ia.cr/2022/347

17. Klemsa, J.: Fast and error-free negacyclic integer convolution using extended fourier transform. In: Dolev, S., Margalit, O., Pinkas, B., Schwarzmann, A. (eds.) Cyber Security Cryptography and Machine Learning: 5th International Symposium, CSCML 2021, Be'er Sheva, Israel, July 8–9, 2021, Proceedings, pp. 282–300. Springer International Publishing, Cham (2021). https://doi.org/10.1007/978-3-030-78086-9_22

18. Klemsa, J., Önen, M., Akın, Y.: A Practical TFHE-Based Multi-Key Homomorphic Encryption with Linear Complexity and Low Noise Growth. Cryptology ePrint Archive, Paper 2023/065 (2023). https://eprint.iacr.org/2023/065
19. Kwak, H., Min, S., Song, Y.: Towards Practical Multi-key TFHE: Parallelizable, Key-Compatible, Quasi-linear Complexity. Cryptology ePrint Archive, Paper 2022/1460 (2022), https://ia.cr/2022/1460
20. López-Alt, A., Tromer, E., Vaikuntanathan, V.: On-the-fly multiparty computation on the cloud via multikey fully homomorphic encryption. In: Proceedings of the Forty-fourth Annual ACM Symposium On Theory Of Computing, pp. 1219–1234 (2012)
21. Lyubashevsky, V., Peikert, C., Regev, O.: On ideal lattices and learning with errors over rings. In: Gilbert, H. (ed.) EUROCRYPT 2010. LNCS, vol. 6110, pp. 1–23. Springer, Heidelberg (2010). https://doi.org/10.1007/978-3-642-13190-5_1
22. Microsoft: SEAL (release 4.1). https://github.com/Microsoft/SEAL (Jan 2023)
23. Mouchet, C., Troncoso-Pastoriza, J., Bossuat, J.P., Hubaux, J.P.: Multiparty homomorphic encryption from ring-learning-with-errors. Proceedings on Privacy Enhancing Technologies, pp. 291–311 (2021)
24. Mouchet, C.V., Bossuat, J.P., Troncoso-Pastoriza, J.R., Hubaux, J.P.: Lattigo: A multiparty homomorphic encryption library in go. In: Proceedings of the 8th Workshop on Encrypted Computing and Applied Homomorphic Cryptography, pp. 64–70. No. CONF (2020)
25. Mukherjee, P., Wichs, D.: Two round multiparty computation via multi-key FHE. In: Fischlin, M., Coron, J.-S. (eds.) Advances in Cryptology – EUROCRYPT 2016: 35th Annual International Conference on the Theory and Applications of Cryptographic Techniques, Vienna, Austria, May 8-12, 2016, Proceedings, Part II, pp. 735–763. Springer Berlin Heidelberg, Berlin, Heidelberg (2016). https://doi.org/10.1007/978-3-662-49896-5_26
26. NuCypher: TFHE.jl. https://github.com/nucypher/TFHE.jl (2022)
27. Peikert, C., Shiehian, S.: Multi-key FHE from LWE, Revisited. In: Hirt, M., Smith, A. (eds.) Theory of Cryptography: 14th International Conference, TCC 2016-B, Beijing, China, October 31-November 3, 2016, Proceedings, Part II, pp. 217–238. Springer Berlin Heidelberg, Berlin, Heidelberg (2016). https://doi.org/10.1007/978-3-662-53644-5_9
28. Regev, O.: On lattices, learning with errors, random linear codes, and cryptography. In: Proceedings of the Thirty-seventh Annual ACM Symposium on Theory of Computing, pp. 84–93 (2005)
29. SNUCrypto: HEAAN (release 1.1). https://github.com/snucrypto/HEAAN (2018)
30. SNUPrivacy: MK-TFHE. https://github.com/SNUPrivacy/MKTFHE (2022)
31. Son, Y., Cheon, J.H.: Revisiting the hybrid attack on sparse secret lwe and application to he parameters. In: Proceedings of the 7th ACM Workshop on Encrypted Computing & Applied Homomorphic Cryptography, pp. 11–20 (2019)

Deniable Cryptosystems: Simpler Constructions and Achieving Leakage Resilience

Zhiyuan An[1,2], Haibo Tian[1,2], Chao Chen[1,2], and Fangguo Zhang[1,2(✉)]

[1] School of Computer Science and Engineering, Sun Yat-sen University,
Guangzhou 510006, China
{anzhy,chench533}@mail2.sysu.edu.cn, {tianhb,isszhfg}@mail.sysu.edu.cn
[2] Guangdong Province Key Laboratory of Information Security Technology,
Guangzhou 510006, China

Abstract. Deniable encryption (Canetti et al. in CRYPTO '97) is an intriguing primitive, which provides security guarantee against coercion by allowing a sender to convincingly open the ciphertext into a fake message. Despite the notable result by Sahai and Waters in STOC '14 and other efforts in functionality extension, all the deniable public key encryption (DPKE) schemes suffer from intolerable overhead due to the heavy building blocks, e.g., translucent sets or indistinguishability obfuscation. Besides, none of them considers the possible damage from leakage in the real world, obstructing these protocols from practical use.

To fill the gap, in this work we first present a simple and generic approach of sender-DPKE from ciphertext-simulatable encryption, which can be instantiated with nearly all the common PKE schemes. The core of this design is a newly-designed framework for flipping a bit-string that offers inverse polynomial distinguishability. Then we theoretically and experimentally expound on how classic side-channel attacks (timing or simple power attacks), can help the coercer break deniability, along with feasible countermeasures.

Keywords: Deniable encryption · Simulatable encryption · Side-channel attacks · Leakage resilience

1 Introduction

DENIABLE ENCRYPTION, firstly introduced by Canetti et al. [6], is a seemingly contradictory primitive which allows a coerced user to produce fake (but valid-looking) random coins that could open the original ciphertext to another message. More detailedly, there is an additional fake algorithm, which on inputting the original plaintext m, used randomness r, and any fake message m^*, returns some fake coins r^*. In this way, the sender can claim the questioned ciphertext to be the encryption of m^* under r^*, and the coercer can not detect the lie.

G. Tsudik et al. (Eds.): ESORICS 2023, LNCS 14344, pp. 24–44, 2024.
https://doi.org/10.1007/978-3-031-50594-2_2

Compared with the traditional encryption notions that provide security against only passive attacks, deniable encryption provides more shields since it is coercion-resistant and non-committing in the context of active attacks. In this sense, deniable public key encryption (DPKE) can be deployed in systems where strong privacy-preserving is required, e.g., electronic voting [12], uncoercible multiparty computation [6,21], cloud storage service [11] and searchable encryption [27].

PRIOR WORKS ON DENIABILITY. Over the last decades, many approaches have been proposed to build deniable encryption. The seminal work [6] provided two schemes for bit encryption using a well-defined primitive called translucent sets (TS). Following this blueprint, O'Neill et al. [32] explored non-interactive bi-deniable encryption under the weak model where both sides can fake simultaneously, along with constructions from lattice-based bi-TS. A notable breakthrough was achieved by Sahai and Waters [33], where they presented the first and only known construction supporting negligible detection probability by use of indistinguishability obfuscation ($i\mathcal{O}$) [20,23] and puncturable PRFs [3]. Recently, Agrawal et al. [1] tackled deniability by equipping fully homomorphic encryption (FHE) [22] (e.g., the BGV scheme [4]) with biased decryption. As extensions of DPKE, Gao et al. [19] studied the stronger notation of CCA-secure DPKE and provided an instantiation from extended hash proof systems; Caro et al. [9,10] built deniable function encryption by combining $i\mathcal{O}$ and delayed trapdoor circuit; Besides, Coladangelo et al. [14] explored the possible quantum setting where the encryption program is implemented under quantum circuits, and gave efficient constructions from LWE. There has also been work on fully interactive DPKE [7], where negligible bi-deniability was achieved based on $i\mathcal{O}$ and OWFs.

CURRENT LIMITATIONS OF DPKE. Although the aforementioned works settled the issue in various aspects, they all bear somewhat heavy building blocks, e.g., TS-based schemes [2,6,32] only support bit-encryption; FHE-derived one [1] has the runtime of encryption being linear of both the inverse detection probability and the size of message space; the only scheme with negligible detection probability [33] is built on the powerful $i\mathcal{O}$ which however requires sub-exponential assumptions and huge storage cost. These facts make them fall short of being deployment-friendly, let alone integrate with other cryptosystems into synthetical programs. Therefore, there has still been a challenging gap between theoretical prototypes and pragmatic systems on *deniability*. In other words, it is more desirable to construct deniable encryption from handy methods and with as practical as possible overhead (ciphertext size or runtime).

On the other side, there has been lots of work paying close attention to another security notion of PKE. Namely, the resilience to the leakage from physical hardware that encapsulates the related algorithms, e.g., side-channel attacks (SCA) from timing or power analysis [17,18,25,26], which are common threats to the cryptographic applications in real-world [5,30]. Previous works have also provided various manners to avoid such leakage including general models or specific countermeasures. However, there has been no headway yet that sheds light on the potential damage to deniable schemes. That is, we have no idea that, with some available side-channel information of programs where the sender operates, can the coercer distinguish the claimed randomness from the real ones, so as to breach the *deniability* of the target system? Thus, towards the practical use of DPKE, it is encouraging to explore *deniability* in the context of SCA.

OUR CONTRIBUTIONS. This work addresses the above two limitations of existing deniable encryption schemes. Our contributions are summarized in the following.

– We propose a generic construction of DPKE from ciphertext-simulatable PKE, an underpinning that can be instantiated with nearly all the common PKE schemes. In particular, we devise a subtle bit-flipping framework within a bit string to support inverse polynomial detection probability.
– We formalize the SCA-equipped coercion model for timing and simple power attacks, under which we show how deniability can be breached, as well as provide suitable countermeasures, we then evidence these results by performing relative experiments.

Table 1. Comparison between known schemes and ours.

Scheme	Methods	Mess. space	Deniability	SCA	Cipher. size	Runtime
[6]	TS	$\{0,1\}$	$\mathcal{O}(\frac{1}{\lambda})$	✗	$\mathcal{O}(\lambda \cdot \tau_l)$	$\mathcal{O}(\lambda \cdot \tau_t)$
[33]	$i\mathcal{O} + $ PKE	$\{0,1\}$	$\mathsf{negl}(\lambda)$	✗	$\mathcal{O}(\tau_l)$	$\mathcal{O}(\tau_t)$
[1]	FHE	$\mathsf{poly}(\lambda)$	$\mathcal{O}(\frac{1}{\lambda})$	✗	$\mathcal{O}(\tau_l)$	$\tau_t \cdot \mathsf{poly}(\lambda)$
Ours	CS-PKE	2^λ	$\mathcal{O}(\frac{1}{\lambda})$	Against	$\mathcal{O}(\lambda \cdot \tau_l)$	$\mathcal{O}(\lambda \cdot \tau_t)$

For security parameter λ, Table 1 gives an overall comparison of some known sender-DPKE and ours, where τ_l and τ_t denote the element size and runtime of the underlying methods, respectively, e.g., the ciphertext size and en/decryption runtime of the PKE used in [33]. As we will expound in Sect. 2, nearly all the common PKE schemes (e.g., ElGamal, Cramer-Shoup, Kyber) are inherently ciphertext-simulatable (CS), which demonstrates the superiority of our scheme in availability. Besides, the notation 2^λ in the third column means that our scheme supports the inherent message space of the used PKE scheme, while [6,33] only admits encryption of bit under whatever methods, and [1] has encryption runtime being linearly dependent of the message space. Finally, our scheme for the first time considers the issue of SCA, along with some basic countermeasures, which is a fundamental guidance towards practical applications of DPKE.

OVERVIEW OF OUR TECHNIQUES. In the following, we provide more technical details of our contributions.

Generic Approach of DPKE. We begin with sketching CS-PKE (see the formal definition in Sect. 2.2), where an oblivious algorithm OEnc samples a random ciphertext ct_r relative to a public key using some randomness r, without knowing the corresponding plaintext. Its inverting algorithm IEnc, on inputting the original message and encryption randomness, simulates the above process by returning a simulated randomness r^*. Our core idea is to utilize the ability of interpreting an encryption as a randomly sampled one in CS-PKE to deceive the coercer. In this sense, we have to make sure that the receiver can distinguish between these two types of ciphertexts. Thus, we tag every ciphertext with an OWF ($\mathcal{H}$) value. Namely, the encryption of a message m is a pair $(\mathsf{Enc}(\mathsf{pk}, m\|u), \mathcal{H}(u))$, while the oblivious sample is $(\mathsf{ct}_r, \mathcal{H}(u))$, where u is a random nonce.

Then we give an abstract of the newly-designed bit-flipping framework. The main layout is that the encryption of a message m contains n sub-ciphertexts $\{\mathsf{ct}_i\}$ binding to the pattern of a random bit-string $s \in \{0,1\}^n$. In particular, for $s[i] = 0$, generate an obliviously sampled pair

$$c_i := (c_i^{(1)}, c_i^{(2)}) \leftarrow (\mathsf{OEnc}(\mathsf{pk}; r_i), \mathcal{H}(u_i)).$$

while for $s[i] = 1$, produce an honest encryption of message m_i as

$$c_i := (c_i^{(1)}, c_i^{(2)}) \leftarrow (\mathsf{Enc}(\mathsf{pk}, m\|u_i; r_i), \mathcal{H}(u_i)),$$

where m_i is random over the valid message space, except for one random index $t = \mathsf{select}(s; v)$ where select is a publicly random map into the "1"-set of the input string and v is an auxiliary nonce, m_t is the real message m. The final ciphertext ct for m is $(\{\mathsf{ct}_i\}, v)$. In this way, the receiver first decodes $\{\mathsf{ct}_i\}$ in sequence to recover s, i.e., set $s[i] = 1$ iff $c_i^{(2)}$ is the OWF image of u_i, which is decrypted from $c_i^{(1)}$; then locates the index $t = \mathsf{select}(s; v)$ to obtain the real message $m_t = m$. The negligible decryption error comes from that for "0"-mode pair, u_i will not be the preimage of $c_i^{(2)}$ due to the *one-wayness* of $\mathcal{H}$.

To fake, the sender first samples from $\mathsf{IEnc}(\mathsf{pk}, m, r_t)$ a simulated randomness r_t^*, which cloaks $c_t^{(1)}$ as a random sample from $\mathsf{OEnc}(\mathsf{pk}; r_t^*)$. Then she/he flips s_t from 1 to 0 to output a faking s^* and provides all the other original randomness $\{m_i, r_i, u_i\}$. In this way, the sender can explain ct as the encryption of m_{t^*} for $t^* = \mathsf{select}(s^*; v)$. Further, the detection probability of a coercer is scaled by the statistical difference of s and s^*, which is essentially the distance between random and one-bit-flipping sampling of a bit-string. We step forward to prove it is bounded by an inverse polynomial $\frac{1}{\sqrt{n}}$ in Theorem 1, thus our scheme shares the same security level of known schemes [1,6,8] from standard assumptions.

SCA *to Deniability*. We mainly consider the basic types of SCA (timing attacks [25] and simple power analysis [26]). The failure of deniability is based on a theoretical observation: there is an inherent disparity between fake opening and honesty of all the known schemes, e.g., the ways of sampling used randomness, the count of times that a subprogram is invoked. This disparity will result in the difference in operating time or power consumption within the encryption program. Then a coercer can first record such side-channel information during the execution of encryption, and demand the sender to rerun the encryption under the claimed randomness and plaintext, then detect the lie if the records of two operations have a significant change. Formally, we model the behaviors of a coercer as two steps: (passively) monitor to collect the target ciphertext ct and its SC information; (actively) coerce to obtain the internal plaintext and randomness, along with the fresh SC information.

Under the above enhanced coercion model, we examine most known DPKE schemes and ours, demonstrating that a *denial* of the original message can always be distinguished with polynomial overhead. To further evidence these theoretical conclusions, we instantiate the schemes of [6] and ours with ElGamal encryption, then compare the consumption of CPU cycles between the honest encryption and fake opening, the experiment results (Fig. 3) show the gap is stable and effective (mostly >54.6 μs). Finally, we provide some countermeasures to such SCA, i.e., we make encryption algorithm conduct some tiny redundancy operations, such that honesty and faking execute the very same instruction stream. Simulations on these updated schemes exhibit that now the variation of time/power consumption changes to be less than 10 ns (Fig. 4), meaning the fixing is indeed feasible. In summary, our work mounts the practical security of deniable encryption when applied in real-world systems.

ORGANIZATION. In the forthcoming sections, we first recall some necessary preliminaries in Sect. 2. Then we provide a generic approach of DPKE from ciphertext-simulatable PKE in Sect. 3. Finally Sect. 4 depicts how to break deniability of known schemes and ours under the SCA-enhanced coercion model, together with suitable countermeasures.

2   Preliminaries

In this section, we define the notation and preliminaries required in this work.

Notations. Let λ denote the security parameter throughout the paper. Function $f(\lambda)$ is said to be negligible if it is $\mathcal{O}(\lambda^{-c})$ for all $c > 0$, and use $\mathsf{negl}(\lambda)$ to denote such a function of λ. $f(\lambda)$ is said to be polynomial if it is $\mathcal{O}(\lambda^{-c})$ for some constant $c > 0$, and use $\mathsf{ploy}(\lambda)$ to denote such a function of λ. Event X is said to occur with overwhelming probability in λ if $\Pr[\mathrm{X}] = 1 - \mathsf{negl}(\lambda)$. Let $\mathcal{F}(x; r)$ denote a randomized algorithm $\mathcal{F}$ runs on input x and randomness r.

Use $[n]$ to denote the integer set $\{1, \ldots, n\}$. Use bold lower-case letters (e.g., s) to denote a bit-string. For s, denote its i-th element as $s[i]$, the index of its $(j + 1)$-th "1" as $\mathsf{L}(s, j)$, its hamming weight as $\mathsf{w}(s)$, its decimal as $\mathsf{dec}(s)$, its 0 and 1-index sets as $\mathcal{S}_0$ and $\mathcal{S}_1$, respectively. For a finite set $\mathcal{X}$, denote by $x \leftarrow \mathcal{X}$ sampling x uniformly from $\mathcal{X}$, and by $y \leftarrow D$ sampling y according to the distribution D. The statistical Distance between two distributions D_1 and D_2 over $\mathcal{X}$ is $\mathsf{SD}(D_1, D_2) = \frac{1}{2} \sum_{x \in \mathcal{S}} |D_1(x) - D_2(x)|$.

2.1   Sender-Deniable Public Key Encryption

We first recall the model of sender-deniable public key encryption introduced in [6], such a scheme $\mathcal{DE} = (\mathsf{KGen}, \mathsf{Enc}, \mathsf{Dec}, \mathsf{Fake})$ has the following syntax:

- KGen(1^λ) → (pk, sk): With the security parameter λ, generate the public and secret key pair (pk, sk).
- Enc(pk, m; r): On inputting the public key pk and a message m, use randomness r to produce a ciphertext ct.
- Dec(sk, ct): On inputting the secret key sk and a ciphertext ct, output a message m or $\bot$.
- Fake(pk, m, r, m^*): On inputting the public key pk, original message m, randomness r, and a fake message m^*, output a fake randomness r^*.

Correctness. $\mathcal{DE}$ is correct if, for any security parameter λ, message m, (pk, sk) ← KGen(1^λ), it holds that $\Pr\left[\mathsf{Dec}(\mathsf{sk}, \mathsf{Enc}(\mathsf{pk}, m; r)) = m\right] = 1 - \mathsf{negl}(\lambda)$.

Definition 1 (IND-CPA). *$\mathcal{DE}$ is IND-CPA secure if for all PPT adversary $\mathcal{A}$, the absolute difference of probability of outputting 1 between experiment* $\mathbf{Exp}_{\mathcal{A}}^{\mathsf{CPA}-0}$ *and* $\mathbf{Exp}_{\mathcal{A}}^{\mathsf{CPA}-1}$ *is negligible.*

Experiment: $\mathbf{Exp}_{\mathcal{A}}^{\mathsf{CPA}-b}(\lambda)$

(pk, sk) ← KGen(1^λ).
(m_0, m_1, st) ← $\mathcal{A}_1$(pk).
Compute ct ← Enc(pk, m_b; r), return ct to $\mathcal{A}$.
$b' \leftarrow \mathcal{A}_2$(pk, ct, st). Output b'.

Definition 2 (Deniability). *$\mathcal{DE}$ satisfies deniability if for any PPT adversary $\mathcal{A}$, the absolute difference of probability of outputting 1 between experiment* $\mathbf{Exp}_{\mathcal{A}}^{\mathsf{De}-0}$ *and* $\mathbf{Exp}_{\mathcal{A}}^{\mathsf{De}-1}$ *is negligible.*

Experiment: $\mathbf{Exp}_{\mathcal{A}}^{\mathsf{De}-b}(\lambda)$

(pk, sk) ← KGen(1^λ).
(m, m^*, st) ← $\mathcal{A}_1$(pk).
Sample r and $r^* \leftarrow$ Fake(pk, m, r, m^*).
If $b = 0$: return $D_0 = (m^*, r, \mathsf{Enc}(\mathsf{pk}, m^*; r))$ to $\mathcal{A}$.
Else if $b = 1$: return $D_1 = (m^*, r^*, \mathsf{Enc}(\mathsf{pk}, m; r))$ to $\mathcal{A}$.
$b' \leftarrow \mathcal{A}_2$(pk, D_b, st). Output b'.

2.2 Ciphertext-Simulatable Public Key Encryption

Ciphertext-simulatable PKE is a relaxed version of simulatable PKE [15], in the sense that 1) it only admits the oblivious sampling of ciphertexts; 2) the corresponding inverting algorithm additionally takes the encryption-used plaintext and randomness as input to return a randomness relative to oblivious sampling.

Formally, such PKE consists of universal algorithms (KGen, Enc, Dec), augmented with (OEnc, IEnc) for obliviously sampling and inverting ciphertexts:

- OEnc(pk; r_o): On inputting the public key pk, use randomness r_o to sample a ciphertext ct.
- IEnc(pk, m, r_e): On inputting the public key pk, message m, randomness r_e used in the original encryption, output a randomness r_o^*.

Definition 3 (Ciphertext-Simulatability [13,15]). *For CS-PKE, it holds that for all PPT distinguisher $\mathcal{D}$, message m, public key* pk $\leftarrow$ KGen(1^λ),

$$\Big| \Pr[\mathcal{D}(\mathsf{Enc}(\mathsf{pk}, m; r_e), \mathsf{IEnc}(\mathsf{pk}, m, r_e)) = 1] - \Pr[\mathcal{D}(\mathsf{OEnc}(\mathsf{pk}; r_o), r_o) = 1] \Big| \leq \mathsf{negl}(\lambda).$$

As noted in [13,32], ciphertext-simulatability implies IND-CPA. Besides, the ongoing works [13,15,16,28,32] have shown that simulatable encryption can be realized from nearly all the standard cryptographic assumptions, e.g., DDH (ElGamal and Cramer-Shoup), RSA (PKE from RSA-based trapdoor permutations), as well as worst-case lattice assumptions (LWE-based encryptions), these results also apply to ciphertext-simulatable PKE as it is a weaker variant.

3   Generic Construction of DPKE

In this section, we give the generic approach of DPKE from any ciphertext-simulatable PKE scheme. The sketchy roadmap is: first sample a uniform random bit-string s, then use another randomness v to select a random index t of "1" in s and encrypt m at t. For $i \in \mathcal{S}_1 \setminus \{t\}$, encrypt a random message m_i; otherwise, obliviously sample a random cipher. In particular, all the encryptions are operated on the message plus a random tag, whose evaluation of an OWF is also dispatched. In this way, the receiver could decrypt all the n ciphers to reassemble s, so as to locate the index t binding to m. To fake, the sender flips s_t to obtain a fake string s^* and index t^*, then invert-samples c_t as a random pair, so to interpret the ciphertext as the encryption of the fake message m_{t^*}.

The faking probability of this design mainly hinges on the statistical distance between s and s^*. Thus, below we first clarify how flipping one bit influences the randomness of a string, then give the description and analysis of our scheme.

3.1   Warm-Up: Bit Flipping

We consider the issue of the remaining randomness of a made string from flipping a "1" of a random string. Specifically, we prove that s and s^* are within an inverse polynomial distance, as the following theorem shows.

Theorem 1 (Randomness of bit-flipping). *Given two distributions U and F for a bit-string, the first is the uniformly random sampling from the finite set $\mathcal{S} = \{0,1\}^n$, and the latter is the flipping case where it first samples s from $\mathcal{S}$, if $s = 0^n$, outputs $\perp$; else it outputs a string from randomly flipping one bit in s from 1 to 0. The statistical distance between U and F is $\Theta(\frac{1}{\sqrt{n}})$.*

Proof. W.l.o.g, assume $n = 2m + 1$. Consider the count k of 1 of s, i.e., $\sum_{i=1}^n x[i] = k$ for $k \in [0, n]$, then the probability of s for each k in R is $\frac{1}{2^n} \cdot \binom{n}{k}$; The probability $F(s)$ is more complicated. Observe that s must be obtained by flipping a "1" (indexed as i) of a string s' from $\mathcal{S}$ whose count of "1" is $k+1$. Thus, there are $n - k$ possible s' when fixing s. Further, the probability of flipping $s[i]$ in s' is $\frac{1}{k+1}$. Therefore, we get $F(s) = \frac{1}{2^n} \cdot \binom{n}{k} \frac{n-k}{k+1}$ and the following equation:

$$
\begin{aligned}
\mathsf{SD}(U, F) &= \frac{1}{2} \cdot \sum_{x \in \mathcal{S}} |U(x) - F(x)| + \frac{1}{2} \cdot F(\bot) \\
&= \frac{1}{2} \cdot \sum_{k=0}^{n} \left| \frac{1}{2^n} \binom{n}{k} \left(1 - \frac{n-k}{k+1} \right) \right| + \frac{1}{2^{n+1}} \\
&= \frac{1}{2^{n+1}} \cdot \left(\sum_{k=m+1}^{n} \binom{n}{k} \left(1 - \frac{n-k}{k+1} \right) + \sum_{k=0}^{m} \binom{n}{k} \left(\frac{n-k}{k+1} - 1 \right) + 1 \right).
\end{aligned}
$$

Note that $\frac{n-k}{k+1} = 1$ for $k = m$ and $\binom{n}{k} = \binom{n}{n-k}$, thus the above equation can be further simplified into

$$
\begin{aligned}
\mathsf{SD}(U, F) &= \frac{1}{2^{n+1}} \cdot \left(\sum_{k=0}^{m} \binom{n}{k} \left(\frac{n-k}{k+1} - \frac{k}{n-k+1} \right) + 1 \right) \\
&= \frac{1}{2^{n+1}} \cdot \left(n + \left(\sum_{k=1}^{m} \binom{n}{k+1} - \binom{n}{k-1} \right) + 1 \right) \qquad (1) \\
&= \frac{1}{2^n} \cdot \binom{n}{m}.
\end{aligned}
$$

By applying Stirling's approximation, we obtain $\mathsf{SD}(U, F) \approx \frac{1}{\sqrt{\pi n}} = \Theta(\frac{1}{\sqrt{n}})$. $\square$

In Appendix A, we further prove the optimality of the above one-bit flipping case, i.e., it reserves the most randomness of s under all the possible flipping manners.

3.2 The New Framework

The underlying methods are an OWF $\mathcal{H} : \mathcal{U} \to \{0,1\}^{\ell_t}$ for $\mathcal{U} = \{0,1\}^{\ell_h}$, and a ciphertext-simulatable PKE $\mathcal{E}$ with message space $\mathcal{M}' = \{0,1\}^{\ell_{m'}}$ where $\ell_{m'} = \ell_m + \ell_h$, randomness space $\mathcal{R}_e \subset \{0,1\}^{\ell_e}$ and $\mathcal{R}_o \subset \{0,1\}^{\ell_o}$ for encryption and oblivious sampling, respectively, w.l.o.g., we assume $\mathcal{R}_o = \mathcal{R}_e = \mathcal{R}$. For ease of notation, we suppress the polynomial dependence on λ of the associated parameters. Our framework of DPKE $\mathcal{DE}$ for message space $\mathcal{M} = \{0,1\}^{\ell_m}$ is as follows:

- KGen(1^λ): Sample (pk, sk) $\leftarrow \mathcal{E}$.KGen(1^λ), and output dpk := pk, dsk := sk.
- Enc(dpk, m): Upon inputting dpk and $m \in \mathcal{M}$, conduct the following:
  1. Sample $s, v \leftarrow \{0,1\}^n$. Abort if $s = 0^n$; Else, determine the index $t = \mathsf{L}(s, \mathsf{dec}(v) \bmod \mathsf{w}(s))$.
  2. For $i \in [n]$: sample $r_i \leftarrow \mathcal{R}, u_i \leftarrow \mathcal{U}$; further if $i \in \mathcal{S}_1$, sample $m_i \leftarrow \mathcal{M}$, except that take $m_t = m$ for $i = t$. The internal randomness is

  $$
  \mathsf{Rand} := (s, \{m_i\}_{i \in \mathcal{S}_1 \setminus \{t\}}, \{r_i, u_i\}_{i \in [n]}).
  $$

3. Finally, generate n ciphertexts $\{c_i\}_{i \in [n]}$ under the pattern of s:
   ① If $i \in \mathcal{S}_0$, set the masking ciphertext as

$$c_i := (c_i^{(1)}, c_i^{(2)}) \leftarrow (\mathcal{E}.\mathsf{OEnc}.(\mathsf{pk}; r_i), \mathcal{H}(u_i)). \tag{1}$$

   ② Else, produce the real encryption of m_i as

$$c_i := (c_i^{(1)}, c_i^{(2)}) \leftarrow (\mathcal{E}.\mathsf{Enc}(\mathsf{pk}, m_i \| u_i; r_i), \mathcal{H}(u_i)). \tag{2}$$

4. Output $\mathsf{dct} := (\{c_i\}_{i \in [n]}, v)$.
- $\mathsf{Dec}(\mathsf{dsk}, \mathsf{dct})$: Parse dct as $(c_1, \ldots, c_n, v)$, for $i \in [n]$, do the following:
  1. Run $\overline{m}_i := \mathcal{E}.\mathsf{Dec}(\mathsf{dsk}, c_i^{(1)})$. If $\overline{m}_i = \perp$, set $e[i] = 0$ and move to $i := i + 1$;
  2. Parse $\overline{m}_i$ as $m_i \| u_i$, set $e[i] = 1$ if $\mathcal{H}(u_i) \stackrel{?}{=} c_i^{(2)}$, or 0 otherwise.
  Output $\perp$ if $\mathsf{w}(e) = 0$. Else, compute $t_e = \mathsf{L}(e, \mathsf{dec}(v) \bmod \mathsf{w}(e))$, and output $m := m_{t_e}$.
- $\mathsf{Fake}(\mathsf{dpk}, m, \mathsf{Rand}, m^*)$: Upon inputting the public key dpk, real message m and used randomness Rand, along with the fake message $m^* \in \{m_i\}_{i \in \mathcal{S}_1 \setminus \{t\}}$, conduct as follows to produce a fake randomness Rand^*:
  1. If $m^* = m$, output $\mathsf{Rand}^* = \mathsf{Rand}$.
  2. Else, set $s^* = (\ldots s[t-1]\ 0\ s[t+1] \ldots)$ and $t^* = \mathsf{L}(s^*, \mathsf{dec}(v) \bmod \mathsf{w}(s^*))$.
  3. For $i \in [n]$: if $i = t$, generate $r_i^* := \mathcal{E}.\mathsf{IEnc}(\mathsf{pk}, m, r_i)$ and set $u_i^* = u_i$; else, set $r_i^* = r_i$ and $u_i^* = u_i$, additionally set $m_i^* = m_i$ if $i \in \mathcal{S}_1 \setminus \{t^*\}$.
  4. Return $\mathsf{Rand}^* = (s^*, \{m_i^*\}_{i \in \mathcal{S}_1 \setminus \{t, t^*\}}, \{r_i^*, u_i^*\}_{i \in [n]})$.

Remark 1. The above scheme is pre-planning, in the sense that the sender must choose the fake message m_{t^*} at the beginning of the encryption.

Theorem 2. *Suppose that $\mathcal{E}$ is correct and $\mathcal{H}$ is one-way, then $\mathcal{DE}$ is correct.*

Proof. We prove the correctness of $\mathcal{DE}$ by showing that the recovered e in Dec is the exact s used in Enc. Note that for any honestly generated ciphertext $\mathsf{dct} : \{c_i\}$, it holds that for $i \in [n]$:

1. If $i \in \mathcal{S}_1$, c_i is produced as Eq. (2), the honest encryption of m_i, then by *correctness* of $\mathcal{E}$ we have that $\mathcal{E}.\mathsf{Dec}(\mathsf{dsk}, c_i^{(1)})$ is equal to $m_i \| u_i$, thus $\mathcal{H}(u_i) = c_i^{(2)}$ and so $e[i] = s[i] = 1$.
2. If $i \in \mathcal{S}_0$, c_i is generated as Eq. (1) from oblivious sampling. Below we expound that if $e[i]$ is assigned as 0 with non-negligible probability ϵ, then we can break the one-wayness of $\mathcal{H}$ with the same probability ϵ. A PPT adversary $\mathcal{A}$ first generates $(\mathsf{pk}_\mathcal{A}, \mathsf{sk}_\mathcal{A}) \leftarrow \mathcal{E}.\mathsf{KGen}(1^\lambda)$, then produces a random cipher $c_\mathcal{A} \leftarrow \mathcal{E}.\mathsf{OEnc}(\mathsf{pk}_\mathcal{A}; r)$. Next, $\mathcal{A}$ requests a challenge for the one-wayness game and receives $\mathcal{H}(u)$ for random $u \in \mathcal{U}$, and decrypts $c_\mathcal{A}$ as $\overline{m}_\mathcal{A}$ using $\mathsf{sk}_\mathcal{A}$. If $\overline{m}_\mathcal{A} = \perp$, $\mathcal{A}$ also outputs $\perp$ and aborts. Else, $\mathcal{A}$ parses $\overline{m}_\mathcal{A}$ as $m' \| u'$ and outputs u'. Note that $(c_\mathcal{A}, \mathcal{H}(u))$ is generated in the same way as Eq. (1), meaning the success of $\mathcal{A}$ in the one-wayness game of $\mathcal{H}$ (i.e., $\mathcal{H}(u') = \mathcal{H}(u)$) is equivalent to assigning $e[i]$ to 1 in this sub-case.

After the above analysis, we have $e = s$ holds with overwhelming probability, so $t_e = t = \mathsf{L}(s, \mathsf{dec}(v) \bmod \mathsf{w}(s))$ and $\mathcal{DE}.\mathsf{Dec}$ always outputs $m_{t_e} = m$. □

3.3   Security Analysis

Below we prove $\mathcal{DE}$ satisfies $IND\text{-}CPA$ and $\frac{1}{\sqrt{n}}$-$deniability$.

Theorem 3. *Suppose that $\mathcal{E}$ is IND-CPA, then $\mathcal{DE}$ is IND-CPA.*

Proof. We prove *CPA security* by contradiction. Suppose that $\mathcal{A}$ succeeds in $\mathbf{Exp}_{\mathcal{A}}^{\mathsf{CPA}-b}$ of $\mathcal{DE}$ with probability $\frac{1}{2} + \epsilon$ for non-negligible ϵ, then we can build a PPT algorithm $\mathcal{B}$ that breaks *CPA security* of $\mathcal{E}$ with also advantage ϵ. Let $(\mathsf{pk}, \mathsf{sk}) \leftarrow \mathcal{E}.\mathsf{KGen}(1^\lambda)$, given pk, $\mathcal{B}$ plays with $\mathcal{A}$ as follows:

- **Setup.** $\mathcal{B}$ sends $\mathsf{dpk} := \mathsf{pk}$ to $\mathcal{A}$.
- **Challenge.** $\mathcal{A}$ picks two different messages $m_0, m_1 \leftarrow \mathcal{M}$ and submits them to $\mathcal{B}$. Then $\mathcal{B}$ samples $u \leftarrow \mathcal{U}$ and sends $(m_0\|u, m_1\|u)$ to the challenger. In this way, the challenger flips a random coin $b \in \{0,1\}$, picks randomness $r \leftarrow \mathcal{R}$ and outputs a challenging ciphertext $c \leftarrow \mathsf{Enc}(\mathsf{pk}, m_b\|u; r)$. Finally, $\mathcal{B}$ performs as $\mathcal{DE}.\mathsf{Enc}$ to produce the trick ciphertexts for $\mathcal{A}$ as follows:
  1. Pick $s, v \leftarrow \{0,1\}^n$. Abort if $s = 0^n$; Else, set $t = \mathsf{L}(s, \mathsf{dec}(v) \bmod \mathsf{w}(s))$.
  2. Set $c_t := (c, \mathcal{H}(u))$, and for $i \in [n] \setminus t$, do the following:
     ① If $i \in \mathcal{S}_0$, pick $r_i, u_i \leftarrow \mathcal{R} \times \mathcal{U}$ and obtain $c_i \leftarrow (\mathcal{E}.\mathsf{OEnc}.(\mathsf{pk}; r_i), \mathcal{H}(u_i))$.
     ② Else, sample $m_i \leftarrow \mathcal{M}$ and $r_i, u_i \leftarrow \mathcal{R} \times \mathcal{U}$, then generate $c_i \leftarrow (\mathcal{E}.\mathsf{Enc} (\mathsf{pk}, m_i\|u_i; r_i), \mathcal{H}(u_i))$.
  3. Return $\mathsf{dct} = (c_1, \ldots, c_n, v)$ to $\mathcal{A}$.
- **Guess.** $\mathcal{A}$ outputs a guess bit b', $\mathcal{B}$ also outputs b' as the guess of b.

From the above construction, we know that the only difference between the distributions of $\mathbf{Exp}_{\mathcal{A}}^{\mathsf{CPA}-0}$ and $\mathbf{Exp}_{\mathcal{A}}^{\mathsf{CPA}-1}$ is the target ciphertext c. Thus, the fact that $\mathcal{A}$ wins with probability $\frac{1}{2} + \epsilon$ implies that $\mathcal{B}$'s advantage of breaking *CPA security* of $\mathcal{E}$ is also ϵ, which concludes the proof.   □

Theorem 4. $\mathcal{DE}$ *is* $\frac{1}{\sqrt{n}}$-*deniable.*

Proof. Let $\mathcal{A}$ and $\mathcal{B}$ be PPT algorithms, playing the role of adversary and challenger in $\mathbf{Exp}_{\mathcal{A}}^{\mathsf{De}-b}$, respectively. For a fake claim under coercion, consider the following hybrid games, where R_i is the output of the adversary in game i.

Game 0. This is the honest encryption case, the distribution from $\mathcal{A}$'s view is

$$D_0 = (\mathsf{dpk}, m^*, \mathsf{Rand}, \mathsf{ct}_0),$$

where $\mathsf{ct}_0 \leftarrow \mathcal{DE}.\mathsf{Enc}(\mathsf{dpk}, m^*; \mathsf{Rand}, v)$, Rand and v are sampled as follows:

1. Pick $s, v \leftarrow \{0,1\}^n$. Abort if $s = 0^n$; Else, set $t = \mathsf{L}(s, \mathsf{dec}(v) \bmod \mathsf{w}(s))$.
2. For $i \in [n]$: sample $r_i \leftarrow \mathcal{R}, u_i \leftarrow \mathcal{U}$; further if $i \in \mathcal{S}_1$, sample $m_i \leftarrow \mathcal{M}$, except that take $m_t = m$ for $i = t$.
3. Return $\mathsf{Rand} := (s, \{m_i\}_{i \in \mathcal{S}_1 \setminus \{t\}}, \{r_i, u_i\}_{i \in [n]})$ and v.

Game 1. This game turns to generate the randomness Rand' and v as follows:

1. Select $s, v \leftarrow \{0,1\}^n$. Abort if $s = 0^n$; Else, set $t = \mathsf{L}(s, \mathsf{dec}(v) \bmod \mathsf{w}(s))$.
2. Flip s into $s' = (\ldots s_{t-1} 0 s_{t+1} \ldots)$, if $s' = 0^n$, which occurs with negligible probability $\frac{n}{2^n}$, abort; else, set $t' = \mathsf{L}(s', \mathsf{dec}(v) \bmod \mathsf{w}(s'))$.
3. For $i \in [n]$: sample $r'_i \leftarrow \mathcal{R}, u'_i \leftarrow \mathcal{U}$, further if $i \in \mathcal{S}'_1 \setminus \{t'\}$, sample $m'_i \leftarrow \mathcal{M}$.
4. Return $\mathsf{Rand}' := (s', \{m'_i\}_{i \in \mathcal{S}'_1 \setminus \{t'\}}, \{r'_i, u'_i\}_{i \in [n]})$ and v.

In this way, the output distribution from $\mathcal{A}$'s view is

$$D_1 = (\mathsf{dpk}, m^*, \mathsf{Rand}', \mathsf{ct}_1),$$

where $\mathsf{ct}_1 \leftarrow \mathcal{DE}.\mathsf{Enc}(\mathsf{dpk}, m^*; \mathsf{Rand}', v)$. Note D_0 and D_1 only differ in the random seed s and s'. Further, the distance between the distribution of s' and F in Theorem 1 is at most $\frac{n}{2^n}$, which is exactly the maximum difference between selecting the flipping index t from random and as $\mathsf{L}(s', \mathsf{dec}(v) \bmod \mathsf{w}(s'))$. In this sense, we conclude that $\mathsf{SD}(s, s')$ is $\Theta(\frac{1}{\sqrt{n}})$. Hence, it holds that $\Pr[R_1 = 1] - \Pr[\mathbf{Exp}_{\mathcal{A}}^{\mathsf{De}-0} = 1] \leq \Theta(\frac{1}{\sqrt{n}})$.

Game 2. This is the faking case, the distribution from $\mathcal{A}$'s view is

$$D_2 = (\mathsf{dpk}, m^*, \mathsf{Rand}^*, \mathsf{ct}_2),$$

where $\mathsf{ct}_2 \leftarrow \mathcal{DE}.\mathsf{Enc}(\mathsf{dpk}, m; \mathsf{Rand}, v)$, the real randomness Rand and v are sampled in the same way as that in Game 0, while the fake randomness Rand^* is sampled as $\mathcal{DE}.\mathsf{Fake}$ operates:

1. Set $s^* = (\ldots s[t-1] 0 s[t+1] \ldots)$ and $t^* = \mathsf{L}(s^*, \mathsf{dec}(v) \bmod \mathsf{w}(s^*))$.
2. For $i \in [n]$: if $i = t$, generate $r^*_i := \mathcal{E}.\mathsf{IEnc}(\mathsf{pk}, m, r_i)$ and set $u_i = u_i$; Else, set $r^*_i = r_i$ and $u^*_i = u_i$, additionally set $m^*_i = m_i$ if $i \in \mathcal{S}_1 \setminus \{t^*\}$.
3. Return $\mathsf{Rand}^* = (s^*, \{m^*_i\}_{i \in \mathcal{S}_1 \setminus \{t, t^*\}}, \{r^*_i, u^*_i\}_{i \in [n]})$.

After the above steps, ct_2 can also be explained as $\mathcal{DE}.\mathsf{Enc}(\mathsf{dpk}, m^*; \mathsf{Rand}^*)$. Therefore, the only difference between D_1 and D_2 is the fake randomness Rand^* and Rand'. To evaluate this distance, consider their components:

a). s is uniformly random over $\{0,1\}^n$, s^* is indeed sampled from one-bit flipping frame F. Thus, $\mathsf{SD}(s, s^*) \leq \frac{n}{2^n} = \mathsf{negl}(\lambda)$, as the above game scales.
b). All the masking messages and the relative randomness are uniformly random over $\mathcal{M} \times \mathcal{R} \times \mathcal{U}$, for $i \in [n] \setminus t$.
c). r^*_t from $\mathcal{E}.\mathsf{IEnc}$ is computationally indistinguishable from $r'_t \in \mathcal{R}$, both u^*_t and u'_t are uniformly random over $\mathcal{U}$.

The above shows Rand^* and Rand' are computationally indistinguishable from each other. Hence, it holds that $\Pr[R_1 = 1] - \Pr[\mathbf{Exp}_{\mathcal{A}}^{\mathsf{De}-1} = 1] = \mathsf{negl}(\lambda)$.

Taking in all the cases, we have $\Pr[\mathbf{Exp}_{\mathcal{A}}^{\mathsf{De}-1} = 1] - \Pr[\mathbf{Exp}_{\mathcal{A}}^{\mathsf{De}-0} = 1] \leq \Theta(\frac{1}{\sqrt{n}})$, so the theorem holds. $\qquad\square$

4 SCA on Deniable Encryption

As noted in Sect. 1, none of the existing DPKE considers the issue of SCA. In this section, we make an initial attempt towards leakage-resilient DPKE. We begin with formalizing the SCA-equipped coercion model for timing and simple power attacks [25, 26, 29, 34], then show how such SCA could break deniability of known schemes and ours, along with giving some heuristic countermeasures.

4.1 SCA-Equipped Coercion Model

In the original attack model [6], the coercer *Eve* first intercepts a dispatched package (ciphertext) from the sender *Alice*, then obtains the claimed plaintext and randomness from *Alice*. In this sense, deniability (Definition 2) asks that *Eve* has no extra advantage in distinguishing between the honest and fake opening. Now, *Eve* can resort to SCA when performing attacks. In particular, *Eve* can additionally collect the SC information (time or power consumption) about the operations of the original encryption and that under the claimed data. Below we formalize this enhanced coercion model for *Eve*.

Definition 4 (SCA-Coercion Model). *For any deniable public key encryption system, a coercer can perform the following attack steps on a system user:*

1. *Passively capture the transmitted ciphertext* ct *and SC information* T *(e.g., time or power consumption) of the encryption execution that produces* ct;
2. *Actively demand the internal message* m *and randomness* r *relative to* ct *and collect new SC information* $\overline{T}$ *of the encryption execution on feeding* (m, r).

Remark 2. We assume that there are no external operations, e.g., ones profiled in more advanced trace [31] or collision attacks [24], are to be executed in running deniable encryption. Besides, to avoid systematic error, a coercer may demand the posterior SC information $\text{poly}(\lambda)$ times.

4.2 Break Deniability of Known Schemes

Below we depict how deniable schemes can be breached under the above enhanced hostile model. The core point is that we observe the internal instruction lines take on some constant difference between the original call of encryption and that of fake opening, which will result in the perceptible gap between T and $\overline{T}$. In this sense, the coercer can use such flavor of distinguishability to tell if a user is lying, details of these attacks to the known schemes are as follows:

- *Translucent-set-based.* Note that the instantiations (e.g., trapdoor permutation [6], simulatable encryption, or lattice-based methods [32]) of translucent set $\mathcal{S}$, are much more complicated than the uniform random set $\mathcal{R}$ which can be built-in. Based on this fact, sampling from $\mathcal{S}$ always takes more operation than sampling from $\mathcal{R}$, indicating more time or power is consumed. Then the coercer can tell that the sender is lying if T is statistically higher than $\overline{T}$. More specifically, consider the pioneering work [6] (Fig. 1) for bit encryption.

– The sender encodes the bit into the parity of the number i of $\mathcal{S}$-elements. To fake, the sender just claims to have chosen $i' = i - 1$. Then the count of $\mathcal{S}$-elements during the rerun of encryption always decreases by 1. Hence, the coercer can first get the prior value $\mathcal{T}$ and many posterior values $\{\overline{\mathcal{T}}\}$, and decides that the claimed randomness is fake if the percentage of $\{\overline{\mathcal{T}}\}$ which is lower than $\mathcal{T}$ is significant, e.g., $>80\%$.

Notations: $\mathcal{R} = \{0,1\}^t$; translucent set $\mathcal{S} \subset \{0,1\}^t$; $\mathcal{S}$'s trapdoor $d_{\mathcal{S}}$

$\mathsf{Enc}(\mathcal{S}, m)$: For $m = 0$ (resp., $m = 1$), pick a random even (resp., odd) number $i \in [n]$, sample $s_1, \ldots, s_i \leftarrow \mathcal{S}$ and $r_{i+1}, \ldots, r_\lambda \leftarrow \mathcal{R}$, output $\mathsf{ct} := (s_1, \ldots, s_i, r_{i+1}, \ldots, r_\lambda)$.

$\mathsf{Dec}(\mathcal{S}, d_{\mathcal{S}}, \mathsf{ct})$: Output the parity of the number of $\mathcal{S}$-element in ct via $d_{\mathcal{S}}$.

$\mathsf{Fake}(\mathcal{S}, m, i, \overline{m})$: If $i = 0$, cheating fail, otherwise output $i - 1$.

Fig. 1. Sketch of the scheme in [6].

- *iO-based* [33]. From Fig. 2, we know that the honest encryption executes step 3 of Encrypt which is a call of the underlying PKE, while the faking randomness leads to step 2 which are just two evaluations of two PRFs. This fact implies that the prior time or power consumption $\mathcal{T}$ is always higher than the posterior one $\overline{\mathcal{T}}$ even under the obfuscated setting (recall that $i\mathcal{O}$ only ensures the obfuscated programs for circuits of the same size and functionality are indistinguishable). Thus, the coercer could apply the same strategy as above, i.e., demand τ posterior values $\{\overline{\mathcal{T}}\}$ with respect to the claimed data $(\overline{m}, r')$ and identify the lie if 80% of $\{\overline{\mathcal{T}}\}$ is lower than $\mathcal{T}$.

Notations: PKE scheme $\mathcal{E}' = \{\mathsf{KGen}, \mathsf{Enc}, \mathsf{Dec}\}$; Puncturable PRFs F_1, F_2, F_3

$\mathsf{DKGen}(1^\lambda)$: Let $(\mathsf{pk}, \mathsf{sk}) \leftarrow \mathsf{KGen}(1^\lambda)$, $P_{enc} = i\mathcal{O}(\mathsf{Encrypt})$, $P_{exp} = i\mathcal{O}(\mathsf{Explain})$, output $\mathsf{dpk} = (P_{enc}, P_{exp})$ and $\mathsf{dsk} = \mathsf{sk}$.
$\mathsf{DEnc}(\mathsf{dpk}, m)$: Sample $r \leftarrow \{0,1\}^{\mathsf{poly}(\lambda)}$, output $\mathsf{dct} \leftarrow P_{enc}(m, r)$.
$\mathsf{DDec}(\mathsf{dsk}, \mathsf{dct})$: Output $m := \mathsf{Dec}(\mathsf{dsk}, \mathsf{dct})$.
$\mathsf{Fake}(\mathsf{dpk}, m, r, \overline{m})$: Output $r' \leftarrow P_{exp}(\mathsf{dct}, m, r)$.

Algorithm $\mathsf{Encrypt}(m, r)$	Algorithm $\mathsf{Explain}(c,m,r)$
1. Parse $r = r_1 \| r_2$. 2. If $F_3(r_1) \oplus r_2 = m\|c\|r'$ and $r_1 = F_2(m\|c\|r')$, output c and stop. 3. Output $c \leftarrow \mathsf{Enc}(\mathsf{pk}, m; F_1(m\|r))$.	– Set $\alpha = F_2(m\|c\|PRG(r))$, $\beta = F_3(\alpha) \oplus m\|c\|PRG(r)$, output $\alpha\|\beta$.

Fig. 2. Sketch of the schemes in [33].

- *FHE-based.* The FHE-based design for bits [1] modifies the line of [6] via building a biased decryption to "0" on random input, while it still encodes the bit message into the parity of the count i of "1"-encryptions in the final ciphertext. To fake, the sender reveals $i' = i - 1$ by randomly interpreting one of "1"-encryptions into "0"-encryption. Further, compared with a "1"-encryption that needs several homomorphic evaluations, a "0"-encryption is done by a random sampling, thus the time consumption of dishonest opening must be less than that of the honest case, implying $\mathcal{T}$ is always higher than $\overline{\mathcal{T}}$.
- *Our schemes.* The issue of $\mathcal{DE}$ is akin to that of [6]. Encryption at "1" invokes a more time (power)-consuming call of the encryption of the underlying CS-PKE, than the single oblivious sampling for encryption at "0". To fake, the sender reveals $\boldsymbol{s}^*$, whose count of "1" always decreases by 1 than that of the real $\boldsymbol{s}$, leading to $\overline{\mathcal{T}}$ being lower than $\mathcal{T}$ with overwhelming probability.

Experimental Results. To evidence that the above attacks are workable, we instantiate the scheme of [6] and ours with ElGamal over $\mathbb{Z}_q$ in Python on the Intel Kaby Lake i7-7700T processor, where we use CPU instruction "rdtsc" to compute the consumption of clock cycles (3.6 GHz) for an encryption execution. More detailedly, for a TS, $\mathcal{S}$-element is a triple $(m, c_1, c_2) \in \mathbb{Z}_q^3$ where (c_1, c_2) is the ElGamal encryption of m, and $\mathcal{R}$-element a random triple over $\mathbb{Z}_q^3$; Our scheme is derived from the ciphertext-simulatability of ElGamal, i.e., OEnc outputs $(c_1, c_2) \leftarrow \mathbb{Z}_q^2$ and IEnc trivially simulates sampling over $\mathbb{Z}_q^2$ (see [15]).

For parameters, we set $\lambda = 128, \log q = 2048, \ell_h = 1024, \ell_t = 512, \ell_m = 1024$, OWF $\mathcal{H}$ as SHA3-512. Then for detecting probability $n = 2^{2k}, k \in [5, 15]$, we take 10^3 times of random encryption execution for both schemes, and term one execution as a success for a coercer if $\mathcal{T} - \overline{\mathcal{T}} \geq \mu + \delta$ ms, where $\mu = 0.0506$ is the expected difference of time consumption between one execution of ElGamal encryption and random sampling from $\mathbb{Z}_q^2$, and $\delta = 0.0040$ is the system error.

Table 2. Success probability (%) of SCA-equipped coercion attacks for different n. **I**: scheme in [6]. **II**: our scheme.

$\log n$	10	12	14	16	18	20	22	24	26	28	30
*succ_prob_*I	87.2	91.0	94.6	91.7	96.6	94.3	92.7	82.5	94.6	91.8	94.2
*cont_prob_*I	3.7	3.4	8.3	5.6	9.2	3.5	1.1	1.3	7.4	4.1	7.3
*succ_prob_*II	92.4	99.5	88.1	80.8	92.3	90.6	86.7	90.2	83.0	91.4	95.1
*cont_prob_*II	8.3	1.5	6.7	12.6	2.1	11.3	6.5	3.8	9.0	10.9	1.2

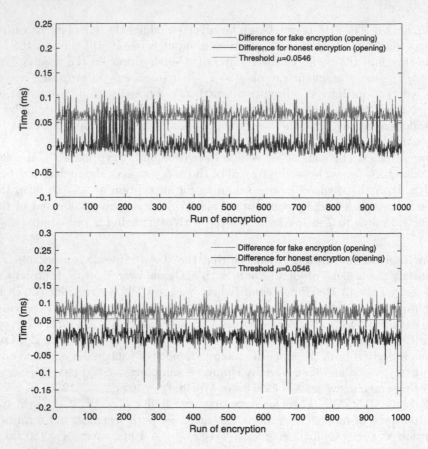

Fig. 3. Distributions of difference in time consumption for $n = 2^{30}$. **Top**: scheme in [6]. **Bottom**: our scheme.

Table 2 lists the running results of a simulated coercer who is equipped with SCA, rows "cont_prob I/II" represent the success probability for the control experiment where each $\overline{T}$ is recorded feeding the real randomness and plaintext used for encryption (i.e., the sender is honest). In particular, for $n = 2^{30}$, Fig. 3 shows the distributions of the difference in time consumption between the original call and the honest/fake opening (black/blue colored) of 10^3 encryption executions, where the trace for fake is apparently under the threshold $\mu = 0.0546$ ms, while the trace for honesty mainly fluctuates around the zero point[1]. Further, from Table 2, we learn that: 1) the success probability for a fake opening is significant ($>80\%$); 2) the success probability for an honest opening (the control group) is inappreciable ($<15\%$). Then we can conclude that the above-described

---

[1] Due to the page limits, we omit the graphics for other values of n that show the similar grades as that of $n = 2^{30}$.

attacks under the enhanced model (Definition 4) are practically effective, signi-fying the damage of deniability from SCA.

4.3 Feasible Therapies

One can take some random and functionless instructions on the hardware layer to perturb SC information. However, as noted in [25], such system noise can be compensated by collecting more records. A more substantial way is to add some redundancy operations into the original encryption algorithm, making hon-esty and faking execute the very same instruction stream, so to eliminate the difference in the context of SC knowledge. Below we give the concrete fixing:

- *Translucent-set-based.* To encrypt a bit m, first sample λ elements $\{s_i\}$ from $\mathcal{S}$ and λ elements $\{r_i\}$ from $\mathcal{R}$, then pick a random even (resp., odd) number $i \in [n]$ for $m = 0$ (resp., $m = 1$) and output $\mathsf{ct} := (s_1, \ldots, s_i, r_{i+1}, \ldots, r_\lambda)$.
- *iO-based.* Let step 2 of Encrypt in Fig. 2 additionally conduct a plain encryp-tion $\mathcal{E}.\mathsf{Enc}(\mathsf{pk}, m; \mathcal{F}_2.\mathsf{Eval}(\mathsf{k}_2, m\|r))$, which is exactly what step 3 executes.
- *FHE-based*: For the scheme [1], always produce n encryptions of bit 1 and sample n random elements from the ciphertext space of the underlying FHE.
- *Our scheme.* Both encryptions at "1" and "0" now conduct a plain encryption and an oblivious sampling. Namely, in algorithm Enc, step 3.① additionally performs $m_i \leftarrow \mathcal{M}, c_i^{(3)} \leftarrow \mathcal{E}.\mathsf{Enc}(\mathsf{pk}, m_i\|u_i; r_i)$, and step 3.① extraly runs $c_i^{(3)} \leftarrow \mathcal{E}.\mathsf{OEnc}.(\mathsf{pk}; r_i)$. The sender will not transmit the auxiliary ciphertexts $\{c_i^{(3)}\}$ and just keep the masks $(\{m_i\}_{i \in \mathcal{S}_0}, \{c_i^{(3)}\}_{i \in [n]})$ in her internal state.

To show the feasibility of these measures, we carry the above experiments to the upgraded variants of the scheme [6] and ours, and profile the results in Table 3 and Fig. 4 below, where we can learn that now the success probability for a fake opening is also reduced to be invisible ($<15\%$), and the time consumptions of honesty and fake are almost the same as that of the original encryption (both traces fluctuate around zero). These facts testify that the redundancy operations really conceal the difference in SC information between the honest encryption and fake opening, so that *deniability* is maintained.

Table 3. Success probability (%) of SCA-equipped coercion attacks for different n. **I**: upgraded variant of scheme in [6]. **II**: upgraded variant of our scheme.

$\log n$	10	12	14	16	18	20	22	24	26	28	30
*succ_prob_*I	1.1	0.8	3.7	4.8	8.5	1.2	5.3	4.9	10.8	2.9	0.8
*cont_prob_*I	2.4	1.6	4.3	3.3	7.2	2.5	4.6	8.3	13.4	4.1	0.6
*succ_prob_*II	3.7	3.9	6.2	8.1	4.6	1.4	8.8	0.7	5.9	7.0	2.7
*cont_prob_*II	5.1	1.7	3.0	11.9	7.3	5.6	7.6	3.9	8.2	3.9	4.4

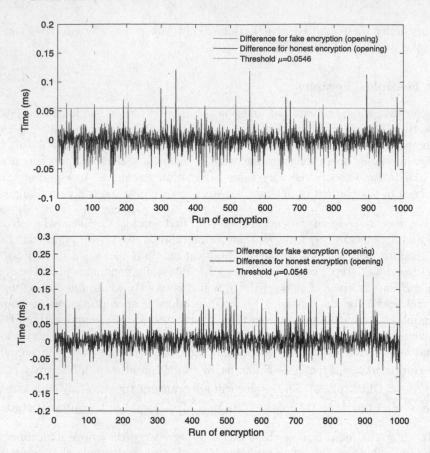

Fig. 4. Distributions of difference in time consumption for $n = 2^{30}$. **Top:** upgraded variant of scheme in [6]. **Bottom:** upgraded variant of our scheme.

Acknowledgments. This work is supported by the National Natural Science Foundation of China (No. 61972429 and No. 62272491) and Guangdong Major Project of Basic and Applied Basic Research (2019B030302008) and the National Key R&D Program of China under Grant (2022YFB2701500).

A   Towards Optimal Flipping Sampling

One natural question raised from the above design of DPKE is: are there any other ways of flipping bits of s that result in a closer distance from U, leveraging which we can devise a DPKE with better deniability? Below we give the negative answer by showing that flipping one bit is actually the optimal way, by proving that it is superior to any t-bit flipping ($t > 1$) or uniformly random flipping. For simplicity, hereafter we assume $\binom{n}{k} = 0$ for $k > n$.

Theorem 5. *For $t \in [1, n]$, let F_t be the flipping case where it first samples s from S, if the count of 1 in s is less than t, outputs $\perp$; else randomly flips t bits in s from 1 to 0. It holds $\mathsf{SD}(U, F_t) > \mathsf{SD}(U, F)$ for $t \geq 2$.*

Proof. Observe that s must be obtained by flipping t bit 1 of some string s' from S whose count of bit 1 is $k + t$. Thus, there are $\binom{n-k}{t}$ possible s' when fixing s. Further, the probability of exactly flipping the corresponding 1 of s' is $1/\binom{k+t}{t}$. Then $\forall s \in S, F(s) = \frac{1}{2^n} \cdot \binom{n}{k}\binom{n-k}{t}/\binom{k+t}{t}$, and the distance between R and F_t is

$$
\mathsf{SD}(R, F_t) = \frac{1}{2} \cdot \sum_{k=0}^{n} \left| \frac{1}{2^n}\binom{n}{k}\left(1 - \frac{\binom{n-k}{t}}{\binom{k+t}{t}}\right)\right| + \frac{1}{2} \cdot F_t(\perp)
$$

$$
= \frac{1}{2^{n+1}} \cdot \left(\sum_{k=0}^{n}\left| \binom{n}{k} - \binom{n}{k+t}\right| + \sum_{k=0}^{t-1}\binom{n}{k}\right).
$$

(2)

To prove $\mathsf{SD}(R, F_t) > \mathsf{SD}(R, F)$ for $t \geq 2$, it suffices to argue that $\mathsf{SD}(R, F_1)$ is the minimum value regarding $\mathsf{SD}(R, F_t)$ as a discrete function of t, for which we consider the following two cases:

– For $1 \leq t \leq m$, Eq. (2) can be simplified into $\frac{1}{2^n} \cdot \sum_{k=\lceil \frac{n-t}{2}\rceil}^{\lceil \frac{n+t}{2}\rceil - 1}\binom{n}{k}$, being monotonically increasing on t. So $t = 1$ is the minimum point in this interval.
– For $m + 1 \leq t \leq n$, Eq. (2) can be simplified into

$$
\frac{1}{2^{n+1}} \cdot \left(\sum_{i=t}^{\lceil \frac{n+t}{2}\rceil - 1}\binom{n}{i} + \sum_{i=\lceil \frac{n-t}{2}\rceil}^{\lceil \frac{n+t}{2}\rceil - 1}\binom{n}{i} - \sum_{i=0}^{\lceil \frac{n-t}{2}\rceil - 1}\binom{n}{i} + \sum_{k=0}^{t-1}\binom{n}{k}\right).
$$

To estimate the scale of the above equation, observe that

$$
\left(\sum_{i=t}^{\lceil \frac{n+t}{2}\rceil - 1}\binom{n}{i} - \sum_{i=0}^{\lceil \frac{n-t}{2}\rceil - 1}\binom{n}{i}\right) \geq 0, \quad \left(\sum_{i=\lceil \frac{n-t}{2}\rceil}^{\lceil \frac{n+t}{2}\rceil - 1}\binom{n}{i} + \sum_{k=0}^{t-1}\binom{n}{k}\right) > 2 \cdot \binom{n}{m}.
$$

Thus we can deduce that $\mathsf{SD}(R, F_t) > \mathsf{SD}(R, F)$ also holds in this interval.

Based on the above analysis, it is clear that $\mathsf{SD}(R, F_t) > \mathsf{SD}(R, F)$ for $t \geq 2$. $\square$

Theorem 6. *Let F' be the flipping case where it first samples s from $S \setminus \{0^n\}$ and then randomly flips some bits of s (not all of 1) from 1 to 0, it holds $\mathsf{SD}(U, F') > \mathsf{SD}(U, F)$.*

Proof. Any s from F' must be obtained by flipping j bits 1 of some s' for $j \in [1, n-k]$, meaning the count of 1 of s' is $k + j$. So the generation of s can be divided into two steps: 1) choose the indexes of i bits 1 to fix s'; 2) flip the target indexes of s'. Hence, the total possible way of sampling s is $\frac{1}{2^n} \cdot \sum\limits_{j=1}^{n-k} \binom{n-k}{j} \cdot 2^{-(k+j)}$.

Then by traversing all the possible s ($\binom{n}{k}$ values), we have that

$$\begin{aligned}
\mathsf{SD}(R, F') &= \frac{1}{2} \cdot \sum_{k=0}^{n} \left| \frac{1}{2^n} \binom{n}{k} \left(1 - \sum_{j=1}^{n-k} \binom{n-k}{j} \cdot 2^{-(k+j)} \right) \right| \\
&= \frac{1}{2^{n+1}} \cdot \sum_{k=0}^{n} \binom{n}{k} \left| 1 - 2^{-k} \cdot \sum_{j=1}^{n-k} \binom{n-k}{j} \cdot 2^{-j} \right|.
\end{aligned} \tag{3}$$

To estimate the relative scale of Eq. (3), we first consider the item of the absolute value $\left| 1 - 2^{-k} \cdot \sum\limits_{j=1}^{n-k} \binom{n-k}{j} \cdot 2^{-j} \right|$. Denote the sum of the involved sequence as $S_m = \sum\limits_{j=0}^{m} \binom{m}{j} \cdot 2^{-j}$, a simple calculation shows that $S_{m+1} = \frac{3}{2} S_m$ (geometric progression), further arriving at the simplified expression $\left| 1 - \frac{3^{n-k}}{2^n} + \frac{1}{2^k} \right|$. For large n, e.g., $n > 2^5$, we obtain the following inequality:

$$\sum_{k=0}^{n} \binom{n}{k} \left| 1 - \frac{3^{n-k}}{2^n} + \frac{1}{2^k} \right| > \sum_{k=0}^{n} \binom{n}{k} \left| 1 - \frac{n-k}{k+1} \right|,$$

which implies that $\mathsf{SD}(R, F') > \mathsf{SD}(R, F)$. □

References

1. Agrawal, S., Goldwasser, S., Mossel, S.: Deniable fully homomorphic encryption from learning with errors. In: Malkin, T., Peikert, C. (eds.) CRYPTO 2021. LNCS, vol. 12826, pp. 641–670. Springer, Cham (2021). https://doi.org/10.1007/978-3-030-84245-1_22
2. Apon, D., Fan, X., Liu, F.-H.: Deniable attribute based encryption for branching programs from LWE. In: Hirt, M., Smith, A. (eds.) TCC 2016. LNCS, vol. 9986, pp. 299–329. Springer, Heidelberg (2016). https://doi.org/10.1007/978-3-662-53644-5_12
3. Boneh, D., Waters, B.: Constrained pseudorandom functions and their applications. In: Sako, K., Sarkar, P. (eds.) ASIACRYPT 2013. LNCS, vol. 8270, pp. 280–300. Springer, Heidelberg (2013). https://doi.org/10.1007/978-3-642-42045-0_15
4. Brakerski, Z., Gentry, C., Vaikuntanathan, V.: (Leveled) fully homomorphic encryption without bootstrapping. ACM Trans. Comput. Theory 6(3), 13:1–13:36 (2014). https://doi.org/10.1145/2633600
5. Canetti, R., Dodis, Y., Halevi, S., Kushilevitz, E., Sahai, A.: Exposure-resilient functions and all-or-nothing transforms. In: Preneel, B. (ed.) EUROCRYPT 2000. LNCS, vol. 1807, pp. 453–469. Springer, Heidelberg (2000). https://doi.org/10.1007/3-540-45539-6_33

6. Canetti, R., Dwork, C., Naor, M., Ostrovsky, R.: Deniable encryption. In: Kaliski, B.S. (ed.) CRYPTO 1997. LNCS, vol. 1294, pp. 90–104. Springer, Heidelberg (1997). https://doi.org/10.1007/BFb0052229
7. Canetti, R., Park, S., Poburinnaya, O.: Fully deniable interactive encryption. In: Micciancio, D., Ristenpart, T. (eds.) CRYPTO 2020. LNCS, vol. 12170, pp. 807–835. Springer, Cham (2020). https://doi.org/10.1007/978-3-030-56784-2_27
8. Cao, Y., Zhang, F., Gao, C., Chen, X.: New practical public-key deniable encryption. In: Meng, W., Gollmann, D., Jensen, C.D., Zhou, J. (eds.) ICICS 2020. LNCS, vol. 12282, pp. 147–163. Springer, Cham (2020). https://doi.org/10.1007/978-3-030-61078-4_9
9. De Caro, A., Iovino, V., O'Neill, A.: Deniable functional encryption. In: Cheng, C.-M., Chung, K.-M., Persiano, G., Yang, B.-Y. (eds.) PKC 2016. LNCS, vol. 9614, pp. 196–222. Springer, Heidelberg (2016). https://doi.org/10.1007/978-3-662-49384-7_8
10. Caro, A.D., Iovino, V., O'Neill, A.: Receiver- and sender-deniable functional encryption. IET Inf. Secur. **12**(3), 207–216 (2018). https://doi.org/10.1049/iet-ifs.2017.0040
11. Chi, P., Lei, C.: Audit-free cloud storage via deniable attribute-based encryption. IEEE Trans. Cloud Comput. **6**(2), 414–427 (2018). https://doi.org/10.1109/TCC.2015.2424882
12. Chillotti, I., Gama, N., Georgieva, M., Izabachène, M.: A homomorphic LWE based e-voting scheme. In: Takagi, T. (ed.) PQCrypto 2016. LNCS, vol. 9606, pp. 245–265. Springer, Cham (2016). https://doi.org/10.1007/978-3-319-29360-8_16
13. Choi, S.G., Dachman-Soled, D., Malkin, T., Wee, H.: Improved non-committing encryption with applications to adaptively secure protocols. In: Matsui, M. (ed.) ASIACRYPT 2009. LNCS, vol. 5912, pp. 287–302. Springer, Heidelberg (2009). https://doi.org/10.1007/978-3-642-10366-7_17
14. Coladangelo, A., Goldwasser, S., Vazirani, U.V.: Deniable encryption in a quantum world. In: Leonardi, S., Gupta, A. (eds.) STOC 2022, pp. 1378–1391. ACM (2022). https://doi.org/10.1145/3519935.3520019
15. Damgård, I., Nielsen, J.B.: Improved non-committing encryption schemes based on a general complexity assumption. In: Bellare, M. (ed.) CRYPTO 2000. LNCS, vol. 1880, pp. 432–450. Springer, Heidelberg (2000). https://doi.org/10.1007/3-540-44598-6_27
16. Dent, A.W.: The Cramer-Shoup encryption scheme is plaintext aware in the standard model. In: Vaudenay, S. (ed.) EUROCRYPT 2006. LNCS, vol. 4004, pp. 289–307. Springer, Heidelberg (2006). https://doi.org/10.1007/11761679_18
17. Dodis, Y., Goldwasser, S., Tauman Kalai, Y., Peikert, C., Vaikuntanathan, V.: Public-key encryption schemes with auxiliary inputs. In: Micciancio, D. (ed.) TCC 2010. LNCS, vol. 5978, pp. 361–381. Springer, Heidelberg (2010). https://doi.org/10.1007/978-3-642-11799-2_22
18. Dziembowski, S., Pietrzak, K.: Leakage-resilient cryptography. In: FOCS 2008, pp. 293–302. IEEE Computer Society (2008). https://doi.org/10.1109/FOCS.2008.56
19. Gao, C., Xie, D., Wei, B.: Deniable encryptions secure against adaptive chosen ciphertext attack. In: Ryan, M.D., Smyth, B., Wang, G. (eds.) ISPEC 2012. LNCS, vol. 7232, pp. 46–62. Springer, Heidelberg (2012). https://doi.org/10.1007/978-3-642-29101-2_4
20. Garg, S., Gentry, C., Halevi, S., Raykova, M., Sahai, A., Waters, B.: Candidate indistinguishability obfuscation and functional encryption for all circuits. In: FOCS 2013, pp. 40–49. IEEE Computer Society (2013). https://doi.org/10.1109/FOCS.2013.13

21. Garg, S., Polychroniadou, A.: Two-round adaptively secure MPC from indistinguishability obfuscation. In: Dodis, Y., Nielsen, J.B. (eds.) TCC 2015. LNCS, vol. 9015, pp. 614–637. Springer, Heidelberg (2015). https://doi.org/10.1007/978-3-662-46497-7_24

22. Gentry, C.: Fully homomorphic encryption using ideal lattices. In: Mitzenmacher, M. (ed.) STOC 2009, pp. 169–178. ACM (2009). https://doi.org/10.1145/1536414.1536440

23. Jain, A., Lin, H., Sahai, A.: Indistinguishability obfuscation from well-founded assumptions. In: Khuller, S., Williams, V.V. (eds.) STOC 2021, pp. 60–73. ACM (2021). https://doi.org/10.1145/3406325.3451093

24. Kaminsky, D., Patterson, M.L., Sassaman, L.: PKI layer cake: new collision attacks against the global X.509 infrastructure. In: Sion, R. (ed.) FC 2010. LNCS, vol. 6052, pp. 289–303. Springer, Heidelberg (2010). https://doi.org/10.1007/978-3-642-14577-3_22

25. Kocher, P.C.: Timing attacks on implementations of Diffie-Hellman, RSA, DSS, and other systems. In: Koblitz, N. (ed.) CRYPTO 1996. LNCS, vol. 1109, pp. 104–113. Springer, Heidelberg (1996). https://doi.org/10.1007/3-540-68697-5_9

26. Kocher, P., Jaffe, J., Jun, B.: Differential power analysis. In: Wiener, M. (ed.) CRYPTO 1999. LNCS, vol. 1666, pp. 388–397. Springer, Heidelberg (1999). https://doi.org/10.1007/3-540-48405-1_25

27. Li, H., Zhang, F., Fan, C.: Deniable searchable symmetric encryption. Inf. Sci. **402**, 233–243 (2017). https://doi.org/10.1016/j.ins.2017.03.032

28. Matsuda, T., Hanaoka, G.: Trading plaintext-awareness for simulatability to achieve chosen ciphertext security. In: Cheng, C.-M., Chung, K.-M., Persiano, G., Yang, B.-Y. (eds.) PKC 2016. LNCS, vol. 9614, pp. 3–34. Springer, Heidelberg (2016). https://doi.org/10.1007/978-3-662-49384-7_1

29. Messerges, T.S.: Using second-order power analysis to attack DPA resistant software. In: Koç, Ç.K., Paar, C. (eds.) CHES 2000. LNCS, vol. 1965, pp. 238–251. Springer, Heidelberg (2000). https://doi.org/10.1007/3-540-44499-8_19

30. Micali, S., Reyzin, L.: Physically observable cryptography. In: Naor, M. (ed.) TCC 2004. LNCS, vol. 2951, pp. 278–296. Springer, Heidelberg (2004). https://doi.org/10.1007/978-3-540-24638-1_16

31. Michalevsky, Y., Schulman, A., Veerapandian, G.A., Boneh, D., Nakibly, G.: PowerSpy: location tracking using mobile device power analysis. In: Jung, J., Holz, T. (eds.) USENIX Security Symposium 2015, pp. 785–800. USENIX Association (2015). https://www.usenix.org/conference/usenixsecurity15/technical-sessions/presentation/michalevsky

32. O'Neill, A., Peikert, C., Waters, B.: Bi-deniable public-key encryption. In: Rogaway, P. (ed.) CRYPTO 2011. LNCS, vol. 6841, pp. 525–542. Springer, Heidelberg (2011). https://doi.org/10.1007/978-3-642-22792-9_30

33. Sahai, A., Waters, B.: How to use indistinguishability obfuscation: deniable encryption, and more. In: Shmoys, D.B. (ed.) STOC 2014, pp. 475–484. ACM (2014). https://doi.org/10.1145/2591796.2591825

34. Silverman, J.H., Whyte, W.: Timing attacks on NTRUEncrypt via variation in the number of hash calls. In: Abe, M. (ed.) CT-RSA 2007. LNCS, vol. 4377, pp. 208–224. Springer, Heidelberg (2006). https://doi.org/10.1007/11967668_14

Threshold Fully Homomorphic Encryption Over the Torus

Yukimasa Sugizaki[1]($\boxtimes$), Hikaru Tsuchida[1]($\boxtimes$), Takuya Hayashi[1], Koji Nuida[2], Akira Nakashima[1], Toshiyuki Isshiki[1], and Kengo Mori[1]

[1] NEC Corporation, Kanagawa, Japan
{yukimasa-sugizaki,h_tsuchida,takuya-hayashi,akira-nakashima,
toshiyuki-isshiki,ke-mori.bx}@nec.com
[2] Kyushu University, Fukuoka, Japan
nuida@imi.kyushu-u.ac.jp

Abstract. Fully homomorphic encryption (FHE) enables arithmetic operations to be performed over plaintext by operations on undecrypted ciphertext. The Chillotti-Gama-Georgieva-Izabachene (CGGI) scheme is a typical FHE scheme, has attracted attention because of its fast bootstrapping and the availability of open-source implementation software.

A threshold FHE (ThFHE) scheme has protocols for distributed key generation and distributed decryption that are executed cooperatively among the parties while keeping the decryption key distributed among them. It is useful for secure computations with inputs from multiple parties. However, a ThFHE scheme based on CGGI has yet to be proposed.

In this paper, we propose a client-aided ThFHE scheme based on CGGI. Our scheme achieves the same bootstrapping as CGGI without affecting the noise analysis or any CGGI parameter. Therefore, existing open-source software implementing CGGI can easily be extended to our scheme, a ThFHE variant of the CGGI scheme, without changing the implementation part regarding homomorphic operations.

Keywords: Threshold fully homomorphic encryption · CGGI · Secret sharing scheme · Multiparty computation · Client-aided model

1 Introduction

1.1 Background

Secure computation (SC) enables parties to compute a function using each party's input and obtain only the computation results without revealing the other parties' inputs. SC has attracted widespread attention because of its usefulness in analysing sensitive data, e.g., secure outsourced computation and cross-organizational data analysis. There are two cryptographic technologies for achieving the SC: *multiparty computation* (MPC) and *fully homomorphic encryption* (FHE).

© The Author(s), under exclusive license to Springer Nature Switzerland AG 2024
G. Tsudik et al. (Eds.): ESORICS 2023, LNCS 14344, pp. 45–65, 2024.
https://doi.org/10.1007/978-3-031-50594-2_3

A typical MPC scheme is a *secret-sharing-based* MPC (SS-MPC) [6,20], in which each party distributes its input among the parties so that it is indistinguishable from a random value in an algebraic structure. The distributed values are called the *shares*. An SS-MPC scheme enables parties to compute a function by computation (without communication) using the shares and communication between parties without revealing the parties' inputs. Some SS-MPC schemes use a helper called *client* to aid in the computation [5,35]. In client-aided SS-MPC schemes, the client participates in the computation only during the *offline* phase, during which the parties and the client can execute computable processes independent of the actual parties' inputs. In the *online* phase, during which the parties run processes dependent on the actual parties' inputs. Since MPC schemes involve a trade-off between the number of communication rounds and the communication volumes, their performance depends on the communication environment among parties.

The FHE scheme [8,13,19] enables arithmetic operations to be performed over plaintext by operations on undecrypted ciphertext. An operation on ciphertext that performs an arithmetic operation over plaintext without decrypting the ciphertext is called a *homomorphic operation*. In SC using an FHE scheme, a user computes a function represented by a circuit by performing homomorphic operations on encrypted inputs gate by gate. Unlike SC with MPC, SC with FHE does not involve any communication dependent on the function to be computed in the computation process. Since it is costly to establish a good communication environment, we focus on FHE schemes.

A typical FHE scheme is the Chillotti-Gama-Georgieva-Izabachene (CGGI) scheme proposed by Chillotti et al. [13]. Compared with other FHE schemes, CGGI has faster *bootstrapping*, which is an operation that refreshes a ciphertext by generating a new ciphertext of the same plaintext, that is, a ciphertext containing less noise than the ciphertext, which contains noise accumulated during homomorphic operations. In addition, various open-source software (OSS) implementing CGGI have been released [4,14,21,27].

A threshold FHE (ThFHE) scheme [3,32,33] has protocols for distributed key generation and distributed decryption that are executed cooperatively among the parties while keeping the decryption key distributed among them. In SC using a ThFHE scheme, each party encrypts its input using the common encryption key. The joint (public) encryption key generation algorithm generates a common encryption key while keeping the decryption key distributed among parties. Each party then sends its encrypted input to a computing serve, which computes a function by homomorphic operations on the encrypted inputs. Finally, the parties decrypt the encrypted results using their share of the decryption key without reconstructing the key. A ThFHE scheme is useful for SC with inputs from multiple parties because only one can reconstruct the decryption key if a certain number of shares of the decryption key are collected.

However, to the best of our knowledge, a CGGI-variant ThFHE scheme has yet to be proposed.

1.2   Our Contributions

We propose a CGGI-variant ThFHE scheme in a client-aided model. Our scheme has the following three features, and a comparison between existing schemes and ours is summarized in Table 1:

1. **CGGI-Based Scheme.** Our scheme is the first ThFHE one based on CGGI. It supports distributed decryption key generation and distributed encryption[1]/decryption protocols with the same bootstrapping of CGGI. Hence, our scheme is useful for SC in the multiparty setting.
2. **Distributed Bootstrapping Key Generation for Binary Decryption Key Distribution.** To the best of our knowledge, our scheme is the only ThFHE scheme supporting distributed bootstrapping key generation for binary decryption key distribution.
3. **Parameters Unaffected by Noise Smudging.** In the distributed decryption protocol of the existing ThFHE schemes, each party needs to add an extra noise to the sending value to prevent leakage of the decryption key. This technique is called *noise smudging* [3]. By the smudging lemma [3], the additional noise is proportional to 2^{λ} where λ is a security parameter. Hence, parameters such as ciphertext modulus size must be increased to prevent noise from affecting the decryption success probability. Then, the difference in error evaluation between the original FHE scheme and its threshold variant when achieving the same security level makes it difficult for developers of SC applications to transparently use the original FHE scheme and its threshold variant.

   To avoid increasing the parameter values, we introduce a *client* into our scheme. The client computes the smudging noise and sends a share of it to each party in the offline phase. Since the client generates the smudging noise instead of each party, the size of the noise is not proportional to the number of parties. We show that it is sufficient to add the noise whose size is the same as the noise in the original ciphertext.

We implement our scheme and compare its execution times for key generation, encryption, decryption and homomorphic NAND computation with those of existing schemes based on CGGI [11,13]. Although our scheme has a longer execution times for key generation, encryption, and decryption, the execution time for homomorphic NAND operation is comparable to that of the original CGGI scheme [13] even when the number of parties is increased. Hence, in the case of SC for a complex function in a multiparty setting, our scheme is superior to existing schemes in terms of execution time.

---

[1] We propose the ThFHE in a private-key setting as well as the original CGGI [13]. Hence, our scheme supports a distributed encryption protocol instead of joint (public) encryption key generation. By using this distributed encryption protocol, parties can generate CGGI-ciphertext in a distributed manner. They can then run the distributed generation of (public) encryption keys by using the conversion method [22]. Our scheme can thus be converted into a scheme in the public-key setting.

Table 1. Comparison of Proposed Scheme with Existing Ones

Schemes	Base Scheme	Distributed Bootstrapping Key Generation	Parameters Unaffected by Noise Smudging
[3,7]	LWE-based scheme	No	No
[33]	BFV [17]	Interactive bootstrapping	No
[15]	CGGI	No	No
[25]	LWE-based scheme	Yes	No
Ours	CGGI	Yes	Yes

1.3   Related Work

FHE. FHEW [16], CGGI [13], and FINAL [8] were designed to provide faster bootstrapping. Among them, the bootstrapping of FINAL is the fastest. However, as far as we know, there is no OSS for implementing FINAL, except for the experimental code[2] implemented by the authors of FINAL. We focus on the CGGI scheme, which has the second fastest bootstrapping, because the method is more mature than FINAL, and it is implemented in several publicly available OSS, including a transpiler [21] to assist developers.

Multi-Key FHE (MK-FHE). An FHE scheme that can perform homomorphic operations between ciphertexts encrypted with different encryption keys is called *multi-key* FHE (MK-FHE) [11,12,26]. MK-FHE based on CGGI (MK-CGGI) has also been proposed [11].

In MK-FHE, the execution time of homomorphic operations and the size of the ciphertext increase as the number of encryption keys involved in the computation increases. Therefore, as the number of parties increases, the less efficient the SC using the MK-FHE becomes. For the efficiency of the SC in a multiparty setting, we focus on ThFHE, not MK-FHE.

ThFHE. Asharov et al. were the first to propose a ThFHE scheme [3]. Mouchet et al. [33] proposed ThFHE schemes based on BFV [17]. Chowdhury et al. recently proposed a CGGI scheme with distributed decryption [15]. Boudgoust and Scholl proposed an LWE-based FHE scheme supporting distributed decryption with polynomial modulus [9]. These schemes do not have a protocol to generate a (public) key for bootstrapping while keeping the decryption key distributed.

Lee et al. proposed a bootstrapping procedure supporting arbitrary decryption key distribution [25]. They applied it to the ThFHE scheme of Asharov et al. [3] and constructed a protocol to generate a (public) key for bootstrapping while keeping the decryption key distributed. However, their scheme and the ThFHE of [3] are affected by noise smudging. If we are to achieve the same level of security in these schemes as the base FHE scheme, we must set the parameters of the security assumption, e.g., ciphertext modulus, larger than those of the base FHE because the noise smudging affects the noise analysis of the scheme.

---

[2] https://github.com/KULeuven-COSIC/FINAL.

2 Preliminaries

2.1 Notations

Let the number of parties and corruptions by an adversary be N' and t, respectively. The i-th party is P_i ($i = 0, \ldots, N' - 1$), and the set of parties is $\mathcal{P} = \{P_i\}_{i=0}^{N'-1}$. $\mathcal{C}$ is the client. We assume that an adversary cannot corrupt $\mathcal{C}$. Let S_M and $\pi \in S_M$ be the set of random permutations for M and a random permutation, respectively. For a distribution denoted as D, sampling the value x in accordance with the distribution is denoted as $x \leftarrow D$. For a set denoted as A, let $a \xleftarrow{U} A$ be a uniformly random sampling of elements a from A. We denote a vector by placing a vector arrow over the character, e.g., $\vec{x}$. We denote an exclusive OR operator as $\oplus$.

Let $\mathbb{T} = \mathbb{R}/\mathbb{Z}$ denote the *torus*, the set of real numbers contained in $[0, 1)$. In other words, $\mathbb{T}$ is the set of real numbers modulo 1. Note that $\mathbb{T}$ has a $\mathbb{Z}$-module structure. Loosely speaking, $\mathbb{T}$ defines additions between elements and integer multiplication of elements, but not the multiplication of elements. For example, $1.5 \cdot 0.3 \bmod 1 \neq (1.5 \bmod 1) \cdot (0.3 \bmod 1)$. We also denote $\{0, 1\}$ and the set of integers as $\mathbb{B}$ and $\mathbb{Z}$, respectively.

We let the set of polynomials modulo $X^N + 1$ with coefficients in $\mathbb{T}$ be $\mathbb{T}_N[X]$ where N is a power of 2. Note that $\mathbb{T}_N[X]$ is a $\mathbb{Z}_N[X]$-module structure where $\mathbb{Z}_N[X]$ is the polynomial ring modulo $X^N + 1$ with coefficients in $\mathbb{Z}$. Loosely speaking, it defines addition between elements of $\mathbb{T}_N[X]$ and multiplication of elements of $\mathbb{T}_N[X]$ by elements of $\mathbb{Z}_N[X]$, but not multiplication of elements of $\mathbb{T}_N[X]$ by each other. We also let the polynomial ring modulo $X^N + 1$ with coefficients in $\mathbb{B}$ and $\mathbb{Z}$ be $\mathbb{B}_N[X] = \mathbb{B}[X]/(X^N + 1)$ and $\mathbb{Z}_N[X] = \mathbb{Z}[X]/(X^N + 1)$, respectively. We denote polynomials in bold, e.g., $\boldsymbol{x}$.

Let $|\mathbb{S}|$ be the bit length of the element of $\mathbb{S}$ where $\mathbb{S} \in \{\mathbb{B}, \mathbb{T}, \mathbb{T}_N[X]\}$. For example, $|\mathbb{B}|$ is 1. $|\mathbb{T}_N[X]|$ is $N|\mathbb{T}|$. If we represent the elements of $\mathbb{T}$ by z bits, then $|\mathbb{T}|$ is z.

Let σ and σ' be positive real values. We denote the error distribution induced by a normal distribution with mean 0 and variance σ^2 (resp. σ'^2) over $\mathbb{T}$ (resp. $\mathbb{T}_N[X]$) as $\chi_{(0,\sigma^2)}$ (resp. $\hat{\chi}_{(0,\sigma'^2)}$).

2.2 Security Assumption

As with CGGI [13], we make the security assumption that LWE problems over $\mathbb{T}$ and $\mathbb{T}_N[X]$ (called TLWE and TRLWE problems, respectively) cannot be solved by any probabilistic polynomial-time adversary. For more details, see Appendix A.

2.3 N'-Out-of-N' Additive Secret Sharing ((N', N')-ASS)

We denote binary operators for the addition and multiplication of shares by $+$ and $\cdot$, respectively, as in the case of the addition and multiplication of values. In (N', N')-ASS, no one can know partial information about the secret value unless N' shares are collected.

For a secret element $x \in \mathbb{S}$, where $\mathbb{S} \in \{\mathbb{B}, \mathbb{T}, \mathbb{T}_N[X]\}$, we denote the (N', N')-ASS share of x over $\mathbb{S}$ as $_\mathbb{S}[x] = (_\mathbb{S}[x]_0, \ldots, _\mathbb{S}[x]_{N'-1})$ where $x = \sum_{i=0}^{N'-1} x_i$ (with performing the modulus operation in accordance with $\mathbb{S}$), $x_i \in \mathbb{S}$, and P_i's share is $_\mathbb{S}[x]_i = x_i$ for $i = 0, \ldots, N' - 1$.

Let $_\mathbb{S}[x]$ and $_\mathbb{S}[y]$ be the shares of (N', N')-ASS over $\mathbb{S}$. Parties can perform addition between shares, $_\mathbb{S}[x + y] = _\mathbb{S}[x] + _\mathbb{S}[y]$ by P_i's setting $_\mathbb{S}[x \oplus y]_i = _\mathbb{S}[x]_i + _\mathbb{S}[y]_i$ for $i = 0, \ldots, N'-1$. Let c_0 and c_1 be the clear constant elements over $\mathbb{S}$ obtained by all parties. Parties can perform scalar addition, $_\mathbb{S}[c_0 + x] = c_0 + _\mathbb{S}[x]$ by P_0's setting $_\mathbb{S}[c_0 + x]_0 = c_0 + _\mathbb{S}[x]_0$ and $P_{i'}$'s setting $_\mathbb{S}[c_0 + x]_{i'} = _\mathbb{S}[x]_{i'}$ for $i' = 1, \ldots, N' - 1$. Parties can perform scalar multiplication on $\mathbb{B}$, $_\mathbb{B}[c_0 \cdot x] = c_0 \cdot _\mathbb{B}[x]$ by P_i's setting $_\mathbb{B}[c_0 \cdot x]_i = c \cdot _\mathbb{B}[x]_i$ for $i = 0, \ldots, N' - 1$.

However, parties cannot perform multiplication of shares and constant elements over $\mathbb{T}$ and $\mathbb{T}_N[X]$ because $\mathbb{T}$ and $\mathbb{T}_N[X]$ have $\mathbb{Z}$-module and $\mathbb{Z}_N[X]$-module structures, respectively. For (N', N')-ASS over $\mathbb{T}$ and $\mathbb{T}_N[X]$, parties can perform multiplication of shares and constant elements over $\mathbb{Z}$ and $\mathbb{Z}_N[X]$, respectively.

2.4   Building Blocks of SS-MPC Based on (N', N')-ASS

We assume an honest majority in our protocol, i.e., $t < N'/2$. We also assume a *semi-honest* adversary who tries to learn as much information about the parties' inputs as possible without deviating from the protocol specifications. Each party is connected via a point-to-point secure and synchronous communication channel. We use the following subprotocols as building blocks.

– $_\mathbb{S}[x] \leftarrow \mathsf{Share}(\mathbb{S}, P_I, x)$: Let P_I be an input dealer. P_I obtains an input element $x \in \mathbb{S}$ where $\mathbb{S} \in \{\mathbb{B}, \mathbb{T}, \mathbb{T}_N[X]\}$. Share takes $\mathbb{S}, P_I$, and x as inputs and outputs $_\mathbb{S}[x]$. In Share, P_I generates $x_1, \ldots, x_{N'-1} \xleftarrow{\mathsf{U}} \mathbb{S}$ and sets $x_0 = x - \sum_{i'=1}^{N'-1} x_{i'}$ with the modulo operation according to $\mathbb{S}$. Then, P_I sends $_\mathbb{S}[x]_i = x_i$ to P_i for $i = 0, \ldots, N' - 1$. If $P_I \in \mathcal{P}$, Share requires one round and $(N' - 1) \cdot |\mathbb{S}|$ bits as communication cost.

– $(P_R, x) \leftarrow \mathsf{Open}(_\mathbb{S}[x])$: Let $P_R \in \mathcal{P}$ be a receiver. Open takes $_\mathbb{S}[x]$ as an input and outputs x to P_R where $\mathbb{S} \in \{\mathbb{B}, \mathbb{T}, \mathbb{T}_N[X]\}$. In Open, the parties in $\mathcal{P} \setminus \{P_R\}$ send their shares to P_R. P_R reconstructs x by using P_R's share and the shares received from the other parties. Hence, Open requires one round and $(N' - 1)|\mathbb{S}|$ bits as communication cost.

– $[r] \leftarrow \mathsf{RandGen}(\mathbb{S}, \mathcal{P})$: RandGen takes $\mathbb{S} \in \{\mathbb{B}, \mathbb{T}, \mathbb{T}_N[X]\}$ and $\mathcal{P}$ as inputs and outputs a share of a random element $r \in \mathbb{S}$, $_\mathbb{S}[r]$. In RandGen, P_i generates $r_i \xleftarrow{\mathsf{U}} \mathbb{S}$ and sets $_\mathbb{S}[r]_i = r_i$ for $i = 0, \ldots, N' - 1$. By setting $r = \sum_{i=0}^{N'-1} r_i$ with the modulus operation in accordance with $\mathbb{S}$, parties get $_\mathbb{S}[r]$.

– $([\vec{x}_0'], \ldots, [\vec{x}_{R-1}']) \leftarrow \mathsf{TableShuffle}(([\vec{x}_0], \ldots, [\vec{x}_{R-1}]))$: Let R and C be the number of rows and columns, respectively. We denote the input share vector and the shuffled share vector as $[\vec{x}_{i'}] = (_{\mathbb{S}_0}[x_{i',0}], \ldots, _{\mathbb{S}_{C-1}}[x_{i',C-1}])$ and $[\vec{x}_{i'}'] = (_{\mathbb{S}_0}[x'_{i',0}], \ldots, _{\mathbb{S}_{C-1}}[x'_{i',C-1}])$ where $x'_{i',j'} = x_{\pi(i'),j'}$, $\mathbb{S}_{i'} \in \{\mathbb{B}, \mathbb{T}, \mathbb{T}_N[X]\}$

(for $i' = 0, \ldots, R - 1$; $j' = 0, \ldots, C - 1$) and $\pi \in S_R$ respectively. Note that no party knows π. TableShuffle takes $([\vec{x}_0], \ldots, [\vec{x}_{R-1}])$ as inputs and outputs $([\vec{x}'_0], \ldots, [\vec{x}'_{R-1}])$. We can construct TableShuffle straightforwardly by running the resharing-based shuffle [24] in parallel. If let $C_\mathbb{S}$ be the number of columns containing the share over $\mathbb{S}$, TableShuffle requires $2 \cdot \binom{N'}{t}$ rounds and $(N' + t - 1)(N' - t)\binom{N'}{t}(C_\mathbb{B} + C_\mathbb{T}|\mathbb{T}| + C_{\mathbb{T}_N[X]}|\mathbb{T}|N)$ bits as communication cost where $\binom{N'}{t}$ is a binomial coefficient, i.e., $\frac{N'!}{(N'-t)!t!}$.

3   Client-Aided ThFHE Based on CGGI

3.1   Naive Methods and Our Approach

Before explaining our approach, we describe three naive methods for constructing a ThFHE scheme on the basis of CGGI and the resulting problems:

1. **Use Additive Homomorphic Property of Keys.** Let $(\mathsf{sk}_i, \mathsf{pk}_{\mathsf{sk}_i})$ be the pair of secret decryption and public encryption keys generated by P_i. In many ThFHE starting with [3], it holds that $\mathsf{pk}_{\sum_{i=0}^{N'-1}\mathsf{sk}_i} = \sum_{i=0}^{N'-1}\mathsf{pk}_{\mathsf{sk}_i}$ because of the additive homomorphic property of keys and those schemes use $\mathsf{pk}_{\sum_{i=0}^{N'-1}\mathsf{sk}_i}$ as a common (public) encryption key. However, we cannot use this approach to construct ThFHE based on CGGI. As explained in [22], the public encryption key of CGGI is on $\mathbb{T}$ while the decryption key of CGGI is on $\mathbb{B}$. Hence, $\mathsf{pk}_{\bigoplus_{i=0}^{N'-1}\mathsf{sk}_i}$ and $\sum_{i=0}^{N'-1}\mathsf{pk}_{\mathsf{sk}_i}$ are not equal in CGGI. For more details, it is impossible to compute the product of the elements on $\mathbb{T}$ with the distributed decryption key on $\mathbb{B}$ in a straightforward manner. For example, we set that $\vec{s} = \vec{s}_0 \oplus \vec{s}_1$ where $\vec{s}$ is the decryption key, $\vec{s}_0$ and $\vec{s}_1$ is the distributed decryption keys, and $\oplus$ is the element-wise XOR of the vector. Then, it holds that $\vec{a} \cdot \vec{s} = \vec{a} \cdot (\vec{s}_0 \oplus \vec{s}_1) \neq \vec{a} \cdot \vec{s}_0 + \vec{a} \cdot \vec{s}_1$.

2. **Use SS-MPC Over $\mathbb{T}$.** To the best of our knowledge, an SS-MPC scheme over $\mathbb{T}$ has not been proposed. Hence, we cannot straightforwardly extend CGGI to a ThFHE scheme on the basis of CGGI by using SS-MPC over $\mathbb{T}$.

3. **Use Ring-Based SS-MPC.** We consider $\mathbb{T}$ as the residue ring of powers of 2, $\mathbb{Z}_{2^k}$ because CGGI is implemented on $\mathbb{Z}_{2^k}$ in OSS [4,14,21,27]. We explain ideas that use Beaver's multiplication triple (BMT), which is correlated randomness for share multiplication, and those that do not use it.

   (a) **Use BMT.** To generate BMT, we need asymmetric-key primitives, e.g. oblivious transfer [34]. It is not desirable to introduce new assumptions other than T(R)LWE problem in constructing a ThFHE scheme on the basis of CGGI. There is another method for computing BMT using CGGI, but it is inefficient. BMT can also be generated by using the client instead of asymmetric-key primitives [5]. However, it is necessary to generate as many BMTs as there are multiplication gates in the computed circuit, which is not desirable because it overly burdens the client.

(b) **Do Not Use BMT.** Maurer proposed SS-MPC by using only secret sharing over arbitrary rings [28]. However, in [28], the size of each party's share increases up to $O(\binom{N'}{t})$. Even when using field-based SS-MPC [6], the sizes of the field and each party's share grow in proportion to N'. In the case of creating a ciphertext for one-bit plaintext, methods that increase the space complexity are inefficient and undesirable.

We propose a new SS-MPC building block to construct a client-aided ThFHE scheme: *bridging multiplexer* (BMUX). As inputs, BMUX takes a share of selector $s \in \mathbb{B}$ of (N', N')-ASS over $\mathbb{B}$ and the shuffled table with two rows of shares of (N', N')-ASS over $\mathbb{T}$ (or $\mathbb{T}_N[X]$). It outputs the shares of either of the two rows in the shuffled table on the basis of selector value. If we use the BMUX by passing the result of the multiplication to the BMUX as a shuffled table, we can compute the share multiplication between the shares of (N', N')-ASS on $\mathbb{B}$ and $\mathbb{T}$ (or $\mathbb{T}_N[X]$) and overcome the problem described in 1 above.

To shuffle the table of shares, we use TableShuffle, which is based on the resharing-based shuffle protocol [24] by assuming $t < N'/2$ and a semi-honest adversary. The shuffle of [24] uses only the (N', N')-ASS, applying the random permutation and resharing shares. Hence, it can deal with the (N', N')-ASS shares on $\mathbb{B}$, $\mathbb{T}$, and $\mathbb{T}_N[X]$ without increasing the size of shares in proportion to N'. Therefore, our approach overcomes the problems of naive methods described in 2, 3(a), and 3(b) above.

In addition, we introduce an honest client $\mathcal{C}$ for efficient noise sampling. Several SS-MPC schemes introduce clients to improve computational efficiency [5,31,35], but we are the first to introduce the client in the ThFHE. Similar to the assumption in [5,31,35], we assume that $\mathcal{C}$ does not collude with parties and is not corrupted by an adversary. In our scheme, $\mathcal{C}$ performs a single noise sampling in distributed decryption and encryption. $\mathcal{C}$ also performs kNt times and $n(k+1)\ell$ times noise sampling in the distributed generation of key-switching and bootstrapping keys, respectively. Compared to [5] in the naive method described in 3(a) above, our protocol reduces the burden on the client. Even if the client of [5] performs noise sampling as in our scheme, the client still needs to generate BMT for the multiplication gates involved in distributed key generation, distributed decryption, and distributed encryption.

3.2   Syntax

Our scheme consists of the following algorithms. Note that our scheme is based on CGGI in the private-key setting.

1. param $\leftarrow$ Setup(1^λ): Let λ be a security parameter. Setup takes 1^λ as inputs and outputs a public parameter param $= (n, N, k, \sigma, \sigma_{\mathsf{ks}}, \sigma', B, B', \ell, t)$. Note that n is the dimension of the vector of the decryption key. N and k is the dimensions of TRLWE problem. σ_{ks} is a standard deviation of the normal distribution with mean 0, $\chi_{(0,\sigma_{\mathsf{ks}}^2)}$ for the key-switching key generation. B and B_g are the base for the gadget decomposition. t and ℓ are the number of digits for the gadget decomposition.

2. $[\vec{s}] \leftarrow \mathsf{DistDKGen}(\mathsf{param}, \mathcal{P})$: The distributed decryption key generation algorithm DistDKGen takes param and $\mathcal{P}$ as inputs and outputs shares of $\vec{s} = (s_0, \ldots, s_{n-1}) \in \mathbb{B}^n$, $_{\mathbb{B}}[\vec{s}] = (_{\mathbb{B}}[s_0], \ldots, _{\mathbb{B}}[s_{n-1}])$.

3. $c \leftarrow \mathsf{DistEnc}(\mathsf{param}, _{\mathbb{B}}[\vec{s}], (m, P_I))$: The distributed encryption algorithm DistEnc takes param, $_{\mathbb{B}}[\vec{s}]$, and (m, P_I) as inputs where $m \in \mathbb{B}$ is the input from the input dealer P_I. DistEnc outputs a ciphertext c.

4. $(\mathsf{ksk}, \mathsf{bsk}) \leftarrow \mathsf{DistEKGen}(\mathsf{param}, _{\mathbb{B}}[\vec{s}])$: The distributed key generation algorithm for key-switching key and bootstrapping key, DistEKGen takes param and $_{\mathbb{B}}[\vec{s}]$ as inputs and outputs $(\mathsf{ksk}, \mathsf{bsk})$ where ksk and bsk are the key-switching key and the bootstrapping key, respectively.

5. $c' \leftarrow \mathsf{Eval}(\mathsf{param}, c_0, c_1, \mathsf{op.}, \mathsf{bsk}, \mathsf{ksk})$: The gate evaluation algorithm, Eval takes param, bsk and ksk as inputs. Eval also takes encrypted inputs c_0 and c_1 and the logic gate op.. Eval outputs the encrypted result from computing op. for c_0 and c_1 by a homomorphic operation.

6. $(P_R, m) \leftarrow \mathsf{DistDec}(\mathsf{param}, c, _{\mathbb{B}}[\vec{s}], P_R)$: The distributed decryption algorithm DistDec takes param, a ciphertext c, $_{\mathbb{B}}[\vec{s}]$, and the receiver P_R as inputs and outputs the plaintext of c, m to P_R.

3.3 Our Protocols

Algorithm 1. BMUX Π_{BMUX}

Input: Share of selector $_{\mathbb{B}}[s]$ and shuffled table of shares $\mathcal{ST}_{\vec{x}_{\mathsf{idx}}, \vec{x}_{\mathsf{idx} \oplus 1}} = ((_{\mathbb{B}}[\mathsf{idx}], _{\mathbb{S}'}[\vec{x}_{\mathsf{idx}}]), (_{\mathbb{B}}[\mathsf{idx} \oplus 1], _{\mathbb{S}'}[\vec{x}_{\mathsf{idx} \oplus 1}]))$ where $s, \mathsf{idx} \in \mathbb{B}$, $_{\mathbb{S}'}[\vec{x}_{\mathsf{idx}}] = (_{\mathbb{S}'}[x_{\mathsf{idx},0}], \ldots, _{\mathbb{S}'}[x_{\mathsf{idx}, C-1}])$, $_{\mathbb{S}'}[\vec{x}_{\mathsf{idx} \oplus 1}] = (_{\mathbb{S}'}[x_{\mathsf{idx} \oplus 1, 0}], \ldots, _{\mathbb{S}'}[x_{\mathsf{idx} \oplus 1, C-1}])$, and $\mathbb{S}' \in \{\mathbb{T}, \mathbb{T}_N[X]\}$

Output: $_{\mathbb{S}'}[\vec{x}_{s \oplus \mathsf{idx}}]$

 1: **for** $i = 0, \ldots, N'-1$ **do in parallel**
 2:     By $\mathsf{Open}(_{\mathbb{B}}[s] \oplus _{\mathbb{B}}[\mathsf{idx}], P_i)$, P_i obtains $s \oplus \mathsf{idx}$. Then, P_i sets $_{\mathbb{S}'}[\mathsf{output}_{j'}]_i = _{\mathbb{S}'}[x_{s \oplus \mathsf{idx}, j'}]_i$ for $j' = 0, \ldots, C-1$.
 3: **end for**
 4: Return $(_{\mathbb{S}'}[\mathsf{output}_0], \ldots, _{\mathbb{S}'}[\mathsf{output}_{C-1}])$.

Intuition of BMUX. Algorithm 1 describes the BMUX Π_{BMUX}. It takes $_{\mathbb{B}}[s]$ and $\mathcal{ST}_{\vec{x}_{\mathsf{idx}}, \vec{x}_{\mathsf{idx} \oplus 1}}$ as inputs and outputs the selected vector of shares $_{\mathbb{S}'}[\vec{x}_{s \oplus \mathsf{idx}}]$ from $\mathcal{ST}_{\vec{x}_{\mathsf{idx}}, \vec{x}_{\mathsf{idx} \oplus 1}}$. To select the vector of shares, parties obtains $s \oplus \mathsf{idx}$ by Share in line 2. Note that $s \oplus \mathsf{idx}$ gives parties only the information whether s matched idx or not because $\mathsf{idx} \in \mathbb{B}$ and $\mathcal{ST}_{\vec{x}_{\mathsf{idx}}, \vec{x}_{\mathsf{idx} \oplus 1}}$ is the table shuffled by rows. That is, $s \oplus \mathsf{idx}$ does not leak confidential information from $\mathcal{ST}_{\vec{x}_{\mathsf{idx}}, \vec{x}_{\mathsf{idx} \oplus 1}}$ or the value of s to parties.

Intuition of Each Algorithm. We describe each algorithm of our scheme. Since Setup and Eval are identical to the setup algorithm and homomorphic operations with the gate-bootstrapping in [13], we omit the explanation. We adopt $\mu = m/4$ ($m \in \mathbb{B}$) as the plaintext encoded on $\mathbb{T}$ as in [11,13].

DistDKGen: By $\mathsf{RandGen}(\mathbb{B}, \mathcal{P})$, parties obtain $_{\mathbb{B}}[s_i]$ for $i = 0, \ldots, n-1$. Parties set $_{\mathbb{B}}[\vec{s}] = (_{\mathbb{B}}[s_0], \ldots, _{\mathbb{B}}[s_{n-1}])$ as shares of the decryption key $\vec{s} \in \mathbb{B}^n$.

Algorithm 2. DistEnc Π_{DistEnc}

Input: Public parameters param, shares of decryption key $_{\mathbb{B}}[\vec{s}] = (_{\mathbb{B}}[s_0], \ldots,$
$_{\mathbb{B}}[s_{n-1}])$, plaintext $m \in \mathbb{B}$, input dealer P_I

Output: Ciphertext $c = (\vec{a} = (a_0, \ldots, a_{n-1}), b = \vec{a} \cdot \vec{s} + \mu + e) \in \mathbb{T}^{n+1}$ where
$\mu = m/4$, $\vec{a} \overset{\mathsf{U}}{\leftarrow} \mathbb{T}^n$, and $e \overset{\mathsf{U}}{\leftarrow} \chi_{(0,\sigma^2)}$

1: (Offline phase)
2: $\mathcal{C}$ samples $e \leftarrow \chi_{(0,\sigma^2)}$. By Share$(\mathbb{T}, e, \mathcal{C})$, $\mathcal{C}$ distributes $_{\mathbb{T}}[e]$ to parties.
3: $_{\mathbb{T}}[a_{i'}] \leftarrow$ RandGen$(\mathbb{T}, \mathcal{P})$ for $i' = 0, \ldots, n - 1$
4: **for** $i = 0, \ldots, N' - 1; i' = 0, \ldots, n - 1$ **do in parallel**
5:     By Open$(_{\mathbb{T}}[a_{i'}], P_i)$, P_i obtains $a_{i'}$.
6: **end for**
7: **for** $i' = 0, \ldots, n - 1$ **do in parallel**
8:     $\mathcal{ST}_{0,a_{i'}} \leftarrow$ TableShuffle$((_{\mathbb{B}}[0], _{\mathbb{T}}[0]), (_{\mathbb{B}}[1], _{\mathbb{T}}[a_{i'}]))$
9:     By $\Pi_{\mathsf{BMUX}}(_{\mathbb{B}}[s_{i'}], \mathcal{ST}_{0,a_{i'}})$, parties obtain $_{\mathbb{T}}[a_{i'} \cdot s_{i'}]$.
10: **end for**
11: $_{\mathbb{T}}[\vec{a} \cdot \vec{s}] = _{\mathbb{T}}[\sum_{i'=0}^{n-1} a_{i'} \cdot s_{i'}] = \sum_{i'=0}^{n-1} {}_{\mathbb{T}}[a_{i'} \cdot s_{i'}]$
12: (Online phase)
13: By Share$(\mathbb{T}, \mu = m/4, P_I)$, P_I distributes $_{\mathbb{T}}[\mu]$ to parties.
14: $_{\mathbb{T}}[b] = _{\mathbb{T}}[\mu] + _{\mathbb{T}}[\vec{a} \cdot \vec{s}] + _{\mathbb{T}}[e]$
15: **for** $i = 0, \ldots, N' - 1$ **do in parallel**
16:     By Open$(_{\mathbb{B}}[b], P_i)$, P_i obtains b and gets $c = (\vec{a}, b)$.
17: **end for**
18: Return $c = (\vec{a}, b)$.

DistEnc: Algorithm 2 describes the distributed encryption algorithm Π_{DistEnc}. We divide Π_{DistEnc} into the offline phase and the online phase and explain it.

The goal of the offline phase is to perform computable processing independent of the actual input, m. In line 2, $\mathcal{C}$ samples the noise contained in the ciphertext of CGGI, e and distributes it to parties as $_{\mathbb{T}}[e]$. In lines 3 to 6, parties compute a part of the ciphertext, $\vec{a}$. Then, in lines 7 to 11, parties compute $_{\mathbb{T}}[\vec{a} \cdot \vec{s}]$ by TableShuffle and Π_{BMUX}. Note that Π_{BMUX} outputs $_{\mathbb{T}}[0]$ if $s_{i'} = 0$ and $_{\mathbb{T}}[a_{i'}]$ otherwise in line 9. That is, Π_{BMUX} outputs $_{\mathbb{T}}[a_{i'} \cdot s_{i'}]$.

The goal of the online phase is to generate the ciphertext by using an actual input m. By Share, P_I distributes the encoded plaintext μ to parties as $_{\mathbb{T}}[\mu]$ in line 13. Then, parties compute $_{\mathbb{T}}[b] = _{\mathbb{T}}[\mu] + _{\mathbb{T}}[\vec{a} \cdot \vec{s}] + _{\mathbb{T}}[e]$ and reconstruct b by Open. Finally, parties set the ciphertext of CGGI as $c = (\vec{a}, b) \in \mathbb{T}^{n+1}$.

Algorithm 3. Distributed key generation for key-switching key Π_{DKSK}

Input: Public parameters param, shares of decryption keys $_{\mathbb{B}}[\vec{s}] = (_{\mathbb{B}}[s_0], \ldots,$
$_{\mathbb{B}}[s_{n-1}])$ and $_{\mathbb{B}}[\vec{K}] = (_{\mathbb{B}}[K_0], \ldots, _{\mathbb{B}}[K_{kN-1}])$

Output: Key-switching key ksk $= \{\mathsf{ksk}_{J,j'}\}_{J=0,j'=0}^{kN-1,t-1}$

1: P_0 sets $_{\mathbb{T}}[1/B^{j'+1}]_0 = 1/B^{j'+1}$ and $P_{i''} \in \mathcal{P} \setminus \{P_0\}$ sets $_{\mathbb{T}}[1/B^{j'+1}]_{i''} = 0$
   for $j' = 0, \ldots, t - 1$ and $i'' = 1, \ldots, N' - 1$.
2: **for** $J = 0, \ldots, kN - 1; j' = 0, \ldots, t - 1$ **do in parallel**

3:    $\mathcal{ST}_{0,1/B^{j'+1}} \leftarrow \mathsf{TableShuffle}((_\mathbb{B}[0], _\mathbb{T}[0]), (_\mathbb{B}[1], _\mathbb{T}[1/B^{j'+1}]))$

4:    By $\Pi_{\mathsf{BMUX}}(_\mathbb{B}[K_J], \mathcal{ST}_{0,1/B^{j'+1}})$, parties obtain $_\mathbb{T}[K_J/B^{j'+1}]$.

5: **end for**

6: Parties consider $_\mathbb{T}[K_J/B^{j'+1}]$ as the share of plaintext in line 13 of Algorithm 2 and generate the ciphertext as in Algorithm 2 with sampling noise from $\chi_{(0,\sigma_{\mathsf{ks}}^2)}$, not from $\chi_{(0,\sigma^2)}$. Then, parties set the generated ciphertext as $\mathsf{ksk}_{J,j'}$ (for $J = 0, \ldots, kN - 1; j' = 0, \ldots, t - 1$ in parallel).

7: Return $\mathsf{ksk} = \{\mathsf{ksk}_{J,j'}\}_{J=0,j'=0}^{kN-1,t-1}$.

Algorithm 4. Distributed key generation for bootstrapping key Π_{DBSK}

Input: Public parameters param, shares of decryption keys $_\mathbb{B}[\vec{s}] = (_\mathbb{B}[s_0], \ldots, _\mathbb{B}[s_{n-1}])$ and $_\mathbb{B}[\vec{K}_h] = (_\mathbb{B}[K_{hN+0}], \ldots, _\mathbb{B}[K_{hN+(N-1)}])$ for $h = 0, \ldots, k - 1$

Output: Bootstrapping key $\mathsf{bsk} = \{\mathsf{bsk}_{i'}\}_{i'=0}^{n-1}$

1: $\mathcal{C}$ samples $e_{i',j'} \leftarrow \hat{\chi}_{(0,\sigma'^2)}$. By $\mathsf{Share}(\mathbb{T}_N[X], \mathcal{C}, e_{i',j'})$, $\mathcal{C}$ distributes $_{\mathbb{T}_N[X]}[e_{i',j'}]$ to parties for $i' = 0, \ldots, n - 1; j' = 0, \ldots, (k+1)\ell - 1$ in parallel.

2: Let $_{\mathbb{T}_N[X]}[B(B_g,\ell)]$ be the vector of shares $(_{\mathbb{T}_N[X]}[B_g^{-1}], \ldots, _{\mathbb{T}_N[X]}[B_g^{-\ell}])^T$. P_0 sets $_{\mathbb{T}_N[X]}[B_g^{-w}]_0 = B_g^{-w}$ and $P_{i''} \in \mathcal{P} \setminus \{P_0\}$ sets $_{\mathbb{T}_N[X]}[B_g^{-w}]_{i''} = 0$ for $i'' = 1, \ldots, N' - 1; w = 1, \ldots, \ell$.

3: P_i sets $_{\mathbb{T}_N[X]}[0]_i = 0$ for $i = 0, \ldots, N' - 1$. Then, parties set $_{\mathbb{T}_N[X]}[\vec{0}] = (_{\mathbb{T}_N[X]}[0], \ldots, _{\mathbb{T}_N[X]}[0])$.

4: **for** $i' = 0, \ldots, n - 1$ **do in parallel**

5:    $\mathcal{ST}_{\vec{0},B(B_g,\ell)} \leftarrow \mathsf{TableShuffle}((_\mathbb{B}[0], _{\mathbb{T}_N[X]}[\vec{0}]), (_\mathbb{B}[1], _{\mathbb{T}_N[X]}[B(B_g,\ell)]))$

6:    By $\Pi_{\mathsf{BMUX}}(_\mathbb{B}[s_{i'}], \mathcal{ST}_{\vec{0},B(B_g,\ell)})$, parties obtain $_{\mathbb{T}_N[X]}[s_{i'} \cdot B(B_g,\ell)]$.

7: **end for**

8: **for** $h = 0, \ldots, k - 1; j = 0, \ldots, N - 1; i' = 0, \ldots, n - 1; j' = 0, \ldots, (k+1)\ell - 1$ **do in parallel**

9:    By $\mathsf{RandGen}(\mathbb{T}_N[X], \mathcal{P})$, parties obtain $_{\mathbb{T}_N[X]}[a_{h,i',j'}]$. Then, parties compute $_{\mathbb{T}_N[X]}[X^j \cdot a_{h,i',j'}] = X^j \cdot {}_{\mathbb{T}_N[X]}[a_{h,i',j'}]$ for $j = 0, \ldots, N - 1$.

10:   $\mathcal{ST}_{0,X^j \cdot a_{h,i',j'}} \leftarrow \mathsf{TableShuffle}((_\mathbb{B}[0], _{\mathbb{T}_N[X]}[0]), (_\mathbb{B}[1], _{\mathbb{T}_N[X]}[X^j \cdot a_{h,i',j'}]))$

11:   By $\Pi_{\mathsf{BMUX}}(_\mathbb{B}[K_{hN+j}], \mathcal{ST}_{0,X^j \cdot a_{h,i',j'}})$, parties obtain $_{\mathbb{T}_N[X]}[K_{hN+j} \cdot X^j \cdot a_{h,i',j'}]$.

12: **end for**

13:   $_{\mathbb{T}_N[X]}[b_{i',j'}] = \sum_{h=0}^{k-1} {}_{\mathbb{T}_N[X]}[K_h \cdot a_{h,i',j'}] + {}_{\mathbb{T}_N[X]}[e_{i',j'}] = \sum_{h=0;j=0}^{k-1;N-1} {}_{\mathbb{T}_N[X]}[K_{hN+j} \cdot X^j \cdot a_{i',j'}] + {}_{\mathbb{T}_N[X]}[e_{i',j'}]$ for $i' = 0, \ldots, n - 1; j' = 0, \ldots, (k+1)\ell - 1$.

14: Parties set $_{\mathbb{T}_N[X]}[z_{i',j'}] = ((_{\mathbb{T}_N[X]}[a_{0,i',j'}], \ldots, _{\mathbb{T}_N[X]}[a_{k-1,i',j'}]), _{\mathbb{T}_N[X]}[b_{i',j'}])$ for $i' = 0, \ldots, n - 1; j' = 0, \ldots, (k+1)\ell - 1$.

15: For $i' = 0, \ldots, n - 1$, $_{\mathbb{T}_N[X]}[\mathsf{bsk}_{i'}] =$

$$\begin{pmatrix} _{\mathbb{T}_N[X]}[s_{i'} \cdot B(B_g,\ell)] & \cdots & 0 \\ \vdots & \ddots & \vdots \\ 0 & \cdots & _{\mathbb{T}_N[X]}[s_{i'} \cdot B(B_g,\ell)] \end{pmatrix} + \begin{pmatrix} _{\mathbb{T}_N[X]}[z_{i',0}] \\ \vdots \\ _{\mathbb{T}_N[X]}[z_{i',(k+1)\ell-1}] \end{pmatrix}$$

16: By Open, parties reconstruct $\mathsf{bsk}_{i'}$ from $_{\mathbb{T}_N[X]}[\mathsf{bsk}_{i'}]$ for $i' = 0, \ldots, n - 1$.

17: Return $\mathsf{bsk} = \{\mathsf{bsk}_{i'}\}_{i'=0}^{n-1}$.

DistEKGen: Since key-switching and bootstrapping keys can be computed only by $\mathcal{P}$ and $\mathcal{C}$, independently of the plaintext, which is the actual input to be computed, we assume that DistEKGen is computed in the offline phase. First, by RandGen$(\mathbb{B}, \mathcal{P})$, parties obtain $_\mathbb{B}[K_J]$ for $J = 0, \ldots, kN - 1$. Parties set $(\boldsymbol{K}_0, \ldots, \boldsymbol{K}_{k-1}) \in (\mathbb{B}_N[X])^k$ as the secret of the TRLWE problem by setting that $\boldsymbol{K}_h = \sum_{j=0}^{N-1} K_{hN+j} \cdot X^j$ for $h = 0, \ldots, k-1; j = 0, \ldots, N-1$.

Next, we describe the distributed key generation for key-switching key Π_{DKSK} in Algorithm 3. In lines 1 to 5, parties compute $_\mathbb{T}[K_J/B^{j'+1}]$ by TableShuffle, Π_{BMUX}, and using $_\mathbb{B}[K_J]$ and $B \in$ param. Π_{BMUX} outputs $_\mathbb{T}[0]$ if $K_J = 0$ and $_\mathbb{T}[1/B^{j'+1}]$ otherwise. That is, Π_{BMUX} outputs $_\mathbb{T}[K_J/B^{j'+1}]$. Then, as described in line 6, parties compute the encryption of $_\mathbb{T}[K_J/B^{j'+1}]$ in the almost same way as Algorithm 2 as $\mathsf{ksk}_{J,j'}$. Finally, parties obtain the key-switching key $\mathsf{ksk} = \{\mathsf{ksk}_{J,j'}\}_{J=0,j'=0}^{kN-1,t-1}$.

Algorithm 4 describes the distributed key generation for bootstrapping key Π_{DBSK}. We set $B(B_g, \ell) = (B_g^{-1}, \ldots, B_g^{-\ell})^T$. Π_{DBSK} is divided into three parts:

1. Computing shares of the product of the decryption key and the gadget matrix (in lines 2 to 7)
2. Computing shares of the TRLWE encryptions of zero (in lines 8 to 14)
3. Merging shares computed in previous parts and generating $\mathsf{bsk} = \{\mathsf{bsk}_{i'}\}_{i'=0}^{n-1}$ by Open (in lines 15 to 17)

Note that parties use TableShuffle and Π_{BMUX} in parts 1 and 2 to compute the product of shares on $\mathbb{B}$ (resp. $\mathbb{B}_N[X]$) and $\mathbb{T}$ (resp. $\mathbb{T}_N[X]$).

Algorithm 5. DistDec Π_{DistDec}

Input: Public parameters param, ciphertext $c = (\vec{a} = (a_0, \ldots, a_{n-1}), b = \vec{a} \cdot \vec{s} + \mu + e) \in \mathbb{T}^{n+1}$, shares of decryption key $_\mathbb{B}[\vec{s}] = (_\mathbb{B}[s_0], \ldots, _\mathbb{B}[s_{n-1}])$, receiver P_R

Output: P_R receives the plaintext of c, $m(= 4 \cdot \mu)$ where $m \in \mathbb{B}$ and $\mu \in \{0, 1/4\}$
1: (Offline phase)
2: $\mathcal{C}$ samples $e' \leftarrow \chi_{(0,\sigma^2)}$. By Share$(\mathbb{T}, e', \mathcal{C})$, $\mathcal{C}$ distributes $_\mathbb{T}[e']$ to parties.
3: (Online phase)
4: P_0 sets $_\mathbb{T}[a_{i'}]_0 = a_{i'}$. $P_{i''} \in \mathcal{P} \setminus \{P_0\}$ sets $_\mathbb{T}[a_{i'}]_{i''} = 0$ for $i'' = 1, \ldots, N' - 1$.
5: In the same way as lines 7 to 11 of Algorithm 2, parties compute $_\mathbb{T}[\vec{a} \cdot \vec{s}]$.
6: $_\mathbb{T}[\mu + e + e'] = b - _\mathbb{T}[\vec{a} \cdot \vec{s}] + _\mathbb{T}[e']$
7: By Open$(_\mathbb{T}[\mu + e + e'], P_R)$, P_R obtains $\mu + e + e'$. Then, P_R rounds $\mu + e + e'$ to the nearest 0 or 1/4, whichever is closer. Let $\hat{\mu}$ be the rounded value.
8: Return $m = 4\hat{\mu}$.

DistDec: Algorithm 5 describes the distributed decryption Π_{DistDec}. In the offline phase of Π_{DistDec} at line 2, $\mathcal{C}$ samples the smudging noise e' from $\chi_{(0,\sigma^2)}$ and distributes it to parties as $_\mathbb{T}[e']$. In the online phase of Π_{DistDec} (in lines 4 to 8), by using $\vec{a}$, parties set $_\mathbb{T}[a_{i'}]$ from $i' = 0 \ldots, n-1$. Then, parties compute $_\mathbb{T}[\vec{a} \cdot \vec{s}]$

in the same way as Algorithm 2. After that, parties compute $_{\mathbb{T}}[\mu + e + e']$ and reconstruct it to P_R by Open. Finally, P_R rounds $\mu + e + e'$ as $\hat{\mu} \in \{0, 1/4\}$ and gets the plaintext of c, $m = 4\hat{\mu}$.

Observations on the Impact of Smudging Noise. Adding the smudging noise e' to b in line 6 of Algorithm 5 is equivalent to adding a trivial ciphertext for a plaintext of 0 where random values are all zero, i.e., $c' = ((0, \ldots, 0), 0 + e') \in \mathbb{T}^{n+1}$ to c. Due to the constraints imposed by the gate-bootstrapping in CGGI [13], it holds that $|e|, |e'| < 1/16$ and $|e + e'| < 1/8$ where $|e|$ and $|e'|$ are the absolute values of e and e', respectively. Note that the plaintext space encoded on $\mathbb{T}$ is $\{0, 1/4\}$. Hence, P_R can correctly perform the rounding at line 7 of Algorithm 5. Therefore, in our scheme, the noise smudging does not affect the decryption or the noise analysis.

Note that P_R can compute $e + e' = (\mu + e + e') - m/4$ by using m at line 8 of Algorithm 5. Even if P_R computes $b - (e + e')$, P_R can only get the ciphertext replacing e by $(-e')$. Since e' is sampled from the same distribution as $\chi_{(0,\sigma^2)}$ from which e was sampled, P_R cannot solve the TLWE problem or break our scheme. Hence, it is sufficient that the smudging noise is sampled from $\chi_{(0,\sigma^2)}$.

Validity of Client-Aided Model. A natural question is which entity will play the role of $\mathcal{C}$ in real-world services. The most straightforward way to assume $\mathcal{C}$ is to add a new entity or server that plays the role of $\mathcal{C}$.

Without adding a new dedicated entity, during DistDec, an honest computing server that does not collude with $\mathcal{P}$ and performs homomorphic operations between ciphertexts can play the role of $\mathcal{C}$. During DistEnc, like the client-server model [2], an input dealer who is not in $\mathcal{P}$ can play it. During DistEKGen, if the computing server (not parties) reconstructs the keys, then one of the parties can play it. In other words, an entity other than the entity that obtains the output of each distributed algorithm can play the role of $\mathcal{C}$. If the noise-making $\mathcal{C}$ gets the output of each distributed protocol, it may leak partial information about the decryption key or plaintext to $\mathcal{C}$ because $\mathcal{C}$ can remove the noise from outputs.

In this way, there are several practical ways to assume $\mathcal{C}$. Hence, we believe that it is reasonable to introduce a client-aided model at our scheme.

Optimization of Round Complexities and Corruption Rate. While the number of communication rounds for distributed key generation and distributed decryption in many ThFHEs is constant, those in our scheme require $O(\binom{N'}{t})$ times of communication rounds. In addition, while most ThFHEs assume $t < N'$, our scheme assumes $t < N'/2$. These drawbacks are caused by using TableShuffle based on the resharing-based shuffle [24] in our scheme.

One way to improve our round complexities and our corruption rate is to have $\mathcal{C}$ shuffle the table of shares in exchange for an increased load on $\mathcal{C}$. As described in Algorithms 2, 3, 4, and 5, the inputs of TableShuffle are the indices and the $B(B_g, \ell)$ or the random values (or random polynomials) of ciphertext. In other words, TableShuffle does not take any secrets as inputs. Hence, instead of TableShuffle, $\mathcal{C}$ can generate and distribute the shares of the shuffled table to $\mathcal{P}$ by Share in exchange for one communication round between $\mathcal{C}$ and $\mathcal{P}$ and for the number of bits communicated about the shares of the shuffled table. This method does not leak secrets and does not affect security unless $\mathcal{C}$ colludes with a party in $\mathcal{P}$. Since this method removes TableShuffle from our scheme, our scheme can achieve constant rounds and assume $t < N'$. Note that if this method is also used for DistDec, $\mathcal{C}$ must also participate in the online phase since it must shuffle the random vector $\vec{a}$ of the input ciphertext.

Security Proof Sketch. The security of Eval and ciphertext is the same as in the CGGI [13]. In other words, our scheme is as secure as the CGGI as long as we assume that any probabilistic polynomial-time adversaries cannot solve the TLWE and TRLWE problems.

In addition, we can prove that the BMUX, DistDKGen, DistEKGen, DistEnc, and DistDec are secure by assuming that (N', N')-ASS and the resharing-based shuffle [24] are secure. Since these protocols are composed of (N', N')-ASS, the resharing-based shuffle [24], and operations without communications, these protocols achieve universal composability (UC) [10] by assuming input availability [23] as long as building blocks are secure. Hence, we can combine these protocols with CGGI and extend CGGI to the ThFHE variant without compromising security. For more details, see Appendix B.

4 Experiments

We evaluate our scheme against the original CGGI [13] and MK-CGGI [11] in terms of execution time.

Experimental Setting. We implement CGGI [13] and our scheme by C++. As an implementation of the MK-CGGI, we use the authors' one that is publicly available. We emphasize that we can only compare the relative execution times because different libraries are used for internal operations, and there is room for optimization. For example, we use the Randen library [36] to generate random numbers, while MK-CGGI uses the C++ standard library function, which is faster but not designed to be cryptographically secure. In addition, we use FFTW library [18] to multiply polynomials, while MK-CGGI uses Spqlios[3], which is optimized for CGGI.

Table 2 shows the ciphertext parameters we used. Our scheme keeps the same parameters as CGGI and, as described earlier, achieves the same security level even if the number of parties is increased.

We measured the execution time for key generation, encryption, decryption, and homomorphic evaluation on a server machine (Intel Xeon Silver 4114 CPU with 96 GB of DDR4-2400 memory). For simplicity, we executed the multiparty operations of all of the parties serially on a single core of this single machine. In a real-world setting, each party may be assigned to a different machine connected to a network. In this case, some of the operations (e.g., decryption key generation) can be processed in parallel, but the parties need to communicate over the network. Therefore, the network's bandwidth and latency may affect the performance. In the results shown below, we also give the estimated communication

---

[3] https://github.com/tfhe/tfhe/tree/master/src/libtfhe/fft_processors/spqlios.

Table 2. Parameter settings derived from the original papers [11,13]. We denote the security level estimated by lattice-estimator [1] (as of 23 Jan. 2023) as λ and λ'. Both schemes use $N = 1024$ and $k = 1$ as TRLWE dimension. For B_g and ℓ in MK-CGGI, values when the maximum allowed number of parties is two, four, and eight, respectively, are shown.

Scheme	TLWE					TRLWE			
	n	σ	B	t	λ	σ'	B_g	ℓ	λ'
CGGI [13] and ours	500	2^{-7}	2	16	150	2.16×10^{-5}	1024	2	191
MK-CGGI [11]	560	3.05×10^{-5}	4	8	107	3.72×10^{-9}	512, 256, 64	3, 4, 5	112

Table 3. Measured execution time and estimated communication time (s) of our implementation of the original CGGI [13] (column #Parties=1 and #Corrupt.=N/A) and our scheme (the other cases).

	Execution						Communication				
#Parties	1	3	4	8				3	4	8	
#Corrupt.	N/A	1	1	1	2	3		1	1	1	2	3
Key gen.	0.85	224	602	5521	18195	33118	LAN	83.9	164	755	2541	4703
							WAN	11649	22840	104905	352967	653251
Enc.	0.00	0.00	0.00	0.01	0.01	0.02	LAN	0.01	0.01	0.06	0.19	0.35
							WAN	0.86	1.73	8.07	27.2	50.4
Dec.	0.00	0.00	0.00	0.01	0.01	0.02	LAN	0.01	0.01	0.06	0.19	0.35
							WAN	0.94	1.81	8.16	27.4	50.6
Eval. (NAND)	0.62						LAN	No comm.				
							WAN					

time. Specifically, we adopt two settings: one is over a local area network (LAN; 10 Gbps throughput and 0.5 ms latency) [29], and the other is over a wide area network (WAN; 72 Mbps throughput and 72 ms latency) [30], which is based on a measurement between the AWS US East and West regions.

Experimental Results. Table 3 shows the time for the original CGGI and our scheme, and Table 4 shows the time for MK-CGGI. In Tables 3 and 4, the key generation time is the sum of decryption key, key-switching key, and bootstrapping key. Values are rounded, thus 0.00 means that the time is less than 5 ms. Execution time for each operation is averaged over multiple runs so that the total time reaches 0.5 s. For ours and MK-CGGI, key generation, encryption, and decryption get slower as the number of parties increases. Notably, our scheme also becomes slower along with a larger number of corruptions since the number of shuffle operations increases. Because the internal operations (e.g. polynomial multiplication) are implemented differently, our CGGI implementation's evaluation is even slower than MK-CGGI's two-party setting. However, the evaluation of MK-CGGI gets slower when the number of parties increases. In contrast, our scheme's evaluation keeps the same time as CGGI, and it becomes faster than MK-CGGI when the number of parties is more than two.

Table 4. Measured execution time and estimated communication time (s) of the authors' implementation in MK-CGGI [11].

	Computation				Communication		
#Parties	2	4	8		2	4	8
Key gen.	3.08	7.08	16.0	LAN	No comm.		
				WAN			
Enc.	0.00	0.00	0.00	LAN	No comm.		
				WAN			
Dec.	0.00	0.00	0.00	LAN	0.00	0.00	0.00
				WAN	0.00	0.00	0.00
Eval. (NAND)	0.28	1.20	5.90	LAN	No comm.		
				WAN			

Note that the key generation of our current implementation is relatively slower in terms of execution and estimated communication time. Quick profiling showed that random number generation by the Randen library occupies more than half of the time, and the shuffle operation follows next. One may offload the shuffle operation onto the client to reduce the execution time and the communication overhead. However, since the number of parties is fixed in the setup phase in the threshold setting, key updates seldom occur. In addition, as suggested earlier, we can generate the keys independently of the input plaintext. Hence, the key generation can be performed in the offline phase and does not affect the response time of the SC in the online phase. Therefore, the performance of the homomorphic operation, of which procedure and execution time are identical to CGGI in our scheme, is more critical for the whole application.

5 Conclusions

We proposed the client-aided ThFHE based on CGGI [13]. By implementing and experimenting with our scheme, we compared the performance between CGGI [13] and MK-CGGI [11] and our scheme.

Our scheme has the same bootstrapping as CGGI and the performance of our homomorphic operations is independent of the number of parties. Hence, in the multiparty setting, our scheme is superior to MK-CGGI, where the performance degrades with the number of keys involved in the homomorphic operation. In addition, the noise analysis and security in our scheme is identical to CGGI because it is not affected by the noise smudging.

Hence, we can extend existing OSS implementing CGGI to our scheme, i.e., ThFHE variant of CGGI without changing the implementation part regarding homomorphic operations. While the standardisation on FHE[4] and threshold

---

[4] https://www.iso.org/standard/83139.html.

cryptography[5] is going on, we believe that our scheme is a good candidate from a standardization perspective, since the discussion of security for CGGI can be applied to our scheme as well.

A   TLWE and TRLWE Problems

Definition 1 (LWE Problem Over $\mathbb{T}$ (TLWE Problem)). *We call the pair of $(\vec{a}, b) \in \mathbb{T}^{n+1}$ TLWE sample where $\vec{a} \xleftarrow{\mathsf{U}} \mathbb{T}^n$, $\vec{s} \xleftarrow{\mathsf{U}} \mathbb{B}^n$, $e \leftarrow \chi_{(0,\sigma^2)}$, and $b = \vec{a} \cdot \vec{s} + e$. For the TLWE sample, we define the following two problems:*

- *Decisional TLWE Problem: The problem of distinguishing between a given TLWE sample $(\vec{a}, b)$ and uniformly randomly sampled elements from $\mathbb{T}^{n+1}$, when the secret $\vec{s}$ is fixed.*
- *Search TLWE Problem: The problem of finding the (common) secret $\vec{s}$ from a given arbitrary number of TLWE samples.*

Definition 2 (LWE Problem Over $\mathbb{T}_N[X]$ (TRLWE Problem)). *We call the pair of $((\boldsymbol{a}_0, \ldots, \boldsymbol{a}_{k-1}), \boldsymbol{b}) \in (\mathbb{T}_N[X])^{k+1}$ TRLWE sample where $(\boldsymbol{a}_0, \ldots, \boldsymbol{a}_{k-1}) \xleftarrow{\mathsf{U}} (\mathbb{T}_N[X])^k$, $(\boldsymbol{K}_0, \ldots, \boldsymbol{K}_{k-1}) \xleftarrow{\mathsf{U}} (\mathbb{B}_N[X])^k$, $e \leftarrow \hat{\chi}_{(0,\sigma'^2)}$, and $\boldsymbol{b} = \sum_{i=0}^{k-1} \boldsymbol{a}_i \cdot \boldsymbol{K}_i + e$. For the TRLWE sample, we can define the decisional and search TRLWE problems as well as the TLWE problem.*

B   Security Definition and Proof

$\boxed{\begin{array}{l} \qquad\qquad \mathcal{F}_{\mathsf{Open}} \text{ - (Ideal functionality for opening } {}_{\mathsf{S}}[x]) \\[6pt] \text{1. Let } P_R \in \mathcal{P} \text{ be the receiver. } P_i \text{ sends the message } (\mathsf{Open}, \ {}_{\mathsf{S}}[x]_i, \ P_i, \ P_R) \\ \quad \text{to } \mathcal{F}_{\mathsf{Open}} \text{ for } i = 0, \ldots, N' - 1. \\ \text{2. } \mathcal{F}_{\mathsf{Open}} \text{ computes } x = \sum_{i=0}^{N'-1} x_i \text{ by performing the modulus operation} \\ \quad \text{according to } \mathbb{S}. \text{ Then, } \mathcal{F}_{\mathsf{Open}} \text{ sends } x \text{ to } P_R. \end{array}}$

Our protocols, BMUX, DistDKGen, DistEKGen, DistEnc, and DistDec are secure in the presence of corrupted parties by a semi-honest adversary if the view of corrupted parties in a real-world protocol execution can be generated by a probabilistic polynomial-time simulator $\mathcal{S}$ given only the corrupted parties' inputs and outputs of a function f. Let x_i and $f_i(\vec{x})$ be P_i's input and output where $\vec{x} = (x_0, \ldots, x_{N'-1})$, respectively. Let $\mathsf{VIEW}_i^{\Pi}(\vec{x})$ and $\mathsf{Output}^{\Pi}(\vec{x})$ be P_i's view (including P_i's inputs, outputs, and random coins) of execution of protocol Π on $\vec{x}$ and the output of all parties from the execution of Π, respectively.

---

[5] https://csrc.nist.gov/Projects/threshold-cryptography.

$\mathcal{F}_{\mathsf{BMUX}}$ - (Ideal functionality for BMUX)

1. We set the share of the selector $_\mathrm{B}[s]$ and the shuffled table of shares $\mathcal{ST}_{\vec{x}_{\mathsf{idx}},\vec{x}_{\mathsf{idx}\oplus 1}} = ((_\mathrm{B}[\mathsf{idx}], _{\mathbb{S}'}[\vec{x}_{\mathsf{idx}}]), (_\mathrm{B}[\mathsf{idx}\oplus 1], _{\mathbb{S}'}[\vec{x}_{\mathsf{idx}\oplus 1}]))$ where $_{\mathbb{S}'}[\vec{x}_{\mathsf{idx}}] = (_{\mathbb{S}'}[x_{\mathsf{idx},0}], \ldots, _{\mathbb{S}'}[x_{\mathsf{idx},C-1}])$, $_{\mathbb{S}'}[\vec{x}_{\mathsf{idx}\oplus 1}] = (_{\mathbb{S}'}[x_{\mathsf{idx}\oplus 1,0}], \ldots, _{\mathbb{S}'}[x_{\mathsf{idx}\oplus 1,C-1}])$, and $\mathbb{S}' \in \{\mathbb{T}, \mathbb{T}_N[X]\}$.
2. P_i sends the message $(\mathsf{BMUX}, _\mathrm{B}[s]_i, _\mathrm{B}[\mathsf{idx}]_i, \{_{\mathbb{S}'}[x_{i',j'}]\}_{i'=0,1;j'=0,\ldots,C-1}$ $P_i)$ to $\mathcal{F}_{\mathsf{BMUX}}$ for $i = 0, \ldots, N'-1$.
3. $\mathcal{F}_{\mathsf{BMUX}}$ computes $\mathsf{idx} \oplus s = \sum_{i=0}^{N'-1} {}_\mathrm{B}[\mathsf{idx}]_i \oplus {}_\mathrm{B}[s]_i \bmod 2$ and $x_{\mathsf{idx}\oplus s,j'} = \sum_{i=0}^{N'-1} {}_{\mathbb{S}'}[x_{\mathsf{idx}\oplus s,j'}]_i$ by performing the modulus operation according to $\mathbb{S}'$ for $j' = 0, \ldots, C-1$. Then, $\mathcal{F}_{\mathsf{BMUX}}$ generates $x_{\mathsf{idx}\oplus s,j',i''} \xleftarrow{\mathsf{U}} \mathbb{S}'$ for $i'' = 1, \ldots, N'-1$ and sets $x_{\mathsf{idx}\oplus s,j',0} = x_{\mathsf{idx}\oplus s,j'} - \sum_{i''=0}^{N'-1} x_{\mathsf{idx}\oplus s,j',i''}$ by performing the modulus operation according to $\mathbb{S}'$ for $j' = 0, \ldots, C-1$.
4. $\mathcal{F}_{\mathsf{BMUX}}$ sets $_{\mathbb{S}'}[x_{\mathsf{idx}\oplus s,j'}]_i = x_{\mathsf{idx}\oplus s,j',i}$ and sends it to P_i for $i = 0, \ldots, N'-1; j' = 0, \ldots, C-1$.

Definition 3 (Perfect Security) . *Let $f : (\{0,1\}^*)^{N'} \to (\{0,1\}^*)^{N'}$ be a probabilistic N'-ary functionality. We say that Π computes f with perfect security in $t(< N'/2)$ corruptions by a semi-honest adversary for f if there exists $\mathcal{S}$ for every corrupted party and every $\vec{x} \in (\{0,1\}^*)^{N'}$ where $|x_0| = \cdots = |x_{N'-1}|$ as follows.*

$$\{(\mathcal{S}(x_i, f_i(\vec{x})), f(\vec{x}))\} \equiv \{(\mathsf{VIEW}_i^\Pi(\vec{x}), \mathsf{Output}^\Pi(\vec{x}))\} \tag{1}$$

We prove that our protocols achieve UC-security [10] by assuming input availability [23] and hybrid model. Loosely speaking, in the hybrid model, a protocol can replace calls to subprotocol by invocations of ideal functionalities $\mathcal{F}$. By replacing the subprotocols with ideal functionalities of subprotocols, we prove that our protocols compute its ideal functionalities with perfect security in t corruptions by a semi-honest adversary in a classic stand-alone setting. Then, as shown in [23], we can prove that our protocols achieve UC-security automatically by assuming input availability (i.e., the property that the inputs of all parties are fixed before protocol executions).

For example, we can prove that Π_{BMUX} in the $\mathcal{F}_{\mathsf{Open}}$-hybrid model computes $\mathcal{F}_{\mathsf{BMUX}}$ with perfect security in t corruptions by a semi-honest adversary. Π_{BMUX} is composed of invoking Open and operations among shares without communications. Hence, if Open computes $\mathcal{F}_{\mathsf{Open}}$ with perfect security in t corruptions by a semi-honest adversary, we can replace Open by $\mathcal{F}_{\mathsf{Open}}$ and $\mathcal{S}$ can be composed in the t corruptions by a semi-honest adversary. Since our other protocols are composed of invoking subprotocols written in Sect. 2.4 and operations among shares without communications, $\mathcal{S}$ for our other protocols can also be composed as long as building blocks are secure, that is, as long as building blocks can compute its ideal functionalities with perfect security in t corruptions by a semi-honest adversary.

References

1. Albrecht, M.R., Player, R., Scott, S.: On the concrete hardness of learning with errors. J. Math. Cryptol. **9**(3), 169–203 (2015). https://doi.org/10.1515/jmc-2015-0016
2. Araki, T., Furukawa, J., Lindell, Y., Nof, A., Ohara, K.: High-throughput semi-honest secure three-party computation with an honest majority. In: Proceedings of the 2016 ACM SIGSAC Conference on Computer and Communications Security (CCS 2016), pp. 805–817. Association for Computing Machinery, New York (2016). https://doi.org/10.1145/2976749.2978331
3. Asharov, G., Jain, A., López-Alt, A., Tromer, E., Vaikuntanathan, V., Wichs, D.: Multiparty computation with low communication, computation and interaction via threshold FHE. In: Pointcheval, D., Johansson, T. (eds.) EUROCRYPT 2012. LNCS, vol. 7237, pp. 483–501. Springer, Heidelberg (2012). https://doi.org/10.1007/978-3-642-29011-4_29
4. Badawi, A.A., et al.: OpenFHE: Open-Source Fully Homomorphic Encryption Library. Cryptology ePrint Archive, Paper 2022/915 (2022). https://eprint.iacr.org/2022/915
5. Beaver, D.: Commodity-based cryptography (extended abstract). In: STOC, pp. 446–455. ACM (1997)
6. Ben-Or, M., Goldwasser, S., Wigderson, A.: Completeness theorems for non-cryptographic fault-tolerant distributed computation (extended abstract). In: STOC, pp. 1–10. ACM (1988)
7. Boneh, D., et al.: Threshold cryptosystems from threshold fully homomorphic encryption. In: Shacham, H., Boldyreva, A. (eds.) CRYPTO 2018. LNCS, vol. 10991, pp. 565–596. Springer, Cham (2018). https://doi.org/10.1007/978-3-319-96884-1_19
8. Bonte, C., Iliashenko, I., Park, J., Pereira, H.V.L., Smart, N.P.: FINAL: faster FHE instantiated with NTRU and LWE. IACR Cryptol. ePrint Arch (2022)
9. Boudgoust, K., Scholl, P.: Simple threshold (fully homomorphic) encryption from lwe with polynomial modulus. Cryptology ePrint Archive, Paper 2023/016 (2023). https://eprint.iacr.org/2023/016
10. Canetti, R.: Universally composable security: a new paradigm for cryptographic protocols. In: FOCS, pp. 136–145. IEEE Computer Society (2001)
11. Chen, H., Chillotti, I., Song, Y.: Multi-key homomorphic encryption from TFHE. In: Galbraith, S.D., Moriai, S. (eds.) ASIACRYPT 2019. LNCS, vol. 11922, pp. 446–472. Springer, Cham (2019). https://doi.org/10.1007/978-3-030-34621-8_16
12. Chen, H., Dai, W., Kim, M., Song, Y.: Efficient multi-key homomorphic encryption with packed ciphertexts with application to oblivious neural network inference. In: CCS, pp. 395–412. ACM (2019)
13. Chillotti, I., Gama, N., Georgieva, M., Izabachène, M.: TFHE: fast fully homomorphic encryption over the torus. J. Cryptol. **33**(1), 34–91 (2020)
14. Chillotti, I., Joye, M., Ligier, D., Orfila, J.B., Tap, S.: Concrete: concrete operates on ciphertexts rapidly by extending TFHE. In: WAHC 2020–8th Workshop on Encrypted Computing and Applied Homomorphic Cryptography, vol. 15 (2020)
15. Chowdhury, S., et al.: Efficient Threshold FHE with Application to Real-Time Systems. Cryptology ePrint Archive, Paper 2022/1625 (2022). https://eprint.iacr.org/2022/1625
16. Ducas, L., Micciancio, D.: FHEW: bootstrapping homomorphic encryption in less than a second. In: Oswald, E., Fischlin, M. (eds.) EUROCRYPT 2015, vol.

9056, pp. 617–640. Springer, Heidelberg (2015). https://doi.org/10.1007/978-3-662-46800-5_24

17. Fan, J., Vercauteren, F.: Somewhat practical fully homomorphic encryption. IACR Cryptol. ePrint Arch. (2012)

18. Frigo, M., Johnson, S.: The design and implementation of FFTW3. Proc. IEEE **93**(2), 216–231 (2005). https://doi.org/10.1109/JPROC.2004.840301

19. Gentry, C.: Fully homomorphic encryption using ideal lattices. In: STOC, pp. 169–178. ACM (2009)

20. Goldreich, O., Micali, S., Wigderson, A.: How to play any mental game or a completeness theorem for protocols with honest majority. In: STOC, pp. 218–229. ACM (1987)

21. Gorantala, S., et al.: A general purpose transpiler for fully homomorphic encryption. Cryptology ePrint Archive, Paper 2021/811 (2021). https://eprint.iacr.org/2021/811

22. Joye, M.: SOK: fully homomorphic encryption over the [discretized] torus. IACR Trans. Cryptogr. Hardw. Embed. Syst. **2022**(4), 661–692 (2022)

23. Kushilevitz, E., Lindell, Y., Rabin, T.: Information-theoretically secure protocols and security under composition. SIAM J. Comput. **39**(5), 2090–2112 (2010)

24. Laur, S., Willemson, J., Zhang, B.: Round-efficient oblivious database manipulation. In: Lai, X., Zhou, J., Li, H. (eds.) Information Security, pp. 262–277. Springer, Heidelberg (2011). https://doi.org/10.1007/978-3-642-24861-0_18

25. Lee, Y., et al.: Efficient fhew bootstrapping with small evaluation keys, and applications to threshold homomorphic encryption. Cryptology ePrint Archive, Paper 2022/198 (2022). https://eprint.iacr.org/2022/198

26. López-Alt, A., Tromer, E., Vaikuntanathan, V.: On-the-fly multiparty computation on the cloud via multikey fully homomorphic encryption. In: STOC, pp. 1219–1234. ACM (2012)

27. Matsuoka, K.: TFHEpp: pure C++ implementation of TFHE cryptosystem (2020). https://github.com/virtualsecureplatform/TFHEpp

28. Maurer, U.: Secure multi-party computation made simple. In: Cimato, S., Persiano, G., Galdi, C. (eds.) SCN 2002. LNCS, vol. 2576, pp. 14–28. Springer, Heidelberg (2003). https://doi.org/10.1007/3-540-36413-7_2

29. Mohassel, P., Rindal, P.: ABY3: a mixed protocol framework for machine learning. In: Proceedings of the 2018 ACM SIGSAC Conference on Computer and Communications Security (CCS 2018), pp. 35–52. Association for Computing Machinery, New York (2018). https://doi.org/10.1145/3243734.3243760

30. Mohassel, P., Zhang, Y.: SecureML: a system for scalable privacy-preserving machine learning. Cryptology ePrint Archive, Paper 2017/396 (2017)

31. Morita, H., Attrapadung, N., Teruya, T., Ohata, S., Nuida, K., Hanaoka, G.: Constant-round client-aided secure comparison protocol. In: Lopez, J., Zhou, J., Soriano, M. (eds.) ESORICS 2018. LNCS, vol. 11099, pp. 395–415. Springer, Cham (2018). https://doi.org/10.1007/978-3-319-98989-1_20

32. Mouchet, C., Bertrand, E., Hubaux, J.: An efficient threshold access-structure for rlwe-based multiparty homomorphic encryption. IACR Cryptol. ePrint Arch. (2022)

33. Mouchet, C., Troncoso-Pastoriza, J.R., Bossuat, J., Hubaux, J.: Multiparty homomorphic encryption from ring-learning-with-errors. Proc. Priv. Enhancing Technol. **2021**(4), 291–311 (2021)

34. Naor, M., Pinkas, B.: Efficient oblivious transfer protocols. In: SODA, pp. 448–457. ACM/SIAM (2001)

35. Ohata, S., Nuida, K.: Communication-efficient (client-aided) secure two-party protocols and its application. In: Bonneau, J., Heninger, N. (eds.) Financial Cryptography and Data Security. LNCS, vol. 12059, pp. 369–385. Springer, Cham (2020). https://doi.org/10.1007/978-3-030-51280-4_20
36. Wassenberg, J., Obryk, R., Alakuijala, J., Mogenet, E.: Randen - fast backtracking-resistant random generator with AES+Feistel+Reverie (2018). https://doi.org/10.48550/ARXIV.1810.02227

Revocable IBE with En-DKER from Lattices: A Novel Approach for Lattice Basis Delegation

Qi Wang[1], Haodong Huang[1], Juyan Li[1(✉)], and Qi Yuan[2]

[1] College of Data Science and Technology, Heilongjiang University, Harbin, China
lijuyan@hlju.edu.cn
[2] College of Telecommunication and Electronic Engineering, Qiqihar university, Qiqihar, China

Abstract. In public key encryption (PKE), anonymity is essential to ensure privacy by preventing the ciphertext from revealing the recipient's identity. However, the literature has addressed the anonymity of PKE under different attack scenarios to a limited extent. Benhamouda et al. (TCC 2020) introduced the first formal definition of anonymity for PKE under corruption, and Huang et al. (ASIACRYPT 2022) made further extensions and provided a generic framework.

In this paper, we introduce a new security notion named enhanced decryption key exposure resistance (En-DKER) for revocable identity-based encryption (RIBE). This notion ensures that the exposure of decryption keys within any time period will not compromise the confidentiality and anonymity of ciphertexts encrypted during different periods. Meanwhile, we construct the first RIBE scheme with En-DKER and prove its security under the learning with errors (LWE) assumption. Our scheme offers several advantages. Firstly, the periodic workload of the key generation center (KGC) in our scheme is nearly zero. Secondly, the encryptor does not need to handle real-time revocation information of users within the system. Thirdly, the size of user secret keys remains constant in multi-bit encryption.

Additionally, we present a novel approach to delegate a lattice basis. Diverging from the work of Cash et al. (J CRYPTOL 2012), our approach allows for the outsourcing of subsequent sampling operations to an untrusted server. Leveraging this approach, our scheme significantly reduces the periodic workload for users to generate decryption keys. Finally, we efficiently implemented our scheme using the number theory library (NTL) and multi-threaded parallel program. The experimental results confirm the advantages of our scheme.

Keywords: Revocable identity-based encryption · Anonymity · Decryption key exposure · Lattice-based cryptography · Lattice basis delegation

G. Tsudik et al. (Eds.): ESORICS 2023, LNCS 14344, pp. 66–85, 2024.
https://doi.org/10.1007/978-3-031-50594-2_4

1   Introduction

Identity-based encryption (IBE) is an advanced form of public key encryption (PKE) that eliminates the need for certificates by allowing any string to serve as a user's public key. This simplifies the traditional PKE process but presents a challenge when it comes to revoking malicious users without a certificate invalidation mechanism. Boneh and Franklin [9] proposed a solution in which the key generation center (KGC) periodically generates and broadcasts keys for all non-revoked users. However, their scheme incurs a periodic workload of $O(N-r)$ for the KGC, which can become the system's bottleneck as the number of users grows, where N is the maximum number of users and r is the number of revoked users. Boldyreva et al. [8] proposed an indirect revocation model, that employs a binary tree structure and subset-cover framework, to reduce the periodic workload of the KGC to $O(r \log(N/r))$.

In order to ensure the comprehensive utilization of the revocable identity-based encryption (RIBE) scheme, it is imperative to consider additional attack scenarios and privacy requirements. Key exposure happens frequently due to external attacks or user errors. Seo and Emura [24] introduced an important security notion called decryption key exposure resistance (DKER), which requires that the exposure of decryption keys for any time period cannot compromise the confidentiality of ciphertexts that are encrypted for different time periods within RIBE schemes. Furthermore, they constructed the first RIBE scheme with DKER by re-randomizing the decryption keys in Boldyreva et al.'s indirect revocation IBE scheme [8]. Subsequently, more efficient and secure schemes have been proposed [13,14,27].

However, the above-mentioned RIBE schemes with DKER are all based on number theoretical assumptions, such as bilinear maps and multilinear maps. The algebraic structure of lattices, which is believed to be resistant against quantum attacks, has traditionally been considered unsuitable for the key re-randomization property. This is because if a user generates a new decryption key that satisfies the correctness without knowledge of the trapdoor, he can also solve the small integer solution (SIS) problem. Therefore, constructing a lattice-based RIBE scheme with DKER without the ability to re-randomize the decryption keys in [8] has become an open problem.

Until 2019, Katsumata et al. [17] combined the first lattice-based indirect revocation IBE scheme by Chen et al. [12] and the lattice basis delegation scheme by Cash et al. [11], thereby achieving a two-level structure and successfully constructing the first lattice-based RIBE scheme with DKER. Specifically, lattice basis delegation scheme allows for the extension of any short basis from a lattice A to a short basis of any higher-dimensional lattice $[A|B]$. In [17], the decryption key of the first level, similar to [12], cannot be re-randomized, while the other level is generated through extended lattice basis sampling and can be reduced to random values over the field during security proofs. This partial key re-randomization ensures the DKER property. By following the idea, Wang et al. [26] constructed a more efficient scheme, and Zhang et al. [28] proposed a lattice-based server-aided RIBE with DKER.

IBE allows using a user's identity information (such as email address or username) as the public key. This eliminates the need for a traditional public key infrastructure (PKI) to distribute and maintain separate key pairs for each user. In this scenario, anonymity becomes crucial because users' identity information is typically sensitive and should not be exposed in the ciphertext [6]. Nevertheless, if the decryption key for any time period is exposed, the two-level structure proposed in [17] fails to ensure the anonymity of ciphertexts encrypted during different time periods. Takayasu and Watanabe [25] explained this point in detail and constructed an anonymity RIBE scheme with bounded decryption key exposure resistance (B-DKER) which is a weaker version of DKER, ensuring the security of RIBE schemes in the case of a-priori bounded number of decryption keys exposure.

Open Problem: *If decryption key exposure for any time period, is it possible to construct an RIBE scheme that ensures the confidentiality and anonymity of ciphertexts encrypted for different time periods?*

Not only under lattice assumptions but also under number theoretical assumptions, Boyen and Waters [10] mentioned that anonymity appears unattainable when re-randomization elements are included in the public parameters. Moreover, the anonymity of PKE under different attack scenarios is less studied in the literature. Recently, Benhamouda et al. [7] introduced the first formal definition of anonymity for PKE under corruption. Then, Huang et al. [16] provided a generic framework of the anonymous PKE scheme under corruption. To the best of our knowledge, there is currently no RIBE scheme that can address the aforementioned problem.

1.1   Related Works

Following the work of Boldyreva et al. [8], Attrapadung and Imai [5] introduced a direct revocation model that eliminates the need for periodic key updates by both the KGC and users. Under this model, data owners can manage the revocation list and generate ciphertext that can only be decrypted by non-revoked users within specific scenarios. However, aside from its limited applicability, this model is restricted to fine-grained revocable encryption schemes, such as revocable attribute encryption (RABE) [19] and revocable predicate encryption (RPE) [18]. For a single recipient, the data owner can verify the non-revocation status of the recipient and share data using IBE schemes without needing RIBE schemes. In 2015, Qin et al. [22] proposed a server-aided revocation model in which almost all user workloads are delegated to an untrusted server. However, the periodic workload of the KGC is still remains logarithmic.

1.2   Technical Overview

Because under lattice assumptions, the decryption keys in the indirect revocation model cannot be re-randomized, our scheme is improved based on the direct revocation model.

First, we need to address the issue of incongruence between the direct revocation model and RIBE schemes. Specifically, in the direct revocation model proposed by Attrapadung and Imai [5], the encryptor uses the revocation list RL_t to generate the set $\mathsf{KUNodes}(RL_t)$ which represents the smallest nodes subset of non-revoked users on time period t. What is interesting is that the set $\mathsf{KUNodes}(RL_t)$ does not reveal any information about the revocation list RL_t since the adversary is unable to determine which user corresponds to each leaf node. Therefore, in our model, the KGC periodically generates and broadcasts the set $\mathsf{KUNodes}(RL_t)$, thereby eliminating the encryptor's need to handle any revocation list information and making our model free from specific scenarios. Moreover, our model inherits the benefits of the direct revocation model, and the periodic workload of the KGC is nearly zero.

Second, by combining the lattice-based delegation algorithm with our improved revocation model, we utilize the extended lattice basis as the user's secret key. Simultaneously, users employ this extended lattice basis for sampling to generate decryption keys, which can be reduced to random values in the field during security proofs. Consequently, we achieve complete re-randomization of decryption keys, thereby ensuring the confidentiality and anonymity of ciphertexts from different time periods in the event of decryption key exposure in any time period.

1.3 Our Contributions

This paper presents three significant contributions.

First, we propose a stronger security notion named enhanced decryption key exposure resistance (En-DKER). Simultaneously, we define the scheme and security model for the RIBE scheme with En-DKER. For details, see Sect. 3.

Second, this paper presents a novel approach to achieving the lattice basis delegation, which enables the outsourcing of subsequent sampling operations to an untrusted server. For details, see Sect. 4.1.

Third, we construct the first RIBE scheme with En-DKER, which is suitable for multi-bit encryption and scenarios where the KGC has a high computational workload. In addition, we outsource the majority of user's workload to an untrusted server. At the same time, we prove the security of our scheme under the LWE assumption. For details, see Sect. 4. Moreover, our scheme is efficiently implemented through the number theory library (NTL) and multi-threaded parallel programming. The experimental results validate the benefits of our revocation model and scheme. See Sect. 5.1 for details.

2 Preliminaries

2.1 Notations

Throughout this paper, we denote λ as the security parameter. For two distributions $\mathcal{D}$ and $\mathcal{D}'$, the statistical distance between $\mathcal{D}$ and $\mathcal{D}'$ is defined as $\mathsf{SD}(\mathcal{D}, \mathcal{D}')$. A family of distributions $\mathcal{D} = \{\mathcal{D}_\lambda\}_{\lambda \in \mathbb{N}}$ and $\mathcal{D}' = \{\mathcal{D}'_\lambda\}_{\lambda \in \mathbb{N}}$ are said to be statistically indistinguishable if there is a negligible function $\mathsf{negl}(\cdot)$ such that $\mathsf{SD}(\mathcal{D}_\lambda, \mathcal{D}'_\lambda) \leq \mathsf{negl}(\lambda)$ for all $\lambda \in \mathbb{N}$, where $\mathsf{negl}(\cdot)$ represents a function that for every constant $c > 0$ there exists an integer N_c satisfying $\mathsf{negl}(\lambda) \leq \lambda^{-c}$ for all $\lambda > N_c$. Let PPT denote probabilistic polynomial time.

If n is a positive integer, we let $[n] = \{1, \ldots, n\}$. For a column vector $\boldsymbol{x} \in \mathbb{Z}_n$, $||\boldsymbol{x}||$ denotes the standard Euclidean norm of $\boldsymbol{x}$. For a matrix $\boldsymbol{A} \in \mathbb{R}^{n \times m}$, denote $\widetilde{\boldsymbol{A}}$ as the Gram-Schmidt orthogonalization of matrix $\boldsymbol{A}$ and denote $||\boldsymbol{A}||$ as the Euclidean norm of the longest column in $\boldsymbol{A}$.

Smudging. The given lemma, originally established in [4], asserts that adding large noise can "smudges out" any small values.

Definition 1 (B-Bounded). *For a family of distributions $\mathcal{D} = \{\mathcal{D}_\lambda\}_{\lambda \in \mathbb{N}}$ over the integers and a bound $\mathcal{B} = \mathcal{B}(\lambda) > 0$, if for every $\lambda \in \mathbb{N}$ it holds that $Pr_{x \leftarrow \mathcal{D}_\lambda}[|x| \leq \mathcal{B}(\lambda)] = 1$, we say that $\mathcal{D}$ is $\mathcal{B}$-bounded.*

Lemma 1 (Smudging Lemma). *Let B_1, B_2 be two polynomials over the integers, and let $\mathcal{D} = \{\mathcal{D}_\lambda\}_\lambda$ be any B_1-bounded distribution family. Let $\mathcal{U} = \{\mathcal{U}_\lambda\}_\lambda$ be the uniform distribution over $[-B_2(\lambda), B_2(\lambda)]$. The family of distributions $\mathcal{D} + \mathcal{U}$ and $\mathcal{U}$ are statistically indistinguishable if there exists a negligible function $\mathsf{negl}(\cdot)$ such that for all $\lambda \in \mathbb{N}$ it holds that $B_1(\lambda)/B_2(\lambda) \leq \mathsf{negl}(\lambda)$.*

Leftover Hash Lemma. Here, we recall the leftover hash lemma from [1].

Lemma 2. *Suppose that $m > (n+1)\log q + \omega(\log n)$, and $k = k(n)$ be some polynomial in n. Then, the distribution $(\boldsymbol{A}, \boldsymbol{AR})$ is statistically indistinguishable to the distribution $(\boldsymbol{A}, \boldsymbol{B})$, where $\boldsymbol{A}$ and $\boldsymbol{B}$ are uniformly matrices in $\mathbb{Z}_q^{n \times m}$ and $\mathbb{Z}_q^{n \times k}$, and $\boldsymbol{R}$ is a uniformly matrix in $\{-1, 1\}^{n \times k}$.*

Full-Rank Different Map. We need this tool to encode identities and time periods as matrices in $\mathbb{Z}_q^{n \times n}$.

Definition 2. *A function $\mathsf{H} : \mathbb{Z}_q^n \to \mathbb{Z}_q^{n \times n}$ is a full-rank different map if the matrix $\mathsf{H}(\boldsymbol{u}) - \mathsf{H}(\boldsymbol{v}) \in \mathbb{Z}_q^{n \times n}$ is full rank, for all distinct $\boldsymbol{u}, \boldsymbol{v} \in \mathbb{Z}_q^n$, and H is computable in $\mathcal{O}(n \log q)$.*

2.2 Background on Lattices

Lattice. An m-dimensional lattice $\mathcal{L}$ is a discrete subgroup of $\mathbb{R}^m$. Let $\mathcal{L}_q^\perp(\boldsymbol{A})$ denote the q-ary lattice $\{\boldsymbol{x} \in \mathbb{Z}^m \mid \boldsymbol{Ax} = \boldsymbol{0} \bmod q\}$, where n, m, q are positive integers and $\boldsymbol{A}$ is a matrix in $\mathbb{Z}_q^{n \times m}$. For any $\boldsymbol{u}$ in $\mathbb{Z}_q^n$, let $\mathcal{L}_q^{\boldsymbol{u}}(\boldsymbol{A})$ denote the coset $\{\boldsymbol{x} \in \mathbb{Z}^m \mid \boldsymbol{Ax} = \boldsymbol{u} \bmod q\}$.

Discrete Gaussians. For any parameter $\sigma > 0$, the discrete Gaussian distribution $\rho_{\mathcal{L},\sigma}(\boldsymbol{x}) = \rho_\sigma(\boldsymbol{x})/\rho_\sigma(\mathcal{L})$, where $\rho_\sigma(\boldsymbol{x}) = \exp(-\pi||x||^2/\sigma^2)$ and $\rho_\sigma(\mathcal{L}) = \sum_{\boldsymbol{x} \in \mathcal{L}} \rho_\sigma(\boldsymbol{x})$. The following lemmas are important properties of discrete Gaussian [15].

Lemma 3. *Let n, m, q be positive integers with $m > n$, $q > 2$, and A be a matrix in $\mathbb{Z}_q^{n \times m}$. Then, there is a negligible function $\mathsf{negl}(\cdot)$ such that $\Pr[\|\|\boldsymbol{x}\| > \sigma\sqrt{m} : \boldsymbol{x} \leftarrow \mathcal{D}_{\mathcal{L}_q^{\perp}(A),\sigma}] \leq \mathsf{negl}(n)$, when $\sigma = \tilde{\Omega}(n)$.*

Lemma 4. *Let n, m, q be positive integers with $m > 2n \log q$. Then, for $A \leftarrow \mathbb{Z}_q^{n \times m}$ and $\boldsymbol{e} \leftarrow \mathcal{D}_{\mathbb{Z}^m,\sigma}$, the distribution of $\boldsymbol{u} = A\boldsymbol{e} \bmod q$ is statistically close to the uniform distribution over $\mathbb{Z}_q^n$.*

Sampling Algorithms. We review some sampling algorithms from [2,3,20].

Lemma 5. *Let $n \geq 1$, $m \geq 2n \lceil \log q \rceil$, $q \geq 2$, we have the following polynomial time algorithms:*

- $\mathsf{TrapGen}(1^n, 1^m, q) \rightarrow (A, T_A)$: *On input n, m, q, output a matrix $A \in \mathbb{Z}_q^{n \times m}$ and its trapdoor $T_A \in \mathbb{Z}^{m \times m}$, satisfying $\|T_A\| \leq O(n \log q)$.*
- $\mathsf{SamplePre}(A, T_A, \sigma, \boldsymbol{u}) \rightarrow \boldsymbol{s}$: *On input a matrix $A \in \mathbb{Z}_q^{n \times m}$ and its trapdoor T_A, a vector $\boldsymbol{u} \in \mathbb{Z}_q^n$, and a parameter $\sigma \geq \|\widetilde{T_A}\| \cdot \omega(\sqrt{\log m})$, output a vector $\boldsymbol{s} \in \mathbb{Z}_q^m$, satisfying $A \cdot \boldsymbol{s}^\top = \boldsymbol{u}^\top$ and $\|\boldsymbol{s}\| \leq \sqrt{m}\sigma$.*
- $\mathsf{SampleLeft}(A, M, T_A, \sigma, \boldsymbol{u}) \rightarrow \boldsymbol{s}$: *On input a matrix $A \in \mathbb{Z}_q^{n \times m}$ and its trapdoor T_A, a matrix $M \in \mathbb{Z}_q^{n \times m_0}$, a vector $\boldsymbol{u} \in \mathbb{Z}_q^n$, and a parameter $\sigma \geq \|\widetilde{T_A}\| \cdot \omega(\sqrt{\log(m + m_0)})$, output a vector $\boldsymbol{s} \in \mathbb{Z}_q^{m+m_0}$ distributed statistically close to $\mathcal{D}_{\mathcal{L}_q^{\boldsymbol{u}}([A|M]),\sigma}$.*
- *There is a gadget matrix G, which is a full rank matrix in $\mathbb{Z}_q^{n \times m}$ and has a publicly known trapdoor T_G with $\|\widetilde{T_G}\| \leq \sqrt{5}$.*
- $\mathsf{SampleRight}(A, G, R, T_G, \sigma, \boldsymbol{u}) \rightarrow \boldsymbol{s}$: *On input a matrix $A \in \mathbb{Z}_q^{n \times m}$, the gadget matrix G and its trapdoor T_G, a uniform random matrix $R \leftarrow \{-1,1\}^{m \times m}$, a vector $\boldsymbol{u} \in \mathbb{Z}_q^n$, and a parameter $\sigma \geq \|\widetilde{T_G}\| \cdot \sqrt{m} \cdot \omega(\sqrt{\log m})$, output a vector $\boldsymbol{s} \in \mathbb{Z}_q^{2m}$ distributed statistically close to $\mathcal{D}_{\mathcal{L}_q^{\boldsymbol{u}}([A|AR+G]),\sigma}$.*

LWE Assumption. Our RIBE scheme is based on the learning with errors (LWE) assumption.

Assumption 1 (Learning with Errors [23]). *Let n, q be positive integers, and a parameter $\sigma \in \mathbb{R}$, for any PPT adversary $\mathcal{A}$, there exists a negligible function $\mathsf{negl}(\cdot)$ that satisfies $|\Pr[\mathcal{A}(\boldsymbol{\alpha}, \boldsymbol{s}^\top \boldsymbol{\alpha} + e) = 1] - \Pr[\mathcal{A}(\boldsymbol{\alpha}, \gamma) = 1]| \leq \mathsf{negl}(\lambda)$, where $\boldsymbol{\alpha} \leftarrow \mathbb{Z}_q^n$, $\boldsymbol{s} \leftarrow \mathbb{Z}_q^n$, $\gamma \leftarrow \mathbb{Z}_q$, and $e \leftarrow \mathcal{D}_{\mathbb{Z},\sigma}$.*

2.3   The Complete Subtree Method

The complete subtree (CS) method, proposed by Naor et al. [21], effectively improves the efficiency of the revocation schemes. In this method, the system will build a complete binary tree BT. For a non-leaf node $\theta \in$ BT, θ_l and θ_r denote the left and right child node of θ, and η denote the leaf node in BT. Path(η) denote the set of nodes on the path from η to the root. Inputting the revocation list RL_t on the time period t, then the KUNodes algorithm proceeds as follows: sets two empty sets X and Y; adds Path(η) to X, for each $\eta \in RL_t$; for each $\theta \in X$, adds θ_l to Y if $\theta_l \notin X$, adds θ_r to Y if $\theta_r \notin X$; if Y is still the empty set, then adds root to Y; finally, outputs Y which is the smallest nodes subset of non-revoked users on the time period t.

3   Formal Definition for RIBE with En-DKER

Definition 3 (En-DKER). *The exposure of users' decryption keys for any time period does not compromise the anonymity and confidentiality of ciphertexts that are encrypted for different time periods.*

It should be noted that En-DKER is different from achieving both DKER and anonymity since current anonymous IBE schemes are constructed under the assumption that the user's decryption keys will not be exposed. In other words, RIBE with En-DKER scheme cannot be constructed by simply combining the RIBE with DKER scheme with an anonymous IBE scheme. Therefore, it is necessary to define a new security notion to avoid confusion for readers.

3.1   Scheme Model of RIBE with En-DKER

Our RIBE scheme consists of the six algorithms (Setup, GenSK, NodesUp, GenDK, Enc, Dec) with associated message space $\mathcal{M}$, identity space $\mathcal{ID}$, and time period space $\mathcal{T}$. The KGC maintains a revocation list RL which is dynamically updated following the time period t.

- **Setup**(λ, N): This algorithm is run by the KGC. Input a security parameter λ and a maximal number N of users, output public parameters PP and a master secret key MSK.
- **GenSK**(PP, MSK, ID): This algorithm is run by the KGC. Input the public parameters PP, the master secret key MSK, and an identity $ID \in \mathcal{ID}$, output a secret key SK_{ID} for the user with the identity ID.
- **NodesUp**(BT, RL_t): This algorithm is run by the KGC. Input the binary tree BT and the revocation list RL_t, the KGC generates and broadcasts a node set $KUNodes(RL_t)$ for the time period t.
- **GenDK**$(PP, SK_{ID}, KUNodes(RL_t))$: This algorithm is run by the receiver. Input the public parameters PP, the secret key SK_{ID}, and the set $KUNodes(RL_t)$, output a decryption key $DK_{ID,t}$.
- **Enc**$(PP, ID, t, KUNodes(RL_t), \mu)$: This algorithm is run by the sender. Input the public parameters PP, an identity $ID \in \mathcal{ID}$, a time period $t \in \mathcal{T}$, the set $KUNodes(RL_t)$, and message μ, output a ciphertext $CT_{ID,t}$.
- **Dec**$(CT_{ID,t}, DK_{ID,t})$: This algorithm is run by the receiver. Input the ciphertext $CT_{ID,t}$ and the decryption key $DK_{ID,t}$, output message $\mu' \in \mathcal{M}$.

Correctness. An RIBE scheme is correct if for all $\lambda \in \mathbb{N}$, $N \in \mathbb{N}$, $(PP, MSK) \leftarrow$ Setup(λ, l, N), $\mu \in \mathcal{M}$, $ID \in \mathcal{ID}$, $t \in \mathcal{T}$ and revocation lists RL it holds that

$$
\Pr\left[\mu' = \mu \middle|
\begin{array}{c}
SK_{ID} \leftarrow \mathbf{GenSK}(PP, MSK, ID) \\
KUNodes(RL_t) \leftarrow \mathbf{NodesUp}(BT, RL_t) \\
DK_{ID,t} \leftarrow \mathbf{GenDK}(PP, SK_{ID}, KUNodes(RL_t)) \\
CT_{ID,t} \leftarrow \mathbf{Enc}(PP, ID, t, KUNodes(RL_t), \mu) \\
\mu' \leftarrow \mathbf{Dec}(CT_{ID,t}, DK_{ID,t})
\end{array}
\right] = 1\text{-negl}(\lambda).
$$

3.2 Security Model of RIBE with En-DKER

Now, we give a formal security definition for RIBE with En-DKER by the game between adversary $\mathcal{A}$ and challenger $\mathcal{C}$. Different from the security definition of RIBE with DKER, we replace the challenge identity ID with $\mathsf{ID}^{(0)}$ and $\mathsf{ID}^{(1)}$. When $\mathcal{C}$ randomly chooses a bit b, the challenge plaintext $\mu^{(b)}$ will be encrypted with the identity $\mathsf{ID}^{(b)}$. Assuming the scheme does not satisfy anonymity, the adversary can distinguish between $\mathsf{ID}^{(0)}$ and $\mathsf{ID}^{(1)}$, then get the value of challenge bit b and win the game. So in this setting, our security definition can verify the anonymity while proving the security of the RIBE schemes.

In addition, since the revocation list RL is dynamically updated following the time period t, so we set a global variable $t_{cu} \in \mathcal{T}$, whose initial value is 1, to assist in generating the decryption key $\mathsf{DK}_{\mathsf{ID},t}$ of any time period queried by $\mathcal{A}$.

Initialize: $\mathcal{A}$ sets the challenge identities $\mathsf{ID}^{(0)}$ and $\mathsf{ID}^{(1)}$, the challenge time period t^*, and the challenge node set $\mathsf{KUNodes}(\mathsf{RL}_{t^*})^*$.

Setup Phase: $\mathcal{C}$ runs Setup and gives the public parameters PP to $\mathcal{A}$.

Query Phase: $\mathcal{A}$ adaptively makes a polynomial number queries to $\mathcal{C}$:

1. $\mathcal{A}$ sets $\mathcal{Q}_0 = \{\mathsf{ID}\}$ for the establishment of the binary tree BT. $\mathcal{C}$ randomly picks an unassigned leaf node η_{ID} for ID.[1] At the end of the quiry, $\mathcal{C}$ obtains $\mathsf{RL}_{t^*}^*$ based on $\mathsf{KUNodes}(\mathsf{RL}_{t^*})^*$ and BT, and sends it to $\mathcal{A}$.

2. $\mathcal{A}$ sets $\mathcal{Q}_1 = \{\mathsf{ID}\}$ for the secret key queries, subject to the restriction: $\mathsf{ID} \in \mathcal{Q}_0$; if $\mathsf{ID} = \mathsf{ID}^{(0)}$ or $\mathsf{ID}^{(1)}$, $\mathsf{ID} \in \mathsf{RL}_{t^*}^*$. $\mathcal{C}$ replies with the corresponding secret key $\mathsf{SK}_{\mathsf{ID}} \leftarrow \mathsf{GenSK}(\mathsf{PP}, \mathsf{MSK}, \mathsf{ID})$.

3. Let $t_{cu} = 1$, and loop through the following steps:

   (a) $\mathcal{A}$ sets $\mathcal{Q}_2 = \{(\mathsf{ID}, t_{cu})\}$ for the decryption key queries, subject to the restriction: $\mathsf{ID} \in \mathcal{Q}_0$; $\mathsf{ID} \notin \mathsf{RL}_{t_{cu}}$; if $t_{cu} = t^*$, $\mathsf{ID} \neq \mathsf{ID}^{(0)}$ and $\mathsf{ID}^{(1)}$. $\mathcal{C}$ replies with the decryption key $\mathsf{DK}_{\mathsf{ID},t} \leftarrow \mathsf{GenDK}(\mathsf{PP}, \mathsf{SK}_{\mathsf{ID}}, \mathsf{KUNodes}(\mathsf{RL}_t))$.

   (b) $\mathcal{A}$ sets $\mathcal{Q}_3 = \{(\mathsf{ID}, t_{cu})\}$ for revocation queries, subject to the restriction: $\mathsf{ID} \in \mathcal{Q}_0$; $\mathsf{ID}^{(0)}$ and $\mathsf{ID}^{(1)}$ are either queried at the same time period t or neither,[2]; $\mathsf{RL}_{t^*} = \mathsf{RL}_{t^*}^*$. $\mathcal{C}$ adds ID to the revocation list RL, and updates $\mathsf{RL}_{t_{cu}+1} = \mathsf{RL}$. Then, $\mathcal{C}$ sent $\mathsf{KUNodes}(\mathsf{RL}_{t_{cu}+1})$ to $\mathcal{A}$.

   (c) $t_{cu} = t_{cu} + 1$.

Challenge Phase: $\mathcal{A}$ outputs the challenge plaintexts $\mu^{(0)}$ and $\mu^{(1)}$. Then $\mathcal{C}$ chooses a random bit $b \leftarrow \{0,1\}$ and replies with the corresponding ciphertext $\mathsf{CT}_{\mathsf{ID}^{(b)},t^*} \leftarrow \mathsf{Enc}(\mathsf{PP}, \mathsf{ID}^{(b)}, t^*, \{\mu_i^{(b)}\}_{i \in [l]})$.

Guess: $\mathcal{A}$ outputs a guess b' of b.

Definition 4. *An RIBE with En-DKER scheme is selectively secure if the advantage $\mathsf{Adv}_{\mathsf{RIBE},\mathcal{A}}^{\mathsf{SEL-En-CPA}}(\lambda)$ is at most negligible for any PPT adversaries $\mathcal{A}$, where $\mathsf{Adv}_{\mathsf{RIBE},\mathcal{A}}^{\mathsf{SEL-En-CPA}}(\lambda) = |\Pr[b = b'] - 1/2|$.*

---

[1] This step moves from the algorithm GenSK to the Query Phase.

[2] If the two challenge identities are revoked at different time periods, the adversary can distinguish them in the subsequent key queries phase.

Remark 1. According to the challenge identities $\mathsf{ID}^{(0)}$ and $\mathsf{ID}^{(1)}$, and the challenge time period t^*, it needs to be divided into two cases:

- If $\mathsf{ID}^{(0)}$ and $\mathsf{ID}^{(1)}$ are revoked before t^*, adversary $\mathcal{A}$ can perform the secret key queries and decryption key queries according to the corresponding restrictions.
- If $\mathsf{ID}^{(0)}$ and $\mathsf{ID}^{(1)}$ have not been revoked before t^*, $\mathcal{A}$ can perform decryption key queries according to the corresponding restrictions. It is important to note that the RIBE without En-DKER schemes cannot support queries in this case.

4   Revocable IBE with En-DKER from Lattices

In this section, we present our proposed lattice-based RIBE scheme with En-DKER. We begin by introducing our approach for lattice basis delegation in Sect. 4.1. We present our scheme in Sect. 4.2 and prove the security in Sect. 4.3.

4.1   Lattice Basis Delegation

Lattice basis delegation enables the extension of a short basis from a lattice A to a short basis of any higher-dimensional lattice $[A|B_{\mathsf{ID}}]$. This extension basis must not disclose any information about the short basis of A. Subsequently, the user ID can employ the extension basis to generate decryption keys. Our novel approach can outsource this sampling calculation to an untrusted server. The details are as follows.

First, the KGC runs the algorithm TrapGen to generate a pair of matrix with trapdoor (A, T_A), where A is the public parameters PP and T_A is the master secret key MSK. Additionally, we need to use a gadget matrix G and a publicly known trapdoor T_G as defined in Lemma 5. Then, by utilizing the SampleLeft algorithm and T_A, the KGC generates K_{ID}, satisfying $[A|B_{\mathsf{ID}}]K_{\mathsf{ID}} = G$. Meanwhile, K_{ID} can serve as the short basis for the user ID, because for any vector $x \in \mathbb{Z}_q^n$, the user can also calculate a bounded small key k by using K_{ID}, satisfying $[A|B_{\mathsf{ID}}]k = x$. The difference is that the majority of the workload to generate k can be outsourced to an untrusted server. Specifically, by utilizing the SampleLeft algorithm and the public trapdoor T_G, the server generates k' and sends it to the user, satisfying $Gk' = x$. Then, the user only needs to calculate $K_{\mathsf{ID}}k'$ as the key k.

However, $K_{\mathsf{ID}}k'$ is only a bounded small key. To make the key k satisfy the re-randomization property, we introduce an important tool called smudging lemma [4]. Specifically, the user first uniformly select an random vector K' in a relatively large distribution, and set $x' = x - [A|B_{\mathsf{ID}}]K'$. Subsequently, by employing the sampling outsourcing approach, the server can generate the key k', satisfying $Gk' = x'$. The user can obtain the key k by adding K' and $K_{\mathsf{ID}}k'$ in a component-wise fashion, satisfying $[A|B_{\mathsf{ID}}]k = x$. Smudging lemma can guarantee the randomness of the decryption key.

Correctness. Now, we analyze the correctness of our approach.

$$[A|B_{\mathsf{ID}}]\,k = [A|B_{\mathsf{ID}}]K' + [A|B_{\mathsf{ID}}]K_{\mathsf{ID}}k'$$
$$= [A|B_{\mathsf{ID}}]K' + Gk'$$
$$= [A|B_{\mathsf{ID}}]K' + x - [A|B_{\mathsf{ID}}]K' = x.$$

Furthermore, given the untrusted nature of the server, users must verify whether Gk' is equal to x' after receiving k'. We will no longer mention this in the subsequent scheme construction.

4.2 Construction

In our scheme, we set the message space $\mathcal{M} = \{0,1\}$, the identity space $\mathcal{ID} \subset \mathbb{Z}_q^n \setminus \{0_n\}$, and the time period space $\mathcal{T} \subset \mathbb{Z}_q^n$. For any $B \in \mathbb{N}$, let $\mathcal{U}_B$ denote the uniform distribution on $\mathbb{Z} \cap [-B, B]$. In addition, our system parameters satisfy the following constraints: $m > 2n \log q$ and $\sigma > \sqrt{m} \cdot \omega(\sqrt{m})$ (for sampling); $O(m^{3/2}B\sigma) < q/4$ (for correctness); $n = O(\lambda)$, $\chi_{\mathsf{LWE}} = \mathcal{D}_{\mathbb{Z},\sigma}$ (for security); $\chi_{\mathsf{big}} = \mathcal{U}_B$, where $B > (m\sigma^2 + 1)2^\lambda$ (for smudging).

Multi-bit Encryption. Agrawal et al. [1] proposed an approach for multi-bit encryption, in which encrypts l bits message using a single random vector $s \in \mathbb{Z}_q^n$. Specifically, they set l vectors $(u_1, \dots, u_l)$ from $\mathbb{Z}_q^n$ into the public parameters PP, as opposed to the basic scheme which utilizes only a single vector u. Message bit number i is encrypted using the vector u_i.

However, in current lattice-based RIBE schemes, changing the vector u from one column to l column results in the size of user secret keys, update keys, and decryption keys growing by a factor of l. The workload for the KGC and users also increases by a factor of l. Fortunately, in our scheme, the size of user secret keys remains constant, periodic workload of the KGC remains nearly zero, and the majority of the workload for generating decryption keys is outsourced to the server with the advantages of our lattice basis delegation approach.

Now, we describe our lattice-based RIBE with En-DKER construction.

Setup(λ, l, N): On input a security parameter λ, number of encryption bits l, and maximum number of users N. The specific process is as follows:
1. Choose an LWE modulus q and dimensions n, m.
2. Run the algorithm $\mathsf{TrapGen}(1^n, 1^m, q)$ to generat a pair of matrix with trapdoor (A, T_A).
3. Select uniformly random matrices B, and W in $\mathbb{Z}_q^{n \times m}$, and uniformly random vectors $\{u_i\}_{i \in [l]}$ in $\mathbb{Z}_q^n$.
4. Build a binary tree BT with at least N leaf nodes. For each node $\theta \in$ BT, select a uniformly random matrix D_θ in $\mathbb{Z}_q^{n \times m}$.
5. Output PP $= \{A, B, W, \{u_i\}_{i \in [l]}, \{D_\theta\}_{\theta \in \mathsf{BT}}\}$, MSK $= \{T_A, \mathsf{BT}\}$.

GenSK(PP, MSK, ID): On input the public parameters PP, the master secret key MSK, and an identity ID $\in \mathcal{ID}$. The specific process is as follows:
1. Randomly pick an unassigned leaf node η_{ID} from BT and store ID in it.

2. Set $B_{\mathsf{ID}} = B + \mathsf{H}(\mathsf{ID})G$, where $\mathsf{H}(\cdot)$ is a full-rank different map defined in Definition 2 and G is a gadget matrix defined in Lemma 5.
3. For each $\theta \in \mathsf{Path}(\eta_{\mathsf{ID}})$, generate $K_{\mathsf{ID},\theta}$ satisfying $[A|B_{\mathsf{ID}}|D_\theta]K_{\mathsf{ID},\theta} = G$.
   (a) Set $Z_{\mathsf{ID}} = [A|B_{\mathsf{ID}}]K'_{\mathsf{ID}}$, where K'_{ID} is a uniformly random matrix selected in $\chi_{\mathsf{LWE}}^{2m \times m}$.
   (b) Sample $K''_{\mathsf{ID},\theta} \leftarrow \mathsf{SampleLeft}(A, D_\theta, T_A, \sigma, G - Z_{\mathsf{ID}})$.
   (c) Split K'_{ID} and $K''_{\mathsf{ID},\theta}$ into two parts, $K'_{1,\mathsf{ID}}$, $K'_{2,\mathsf{ID}}$ and $K''_{1,\mathsf{ID},\theta}$, $K''_{2,\mathsf{ID},\theta}$, m rows per part. Then, generate

$$K_{\mathsf{ID},\theta} = \left[\left(K'_{1,\mathsf{ID}} + K''_{1,\mathsf{ID},\theta}\right)^\top \middle| \left(K'_{2,\mathsf{ID}}\right)^\top \middle| \left(K''_{2,\mathsf{ID},\theta}\right)^\top \right]^\top \in \mathbb{Z}_q^{3m \times m}.$$

4. Output $\mathsf{SK}_{\mathsf{ID}} = \{K_{\mathsf{ID},\theta}\}_{\theta \in \mathsf{Path}(\eta_{\mathsf{ID}})}$.

NodesUp$(\mathsf{BT}, \mathsf{RL}_t)$: On input the binary tree BT and the revocation list RL_t, the KGC generates and broadcasts a set $\mathsf{KUNodes}(\mathsf{RL}_t)$ for the time period t.

GenDK$(\mathsf{PP}, \mathsf{SK}_{\mathsf{ID}}, \mathsf{KUNodes}(\mathsf{RL}_t))$: On input the public parameters PP, the secret key $\mathsf{SK}_{\mathsf{ID}}$, and the node set $\mathsf{KUNodes}(\mathsf{RL}_t)$. The specific process is as follows:

1. Perform node matching, and let $\theta^* = \mathsf{Path}(\eta_{\mathsf{ID}}) \cap \mathsf{KUNodes}(\mathsf{RL}_t)$. If $\theta^* = \emptyset$, outputs $\bot$. Otherwise, continue the following steps.
2. For $i \in [l]$, generate $dk_{i,\mathsf{ID},\theta^*,t}$ satisfying $[A|B_{\mathsf{ID}}|D_{\theta^*}|W_t]dk_{i,\mathsf{ID},\theta^*,t} = u_i$, where $dk_{i,\mathsf{ID},\theta^*,t} \in \mathbb{Z}_q^{4m}$.
   (a) Set $h_{i,\mathsf{ID},t} = [A|B_{\mathsf{ID}}|D_{\theta^*}|W_t]k_{i,t}$ and send to the server, where $k_{i,t}$ is a uniformly random vector selected in χ_{big}^{4m}, $W_t = W + \mathsf{H}(t)G$.
   (b) The server samples $k'_{i,\mathsf{ID},t} \leftarrow \mathsf{SamplePre}(G, T_G, \sigma, u_i - h_{i,\mathsf{ID},t})$ and sends to the user.
   (c) Compute $k''_{i,\mathsf{ID},\theta^*,t} = K_{\mathsf{ID},\theta^*}k'_{i,\mathsf{ID},t}$, satisfying $[A|B_{\mathsf{ID}}|D_{\theta^*}]k''_{i,\mathsf{ID},\theta^*,t} = u_i - h_{i,\mathsf{ID},t}$, where $k''_{i,\mathsf{ID},\theta^*,t} \in \mathbb{Z}_q^{3m}$.
   (d) Split $k_{i,t}$ into four parts, $k_{1,i,t}$, $k_{2,i,t}$, $k_{3,i,t}$, $k_{4,i,t}$, and $k''_{i,\mathsf{ID},\theta^*,t}$ into three parts $k''_{1,i,\mathsf{ID},\theta^*,t}$, $k''_{2,i,\mathsf{ID},\theta^*,t}$, $k''_{3,i,\mathsf{ID},\theta^*,t}$, m rows per part. Then, generate

$$dk_{i,\mathsf{ID},\theta^*,t} = \left[\left(\begin{matrix} k_{1,i,t} + k''_{1,i,\mathsf{ID},\theta^*,t} \\ k_{2,i,t} + k''_{2,i,\mathsf{ID},\theta^*,t} \end{matrix}\right)^\top \middle| \left(\begin{matrix} k_{3,i,t} + k''_{3,i,\mathsf{ID},\theta^*,t} \\ k_{4,i,t} \end{matrix}\right)^\top \right]^\top \in \mathbb{Z}_q^{4m}.$$

3. Output $\mathsf{DK}_{\mathsf{ID},t} = \{dk_{i,\mathsf{ID},\theta^*,t}\}_{i \in [l]}$.

Enc$(\mathsf{PP}, \mathsf{ID}, t, \mathsf{KUNodes}(\mathsf{RL}_t), \{\mu_i\}_{i \in [l]})$: On input the public parameters PP, an identity $\mathsf{ID} \in \mathcal{ID}$, a time period $t \in \mathcal{T}$, the set $\mathsf{KUNodes}(\mathsf{RL}_t)$, and message $\mu_i \in \mathcal{M}$, where $i \in [l]$. The specific process is as follows:

1. Select uniformly random matrices R, S_θ, and V in $\{-1,1\}^{m \times m}$, where $\theta \in \mathsf{KUNodes}(\mathsf{RL}_t)$, and a uniformly random vector s in $\mathbb{Z}_q^n$.
2. Choose noise $e_i \leftarrow \chi_{\mathsf{LWE}}$ and a noise vector $e' \leftarrow \chi_{\mathsf{LWE}}^m$, where $i \in [l]$.
3. Set $C_i = s^\top u_i + \lfloor \frac{q}{2} \rfloor \cdot \mu_i + e_i$, where $i \in [l]$.
4. Set $c_{\mathsf{ID},\theta,t} = s^\top [A|B_{\mathsf{ID}}|D_\theta|W_t] + e'^\top [I_m|R|S_\theta|V]$, where I_m is an identity matrix, $\theta \in \mathsf{KUNodes}(\mathsf{RL}_t)$.

5. Output $\mathsf{CT}_{\mathsf{ID},t} = \{\{C_i\}_{i\in[l]}, \{c_{\mathsf{ID},\theta,t}\}_{\theta\in\mathsf{KUNodes}(\mathsf{RL}_t)}\}$.

$\mathsf{Dec}(\mathsf{CT}_{\mathsf{ID},t}, \mathsf{DK}_{\mathsf{ID},t})$: On input the ciphertext $\mathsf{CT}_{\mathsf{ID},t}$ and the decryption key $\mathsf{DK}_{\mathsf{ID},t}$. The specific process is as follows:

1. Compute $C_i' = C_i - c_{\mathsf{ID},\theta^*,t}dk_{i,\mathsf{ID},\theta^*,t}$, where $i \in [l]$.
2. For each $i \in [l]$, output $\mu_i = 1$ if $|C_i' - \lfloor\frac{q}{2}\rfloor| < \lfloor\frac{q}{4}\rfloor$, otherwise $\mu_i = 0$.

Correctness. Now, we analyze the correctness of our scheme,

$$
\begin{aligned}
C_i' &= C_i - c_{\mathsf{ID},\theta^*,t}dk_{i,\mathsf{ID},\theta^*,t}\\
&= s^\top u_i + \left\lfloor\frac{q}{2}\right\rfloor \cdot \mu_i - s^\top[A|B_{\mathsf{ID}}|D_{\theta^*}|W_t]dk_{i,\mathsf{ID},\theta^*,t} + \mathsf{noise}_i\\
&= \left\lfloor\frac{q}{2}\right\rfloor \cdot \mu_i + \mathsf{noise}_i,
\end{aligned}
$$

for each $i \in [l]$, where

$$
\begin{aligned}
\mathsf{noise}_i &= e_i - e'^\top[I_m|R|S_{\theta^*}|V]dk_{i,\mathsf{ID},\theta^*,t}\\
&= e_i - e'^\top[I_m|R|S_{\theta^*}|V]\begin{bmatrix} k_{1,i,t} + K'_{1,\mathsf{ID}}k'_{i,\mathsf{ID},t} + K''_{1,\mathsf{ID},\theta^*}k'_{i,\mathsf{ID},t}\\ k_{2,i,t} + K'_{2,\mathsf{ID}}k'_{i,\mathsf{ID},t}\\ k_{3,i,t} + K''_{2,\mathsf{ID},\theta^*}k'_{i,\mathsf{ID},t}\\ k_{4,i,t} \end{bmatrix}.
\end{aligned}
$$

Correctness now follows since noise_i is small and should not affect $\lfloor\frac{q}{2}\rfloor \cdot \mu_i$. Moreover, the following inequalities hold except with negligible probability:

- From Lemma 2, we have $||R||$, $||S_{\theta^*}||$, and $||V|| \leq O(\sqrt{m})$.
- From Lemma 1, we have $||k_{1,i,t}||$, $||k_{2,i,t}||$, $||k_{3,i,t}||$, and $||k_{4,i,t}|| \leq \sqrt{m}\mathsf{B}$.
- From Lemma 5, we have $||K'_{1,\mathsf{ID}}k'_{i,\mathsf{ID},t}||$, $||K''_{1,\mathsf{ID},\theta^*}k'_{i,\mathsf{ID},t}||$, $||K'_{2,\mathsf{ID}}k'_{i,\mathsf{ID},t}||$, and $||K''_{2,\mathsf{ID},\theta^*}k'_{i,\mathsf{ID},t}|| \leq m^{3/2}\sigma$, and $||e_i|| \leq \sigma$, $||e'|| \leq \sqrt{m}\sigma$.

$$
\begin{aligned}
||\mathsf{noise}_i|| &= ||e_i - e'^\top[I_m|R|S_{\theta^*}|V]dk_{i,\mathsf{ID},\theta^*,t}||\\
&\leq ||e_i|| + ||e'^\top|| \cdot ||[I_m|R|S_{\theta^*}|V]dk_{i,\mathsf{ID},\theta^*,t}||\\
&\leq \sigma + (\sqrt{m}\sigma)[(2m^{3/2}\sigma + \sqrt{m}\mathsf{B}) + (2m^{3/2}\sigma + 3\sqrt{m}\mathsf{B})O(\sqrt{m})]\\
&\leq O(m^{3/2}\mathsf{B}\sigma) < q/4,
\end{aligned}
$$

and we can get μ_i by judging $|C_i' - \lfloor\frac{q}{2}\rfloor| = ||\lfloor\frac{q}{2}\rfloor \cdot \mu_i + \mathsf{noise}_i - \lfloor\frac{q}{2}\rfloor| < \lfloor\frac{q}{4}\rfloor$.

4.3 Security Analysis

Theorem 1. *If the* LWE *assumption holds, the proposed RIBE scheme with En-DKER is selectively secure.*

Proof. We set a series of games, and $\mathcal{A}$'s advantage changes only by a negligible amount between each adjacent games. The first game corresponds to the real selective security for the proposed RIBE scheme, and the final game's ciphertext is independent of the bit b, whereby the advantage of $\mathcal{A}$ is zero. The proof of Theorem 1 is completed.

The Series of Games. Let $\mathcal{A}$ be the adversary in the security definition of the RIBE with En-DKER. We consider the following series of games.

Game$_0^{(b)}$: This game corresponds to the real selective security game for the proposed RIBE scheme. $\mathcal{B}$ chooses a random bit $b \leftarrow \{0,1\}$.

Game$_1^{(b)}$: This game is analogous to Game$_0^{(b)}$ except the generation of matrices B, $\{D_\theta\}_{\theta \in \mathsf{BT}}$, and W during the Setup phase.

1. Select uniformly random matrices R^*, S_θ^* and V^* in $\{-1,1\}^{m \times m}$, where $\theta \in \mathsf{BT}$.[3]
2. Set $B = AR^* - \mathsf{H}(\mathsf{ID}^{(b)})G$, $W = AV^* - \mathsf{H}(t^*)G$, and

$$D_\theta = \begin{cases} AS_\theta^*, & \text{if } \theta \in \mathsf{KUNodes}(\mathsf{RL}_{t^*})^*, \\ AS_\theta^* + G, & \text{otherwise}. \end{cases}$$

Game$_2^{(b)}$: This game is analogous to Game$_1^{(b)}$ except the generation of the secret key $\mathsf{SK}_{\mathsf{ID}}$ while answering the $\mathcal{Q}_1$ key queries during the Query phase. We divide the generation of K'_{ID} and $K''_{\mathsf{ID},\theta}$ into the following cases, and other steps are the same as Game$_1^{(b)}$.

- **Case 1**: $\mathsf{ID} = \mathsf{ID}^{(b)}$. In this case, due to the $\mathcal{Q}_1$ key queries restriction in the security definition, the user with the identity ID must have been revoked before the challenge time period t^*. So $\mathsf{Path}(\eta_{\mathsf{ID}}) \cap \mathsf{KUNodes}(\mathsf{RL}_{t^*})^* = \emptyset$, and $D_\theta = AS_\theta^* + G$ for each node $\theta \in \mathsf{Path}(\eta_{\mathsf{ID}})$.
    1. Perform the operation 3.(a) in algorithm **GenSK**.
    2. Sample $K''_{\mathsf{ID},\theta} \leftarrow \mathsf{SampleRight}(A, S_\theta^*, G, T_G, \sigma, G - Z_{\mathsf{ID}})$, $\theta \in \mathsf{Path}(\eta_{\mathsf{ID}})$.
- **Case 2**: $\mathsf{ID} \neq \mathsf{ID}^{(b)}$ and $\mathsf{Path}(\eta_{\mathsf{ID}}) \cap \mathsf{KUNodes}(\mathsf{RL}_{t^*})^* \neq \emptyset$.
    1. Sample $K''_{\mathsf{ID},\theta^*} \leftarrow \chi_{\mathsf{LWE}}^{2m \times m}$ and set $Z_{\mathsf{ID}} = [A|D_{\theta^*}]K''_{\mathsf{ID},\theta^*}$.
    2. $K''_{\mathsf{ID},\theta} \leftarrow \mathsf{SampleRight}(A, S_\theta^*, G, T_G, \sigma, Z_{\mathsf{ID}})$, where $\theta \in \mathsf{Path}(\eta_{\mathsf{ID}})(\neq \theta^*)$.
    3. $K'_{\mathsf{ID}} \leftarrow \mathsf{SampleRight}(A, R^*, (\mathsf{H}(\mathsf{ID}) - \mathsf{H}(\mathsf{ID}^{(b)}))G, T_G, \sigma, G - Z_{\mathsf{ID}})$.
- **Case 3**: $\mathsf{ID} \neq \mathsf{ID}^{(b)}$ and $\mathsf{Path}(\eta_{\mathsf{ID}}) \cap \mathsf{KUNodes}(\mathsf{RL}_{t^*})^* = \emptyset$. In this case, $D_\theta = AS_\theta^* + G$ for each node $\theta \in \mathsf{Path}(\eta_{\mathsf{ID}})$.
    1. Select uniformly random matrix Z_{ID} in $\mathbb{Z}_q^{n \times m}$ for the identity ID.
    2. Sample $K''_{\mathsf{ID},\theta} \leftarrow \mathsf{SampleRight}(A, S_\theta^*, G, T_G, \sigma, Z_{\mathsf{ID}})$, where $\theta \in \mathsf{Path}(\eta_{\mathsf{ID}})$.
    3. $K'_{\mathsf{ID}} \leftarrow \mathsf{SampleRight}(A, R^*, (\mathsf{H}(\mathsf{ID}) - \mathsf{H}(\mathsf{ID}^{(b)}))G, T_G, \sigma, G - Z_{\mathsf{ID}})$.

Game$_3^{(b)}$: This game is analogous to Game$_2^{(b)}$ except the generation of the decryption key $\mathsf{DK}_{\mathsf{ID},t}$ while answering the $\mathcal{Q}_2$ key queries during the **Query** phase when $\mathsf{ID} = \mathsf{ID}^{(b)}$, $\mathsf{Path}(\eta_{\mathsf{ID}}) \cap \mathsf{KUNodes}(\mathsf{RL}_{t^*})^* \neq \emptyset$ and $t \neq t^*$.[4]

1. Sample $\widetilde{K}_t \leftarrow \mathsf{SampleRight}(A, V^*, (\mathsf{H}(t) - \mathsf{H}(t^*))G, T_G, \sigma, G)$.
2. Perform the operation 2.(a) and 2.(b) in algorithm **GenDK**.

---

[3] This step moves from the algorithm Enc to the Setup phase.

[4] In this case, challenger $\mathcal{C}$ cannot simulate the secret key $\{K_{\mathsf{ID},\theta}\}_{\theta \in \mathsf{Path}(\eta_{\mathsf{ID}})}$, but $\mathcal{C}$ can construct a secret key $\widetilde{K}_t$ that satisfies $[A|W_t]\widetilde{K}_t = G$.

3. Compute $\widetilde{k}''_{i,\mathsf{ID},t} = \widetilde{K}_t k'_{i,\mathsf{ID},t}$, satisfying $[A|W_t]\widetilde{k}''_{i,\mathsf{ID},t} = u_i - h_{i,\mathsf{ID},t}$, where $\widetilde{k}''_{i,\mathsf{ID},t} \in \mathbb{Z}_q^{2m}$.

4. Split $k_{i,t}$ into four parts, $k_{1,i,t}$, $k_{2,i,t}$, $k_{3,i,t}$, $k_{4,i,t}$, and $\widetilde{k}''_{i,\mathsf{ID},t}$ into two parts $\widetilde{k}''_{1,i,\mathsf{ID},t}$, $\widetilde{k}''_{2,i,\mathsf{ID},t}$, m rows per part. Then, generate

$$dk_{i,\mathsf{ID},\theta^*,t} = \left[\begin{pmatrix} k_{1,i,t} + \widetilde{k}''_{1,i,\mathsf{ID},t} \\ k_{2,i,t} \end{pmatrix}^\top \middle| \begin{pmatrix} k_{3,i,t} \\ k_{4,i,t} + \widetilde{k}''_{2,i,\mathsf{ID},t} \end{pmatrix}^\top \right]^\top \in \mathbb{Z}_q^{4m}.$$

$\mathsf{Game}_4^{(b)}$: This game is analogous to $\mathsf{Game}_3^{(b)}$ except the generation of the matrix A and the ciphertexts.

1. Select a uniformly random matrix A in $\mathbb{Z}_q^{n \times m}$.

2. Choose $C'_i \leftarrow \mathbb{Z}_q$ and $c_{\mathsf{ID}^{(b)},\theta,t^*} \leftarrow \mathbb{Z}_q^{4m}$, where $\theta \in \mathsf{KUNodes}(\mathsf{RL}_{t^*})^*$, $i \in [l]$.

Analysis. Set function $\mathcal{P}_{\mathcal{A},x}(\lambda)\colon \mathbb{N} \to [0,1]$ denote the probability that $\mathcal{A}$ correctly guesses the challenge bit b on input the security parameter $\lambda \in \mathbb{N}$ in the game $\mathsf{Game}_x^{(b)}$. From the definition of $\mathsf{Game}_0^{(b)}$, it follows that the advantage of $\mathcal{A}$ is $\mathsf{Adv}_{\mathsf{RIBE},\mathcal{A}}^{\mathsf{SEL-En-CPA}}(\lambda) = |\mathcal{P}_{\mathcal{A},0}(\lambda) - 1/2|$. In addition, $\mathcal{P}_{\mathcal{A},4}(\lambda) = 1/2$ since we make the ciphertext independent of bit b through the LWE assumption in $\mathsf{Game}_4^{(b)}$. So for all $\lambda \in \mathbb{N}$, we have

$$\mathsf{Adv}_{\mathsf{RIBE},\mathcal{A}}^{\mathsf{SEL-En-CPA}}(\lambda) \le \sum_{x \in [4]} |\mathcal{P}_{\mathcal{A},x-1}(\lambda) - \mathcal{P}_{\mathcal{A},x}(\lambda)| \le \sum_{x \in [4]} \mathsf{negl}_x(\lambda)$$

We will demonstrate that the difference between successive games is only by a negligible amount $\mathsf{negl}_x(\lambda)$, as proven in a series of lemmas in Appendix A.

5 Implementation and Evaluation

In this section, we first compare our scheme with existing revocation models in theory. Then, the performance of our scheme is further evaluated by using simulation experiments.

Table 1. Revocation model comparison. Where SK and CT represent the size of secret key and ciphertext, KGC's pw represents the KGC's periodic workload, and RL permission refers to the entity responsible for managing real-time revocation information of users in the system.

Revocation model	SK	KGC's pw	CT	RL permission
Indirect [8]	$O(logN)$	$O(r\log(N/r))$	$O(1)$	KGC
Direct [5]	$O(logN)$	–	$O(r\log(N/r))$	Encryptor
Server-aided [22]	$O(1)$	$O(r\log(N/r))$	$O(1)$	KGC
Ours	$O(logN)$	≈ 0	$O(r\log(N/r))$	KGC

5.1   Theoretical Evaluation

As shown in Table 1, we compare our scheme with three existing revocation models, indirect revocation [8], direct revocation [5], and server-aided revocation [22]. It can be observed that our scheme has two main advantages, periodic workload of the KGC is nearly zero, and the encryptor is not required to handle real-time revocation information of users within the system.

5.2   Experimental Evaluation

Our scheme runs on a Ubuntu laptop with an AMD Ryzen7 6800HS CPU and 16GB of memory. For better portability, we implement our program using the NTL library and C++ language. Based on the limitations of $m > 2n \log q$, $O(m^{3/2}B\sigma) < q/4$, and $B > (m\sigma^2 + 1)2^\lambda$, we set two sets of parameters: $n = 64$, $m = 390$, $q = 2^{20}$, and $n = 128$, $m = 774$, $q = 2^{23}$.

The Sampling Algorithms. This paper mainly employs three sampling algorithms: TrapGen, SamplePre, and SampleLeft, which are the cornerstone of our scheme and also the most time-consuming in the implementation. To ensure efficient algorithm execution, we concentrate on two optimizations: extracting the Schmidt orthogonalization operation as a preprocessing step to eliminate redundant calculations during each sampling, and harnessing parallel programming to improve computational efficiency. As shown in Table 2, we provide the average runtime of these algorithms over ten executions.

Our Scheme. Now, we compare the runtime overhead of our scheme with Katsumata et al.'s lattice-based RIBE scheme with DKER [17]. Our scheme consists of the six algorithms (Setup, GenSK, NodesUp, GenDK, Enc, Dec), where Setup and Dec is similar to other schemes, and we record the runtime in Table 2. The NodesUp algorithm only involves one KUNodes operation, so the runtime is nearly zero.

As shown in Fig. 1a, the runtime overhead for the KGC to generate secret keys remains constant in multi-bit encryption. Referring to Fig. 1b, as the number of encrypted bits increases, the workload for users to generate decryption

Table 2. The running time of sampling, Setup, and Dec algorithms.

Time(ms)	TrapGen	SamplePre	SampleLeft	Setup	Dec
$n = 64$	114	159	167	323	0.1386
$n = 128$	396	314	330	1362	0.342

keys in our system grows slowly. It only involves some matrix operations, while the time-consuming sampling process is completely outsourced to the server.

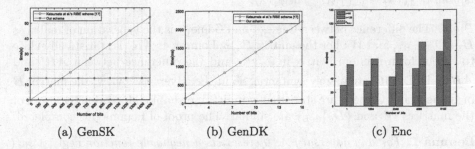

(a) GenSK   (b) GenDK   (c) Enc

Fig. 1. The main runtime of our scheme.

In our scheme, the runtime overhead of the Enc algorithm can be divided into two parts: C_i, which is related to the plaintext, and $c_{\mathsf{ID},\theta,t}$, which is unrelated to the plaintext. As shown in Fig. 1c, we set the maximum number of users N is 5000, and the number of revoked users r is 100, the shaded area represents the time overhead of the $c_{\mathsf{ID},\theta,t}$ part of the encryption, which remains constant as the number of encrypted bits increases. Moreover, C_i part takes 0.006ms when encrypting one bit.

6   Conclusion

In this paper, we propose a lattice-based RIBE scheme with En-DKER, which is the first RIBE scheme to ensure confidentiality and anonymity under decryption key exposure. Additionally, we introduce a novel approach to delegate a lattice basis. Leveraging this approach, our scheme significantly reduces the periodic workload for users to generate decryption keys. We prove the security of our scheme under the LWE assumption and efficiently implemented through the NTL and multi-threaded parallel program. The experimental results show that our scheme is suitable for multi-bit encryption and scenarios where the KGC has a high computational workload. Lastly, how to construct an adaptive secure RIBE with En-DKER is the direction of our future research.

Acknowledgements. We thank Qiqi Lai (School of Computer Science, Shaanxi Normal University, Xi'an, China) for his valuable contribution to the revision of our paper and for pointing out the need to enhance the verification of results returned by untrusted servers in our lattice basis delegation approach. This research was funded by National Natural Science Foundation of China (No. 61872204), Natural Science Foundation of Heilongjiang Province of China (No. LH2020F050), Fundamental Research Funds for Heilongjiang Universities of China (No. 2021-KYYWF-0016), Research Project on Reform of Undergraduate Education of Heilongjiang Province of China (No. SJGZ20220050).

A   The Series of Lemmas

Lemma 6. *For any adversary $\mathcal{A}$, there exists a negligible function $\mathsf{negl}_1(\cdot)$ satisfying $|\mathcal{P}_{\mathcal{A},0}(\lambda) - \mathcal{P}_{\mathcal{A},1}(\lambda)| \leq \mathsf{negl}_1(\lambda)$.*

Proof. The difference between $\mathsf{Game}_0^{(b)}$ and $\mathsf{Game}_1^{(b)}$ is the generation of matrices $\boldsymbol{B}, \{\boldsymbol{D}_\theta\}_{\theta \in \mathsf{BT}}$, and $\boldsymbol{W}$. For the matrix $\boldsymbol{B}$, by Lemma 4, $\boldsymbol{AR}^*$ is statistically close to the uniform random matrix in $\mathbb{Z}_q^{n \times m}$, and the difference between $\boldsymbol{AR}^*$ and $\boldsymbol{AR}^* - \mathsf{H}(\mathsf{ID}^{(b)})\boldsymbol{G}$ are merely syntactic. So in the adversary's view, the matrix $\boldsymbol{B}$ in $\mathsf{Game}_0^{(b)}$ and $\mathsf{Game}_1^{(b)}$ are statistically indistinguishable. Moreover, the proof of the matrices $\boldsymbol{W}$ and $\{\boldsymbol{D}_\theta\}_{\theta \in \mathsf{BT}}$ are similar. The proof of Lemma 6 is completed.

Lemma 7. *For any adversary $\mathcal{A}$, there exists a negligible function $\mathsf{negl}_2(\cdot)$ satisfying $|\mathcal{P}_{\mathcal{A},1}(\lambda) - \mathcal{P}_{\mathcal{A},2}(\lambda)| \leq \mathsf{negl}_2(\lambda)$.*

Proof. The difference between $\mathsf{Game}_1^{(b)}$ and $\mathsf{Game}_2^{(b)}$ is the generation of matrices $\boldsymbol{K}'_{\mathsf{ID}}$, $\boldsymbol{K}''_{\mathsf{ID},\theta}$ and $\boldsymbol{Z}_{\mathsf{ID}}$. For the matrix $\boldsymbol{K}'_{\mathsf{ID}}$, by the properties of sampling algorithms, sampled via algorithm $\mathsf{SampleLeft}$ is statistically close to randomly chosen in $\chi_{\mathsf{LWE}}^{2m \times m}$ and also statistically close to sampled via algorithm $\mathsf{SampleRight}$. So in the adversary's view, the matrix $\boldsymbol{K}'_{\mathsf{ID}}$ in $\mathsf{Game}_1^{(b)}$ and the three cases in $\mathsf{Game}_2^{(b)}$ are statistically indistinguishable. The proof of the matrix $\boldsymbol{K}''_{\mathsf{ID},\theta}$ is similar. So we can also derive that $\boldsymbol{Z}_{\mathsf{ID}} = [\boldsymbol{A}|\boldsymbol{B}_{\mathsf{ID}}]\boldsymbol{K}'_{\mathsf{ID}}$ and $\boldsymbol{Z}_{\mathsf{ID}} = [\boldsymbol{A}|\boldsymbol{D}_{\theta^*}]\boldsymbol{K}''_{\mathsf{ID},\theta^*}$ are statistically indistinguishable from a uniformly random matrix selected in $\mathbb{Z}_q^{n \times m}$. The proof of Lemma 7 is completed.

Lemma 8. *For any adversary $\mathcal{A}$, there exists a negligible function $\mathsf{negl}_3(\cdot)$ satisfying $|\mathcal{P}_{\mathcal{A},2}(\lambda) - \mathcal{P}_{\mathcal{A},3}(\lambda)| \leq \mathsf{negl}_3(\lambda)$.*

Proof. The difference between $\mathsf{Game}_2^{(b)}$ and $\mathsf{Game}_3^{(b)}$ is the generation of the decryption key $\mathsf{DK}_{\mathsf{ID},t}$. In $\mathsf{Game}_2^{(b)}$ and $\mathsf{Game}_3^{(b)}$,

$$\boldsymbol{dk}_{i,\mathsf{ID},\theta^*,t} = \left[\left(\begin{matrix} \boldsymbol{k}_{1,i,t} + \boldsymbol{k}''_{1,i,\mathsf{ID},\theta^*,t} \\ \boldsymbol{k}_{2,i,t} + \boldsymbol{k}''_{2,i,\mathsf{ID},\theta^*,t} \end{matrix} \right)^{\top} \middle| \left(\begin{matrix} \boldsymbol{k}_{3,i,t} + \boldsymbol{k}''_{3,i,\mathsf{ID},\theta^*,t} \\ \boldsymbol{k}_{4,i,t} \end{matrix} \right)^{\top} \right]^{\top} \in \mathbb{Z}_q^{4m},$$

$$\boldsymbol{dk}_{i,\mathsf{ID},\theta^*,t} = \left[\left(\begin{matrix} \boldsymbol{k}_{1,i,t} + \widetilde{\boldsymbol{k}}''_{1,i,\mathsf{ID},t} \\ \boldsymbol{k}_{2,i,t} \end{matrix} \right)^{\top} \middle| \left(\begin{matrix} \boldsymbol{k}_{3,i,t} \\ \boldsymbol{k}_{4,i,t} + \widetilde{\boldsymbol{k}}''_{2,i,\mathsf{ID},t} \end{matrix} \right)^{\top} \right]^{\top} \in \mathbb{Z}_q^{4m},$$

respectively. By the triangle inequality for statistical distance and Lemma 1, since $B > (m\sigma^2 + 1)2^\lambda$ holds, we can argue that there exists a negligible function $\mathsf{negl}_{smudge}(\cdot)$ such that for all $\lambda \in \mathbb{N}$,

$$\begin{aligned}
&\mathsf{SD}(\boldsymbol{k}_{1,i,t} + \boldsymbol{k}''_{1,i,\mathsf{ID},\theta^*,t}, \boldsymbol{k}_{1,i,t} + \widetilde{\boldsymbol{k}}''_{1,i,\mathsf{ID},t}) \\
&\leq \mathsf{SD}(\boldsymbol{k}_{1,i,t} + \boldsymbol{k}''_{1,i,\mathsf{ID},\theta^*,t}, \boldsymbol{k}_{1,i,t}) + \mathsf{SD}(\boldsymbol{k}_{1,i,t}, \boldsymbol{k}_{1,i,t} + \widetilde{\boldsymbol{k}}''_{1,i,\mathsf{ID},t}) \\
&\leq m \cdot \mathsf{negl}_{smudge}(\cdot) + m \cdot \mathsf{negl}_{smudge}(\cdot) \\
&= 2m \cdot \mathsf{negl}_{smudge}(\cdot).
\end{aligned}$$

Other $3m$ dimensional vector proves the same. So in the adversary's view,

$$|\mathcal{P}_{\mathcal{A},2}(\lambda) - \mathcal{P}_{\mathcal{A},3}(\lambda)| \leq 5m \cdot \mathsf{negl}_{smudge}(\cdot).$$

The proof of Lemma 8 is completed.

Lemma 9. *If the* LWE *assumption holds, for any adversary* $\mathcal{A}$, *there exists a negligible function* $\mathsf{negl}_4(\cdot)$ *satisfying* $|\mathcal{P}_{\mathcal{A},3}(\lambda) - \mathcal{P}_{\mathcal{A},4}(\lambda)| \leq \mathsf{negl}_4(\lambda)$.

Proof. Proof by contradiction, assuming there exists a non-negligible function $\delta(\cdot)$ such that $|\mathcal{P}_{\mathcal{A},3}(\lambda) - \mathcal{P}_{\mathcal{A},4}(\lambda)| \geq \delta(\cdot)$. We can use $\mathcal{A}$ to construct an LWE algorithm $\mathcal{B}$ such that $\mathsf{Adv}_{\mathcal{B}}^{\mathsf{LWE}}(\lambda) \geq \delta(\lambda)$ for all $\lambda \in \mathbb{N}$.

Initialize: $\mathcal{A}$ sets the challenge identities $\mathsf{ID}^{(0)}$ and $\mathsf{ID}^{(1)}$, the challenge time period t^*, and the challenge node set $\mathsf{KUNodes}(\mathsf{RL}_{t^*})^*$.

Setup Phase: $\mathcal{B}$ uses $\mathsf{LWE}_{n,q,\sigma}$ challenger to define the matrix $\boldsymbol{A} \in \mathbb{Z}_q^{n \times m}$ and the vector $\boldsymbol{u} \in \mathbb{Z}_q^n$ in public parameters PP. $\mathcal{B}$ makes $m + l$ times queries and receives $\{\boldsymbol{\alpha}_i, \gamma_i\}_{i \in [m+l]} \subset \mathbb{Z}_q^n \times \mathbb{Z}_q$ from $\mathsf{LWE}_{n,q,\sigma}$ challenger, where $\gamma_i = \boldsymbol{s}^\top \boldsymbol{\alpha}_i + e_i \bmod q$, $e_i \leftarrow \chi_{\mathsf{LWE}}$. Then set the matrix $\boldsymbol{A} = (\boldsymbol{\alpha}_1 | \cdots | \boldsymbol{\alpha}_m)$ and the vector $\boldsymbol{u}_i = \boldsymbol{\alpha}_{m+i}$, where $i \in [l]$. Other steps are the same as $\mathsf{Game}_3^{(b)}$.

Query Phase: $\mathcal{B}$ replies to the corresponding secret key, decryption key, and revocation queries as in $\mathsf{Game}_3^{(b)}$.

Challenge Phase: $\mathcal{B}$ performs the following computation and replies. $C_i = \gamma_{m+i} + \lfloor \frac{q}{2} \rfloor \cdot \mu_i^{(b)}$ and $\boldsymbol{c}_{\mathsf{ID}^{(b)},\theta,t^*} = \boldsymbol{\gamma}^\top [\boldsymbol{I}_m | \boldsymbol{R}^* | \boldsymbol{S}_\theta^* | \boldsymbol{V}^*]$, where $\boldsymbol{\gamma} = (\gamma_1, \dots, \gamma_m) \in \mathbb{Z}_q^m$, $i \in [l]$, and $\theta \in \mathsf{KUNodes}(\mathsf{RL}_{t^*})^*$.

Guess: $\mathcal{A}$ outputs a guess b' of b. Then $\mathcal{B}$ outputs $\mathcal{A}$'s guess as the answer to the $\mathsf{LWE}_{n,q,\sigma}$ challenge. Note that

$$C_i = \gamma_{m+i} + \left\lfloor \frac{q}{2} \right\rfloor \cdot \mu_i^{(b)} = \boldsymbol{s}^\top \boldsymbol{u}_i + \left\lfloor \frac{q}{2} \right\rfloor \cdot \mu_i^{(b)} + e_i,$$

$$\boldsymbol{c}_{\mathsf{ID}^{(b)},\theta,t^*} = \boldsymbol{\gamma}^\top [\boldsymbol{I}_m | \boldsymbol{R}^* | \boldsymbol{S}_\theta^* | \boldsymbol{V}^*] = \boldsymbol{s}^\top [\boldsymbol{A} | \boldsymbol{B}_{\mathsf{ID}^{(b)}} | \boldsymbol{D}_\theta | \boldsymbol{W}_{t^*}] + \boldsymbol{e}'^\top [\boldsymbol{I}_m | \boldsymbol{R}^* | \boldsymbol{S}_\theta^* | \boldsymbol{V}^*],$$

where $e_i = e_{m+i}$ and $\boldsymbol{e}' = (e_1, \dots, e_m)$. So the game simulated by the reduction algorithm $\mathcal{B}$ coincides with $\mathsf{Game}_3^{(b)}$. Simultaneously, based on LWE assumption, C_i and $\boldsymbol{c}_{\mathsf{ID}^{(b)},\theta,t^*}$ are uniformly and independently distributed over $\mathbb{Z}_q$ and $\mathbb{Z}_q^m$, so the game simulated by the reduction algorithm $\mathcal{B}$ coincides with $\mathsf{Game}_4^{(b)}$. Hence, the advantage of $\mathcal{B}$ in solving $\mathsf{LWE}_{n,q,\sigma}$ problem is the same as the advantage of $\mathcal{A}$ in distinguishing $\mathsf{Game}_3^{(b)}$ and $\mathsf{Game}_4^{(b)}$. The proof of Lemma 9 is completed.

References

1. Agrawal, S., Boneh, D., Boyen, X.: Efficient Lattice (H)IBE in the standard model. In: Gilbert, H. (ed.) EUROCRYPT 2010. LNCS, vol. 6110, pp. 553–572. Springer, Heidelberg (2010). https://doi.org/10.1007/978-3-642-13190-5_28

2. Ajtai, M.: Generating hard instances of the short basis problem. In: Wiedermann, J., van Emde Boas, P., Nielsen, M. (eds.) ICALP 1999. LNCS, vol. 1644, pp. 1–9. Springer, Heidelberg (1999). https://doi.org/10.1007/3-540-48523-6_1
3. Alwen, J., Peikert, C.: Generating shorter bases for hard random lattices. Theory Comput. Syst. **48**, 535–553 (2011)
4. Asharov, G., Jain, A., López-Alt, A., Tromer, E., Vaikuntanathan, V., Wichs, D.: Multiparty computation with low communication, computation and interaction via threshold FHE. In: Pointcheval, D., Johansson, T. (eds.) EUROCRYPT 2012. LNCS, vol. 7237, pp. 483–501. Springer, Heidelberg (2012). https://doi.org/10.1007/978-3-642-29011-4_29
5. Attrapadung, N., Imai, H.: Attribute-based encryption supporting direct/indirect revocation modes. In: Parker, M.G. (ed.) IMACC 2009. LNCS, vol. 5921, pp. 278–300. Springer, Heidelberg (2009). https://doi.org/10.1007/978-3-642-10868-6_17
6. Bellare, M., Boldyreva, A., Desai, A., Pointcheval, D.: Key-privacy in public-key encryption. In: Boyd, C. (ed.) ASIACRYPT 2001. LNCS, vol. 2248, pp. 566–582. Springer, Heidelberg (2001). https://doi.org/10.1007/3-540-45682-1_33
7. Benhamouda, F., Gentry, C., Gorbunov, S., Halevi, S., Krawczyk, H., Lin, C., Rabin, T., Reyzin, L.: Can a public blockchain keep a secret? In: Pass, R., Pietrzak, K. (eds.) TCC 2020. LNCS, vol. 12550, pp. 260–290. Springer, Cham (2020). https://doi.org/10.1007/978-3-030-64375-1_10
8. Boldyreva, A., Goyal, V., Kumar, V.: Identity-based encryption with efficient revocation. In: Proceedings of the 15th ACM Conference on Computer and Communications Security, pp. 417–426 (2008)
9. Boneh, D., Franklin, M.: Identity-based encryption from the weil pairing. SIAM J. Comput. **32**(3), 586–615 (2003)
10. Boyen, X., Waters, B.: Anonymous hierarchical identity-based encryption (without random oracles). In: Dwork, C. (ed.) CRYPTO 2006. LNCS, vol. 4117, pp. 290–307. Springer, Heidelberg (2006). https://doi.org/10.1007/11818175_17
11. Cash, D., Hofheinz, D., Kiltz, E., Peikert, C.: Bonsai trees, or how to delegate a lattice basis. J. Cryptol. **25**, 601–639 (2012)
12. Chen, J., Lim, H.W., Ling, S., Wang, H., Nguyen, K.: Revocable identity-based encryption from lattices. In: Susilo, W., Mu, Y., Seberry, J. (eds.) ACISP 2012. LNCS, vol. 7372, pp. 390–403. Springer, Heidelberg (2012). https://doi.org/10.1007/978-3-642-31448-3_29
13. Emura, K., Takayasu, A., Watanabe, Y.: Adaptively secure revocable hierarchical ibe from k-linear assumption. Des. Codes Crypt. **89**(7), 1535–1574 (2021)
14. Ge, A., Wei, P.: Identity-based broadcast encryption with efficient revocation. In: Lin, D., Sako, K. (eds.) PKC 2019. LNCS, vol. 11442, pp. 405–435. Springer, Cham (2019). https://doi.org/10.1007/978-3-030-17253-4_14
15. Gentry, C., Peikert, C., Vaikuntanathan, V.: Trapdoors for hard lattices and new cryptographic constructions. In: Proceedings of the Fortieth Annual ACM Symposium on Theory of Computing, pp. 197–206 (2008)
16. Huang, Z., Lai, J., Han, S., Lyu, L., Weng, J.: Anonymous public key encryption under corruptions. In: Advances in Cryptology-ASIACRYPT 2022: 28th International Conference on the Theory and Application of Cryptology and Information Security, Taipei, Taiwan, December 5–9, 2022, Proceedings, Part III. pp. 423–453. Springer (2023)
17. Katsumata, S., Matsuda, T., Takayasu, A.: Lattice-based revocable (hierarchical) IBE with decryption key exposure resistance. In: Lin, D., Sako, K. (eds.) PKC 2019. LNCS, vol. 11443, pp. 441–471. Springer, Cham (2019). https://doi.org/10.1007/978-3-030-17259-6_15

18. Ling, S., Nguyen, K., Wang, H., Zhang, J.: Revocable predicate encryption from lattices. In: Okamoto, T., Yu, Y., Au, M.H., Li, Y. (eds.) ProvSec 2017. LNCS, vol. 10592, pp. 305–326. Springer, Cham (2017). https://doi.org/10.1007/978-3-319-68637-0_19
19. Luo, F., Al-Kuwari, S., Wang, H., Wang, F., Chen, K.: Revocable attribute-based encryption from standard lattices. Comput. Stand. Interfaces **84**, 103698 (2023)
20. Micciancio, D., Peikert, C.: Trapdoors for lattices: simpler, tighter, faster, smaller. In: Pointcheval, D., Johansson, T. (eds.) EUROCRYPT 2012. LNCS, vol. 7237, pp. 700–718. Springer, Heidelberg (2012). https://doi.org/10.1007/978-3-642-29011-4_41
21. Naor, D., Naor, M., Lotspiech, J.: Revocation and tracing schemes for stateless receivers. In: Kilian, J. (ed.) CRYPTO 2001. LNCS, vol. 2139, pp. 41–62. Springer, Heidelberg (2001). https://doi.org/10.1007/3-540-44647-8_3
22. Qin, B., Deng, R.H., Li, Y., Liu, S.: Server-aided revocable identity-based encryption. In: Pernul, G., Ryan, P.Y.A., Weippl, E. (eds.) ESORICS 2015. LNCS, vol. 9326, pp. 286–304. Springer, Cham (2015). https://doi.org/10.1007/978-3-319-24174-6_15
23. Regev, O.: On lattices, learning with errors, random linear codes, and cryptography. J. ACM (JACM) **56**(6), 1–40 (2009)
24. Seo, J.H., Emura, K.: Revocable identity-based encryption revisited: security model and construction. In: Kurosawa, K., Hanaoka, G. (eds.) PKC 2013. LNCS, vol. 7778, pp. 216–234. Springer, Heidelberg (2013). https://doi.org/10.1007/978-3-642-36362-7_14
25. Takayasu, A., Watanabe, Y.: Revocable identity-based encryption with bounded decryption key exposure resistance: Lattice-based construction and more. Theoret. Comput. Sci. **849**, 64–98 (2021)
26. Wang, S., Zhang, J., He, J., Wang, H., Li, C.: Simplified revocable hierarchical identity-based encryption from lattices. In: Mu, Y., Deng, R.H., Huang, X. (eds.) CANS 2019. LNCS, vol. 11829, pp. 99–119. Springer, Cham (2019). https://doi.org/10.1007/978-3-030-31578-8_6
27. Watanabe, Y., Emura, K., Seo, J.H.: New Revocable IBE in prime-order groups: adaptively secure, decryption key exposure resistant, and with short public parameters. In: Handschuh, H. (ed.) CT-RSA 2017. LNCS, vol. 10159, pp. 432–449. Springer, Cham (2017). https://doi.org/10.1007/978-3-319-52153-4_25
28. Zhang, Y., Liu, X., Hu, Y.: Simplified server-aided revocable identity-based encryption from lattices. In: Provable and Practical Security: 16th International Conference, ProvSec 2022, Nanjing, China, November 11–12, 2022, Proceedings. pp. 71–87. Springer, Cham (2022). https://doi.org/10.1007/978-3-031-20917-8_6

Arithmetic Circuit Implementations of S-boxes for SKINNY and PHOTON in MPC

Aysajan Abidin⬤, Erik Pohle(✉)⬤, and Bart Preneel⬤

COSIC, KU Leuven, Leuven, Belgium
{aysajan.abidin,erik.pohle,bart.preneel}@esat.kuleuven.be

Abstract. Secure multi-party computation (MPC) enables multiple distrusting parties to compute a function while keeping their respective inputs private. In a threshold implementation of a symmetric primitive, e.g., of a block cipher, each party holds a share of the secret key or of the input block. The output block is computed without reconstructing the secret key. This enables the construction of distributed TPMs or transciphering for secure data transmission in/out of the MPC context.

This paper investigates implementation approaches for the lightweight primitives SKINNY and PHOTON in arithmetic circuits. For these primitives, we identify arithmetic expressions for the S-box that result in smaller arithmetic circuits compared to the Boolean expressions from the literature. We validate the optimization using a generic actively secure MPC protocol and obtain 18% faster execution time with 49% less communication data for SKINNY-64-128 and 27% to 74% faster execution time with 49% to 81% less data for PHOTON P_{100} and P_{288}. Furthermore, we find a new set of parameters for the heuristic method of polynomial decomposition, introduced by Coron, Roy and Vivek, specialized for SKINNY's 8-bit S-box. We reduce the multiplicative depth from 9 to 5.

Keywords: S-box · SKINNY · PHOTON · Secure Multi-Party Computation · Arithmetic Circuit

1 Introduction

Recent improvements in advanced cryptographic protocols, such as secure multi-party computation (MPC), fully homomorphic encryption (FHE), or zero-knowledge proof systems, made computation on encrypted data practical. This development enables privacy-preserving and GDPR compliant data processing and utilization in many areas, such as in public sector services, in smart cities, or healthcare. With added privacy benefits for users and data providers, various use cases emerge where cryptographic primitives are needed, including proofs

This work is supported by the Flemish Government through FWO SBO project MOZAIK S003321N.

© The Author(s), under exclusive license to Springer Nature Switzerland AG 2024
G. Tsudik et al. (Eds.): ESORICS 2023, LNCS 14344, pp. 86–105, 2024.
https://doi.org/10.1007/978-3-031-50594-2_5

over correct hashing, ciphertext-compression for FHE schemes, and secure out-sourcing of computation and data storage for MPC.

Applications of Symmetric Primitive Evaluation in MPC. The applications of MPC evaluation of symmetric-key primitives are numerous. We briefly sketch a selection of them. In a **distributed TPM**, instead of relying on trusted hardware, trust is distributed among multiple servers. Generation of secret keys is distributed and each server only ever obtains a secret share. The key shares are used in collaborative (or distributed) computations, e.g., encryption or signing, using MPC without reconstructing the secret key. Symmetric-key encryption can also be paired with MPC to enable flexible, secure and **privacy-preserving data collection and processing** [1]. Collected data can be encrypted at the source, stored and once MPC-based processing is desired, the data is decrypted in MPC and then processed. Since MPC creates a secure context for data processing, the input that is moved into this context and the output data that is moved out of this context may be encrypted to **facilitate secure input/output with parties that do not participate in the MPC protocol** [23,24]. Additionally, in the same way, MPC computation can be paused and continued later by encrypting intermediate data for secure storage. Finally, symmetric primitives in MPC may be used as **oblivious PRFs**, to bootstrap **secure database queries** or to create **MPC-in-the-head zero-knowledge proofs** and **post-quantum signatures** [10].

Related Work. Dedicated PRFs [18,23,24], block and stream ciphers [2–4,9,17,21,32], and hash functions [20,22] have been proposed that focus on minimizing multiplicative depth. However, in a real-world scenario, cryptographic mechanisms and constructions need to interoperate between traditional computing systems (e.g., IoT devices, mobile phones, commodity and server CPUs) and these advanced cryptographic protocols. Traditional symmetric primitives, such as AES [33] and SHA-2 [34], are widely used in real-world applications and are widespread in internet and industry standards. For instance, the correct processing of financial transaction data in MPC requires the usage of standardized constructions from that real-world domain since the information is not protected under non-standard cryptographic mechanisms that are MPC-friendly. These standards almost exclusively specify traditional symmetric primitives at the core. Further, thresholdization of primitives, i.e., where the secret key is split among multiple parties who then jointly compute the relevant operation without reconstructing the secret key, is recently being investigated by NIST for standardization [8]. The important key part of thresholdization is that a threshold and a non-threshold implementation have to be interoperable, such that, e.g., systems managing keys in a threshold fashion can seamlessly interact with systems not using thresholdization.

While thresholdized AES implementations have been studied, e.g., [12,13, 16,19,27], other traditional primitives have not received that much attention. In this work, we want to study threshold implementations of lightweight primitives that may be used in applications where AES is undesirable. Lorünser and Wohner [30] implement several symmetric ciphers using two MPC frameworks, namely, MP-SPDZ and MPyC, to facilitate a better understanding of the two MPC frameworks. However, they treat the primitives as black boxes with little optimization of the primitive's performance. Motivated partly by the interoperability of privacy-enhancing protocols and lightweight cryptography, Mandal and Gong [31] study the Boolean circuit complexity of the core primitives in the NIST Lightweight Cryptography Competition (LWC)[1] round 2 candidates. However, their study is limited to Boolean circuits using the two-party garbling scheme HalfGates [35] for the MPC evaluation of the ciphers.

Contribution. To complement this effort, we move to the arithmetic circuit setting where variables are elements of, e.g., a finite field or ring, and basic gates are addition and multiplication gates. We investigate whether such a representation results in benefits, such as reduced circuit size, faster execution, or less communication data, over a straight-forward emulation of Boolean arithmetic paired with known Boolean circuits of lightweight primitives. A possible avenue in the arithmetic setting is to identify operations and structure in the primitive where groups of bits can be encoded as field/ring elements and equivalent arithmetic operations can replace bit-oriented functionality. For this purpose, we analyze the ten LWC finalists, but we limit our study to substitution-permutation network (SPN) designs of the underlying primitives which excludes SPARKLE, Grain-128AEAD, and TinyJambu. Moreover, we rule out the permutations used in sponge-based AEADs (Ascon, ISAP, and Xoodyak) for two reasons. First, the sponge structure creates highly serial circuits with high multiplicative depth that results in poor performance in non-constant round MPC protocols. Second, the permutation's round function operates over lanes, sheets, and columns of the state, mixing bits over all dimensions. This makes grouping bits within the state costly without a foreseeable benefit for arithmetic purposes. Further, the SPN primitives of Elephant and GIFT-COFB involve a bit-level permutation making the linear layer costly (when grouped). Ultimately, we identify two primitives, SKINNY and PHOTON, stemming from the finalists Romulus and PHOTON-Beetle, respectively, where all operations on the state can be expressed as cellwise operations and no intra-cell operations occur. We can therefore group the bits of each cell into one field/ring element and then investigate the cost of all operations in the arithmetic circuit. While SKINNY serves as the main demonstration example, we also apply our findings to PHOTON. Our contributions can be summarized as follows:

– We provide several program representations for the SKINNY primitive in arithmetic circuits over $\mathbb{F}_{2^k}$ (see Sect. 3) optimized for usage in MPC protocols. We identify a trade-off between multiplications and pre-processed random bits for the evaluation of polynomials, resulting in a reduced number of multiplications for all 4-bit S-boxes.

---

[1] https://csrc.nist.gov/Projects/Lightweight-Cryptography.

- We benchmark the promising candidates of the trade-off in the secret sharing based "SPDZ-like" protocol MASCOT in the active security setting (see Sect. 4). We confirm the trade-off in practice and obtain improved performance for SKINNY variants with 64-bit block size, i.e., faster execution and lower communication cost, compared to the baseline.
- We show how the results for SKINNY carry over to a threshold implementation of PHOTON (see Sect. 4.3). We obtain similar performance improvements for 4-bit S-boxes and can apply well-known optimizations of the AES S-box used in the 8-bit PHOTON instance.

The rest of this paper is organized as follows. We give an introduction and background information on SKINNY, PHOTON and on the MPC protocol in Sect. 2. Then, we investigate the representation of SKINNY in arithmetic circuits in Sect. 3. The results of the experimental benchmark are detailed and discussed in Sect. 4. We conclude the paper in Sect. 5.

2 Background on Primitives and MPC

In the following, we give background details on the SKINNY lightweight block cipher family (Sect. 2.1), the permutations defined in PHOTON (Sect. 2.2) and discuss one MPC protocol for arithmetic circuits (Sect. 2.3).

2.1 SKINNY

SKINNY [6] is a lightweight tweakable block cipher with a SPN structure similar to AES. Its different variants process 64-bit or 128-bit blocks, and 64–384-bit tweakeys which is the concatenation of a (secret), e.g., 64- or 128-bit key and a (public) tweak. Table 1 lists the number of rounds specified for each variant. The round function alters the internal state, a 4×4 array of s-bit cells. For a block size of 64-bit, $s = 4$, for 128-bit block size, $s = 8$. The initial state is the message block. Let the message be a sequence of s-bit values $s_0 \, s_1 \, \ldots \, s_{15}$, then the 4×4 array is filled row-wise:

$$\begin{pmatrix} s_0 & s_1 & s_2 & s_3 \\ s_4 & s_5 & s_6 & s_7 \\ s_8 & s_9 & s_{10} & s_{11} \\ s_{12} & s_{13} & s_{14} & s_{15} \end{pmatrix}.$$

The resulting ciphertext is the state after all rounds have been computed. The tweakeys are loaded into 4×4 arrays, TK1, TK2, TK3, in the same manner. TK1, present in all variants, is loaded with tweakey bits $0 \cdots (16s - 1)$. TK2 and TK3 are loaded with tweakey bits $16s \cdots (32s - 1)$ and $32s \cdots (48s - 1)$ respectively, if needed. The round function applies five steps in series: SubCells, AddRoundConstants, AddRoundKey, ShiftRows and MixColumns.

SubCells. SubCells applies the S-box to each cell in the state. For $s = 4$, the 4-bit S-box is used (see Fig. 1a), for $s = 8$, the 8-bit S-box is used (see Fig. 1b). Both S-boxes are computed by repeating XOR and NOR operations, and bit permutations. For the S-box definition as a truth table, we refer the reader to the original specification document [6].

AddRoundConstants. This step XORs public constants to three cells:

$$s_0' \leftarrow s_0 \oplus c_0, \quad s_4' \leftarrow s_4 \oplus c_1, \quad s_8' \leftarrow s_8 \oplus \text{0x2}.$$

The constants c_0 and c_1 are defined for each round, whereas the operand for s_8 remains 0x2.

AddRoundKey. In each round, the first two rows of the state are XORed cell-wise with the first rows of each available round tweakey. Let $a_{i..j} \oplus b_{i..j}$ be a short-hand notation for $a_i \oplus b_i \ldots a_j \oplus b_j$, then

$$s_{0..3}' \leftarrow s_{0..3} \oplus \text{TK1}_{0..3} \oplus \text{TK2}_{0..3} \oplus \text{TK3}_{0..3},$$
$$s_{4..7}' \leftarrow s_{4..7}' \oplus \text{TK1}_{4..7} \oplus \text{TK2}_{4..7} \oplus \text{TK3}_{4..7}.$$

ShiftRows. Shift rows applies a cell-wise permutation P_S on the state where

$$P_S(0,...,15) = (0,1,2,3,7,4,5,6,10,11,8,9,13,14,15,12).$$

This rotates each row by $0,1,2$ and 3 elements to the right.

MixColumns. The MixColumns step multiplies the state with the matrix

$$\begin{pmatrix} s_0' & s_1' & s_2' & s_3' \\ s_4' & s_5' & s_6' & s_7' \\ s_8' & s_9' & s_{10}' & s_{11}' \\ s_{12}' & s_{13}' & s_{14}' & s_{15}' \end{pmatrix} \leftarrow \begin{pmatrix} 1 & 0 & 1 & 1 \\ 1 & 0 & 0 & 0 \\ 0 & 1 & 1 & 0 \\ 1 & 0 & 1 & 0 \end{pmatrix} \begin{pmatrix} s_0 & s_1 & s_2 & s_3 \\ s_4 & s_5 & s_6 & s_7 \\ s_8 & s_9 & s_{10} & s_{11} \\ s_{12} & s_{13} & s_{14} & s_{15} \end{pmatrix}.$$

Key Schedule. The key schedule describes how a round key is derived from the cipher's key. The first round key is the tweakey itself. Round keys for subsequent rounds are obtained by applying the permutation P_T cell-wise on the 4×4 array representation of each tweakey. Each cell in TK2 and TK3 is further updated by a linear feedback shift register (LFSR). In short, denoting the round key for the next round by $\text{TK}i', i = 1, 2, 3$, we have

$$\text{TK1}' \leftarrow P_T(\text{TK1}), \quad \text{TK2}' \leftarrow \text{LFSR2} \circ P_T(\text{TK2}), \quad \text{TK3}' \leftarrow \text{LFSR3} \circ P_T(\text{TK3}),$$

where $P_T(0,..,15) = (9,15,8,13,10,14,12,11,0,1,2,3,4,5,6,7)$ and LFSR2/ LFSR3 are defined in Table 2. P_T swaps the first two rows with the last two rows of the state and applies a permutation to the now first two rows.

Table 1. The number of rounds for each variant of SKINNY. Variants are denoted by SKINNY-b-tk where b is the block size in bits and tk is the tweakey size in bits. Note that the key size equals the block size in all variants.

Variant	Block Size	Rounds	Variant	Block Size	Rounds
SKINNY-64-64		32	SKINNY-128-128		40
SKINNY-64-128	64	36	SKINNY-128-256	128	48
SKINNY-64-192		40	SKINNY-128-384		56

Table 2. Linear feedback shift registers LFSR2 and LFSR3 defined in the key schedule of SKINNY for tweakeys TK2 and TK3, respectively.

	Cell size			
LFSR2	4-bit	(x_3, x_2, x_1, x_0)	$\rightarrow$	$(x_2, x_1, x_0, x_3 \oplus x_2)$
	8-bit	$(x_7, x_6, x_5, x_4, x_3, x_2, x_1, x_0)$	$\rightarrow$	$(x_6, x_5, x_4, x_3, x_2, x_1, x_0, x_7 \oplus x_5)$
LFSR3	4-bit	(x_3, x_2, x_1, x_0)	$\rightarrow$	$(x_0 \oplus x_3, x_3, x_2, x_1)$
	8-bit	$(x_7, x_6, x_5, x_4, x_3, x_2, x_1, x_0)$	$\rightarrow$	$(x_0 \oplus x_6, x_7, x_6, x_5, x_4, x_3, x_2, x_1)$

2.2 PHOTON

We briefly describe the internal permutations P_t, $t \in \{100, 144, 196, 256, 288\}$, of the PHOTON hash function [25]. Similarly to SKINNY, the internal state is a $d \times d$ array of s-bit cells that is transformed by applying the following round function steps 12 times: AddConstant, SubCells, ShiftRows, MixColumnsSerial. Since P_t is a permutation, it has no secret key addition layer. Table 3 lists the parameters for each variant.

AddConstant. Public round constants and instance-specific internal constants are XORed to the first column of the state.

SubCells. If $s = 4$, the PRESENT S-box [7] is applied to each cell in the state. If $s = 8$, the AES S-box is applied.

ShiftRows. This applies a cell-wise permutation on the state where row i is rotated by i columns to the left.

MixColumnsSerial. Each column of the state is multiplied with a matrix A_t d times. The multiplication is defined over $\mathbb{F}_2[X]/X^4 + X + 1$ for $s = 4$ and over $\mathbb{F}_2[X]/X^8 + X^4 + X^3 + X + 1$ for $s = 8$.

Table 3. State size d, cell size s and modulus of PHOTON P_t.

Instance	d	s	Modulus
P_{100}	5	4	
P_{144}	6	4	$X^4 + X + 1$
P_{196}	7	4	
P_{256}	8	4	
P_{288}	6	8	$X^8 + X^4 + X^3 + X + 1$

2.3 A Multi-party Computation Protocol for Arithmetic Circuits

In this and the following sections, we denote a uniform random sampling from a finite set A with $\xleftarrow{\$} A$. We now briefly discuss the SPDZ-style, dishonest-majority MPC protocol on arithmetic circuits that achieves active security using information-theoretically secure MACs. The communication model in the protocol assumes secure point-to-point channels and a synchronous network. If we later refer to a round of communication, this means each party broadcasts one or more local values to all other parties. In this model, the broadcast based on point-to-point connections costs $\mathcal{O}(n^2)$ values to send for n players. In the protocol, the computation is split into a pre-processing, a.k.a. offline, phase and an online phase. In the offline phase, the players jointly create correlated randomness for multiplication and bit-decomposition. Since neither the individual party's inputs nor the concrete function to compute[2] have to be known, this phase can take place well before the online phase and is usually computationally much heavier. In the online phase, the parties know their own inputs and the arithmetic circuit. This phase consumes the correlated randomness from the offline phase. Since we only consider binary extension fields in this paper, we adapt the notation for the MPC protocol accordingly. Recall that $\mathbb{F}_{2^k} = \mathbb{F}_2[X]/Q(X)$ is a finite field with 2^k elements, where $k > 0$. Each element can be represented as a polynomial of degree at most $k - 1$ whose coefficients are in $\mathbb{F}_2$ and $Q(X)$ is an irreducible polynomial of degree k. Addition $g(X) + h(X)$, for $g(X), h(X) \in \mathbb{F}_{2^k}$, is performed coefficient-wise. Multiplication $g(X)h(X)$ is the ordinary polynomial multiplication modulo $Q(X)$. Every variable in the arithmetic circuit is an element in $\mathbb{F}_{2^k}$. During execution, each player holds or obtains an additive secret share of every variable. We denote the additive share of $x \in \mathbb{F}_{2^k}$ of player i with $x^{(i)}$, i.e., $\sum x^{(i)} = x$. A SPDZ-like share of the same player is denoted with $[\![x]\!]_i = \langle x^{(i)}, m^{(i)} \rangle$ which carries a MAC share $m^{(i)}$ that authenticates the secret share to enable active security where m is created using the global secret MAC key $\Delta \in \mathbb{F}_{2^k}$.

Offline Phase. The offline phase implements the functionalities $\mathcal{F}_{\text{Triple}}$ and $\mathcal{F}_{\text{Bit}}$ by using somewhat homomorphic encryption SHE (e.g. in [14,15,29]) or oblivious transfer [28]. While the offline phase dominates the total runtime of the MPC protocol, its details are less important for the purpose of this paper. We invite the reader to consult the aforementioned references for further details.

The functionality $\mathcal{F}_{\text{Triple}}$ produces Beaver multiplication triples [5] of the form $([\![a]\!], [\![b]\!], [\![c]\!])$ where $c = ab$ and $a, b \xleftarrow{\$} \mathbb{F}_{2^k}$. The functionality $\mathcal{F}_{\text{Bit}}$ produces random bits $[\![r]\!]$ with $r \xleftarrow{\$} \{0, 1\}$.

Online Phase. Before detailing the addition and multiplication of shares, we have to describe the concept of (partially) opening a share. In general, if a share $[\![x]\!]$ is opened, each player i broadcasts $x^{(i)}$ and then sums up all shares to obtain x. For active security, the players first commit to the MAC shares $m^{(i)} - \Delta^{(i)} x^{(i)}$ before opening them. Later it is checked whether $m - \Delta x = 0$. The core idea of SPDZ is to defer the checking of the MAC values to the very end of the protocol, resulting in a so-called partial open. Before the final output is revealed, all MACs

---

[2] However, the players must know an upper bound on the number of required multiplication triples resp. random bits.

of partially opened shares are checked in one go. If this check passes, the output value is reconstructed.

Let $[\![x]\!] = \langle x^{(i)}, m_x^{(i)} \rangle$, $[\![y]\!] = \langle y^{(i)}, m_y^{(i)} \rangle$ be shares and $e \in \mathbb{F}_{2^k}$ a public constant, then addition of shares, public constants and multiplication by public constants can be performed locally by each player:

$$e + [\![x]\!] = [\![e + x]\!] : \begin{cases} \langle x^{(0)} + e, m_x^{(0)} + e\Delta^{(0)} \rangle & \text{if } i = 0, \\ \langle x^{(i)}, m_x^{(i)} + e\Delta^{(i)} \rangle & \text{else,} \end{cases}$$

$$e \cdot [\![x]\!] = [\![e \cdot x]\!] : \langle e \cdot x^{(i)}, e \cdot m_x^{(i)} \rangle,$$

$$[\![x]\!] + [\![y]\!] = [\![x + y]\!] : \langle x^{(i)} + y^{(i)}, m_x^{(i)} + m_y^{(i)} \rangle.$$

Given a multiplication triple $([\![a]\!], [\![b]\!], [\![c]\!])$ from $\mathcal{F}_{\mathsf{Triple}}$, we compute the multiplication $[\![x]\!] \cdot [\![y]\!] = [\![x \cdot y]\!]$ in two steps.

1. The players partially open $[\![x - a]\!]$ as γ and $[\![y - b]\!]$ as ϵ.
2. Each player computes locally $[\![x \cdot y]\!]_i = [\![c]\!]_i + \gamma \cdot [\![b]\!]_i + \epsilon \cdot [\![a]\!]_i + \gamma \cdot \epsilon$.

The partial open requires one round of communication, unlike the linear operations mentioned before.

We can also compute a bit-decomposition of a shared $x \in \mathbb{F}_{2^k}$ into k shares of the bits of x, $b_0, \ldots, b_{k-1}$ where $x = \sum_{j=0}^{k-1} b_j X^j$. Note that the resulting bit b_i is still shared over $\mathbb{F}_{2^k}$. Given k random bits $[\![r_0]\!], \ldots, [\![r_{k-1}]\!]$ from $\mathcal{F}_{\mathsf{Bit}}$,

1. The players locally compute $[\![r]\!] = \sum_{j=0}^{k-1} [\![r_j]\!] X^j$ and partially open $[\![x - r]\!]$ as γ.
2. Let $\gamma_0, \ldots, \gamma_{k-1} \in \{0, 1\}$ be the (clear text) decomposition of γ. Each player then computes $[\![b_0]\!] = [\![\gamma_0 + r_0]\!], \ldots, [\![b_{k-1}]\!] = [\![\gamma_{k-1} + r_{k-1}]\!]$.

In summary, multiplying two secret-shared values, i.e., $[\![x \cdot y]\!] \leftarrow [\![x]\!] \cdot [\![y]\!]$, requires one multiplication triple from $\mathcal{F}_{\mathsf{Triple}}$ and one round of communication. A bit-decomposition of $[\![x]\!]$ into k bits $[\![b_0]\!], \ldots, [\![b_{k-1}]\!]$ requires k random bits from $\mathcal{F}_{\mathsf{Bit}}$ and one round of communication. Note that both for multiplication and bit-decomposition, data of independent operations can be sent in the same round.

3 Arithmetic Circuit Implementation

We aim to explore possible performance gains of an arithmetic representation of the circuit where we utilize properties of the underlying field over an emulation of Boolean arithmetic. Thus in the following, variables are elements of a finite field. The cell-focused nature of SKINNY allows the representation of each cell as a finite field element. Thus, the state consists of 16 field elements.

Concretely, we define two fields[3] of size 2^4 and 2^8,

$$\mathbb{F}_{2^4} = \mathbb{F}_2[X]/(X^4 + X^3 + 1),$$
$$\mathbb{F}_{2^8} = \mathbb{F}_2[X]/(X^8 + X^7 + X^6 + X^5 + X^4 + X^2 + 1). \tag{1}$$

---

[3] Since the SKINNY reference does not specify operations in a field, we are free to pick a suitable one.

For SKINNY versions with a 64-bit state, we pick the field $\mathbb{F}_{2^4}$ and for a 128-bit state, we use $\mathbb{F}_{2^8}$. We encode s-bit cell values $b_{s-1} \ldots b_0$ into field elements as $b_{s-1} \ldots b_0 \leftrightarrow \sum_{i=0}^{s-1} b_i X^i$. We express values from this correspondence as hexadecimal literals, e.g., $\texttt{0xa3} \leftrightarrow X^7 + X^5 + X + 1$. With this correspondence, XOR of two s-bit values translates to addition of two field elements in $\mathbb{F}_{2^s}$. As a result, all parts of the round function except for SubCells become linear and can be computed locally by each player. The fields defined in Eq. (1) entail a minimal number of multiplications to implement the respective S-box via polynomial interpolation. We give more details later in Sect. 3.2. From Table 2, we can see that if the tweakey is available in shared bits, the LFSR computation, and thus the whole key schedule, is also linear and incurs no communication rounds.

Furthermore, we recall that squaring is a linear operation in fields of characteristic two, i.e.,

$$\left(\sum_{i=0}^{s-1} b_i X^i\right)^2 = \sum_{i=0}^{s-1} (b_i X^i)^2. \tag{2}$$

Given the bits of such a field element as vector $\boldsymbol{b} = (b_0, \ldots, b_{s-1})$, the output bit vector for squaring is $\mathsf{sq} : \{0,1\}^s \mapsto \{0,1\}^s = \boldsymbol{Mb}$ where $\boldsymbol{M} \in \mathbb{F}_2^{s \times s}$ is a matrix depending on the irreducible polynomial. Thus, given the bit-decomposition $\boldsymbol{b}$ of $x \in \mathbb{F}_{2^s}$, any power of the form x^{2^j} can be computed without any multiplication triples since sq is a linear function. We stress, however, that the initial bit-decomposition requires one opening in the online phase, so computing any number of squares in $\{x^2, x^4, x^8, \ldots\}$ costs one round of communication and s random bits.

In the following, we describe approaches to express the non-linear part of SubCells, the S-box. Section 3.1 describes the baseline approach that emulates Boolean arithmetic. Then, we study approaches via polynomial interpolation. Section 3.2 details the interpolation and Sect. 3.3 improves the evaluation by utilizing the free squaring property. In Sect. 3.4, we apply a polynomial decomposition to compute the S-box. Table 4 lists the cost of each S-box implementation approach in terms of multiplication triples, random bits and communication rounds.

3.1   Binary S-box

The Boolean operations AND, XOR and NOT can be naturally emulated in any field with characteristic two. If the values are a sharing of 0 or 1, AND is expressed as multiplication, XOR as addition and NOT is addition with the constant $\texttt{0x1}$. In this approach, each bit in an s-bit cell is encoded as a field element and we compute the S-box as given in the SKINNY specification [6] emulating Boolean operations (see Fig. 1). We will further use this approach as baseline for the comparison.

$$x_0' \leftarrow x_1 \oplus (\neg x_3' \wedge \neg x_2')$$
$$x_1' \leftarrow x_2 \oplus (\neg x_1 \wedge \neg x_3')$$
$$x_2' \leftarrow x_3 \oplus (\neg x_2 \wedge \neg x_1)$$
$$x_3' \leftarrow x_0 \oplus (\neg x_3 \wedge \neg x_2)$$

$$x_0' \leftarrow x_2 \oplus (\neg x_3' \wedge \neg x_1') \quad x_4' \leftarrow x_3 \oplus (\neg x_7' \wedge \neg x_6')$$
$$x_1' \leftarrow x_7 \oplus (\neg x_7' \wedge \neg x_2') \quad x_5' \leftarrow x_0 \oplus (\neg x_3 \wedge \neg x_2)$$
$$x_2' \leftarrow x_6 \oplus (\neg x_2 \wedge \neg x_1) \quad x_6' \leftarrow x_4 \oplus (\neg x_7 \wedge \neg x_6)$$
$$x_3' \leftarrow x_1 \oplus (\neg x_5' \wedge \neg x_3) \quad x_7' \leftarrow x_5 \oplus (\neg x_6' \wedge \neg x_5')$$

(a) The 4-bit S-box.   (b) The 8-bit S-box.

Fig. 1. The 4-bit and 8-bit S-box of the SKINNY cipher. The cell bit x_i is transformed into x_i'.

3.2 S-box via Polynomial Interpolation

Another representation of the (s-bit) S-box is via a polynomial $P_s(z) = \sum_{i=0}^{2^s-1} a_i z^i$, where $a_i \in \mathbb{F}_{2^s}$. Then, the computation of the S-box on a given value x is the evaluation of P_s at x. We can obtain the coefficients a_i by associating $(x, \mathcal{S}_s(x))$ for all $x \in \mathbb{F}_{2^s}$ and computing the interpolating polynomial by means of Lagrange interpolation, or by solving the following linear system of equations

$$\begin{pmatrix} 0x1 \ 0x0^1 \ \dots \ 0x0^{2^s-1} \\ 0x1^0 \ 0x1^1 \ \dots \ 0x1^{2^s-1} \\ \vdots \end{pmatrix} \begin{pmatrix} a_0 \\ \vdots \\ a_{2^s-1} \end{pmatrix} = \begin{pmatrix} \mathcal{S}_s(0x0) \\ \mathcal{S}_s(0x1) \\ \vdots \end{pmatrix}. \tag{3}$$

This approach primarily motivated the choice for the irreducible polynomials in Eq. (1). The chosen modulus entails a maximally sparse interpolating polynomial for the respective S-box, i.e., for this modulus, $P_s(z)$ contains the maximal number of coefficients $a_i = 0x0$.

The interpolating polynomial for SKINNY's 4-bit S-box $\mathcal{S}_4$ is

$$P_4(z) = 0xc + 0x8z + 0x3z^2 + 0xdz^3 + 0xfz^4 + 0x4z^5 + 0x8z^6 + 0x6z^7$$
$$+ 0x1z^8 + 0x9z^9 + 0x8z^{10} + 0xez^{12} + 0xcz^{13} + 0xbz^{14}. \tag{4}$$

The inverse $\mathcal{S}_4^{-1}$ is slightly sparser, with one less non-zero coefficient. For the 8-bit S-box $\mathcal{S}_8$, $P_8(z)$ is more unwieldy with degree 252 and 244 non-zero coefficients. Its inverse $\mathcal{S}_8^{-1}$ has degree 252 with 241 non-zero coefficients.

For a direct evaluation of $P(z)$, we need to compute the powers z^i that occur in $P(z)$. The remaining linear combination $\sum a_i z^i$ is free. In order to minimize the number of sequential multiplications, we express the computation through the shortest addition chain of the set $\{1, 2, 3, 4, 5, 6, 7, 8, 9, 10, 13, 14\}$ for P_4 (see Fig. 2a). This approach is marked as MUL in Table 4. Analogously for $\mathcal{S}_8$, we find a chain that requires 242 multiplications in 8 rounds and for $\mathcal{S}_8^{-1}$, we use 239 multiplications in 8 rounds.

3.3 S-box via Polynomial Interpolation with Free Squaring

We may use bit-decomposition and then repeated free squaring to compute more powers in a single round. This creates a trade-off between multiplicative depth,

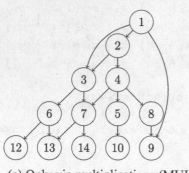
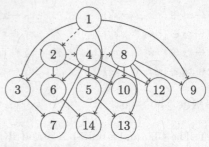

(a) Only via multiplications (MUL).

(b) Using free squares 2,4,8 (SQ1). Dashed arrows denote free squaring via bit-decomposition.

Fig. 2. Shortest addition chain for powers in the interpolating polynomial for SKINNY's 4-bit S-box. Each level in the tree denotes one communication round.

the number of multiplications and the number of required pre-processed random bits for the bit-decomposition. We explore this trade-off for the 4-bit S-box in detail since the number of powers to compute is significantly smaller than for the 8-bit S-box. We denote this approach SQ1, SQ2, ... where one, two, ... base values are used for free squaring. Table 4 lists the cost for each combination. For S_4 and SQ1, we first square z^1 to obtain z^2, z^4, z^8. This is illustrated in Fig. 2b. For SQ2, we compute z^3 normally and also square it to obtain z^6, z^{12}, z^9 for free. For SQ3, z^5 is squared to obtain z^{10} and for SQ4 squaring z^7 yields z^{14}, z^{13}, z^{11}. While squaring once/twice, e.g., SQ1 and SQ2, decreases the number of rounds that are necessary for the computation, SQ3 and SQ4 require one more round. The reason for the additional required round is that some powers can no longer be computed in the original round since the prerequisite powers are no longer both available in the previous round because they are computed later for free. Concretely, power 14 can no longer be computed in round 3 by using powers 6 and 8 since power 6 is computed for free at the earliest in round 3. Figure 5a in Appendix A illustrates this by showing the addition chain for SQ3.

We visualize the trade-off in the 8-bit case in Fig. 5b in Appendix A. Three configurations may be of interest. The plain multiplication approach requires 242 multiplications in 8 rounds but no random bits. Using only the square chain $1 \rightarrow 2 \rightarrow 4 \rightarrow 8 \rightarrow \ldots$ requires 236 multiplications, 8 random bits in 4 rounds. On the other end, if as many values are computed via squaring as possible, the computation requires 33 multiplications and 264 random bits in 5 rounds.

3.4   Decomposition

We can use the decomposition method, CRV, by Coron, Roy and Vivek [11] to reduce the number of multiplications to evaluate the interpolating polynomial $P(z)$. In short, $P(z)$ is decomposed into the sum of products of polynomials $p_i(z)$

Table 4. Cost of implementation approaches for SKINNY's 4-bit and 8-bit S-boxes. MUL denotes the direct evaluation of the interpolating polynomial, BIN is the emulation of Boolean arithmetic, SQi denotes utilization of i free square chains and CRV denotes the polynomial decomposition.

	$\mathcal{S}_4$			$\mathcal{S}_4^{-1}$		
	Mult.	Bits	Depth	Mult.	Bits	Depth
MUL	12	0	4	11	0	4
BIN	4	0	2	4	0	4
SQ1	9	4	3	8	4	3
SQ2	6	8	3	6	8	3
SQ3	5	12	4	5	12	4
SQ4	3	16	4	3	16	4
CRV	2	8	4	2	8	4

	$\mathcal{S}_8$			$\mathcal{S}_8^{-1}$		
	Mult.	Bits	Depth	Mult.	Bits	Depth
MUL	242	0	8	239	0	8
BIN	8	0	4	8	0	4
SQ1	236	8	4	233	8	4
SQ33	33	264	5	32	256	5
CRV	10	40	5	10	40	5

and $q_i(z)$,

$$P(z) = \sum_{i=1}^{t-1} p_i(z)q_i(z) + p_t(z), \tag{5}$$

where each polynomial p_i, q_i only has monomials z^a with $a \in L$ where

$$L = C_{\alpha_1} \cup \cdots \cup C_{\alpha_l}. \tag{6}$$

The set L is constructed from a number of cyclotomic bases C_{α_j} constructs the consecutive squares starting from α_j: $C_{\alpha_j} = \{2^i \alpha_j \mod 2^s - 1 \mid \forall 0 \le i < 2^s\}$.

With a good choice of l cyclotomic bases, all powers z^a for $a \in L$ can be computed with $l - 2$ multiplications. Naturally, $\alpha_1 = 0$ and $\alpha_2 = 1$, i.e., z^0 and z^1, which don't require any computation. Essentially, z^{α_j} is computed as the product of previous values, while $z^{2^i \alpha_j}$ is computed for free since squaring is linear in our chosen field. Therefore, the entire polynomial can be evaluated with $l - 2 + t - 1$ multiplications by first computing the monomials defined by L and then computing the product $p_i(z)q_i(z)$.

The CRV method is heuristic as one chooses the cyclotomic bases and coefficients for polynomials q_i to solve the resulting linear system for coefficients of p_i. The authors of [11] give α values for 4- and 8-bit polynomials for which random choices for q_i lead to a system with a solution.

Their parameter choice was motivated by finding higher-order masking to protect implementations against side-channel attacks and has a minimal number of multiplications. For our scenario, we also attempt to reduce the multiplicative depth since this reduces the number of communication rounds in the protocol. Table 5 lists our parameter choice and the heuristics given in [11]. For the 4-bit case, the choice $\alpha_j \in \{0, 1, 3\}$ is also minimal in terms of communication rounds. For the specific S-boxes $\mathcal{S}_8$ and $\mathcal{S}_8^{-1}$, we find a new set of cyclotomic bases with a lower multiplicative depth and less random bits which only increases the number of linear operations.

Table 5. Parameter choices for the polynomial decomposition in $\mathbb{F}_{2^s}$ and the evaluation cost in terms of multiplication triples, random bits and multiplicative depth. The parameter t denotes the number of p_i/q_i polynomials in Eq. (5).

	s	t	Base α	Mult	Bits	Depth
CRV [11]	4	2	$\{0,1,3\}$	2	8	4
CRV [11]	8	6	$\{0,1,3,7,29,87,251\}$	10	48	9
Ours for $\mathcal{S}_8$ and $\mathcal{S}_8^{-1}$	8	7	$\{0,1,3,5,7,11\}$	10	40	5

Using this approach, *any* 4-bit S-box can be implemented requiring 2 multiplications and 8 random bits in 4 rounds. Our new parameters implement SKINNY's 8-bit S-boxes with 10 multiplications and 40 random bits in 5 rounds, however, they don't allow the implementation of any 8-bit S-box[4].

4 Experimental Results

We implemented two cipher variants, SKINNY-64-128 and SKINNY-128-256, in the forward and inverse direction. In Sect. 4.1 we evaluate all S-box approaches for SKINNY's 4-bit S-box and in Sect. 4.2, we investigate the BIN and CRV variant for SKINNY's 8-bit S-box. Finally, we apply the results to PHOTON in Sect. 4.3. Table 6 shows the gate counts for the complete primitives. In all comparisons, BIN denotes the baseline.

We benchmark in a three-party LAN setting[5] using the MASCOT MPC protocol [28] in the MP-SPDZ framework [26]. MASCOT provides active security for a dishonest majority. In the MP-SPDZ implementation, shares are elements of the field $\mathbb{F}_{2^{40}}$ defined as $\mathbb{F}_{2^{40}} = \mathbb{F}_2[Y]/(Y^{40}+Y^{20}+Y^{15}+Y^{10}+1)$. We therefore embed both $\mathbb{F}_{2^4}$ and $\mathbb{F}_{2^8}$ into $\mathbb{F}_{2^{40}}$. This also achieves 40-bit statistical security. Let $\mathcal{E}_4$ and $\mathcal{E}_8$ denote the embedding $\mathbb{F}_{2^4} \hookrightarrow \mathbb{F}_{2^{40}}$ and $\mathbb{F}_{2^8} \hookrightarrow \mathbb{F}_{2^{40}}$, respectively. We use $\mathcal{E}_4(Y) = Y^{35}+Y^{20}+Y^5+1$ and $\mathcal{E}_8(Y) = Y^{35}+Y^{30}+Y^{25}+Y^{20}+Y^{10}+Y^5$ as they require the lowest number of linear operations to be computed among all available embeddings. Note that decomposing an embedded element from $\mathbb{F}_{2^s}$ still only costs s random bits (see Table 7 in Appendix A for more details). A different modulus for $\mathbb{F}_{2^{40}}$ would require different embeddings from $\mathbb{F}_{2^4}$ and $\mathbb{F}_{2^8}$ but has otherwise no impact on the performance.

We compute 100 circuits (key schedule, if applicable, and block encryption/decryption) in parallel to allow for amortization effects in the pre-processing phase. Both the input block and the key are secret inputs and not entirely known by any party. Note that if one party fully knows the key, it may be more efficient to compute the key schedule locally and input each round key separately. We compute the key schedule within the MPC protocol to make our

---

[4] The parameters cannot be used to decompose the AES S-box, for instance.

[5] Each party runs on a separate machine with 4 cores and 16 GB RAM connected with a bandwidth of 10 Gbit/sec and <1 ms latency.

Table 6. Gate counts of SKINNY-64-128, SKINNY-128-256, PHOTON P_{100}, PHO-
TON P_{288} and AES-128 (for context). Add/Cmul denote the number of local linear
operations.

	Mult.	Random Bits	Add/Cmul	Comm. Rounds
SKINNY-64-128 (BIN)	2304	0	10238	72
SKINNY-64-128 (CRV)	1152	4608	82764	144
SKINNY-128-256 (BIN)	6144	0	27465	145
SKINNY-128-256 (CRV)	7680	30720	1545744	240
PHOTON P_{100} (BIN)	1200	0	13862	48
PHOTON P_{100} (CRV)	600	2400	56520	48
PHOTON P_{288} (BIN)	13824	0	135648	72
PHOTON P_{288} (AES)	2592	6912	207072	60
AES-128 [13]	1200	3200	45149	53

experiments more broadly usable, if, e.g., the key is the result of a previous MPC
computation or each party inputs a key share as in the case for transciphering
or OPRF evaluation.

4.1   SKINNY-64-128

We choose the SKINNY-64-128 variant to assess the performance of all 4-bit
S-box implementation approaches. Any performance gains for SKINNY-64-64 or
SKINNY-64-192 will be similar since these variants only differ in the number of
rounds and the linear key schedule.

Figure 3a visualizes the total, i.e., pre-processing and online, runtime and
total communication data per player per encryption/decryption and S-box implementation approach for SKINNY-64-128. We note that the number of multiplications in the circuit seems to dominate the total performance regarding time
and data. The more free squares are used, the lower the time and data.

While the SQ4 approach uses fewer multiplications than BIN, we measure
fewer data but a slower total time, presumably due to the two additional rounds
and four bit-decompositions. The CRV implementation performs best in time
and data compared to all other approaches, including the baseline Boolean arithmetic emulation BIN. At least in our setting, trading-off two multiplications with
two bit-decompositions (and thus eight random bits) leads to better overall performance. SQ4 is around 24% slower but uses 23% less data than BIN. CRV is
approx. 18% faster and uses 49% less data than BIN.

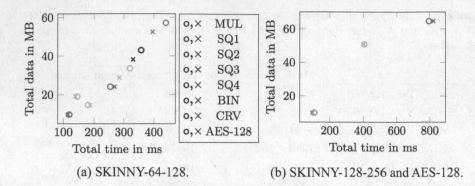

(a) SKINNY-64-128.   (b) SKINNY-128-256 and AES-128.

Fig. 3. Total, i.e., pre-processing and online, execution time and communication data for multiple S-box implementation approaches of SKINNY-64-128 and SKINNY-128-256 amortized with 100 executions in parallel. The legend symbol o denotes the forward direction while × denotes the inverse direction.

4.2 SKINNY-128-256

We implemented the BIN and CRV approach for the 8-bit S-boxes since the MUL or SQ1/SQ33 approaches are not better than CRV or BIN in any metric, i.e., number of multiplications, number of random bits or multiplicative depth. We evaluate BIN and CRV in SKINNY-128-256 and report the total time and communication data per player in Fig. 3b. In the same figure, we also give total time and communication data of an AES forward and inverse computation in the same setting following the implementation from Damgård et al. [13].

As already visible in the gate counts (cf. Table 4), the CRV approach does not create a favourable trade-off for the 8-bit S-box. This means that the BIN baseline approach is faster and uses less data than CRV. Furthermore, for the block size of 128 bits, AES outperforms SKINNY-128-256. The S-box of AES is much cheaper to implement arithmetically, via 6 multiplications and two bit-decompositions than the Boolean implementation that would require 32 multiplications. In addition, AES only has ten rounds while SKINNY-128-256 has more than four times more rounds.

4.3 PHOTON

Finally, we transferred the results to PHOTON. The four defined permutations $P_{100}, P_{144}, P_{196}$ and P_{256} use the 4-bit S-box of PRESENT [7] while P_{288} uses the AES S-box. The PHOTON permutations have mixing layers where the state is multiplied with a mixing matrix in a pre-defined finite field. While it may seem that this complicates the implementation approaches, a fixed modulus is not a problem since the CRV method (for the 4-bit case) applies to any field with the same cost. Further, any AES S-box implementation may be applied to P_{288}. To illustrate how our results carry over, we implemented P_{100} and P_{288}. For P_{100}, we apply the CRV decomposition approach, and for P_{288} we apply the

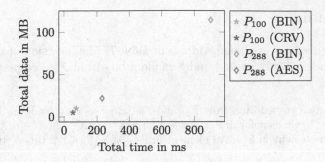

Fig. 4. Total, i.e., pre-processing and online, execution time and communication data for PHOTON P_{100} and P_{288} amortized with 100 executions in parallel.

known AES S-box optimizations from [13]. Figure 4 illustrates the benchmark results. For P_{100}, we note a 27% faster execution with 49% less data. For P_{288}, we observe a 74% faster execution with 81% less data.

5 Conclusion

We investigated and identified improvements of an arithmetic circuit representation of the most costly component of the SKINNY cipher, namely, the S-box, over an emulation of its Boolean circuit for MPC evaluation. Our approaches implement SKINNY's S-boxes over $\mathbb{F}_{2^4}$ and $\mathbb{F}_{2^8}$.

In the 4-bit case, we identified a favourable trade-off between the Boolean implementation, a direct interpolation of the S-box with squaring, and a polynomial decomposition approach. Choosing the decomposition approach saves 50% of multiplications in the circuit, traded-off with pre-processed random bits, compared to the Boolean implementation. Our practical benchmark confirms the trade-off. Moving to the arithmetic circuit setting indeed offers increased performance benefits of ≈18% faster execution with ≈49% less data.

In the 8-bit case, we observe that the S-box cannot be more efficiently expressed using our techniques. Our benchmark shows no improvement over the baseline Boolean circuit approach. Nonetheless, we find new parameters for the polynomial decomposition approach specific to SKINNY's 8-bit S-boxes that reduces the multiplicative depth of an evaluation from 9 to 5.

Further, we apply our technique to PHOTON and obtain an improved circuit representation with 50% fewer multiplications for the variants with 4-bit cells. For the 8-bit cell-based variant P_{288} with the AES S-box optimization, we achieve a circuit with ≈81% fewer multiplications. A practical benchmark confirms the optimization effort over a Boolean circuit emulation with 27% and 74% faster execution and 49% and 81% less data for P_{100} and P_{288}, respectively.

Finally, we note that the identified polynomial decomposition approach will likely achieve similar improvements for other primitives with 4-bit S-boxes, such as Midori, TWINE, LED, KLEIN, QARMA, or KNOT.

A Appendix

We detail the used (inverse) embeddings in Table 7. The inversion of the embedding of $\mathbb{F}_{2^4}$ and $\mathbb{F}_{2^8}$ only costs 4 and 8 random bits from $\mathcal{F}_{\mathsf{Bit}}$, respectively.

Table 7. The used embeddings from $\mathbb{F}_{2^4}$ and $\mathbb{F}_{2^8}$ into $\mathbb{F}_{2^{40}}$ on a bit level. Let $b_3 X^3 + b_2 X^2 + b_1 X + b_0$ be an element in $\mathbb{F}_{2^4}$ and $b_7 X^7 + b_6 X^6 + b_5 X^5 + b_4 X^4 + b_3 X^3 + b_2 X^2 + b_1 X + b_0$ be an element in $\mathbb{F}_{2^8}$. An element in $\mathbb{F}_{2^{40}}$ is $\sum_{i=0}^{39} b_i' Y^i$. Bits b_i' that are not set below are 0.

Embedding	$\mathbb{F}_{2^4}/\mathbb{F}_{2^8}$ to $\mathbb{F}_{2^{40}}$	$\mathbb{F}_{2^{40}}$ to $\mathbb{F}_{2^4}/\mathbb{F}_{2^8}$
$\mathbb{F}_{2^4} \hookrightarrow \mathbb{F}_{2^{40}}$ via $Y^{35} + Y^{20} + Y^5 + 1$	$\begin{pmatrix} b_0' \\ b_5' \\ b_{10}' \\ b_{15}' \\ b_{20}' \\ b_{30}' \\ b_{35}' \end{pmatrix} = \begin{pmatrix} 1&1&1&0 \\ 0&1&1&0 \\ 0&0&0&1 \\ 0&0&1&0 \\ 0&1&0&0 \\ 0&0&0&1 \\ 0&1&0&0 \end{pmatrix} \begin{pmatrix} b_0 \\ b_1 \\ b_2 \\ b_3 \end{pmatrix}$	$\begin{pmatrix} b_0 \\ b_1 \\ b_2 \\ b_3 \end{pmatrix} = \begin{pmatrix} 1&1&0&0 \\ 0&1&0&1 \\ 0&0&0&1 \\ 0&0&1&0 \end{pmatrix} \begin{pmatrix} b_0' \\ b_5' \\ b_{10}' \\ b_{15}' \end{pmatrix}$
$\mathbb{F}_{2^8} \hookrightarrow \mathbb{F}_{2^{40}}$ via $Y^{35} + Y^{30} + Y^{25} + Y^{20} + Y^{10}$	$\begin{pmatrix} b_0' \\ b_5' \\ b_{10}' \\ b_{15}' \\ b_{20}' \\ b_{25}' \\ b_{30}' \\ b_{35}' \end{pmatrix} = \begin{pmatrix} 1&0&1&0&0&1&1&1 \\ 0&1&1&1&1&0&0&0 \\ 0&1&0&0&0&0&1&0 \\ 0&0&0&1&0&0&1&0 \\ 0&1&0&1&0&1&0&0 \\ 0&1&1&1&1&0&1&0 \\ 0&1&0&0&1&0&0&1 \\ 0&1&1&0&0&0&0&0 \end{pmatrix} \begin{pmatrix} b_0 \\ b_1 \\ b_2 \\ b_3 \\ b_4 \\ b_5 \\ b_6 \\ b_7 \end{pmatrix}$	$\begin{pmatrix} b_0 \\ b_1 \\ b_2 \\ b_3 \\ b_4 \\ b_5 \\ b_6 \\ b_7 \end{pmatrix} = \begin{pmatrix} 1&1&1&0&1&0&1&0 \\ 0&1&1&0&0&1&0&0 \\ 0&1&1&0&0&1&0&1 \\ 0&1&0&1&0&1&0&0 \\ 0&0&0&1&0&1&0&1 \\ 0&0&1&1&1&0&0&0 \\ 0&1&0&0&0&1&0&0 \\ 0&1&1&1&0&0&1&1 \end{pmatrix} \begin{pmatrix} b_0' \\ b_5' \\ b_{10}' \\ b_{15}' \\ b_{20}' \\ b_{25}' \\ b_{30}' \\ b_{35}' \end{pmatrix}$

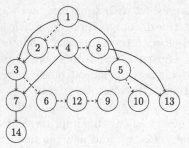

(a) Shortest addition chain for powers in the interpolating polynomial for S_4 suing free squares (2,4,8), (6,12,9) and (10) (SQ3). Note that since 6 is no longer available in round 2, 14 has to be computed in round 4.

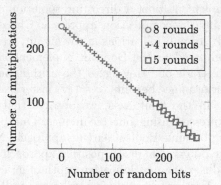

(b) Trade-off between the number of multiplications and free squares for the interpolation polynomial of S_8.

Fig. 5. Additional figures for shortest addition chain and the trade-off between multiplication and free squares.

References

1. Abidin, A., et al.: MOZAIK: an end-to-end secure data sharing platform. In: Second ACM Data Economy Workshop (DEC 2023), Seattle, WA, USA, 18 June 2023, p. 7. ACM (2023)
2. Albrecht, M., Grassi, L., Rechberger, C., Roy, A., Tiessen, T.: MiMC: efficient encryption and cryptographic hashing with minimal multiplicative complexity. In: Cheon, J.H., Takagi, T. (eds.) ASIACRYPT 2016. LNCS, vol. 10031, pp. 191–219. Springer, Heidelberg (2016). https://doi.org/10.1007/978-3-662-53887-6_7
3. Albrecht, M.R., Rechberger, C., Schneider, T., Tiessen, T., Zohner, M.: Ciphers for MPC and FHE. In: Oswald, E., Fischlin, M. (eds.) EUROCRYPT 2015. LNCS, vol. 9056, pp. 430–454. Springer, Heidelberg (2015). https://doi.org/10.1007/978-3-662-46800-5_17
4. Aly, A., Ashur, T., Ben-Sasson, E., Dhooghe, S., Szepieniec, A.: Design of symmetric-key primitives for advanced cryptographic protocols. IACR Trans. Symmetric Cryptol. **2020**(3), 1–45 (2020)
5. Beaver, D.: Efficient multiparty protocols using circuit randomization. In: Feigenbaum, J. (ed.) CRYPTO 1991. LNCS, vol. 576, pp. 420–432. Springer, Heidelberg (1992). https://doi.org/10.1007/3-540-46766-1_34
6. Beierle, C., et al.: The SKINNY family of block ciphers and its low-latency variant MANTIS. In: Robshaw, M., Katz, J. (eds.) CRYPTO 2016. LNCS, vol. 9815, pp. 123–153. Springer, Heidelberg (2016). https://doi.org/10.1007/978-3-662-53008-5_5
7. Bogdanov, A., et al.: PRESENT: an ultra-lightweight block cipher. In: Paillier, P., Verbauwhede, I. (eds.) CHES 2007. LNCS, vol. 4727, pp. 450–466. Springer, Heidelberg (2007). https://doi.org/10.1007/978-3-540-74735-2_31
8. Brandão, L.T.A.N., Peralta, R.: NIST IR 8214C ipd NIST First Call for Multi-Party Threshold Schemes (Initial Public Draft) (2023)
9. Canteaut, A., et al.: Stream ciphers: a practical solution for efficient homomorphic-ciphertext compression. J. Cryptol. **31**(3), 885–916 (2018)
10. Chase, M., et al.: Post-quantum zero-knowledge and signatures from symmetric-key primitives. In: Proceedings of the 2017 ACM SIGSAC Conference on Computer and Communications Security, CCS 2017, pp. 1825–1842. Association for Computing Machinery (2017)
11. Coron, J.-S., Roy, A., Vivek, S.: Fast evaluation of polynomials over binary finite fields and application to side-channel countermeasures. In: Batina, L., Robshaw, M. (eds.) CHES 2014. LNCS, vol. 8731, pp. 170–187. Springer, Heidelberg (2014). https://doi.org/10.1007/978-3-662-44709-3_10
12. Damgård, I., Keller, M.: Secure multiparty AES. In: Sion, R. (ed.) FC 2010. LNCS, vol. 6052, pp. 367–374. Springer, Heidelberg (2010). https://doi.org/10.1007/978-3-642-14577-3_31
13. Damgård, I., Keller, M., Larraia, E., Miles, C., Smart, N.P.: Implementing AES via an actively/covertly secure dishonest-majority MPC protocol. In: Visconti, I., De Prisco, R. (eds.) SCN 2012. LNCS, vol. 7485, pp. 241–263. Springer, Heidelberg (2012). https://doi.org/10.1007/978-3-642-32928-9_14
14. Damgård, I., Keller, M., Larraia, E., Pastro, V., Scholl, P., Smart, N.P.: Practical covertly secure MPC for dishonest majority – or: breaking the SPDZ limits. In: Crampton, J., Jajodia, S., Mayes, K. (eds.) ESORICS 2013. LNCS, vol. 8134, pp. 1–18. Springer, Heidelberg (2013). https://doi.org/10.1007/978-3-642-40203-6_1

15. Damgård, I., Pastro, V., Smart, N., Zakarias, S.: Multiparty computation from somewhat homomorphic encryption. In: Safavi-Naini, R., Canetti, R. (eds.) CRYPTO 2012. LNCS, vol. 7417, pp. 643–662. Springer, Heidelberg (2012). https://doi.org/10.1007/978-3-642-32009-5_38

16. Damgård, I., Zakarias, R.: Fast oblivious AES a dedicated application of the MiniMac protocol. In: Pointcheval, D., Nitaj, A., Rachidi, T. (eds.) AFRICACRYPT 2016. LNCS, vol. 9646, pp. 245–264. Springer, Cham (2016). https://doi.org/10.1007/978-3-319-31517-1_13

17. Dobraunig, C., et al.: Rasta: a cipher with low ANDdepth and few ANDs per bit. In: Shacham, H., Boldyreva, A. (eds.) CRYPTO 2018. LNCS, vol. 10991, pp. 662–692. Springer, Cham (2018). https://doi.org/10.1007/978-3-319-96884-1_22

18. Dobraunig, C., Grassi, L., Guinet, A., Kuijsters, D.: CIMINION: symmetric encryption based on Toffoli-gates over large finite fields. In: Canteaut, A., Standaert, F.-X. (eds.) EUROCRYPT 2021. LNCS, vol. 12697, pp. 3–34. Springer, Cham (2021). https://doi.org/10.1007/978-3-030-77886-6_1

19. Durak, F.B., Guajardo, J.: Improving the efficiency of AES protocols in multi-party computation. In: Borisov, N., Diaz, C. (eds.) FC 2021. LNCS, vol. 12674, pp. 229–248. Springer, Heidelberg (2021). https://doi.org/10.1007/978-3-662-64322-8_11

20. Grassi, L., Khovratovich, D., Rechberger, C., Roy, A., Schofnegger, M.: Poseidon: a new hash function for zero-knowledge proof systems. In: Bailey, M., Greenstadt, R. (eds.) 30th USENIX Security Symposium, USENIX Security 2021, pp. 519–535. USENIX Association (2021)

21. Grassi, L., Lüftenegger, R., Rechberger, C., Rotaru, D., Schofnegger, M.: On a generalization of substitution-permutation networks: the HADES design strategy. In: Canteaut, A., Ishai, Y. (eds.) EUROCRYPT 2020. LNCS, vol. 12106, pp. 674–704. Springer, Cham (2020). https://doi.org/10.1007/978-3-030-45724-2_23

22. Grassi, L., Onofri, S., Pedicini, M., Sozzi, L.: Invertible quadratic non-linear layers for MPC-/FHE-/ZK-friendly schemes over Fnp application to Poseidon. IACR Trans. Symmetric Cryptol. **2022**(3), 20–72 (2022)

23. Grassi, L., Øygarden, M., Schofnegger, M., Walch, R.: From Farfalle to Megafono via Ciminion: the PRF hydra for MPC applications. In: Hazay, C., Stam, M. (eds.) EUROCRYPT 2023. LNCS, vol. 14007, pp. 255–286. Springer, Cham (2023). https://doi.org/10.1007/978-3-031-30634-1_9

24. Grassi, L., Rechberger, C., Rotaru, D., Scholl, P., Smart, N.P.: MPC-friendly symmetric key primitives. In: Weippl, E.R., Katzenbeisser, S., Kruegel, C., Myers, A.C., Halevi, S. (eds.) Proceedings of the 2016 ACM SIGSAC Conference on Computer and Communications Security, pp. 430–443. ACM (2016)

25. Guo, J., Peyrin, T., Poschmann, A.: The PHOTON family of lightweight hash functions. In: Rogaway, P. (ed.) CRYPTO 2011. LNCS, vol. 6841, pp. 222–239. Springer, Heidelberg (2011). https://doi.org/10.1007/978-3-642-22792-9_13

26. Keller, M.: MP-SPDZ: a versatile framework for multi-party computation. In: Ligatti, J., Ou, X., Katz, J., Vigna, G. (eds.) 2020 ACM SIGSAC Conference on Computer and Communications Security, CCS 2020, pp. 1575–1590. ACM (2020)

27. Keller, M., Orsini, E., Rotaru, D., Scholl, P., Soria-Vazquez, E., Vivek, S.: Faster secure multi-party computation of AES and DES using lookup tables. In: Gollmann, D., Miyaji, A., Kikuchi, H. (eds.) ACNS 2017. LNCS, vol. 10355, pp. 229–249. Springer, Cham (2017). https://doi.org/10.1007/978-3-319-61204-1_12

28. Keller, M., Orsini, E., Scholl, P.: MASCOT: faster malicious arithmetic secure computation with oblivious transfer. In: Weippl, E.R., Katzenbeisser, S., Kruegel, C., Myers, A.C., Halevi, S. (eds.) Proceedings of the 2016 ACM SIGSAC Conference on Computer and Communications Security, pp. 830–842. ACM (2016)

29. Keller, M., Pastro, V., Rotaru, D.: Overdrive: making SPDZ great again. In: Nielsen, J.B., Rijmen, V. (eds.) EUROCRYPT 2018. LNCS, vol. 10822, pp. 158–189. Springer, Cham (2018). https://doi.org/10.1007/978-3-319-78372-7_6

30. Lorünser, T., Wohner, F.: Performance comparison of two generic MPC-frameworks with symmetric ciphers. In: Samarati, P., di Vimercati, S.D.C., Obaidat, M.S., Ben-Othman, J. (eds.) Proceedings of the 17th International Joint Conference on e-Business and Telecommunications, ICETE 2020, SECRYPT, vol. 2, pp. 587–594. ScitePress (2020)

31. Mandal, K., Gong, G.: Can LWC and PEC be friends?: evaluating lightweight ciphers in privacy-enhancing cryptography. In: Fourth Lightweight Cryptography Workshop. NIST (2020)

32. Méaux, P., Journault, A., Standaert, F.-X., Carlet, C.: Towards stream ciphers for efficient FHE with low-noise ciphertexts. In: Fischlin, M., Coron, J.-S. (eds.) EUROCRYPT 2016. LNCS, vol. 9665, pp. 311–343. Springer, Heidelberg (2016). https://doi.org/10.1007/978-3-662-49890-3_13

33. National Institute of Standards and Technology: Specification for the ADVANCED ENCRYPTION STANDARD (AES). Federal Information Processing Standards Publications 197 (2001)

34. National Institute of Standards and Technology: Secure Hash Standard (SHS). Federal Information Processing Standards Publications 180-4, August 2015

35. Zahur, S., Rosulek, M., Evans, D.: Two halves make a whole - reducing data transfer in garbled circuits using half gates. In: Oswald, E., Fischlin, M. (eds.) EUROCRYPT 2015. LNCS, vol. 9057, pp. 220–250. Springer, Heidelberg (2015). https://doi.org/10.1007/978-3-662-46803-6_8

Code-Based Secret Handshake Scheme, Revisited

Minkyu Kim[1] and Hyung Tae Lee[2(✉)]

[1] The Affiliated Institute of ETRI, Daejeon, Republic of Korea
`mkkim@nsr.re.kr`
[2] School of Computer Science and Engineering, Chung-Ang University, Seoul,
Republic of Korea
`hyungtaelee@cau.ac.kr`

Abstract. Secret handshake (SH) allows two users to authenticate each
other anonymously only when they are in the same group. Recently,
due to the concern of developments on large-scale quantum computers,
designing post-quantum SH has been investigated and three constructions were proposed: One is code-based [21] and two others are lattice-
based [1,2]. However, it turns out that the code-based construction [21]
has a security flaw that the adversary easily impersonates an honest user
to activate a handshake.

In this paper, we show how to construct a code-based SH scheme in the
framework of CA-oblivious encryption by utilizing the recently proposed
code-based signature scheme, called LESS-FM, whose security is based
on the hardness of the code equivalence problem. Our proposed scheme
is the first *secure* code-based SH and has the smallest communication
cost among all known post-quantum SH schemes. For example, for 80-
bit security, our scheme has communication costs of about 260 KB and
3.4 KB when instantiated with Classic McEliece and BIKE, respectively,
while other existing post-quantum constructions have communication
costs of megabytes or gigabytes.

Keywords: secret handshake · CA-oblivious encryption · code-based
construction · code equivalence problem · LESS-FM signatures

1 Introduction

A secret handshake scheme (SHS) allows two users to authenticate each other
anonymously if they belong to the same group, but does not learn any other
information than the result, otherwise. For example, suppose that Alice is a
CIA agent and wants to communicate securely with Bob if he is also a CIA
agent. On the other hand, if Bob is not a CIA agent, Alice may not want to leak
any information that she is a CIA agent. The solution to this problem was firstly
introduced by Balfanz et al. [4] in 2003. They formalized a notion of the SHS
and then provided an instantiation of the SHS based on bilinear maps. Later, by
considering its diverse application scenarios, there have been proposed various

© The Author(s), under exclusive license to Springer Nature Switzerland AG 2024
G. Tsudik et al. (Eds.): ESORICS 2023, LNCS 14344, pp. 106–125, 2024.
https://doi.org/10.1007/978-3-031-50594-2_6

SHSs [11,14–16,19,20,22] under different cryptographic primitives. We refer to [1,21] for the details of related work on SHSs.

However, to the best of our knowledge, all existing solutions are not secure against quantum attacks by Shor's algorithm [18], except three constructions: One is in the code-based setting [21] and the other two are in the lattice-based setting [1,2]. Among them, unfortunately, the security flaw [2] was found in the code-based construction that the adversary can easily impersonates an honest user to activate a handshake. In [2], the authors discussed how to prevent an impersonating attack for the code-based construction [21], but they did not provide a concrete description of modification and its detailed security analysis. In particular, their solution needs a Diffie-Hellman-style key exchange, but as far as we know, there is no known way to design it in the code-based setting.

In this paper, we provide the first *secure* code-based SHS using the generic approach from certificate authority (CA)-oblivious encryption, proposed by Castelluccia et al. [11], where a certificate for each identity is issued by the CA and other users send ciphertexts to the receiver of that identity by recovering the public key from the certificate. To that end, we first design a new CA-oblivious encryption scheme that achieves the one-wayness under chosen plaintext attacks (OW-CPA) by combining a public key encryption scheme and a modification of the recently proposed code-based signature scheme, called LESS-FM [5]. In CA-oblivious encryption, it is required to not only achieve the OW-CPA security, but also hide any information about the CA to sender and receiver: (1) the sender does not get any information about the CA who certified the receiver from the receiver's identity and certificate, (2) the receiver does not learn any information about the CA that the sender took in generating the ciphertext.

For the former, i.e., to hide any information about the CA from the receiver's identity and certificate, the CA in our construction issues a certificate by generating a signature of given identity using the modified LESS-FM. In our modification, the public key pk_{PKE} of the receiver which is independent from the CA is concealed in the certificate, and the sender just recovers the public key pk_{PKE} from the certificate, but cannot check the validity of the recovered outcome. For the latter, i.e., to hide any information about the CA that the receiver took in generating the ciphertext, we exploit a public key encryption scheme that achieves the indistinguishability of key under chosen plaintext attacks (IK-CPA) [8]. Informally, the IK-CPA security means that the adversary cannot distinguish between two ciphertexts of the same message generated by different public keys. Thus, the adversary cannot obtain any information about the CA who certified as well as the public key from the target ciphertext.

In order to complete obtaining *code-based* CA-oblivious encryption schemes, we employ a code-based public key encryption scheme for our CA-oblivious construction. For this purpose, we identify that Classic McEliece [9] and BIKE [3], which are the 4th round candidate algorithms of the NIST Post-Quantum Cryptography Standardization project, are appropriate candidates for our construction by confirming that both they achieve the IK-CPA security as well as the OW-CPA security, as already known.

Finally, we obtain a new code-based SHS by instantiating Castelluccia et al.'s generic construction with our new code-based CA-oblivious encryption schemes. Our instantiations have the smallest communication costs among all known post-quantum SHS. For 80-bit security, our SHS instantiating with Classic McEliece [9] has 56.96 KB, 261.4 KB, and 261.5 KB for the group public key, a credential, and a transcript of handshake, respectively. By instantiating with BIKE [3], the sizes of credential and transcript of handshake can be further reduced to 1.85 KB and 3.41 KB, respectively. It improves by about 1923 and 655 times with Classic McEliece, and about 1923 and 50234 times with BIKE, for the sizes of the group key and a transcript of handshake, respectively, compared to the existing (insecure) code-based SHS, while the size of our credential with Classic McEliece is about 4 times longer. Ours instantiating with Classic McEliece and BIKE also outperform the recent lattice-based construction [1] by about 27.8 and 2137 times, respectively, in the size of transcript of handshake, while the sizes of group public key and credential are comparable.

Organization of the Paper. The next section introduces some preliminaries, including definitions for SHS and CA-oblivious encryption, and the description of LESS-FM signatures. Section 3 provides a new CA-oblivious encryption with its security analysis. In Sect. 4, we review Castelluccia et al.'s generic construction and investigate our instantiations of SHS obtained by instantiating the generic construction with our new CA-oblivious encryption. Some supplementary materials for readers are presented in Appendices.

2   Preliminaries

In this section, we first introduce several definitions for SHS and CA-oblivious encryption. Next, we recall the recently proposed code-based signature scheme, called LESS-FM, which will be used in our new CA-oblivious encryption scheme.

Notations. Throughout the paper, matrices and vectors are denoted by boldface uppercase and lowercase letters, respectively. $A \to a$ denotes that an algorithm A outputs a. Let $[a, b]$ denote the set of all integers x satisfying $a \leq x \leq b$. Let $wt(\mathbf{x})$ denote the number of nonzero components of vector $\mathbf{x}$. For a set S, $s \xleftarrow{\$} S$ denotes that an element s is sampled uniformly at random from S. In a two-party protocol P executing between A and B, by the notation $P(x_A; x_B) \to (y_A; y_B)$ we mean that x_A and x_B are A's input and B's input, respectively, and at the end of executing the protocol y_A and y_B are given to A and B, respectively, as their outputs.

2.1   Definition for Secret Handshake Schemes

We first look at the definition of SHS. The SHS consists of the following four polynomial time algorithms and two protocols:

- SHS.Setup: This takes a security parameter λ as an input and generates the public parameter params common to all subsequently generated groups.

- SHS.CreateGroup: This can be seen as a key generation algorithm for group authority (GA) to establish a group G. It takes the public parameter params and returns a pair of group public key and secret key $(\text{gpk}_G, \text{gsk}_G)$.
- SHS.AddMember: This is a two-party protocol between a user and the GA. A user and the GA participate in the protocol with an identity ID and $(\text{gpk}_G, \text{gsk}_G)$, respectively. After executing the protocol, the user obtains the user's group credential cred_{ID} and group public key gpk_G.
- SHS.Handshake: This is a two-party authenticating protocol run by two users (A, B). Each party joins the protocol with his/her secret credential and some other public parameters. After executing the protocol, each party has 1 (*accept*) and a session key K between two participating users if they belong to the same group. Otherwise, they have 0 (*reject*) each.
- SHS.TraceMember: This is a polynomial time algorithm executed by the GA. It outputs the identity of the user A once a transcript of secret handshake between the user A and the other user is submitted.
- SHS.RemoveMember: This is also a polynomial time algorithm executed by the GA. It takes its current credential revocation list (CRL) and a user's revocation token as inputs and returns an updated CRL.

In general, an SHS is required to satisfy four security properties, completeness, impersonator resistance, detector resistance, and unlinkability. Informally, the completeness is that two users in the SHS.Handshake protocol should have 1 (accept) and the same session key if they belong to the same group. The impersonator resistance is that an adversary who is not legitimate cannot impersonate a legitimate user. The detector resistance is that an adversary cannot identity an honest user's affiliation by executing the SHS.Handshake protocol. Finally, the unlinkability is that an adversary cannot associate two executions of the SHS.Handshake protocol involving the same honest user. See [2,11,21] for the formal security definitions for SHS.

2.2 Definitions for PKI-Enabled CA-Oblivious Encryption

Now, we present the definition of PKI-enabled encryption scheme, and review its security notions, including correctness, one-wayness, and CA-obliviousness.

PKI-Enabled Encryption. A PKI-enabled encryption scheme consists of the following five polynomial time algorithms and one protocol:

- Initialize(λ) $\rightarrow$ params: It takes a security parameter λ as an input and generates the public parameter params common to all subsequently generated CAs. It is assumed that all other algorithms and protocol below take params as input, even though it is not clearly stated.
- CAInit(params) $\rightarrow$ $(\text{pk}_{\text{CA}}, \text{sk}_{\text{CA}})$: It takes the public parameter params as an input, and returns a pair of public key and secret key $(\text{pk}_{\text{CA}}, \text{sk}_{\text{CA}})$ for CA.
- Certify$((\text{pk}_{\text{CA}}, \text{sk}_{\text{CA}}); \text{ID})$ $\rightarrow$ $(\emptyset; (\text{tr}_{\text{ID}}, \text{cert}_{\text{ID}}))$: This protocol is executed between a CA and a user. The CA and the user join the protocol with inputs

the pair of public key and secret key $(\mathsf{pk_{CA}}, \mathsf{sk_{CA}})$ and the ID string ID, respectively. After executing the protocol, the user obtains a trapdoor $\mathsf{tr_{ID}}$ and a certificate $\mathsf{cert_{ID}}$ as outputs.

- $\mathsf{Recover}(\mathsf{pk_{CA}}, \mathsf{ID}, \mathsf{cert_{ID}}) \rightarrow \mathsf{pk_{ID}}$: It is executed by a sender, who wants to send a message as encrypted to a user ID, to obtain a public key of ID. It takes a public key $\mathsf{pk_{CA}}$ of CA, a receiver's identity ID and certificate $\mathsf{cert_{ID}}$, and returns the public key of ID, $\mathsf{pk_{ID}}$.
- $\mathsf{Enc}(\mathsf{pk_{ID}}, m) \rightarrow \mathsf{CT}$: It takes the public key $\mathsf{pk_{ID}}$ of ID and a message $m \in \mathcal{M}$ as inputs for the message space $\mathcal{M}$. It returns a ciphertext CT.
- $\mathsf{Dec}(\mathsf{tr_{ID}}, \mathsf{CT}) \rightarrow m$: It takes the trapdoor $\mathsf{tr_{ID}}$ of ID and the ciphertext CT as inputs, and returns a message m.

Correctness. A PKI-enabled encryption scheme is *correct* if for any security parameter λ, certificate authority CA, ID string ID, and message $m \in \mathcal{M}$, it always holds that

$$\mathsf{Dec}(\mathsf{tr_{ID}}, \mathsf{Enc}(\mathsf{pk_{ID}}, m)) = m$$

where $\mathsf{Initialize}(\lambda) \rightarrow \mathsf{params}$, $\mathsf{CAInit}(\mathsf{params}) \rightarrow (\mathsf{pk_{CA}}, \mathsf{sk_{CA}})$, $\mathsf{Certify}((\mathsf{pk_{CA}}, \mathsf{sk_{CA}}); \mathsf{ID}) \rightarrow (\emptyset; (\mathsf{tr_{ID}}, \mathsf{cert_{ID}}))$ and $\mathsf{Recover}(\mathsf{pk_{CA}}, \mathsf{ID}, \mathsf{cert_{ID}}) \rightarrow \mathsf{pk_{ID}}$.

One-Wayness. Next, we adapt the standard security notation for public key encryption to PKI-enabled encryption schemes. A PKI-enabled encryption scheme is *one-way* under chosen plaintext attacks (OW-CPA) if for any probabilistic polynomial time (PPT) adversary $\mathcal{A}$, its advantage in the following experiment is negligible in the security parameter λ:

$\underline{\mathsf{Exp}_{\mathcal{A}}^{\mathrm{OW\text{-}CPA}}(\lambda)}$

$\mathsf{Initialize}(\lambda) \rightarrowtail \mathsf{params}$, $\mathsf{CAInit}(\mathsf{params}) \rightarrow (\mathsf{pk_{CA}}, \mathsf{sk_{CA}})$

$\mathcal{A}^{\mathcal{O}^{\mathsf{Certify}((\mathsf{pk_{CA}}, \mathsf{sk_{CA}}); \cdot)}}(\mathsf{params}, \mathsf{pk_{CA}}) \rightarrow (\mathsf{ID}_{\mathcal{A}}, \mathsf{cert}_{\mathsf{ID}_{\mathcal{A}}})$

$m \xleftarrow{\$} \mathcal{M}$, $\mathsf{Recover}(\mathsf{pk_{CA}}, \mathsf{ID}_{\mathcal{A}}, \mathsf{cert}_{\mathsf{ID}_{\mathcal{A}}}) \rightarrow \mathsf{pk}_{\mathsf{ID}_{\mathcal{A}}}$, $\mathsf{Enc}(\mathsf{pk}_{\mathsf{ID}_{\mathcal{A}}}, m) \rightarrow \mathsf{CT}^*$

$\mathcal{A}^{\mathcal{O}^{\mathsf{Certify}((\mathsf{pk_{CA}}, \mathsf{sk_{CA}}); \cdot)}}(\mathsf{CT}^*) \rightarrow m'$

where $\mathcal{O}^{\mathsf{Certify}((\mathsf{pk_{CA}}, \mathsf{sk_{CA}}); \cdot)}$ indicates the Certify oracle that takes an identity ID_i as an input, and returns the corresponding pair of trapdoor and certificate $(\mathsf{tr}_{\mathsf{ID}_i}, \mathsf{cert}_{\mathsf{ID}_i})$ under the public key $\mathsf{pk_{CA}}$ and secret key $\mathsf{sk_{CA}}$ for CA. In the above experiment, there is a restriction for $\mathcal{A}$ that $\mathsf{ID}_{\mathcal{A}}$ cannot be queried to $\mathcal{O}^{\mathsf{Certify}((\mathsf{pk_{CA}}, \mathsf{sk_{CA}}); \cdot)}$. The advantage of $\mathcal{A}$ in the above experiment is defined as $\mathbf{Adv}_{\mathcal{A}}^{\mathrm{OW\text{-}CPA}}(\lambda) := \Pr[m = m']$.

CA-Obliviousness. The CA-obliviousness can be considered by dividing into two categories, (1) receiver CA-obliviousness and (2) sender CA-obliviousness. On the one hand, informally speaking, the receiver CA-obliviousness means that the receiver's message $(\mathsf{ID}_R, \mathsf{cert}_{\mathsf{ID}_R})$ to the sender does not reveal the identity of the CA who certified ID_R. On the other hand, the sender CA-obliviousness means that the sender's message, i.e., ciphertext, to the receiver does not leak any information about the CA that the sender took in computing the receiver's public key and the ciphertext.

We first look at the receiver CA-obliviousness. A PKI-enabled encryption scheme is *receiver* CA-oblivious if for any PPT adversary $\mathcal{A}$, its advantage in the following experiment is negligible in the security parameter λ:

$\underline{\mathsf{Exp}_{\mathcal{A}}^{\mathsf{RCA}}(\lambda)}$

$\mathsf{Initialize}(\lambda) \to \mathsf{params}, \mathsf{CAInit}(\mathsf{params}) \to (\mathsf{pk}_{\mathsf{CA}}, \mathsf{sk}_{\mathsf{CA}})$

$\mathcal{A}^{\mathcal{O}^{\mathsf{Certify}((\mathsf{pk}_{\mathsf{CA}}, \mathsf{sk}_{\mathsf{CA}});\cdot)}}(\mathsf{params}, \mathsf{pk}_{\mathsf{CA}}) \to \mathsf{ID}_{\mathcal{A}}$

$b \xleftarrow{\$} \{0,1\}$

if $b = 0$: $\mathsf{Certify}((\mathsf{pk}_{\mathsf{CA}}, \mathsf{sk}_{\mathsf{CA}}); \mathsf{ID}_{\mathcal{A}}) \to (\emptyset; \mathsf{cert}_{\mathsf{ID}_{\mathcal{A}}})$

if $b = 1$: $\mathsf{CAInit}(\mathsf{params}) \to (\mathsf{pk}_{\mathsf{CA}'}, \mathsf{sk}_{\mathsf{CA}'}), \mathsf{Certify}((\mathsf{pk}_{\mathsf{CA}'}, \mathsf{sk}_{\mathsf{CA}'}); \mathsf{ID}_{\mathcal{A}}) \to (\emptyset; \mathsf{cert}_{\mathsf{ID}_{\mathcal{A}}})$

$\mathcal{A}^{\mathcal{O}^{\mathsf{Certify}((\mathsf{pk}_{\mathsf{CA}}, \mathsf{sk}_{\mathsf{CA}});\cdot)}}(\mathsf{cert}_{\mathsf{ID}_{\mathcal{A}}}) \to b'$

The definition of $\mathcal{O}^{\mathsf{Certify}((\mathsf{pk}_{\mathsf{CA}}, \mathsf{sk}_{\mathsf{CA}});\cdot)}$ and the restriction on $\mathsf{ID}_{\mathcal{A}}$ for $\mathcal{A}$ are the same as in the experiment $\mathsf{Exp}_{\mathcal{A}}^{\mathsf{OW\text{-}CPA}}(\lambda)$. The advantage of $\mathcal{A}$ in the above experiment is defined as $\mathbf{Adv}_{\mathcal{A}}^{\mathsf{RCA}}(\lambda) := \left|\Pr[b = b'] - \frac{1}{2}\right|$.

Next, we define the sender CA-obliviousness. A PKI-enabled encryption scheme is *sender* CA-oblivious if for any PPT adversary $\mathcal{A}$, its advantage in the following experiment is negligible in the security parameter λ:

$\underline{\mathsf{Exp}_{\mathcal{A}}^{\mathsf{SCA}}(\lambda)}$

$\mathsf{Initialize}(\lambda) \to \mathsf{params}, \mathsf{CAInit}(\mathsf{params}) \to (\mathsf{pk}_{\mathsf{CA}}, \mathsf{sk}_{\mathsf{CA}})$

$\mathcal{A}^{\mathcal{O}^{\mathsf{Certify}((\mathsf{pk}_{\mathsf{CA}}, \mathsf{sk}_{\mathsf{CA}});\cdot)}}(\mathsf{params}, \mathsf{pk}_{\mathsf{CA}}) \to (\mathsf{ID}_{\mathcal{A}}, \mathsf{cert}_{\mathsf{ID}_{\mathcal{A}}})$

$b \xleftarrow{\$} \{0,1\}, m \xleftarrow{\$} \mathcal{M}$

if $b = 0$: $\mathsf{Recover}(\mathsf{pk}_{\mathsf{CA}}, \mathsf{ID}_{\mathcal{A}}, \mathsf{cert}_{\mathsf{ID}_{\mathcal{A}}}) \to \mathsf{pk}_{\mathsf{ID}_{\mathcal{A}}}, \mathsf{Enc}(\mathsf{pk}_{\mathsf{ID}_{\mathcal{A}}}, m) \to \mathsf{CT}_b^*$

if $b = 1$: $\mathsf{CAInit}(\mathsf{params}) \to (\mathsf{pk}_{\mathsf{CA}'}, \mathsf{sk}_{\mathsf{CA}'}), \mathsf{Recover}(\mathsf{pk}_{\mathsf{CA}'}, \mathsf{ID}_{\mathcal{A}}, \mathsf{cert}_{\mathsf{ID}_{\mathcal{A}}}) \to \mathsf{pk}_{\mathsf{ID}_{\mathcal{A}}}'$,

$\qquad\qquad \mathsf{Enc}(\mathsf{pk}_{\mathsf{ID}_{\mathcal{A}}}', m) \to \mathsf{CT}_b^*$

$\mathcal{A}^{\mathcal{O}^{\mathsf{Certify}((\mathsf{pk}_{\mathsf{CA}}, \mathsf{sk}_{\mathsf{CA}});\cdot)}}(\mathsf{CT}_b^*) \to b'$

Similarly, the definition of $\mathcal{O}^{\mathsf{Certify}((\mathsf{pk}_{\mathsf{CA}}, \mathsf{sk}_{\mathsf{CA}});\cdot)}$ and the restriction on $\mathsf{ID}_{\mathcal{A}}$ for $\mathcal{A}$ are the same as in the experiment $\mathsf{Exp}_{\mathcal{A}}^{\mathsf{OW\text{-}CPA}}(\lambda)$. The advantage of $\mathcal{A}$ in the above experiment is defined as $\mathbf{Adv}_{\mathcal{A}}^{\mathsf{SCA}}(\lambda) := \left|\Pr[b = b'] - \frac{1}{2}\right|$.

2.3   LESS-FM: Code-Based Signature Schemes

Recently, there have been proposed new code-based signature schemes based on the hardness of the code equivalence problem (CEP) [5,10]. Biasse et al. [10] designed a new zero-knowledge identification scheme, where the secret information that the prover has is a solution to an instance of the CEP. Then, they obtained signature schemes, called LESS, by applying the Fiat-Shamir transformation [13] to the proposed zero-knowledge identification scheme. Later, Barenghi et al. [5] considered several variants of LESS signature schemes for performance optimizations by either extending the challenge string part from a bit to a multi-bit, or changing the range of the challenge strings into the set of fixed low Hamming weight vectors, and combining both optimization techniques. Among them, in this paper, we will exploit LESS-FM signature schemes, which are obtained by applying the above two optimization techniques both. However, one can easily obtain several variants of our CA-oblivious encryption and SHS by replacing LESS-FM signature schemes with their variants.

Before looking at the details of LESS-FM signature schemes, we introduce several definitions and notations first. An $[n, k]$-linear code $\mathfrak{C}$ of length n and dimension k over $\mathbb{F}_q$ is a k-dimensional subspace of $\mathbb{F}_q^n$. A linear code $\mathfrak{C}$ has a generator matrix $\mathbf{G} \in \mathbb{F}_q^{k \times n}$ whose rows consist of a basis of $\mathfrak{C}$. Let us write $\mathbf{G}$ as $\mathbf{G} = [\mathbf{G}_1 | \mathbf{G}_2]$ where $\mathbf{G}_1 \in \mathbb{F}_q^{k \times k}$, $\mathbf{G}_2 \in \mathbb{F}_q^{k \times (n-k)}$ and assume that $\mathbf{G}_1$ is invertible. It then can be transformed into a matrix of form $[\mathbf{I}_k | \mathbf{M}]$ for $k \times k$ identity matrix $\mathbf{I}_k$ and some $k \times (n-k)$ matrix $\mathbf{M}$ by calculating the row-reduced echelon form of the generator matrix. We call this type of matrices *systematic form* and denote by SF an algorithm that returns the systematic form of an input matrix. Let Perm_n denote the set of all $n \times n$ permutation matrices and $\mathsf{Mono}_{n,q}$ denote the set of all matrices of the form $\mathbf{Q} = \mathbf{DP}$ where $\mathbf{D}$ is an invertible diagonal matrix in $\mathbb{F}_q^{n \times n}$ and $\mathbf{P} \in \mathsf{Perm}_n$. We say that a matrix in $\mathsf{Mono}_{n,q}$ is monomial. We also write $\mathsf{GL}_{k,q}$ for the set of all invertible matrices in $\mathbb{F}_q^{k \times k}$. The following lemma introduces a useful property about the distribution of monomial matrices and will be used in the proof of our CA-oblivious encryption.

Lemma 1 (Lemma 3.3 of [6]). *If $\mathbf{A} \in \mathsf{Mono}_{n,q}$ is fixed and $\mathbf{B}$ is selected uniformly at random from $\mathsf{Mono}_{n,q}$, then $\mathbf{AB}$ is uniformly distributed over $\mathsf{Mono}_{n,q}$.*

It is clear that the above lemma is also true if $\mathsf{Mono}_{n,q}$ is replaced by Perm_n.

Now, we introduce the linear code equivalence problem (LEP) below. For more general definition for code equivalence, we refer to [10]. We say that two linear codes $\mathfrak{C}_1, \mathfrak{C}_2$ are linearly equivalent if there exists $\mathbf{Q} \in \mathsf{Mono}_{n,q}$ such that $\mathfrak{C}_2 = \{\mathbf{xQ} : \mathbf{x} \in \mathfrak{C}_1\}$.

Definition 1 (Linear Code Equivalence Problem). *Given two generator matrices $\mathbf{G}_1, \mathbf{G}_2 \in \mathbb{F}_q^{k \times n}$ for linearly equivalent codes $\mathfrak{C}_1, \mathfrak{C}_2$, respectively, find $\mathbf{S} \in \mathsf{GL}_{k,q}$ and $\mathbf{Q} \in \mathsf{Mono}_{n,q}$ such that $\mathbf{G}_2 = \mathbf{SG}_1\mathbf{Q}$.*

We note that the permutation code equivalence problem (PEP) is defined similarly by restricting $\mathbf{Q} \in \mathsf{Perm}_n$.

LESS-FM Signatures. Recently, Barenghi et al. presented a new code-based signature scheme, LESS-FM [5], obtained by constructing a new code-based zero-knowledge identification scheme under the hardness of the CEP and then applying the Fiat-Shamir transformation [13] to the new identification scheme. Below is the detailed description of the LESS-FM signature scheme. We assume that parameters $\mathsf{pp} = (q, n, k, r, t, w)$, a generator matrix $\mathbf{G} \in \mathbb{F}_q^{k \times n}$, and a weight-restricted hash function $\widehat{\mathcal{H}} : \{0,1\}^* \to \mathbb{Z}_{r+1,w}^t$ are publicly given where $\mathbb{Z}_{r+1,w}^t$ denotes the set of all vectors in $\mathbb{Z}_{r+1}^t$ that have exactly w nonzero components for $w \in [0, n]$ and $\mathbb{Z}_{r+1,w}^t = \mathbb{Z}_{r+1}^t$ for $w = \bot$. We also denote $\mathbf{G}_0 = \mathbf{G}$ and $\mathbf{Q}_0 = \mathbf{I}_n$.

- LESSFM.KeyGen(pp, $\mathbf{G}$, λ) $\rightarrow$ (sk, pk): On input a public parameter pp = (q, n, k, r, t, w), a generator matrix $\mathbf{G}$, and a security parameter λ, it performs as follows:
  1. For each $i = 1, \ldots, r$, select $\mathbf{Q}_i \xleftarrow{\$} \mathsf{Mono}_{n,q}$ and compute $\mathbf{G}_i = \mathsf{SF}(\mathbf{GQ}_i)$.
  2. Output sk = $(\mathbf{Q}_1, \ldots, \mathbf{Q}_r)$ and pk = $(\mathbf{G}_1, \ldots, \mathbf{G}_r)$.
- LESSFM.Sign(sk, msg) $\rightarrow$ σ: Given a secret key sk = $(\mathbf{Q}_1, \ldots, \mathbf{Q}_r)$ and a message msg, it performs as follows:
  1. For each $i = 1, \ldots, t$, select $\tilde{\mathbf{Q}}_i \xleftarrow{\$} \mathsf{Mono}_{n,q}$ and compute $\tilde{\mathbf{G}}_i = \mathsf{SF}(\mathbf{G}\tilde{\mathbf{Q}}_i)$.
  2. Compute $\mathbf{h} = (h_1, \ldots, h_t) := \widehat{\mathcal{H}}(\tilde{\mathbf{G}}_1, \ldots, \tilde{\mathbf{G}}_t, \mathsf{msg}) \in \mathbb{Z}^t_{r+1,w}$.
  3. For each $i = 1, \ldots, t$, compute $\mathbf{R}_i = \mathbf{Q}_{h_i}^{-1}\tilde{\mathbf{Q}}_i$.
  4. Output $\sigma = (\mathbf{R}_1, \ldots, \mathbf{R}_t, \mathbf{h})$.
- LESSFM.Verify(pk, σ, msg) $\rightarrow$ 1/0: Given a public key pk = $(\mathbf{G}_1, \ldots, \mathbf{G}_r)$, a signature σ, and a message msg, it performs as follows:
  1. Parse σ as $(\mathbf{R}_1, \ldots, \mathbf{R}_t, \mathbf{h})$ and then $\mathbf{h}$ as $(h_1, \ldots, h_t)$.
  2. For each $i = 1, \ldots, t$, compute $\tilde{\mathbf{G}}'_i = \mathsf{SF}(\mathbf{G}_{h_i}\mathbf{R}_i)$.
  3. Output 1 if $\mathbf{h} = \widehat{\mathcal{H}}(\tilde{\mathbf{G}}'_1, \ldots, \tilde{\mathbf{G}}'_t, \mathsf{msg})$. Otherwise, output 0.

The LESS-FM signature is EUF-CMA secure under the hardness of LEP in the random oracle model. In the above description of the LESS-FM signature, if $\mathsf{Mono}_{n,q}$ is replaced by Perm_n, then it is EUF-CMA secure under the hardness of PEP. Due to the space limitation, we relegate the definition for EUF-CMA to Appendix A and refer to [5] for the detailed security analysis of LESS-FM.

3   New CA-Oblivious Encryption from Codes

In this section, we provide a new CA-oblivious encryption scheme that will be utilized in our SHS and analyze its security.

3.1   Our New CA-Oblivious Encryption from Codes

Now, we present a new CA-oblivious encryption scheme from codes. Our new CA-oblivious encryption employs a public key encryption that is OW-CPA and IK-CPA secure. A public key encryption scheme PKE = (PKE.KeyGen, PKE.Enc, PKE.Dec) consists of the following three polynomial-time algorithms:

- PKE.KeyGen(λ) $\rightarrow$ (pk, sk): On input the security parameter λ, it returns a pair of public and secret keys (pk, sk).
- PKE.Enc(pk, m) $\rightarrow$ CT: On input the public key pk and a message m, it returns a ciphertext CT.
- PKE.Dec(sk, CT) $\rightarrow$ m: On input the secret key sk and the ciphertext CT, it returns a message m.

A public key encryption scheme is OW-CPA secure if for any PPT adversary $\mathcal{A}$, its advantage in the following experiment is negligible in the security parameter λ:

$\mathsf{Exp}_{\mathcal{A},\mathsf{PKE}}^{\mathrm{OW\text{-}CPA}}(\lambda)$

PKE.KeyGen$(\lambda) \to (\mathsf{pk},\mathsf{sk})$, $m \xleftarrow{\$} \mathcal{M}$, PKE.Enc$(\mathsf{pk},m) \to \mathsf{CT}^*$
$\mathcal{A}(\mathsf{pk},\mathsf{CT}^*) \to m'$

The advantage of $\mathcal{A}$ in the above experiment is defined as $\mathbf{Adv}_{\mathcal{A},\mathsf{PKE}}^{\mathrm{OW\text{-}CPA}}(\lambda) :=$ $\Pr[m = m']$.

We also define the IK-CPA0 security of the public key encryption. Informally, the IK-CPA0 security means that the adversary cannot distinguish between two ciphertexts of the same message generated by two different public keys. We say that a public key encryption scheme is IK-CPA0 secure if for any PPT adversary $\mathcal{A}$, its advantage in the following experiment is negligible in the security parameter λ:

$\mathsf{Exp}_{\mathcal{A},\mathsf{PKE}}^{\mathrm{IK\text{-}CPA0}}(\lambda)$

PKE.KeyGen$(\lambda) \to (\mathsf{pk}_0,\mathsf{sk}_0)$, PKE.KeyGen$(\lambda) \to (\mathsf{pk}_1,\mathsf{sk}_1)$
$b \xleftarrow{\$} \{0,1\}$, $m \xleftarrow{\$} \mathcal{M}$, PKE.Enc$(\mathsf{pk}_b,m) \to \mathsf{CT}_b^*$
$\mathcal{A}(\mathsf{pk}_0,\mathsf{pk}_1,\mathsf{CT}_b^*) \to b'$

The advantage of $\mathcal{A}$ in the above experiment is defined as $\mathbf{Adv}_{\mathcal{A},\mathsf{PKE}}^{\mathrm{IK\text{-}CPA0}}(\lambda) :=$ $\left|\Pr[b = b'] - \frac{1}{2}\right|$. Note that the IK-CPA0 security notion is a relaxed version of the original IK-CPA security [8] where the plaintext m of the challenge ciphertext CT^* is chosen by the adversary. In particular, the IK-CPA security implies the IK-CPA0 security.

We note that any (OW-CPA and IK-CPA0 secure) public key encryption scheme can be exploited in our proposed scheme. However, the goal of this work is to design a new code-based CA-oblivious encryption and we will employ appropriate public key encryption schemes from codes in our instantiation.

Description of Our CA-oblivious Encryption. Below we provide the full description of our CA-oblivious encryption scheme.

– Initialize(λ): On input the security parameter λ,
  1. Set a parameter $\mathsf{pp} = (q,n,k,r,t,w)$ for the LESS-FM scheme.
  2. Pick a generator matrix $\mathbf{G} \in \mathbb{F}_q^{k \times n}$.
  3. Generate a hash function $\mathcal{H}_1 : \{0,1\}^* \to \{0,1\}^\ell$ where the set of all possible public keys of the exploited PKE is included in $\{0,1\}^\ell$.
  4. Generate a weight-restricted hash function $\mathcal{H}_2 : \{0,1\}^* \to \mathbb{Z}_{r+1,w}^t$.
  5. Output the public parameter $\mathsf{params} = (\lambda,\mathsf{pp},\mathbf{G},\mathcal{H}_1,\mathcal{H}_2)$.
– CAInit(params): Given the public parameter params, it performs as follows:
  1. For each $1 \le i \le r$, select $\mathbf{Q}_i \xleftarrow{\$} \mathsf{Mono}_{n,q}$ and compute $\mathbf{G}_i = \mathsf{SF}(\mathbf{G}\mathbf{Q}_i)$.
  2. Set and output $\mathsf{sk}_{\mathsf{CA}} = (\mathbf{Q}_i)_{1 \le i \le r}$ and $\mathsf{pk}_{\mathsf{CA}} = (\mathbf{G}_i)_{1 \le i \le r}$.

- Certify$((\mathsf{pk}_{\mathsf{CA}}, \mathsf{sk}_{\mathsf{CA}}); \mathsf{ID})$: On input a pair of public and secret keys $(\mathsf{pk}_{\mathsf{CA}}, \mathsf{sk}_{\mathsf{CA}})$ from the CA and an identity ID from the user,
  1. Run PKE.KeyGen$(\lambda) \rightarrow (\mathsf{pk}_{\mathsf{ID}}, \mathsf{sk}_{\mathsf{ID}})$.
  2. For each $1 \leq i \leq t$, pick $\tilde{\mathbf{Q}}_i \xleftarrow{\$} \mathsf{Mono}_{n,q}$ and compute $\tilde{\mathbf{G}}_i = \mathsf{SF}(\mathbf{G}\tilde{\mathbf{Q}}_i)$.
  3. Compute $c = \mathsf{pk}_{\mathsf{ID}} \oplus \mathcal{H}_1((\tilde{\mathbf{G}}_i)_{1 \leq i \leq t}, \mathsf{ID})$.
  4. Compute $\mathbf{h} = (h_i)_{1 \leq i \leq t} = \mathcal{H}_2(c, \mathsf{ID})$.
  5. Compute $\mathbf{R}_i = \mathbf{Q}_{h_i}^{-1}\tilde{\mathbf{Q}}_i$ for all $1 \leq i \leq t$.
  6. Output $\mathsf{tr}_{\mathsf{ID}} = \mathsf{sk}_{\mathsf{ID}}$ and $\mathsf{cert}_{\mathsf{ID}} = (c, (\mathbf{R}_i)_{1 \leq i \leq t})$.
- Recover$(\mathsf{pk}_{\mathsf{CA}}, \mathsf{ID}, \mathsf{cert}_{\mathsf{ID}})$: On input a public key $\mathsf{pk}_{\mathsf{CA}}$ for the CA, an identity ID, and a certificate $\mathsf{cert}_{\mathsf{ID}}$ for ID, it performs as follows:
  1. Calculate $\mathbf{h} = (h_i)_{1 \leq i \leq t} = \mathcal{H}_2(c, \mathsf{ID})$.
  2. For each $1 \leq i \leq t$, compute $\tilde{\mathbf{G}}_i = \mathsf{SF}(\mathbf{G}_{h_i}\mathbf{R}_i)$.
  3. Compute and output $\mathsf{pk}_{\mathsf{ID}} = c \oplus \mathcal{H}_1((\tilde{\mathbf{G}}_i)_{1 \leq i \leq t}, \mathsf{ID})$.
- Enc$(\mathsf{pk}_{\mathsf{ID}}, m) \rightarrow \mathsf{CT}$: On input the public key $\mathsf{pk}_{\mathsf{ID}}$ for identity ID and a message m, run PKE.Enc$(\mathsf{pk}_{\mathsf{ID}}, m) \rightarrow \mathsf{CT}$ and output CT.
- Dec$(\mathsf{tr}_{\mathsf{ID}}, \mathsf{CT}) \rightarrow m$: On input the secret key $\mathsf{tr}_{\mathsf{ID}}$ for identity ID and the ciphertext CT, run PKE.Dec$(\mathsf{tr}_{\mathsf{ID}}, \mathsf{CT}) \rightarrow m$ and return m.

Correctness of Our CA-Oblivious Encryption. Since the Enc and Dec algorithms are the same as PKE.Enc and PKE.Dec, respectively, it is sufficient to show that the Recover algorithm returns $\mathsf{pk}_{\mathsf{ID}}$ correctly from $\mathsf{cert}_{\mathsf{ID}}$ that is corresponding to $\mathsf{tr}_{\mathsf{ID}} = \mathsf{sk}_{\mathsf{ID}}$, if the exploited PKE is correct. Suppose that $(\mathsf{tr}_{\mathsf{ID}}, \mathsf{cert}_{\mathsf{ID}})$ is generated by the Certify protocol with inputs $(\mathsf{pk}_{\mathsf{CA}}, \mathsf{sk}_{\mathsf{CA}})$ and ID. Then it has the form of

$$c = \mathsf{pk}_{\mathsf{ID}} \oplus \mathcal{H}_1((\tilde{\mathbf{G}}_i)_{1 \leq i \leq t}, \mathsf{ID}) \quad \text{and} \quad \mathbf{R}_i = \mathbf{Q}_{h_i}^{-1}\tilde{\mathbf{Q}}_i \text{ for all } 1 \leq i \leq t$$

where $\tilde{\mathbf{Q}}_i$'s are randomly selected from $\mathsf{Mono}_{n,q}$ in the Certify protocol, $\tilde{\mathbf{G}}_i = \mathsf{SF}(\mathbf{G}\tilde{\mathbf{Q}}_i)$, and $\mathbf{h} = (h_1, \ldots, h_t) = \mathcal{H}_2(c, \mathsf{ID})$. Then, in the Recover algorithm, it first has the same $\mathbf{h} = (h_1, \ldots, h_t) = \mathcal{H}_2(c, \mathsf{ID})$ and recovers the same $\mathsf{pk}_{\mathsf{ID}}$ from computing $c \oplus \mathcal{H}_1((\tilde{\mathbf{G}}_i)_{1 \leq i \leq t}, \mathsf{ID})$ by the relation

$$\mathsf{SF}(\mathbf{G}_{h_i}\mathbf{R}_i) = \mathsf{SF}(\mathbf{G}_{h_i}\mathbf{Q}_{h_i}^{-1}\tilde{\mathbf{Q}}_i) = \mathsf{SF}(\mathsf{SF}(\mathbf{G}\mathbf{Q}_{h_i})\mathbf{Q}_{h_i}^{-1}\tilde{\mathbf{Q}}_i) = \mathsf{SF}(\mathbf{G}\tilde{\mathbf{Q}}_i) = \tilde{\mathbf{G}}_i$$

for all $1 \leq i \leq t$. We remark that $\mathsf{SF}(\mathbf{G}\mathbf{Q}_{h_i}) = \mathbf{S}\mathbf{G}\mathbf{Q}_{h_i}$ for some matrix $\mathbf{S} \in \mathsf{GL}_{k,q}$ and $\mathsf{SF}(\mathbf{A}\mathbf{G}\tilde{\mathbf{Q}}_i) = \mathsf{SF}(\mathbf{B}\mathbf{G}\tilde{\mathbf{Q}}_i)$ for any $\mathbf{A}, \mathbf{B} \in \mathsf{GL}_{k,q}$.

3.2 Security Analysis of Our CA-Oblivious Encryption from Codes

Now, we look into the OW-CPA security and CA-obliviousness of our proposed PKI-enabled encryption scheme.

Theorem 1. *The proposed PKI-enabled encryption scheme in Sect. 3.1 is OW-CPA secure in the random oracle model under the assumptions that the underlying public key encryption PKE is OW-CPA secure and LESS-FM signature scheme is EUF-CMA secure.*

Proof. Suppose there exists a PPT adversary $\mathcal{A}$ who breaks the OW-CPA security of the proposed PKI-enabled encryption scheme described in Sect. 3.1 with non-negligible probability. We construct a PPT adversary $\mathcal{B}$ using $\mathcal{A}$ that breaks the OW-CPA security of the public key encryption PKE used in the proposed scheme.

1. Once the target public key pk^* of PKE is given to $\mathcal{B}$, it runs $\mathsf{Initialize}(\lambda) \rightarrow$ params and $\mathsf{CAInit}(\mathsf{params}) \rightarrow (pk_{CA}, sk_{CA})$. It passes params and pk_{CA} to $\mathcal{A}$.
2. For $\mathcal{A}$'s queries, $\mathcal{B}$ responds as follows: The lists $List^{\mathcal{H}_1}$ and $List^{\mathcal{H}_2}$ are initialized as empty sets.
   - $\mathcal{H}_1$ queries: On input $((\tilde{\mathbf{G}}_{j,i})_{1 \leq i \leq t}, \mathsf{ID}_j)$, if it is in $List^{\mathcal{H}_1}$, it returns the corresponding rv_j. Otherwise, it selects a random rv_j from $\{0,1\}^\ell$, stores $\langle (\tilde{\mathbf{G}}_{j,i})_{1 \leq i \leq t}, \mathsf{ID}_j, rv_j \rangle$ at $List^{\mathcal{H}_1}$ and returns rv_j.
   - $\mathcal{H}_2$ queries: On input (c_j, ID_j), if it is in $List^{\mathcal{H}_2}$, it returns the corresponding $\mathbf{rv}_j$. Otherwise, it selects a random $\mathbf{rv}_j$ from $\mathbb{Z}_{r+1,w}^t$, stores $\langle c_j, \mathsf{ID}_j, \mathbf{rv}_j \rangle$ at $List^{\mathcal{H}_2}$ and returns $\mathbf{rv}_j$.
   - Certify queries: For $\mathcal{A}$'s request on $(\mathsf{tr}_{\mathsf{ID}_j}, \mathsf{cert}_{\mathsf{ID}_j})$ of any ID string ID_j under pk_{CA}, it runs the protocol $\mathsf{Certify}((pk_{CA}, sk_{CA}); \mathsf{ID}_j)$ to obtain $(\mathsf{tr}_{\mathsf{ID}_j}, \mathsf{cert}_{\mathsf{ID}_j})$. $\mathcal{B}$ returns it to $\mathcal{A}$.
3. Once $\mathcal{A}$ submits a pair of target ID string and certificate $(\mathsf{ID}_{\mathcal{A}}, \mathsf{cert}_{\mathsf{ID}_{\mathcal{A}}})$ where $\mathsf{cert}_{\mathsf{ID}_{\mathcal{A}}} = (c_{\mathsf{ID}_{\mathcal{A}}}, (\mathbf{R}_{\mathsf{ID}_{\mathcal{A}},i})_{1 \leq i \leq t})$, $\mathcal{B}$ first obtains the challenge ciphertext CT^* by requesting to the challenger of the OW-CPA security experiment for PKE. Then,
   (a) Check whether $(c_{\mathsf{ID}_{\mathcal{A}}}, \mathsf{ID}_{\mathcal{A}})$ is in $List^{\mathcal{H}_2}$. If it does not exist, select a random $\mathbf{rv}_{\mathcal{A}}$ from $\mathbb{Z}_{r+1,w}^t$ and store $\langle c_{\mathsf{ID}_{\mathcal{A}}}, \mathsf{ID}_{\mathcal{A}}, \mathbf{rv}_{\mathcal{A}} \rangle$ at $List^{\mathcal{H}_2}$.
   (b) Let $\mathbf{rv}_{\mathcal{A}} = (h_1, \ldots, h_t)$ be the corresponding hash value to $(c_{\mathcal{A}}, \mathsf{ID}_{\mathcal{A}})$ stored at $List^{\mathcal{H}_2}$. Compute $\tilde{\mathbf{Q}}_i = \mathbf{R}_{\mathsf{ID}_{\mathcal{A}},i} \mathbf{Q}_{h_i}$ and $\tilde{\mathbf{G}}_i = \mathsf{SF}(\mathbf{G}\tilde{\mathbf{Q}}_i)$ for all $1 \leq i \leq t$. Then, search $((\tilde{\mathbf{G}}_i)_{1 \leq i \leq t}, \mathsf{ID}_{\mathcal{A}})$ from $List^{\mathcal{H}_1}$. If $((\tilde{\mathbf{G}}_i)_{1 \leq i \leq t}, \mathsf{ID}_{\mathcal{A}}, rv_{\mathcal{A}})$ already exists and $rv_{\mathcal{A}}$ is different from $c_{\mathsf{ID}_{\mathcal{A}}} \oplus pk^*$, then $\mathcal{B}$ aborts this experiment, selects and returns a random message m'. Otherwise, continue to proceed with $\mathcal{A}$.
4. For $\mathcal{A}$'s queries, $\mathcal{B}$ responds as Step 2.
5. Finally, once $\mathcal{A}$ outputs m', $\mathcal{B}$ forwards it to the challenger of the OW-CPA experiment for PKE.

Let us calculate the advantage of $\mathcal{B}$. It is clear that $\mathcal{B}$ breaks the OW-CPA security of PKE if $\mathcal{A}$ succeeds in breaking the OW-CPA security of our PKI-enabled encryption scheme unless $\mathcal{B}$ aborts in the above simulation. Thus, the advantage of $\mathcal{B}$ is the same as that of $\mathcal{A}$ if $\mathcal{B}$ does not abort.

Suppose that the event that $\mathcal{B}$ aborts at Step 3 (b) occurs. Then, there exists $((\tilde{\mathbf{G}}_i)_{1 \leq i \leq t}, \mathsf{ID}_{\mathcal{A}})$ such that $\tilde{\mathbf{Q}}_i = \mathbf{R}_{\mathsf{ID}_{\mathcal{A}},i} \mathbf{Q}_{h_i}$ and $\tilde{\mathbf{G}}_i = \mathsf{SF}(\mathbf{G}\tilde{\mathbf{Q}}_i)$ for some $\mathbf{h} = (h_1, \ldots, h_t)$. Here, $((\mathbf{R}_{\mathsf{ID}_{\mathcal{A}},i})_{1 \leq i \leq t}, \mathbf{h})$ has the form of the LESS-FM signature of message $\mathsf{ID}_{\mathcal{A}}$, except that $\mathbf{h}$ is $\mathcal{H}_2(c, \mathsf{ID}_{\mathcal{A}})$, not $\mathcal{H}_1((\tilde{\mathbf{G}}_i)_{1 \leq i \leq t}, \mathsf{ID}_{\mathcal{A}})$. However, we can construct a PPT adversary that breaks the EUF-CMA security of the LESS-FM signature scheme using this event by adjusting hash queries appropriately. The following lemma shows it and the full proof of this lemma is given in Appendix B.

Lemma 2. *The probability that $\mathcal{B}$ aborts is negligible in the security parameter if LESS-FM is EUF-CMA secure.*

To sum up, our proposed PKI-enabled encryption scheme is OW-CPA secure if the exploited PKE is OW-CPA secure and LESS-FM is EUF-CMA secure. □

Theorem 2. *The proposed PKI-enabled encryption scheme in Sect. 3.1 is CA-oblivious in the random oracle model under the assumption that the employed public key encryption PKE is IK-CPA0 secure.*

Proof of Sketch. (Receiver CA-oblivious) We can easily confirm that $\mathsf{cert}_{\mathsf{ID}}$ does not reveal any information about the CA who certified ID. Recall that $\mathsf{cert}_{\mathsf{ID}}$ is the form of

$$c = \mathsf{pk}_{\mathsf{ID}} \oplus \mathcal{H}_1((\tilde{\mathbf{G}}_i)_{1 \le i \le t}, \mathsf{ID}) \quad \text{and} \quad \mathbf{R}_i = \mathbf{Q}_{h_i}^{-1} \tilde{\mathbf{Q}}_i$$

where $\mathsf{pk}_{\mathsf{ID}}$ is a public key of PKE for ID generated in the Certify protocol, $\mathbf{Q}_{h_i}$ is included in the secret key $\mathsf{sk}_{\mathsf{CA}}$ of CA, each $\tilde{\mathbf{Q}}_i$ was randomly selected in the Certify protocol, and $\tilde{\mathbf{G}}_i = \mathsf{SF}(\mathbf{G}\tilde{\mathbf{Q}}_i)$ for $1 \le i \le t$. Since we assume random oracle heuristics, c looks random. In addition, for each $1 \le i \le t$, $\mathbf{R}_i$ is uniformly distributed over $\mathsf{Mono}_{n,q}$ from Lemma 1. Thus, $\mathsf{cert}_{\mathsf{ID}} = (c, (\mathbf{R}_i)_{1 \le i \le t})$ is indistinguishable from $(c', (\mathbf{R}'_i)_{1 \le i \le t})$ where c' is randomly selected from $\{0,1\}^\ell$ and each $\mathbf{R}'_i$ is randomly selected from $\mathsf{Mono}_{n,q}$ for $1 \le i \le t$.

(Sender CA-oblivious) At the challenge phase of the sender CA-oblivious security experiment, $\mathcal{C}$ first tosses the unbiased coin $b \in \{0,1\}$ and selects a random message $m \in \mathcal{M}$. If $b = 0$, then $\mathcal{C}$ runs $\mathsf{PKE.Enc}(\mathsf{pk}_{\mathsf{ID}_{\mathcal{A}}}, m) \to \mathsf{CT}_b^*$ where $\mathsf{Recover}(\mathsf{pk}_{\mathsf{CA}}, \mathsf{ID}_{\mathcal{A}}, \mathsf{cert}_{\mathsf{ID}_{\mathcal{A}}}) \to \mathsf{pk}_{\mathsf{ID}_{\mathcal{A}}}$ and returns CT_b^* to $\mathcal{A}$. Otherwise, $\mathcal{C}$ generates a new public key pk' by running $\mathsf{PKE.KeyGen}(\lambda) \to (\mathsf{pk}', \mathsf{sk}')$ and returns CT_b^* by running $\mathsf{PKE.Enc}(\mathsf{pk}', m) \to \mathsf{CT}_b^*$. Since it is assumed that the employed PKE is IK-CPA0 secure, in the sender CA-oblivious security experiment, $\mathcal{A}$ cannot distinguish between these two cases. Thus, our proposed encryption is sender CA-oblivious. □

4 New Code-Based Secret Handshake Scheme

In this section, we first introduce a generic construction for SHS from a CA-oblivious encryption scheme, proposed by Castelluccia et al. [11]. We then adapt our CA-oblivious encryption to this generic construction to obtain a code-based SHS.

4.1 Generic Construction for SHS from CA-Oblivious Encryption

We review Castelluccia et al.'s generic construction for SHS from CA-oblivious encryption. Assume that a CA-oblivious encryption (Initialize, CAInit, Certify, Recover, Enc, Dec) and a hash function $\mathcal{H} : \{0,1\}^* \to \{0,1\}^\lambda$ are given. Algorithms SHS.Setup, SHS.CreateGroup, SHS.AddMember are executed by running

Initialize, CAInit, and Certify, respectively. We additionally assume that in the Certify protocol the CA also has the same output as the user and the GA in the SHS.AddMember protocol records it to the CRL whenever executing the protocol. The SHS.Handshake protocol between users A and B works as follows (here we regard that cert in the CA-oblivious encryption is the same as cred in SHS):

1. Once A receives ID_B and $cred_{ID_B}$ from B, A does as follows:
   (a) Obtain pk_{ID_B} by running $\mathsf{Recover}(pk_{CA}, ID_B, cred_{ID_B}) \to pk_{ID_B}$.
   (b) Select $r_{ID_A} \overset{\$}{\leftarrow} \mathcal{M}$ and $ch_{ID_A} \overset{\$}{\leftarrow} \{0,1\}^\lambda$.
   (c) Compute CT_{ID_A} by running $\mathsf{Enc}(pk_{ID_B}, r_{ID_A}) \to CT_{ID_A}$.
   (d) Send $ID_A, cred_{ID_A}, CT_{ID_A}, ch_{ID_A}$ to B.
2. Once B receives $ID_A, cred_{ID_A}, CT_{ID_A}, ch_{ID_A}$ from A, B does as follows:
   (a) Obtain pk_{ID_A} by running $\mathsf{Recover}(pk_{CA}, ID_A, cred_{ID_A}) \to pk_{ID_A}$.
   (b) Obtain r_{ID_A} by running $\mathsf{Dec}(tr_{ID_B}, CT_{ID_A}) \to r_{ID_A}$.
   (c) Select $r_{ID_B} \overset{\$}{\leftarrow} \mathcal{M}$ and $ch_{ID_B} \overset{\$}{\leftarrow} \{0,1\}^\lambda$.
   (d) Compute CT_{ID_B} by running $\mathsf{Enc}(pk_{ID_A}, r_{ID_B}) \to CT_{ID_B}$.
   (e) Compute $resp_{ID_B} = \mathcal{H}(r_{ID_A}, r_{ID_B}, ch_{ID_A})$.
   (f) Send $CT_{ID_B}, resp_{ID_B}, ch_{ID_B}$ to A.
3. Once A receives $CT_{ID_B}, resp_{ID_B}, ch_{ID_B}$ from B, A does as follows:
   (a) Obtain r_{ID_B} by running $\mathsf{Dec}(tr_{ID_A}, CT_{ID_B}) \to r_{ID_B}$.
   (b) Check if $resp_{ID_B} = \mathcal{H}(r_{ID_A}, r_{ID_B}, ch_{ID_A})$. If it does not hold, output 0.
   (c) Otherwise, compute $resp_{ID_A} = \mathcal{H}(r_{ID_A}, r_{ID_B}, ch_{ID_B})$, set $K = \mathcal{H}(r_{ID_A}, r_{ID_B})$.
   (d) Send $resp_{ID_A}$, and output 1 (accept) and K.
4. Once B receives $resp_{ID_A}$ from A, B does as follows:
   (a) Check if $resp_{ID_A} = \mathcal{H}(r_{ID_A}, r_{ID_B}, ch_{ID_B})$. If it does not hold, output 0.
   (b) Set $K = \mathcal{H}(r_{ID_A}, r_{ID_B})$, and output 1 (accept) and K.

   Castelluccia et al.'s generic construction does not consider SHS.TraceMember and SHS.RemoveMember algorithms. Beyond their generic construction, we provide those algorithms as follows:

- SHS.TraceMember: Given a transcript of secret handshake, it extracts an identity of users from the input and returns it.
- SHS.RemoveMember: On input a user's revocation token and the current CRL, it updates the CRL by removing the corresponding identity of user, and returns the updated CRL.

   As in [4,20,21], we follow the fundamental strategy to achieve the unlinkability that allows to use the credential only once in this paper. We leave it as a future work to design efficient code-based SHSs that allow to reuse credentials.

4.2   Concrete Instances

In this subsection, we present concrete instances of the proposed SHS as well as a comparison with the existing post-quantum SHSs [1,2,21]. We select parameter sets for 80-bit quantum security such that the code parameters n, k, q achieve the 160-bit *classical* security for solving the code equivalence problem (CEP). We consider quantum algorithms for solving the CEP by just doubling the classical security. One reason is that not enough research has been done for quantum algorithms for solving the CEP: As far as we know, the only known quantum solvers for the CEP were presented in the extended version [6] of [7]. More seriously, it is unclear how much quantum speedup is possible in practice, due to heavy overhead from quantum walk or Grover search. As a result, the proposed parameter sets are very conservative and far from optimal, but these excessive parameter sets are enough to demonstrate that our construction is superior to other post-quantum constructions.

Parameter Sets for CEP. The code parameters n, k, q are determined based on the security estimates for the CEP proposed in [7]. We suggest two kinds of parameter sets in Table 1: One is based on the PEP for weakly self-dual codes, and the other is based on the LEP.

Performance Evaluation. Let $Q = \lfloor \log_2 q \rfloor + 1$, $N = \lfloor \log_2 n \rfloor + 1$, and $|\cdot|$ denote the bit-length of input argument. A matrix in systematic form can be represented by $k(n-k)Q$ bits by storing the non-identity part only. A permutation matrix in $\mathbb{F}_q^{n \times n}$ can be encoded with nN bits, and a monomial matrix in $\mathbb{F}_q^{n \times n}$ can be encoded with $n(N + Q)$ bits by additionally storing n elements in $\mathbb{F}_q$. When $h_i = 0$, we send λ-bit seeds used to generate monomial matrices $\mathbf{R}_i = \tilde{\mathbf{Q}}_i$ instead of sending $\mathbf{R}_i$ itself.

The following shows the (expected) bit-size of group public key, trapdoor, and credentials.

- $|\mathsf{gpk}| = rk(n-k)Q$
- $|\mathsf{tr}| = |\mathsf{sk_{PKE}}|$
- $|\mathsf{cred}| = \sum_{i=1}^{t} |\mathbf{R}_i| + |\mathsf{pk_{PKE}}|$ where

$$\sum_{i=1}^{t} |\mathbf{R}_i| - \begin{cases} \frac{t}{r+1}\lambda + (t - \frac{t}{r+1})nN & \text{if } w = \bot, \text{PEP} \\ \frac{t}{r+1}\lambda + (t - \frac{t}{r+1})n(N + Q) & \text{if } w = \bot, \text{LEP} \\ (t - w)\lambda + wnN & \text{if } w \neq \bot, \text{PEP} \\ (t - w)\lambda + wn(N + Q) & \text{if } w \neq \bot, \text{LEP} \end{cases}$$

Note that $\binom{t}{\omega}r^\omega \geq 2^\lambda$ for $\omega \neq \bot$ and $(r+1)^t \geq 2^\lambda$ for $\omega = \bot$, and we set $|\mathsf{ID}| = \lambda$. Table 1 reports the relevant result.

Table 1. Parameter sets and sizes for our SHS ($r = 3$, $t = 113$, $w = 14$)

n	k	q	$|\mathsf{gpk}|$	$\sum_i |\mathbf{R}_i|$	Type	Security level
322	152	127	67.83 KB	184 Bytes	PEP	80
295	140	127	56.96 KB	297 Bytes	LEP	80

Combined Public Key Encryption. We present two encryption algorithms as examples of combined public key encryption schemes: One is from Classic McEliece [9] and the other is from BIKE [3]. Both are the 4th round candidate algorithms of the NIST Post-Quantum Cryptography Standardization project. Below we describe the encryption algorithm only, and refer to [3,9] for more detailed information.

For the Classic McEliece case, we use the underlying trapdoor one-way function and so the encryption algorithm works as $\mathsf{PKE.Enc}(\mathsf{pk}, \mathbf{m}) = \mathbf{Hm}$ where $\mathsf{pk} = \mathbf{H} = [\mathbf{I}_{n'-k'}|\mathbf{T}], \mathbf{T} \in \mathbb{F}_2^{k' \times (n'-k')}$ and $\mathbf{m} \in \mathcal{M} = \{\mathbf{e} \in \mathbb{F}_2^{n'} : \mathsf{wt}(\mathbf{e}) = t'\}$. Assuming that $\mathbf{T}$ is random which is in general stated in the form of the Goppa Code Distinguishing (GCD) problem and combining it with the pseudo-randomness of $[\mathbf{I}_{n'-k'}|\mathbf{R}]\mathbf{m}$ which can be derived from [17, Theorem 1], we can show that the described encryption scheme is IK-CPA0 secure. Note that there is no known efficient algorithms for solving the GCD problem unless the Goppa code is high-rate [12], i.e., $\frac{k'}{n'}$ is very close to 1. For 80-bit quantum security, we use a parameter set `mceliece348864` where $n' = 3488$, $k' = 2720$, $t' = 64$, and in this case we have $|\mathsf{pk_{PKE}}| = 255 \cdot 2^{13}$ and $|\mathsf{CT_{PKE}}| = 768$, and the code rate is $\frac{k'}{n'} \approx 0.78$ which is far from 1.

As Classic McEliece, BIKE is also a Niederreiter-type encryption scheme, and in particular it is instantiated with QC-MDPC codes. Here are some notations relevant to BIKE:

- $\mathcal{R} = \mathbb{F}_2[X]/(X^{r''}- 1)$,
- $\mathcal{HW}_w = \{(\mathbf{h}_0, \mathbf{h}_1) \in \mathcal{R}^2 : \mathsf{wt}(\mathbf{h}_i) = w''/2\}$,
- $\mathcal{M} = \{(\mathbf{e}_0, \mathbf{e}_1) \in \mathcal{R}^2 : \mathsf{wt}(\mathbf{e}_0) + \mathsf{wt}(\mathbf{e}_1) = t''\}$.

We take the encryption algorithm PKE_0 described in [3, Appendix C.1] which is proved to be OW-CPA secure under appropriate assumptions. The encryption algorithm works as $\mathsf{PKE}_0(\mathsf{pk}, \mathbf{m} = (\mathbf{m}_0, \mathbf{m}_1)) = \mathbf{m}_0 + \mathbf{m}_1\mathbf{h}$ where $\mathsf{pk} = \mathbf{h} = \mathbf{h}_1\mathbf{h}_0^{-1}$, $(\mathbf{h}_0, \mathbf{h}_1) \in \mathcal{HW}_w$, and $\mathbf{m} \in \mathcal{M}$. Similar to Classic McEliece, we can show that PKE_0 is IK-CPA0 secure by assuming that $\mathbf{h}_1\mathbf{h}_0^{-1}$ and $\mathbf{m}_0+\mathbf{m}_1\mathbf{h}$ are random, which are also assumed in [3, Appendix B-C] as QCCF indistinguishability and QCSD indistinguishability, respectively. For 80-bit quantum security, we use the Level 1 parameter where $r'' = 12323$, $w'' = 142$, $t'' = 134$, and so $|\mathsf{pk_{PKE}}| = |\mathsf{CT_{PKE}}| = 12323$.

Comparison. Table 2 reports a comparison of the data sizes between known post-quantum SHSs. There are only three post-quantum SHSs: One is code-based and the other two are lattice-based. In Table 2, |handshake| denotes the bit-length of all outgoing transcripts generated by a user in the SHS.Handshake protocol. In our scheme, |handshake| is computed as $|\mathsf{handshake}| = |\mathsf{ID}| + |\mathsf{cred}| + |\mathsf{CT_{PKE}}| + |resp| + |ch| = \sum_i |\mathbf{R}_i| + |\mathsf{pk_{PKE}}| + |\mathsf{CT_{PKE}}| + 3\lambda$.

The only known code-based SH construction which is known to be *insecure* has much larger communication costs in all aspects than ours, and it is not changed even if it is possible to fix the SHS as proposed in [2]. This is the same for a lattice-based construction in [2]. Our scheme instantiated with Classic McEliece

Table 2. Communication costs among known post-quantum SHSs and ours

Scheme	|gpk|	|cred|	|handshake|	Security level
[21]	109.58 MB	64.1 KB	171.3 MB	80 (classic)
[2]	947.69 MB	579 KB	7.8 GB	80 (quantum)
[1]	0.53 KB	1.54 KB	7.29 MB	80 (quantum)
Ours (PEP)^c	67.83 KB	261.3 KB	261.4 KB	80 (quantum)
Ours (LEP)^c	56.96 KB	261.4 KB	261.5 KB	80 (quantum)
Ours (PEP)^b	67.83 KB	1.73 KB	3.29 KB	80 (quantum)
Ours (LEP)^b	56.96 KB	1.85 KB	3.41 KB	80 (quantum)

^{c} instantiated with Classic McEliece, ^{b} instantiated with BIKE

has larger credential size than [1], but it can be reduced to be comparable by using other code-based encryption schemes, such as BIKE. On the other hand, two lattice-based constructions offer additional properties like dynamicity.

5   Conclusion

In this paper, we presented the first secure code-based SHS by using Castelluccia et al.'s generic construction from CA-oblivious encryption [11]. For this purpose, we provided a new CA-oblivious encryption scheme by combining a public key encryption scheme and a modification of the recently proposed code-based signature scheme. Then, we instantiated the code-based CA-oblivious encryption by exploiting the recent code-based public key encryption schemes. Our instantiations of SHS have the smallest communication costs among the existing post-quantum SHSs.

To achieve the unlinkability in our SHS, the credential should be used only once and it is quite inefficient in practice. It would be worthwhile to construct code-based SHSs that allow to reuse the credential. Furthermore, our CA-oblivious encryption can be obtained by exploiting any (OW-CPA and IK-CPA0 secure) public key encryption. Based on this feature, it would be also interesting to develop generic approaches to design new CA-oblivious encryption and SHS.

Acknowledgements. The authors thank the anonymous reviewers for their helpful comments. H. T. Lee was supported by the National Research Foundation of Korea (NRF) grant funded by the Korea government (MSIT) (No. NRF-2021R1A2C1007484, NRF-2022R1A4A5034130).

A   Definitions for Digital Signatures

A signature scheme Sig = (KeyGen, Sign, Verify) consists of the following three polynomial-time algorithms:

- KeyGen(λ) $\rightarrow$ (sk, pk): On input a security parameter λ, it returns a pair of secret and public keys (sk, pk).
- Sign(sk, msg) $\rightarrow$ σ: Given the secret key sk and a message msg, it returns a signature σ.
- Verify(pk, σ, msg) $\rightarrow$ 1/0: Given the public key pk, a signature σ, and a message msg, it returns 1 (accept) or 0 (reject).

We say that a signature scheme Sig = (KeyGen, Sign, Verify) is *correct* if for any security parameter λ and message msg, it always holds that

$$\text{Verify}(\text{pk}, \sigma, \text{msg}) = 1$$

where KeyGen(λ) $\rightarrow$ (sk, pk) and Sign(sk, msg) $\rightarrow$ σ.

EUF-CMA Security. A digital signature scheme is existentially unforgeable against chosen message attacks (EUF-CMA) if for any PPT adversary $\mathcal{A}$ its advantage in the following experiment is negligible in the security parameter λ:

$$\underline{\text{Exp}_{\mathcal{A},\text{Sig}}^{\text{EUF-CMA}}(\lambda)}$$

KeyGen(λ) $\rightarrow$ (sk, pk)
$\mathcal{A}^{\mathcal{O}^{\text{Sign}(\text{sk},\cdot)}}$(pk) $\rightarrow$ (msg*, σ^*)

where $\mathcal{O}^{\text{Sign}(\text{sk},\cdot)}$ is the signing oracle that takes a message as an input and returns a signature of input message under the secret key sk. There is a restriction that msg* should not be queried to $\mathcal{O}^{\text{Sign}(\text{sk},\cdot)}$. The advantage of $\mathcal{A}$ in the above experiment is defined as $\mathbf{Adv}_{\mathcal{A},\text{Sig}}^{\text{EUF-CMA}}(\lambda) := \Pr[\text{Verify}(\text{pk}, \sigma^*, \text{msg}^*) \rightarrow 1]$.

B   Proof of Lemma 2

Consider the OW-CPA security experiment between $\mathcal{A}$ and $\mathcal{S}$ where $\mathcal{A}$ may generate the event that $\mathcal{B}$ aborts as in the security game of the proof of Theorem 1 and $\mathcal{S}$ is a PPT adversary who wants to break the EUF-CMA security of LESS-FM. Let $\mathcal{C}_L$ be the challenger who interacts with $\mathcal{S}$ in the EUF-CMA security experiment of LESS-FM.

1. Once the target parameter pp, $\mathbf{G}$ and public key pk* = ($\mathbf{G}_1, \ldots, \mathbf{G}_r$) of LESS-FM are given to $\mathcal{S}$, set params = (λ, pp, $\mathbf{G}$) and pk$_{\text{CA}}$ = pk*. Then, $\mathcal{S}$ passes params and pk$_{\text{CA}}$ to $\mathcal{A}$.
2. For $\mathcal{A}$'s queries, $\mathcal{S}$ responds as follows:
   - $\mathcal{H}_1$ and $\mathcal{H}_2$ queries: For $\mathcal{H}_1$ and $\mathcal{H}_2$ queries, the list *List* is initialized as an empty set and $\mathcal{S}$ performs as follows:
     - $\mathcal{H}_1$ queries: On input $((\tilde{\mathbf{G}}_{j,i})_{1 \leq i \leq t}, \text{ID}_j)$,
       (a) Request a $\widehat{\mathcal{H}}$ query on $((\tilde{\mathbf{G}}_{j,i})_{1 \leq i \leq t}, \text{ID}_j)$ to $\mathcal{C}_L$ and obtain $\mathbf{h}_j$ which is corresponded to $\widehat{\mathcal{H}}((\tilde{\mathbf{G}}_{j,i})_{1 \leq i \leq t}, \text{ID}_j)$ in LESS-FM.
       (b) Search the list *List* if a pair of (pk$_{\text{ID}_j}$, sk$_{\text{ID}_j}$) was already generated. If it exists, take and use it for the following steps. Otherwise, run and use PKE.KeyGen(λ) $\rightarrow$ (pk$_{\text{ID}_j}$, sk$_{\text{ID}_j}$).

  (c) Pick a random rv_j from $\{0,1\}^\ell$ and compute $c_j = rv_j \oplus \mathsf{pk}_{\mathsf{ID}_j}$.

  (d) Store $\langle \mathsf{ID}_j, \mathsf{pk}_{\mathsf{ID}_j}, \mathsf{sk}_{\mathsf{ID}_j}, (\mathbf{G}_{j,i})_{1 \le i \le t}, c_j, rv_j, \mathbf{h}_j \rangle$ at $List$ and return rv_j to $\mathcal{A}$.

  We note that at this point $\mathcal{H}_2(c_j, \mathsf{ID}_j)$ is determined as $\mathbf{h}_j$ as well as $\mathcal{H}_1((\tilde{\mathbf{G}}_{j,i})_{1 \le i \le t}, \mathsf{ID}_j)$ is determined as rv_j.

- $\mathcal{H}_2$ queries: On input (c_j, ID_j), $\mathcal{S}$ checks if a tuple $\langle \mathsf{ID}_j, \cdot, \cdot, \cdot, c_j, \cdot, \mathbf{h}_j \rangle$ already exists. If it exists, return the corresponding $\mathbf{h}_j$. Otherwise, $\mathcal{S}$ performs as follows:

  (a) Check the list $List$ if a pair of $(\mathsf{pk}_{\mathsf{ID}_j}, \mathsf{sk}_{\mathsf{ID}_j})$ was already generated. If it exists, take and use it for the following step. Otherwise, run and use $\mathsf{PKE.KeyGen}(\lambda) \to (\mathsf{pk}_{\mathsf{ID}_j}, \mathsf{sk}_{\mathsf{ID}_j})$.

  (b) Pick $\mathbf{h}_j \xleftarrow{\$} \mathbb{Z}_{r+1,w}^t$, store $\langle \mathsf{ID}_j, \mathsf{pk}_{\mathsf{ID}_j}, \mathsf{sk}_{\mathsf{ID}_j}, -, c_j, -, \mathbf{h}_j \rangle$ at $List$ where $-$ indicates an empty string, and return $\mathbf{h}_j$ to $\mathcal{A}$.

- Certify queries: For $\mathcal{A}$'s request on $(\mathsf{tr}_{\mathsf{ID}_j}, \mathsf{cert}_{\mathsf{ID}_j})$ of any ID string ID_j under $\mathsf{pk}_{\mathsf{CA}}$, $\mathcal{S}$ performs as follows:

  (a) Request a signing query on message ID_j to obtain the LESS-FM signature $((\mathbf{R}_{j,i})_{1 \le i \le t}, \mathbf{h}_j)$ for message ID_j.

  (b) Check the list $List$ if a tuple $\langle \mathsf{ID}_j, \mathsf{pk}_{\mathsf{ID}_j}, \mathsf{sk}_{\mathsf{ID}_j}, \cdot, \cdot, \cdot, \cdot \rangle$ is stored. If it exists, take and use $(\mathsf{pk}_{\mathsf{ID}_j}, \mathsf{sk}_{\mathsf{ID}_j})$ for the following steps. Otherwise, run and use $\mathsf{PKE.KeyGen}(\lambda) \to (\mathsf{pk}_{\mathsf{ID}_j}, \mathsf{sk}_{\mathsf{ID}_j})$.

  (c) Pick a random rv_j from $\{0,1\}^\ell$ and compute $c_j = \mathsf{pk}_{\mathsf{ID}_j} \oplus rv_j$.

  (d) Store $\langle \mathsf{ID}_j, \mathsf{pk}_{\mathsf{ID}_j}, \mathsf{sk}_{\mathsf{ID}_j}, -, c_j, rv_j, \mathbf{h}_j \rangle$ at $List$. Set and return $\mathsf{tr}_{\mathsf{ID}_j} = \mathsf{sk}_{\mathsf{ID}_j}$, $\mathsf{cert}_{\mathsf{ID}_j} = (c_j, (\mathbf{R}_{j,i})_{1 \le i \le t})$.

3. Once $\mathcal{A}$ submits a pair of target ID string and certificate $(\mathsf{ID}_{\mathcal{A}}, \mathsf{cert}_{\mathsf{ID}_{\mathcal{A}}})$ where $\mathsf{cert}_{\mathsf{ID}_{\mathcal{A}}} = (c_{\mathsf{ID}_{\mathcal{A}}}, (\mathbf{R}_{\mathsf{ID}_{\mathcal{A}},i})_{1 \le i \le t})$, $\mathcal{S}$ performs as follows:

  (a) Check the list $List$ if $\langle \mathsf{ID}_{\mathcal{A}}, \mathsf{pk}_{\mathsf{ID}_{\mathcal{A}}}, \mathsf{sk}_{\mathsf{ID}_{\mathcal{A}}}, \cdot, \cdot, \cdot, \cdot \rangle$ is stored. If it exists, take and use $(\mathsf{pk}_{\mathsf{ID}_{\mathcal{A}}}, \mathsf{sk}_{\mathsf{ID}_{\mathcal{A}}})$ for the following steps. Otherwise, run and use $\mathsf{PKE.KeyGen}(\lambda) \to (\mathsf{pk}_{\mathsf{ID}_{\mathcal{A}}}, \mathsf{sk}_{\mathsf{ID}_{\mathcal{A}}})$.

  (b) Store $\langle \mathsf{ID}_{\mathcal{A}}, \mathsf{pk}_{\mathsf{ID}_{\mathcal{A}}}, \mathsf{sk}_{\mathsf{ID}_{\mathcal{A}}}, -, c_{\mathsf{ID}_{\mathcal{A}}}, -, - \rangle$ at $List$.

  (c) Select a random message $m \in \mathcal{M}$ and run $\mathsf{PKE.Enc}(\mathsf{pk}_{\mathsf{ID}_{\mathcal{A}}}, m) \to \mathsf{CT}^*$. Return CT^* to $\mathcal{A}$.

4. For $\mathcal{A}$'s queries, $\mathcal{S}$ responds as Step 2.

5. Finally, once $\mathcal{A}$ outputs m', $\mathcal{S}$ selects $\mathbf{h}$ randomly in the last column of $List$ and returns a message $\mathsf{ID}_{\mathcal{A}}$ and a pair of $((\mathbf{R}_{\mathsf{ID}_{\mathcal{A}},i})_{1 \le i \le t}, \mathbf{h})$ as the corresponding signature.

We first consider the case that the above simulation fails. It may occurs when $\mathcal{H}_1$ and $\mathcal{H}_2$ queries are operated incorrectly. In the simulation, suppose that (c_j, ID_j) was requested to the $\mathcal{H}_2$ oracle first, and a value for $\mathcal{H}_2(c_j, \mathsf{ID}_j)$ was assigned. Later, once $((\mathbf{G}_{j,i})_{1 \le i \le t}, \mathsf{ID}_j)$ is requested to the $\mathcal{H}_1$ oracle, $\mathcal{S}$ requests a value to $\mathcal{C}_L$ and receives $\mathbf{h}'$. Then, $\mathcal{S}$ selects a random rv_j, computes $c_j = rv_j \oplus \mathsf{pk}_{\mathsf{ID}_j}$, and returns rv_j. In this process, if (c_j, ID_j) was already stored and the value for $\mathcal{H}_2(c_j, \mathsf{ID}_j)$ is different from $\mathbf{h}'$, then the simulation fails. On the one hand, rv_j's are randomly selected from $\{0,1\}^\ell$ whose cardinality 2^ℓ is exponential in the security parameter λ and so the probability that a collision occurs among up to $2^{\ell/2}$ randomly selected elements is less than $1/2$. On the other hand, the number of queries allowed to $\mathcal{A}$ is polynomial in the security parameter. Thus, the probability that the above simulation fails is less than $1/2$.

Suppose that the event that $\mathcal{B}$ aborts occurs in the previous OW-CPA security experiment between $\mathcal{A}$ and $\mathcal{B}$. That is, when $\mathcal{A}$ submits a pair of target ID string and certificate $(\mathsf{ID}_\mathcal{A}, \mathsf{cert}_{\mathsf{ID}_\mathcal{A}})$ where $\mathsf{cert}_{\mathsf{ID}_\mathcal{A}} = (c_{\mathsf{ID}_\mathcal{A}}, (\mathbf{R}_{\mathsf{ID}_\mathcal{A},i})_{1 \leq i \leq t})$, each $\mathbf{R}_{\mathsf{ID}_\mathcal{A},i}$ satisfies $\tilde{\mathbf{Q}}_i = \mathbf{R}_{\mathsf{ID}_\mathcal{A},i}\mathbf{Q}_{h_i}$ and $\tilde{\mathbf{G}}_i = \mathsf{SF}(\mathbf{G}\tilde{\mathbf{Q}}_i)$ where $\mathbf{Q}_{h_i}$'s are in the target secret key of LESS-FM and $\mathbf{h} = (h_1, \ldots, h_t) = \mathcal{H}_2(c_{\mathsf{ID}_\mathcal{A}}, \mathsf{ID}_\mathcal{A})$. So, it holds that

$$\tilde{\mathbf{G}}'_i := \mathsf{SF}(\mathbf{G}_{h_i}\mathbf{R}_{\mathsf{ID}_\mathcal{A},i}) \quad \text{and} \quad \mathbf{h} = \mathcal{H}_1(\tilde{\mathbf{G}}'_1, \ldots, \tilde{\mathbf{G}}'_t, \mathsf{ID}_\mathcal{A})$$

for some $\mathbf{h} = (h_1, \ldots, h_t)$, which is the same as the verification algorithm of LESS-FM with input signature $((\mathbf{R}_{\mathsf{ID}_\mathcal{A},i})_{1 \leq i \leq t}, \mathbf{h})$ of message $\mathsf{ID}_\mathcal{A}$. Such the $\mathbf{h}$ should appear in *List* since $\mathbf{h}$ is a hash value if the simulation does not fail.

Now, let us calculate the advantage of $\mathcal{S}$. Let E be the event that $\mathcal{B}$ aborts and F be the event that the simulation fails. Then, the advantage of $\mathcal{S}$ is

$$\mathbf{Adv}_{\mathcal{S},\text{LESS-FM}}^{\text{EUF-CMA}}(\lambda) = \frac{1}{q_{\mathcal{H}_1} + q_{\mathcal{H}_2}} \left(\Pr[E|F]\Pr[F] + \Pr[E|F^c]\Pr[F^c] \right)$$

$$\geq \frac{1}{q_{\mathcal{H}_1} + q_{\mathcal{H}_2}} \Pr[E|F^c]\Pr[F^c] \geq \frac{1}{2(q_{\mathcal{H}_1} + q_{\mathcal{H}_2})}\varepsilon_\mathcal{A}$$

where $\varepsilon_\mathcal{A}$ is the probability of the event that $\mathcal{B}$ aborts, and $q_{\mathcal{H}_1}$ and $q_{\mathcal{H}_2}$ are the numbers of queries on $\mathcal{H}_1$ and $\mathcal{H}_2$ oracles, respectively. Thus, if LESS-FM is EUF-CMA secure, the probability that the event that $\mathcal{B}$ aborts is negligible in the security parameter.

References

1. An, Z., Pan, J., Wen, Y., Zhang, F.: Secret handshakes: Full dynamicity, deniability and lattice-based design. Theoret. Comput. Sci. **940**, 14–35 (2023)
2. An, Z., Zhang, Z., Wen, Y., Zhang, F.: Lattice-based secret handshakes with reusable credentials. In: Gao, D., Li, Q., Guan, X., Liao, X. (eds.) ICICS 2021. LNCS, vol. 12919, pp. 231–248. Springer, Cham (2021). https://doi.org/10.1007/978-3-030-88052-1_14
3. Aragon, N.m et al.: BIKE. Technical report, National Institute of Standards and Technology, 2022. https://csrc.nist.gov/Projects/post-quantum-cryptography/round-4-submissions
4. Balfanz, D., Durfee, G., Shankar, N., Smetters, D.K., Staddon, J., Wong, H.: Secret handshakes from pairing-based key agreements. In: IEEE Symposium on Security and Privacy (S&P 2003), pp. 180–196. IEEE Computer Society (2003)
5. Barenghi, A., Biasse, J.-F., Persichetti, E., Santini, P.: LESS-FM: fine-tuning signatures from the code equivalence problem. In: Cheon, J.H., Tillich, J.-P. (eds.) PQCrypto 2021 2021. LNCS, vol. 12841, pp. 23–43. Springer, Cham (2021). https://doi.org/10.1007/978-3-030-81293-5_2
6. Barenghi, A., Biasse, J.-F., Persichetti, E., Santini, P.: On the computational hardness of the code equivalence problem in cryptography. Cryptology ePrint Archive, Paper 2022/967 (2022). https://eprint.iacr.org/2022/967

7. Barenghi, A., Biasse, J.-F., Persichetti, E., Santini, P.: On the computational hardness of the code equivalence problem in cryptography. Adv. Math. Commun. **17**(1), 23–55 (2023)
8. Bellare, M., Boldyreva, A., Desai, A., Pointcheval, D.: Key-privacy in public-key encryption. In: Boyd, C. (ed.) ASIACRYPT 2001. LNCS, vol. 2248, pp. 566–582. Springer, Heidelberg (2001). https://doi.org/10.1007/3-540-45682-1_33
9. Bernstein, D.J.: Classic McEliece. Technical report, National Institute of Standards and Technology (2022). https://csrc.nist.gov/Projects/post-quantum-cryptography/round-4-submissions
10. Biasse, J.-F., Micheli, G., Persichetti, E., Santini, P.: LESS is more: code-based signatures without syndromes. In: Nitaj, A., Youssef, A. (eds.) AFRICACRYPT 2020. LNCS, vol. 12174, pp. 45–65. Springer, Cham (2020). https://doi.org/10.1007/978-3-030-51938-4_3
11. Castelluccia, C., Jarecki, S., Tsudik, G.: Secret handshakes from ca-oblivious encryption. In: Lee, P.J. (ed.) ASIACRYPT 2004. LNCS, vol. 3329, pp. 293–307. Springer, Heidelberg (2004). https://doi.org/10.1007/978-3-540-30539-2_21
12. Faugère, J.-C., Gauthier-Umañá, V., Otmani, A., Perret, L., Tillich, J.-P.: A distinguisher for high rate McEliece cryptosystems. In: 2011 IEEE Information Theory Workshop, pp. 282–286 (2011)
13. Fiat, A., Shamir, A.: How to prove yourself: practical solutions to identification and signature problems. In: Odlyzko, A.M. (ed.) CRYPTO 1986. LNCS, vol. 263, pp. 186–194. Springer, Heidelberg (1987). https://doi.org/10.1007/3-540-47721-7_12
14. Jarecki, S., Kim, J., Tsudik, G.: Authentication for paranoids: multi-party secret handshakes. In: Zhou, J., Yung, M., Bao, F. (eds.) ACNS 2006. LNCS, vol. 3989, pp. 325–339. Springer, Heidelberg (2006). https://doi.org/10.1007/11767480_22
15. Jarecki, S., Kim, J., Tsudik, G.: Group secret handshakes or affiliation-hiding authenticated group key agreement. In: Abe, M. (ed.) CT-RSA 2007. LNCS, vol. 4377, pp. 287–308. Springer, Heidelberg (2006). https://doi.org/10.1007/11967668_19
16. Jarecki, S., Liu, X.: Unlinkable secret handshakes and key-private group key management schemes. In: Katz, J., Yung, M. (eds.) ACNS 2007. LNCS, vol. 4521, pp. 270–287. Springer, Heidelberg (2007). https://doi.org/10.1007/978-3-540-72738-5_18
17. Nojima, R., Imai, H., Kobara, K., Morozov, K.: Semantic security for the McEliece cryptosystem without random oracles. Des. Codes Crypt. **49**(1), 289–305 (2008)
18. Shor, P.W.: Algorithms for quantum computation: Discrete logarithms and factoring. In: 35th Annual Symposium on Foundations of Computer Science (FOCS) 1994, pp. 124–134. IEEE Computer Society (1994)
19. Wen, Y., Zhang, F., Wang, H., Gong, Z., Miao, Y., Deng, Y.: A new secret handshake scheme with multi-symptom intersection for mobile healthcare social networks. Inf. Sci. **520**, 142–154 (2020)
20. Wen, Y., Zhang, F., Xu, L.: Secret handshakes from ID-based message recovery signatures: a new generic approach. Comput. Elect. Eng. **38**(1), 96–104 (2012)
21. Zhang, Z., Zhang, F., Tian, H.: CSH: a post-quantum secret handshake scheme from coding theory. In: Chen, L., Li, N., Liang, K., Schneider, S. (eds.) ESORICS 2020. LNCS, vol. 12309, pp. 317–335. Springer, Cham (2020). https://doi.org/10.1007/978-3-030-59013-0_16
22. Zhou, L., Susilo, W., Mu, Y.: Three-round secret handshakes based on ElGamal and DSA. In: Chen, K., Deng, R., Lai, X., Zhou, J. (eds.) ISPEC 2006. LNCS, vol. 3903, pp. 332–342. Springer, Heidelberg (2006). https://doi.org/10.1007/11689522_31

Beyond Volume Pattern: Storage-Efficient Boolean Searchable Symmetric Encryption with Suppressed Leakage

Feng Li[1], Jianfeng Ma[1], Yinbin Miao[1], Pengfei Wu[2], and Xiangfu Song[2(✉)]

[1] Xidian University, Xi'an 710071, China
feng.li@stu.xidian.edu.cn, {jfma,ybmiao}@xidian.edu.cn
[2] School of Computing, National University of Singapore, Singapore 119391, Singapore
{wupf,songxf}@comp.nus.edu.sg

Abstract. Boolean Searchable Symmetric Encryption (BSSE) enables users to perform retrieval operations on the encrypted data while supporting complex query capabilities. This paper focuses on addressing the storage overhead and privacy concerns associated with existing BSSE schemes. While Patel *et al.* (ASIACRYPT'21) and Bag *et al.* (PETS'23) introduced BSSE schemes that conceal the number of single keyword results, both of them suffer from quadratic storage overhead and neglect the privacy of search and access patterns. Consequently, an open question arises: Can we design a storage-efficient Boolean query scheme that effectively suppresses leakage, covering not only the volume pattern for singleton keywords, but also search and access patterns?

In light of the limitations of existing schemes in terms of storage overhead and privacy protection, this work presents a novel solution called **SESAME**. It realizes efficient storage and privacy preserving based on Bloom filter and functional encryption. Moreover, we propose an enhanced version, **SESAME+**, which offers improved search performance. By rigorous security analysis on the leakage functions of our schemes, we provide a formal security proof. Finally, we implement our schemes and demonstrate that **SESAME+** achieves superior search efficiency and reduced storage overhead.

Keywords: Searchable symmetric encryption · Boolean search · Volume pattern · Search pattern

1 Introduction

Amidst the current explosive growth of data, outsourcing data to a cloud server is considered as a judicious choice for resource-constrained individuals or organizations. It provides them access to professional, efficient, reliable, and cost-effective computing and storage services, while also providing ubiquitous data accessibility. However, a crucial concern is how to effectively protect sensitive information while maintaining the utility.

© The Author(s), under exclusive license to Springer Nature Switzerland AG 2024
G. Tsudik et al. (Eds.): ESORICS 2023, LNCS 14344, pp. 126–146, 2024.
https://doi.org/10.1007/978-3-031-50594-2_7

Searchable Symmetric Encryption (SSE) [14, 20, 32] plays a vital role in secure search over encrypted data and facilitates data outsourcing by individuals and organizations. It allows users to retrieve interested documents stored on the cloud server while preserving the privacy of both queries and document contents. Thus far, the SSE research community has proposed many practical approaches, ranging from efficient and expressive query functionality [6, 12, 13, 15] to secure searching using privacy-preserving methods capable of withstanding security threats [9, 10, 25, 31].

One of the most attractive features of SSE functionality is Boolean query. A naive Boolean query construction can be derived from a single keyword scheme, where the user receives all single keyword results in a Boolean formula Φ and evaluates Φ locally using union and intersection operations. However, such a scheme has the worst performance in terms of efficiency and leakage. That is, it requires returning all query results for each single keyword and revealing the result sizes for all keywords. The Boolean query scheme with sub-linear search complexity was originally proposed by Cash *et al.* [12], however, it requires the Boolean formula to be in a searchable normal form $(w_1 \wedge \Phi(w_2, \cdots, w_q))$. Kamara *et al.* [21] proposed a non-interactive SSE scheme that enables the processing of arbitrary Boolean queries with worst-case sub-linear search complexity. Unfortunately, these schemes failed to consider the leakage of some sensitive information, including the disclosure of volume pattern for some keywords.

Recently, Patel *et al.* [29] made advancements regarding the security of Boolean queries by introducing a novel construction that specifically addresses the protection of the volume pattern for any singleton keywords. Bag *et al.* [6] developed a general Boolean query scheme from any conjunctive schemes. But both of them come with significant storage overhead and do not consider the potential leakage of search and access patterns.

Leakage-Abuse Attacks. Numerous studies have extensively investigated leakage abuse attacks in SSE. For instance, access pattern leakage [19, 27, 30] or search pattern leakage [24, 26, 28] has been shown to enable adversaries to infer the underlying keyword based on prior knowledge. Furthermore, when equipped with knowledge of volume pattern, adversaries can even reconstruct the range query database [17, 18, 22]. Although these works primarily concentrate on single keyword or range queries, it is possible to apply them to Boolean queries as well.

In scenarios where a Boolean query reveals search pattern for certain keywords, adversaries can potentially employ inference attacks to recover the underlying keywords. For example, in the case of BIEX [21], the search pattern for each singleton keyword in the first clause can be exposed. Similarly, even in the case of CNFFilter [29], where tokens are constructed using keyword pairs, the access pattern could still be exploited to compromise the confidentiality of the underlying keyword pairs. Furthermore, existing attacks targeting exact or range queries can also potentially exploit the leakage of access and volume patterns to infer sensitive information or even the underlying keywords.

This naturally leads us to pose the following question: *Can we design a storage-efficient Boolean query scheme that effectively suppresses leakage, cov-*

ering not only the volume pattern for singleton keywords, but also search and access patterns?

Challenges. This paper focuses on addressing privacy concerns and storage overhead related to Boolean queries. Specifically, the proposed construction aims to prevent the leakage of the result size (*i.e.*, volume pattern) of any single keyword in a Boolean formula. For example, in the case of the Boolean formula $\Phi = (w_1 \wedge w_2) \vee (w_3 \wedge w_4)$, the volume pattern of any keyword w_i in Φ is protected. We are also concerned about the leakage of access and search patterns, which are often neglected by existing schemes, yet they pose comparable threats. Furthermore, the construction should exhibit linear growth in storage overhead instead·of quadratic growth.

Solutions Overview. In order to conceal the volume pattern associated with any single keyword in a Boolean query, we have to avoid operations that reveal information about a single keyword within a Boolean query. To accomplish this, we utilize a forward index based on a vector representation. In particular, each document is encoded as a Bloom filter, encompassing all the keywords it contains. Each plaintext Boolean query is represented as a Disjunctive Normal Form (DNF). Such a DNF query consists of a disjunction of several conjunctive queries, where each conjunctive query can be represented as a Bloom filter as well. In doing this, Boolean query can be divided into several conjunctive queries where each conjunctive query can be done by computing the inner product between two Bloom filters and checking if the result is over a threshold.

To protect the forward indexes, we leverage inner product functional encryption (IPFE). An IPFE scheme enables a party, who holds a decryption key sk_x corresponding to a vector x, to decrypt a ciphertext $\mathsf{Enc}(y)$ encrypted from a vector y and learn the inner product $\langle x, y \rangle$. We use IPFE to encrypt the forward indexes and the server stores the encrypted ciphertexts of all documents. During a search, the client generates an IPFE decryption key for the Bloom filter associated with a conjunctive query and sends the decryption key to the server. Using the key, the server, for each encrypted forward index, computes the inner product by decryption and compares it with a threshold to find matches.

It is possible to use a *function hiding* IPFE [7,23] to protect the query further, which reveals no information about the query x at the cost of heavy computing overhead. In our constructions, we adopt a more practical approach. Our idea is that the client can add dummy keywords when generating a Bloom filter associated with a conjunctive query. This approach not only fulfills the aforementioned security requirements but also circumvents the use of function hiding functional encryption for the inner product computation.

Our Contribution. We present a novel storage-efficient Boolean searchable symmetric encryption scheme that effectively mitigates the leakage of volume, search, and access patterns. Meanwhile, it incurs small communication and linear storage overheads. Compared with prior works, our scheme demonstrates a smaller *base query set of leakage*, which refers to the disclosure of the result set of Boolean queries, as introduced by Patel *et al.* [29]. This leakage only includes the result set of each clause within the Boolean formula, rather than keywords or keyword pairs. Specifically, our contributions can be summarized as follows:

- We propose a basic Boolean SSE scheme based on forward indexing structure of vector representation and inner product functional encryption, which restricts the *base query set of leakage* to the clauses within the Boolean formula, and improves the security by introducing dummy keywords.
- We enhance the basic scheme with optimizations. Typically, queries involve a small number of keywords, but the requirement for token length to match the index length during computations can introduce substantial computational overhead without meaningful contributions. To mitigate this issue, we employ a token pruning technique, improving efficiency by over tenfold.
- We provide a formal security analysis of our proposed scheme and substantiate its superior security compared to existing schemes that support Boolean queries. Additionally, we implement a series of experiments to empirically demonstrate the enhanced efficiency of our scheme in terms of search and storage capabilities.

1.1   Related Works

Curtmola *et al.* [14] were the first to provide a formal definition of SSE and establish *indistinguishability* and *simulation-based* security definitions in the static setting. Subsequently, Kamara *et al.* [20] extended the work of [14] by introducing the capability of efficient addition and deletion of files, commonly referred to as dynamic SSE (DSSE). To enhance the query function of SSE, Cao *et al.* [11] proposed a scheme based on TF-IDF to support multi-keyword ranking. Wang *et al.* [33] introduced multi-keyword fuzzy search that can tolerate minor typos in keywords. Fu *et al.* [16] presented a scheme to enable content-aware search by constructing conceptual graphs. Moreover, Cash *et al.* [12] designed a general Boolean query scheme with sub-linear search time complexity.

While [12] efficiently handles queries in searchable normal form, it exhibits linear time complexity for processing arbitrary Boolean queries. In response to this limitation, Kamara *et al.* [21] proposed a generic Boolean query scheme with worst-case sub-linear search. This scheme constructs a global multi-map and a dictionary as an index structure, where each multi-map maps each keyword v that co-occurs with a given keyword $w \in W$ to a tuple of $\mathsf{DB}(w) \cap \mathsf{DB}(v)$. However, this scheme inadvertently reveals the result size for each singleton keyword in the first clause of the Boolean formula. To address this vulnerability, Patel *et al.* [29] presented an improved construction with significantly reduced leakage by building indexes using any combination of two keywords as meta-keywords. Bag *et al.* [6] also employed the construction of meta-keywords to build indexes and allowed any scheme supporting conjunctive queries could be smoothly scaled to support any Boolean queries. Regrettably, these schemes entail substantial storage overhead and expose noteworthy information leakages.

The study of access pattern leakage was first initiated by Islam *et al.* [19] who proposed inference attacks for recovering the underlying keywords given prior knowledge. Pouliot *et al.* [30] presented a combinatorial optimization problem based on graph matching to attack access pattern leakage. Ning *et al.* [27] further designed attacks under different types of assumptions. Grubbs *et al.* [17] exploited the leakage of volume pattern in range queries to reconstruct the database. Gui *et al.* [18] further investigated attacks on volume pattern leakage and reduced the required prior knowledge. Kornaropoulos *et al.* [24] exploited search pattern leakage to develop value reconstruction attacks that succeeded without any knowledge about the query or data distribution. Oya *et al.* [28] proposed an attack on SSE against hidden access pattern and leaked search pattern, which successfully recovered the underlying keywords.

1.2   Organization

This paper is organized as follows. In Sect. 2, we introduce the cryptographic primitives that underpin our construction. Section 3 provides definitions for Boolean searchable symmetric encryption and security notions. In Sect. 4, we present the details of our constructions, SESAME and SESAME+. Security analysis and experimental analysis are presented in Sect. 5 and Sect. 6, respectively. Finally, Sect. 7 concludes this paper.

2   Preliminaries

This section presents cryptographic primitives utilized in our constructions. Table 1 summarizes commonly used symbols.

2.1   Bloom Filter

Bloom filter is a data structure used to represent a set, which is a bit vector of length l with a family of hash functions $\mathcal{H} = \{h_i \mid h_i : \{0,1\}^* \to [l], 1 \leq i \leq s\}$. Specifically, given a set $S = \{a_1, \cdots, a_n\}$ of elements, initialize a bit vector of length l and set all positions in the vector to 0. Use s independent hash functions h_i to map each element in the set S to the vector by setting the corresponding positions to 1. To verify if a given element a exists in the set S, compute the mapping positions of a using the s hash functions h_i. If all corresponding positions in the vector are 1, then a is possibly in the set (with some false positive probability), otherwise a is definitely not in the set. The false positive rate for an l-bit Bloom filter is approximately $(1 - e^{-\frac{sn}{l}})^s$.

2.2   Functional Encryption for Inner Product

Functional Encryption (FE) [8] extends traditional public key encryption, enabling the retrieval of partial information from ciphertexts without the need to decrypt them entirely. Specifically, by leveraging a decryption key associated with a designated function F and a ciphertext $\mathsf{Enc}(x)$, an authorized user can retrieve the value of $F(x)$ using a decryption key corresponding to F, without revealing the underlying message x itself.

Table 1. Summary of Notations

Notation	Description
λ	The computational security parameter
l	The length of a vector (*i.e.*, Bloom filter)
ind_i	The identifier of the i-th document
W_i	The list of keywords for the i-th document
α	The number of non-zero elements in the token q
β	The positions of all non-zero elements in the token q
w'	Dummy keyword, which satisfies $w' \notin \bigcup_{i=1}^{d} W_i$
sk_q	The decryption key of vector q for functional encryption
$\mathcal{R}$	The result set
Q	A Boolean query in the disjunctive normal form
v_i	The Bloom filter (or vector) corresponding to the i-th document
ev_i	The encrypted Bloom filter (or vector) corresponding to the v_i
A	A matrix consisting of encrypted vectors
q	The search token corresponding to the conjunctive query q
r	The result vector
R	The result matrix
Q	A matrix consisting of tokens
U	A token set that has been pruned

Functional encryption for inner product [4,5] is a form of functional encryption that restricts F to the inner product operation, enabling the decryption key holder with a vector x to decrypt the ciphertext vector $\mathsf{Enc}(y)$ and obtain $\langle x, y \rangle$ without revealing any other information about y. Next, we introduce a functional encryption for inner product based on the Decisional Diffie-Hellman (DDH) assumption, which serves as a fundamental building block in our construction. Formally, the cryptographic scheme [5] consists of four algorithms, denoted as $\mathsf{IPFE} = (\mathsf{Setup}, \mathsf{Keygen}, \mathsf{Encrypt}, \mathsf{Decrypt})$, formally defined as follows:

- $(\mathsf{msk}, \mathsf{mpk}) \leftarrow \mathsf{Setup}(1^\lambda, 1^l)$: Choose a cyclic group $\mathbb{G}$ with a prime order $p > 2^\lambda$ and generate two generators $g, h \leftarrow \mathbb{G}$. Then randomly sample $s_i, t_i \leftarrow \mathbb{Z}_p$ for each $i \in \{1, \cdots, l\}$, and compute $h_i = g^{s_i} \cdot h^{t_i}$. The msk and the mpk are defined as, $\mathsf{msk} := \{(s_i, t_i)\}_{i=1}^{l}$ and $\mathsf{mpk} := (\mathbb{G}, g, h, \{h_i\}_{i=1}^{l})$, respectively.
- $\mathsf{sk}_x \leftarrow \mathsf{Keygen}(\mathsf{msk}, x)$: Take the msk and the vector $x = (x_1, \cdots, x_l)$ as input, where $x_i \in \mathbb{Z}_q$, compute the decryption key $\mathsf{sk}_x = (s_x, t_x) = (\sum_{i=1}^{l} s_i \cdot x_i, \sum_{i=1}^{l} t_i \cdot x_i) = (\langle s, x \rangle, \langle t, x \rangle)$.
- $C_y \leftarrow \mathsf{Encrypt}(\mathsf{mpk}, y)$: Given the mpk and a vector $y = (y_1, \cdots, y_l)$ as input, where $y_i \in \mathbb{Z}_q$, the algorithm randomly samples $r \leftarrow \mathbb{Z}_p$ and encrypts the vector y as $C = g^r, D = h^r, \{E_i = g^{y_i} \cdot h_i^r\}_{i=1}^{l}$. The resulting ciphertext is denoted as $C_y = (C, D, \{E_i\}_{i=1}^{l})$.

– $\langle x, y \rangle \leftarrow$ Decrypt(mpk, sk$_x$, C_y) : Given the input of mpk, the decryption key sk$_x$, and the ciphertext C_y, the algorithm proceeds to compute $E_x = (\prod_{i=1}^{l} E_i^{x_i})/(C^{s_x} \cdot D^{t_x})$. The inner product of the vectors x and y can be recovered from computing the discrete logarithm of E_x as regards the base g.

2.3 Pseudorandom Function

A keyed function $F : \mathcal{K} \times \mathcal{X} \to \mathcal{Z}$ is a two-input function, where the first input is referred to as the *key*. If there exists a polynomial time algorithm that can compute $F(k, x)$ for any given $k \in \mathcal{K}$ and $x \in \mathcal{X}$, and for all probabilistic polynomial time adversaries $\mathcal{A}$ satisfy $|\Pr[\mathcal{A}^{F(k,\cdot)}(1^\lambda) = 1] - \Pr[\mathcal{A}^{f(\cdot)}(1^\lambda) = 1]| \leq$ negl(λ), where negl(λ) is negligible in the security parameter λ, $k \xleftarrow{\$} \mathcal{K}$ and f is a random function from $\mathcal{X}$ to $\mathcal{Z}$, then it is called Pseudorandom Function (PRF).

3   Boolean Searchable Symmetric Encryption

Boolean Searchable Symmetric Encryption (BSSE) supports arbitrary Boolean queries on encrypted data. Typically, BSSE involves three entities: the Data Owner (DO), the Data User (DU)[1], and the Cloud Service Provider (CSP). The DO encrypts the database DB = $\{(\text{ind}_i, W_i)\}_{i=1}^{d}$ and generates the corresponding encrypted index. The CSP stores the encrypted data and index and handles query requests. The DU generates a query request and transmits it to the CSP. A generic BSSE scheme can be outlined with three algorithms:

– (msk, EDB) ← Setup(1^λ, DB): The Setup algorithm takes a security parameter 1^λ and a database DB as input and produces the master secret key msk as well as the encrypted database EDB, which encompasses both encrypted data and index.
– tok$_Q$ ← Token(Q, msk): The Token algorithm receives the master secret key msk and a Boolean query Q as input and generates the search token tok$_Q$.
– $\mathcal{R}$ ← Search(tok$_Q$, EDB): This algorithm takes the search token tok$_Q$ and the encrypted database EDB as input. It performs a search on the encrypted index and retrieves the documents that satisfy the given Boolean query Q. The results are stored in the result set $\mathcal{R}$ and returned as the output.

3.1   Security Notions

We provide a security model for BSSE following the definition of Curtmola *et al.* [14]. The adversary's knowledge of leakage is defined as $\mathcal{L} = (\mathcal{L}_{\text{Setup}}, \mathcal{L}_{\text{Token}}, \mathcal{L}_{\text{Search}})$, where the leakage function of $\mathcal{L}_{\text{Setup}}$ captures the leakage information of BSSE in the Setup stage, the leakage function of $\mathcal{L}_{\text{Token}}$ captures the leakage information from the token learned by the adversary (*i.e.*, the server), and the leakage function $\mathcal{L}_{\text{Search}}$ captures the leakage in the Search stage.

---

[1] The data owner and the data user can be the same entity.

To formally describe the security notion of BSSE, we present a simulation-based Real-Ideal game against adversaries. In this game, $\mathcal{A}$ represents the adversary and $\mathcal{S}$ represents the simulator.

- **Real$_{\mathcal{A}}^{\text{BSSE}}(\lambda)$**: The stateful adversary $\mathcal{A}$ chooses a database DB and sends it to the challenger $\mathcal{C}$. $\mathcal{C}$ runs Setup$(1^\lambda, \text{DB}; \text{msk}, \text{EDB})$ and returns EDB to $\mathcal{A}$. Then $\mathcal{A}$ randomly selects a series of Boolean queries $\{Q_1, \cdots\}$ at once and sends them to $\mathcal{C}$. For each Q_i, $\mathcal{C}$ runs the Token$(Q_i, \text{msk}; \text{tok}_{Q_i})$ and returns tok_{Q_i} to $\mathcal{A}$. $\mathcal{A}$ sends tok_{Q_i} to $\mathcal{C}$, who performs the Search$(\text{tok}_{Q_i}, \text{EDB}; \mathcal{R}_i)$ and returns the result set $\mathcal{R}_i$ to $\mathcal{A}$. Finally, $\mathcal{A}$ outputs a bit $b \in \{0,1\}$.
- **Ideal$_{\mathcal{A},\mathcal{S}}^{\text{BSSE}}(\lambda)$**: The stateful adversary $\mathcal{A}$ chooses a database DB and sends it to the challenger $\mathcal{C}$. The simulator $\mathcal{S}$ runs Sim$_{\text{Setup}}(\mathcal{L}; \text{EDB})$ based on the leakage information $\mathcal{L}$ and returns EDB to $\mathcal{A}$. Subsequently, $\mathcal{A}$ randomly selects a series of Boolean queries $\{Q_1, \cdots\}$ at once and sends them to $\mathcal{C}$, which $\mathcal{S}$ processes through Sim$_{\text{Token}}(\mathcal{L}; \text{tok}_{Q_i})$, returning the corresponding token tok_{Q_i} to $\mathcal{A}$. After $\mathcal{A}$ forwards the token tok_{Q_i} to $\mathcal{C}$, $\mathcal{S}$ executes Sim$_{\text{Search}}(\mathcal{L}; \mathcal{R}_i)$ to obtain the result set $\mathcal{R}_i$, which is returned to $\mathcal{A}$. Finally, $\mathcal{A}$ produces a bit $b \in \{0,1\}$ to complete the experiment.

The security of BSSE is defined as the advantage of $\mathcal{A}$ in distinguishing between two worlds: in the real world, $\mathcal{A}$ interacts with a real BSSE system, and in the ideal world, $\mathcal{A}$ interacts with a stateful simulator $\mathcal{S}$ that receives the same input as $\mathcal{A}$ and simulates the response of the ideal functionality. BSSE is $\mathcal{L}$-secure if for any probabilistic polynomial-time (PPT) adversary $\mathcal{A}$, there exists a PPT simulator $\mathcal{S}$ such that $|\Pr[\textbf{Real}_{\mathcal{A}}^{\text{BSSE}}(\lambda) = 1] - \Pr[\textbf{Ideal}_{\mathcal{A},\mathcal{S}}^{\text{BSSE}}(\lambda) = 1]| \leq \text{negl}(\lambda)$.

Definition 1 (Search Pattern). *The search pattern is a sequence over n queries $\mathcal{Q}$ that can be inferred whether two queries are the same, and is defined as $sp(Q_i) = \{u_i \mid (u_i, Q_i) \in \mathcal{Q}\}$.*

Definition 2 (Access Pattern). *The access pattern is a sequence over n queries $\mathcal{Q}$ that reveals the results of the queries (including the number of results, named volume pattern) and is defined as $ap(Q_i) = \{DB(Q_i)\}$.*

4 Constructions

In this section, we present our fundamental scheme, SESAME (Storage-Efficient Boolean SeArchable SyMmetric Encryption with Suppressed Leakage)[2], as well as its enhancement SESAME+. We first introduce a construction that facilitates conjunctive queries, and subsequently extend it to support arbitrary Boolean queries. Finally, we propose an enhanced construction with improved efficiency.

4.1 Overview

Before presenting our constructions, we provide an overview of the core ideas behind them. As mentioned, the focus of this paper is to balance storage overhead

---

[2] SESAME implies a mystical code that unlocks the treasure.

and privacy protection while maintaining search efficiency and single-keyword search ability. To achieve linear storage overhead, we utilize the Bloom filter to represent the forward index structure of the document and protect the number of single keyword results. To address functional encryption leakage from queries and protect the search pattern, we introduce dummy keywords in the token generation process, which also safeguards the access pattern of the query. Lastly, to improve search efficiency, we prune tokens as the number of keywords in a query is usually small.

4.2   Basic Construction

Conjunctive Protocol. We start by describing our building block for conjunctive queries, which comprises a tuple of algorithms, denoted as $\Sigma_{\mathsf{Conj}} =$ (Setup, Token, Search). The formal description of Σ_{Conj} is presented in Algorithm 1.

Setup. Given an input database DB, the Setup algorithm initializes and generates master public key mpk and the master secret key msk, with inputs of the

---

Algorithm 1: Conjunctive Protocol Σ_{Conj}

@ **Setup**(1^λ, 1^l, DB; mpk, msk, EDB)

1 Choose a cyclic group $\mathbb{G}$ with a prime order $p > 2^\lambda$ and parse DB as $\{(\mathrm{ind}_i, W_i)\}_{i=1}^d$;

2 Generate two generators $g, h \leftarrow \mathbb{G}$ and randomly sample $s_i, t_i \leftarrow \mathbb{Z}_p$ for each $i \in \{1, \cdots, l\}$ and $k \leftarrow \{0,1\}^\lambda$, then compute $h_i = g^{s_i} \cdot h^{t_i}$. Finally, let $\mathsf{msk} := (\mathsf{sk}_{\mathsf{IPFE}} = \{(s_i, t_i)\}_{i=1}^l, k)$ and $\mathsf{mpk} := (\mathbb{G}, g, h, \{h_i\}_{i=1}^l)$;

3 **for** $i \in \{1, \cdots, d\}$ **do**

4 $\quad$ Construct a Bloom filter $\boldsymbol{v}_i$ by mapping each kw_j into $\boldsymbol{v}_i$, where $kw_j \leftarrow F(k, w_j)$ and $w_j \in W_i$;

5 $\quad$ Encrypt the Bloom filter $\boldsymbol{v}_i$ by using functional encryption for inner product, $\boldsymbol{ev}_i = \mathsf{IPFE.Encrypt}(\mathsf{mpk}, \boldsymbol{v}_i)$;

6 Combine all encrypted Bloom filters into a matrix $\boldsymbol{A} = \{\boldsymbol{ev}_1, \cdots, \boldsymbol{ev}_d\}$;

7 Define $\mathsf{EDB} = \boldsymbol{A}$, then output $(\mathsf{mpk}, \mathsf{msk}, \mathsf{EDB})$.

@ **Token**(msk, q; $\boldsymbol{q}$, sk_q, α)

1 Construct a Bloom filter $\boldsymbol{q}$ by mapping each kw_j into $\boldsymbol{q}$ and count the number of non-zero elements α, where $kw_j \leftarrow F(k, w_j)$ and $w_j \in q$;

2 Add an extra kw' into $\boldsymbol{q}$, where $kw' \leftarrow F(k, w')$ and w' is a dummy keyword;

3 Generate a key for the vector $\boldsymbol{q}$, $\mathsf{sk}_q = \mathsf{IPFE.Keygen}(\mathsf{sk}_{\mathsf{IPFE}}, \boldsymbol{q})$;

4 Send $(\boldsymbol{q}, \mathsf{sk}_q, \alpha)$ to the server.

@ **Search**(EDB, mpk, $\boldsymbol{q}$, sk_q, α; $\mathcal{R}$)

1 Compute the inner product between the vector $\boldsymbol{q}$ and the matrix $\boldsymbol{A}$, $\boldsymbol{r} = \mathsf{IPFE.Decrypt}(\mathsf{mpk}, \mathsf{sk}_q, \boldsymbol{A})$;

2 **for** $e_i \in \boldsymbol{r}$ **do**

$\quad$ **if** $e_i \geq \alpha$ **then** put corresponding document identifier ind_i into the result set $\mathcal{R}$;

3 **return** query result set $\mathcal{R}$.

---

security parameter λ and the predefined vector length l. Then the algorithm parses the DB as $\{(\text{ind}_i, W_i)\}_{i=1}^{d}$.

For each document ind_i, the algorithm initializes a Bloom filter $\boldsymbol{v}_i$ of length l by mapping each masked keyword kw_j into corresponding bit positions in the filter, and then encrypts it using functional encryption. All encrypted Bloom filters are combined into a matrix $\boldsymbol{A}$ to form the encrypted database EDB. The output of the algorithm is denoted as $(\mathsf{mpk}, \mathsf{msk}, \mathsf{EDB})$.

Token. The Token algorithm takes the master secret key msk and a conjunctive query $q = (w_1 \wedge \cdots \wedge w_q)$ as input. To compute the inner product with $\boldsymbol{ev}_i$, the length of the token needs to match that of $\boldsymbol{v}_i$. The algorithm initializes a Bloom filter of length l, maps each keyword in q to the Bloom filter using the same method as in the Setup algorithm, and records the number of non-zero elements in the Bloom filter $\boldsymbol{q}$. Essentially, the client can generate the decryption key sk_q from the vector $\boldsymbol{q}$ and then send it to the server for retrieval.

However, it exposes the $\boldsymbol{q}$ in plaintext during the decryption of the functional encryption, which requires both the decryption key sk_q and $\boldsymbol{q}$. Even though $\boldsymbol{q}$ is a Bloom filter that does not reveal the underlying keywords to an adversary, it still leaks the search pattern, allowing the adversary to distinguish whether the same query is repeated or not. To protect the search pattern, we incorporate the addition of random dummy keywords during token generation that do not correspond to any document. It is worth noting that the client has the flexibility to choose the dummy keyword and its quantity randomly, or has them randomly generated by the protocol when generating the token, so the protocol does not explicitly take the dummy keyword as input. Adding more dummy keywords increases query obfuscation but also raises the false positive matching probability; so, we note there is a trade-off between security and accuracy.

Search. The Search algorithm takes as input the encrypted database EDB, the master public key mpk, the search token $\boldsymbol{q}$, the decryption key sk_q and the number of non-zero elements α. The server begins by computing the inner product between the vector $\boldsymbol{q}$ and the matrix $\boldsymbol{A}^3$, resulting in the vector $\boldsymbol{r}$. It then scans each element of $\boldsymbol{r}$ and checks whether the value exceeds or equals to a threshold α. If the condition is satisfied, the corresponding document identifier is added to the result set $\mathcal{R}$.

Boolean Protocol. We extend conjunctive construction to support arbitrary Boolean queries. We now give a description of an extended variant that supports arbitrary Boolean queries and refer to it as SESAME. Algorithm 2 provides a more detailed illustration of the extended version.

Recall that any Boolean query can be written as a DNF query $Q = q_1 \vee \cdots \vee q_m$, where each $q_i = w_{i,1} \wedge \cdots \wedge w_{i,m_i}$ is a conjunction. Therefore, for any Boolean query, the client first parses it as disjunctive normal form, and then uses $\Sigma_{\mathsf{Conj}}.\mathsf{Token}$ to generate the token and the decryption key for each q_i. To obtain the resulting matrix $\boldsymbol{R}$, we treat all tokens as a matrix $\boldsymbol{Q}$ and multiply

---

[3] Representing all encrypted vectors as a matrix is a matter of convenience for notation purposes, and the actual computation still relies on the inner product operation of vectors.

them by A^4. For each column r_i in R, if any element is greater than or equal to the threshold α_j, the corresponding document ind_i is added to the result set $\mathcal{R}$.

Algorithm 2: SESAME

@ **Token**(msk, Q; Q, sk$_Q$, α)

1 **for** $q_i \in Q$ **do**

2   Construct a Bloom filter q_i by mapping each kw_j into q_i and count the number of non-zero elements α_i, where $kw_j \leftarrow F(k, w_j)$ and $w_j \in q_i$;

3   Add an extra kw' into q_i, where $kw' \leftarrow F(k, w')$ and w' is a dummy keyword;

4   Generate a key for the vector q_i, sk$_{q_i}$ = IPFE.Keygen(sk$_{\mathsf{IPFE}}$, q_i);

5 Define $Q = \{q_1, \cdots q_m\}$, sk$_Q$ = {sk$_{q_1}$, $\cdots$, sk$_{q_m}$}, $\alpha = \{\alpha_1, \cdots, \alpha_m\}$;

6 Send $(Q, \mathrm{sk}_Q, \alpha)$ to the server.

@ **Search**(EDB, mpk, Q, sk$_Q$, α; $\mathcal{R}$)

1 Compute the matrix multiplication between the matrix Q and the matrix A, $R =$ IPFE.Decrypt(mpk, sk$_Q$, A);

2 **for** $r_i \in R$ **do**

    if $\exists e_j \in r_i, e_j \geq \alpha_j$ **then** put document identifier ind_i into the result set $\mathcal{R}$;

3 **return** query result set $\mathcal{R}$.

4.3   Enhanced Construction

We observe that the number of queried keywords is typically much smaller than the total number of keywords in the universal keyword set, i.e., $|q_i| \ll |\cup_{i=1}^d W_i|$. Consequently, a significant amount of unnecessary computational overhead arises since the 0 elements in the query vector are meaningless for the computation. Therefore, the primary objective of the SESAME+ enhancement construction is to improve query efficiency. The extended version of the proposed scheme is illustrated in more detail in Algorithm 3, which depicts the various components and operations involved in supporting arbitrary Boolean queries.

To improve the efficiency of the scheme, SESAME+ eliminates all the 0 elements in the vector q_i, which is a straightforward yet effective approach. However, directly removing the 0 elements from the vector q_i would render encryption and decryption infeasible. SESAME+ makes changes to the Token and Search algorithms, where the setup phase remains the same as that of SESAME. In the Token algorithm, it is necessary to record the number of non-zero elements, denoted as α_i, for clause q_i before adding the dummy keyword w' and the position set β_i of the non-zero elements for the modified query $q_i' = q_i \wedge w'$ after adding the dummy keyword (line 3, Algorithm 3); suppose there are α_i' non-zero elements after adding the dummy keyword and $\alpha_i' \geq \alpha_i$, then the server doesn't know which α_i non-zero elements out of α_i' are introduced by non-dummy keywords, hence reducing leakage. Then, the 0 elements in q_i are removed to obtain

---

[4] Similarly, it is represented as a matrix solely for descriptive purposes.

the pruned vector $\boldsymbol{u}_i$ and generate the corresponding decryption key. Similarly, in the Search algorithm, the server needs to prune $\boldsymbol{A}$ according to the received β_i to obtain the matrix $\boldsymbol{A}'$ corresponding to $\boldsymbol{u}_i$. The inner product $\boldsymbol{r}_i$ from $\boldsymbol{u}_i$ and $\boldsymbol{A}'$ is then computed to filter the documents that satisfy the query condition.

Algorithm 3: SESAME+

@ **Token**(msk, Q; $\boldsymbol{U}$, sk$_U$, $\boldsymbol{\alpha}$, $\boldsymbol{\beta}$)

1 **for** $q_i \in Q$ **do**

2 $\quad$ Construct a Bloom filter $\boldsymbol{q}_i$ by mapping each kw_j into $\boldsymbol{q}_i$ and count the number of non-zero elements α_i, where $kw_j \leftarrow F(k, w_j)$ and $w_j \in q_i$;

3 $\quad$ Add an extra kw' into $\boldsymbol{q}_i$, where $kw' \leftarrow F(k, w')$ and w' is a dummy keyword, record the positions of all non-zero elements in $\boldsymbol{q}_i$, denoted as β_i, and then remove the $0s$ in $\boldsymbol{q}_i$ to get a new vector $\boldsymbol{u}_i$ with all $1s$;

4 $\quad$ Generate a key for the vector $\boldsymbol{u}_i$,
$$\text{sk}_{\boldsymbol{u}_i} = (s_{\boldsymbol{u}_i}, t_{\boldsymbol{u}_i}) = (\Sigma_{j=1}^{|\boldsymbol{u}_i|} s_{\beta_{i,j}} \cdot \boldsymbol{u}_{i,j}, \Sigma_{j=1}^{|\boldsymbol{u}_i|} t_{\beta_{i,j}} \cdot \boldsymbol{u}_{i,j});$$

5 Define $\boldsymbol{U} = \{\boldsymbol{u}_1, \cdots \boldsymbol{u}_m\}$, sk$_U = \{\text{sk}_{\boldsymbol{u}_1}, \cdots, \text{sk}_{\boldsymbol{u}_m}\}$, $\boldsymbol{\alpha} = \{\alpha_1, \cdots, \alpha_m\}$, $\boldsymbol{\beta} = \{\beta_1, \cdots, \beta_m\}$;

6 Send $(\boldsymbol{U}, \text{sk}_U, \boldsymbol{\alpha}, \boldsymbol{\beta})$ to the server.

@ **Search**(EDB, mpk, $\boldsymbol{U}$, sk$_U$, $\boldsymbol{\alpha}$, $\boldsymbol{\beta}$; $\mathcal{R}$)

1 **for** $\boldsymbol{u}_i \in \boldsymbol{U}$ **do**

2 $\quad$ Select the corresponding rows from matrix $\boldsymbol{A}$ according to β_i to form a new matrix $\boldsymbol{A}'$;

3 $\quad$ Compute the inner product between the vector $\boldsymbol{u}_i$ and the matrix $\boldsymbol{A}'$, $\boldsymbol{r}_i = \text{IPFE.Decrypt}(\text{mpk}, \text{sk}_{\boldsymbol{u}_i}, \boldsymbol{A}')$;

4 $\quad$ **for** $e_j \in \boldsymbol{r}_i$ **do**
$\qquad$ **if** $e_j \geq \alpha_i$ **then** put corresponding document identifier ind$_j$ into the result set $\mathcal{R}$;

5 **return** query result set $\mathcal{R}$.

---

5   Security Analysis

We overview the security of our enhanced construction SESAME+. We only provide the security of SESAME+ since all optimizations in SESAME+ do not downgrade the security of SESAME. We first present an informal discussion of the leakage functions, and then show the security of SESAME+ in Theorem 1, with the proof from Appendix A.

The Setup protocol securely encrypts the input database DB and subsequently outsources it to the server for storage. As the adversary only has access to the stored data, the leakage function $\mathcal{L}_{\text{Setup}}$ is defined as $\mathcal{L}_{\text{Setup}} = (d, l)$, where d denotes the number of vectors and l denotes the length of each vector.

For the Token protocol, the input Boolean query Q is converted into a token that can be computed on the encrypted database and sent to the server. Hence, the adversary's view includes $\boldsymbol{U}$, sk$_U$, $\boldsymbol{\alpha}$, and $\boldsymbol{\beta}$. However, since $\boldsymbol{\beta}$ reveals the positions of all non-zero elements and the number of Boolean query clauses, the leakage function can be defined as $\mathcal{L}_{\mathsf{Token}} = (m, \boldsymbol{\alpha}, \boldsymbol{\beta})$, where m represents the number of clauses in the query Q.

For Search protocol, the server computes the inner product between the token and the encrypted database to determine whether a document satisfies the search criteria, enabling the server to learn this information. The leakage function can be defined as $\mathcal{L}_{\mathsf{Search}} = (\{r_1, \cdots, r_m\}, \mathcal{R})$, which contains the inner-product result r_i for the i-th clause and the final search result $\mathcal{R}$.

Theorem 1. SESAME+ *is an $\mathcal{L}$-secure Boolean Searchable Symmetric Encryption scheme with non-adaptive security[5] that supports arbitrary Boolean queries, if the inner-product functional encryption is secure.*

6   Experimental Evaluation

In this section, we report the implementation and performance of SESAME and SESAME+. We evaluate the performance on real-world data set and compare the storage overhead and search efficiency of SESAME+ with those of TWINSSE$_{\mathsf{OXT}}$[6] [6] in conjunctive normal form. Furthermore, we evaluate the storage overhead of CNFFilter [29] and present an efficiency comparison with TWINSSE$_{\mathsf{OXT}}$ (in CNF and DNF form) and SESAME+.

Data Set and Platform. We utilize the Enron email data set [1], comprising a total of 515,705 documents (emails). To ensure a more enriched and meaningful set of keywords in each document, we chose 17,006 documents that are greater than 10 KB in size. The experiments are conducted using Python3 on a system running macOS Monterey 12.4 with an Intel Core i7 2.9 GHz CPU.

Implementation Details. We extract 500 keywords from the Enron dataset with a total of 2,553,585 document-keyword pairs. For cryptographic primitives, we implement PRF and encryption using HMAC and AES algorithms, respectively, as provided by the Crypto library [2]. In our implementation, we set the prime order p of functional encryption to 256 bits. In the implementation of scheme TWINSSE$_{\mathsf{OXT}}$, we use the Pairing-Based Cryptography Library [3] and set both *qbits* and *rbits* to 256. Additionally, we set the bucket size to 10, which is consistent with the configuration used in [6]. For CNFFilter, we take the first 8 bytes for the output of PRFs, which is the same as the setting in [29].

6.1   Evaluation of Our Constructions

We present the performance evaluation of both our basic construction, SESAME, and its enhanced version, SESAME+, in terms of search efficiency and accuracy.

---

[5] Adaptive security denotes that the adversary can issue queries depending on previous queries, whereas non-adaptive security means that the adversary must prepare all the queries at the beginning of the BSSE security game.

[6] In this paper, unless explicitly specified, TWINSSE$_{\mathsf{OXT}}$ is used to represent a scheme specifically designed for processing Boolean queries in CNF form.

This evaluation includes various configurations of Bloom filters, where we vary the filter length and the number of hash functions. The results are summarized in Table 2. In the experimental setting, we consider Boolean queries of the form $D_1 \vee D_2$, where D_i represents a conjunction of three labels.

Table 2. Performance Comparison: Search Efficiency and Accuracy

	1200				1800				2400			
	SESAME		SESAME+		SESAME		SESAME+		SESAME		SESAME+	
	time	acc	time	acc	time	acc	time	acc	time	acc	time	acc
2	78.678	0.942	3.256	0.942	115.477	0.947	3.290	0.947	156.806	0.989	3.326	0.989
3	79.770	0.739	4.157	0.739	118.784	0.957	4.269	0.957	160.209	0.827	4.328	0.827
4	77.025	0.587	5.000	0.587	118.532	0.878	5.105	0.878	163.714	0.844	5.273	0.844
5	73.810	0.503	5.679	0.503	119.807	0.827	6.053	0.827	162.508	0.807	6.174	0.807

[1] Search time is measured in seconds and "acc" stands for "accuracy".
[2] The leftmost column corresponds to the number of hash functions, while the top row denotes the length of the Bloom filter.

Within our proposed schemes, alongside the documents that satisfy the query, the query results also encompass certain erroneous documents, which are evaluated using accuracy as a metric. The occurrence of errors can be attributed to two factors. Firstly, the utilization of the Bloom filter as an indexing mechanism inherently introduces errors, which can be adjusted through parameter modifications. Secondly, to protect access and search patterns, we have incorporated a dummy keyword, which simultaneously increases the false positive rate.

Based on the empirical findings presented in Table 2, we observe that when the length of the Bloom filter remains constant, the accuracy of the query results decreases with an increasing number of hash functions. On the other hand, increasing the length of the Bloom filter improves the performance of our constructions. Therefore, our proposed constructions allow for parameter adjustments within the Bloom filter to achieve the desired level of accuracy.

Through a comparative analysis of SESAME and SESAME+, notable distinctions emerge. SESAME+ demonstrates a search time that is at least ten times faster than that of SESAME and is unaffected by the length of the Bloom filter. In contrast, the search time of SESAME escalates with the expansion of the Bloom filter's length. The discrepancy arises from SESAME+ selectively computing relevant vector elements, ignoring nonsensical ones, compared to SESAME that calculates the entire vector regardless of element relevance. This enhancement in our construction leads to a substantial improvement in search efficiency.

6.2 Performance Comparison

We evaluate and compare the search and accuracy performance of SESAME+ and TWINSSE$_{OXT}$ by varying queries. Each query is composed of two clauses, with each clause containing 2 or 3 keywords, as depicted in Fig. 1(a) and (b), respectively. The resulting size is varied by carefully selecting the keywords. For our implementation, we employ a Bloom filter with a length of 2400 bits and a hash family with two hash functions.

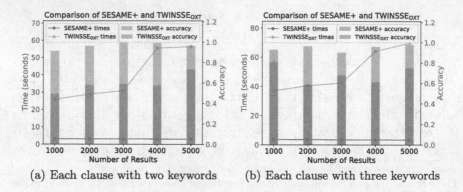

(a) Each clause with two keywords   (b) Each clause with three keywords

Fig. 1. Search Efficiency and Accuracy Performance

Our proposed construction, SESAME+, exhibits superior performance compared to TWINSSE$_{OXT}$ in terms of both search efficiency and result accuracy. In terms of search efficiency, SESAME+ achieves a more than tenfold improvement, which remains consistent regardless of the number of results or changes in query formulas. This is attributed to the linear search nature of our construction, where the number of elements involved in the computation is typically small. In contrast, TWINSSE$_{OXT}$ utilizes meta-keywords that often contain numerous elements, requiring individual verification and resulting in search times that fluctuate with the number of results or changes in query formula. Our construction also outperforms in result accuracy, as our scheme allows for enhanced accuracy by adjusting the parameters of the Bloom filter. On the other hand, TWINSSE$_{OXT}$ introduces errors through meta-keywords, which are query-dependent and consequently limit improvements in accuracy across all queries. Figure 2 illustrates the comparison of our scheme with TWINSSE$_{OXT}$ and CNFFilter in terms of search time. CNFFilter achieves faster search efficiency at the expense of storage overhead and information leakage.

In addition, we conduct a comparison of storage overhead and token size, as illustrated in Table 3. The storage overhead is determined by serializing the encrypted database using the *pickle* library, while the token size is computed using the `getsizeof()` function from the *sys* library. It is important to note that the token size solely captures the information transmitted from the client to the server and does not account for any information returned by the server.

From the comparison, we observe that SESAME+ demonstrates significantly lower storage overhead compared to other constructions. This is attributed to the linear relationship between the storage overhead of SESAME+ and the number

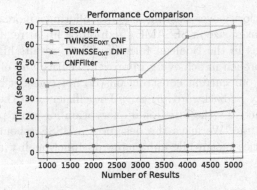

Fig. 2. Efficiency Comparison

of documents, which is independent of the number of keywords present in each document. In contrast, the storage overhead of the other two constructions is influenced by the number of document-key pairs, and the generation of meta-keywords results in an expansion of storage space.

Table 3. Performance Comparison: Storage Overhead and Token Size

	Storage Size (GB)	Token Size (KB)				
		1000	2000	3000	4000	5000
SESAME+	1.55	416	416	416	416	416
TWINSSE$_{OXT}$	6.69	147816	295264	295264	295264	295264
CNFFilter	23.0	208	208	208	208	208

Furthermore, we observe SESAME+ shows a smaller token size due to its linear relationship with the number of keywords in the Boolean formula. In contrast, the token size of CNFFilter is quadratically related to the number of keywords in the Boolean formula, as it necessitates the generation of double tag seeds. The search protocol of TWINSSE$_{OXT}$ involves two rounds of interaction, resulting in a token size that is influenced not only by the number of keywords in the Boolean formula but also by the number of results in the first clause.

7 Conclusion

This paper further advanced the design of Boolean Searchable Symmetric Encryption (BSSE) schemes with a focus on reducing leakage and improving storage efficiency. Our proposed scheme, SESAME+, addresses the issue of volume leakage and provides enhanced protection for search and access pattern leakage that previous works have overlooked. Regarding storage overhead, SESAME+

demonstrates superiority over existing schemes, offering a more efficient solution. Additionally, the token size in SESAME+ exhibits a linear relationship with the number of keywords in the Boolean formula. These results highlight the effectiveness of our approach in achieving improved security and efficiency in BSSE schemes. However, our current constructions do not consider dynamic aspects, nor forward privacy or backward privacy. The efficiency of these constructions is primarily influenced by the functional encryption for inner product primitive and linear search time. We leave the design of a BSSE scheme with the same merits and properties meanwhile enhancing its functionality and efficiency, as our future work.

Acknowledgement. This work was supported in part by the National Key Research and Development Program of China under Grant No. 2021YFB3101100; in part by China Scholarship Council.

Appendix A   Proof of Theorem 1

We provide a formal security proof of our construction SESAME+. We consider a database DB and a sequence of DNF queries $\mathcal{Q} = \{Q_1, \cdots, Q_n\}$, where $Q_i = q_{i,1} \vee \cdots \vee q_{i,m}$ consists of m conjunctions.

The leakage function $\mathcal{L}_{\mathsf{Setup}}$ captures information that is leaked from the Setup algorithm. In our construction, we use Bloom filters to represent documents and encrypt them using functional encryption. As the adversary is restricted to access only the encrypted vectors, the acquired information is confined to the total number of encrypted vectors and their respective lengths, represented as d and l, respectively. Hence, the Setup leakage function is defined as $\mathcal{L}_{\mathsf{Setup}} = (d, l)$.

The leakage function $\mathcal{L}_{\mathsf{Token}}$ is a summary of the information that an adversary can acquire in the context of the Token algorithm. It is noteworthy that both the vector $\boldsymbol{\alpha}$, which records the number of non-zero elements, and the vector $\boldsymbol{\beta}$, which records the positions of non-zero elements, are sent to the server as auxiliary query information, thereby making them susceptible to the adversary. Additionally, U can be derived from $\boldsymbol{\beta}$, which means that it is not part of $\mathcal{L}_{\mathsf{Token}}$. Furthermore, $\boldsymbol{\beta}$ discloses the number of clauses in the query Q as m. Consequently, the Token leakage function is represented as $\mathcal{L}_{\mathsf{Token}} = (m, \boldsymbol{\alpha}, \boldsymbol{\beta})$.

Regarding the information that is leaked in the Search algorithm, it is important to note that the output from the Token is received by the server, and this output has already been included in the $\mathcal{L}_{\mathsf{Token}}$. During query execution, the server prunes the matrix $\boldsymbol{A}$ based on β_i to derive $\boldsymbol{A}'$ for each clause in Q, where $\boldsymbol{A}$ represents the ciphertext vectors encrypted by functional encryption generated in the Setup, and its security is guaranteed by functional encryption. Subsequently, the server decrypts $\boldsymbol{A}'$ to obtain the inner product result r_i, which can be acquired by the adversary. Additionally, the server discloses the query's result set $\mathcal{R}$, which constitutes information accessible to the adversary. Therefore, the Search leakage function is defined as $\mathcal{L}_{\mathsf{Search}} = (\{r_1, \cdots, r_m\}, \mathcal{R})$.

Proof. To demonstrate that $\mathbf{Real}_{\mathcal{A}}^{\mathsf{SESAME+}}(\lambda)$ and $\mathbf{Ideal}_{\mathcal{A},\mathcal{S}}^{\mathsf{SESAME+}}(\lambda)$ are computationally indistinguishable, we characterize a probabilistic polynomial-time simulator $\mathcal{S}$ capable of simulating the three protocols in our SESAME+ scheme. The simulator $\mathcal{S}$ must be able to regenerate the encrypted database and tokens from the leakage information $\mathcal{L}$, with the regenerated tokens satisfying the dependencies among the leakage functions $\mathcal{L}_{\mathsf{Setup}}$, $\mathcal{L}_{\mathsf{Token}}$, and $\mathcal{L}_{\mathsf{Search}}$, in order to prevent the adversary $\mathcal{A}$ from distinguishing between the real world and ideal world scenarios. The adversary $\mathcal{A}$ has access to the simulated encrypted database and can retrieve data using the simulated tokens.

Provided the leakage information $\mathcal{L} = (\mathcal{L}_{\mathsf{Setup}}, \mathcal{L}_{\mathsf{Token}}, \mathcal{L}_{\mathsf{Search}})$, the simulations can be formulated as follows:

To simulate the Setup protocol, $\mathcal{S}$ selects a cyclic group $\mathbb{G}$ of prime order $p > 2^{\lambda}$. Then, $\mathcal{S}$ randomly samples $s_i, t_i \leftarrow \mathbb{Z}_p$ for each $i \in \{1, \cdots, l\}$, where l is determined by $\mathcal{L}_{\mathsf{Setup}}$, randomly samples $k \leftarrow \{0,1\}^{\lambda}$ and computes $h_i = g^{s_i} \cdot h^{t_i}$, where g and h are two randomly generated generators in $\mathbb{G}$. As a result, $\mathcal{S}$ simulates the master secret key and master public key as $\mathsf{msk} := (\mathsf{sk}_{\mathsf{IPFE}} = \{(s_i, t_i)\}_{i=1}^{l}, k)$ and $\mathsf{mpk} := (\mathbb{G}, g, h, \{h_i\}_{i=1}^{l})$, respectively.

For simulating the EDB, $\mathcal{S}$ generates d Bloom filters $\boldsymbol{v}_i$ of length l. These vectors are constructed to maintain dependencies with the leakage functions $\mathcal{L}_{\mathsf{Token}}$ and $\mathcal{L}_{\mathsf{Search}}$, ensuring that the adversary's verification using simulated tokens remains valid. The adversary can only learn the length l of the vectors and the number of vectors d, as they only have access to the encrypted vectors. Finally, the simulator $\mathcal{S}$ employs functional encryption for inner product with the mpk to encrypt the vectors and simulate the encrypted database EDB.

In the context of the Setup protocol, given the leakage information $\mathcal{L}$, the simulator $\mathcal{S}$ generates simulated outputs, including the encrypted database EDB, the master public key mpk, and the master secret key msk. The difference between the simulated EDB and the real-world scenario lies in the selection of $\boldsymbol{v}_i$. Instead of obtaining $\boldsymbol{v}_i$ based on the document mapping, $\mathcal{S}$ selects $\boldsymbol{v}_i$ using the leakage functions $\mathcal{L}_{\mathsf{Token}}$ and $\mathcal{L}_{\mathsf{Search}}$, followed by its encryption. The advantage of distinguishing them is negligible if functional encryption is fully secure. The simulations of the mpk and msk are equivalent with those of the real world.

In the simulation of the Token protocol, $\mathcal{S}$ simulates tokens for Boolean queries based on the leakage function $\mathcal{L}_{\mathsf{Token}}$ and ensures that these tokens can operate on the simulated encrypted database EDB. The leakage information provided by $\mathcal{L}_{\mathsf{Token}}$ reveals the positions of non-zero elements in the vector for each Boolean query clause, as well as the number of clauses for each Boolean query. Consequently, $\mathcal{S}$ can generate tokens that are identical to those in the real experiment. For simulating the decryption key, $\mathcal{S}$ leverages the leaked positions information to simulate the decryption key using the Keygen algorithm of functional encryption. The advantage of $\mathcal{A}$ in distinguishing between the real world and the ideal world becomes negligible if the functional encryption is secure.

When simulating the Search protocol, $\mathcal{S}$ retrieves documents from the encrypted database EDB based on a given Boolean query. Upon receiving the simulated token tok, $\mathcal{S}$ prunes the simulated EDB according to the corresponding β, then performs the decryption process on the pruned EDB to obtain the identifiers of documents that satisfy the query. Since both EDB and tok are simulated based on the leakage function $\mathcal{L}$, the search process performed on the simulated token leaks the same information as $\mathcal{L}_{\text{Search}}$. Consequently, $\mathcal{A}$ cannot distinguish between the real world and the ideal world with more than negligible probability.

In the above proof, we describe a probabilistic polynomial-time simulator $\mathcal{S}$ that simulates the real experiment by using a given leakage information from $\mathcal{L}$. Assuming that functional encryption for inner product is secure, then our scheme SESAME+ achieves $\mathcal{L}$-secure, that is

$$|\Pr[\mathbf{Real}_{\mathcal{A}}^{\text{SESAME+}}(\lambda) = 1] - \Pr[\mathbf{Ideal}_{\mathcal{A},\mathcal{S}}^{\text{SESAME+}}(\lambda) = 1]| \leq \text{negl}(\lambda).$$

Remark. Due to subtle issues from the underlying inner product functional encryption, we prove SESAME+ with *non-adaptive* security, *i.e.*, the adversary issues all queries before running the game. Designing an adaptively secure BSSE scheme with similar properties as SESAME+ seems to require fundamentally different primitives and proof techniques, for which we leave as a future work.

References

1. Enron Email Dataset. https://www.cs.cmu.edu/~enron/. Accessed May 2015
2. PyCryptodome. https://pycryptodome.readthedocs.io/en/latest/index.html
3. The Pairing-Based Cryptography Library. https://crypto.stanford.edu/pbc/
4. Abdalla, M., Bourse, F., De Caro, A., Pointcheval, D.: Simple functional encryption schemes for inner products. In: Katz, J. (ed.) PKC 2015. LNCS, vol. 9020, pp. 733–751. Springer, Heidelberg (2015). https://doi.org/10.1007/978-3-662-46447-2_33
5. Agrawal, S., Libert, B., Stehlé, D.: Fully secure functional encryption for inner products, from standard assumptions. In: Robshaw, M., Katz, J. (eds.) CRYPTO 2016. LNCS, vol. 9816, pp. 333–362. Springer, Heidelberg (2016). https://doi.org/10.1007/978-3-662-53015-3_12
6. Bag, A., Talapatra, D., et al.: TWo-IN-one-SSE: fast, scalable and storage-efficient searchable symmetric encryption for conjunctive and disjunctive boolean queries. Proc. Priv. Enhancing Technol. **2023**(1), 115–139 (2023)
7. Bishop, A., Jain, A., Kowalczyk, L.: Function-hiding inner product encryption. In: Iwata, T., Cheon, J.H. (eds.) ASIACRYPT 2015. LNCS, vol. 9452, pp. 470–491. Springer, Heidelberg (2015). https://doi.org/10.1007/978-3-662-48797-6_20
8. Boneh, D., Sahai, A., Waters, B.: Functional encryption: definitions and challenges. In: Ishai, Y. (ed.) TCC 2011. LNCS, vol. 6597, pp. 253–273. Springer, Heidelberg (2011). https://doi.org/10.1007/978-3-642-19571-6_16
9. Bost, R.: $\sum o\varphi o\varsigma$: forward secure searchable encryption. In: 2016 ACM SIGSAC Conference on Computer and Communications Security, CCS 2016, Vienna, Austria, pp. 1143–1154. ACM (2016)
10. Bost, R., Minaud, B., et al.: Forward and backward private searchable encryption from constrained cryptographic primitives. In: 2017 ACM SIGSAC Conference on Computer and Communications Security, CCS 2017, pp. 1465–1482. ACM (2017)
11. Cao, N., et al.: Privacy-preserving multi-keyword ranked search over encrypted cloud data. IEEE Trans. Parallel Distrib. Syst. **25**(1), 222–233 (2014)

12. Cash, D., Jarecki, S., Jutla, C., Krawczyk, H., Roşu, M.-C., Steiner, M.: Highly-scalable searchable symmetric encryption with support for Boolean queries. In: Canetti, R., Garay, J.A. (eds.) CRYPTO 2013. LNCS, vol. 8042, pp. 353–373. Springer, Heidelberg (2013). https://doi.org/10.1007/978-3-642-40041-4_20

13. Cash, D., et al.: Dynamic searchable encryption in very-large databases: data structures and implementation. In: 21st Annual Network and Distributed System Security Symposium, NDSS 2014. The Internet Society (2014)

14. Curtmola, R., Garay, J., Kamara, S., Ostrovsky, R.: Searchable symmetric encryption: improved definitions and efficient constructions. In: 2006 ACM Conference on Computer and Communications Security, CCS 2006, pp. 79–88. ACM (2006)

15. Demertzis, I., Papadopoulos, D., Papamanthou, C.: Searchable encryption with optimal locality: achieving sublogarithmic read efficiency. In: Shacham, H., Boldyreva, A. (eds.) CRYPTO 2018. LNCS, vol. 10991, pp. 371–406. Springer, Cham (2018). https://doi.org/10.1007/978-3-319-96884-1_13

16. Fu, Z., Huang, F., Ren, K., Weng, J., Wang, C.: Privacy-preserving smart semantic search based on conceptual graphs over encrypted outsourced data. IEEE Trans. Inf. Forensics Secur. **12**(8), 1874–1884 (2017)

17. Grubbs, P., Lacharité, M.-S., Minaud, B., Paterson, K.G.: Pump up the volume: practical database reconstruction from volume leakage on range queries. In: 2018 ACM Conference on Computer and Communications Security, CCS 2018, pp. 315–331. ACM (2018)

18. Gui, Z., Johnson, O., Warinschi, B.: Encrypted databases: new volume attacks against range queries. In: 2019 ACM Conference on Computer and Communications Security, CCS 2019, pp. 361–378. ACM (2019)

19. Islam, M.S., Kuzu, M., et al.: Access pattern disclosure on searchable encryption: ramification, attack and mitigation. In: 19th Annual Network and Distributed System Security Symposium, NDSS 2012, p. 12. The Internet Society (2012)

20. Kamara, S., Papamanthou, C., Roeder, T.: Dynamic searchable symmetric encryption. In: 2012 ACM Conference on Computer and Communications Security, CCS 2012, pp. 965–976. ACM (2012)

21. Kamara, S., Moataz, T.: Boolean searchable symmetric encryption with worst-case sub-linear complexity. In: Coron, J.-S., Nielsen, J.B. (eds.) EUROCRYPT 2017. LNCS, vol. 10212, pp. 94–124. Springer, Cham (2017). https://doi.org/10.1007/978-3-319-56617-7_4

22. Kellaris, G., Kollios, G., Nissim, K., O'Neill, A.: Generic attacks on secure outsourced databases. In: 2016 ACM Conference on Computer and Communications Security, CCS 2016, pp. 1329–1340. ACM (2016)

23. Kim, S., Lewi, K., Mandal, A., Montgomery, H., Roy, A., Wu, D.J.: Function-hiding inner product encryption is practical. In: Catalano, D., De Prisco, R. (eds.) SCN 2018. LNCS, vol. 11035, pp. 544–562. Springer, Cham (2018). https://doi.org/10.1007/978-3-319-98113-0_29

24. Kornaropoulos, E.M., Papamanthou, C., Tamassia, R.: The state of the uniform: attacks on encrypted databases beyond the uniform query distribution. In: 2020 IEEE Symposium on Security and Privacy, S&P 2020, pp. 1223–1240. IEEE (2020)

25. Lai, S., Patranabis, S., et al.: Result pattern hiding searchable encryption for conjunctive queries. In: 2018 ACM SIGSAC Conference on Computer and Communications Security, CCS 2018, pp. 745–762. ACM (2018)

26. Liu, C., Zhu, L., Wang, M., Tan, Y.: Search pattern leakage in searchable encryption: attacks and new construction. Inf. Sci. **265**, 176–188 (2014)

27. Ning, J., Xu, J., Liang, K., Zhang, F., Chang, E.-C.: Passive attacks against searchable encryption. IEEE Trans. Inf. Forensics Secur. **14**(3), 789–802 (2019)

28. Oya, S., Kerschbaum, F.: Hiding the access pattern is not enough: exploiting search pattern leakage in searchable encryption. In: 30th USENIX Security Symposium, USENIX Security 2021, pp. 127–142. USENIX Association (2021)

29. Patel, S., Persiano, G., Seo, J.Y., Yeo, K.: Efficient Boolean search over encrypted data with reduced leakage. In: Tibouchi, M., Wang, H. (eds.) ASIACRYPT 2021. LNCS, vol. 13092, pp. 577–607. Springer, Cham (2021). https://doi.org/10.1007/978-3-030-92078-4_20

30. Pouliot, D., Wright, C.V.: The shadow nemesis: inference attacks on efficiently deployable, efficiently searchable encryption. In: 2016 ACM Conference on Computer and Communications Security, CCS 2016, pp. 1341–1352. ACM (2016)

31. Shang, Z., Oya, S., Peter, A., Kerschbaum, F.: Obfuscated access and search patterns in searchable encryption. In: 28th Annual Network and Distributed System Security Symposium, NDSS 2021. The Internet Society (2021)

32. Song, D.X., Wagner, D.A., Perring A.: Practical techniques for searches on encrypted data. In: 2000 IEEE Symposium on Security and Privacy, S&P 2000, pp. 44–55. IEEE Computer Society (2000)

33. Wang, B., Yu, S., Lou, W., Hou, Y.T.: Privacy-preserving multi-keyword fuzzy search over encrypted data in the cloud. In: 2014 IEEE Conference on Computer Communications, INFOCOM 2014, pp. 2112–2120. IEEE (2014)

Password-Based Credentials
with Security Against Server Compromise

Dennis Dayanikli[✉] and Anja Lehmann

Hasso-Plattner-Institute, University of Potsdam, Potsdam, Germany
{dennis.dayanikli,anja.lehmann}@hpi.de

Abstract. Password-based credentials (PBCs), introduced by Zhang
et al. (NDSS'20), provide an elegant solution to secure, yet convenient
user authentication. Therein the user establishes a strong cryptographic
access credential with the server. To avoid the assumption of secure storage on the user side, the user does not store the credential directly, but
only a password-protected version of it. The ingenuity of PBCs is that
the password-based credential cannot be offline attacked, offering essentially the same strong security as standard key-based authentication.
This security relies on a secret key of the server that is needed to verify
whether an authentication token derived from a password-based credential and password is correct. However, the work by Zhang et al. assumes
that this server key never gets compromised, and their protocol loses all
security in case of a breach. As such a passive leak of the server's stored
verification data is one of the main threats in user authentication, our
work aims to strengthen PBC to remain secure even when the server's key
got compromised. We first show that the desired security against server
compromise is impossible to achieve in the original framework. We then
introduce a modified version of PBCs that circumvents our impossibility
result and formally define a set of security properties, each being optimal
for the respective corruption setting. Finally, we propose a surprisingly
simple construction that provably achieves our stronger security guarantees, and is generically composed from basic building blocks.

1 Introduction

Password-based authentication is still the most common form of user authentication online. Their main benefit is convenience: users can access their accounts
from any device based on human-memorizable information only. On the down-
side, passwords provide weak security guarantees. The biggest threats are server
compromise, i.e., an attacker gaining access to the password data stored on the
server side, and weak passwords that can be (online) guessed.

To provide better security for users, strong authentication solutions such as
FIDO [18,23] see an increasing interest in the industry and among standardization communities. In these solutions, the user typically owns a cryptographically
strong signing key, and authenticates by signing a challenge provided by the
server who stores the corresponding public key. This solution eliminates both

G. Tsudik et al. (Eds.): ESORICS 2023, LNCS 14344, pp. 147–167, 2024.
https://doi.org/10.1007/978-3-031-50594-2_8

the risk of guessing attacks (the user now has a high-entropy key) and server compromise (the information on the server side is only the user's public key, i.e., not sensitive). However, this strong security comes for the price of reduced usability, as the user must securely manage cryptographic key material. This is particularly challenging when users want to access the key from many, and possibly low-security, devices. A common approach therefore is to rely on tamper-resistant hardware tokens, e.g. Yubikey [25], which is desirable from a security perspective, but clearly not ideal in terms of usability [19].

Password-Based Credentials. To combine the best of both worlds, Zhang et al. [26] recently proposed the concept of *password-based credentials* (PBC) that provide similarly strong security as the key-based solution, but without having to store sensitive key material on the user side. In the PBC-system, the user establishes a cryptographically strong access credential with the server upon registration. To avoid the need of secure hardware on the user side, the user does not store the sensitive credential directly, but only a password-protected version of it. When authenticating to the server, the user needs both the credential and her password. The twist of their solution is that this password-based credential is resistant to offline brute-force attacks against the password, and thus could even be synced via (untrusted) cloud providers or simply copied on many (low-security) devices. This offline-attack resistance is achieved by relying on a high-entropy key of the server for verifying whether an authentication token derived from the credential and password is correct. Thus, verifying whether a password guess was correct requires interaction with the server, which reduces the attack surface from offline to online attacks if an attacker knows the password-based credential. If the adversary does not possess the user's password-based credential, the security is essentially equivalent to strong authentication. Their security comes with one significant limitation though – it assumes the server never gets compromised.

Importance of Server Compromise. Server compromise is a major threat to password-based authentication, and refers to an attack where the adversary gains access to the authentication information maintained by the server, such as password hashes. The server itself is considered to be honest, but an attacker can now recover the users' access details to either gain access to a user's account at the compromised server or, if the same password is re-used across multiple services, even impersonate the user on different sites. Even major companies such as Yahoo [24], PayPal [10], Linkedin [1], Blizzard [20] or LastPass [22] have suffered from such attacks, resulting in millions of password hashes or password-protected files being compromised.

Thus, considering the threat of server compromise and building solutions that maintain security in such scenarios is crucial for end-user authentication. Surprisingly, despite having server compromise as a core motivation for their work, Zhang et al. [26] do not include server compromise attacks in their model. In fact, their PBC protocol loses all security if the server's data gets compromised, as the attacker can then impersonate any user who has registered with the server. This even holds regardless of the user's chosen password, as it does not require any additional offline attack to recover the password.

1.1 Our Contributions

We address the problem of password-based credentials that remain secure in the presence of server compromise. We show that the desired security is impossible to achieve in the framework proposed by Zhang, Wang and Yang [26] (henceforth called the ZWY framework). We adapt this framework to circumvent the impossibility result and propose a generic protocol that provably satisfies our stronger notion – and is even simpler than the one by Zhang et al.

Following the work by Zhang et al. [26], we formalize PBC as a password-based token scheme, i.e., the actual authentication protocol is abstracted away. On a high-level, the user registers with the server, obtaining a credential that is protected under her password. After registration, the user can generate a token by "signing" her username and message (which typically will be a fresh nonce in the actual authentication protocol) using the credential and password as a secret key input. The server verifies that token using it's *secret* verification key.

We extend and strengthen the ZWY security framework to capture the following high-level security guarantees:

Strong Unforgeability: An attacker without knowledge of the user's credential should not be able to forge an authentication token – thus essentially guaranteeing the same level as classic key-based strong authentication. This property must also hold when the adversary knows the user's password, and when the server is compromised, i.e., even if the adversary knows the server's verification key.

Online Unforgeability: When the adversary knows the user's credential (but not the server's verification key), tokens remain unforgeable as long as the adversary has not guessed the correct password. The strength of this property is that the adversary must not be able to offline attack the password but run an online attack against the honest server. Requiring participation of the server for each password guess, enables the server to notice suspicious access patterns and impose throttling on the affected account.

Offline Unforgeability: If both the user's credential and the server's key are compromised, the attacker can unavoidably test passwords in an offline way. However, we require the attacker to perform such an offline attack on *each* password. This adds a last layer of security for users with strong passwords.

The ZWY framework captures a security definition for a combined version of online unforgeability and a weaker form of strong unforgeability where the server could not be compromised. Their work did not cover or achieve offline unforgeability.

Impossibility of Security Against Server-Compromise in Single-Key Setting. In the ZWY framework [26], the server only has a single verification key for *all* users. The high-level idea of their concrete construction is as follows: the server has a global MAC key, and the credential is essentially a server's (algebraic) MAC on the username which the user encrypts under her password. The core idea of authentication is decrypting the credential with the password, recovering the MAC and sending it back to server (and bound to the message). Without knowing the server's high-entropy key, one cannot verify if the decrypted value is indeed a correct MAC, ensuring the desired online unforgeability. It is easy to see that this construction is not secure if the server's key got compromised, as the adversary can simply create MACs for all users he wants to impersonate.

In fact, we show that this is not merely a weakness of their scheme but inherent in the overall *single*-key setting. That is, we show that strong unforgeability and offline unforgeability are impossible to achieve when the server owns a single verification key for all users.

Framework for Multi-key Password-Based Credentials. As two of the three desired security properties are impossible to achieve in the single-key ZWY framework [26], we propose a new variant – *Multi-key Password-based Credentials* (mkPBC) – where the server maintains an individual verification key for every user. Moving to a setting where the server maintains individual verification information for each user requires an additional property also concerned with server compromise, yet not captured by any of the three properties listed above:

Pw-Hiding: The server's verification key for a user should not leak any information about the user's password.

The reason this property is not covered by the unforgeability notions discussed above is that learning the password in the mkPBC scheme does not allow the server to impersonate the user (this still requires the user credential). However, as users tend to reuse their passwords across different sites, we want the password to remain fully hidden in case the server gets compromised.

We formally define all four properties through game-based security definitions, capturing the optimal security guarantees for a mkPBC scheme.

Simple Construction From Standard Building Blocks. Finally, we present a surprisingly simple generic mkPBC scheme (PBC$_{StE}$) constructed from standard building blocks – a pseudorandom function, public-key encryption and signature scheme. The challenge is in formally proving that it achieves all our security notions. To do so, we require the signature scheme to satisfy two properties in addition to unforgeability – *complete robustness* and *randomness injectivity*. Both are natural properties, and we show that they are achieved by standard signature schemes, such as Schnorr and DSA.

Interestingly, our construction does not only provide stronger security than the original scheme, but is also much simpler and generic: Whereas Zhang et al. [26] gave a concrete discrete-logarithm based construction that required the q-SDH and q-DDHI assumptions, our PBC$_{StE}$ only requires basic building blocks, and thus can be easily implemented using standard cryptographic libraries. The generic approach also allows to obtain a quantum-safe variant of our scheme if the generic building blocks are instantiated with PQC-variants.

2   Single-Key Password-Based Credentials

This section presents the idea and security of the ZWY framework by Zhang et al. [26], to which we refer to as *single-key* password-based credentials (skPBC). We show that no skPBC can achieve security in the presence of server compromise, which we consider a crucial goal and which motivates our switch to *multi-key* PBCs in the following section.

We start by presenting the definition of single-key PBCs before we present the impossibility result. We adopted the ZWY framework to our notation for consistency with our main result. For completeness, we summarize our editorial changes to the ZWY syntax and security definitions in Appendix A and explain that they do not change the technical aspects of [26].

Syntax. A (single-key) password-based credential system skPBC consists of five algorithms (KGen, ⟨RegU, RegS⟩, Sign, Vf) used in two main phases – a *registration phase* and an *authentication phase* – and involves two parties: a server S and a user U who wishes to authenticate to the server. In the single-key setting, the server is assumed to have a single long-term key $\mathsf{KGen}(1^\lambda) \to (ssk, spk)$ that is used to register and verify all users. In the interactive registration protocol ⟨RegU(spk, uid, pw), RegS(ssk, uid)⟩ $\to (ask; -)$ the user registers herself at the server with a username uid and password pw from password space $\mathcal{D}_{\mathsf{pw}}$. The server issues her a credential ask (= authenticated secret key) using a server key ssk and stores her username in his database.

While the overall goal is to use PBC for user authentication, where U and S engage in a challenge-response protocol, this is abstracted away in PBCs by modelling a special type of authentication token τ. This token is created through $\mathsf{Sign}(uid, ask, pw, m) \to \tau$ by the user for a (challenge) message m and username uid, using the user's credential ask and password pw. Verification is a secret-key operation and allows the server with key ssk to verify whether the message m was indeed signed by user uid. This is defined through $\mathsf{Vf}(ssk, uid, m, \tau) \to 0/1$.

2.1   Security Model of ZWY [26]

Zhang et al. [26] proposed the security definition *Existential Unforgeability under Chosen Message and Chosen Verification Queries Attack* (EUF-CMVA). This definition comes with two independent winning conditions and guarantees, (1) classic unforgeability if the adversary only knows the user's password but none of the keys (neither of server nor user) and (2) online unforgeability if the user's key got compromised.

Thus, this can be seen as a combined version of the strong and online unforgeability we described in the introduction, with one significant limitation though: the ZWY model does not allow for server compromise in the strong unforgeability game, thus we refer to their version as *weak unforgeability*. In fact, we show that strong unforgeability is impossible in their setting.

Furthermore, their work does not capture offline unforgeability, again due to the absence of server compromise, and we show that this is also impossible in

Oracle $\mathcal{O}_{\text{Vf}}(i, m, \tau)$	Oracle $\mathcal{O}_{\text{Sign}}(i, m)$	Oracle $\mathcal{O}_{\text{RevCred}}(i)$
Return $\text{Vf}(ssk, uid_i, m, \tau)$	$\tau \leftarrow \text{Sign}(uid_i, ask_i, pw_i, m)$	Add i to RevCred
	Add (i, m) to Q, **Return** τ	**Return** ask_i

Experiment $\text{Exp}_{\mathcal{A},\text{skPBC}}^{x\text{UNF}}(\lambda)$ for $x \in \{\text{weak}, \boxed{\text{strong}}\}$

$(ssk, spk) \leftarrow \text{KGen}(1^\lambda)$, $\quad$ RevCred $\leftarrow \emptyset$, $\quad Q \leftarrow \emptyset$

$(uid_1, \dots, uid_n, st) \leftarrow \mathcal{A}(spk)$, $\quad$ for $\ i = 1, \dots n : pw_i \xleftarrow{r} \mathcal{D}_{\text{pw}}$

$(ask_i; -) \leftarrow \langle \text{RegU}(spk, uid_i, pw_i), \text{RegS}(ssk, uid_i) \rangle$

$(uid_j, m^*, \tau^*) \leftarrow \mathcal{A}^{\mathcal{O}_{\text{RevCred}}, \mathcal{O}_{\text{Sign}}, \mathcal{O}_{\text{Vf}}}(st, pw_1, \dots, pw_n, \boxed{ssk})$

Return 1 if $\text{Vf}(ssk, uid_j, m^*, \tau^*) = 1 \land j \in [n] \land j \notin \text{RevCred} \land (j, m^*) \notin Q$

Fig. 1. Weak and Strong (including the highlighted text) Unforgeability for skPBC. The oracles use the values (i, uid_i, ask_i, pw_i) established during registration.

their setting. Note that the pw-hiding property is not needed in skPBC, as the server does not maintain user-specific state which could depend on the password.

For consistency and ease of presentation, we split the EUF-CMVA game along the two independent winning conditions which correspond to weak and online unforgeability. In the following we only focus on the weak unforgeability and the impossibility of strong unforgeability.

Weak Unforgeability. Weak unforgeability guarantees that the adversary cannot forge a valid authentication token for a user if he does not know the user's credential ask. This provides standard security for users whose credential have not been compromised.

This property is modelled as a game played between a challenger and an adversary. The adversary chooses the usernames of all users. The challenger registers them with randomly chosen passwords with the honest server. The adversary is given the passwords of all users and can then ask arbitrary honest users to sign messages of his choice (via $\mathcal{O}_{\text{Sign}}$) and ask the server to verify tokens of his choice (via $\mathcal{O}_{\text{Vf}}$, recall that this is necessary as verify is a secret-key operation). He can also corrupt users via the $\mathcal{O}_{\text{RevCred}}$ oracle, which returns the credential ask_i of a user i of his choice. The adversary wins if he can forge an authentication token on a fresh message for a user whose credential he has not obtained. The security experiment $\text{Exp}_{\mathcal{A},\text{skPBC}}^{\text{weakUNF}}(\lambda)$ is given in Fig. 1 and the security definition is as follows:

Definition 1 (skPBC Weak/Strong Unforgeability). *A skPBC scheme is x-unforgeable, for $x \in \{weakly, strongly\}$, if for all PPT adversaries $\mathcal{A}$, it holds that $\Pr[\text{Exp}_{\mathcal{A},\text{skPBC}}^{x\text{UNF}}(\lambda) = 1] \leq \text{negl}(\lambda)$.*

2.2 Impossibility of Strong (and Offline) Unforgeability

Lifting the security definition from weak to strong unforgeability is straightforward: to model server compromise, we give the adversary access to the server's secret state – here ssk – after registering honest users. We require the same unforgeability for users whose individual credentials he never learned (see Fig. 1).

However, we now show that achieving this notion is impossible in the single-key setting. The idea of the attack is simple: once the adversary has learned the server's secret key, he re-runs the registration of an arbitrary honest user with a password of his choice to obtain a valid user credential and creates tokens in her name. More precisely, the following adversary $\mathcal{A}$ wins the strong unforgeability game for skPBC with probability 1:

$\underline{\mathcal{A}(spk)}$

Pick $uid_1 \xleftarrow{r} \mathcal{D}_{\mathsf{uid}}$, send (uid_1, st) to the challenger, receive (st, pw_1, ssk);

Pick $pw' \xleftarrow{r} \mathcal{D}_{\mathsf{pw}}$ and run $(ask'; -) \leftarrow \langle \mathsf{RegU}(spk, uid_1, pw'), \mathsf{RegS}(ssk, uid_1) \rangle$

Choose $m^* \xleftarrow{r} \mathcal{M}$; compute $\tau^* \leftarrow \mathsf{Sign}(uid_1, ask', pw', m^*)$ and $\mathbf{output}(uid_1, m^*, \tau^*)$

Success Analysis of $\mathcal{A}$: By the correctness definition it holds that $\mathsf{Vf}(ssk, uid_1, m^*, \mathsf{Sign}(uid_1, ask', pw', m^*)) = 1$ since ask' is obtained by running the registration protocol with (uid_1, pw') and the correct issuer secret key ssk. The adversary did neither query $\mathcal{O}_{\mathsf{Sign}}(1, m^*)$ nor $\mathcal{O}_{\mathsf{RevCred}}(1)$, and thus wins the security experiment $\mathsf{Exp}^{\mathsf{strongUNF}}_{\mathcal{A}, \mathsf{skPBC}}(\lambda)$ with probability 1.

The attack exploits the fact that a single key ssk is used to both register users and verify their tokens, and never gets updated when a user registers. Hence, the authentication cannot depend on any user-provided input, but solely on the server key (and the secrecy thereof). This attack also extends to the context of offline unforgeability since an adversary who knows ssk can forge authentication tokens for any user without offline dictionary attacks.

3   Multi-key Password-Based Credentials

Motivated by the impossibility of strong unforgeability in the single-key setting, we now introduce our concept of multi-key password-based credentials. The crucial difference is that the server no longer has a single secret key to issue user credentials and verify their tokens. Instead, he generates a user-specific verification key for each registered user and uses that user-specific key when verifying a user's token. We modify the original PBC syntax to the multi-key setting and then formalize the desired security properties.

Syntax. While the overall idea and concept remain the same in the multi-key setting, we change how the server stores user-specific verification information. We do not assume that the server has a single key pair (ssk, spk). Instead, in the registration phase, the server will output a user-specific verification key avk which allows him to verify the user's authentication token.

Definition 2 (Multi-key Password-based Credential). *A multi-key PBC scheme* $\mathsf{mkPBC} = (\mathsf{Setup}, \langle \mathsf{RegU}, \mathsf{RegS} \rangle, \mathsf{Sign}, \mathsf{Vf})$ *with message space $\mathcal{M}$, username space $\mathcal{D}_{\mathsf{uid}}$ and password space $\mathcal{D}_{\mathsf{pw}}$ is defined as follows.*

Setup(1^λ) $\to$ pp: *Outputs public parameters pp. We assume all algorithms get the public parameters pp as implicit input.*

$\langle$RegU(uid, pw), RegS(uid)$\rangle$ $\to$ ($ask; avk$): *An interactive protocol between $\mathcal{U}$ with (uid, pw) $\in \mathcal{D}_{\mathsf{uid}} \times \mathcal{D}_{\mathsf{pw}}$ and $\mathcal{S}$. After successful registration, the user outputs a credential ask, and the server outputs a user-specific verification key avk.*

Sign(uid, ask, pw, m) $\to \tau$: *Generates an authentication token τ on message $m \in \mathcal{M}$ and username uid, using ask and pw.*

Vf(uid, avk, m, τ) $\to$ 0/1: *Outputs 1 if authentication token τ is valid on uid and m under avk and 0 otherwise.*

We require all honestly generated authentication tokens using the correct combination of *ask* and *pw* to pass validation under the corresponding *avk*. A formal correctness definition is given in Appendix C.

3.1 Security Model

We now provide a formal model for the following security properties motivated in Sect. 1.1 and partially inspired by the ZWY model [26].

Strong Unforgeability: An adversary who does not know a user's *ask* cannot forge an authentication token for that user, even when he knows the user's password *pw* and the server's verification key *avk*.

Online Unforgeability: An adversary who knows *ask* but not *pw* or *avk* cannot forge an authentication token more efficiently than through online guessing attacks, interacting with the server who has *avk*.

Offline Unforgeability: If the adversary knows both *ask* and *avk* of a user, he has to conduct a brute-force offline dictionary attack on the password *pw* in order to forge an authentication token.

Pw-Hiding: The *avk* does not leak any information about the underlying *pw*.

Optimal Security. We stress that all security guarantees are optimal for the respective corruption setting, i.e., achieve the strongest level of full/online/offline attack-resistance for each combination of corrupted keys and passwords. When defining these properties through formal security models, it is important to give the adversary therein as much "access" to honest parties as possible. In fact, this was not properly captured in the ZWY model: therein corrupt users where not allowed to register with an honest server, which allows entirely insecure schemes to be proven secure. See Appendix A for a discussion of that shortcoming. Interestingly, our choice of letting the server maintain *independent* key material for all users, simplifies the modelling significantly: since the server in mkPBC does not have any long-term secret key used during registration or verification, the adversary can internally simulate the registration of any corrupt user (expressed through any combination of *uid* and *pw*) that he wants. Thus, for our security model (Fig. 2), it suffices to consider only a single honest target user and let the adversary (internally) handle all other (corrupt) users in the system.

$\text{Exp}^{\text{xUNF}}_{\mathcal{A},\text{mkPBC}}(\lambda)$ for $x \in \{\text{strong}, \text{online}, \text{offline}\}$	**Oracles** init. with (uid, ask, avk, pw)
$pp \leftarrow \text{Setup}(1^{\lambda}), \quad Q \leftarrow \emptyset$	$\mathcal{O}_{\text{Sign}}(m_i)\colon \tau_i \leftarrow \text{Sign}(uid, ask, pw, m_i)$
$(uid, st) \leftarrow \mathcal{A}(pp), \quad pw \xleftarrow{r} \mathcal{D}_{\text{pw}}$	$Q \leftarrow Q \cup m_i, \textbf{ Return } \tau_i$
$(ask; avk) \leftarrow \langle \text{RegU}(uid, pw), \text{RegS}(uid)\rangle$	$\mathcal{O}_{\text{Vf}}(m_i, \tau_i)\colon \textbf{Return } \text{Vf}(uid, avk, m_i, \tau_i)$
$(m^*, \tau^*) \leftarrow \mathcal{A}^{\mathcal{O}}(\text{keys}, st)$	$\mathcal{O}_{\text{TestPW}}(pw_i)\colon \textbf{Return } pw = pw_i$
Return 1 if $\text{Vf}(uid, avk, m^*, \tau^*) = 1 \wedge m^* \notin Q$

With keys and $\mathcal{O}$ defined as:

x	keys	Oracles $\mathcal{O}$
strong	avk, pw	$\mathcal{O}_{\text{Sign}}$
online	ask	$\mathcal{O}_{\text{Sign}}, \mathcal{O}_{\text{Vf}}$
offline	ask, avk	$\mathcal{O}_{\text{Sign}}, \mathcal{O}_{\text{TestPW}}$

$\text{Exp}^{\text{PW}-\text{Hiding}}_{\mathcal{A},\text{mkPBC}}(\lambda)$

$(uid, pw_0, pw_1, st) \leftarrow \mathcal{A}(pp); b \xleftarrow{r} \{0,1\}$

$(ask; avk) \leftarrow \langle \text{RegU}(uid, pw_b), \text{RegS}(uid)\rangle$

$b' \leftarrow \mathcal{A}^{\mathcal{O}_{\text{Sign}}}(avk, st)$ with $\mathcal{O}_{\text{Sign}}$ using $pw := pw_b$

Return 1 if $b = b'$

Fig. 2. Security experiments and oracles for mkPBC. The overall goal of the adversary in our three unforgeability games is the same, and is shown in the combined xUNF experiment, where only the set of revealed keys and oracles differ depending on x.

Strong Unforgeability. Without knowing the user's credential ask, we want the strongest security in the sense that an adversary can forge tokens in the name of an honest user uid with *negligible* probability only. This is modelled by letting the challenger run the registration for an honest user uid with password pw, obtaining ask and avk. It then hands avk, pw to the adversary, and grants $\mathcal{A}$ access to a sign oracle $\mathcal{O}_{\text{Sign}}$, which returns tokens created with ask (and pw) for messages m_i of his choice. The adversary wins if he can produce a valid token τ^* for a fresh message m^* that verifies for the honest users uid and avk.

Definition 3 (Strong Unforgeability). *A* mkPBC *scheme is strongly unforgeable, if for all PPT adversaries* $\mathcal{A}$*:* $\Pr[\text{Exp}^{\text{strongUNF}}_{\mathcal{A},\text{mkPBC}}(\lambda) = 1] \leq \text{negl}(\lambda)$.

Online Unforgeability. If the adversary knows the user's high-entropy credential ask it is impossible to achieve strong unforgeability anymore. As soon as $\mathcal{A}$ has correctly guessed the user's password, there is no security. The best we can hope for is security against online attacks, relying on the server's user-specific verification key avk as a second defense, i.e. the honest server's participation must be required to verify each of $\mathcal{A}$'s password guesses.

In the security game, this is modelled by giving $\mathcal{A}$ the credential ask of the honestly registered user uid, but neither avk nor pw. Consequently, we grant $\mathcal{A}$ access to avk through a verify oracle $\mathcal{O}_{\text{Vf}}$ that allows the adversary to verify message-token pairs (m_i, σ_i) of his choice under the server's avk. Given that the adversary knows ask, he can use $\mathcal{O}_{\text{Vf}}$ as a password test oracle, submitting tokens generated for the correct ask and different password guesses pw'.

It might look surprising that we grant $\mathcal{A}$ access to a sign oracle too – as he does know ask here – but this oracle is necessary since he does not know the corresponding pw and must be able to observe valid tokens by the honest user.

The adversary's goal is still to forge an authentication token for the honest user. The security definition needs to be weakened to online attacks though, and states that the adversary cannot win the experiment significantly better than through testing $q_{Vf} + 1$ of the $|\mathcal{D}_{pw}|$ passwords where q_{Vf} is the number of queries made to the $\mathcal{O}_{Vf}$ oracle. The additional constant 1 is added because the forgery which $\mathcal{A}$ outputs in the end, can itself be seen as a password guess.

Definition 4 (Online Unforgeability). *A* mkPBC *scheme is online unforgeable, if for all PPT adversaries $\mathcal{A}$ it holds that* $\Pr[\text{Exp}_{\mathcal{A},\text{mkPBC}}^{\text{onlineUNF}}(\lambda) = 1] \leq \frac{q_{Vf}+1}{|\mathcal{D}_{pw}|} + \text{negl}(\lambda)$, *where q_{Vf} is the number of queries to the $\mathcal{O}_{Vf}$ oracle.*

Offline Unforgeability. If both keys, *ask* and *avk*, related to an honest user are compromised, the unforgeability solely relies on the strength of the user password *pw*. The best we can hope for in this setting are offline attacks: the adversary can test passwords by signing a message using the corrupted *ask* and password guess *pw'* and verify the resulting token using the key *avk*. As soon as the adversary has correctly guessed *pw*, there is no secret left, and he can create tokens for arbitrary messages. Offline attacks are unavoidable in this case, but we also want them to be the best possible attack. This means that choosing a strong password adds an additional (albeit weak) layer of security for the user.

To quantify the offline amount of work the adversary has to perform, we took inspiration from security models of other password-based protocols [6–8] and introduce an oracle $\mathcal{O}_{\text{TestPW}}$ which takes the adversaries password guess *pw'* and returns 1 if $pw = pw'$ and 0 else. The adversary's goal stays the same – forging an authentication token for the honest user – which he must not be able to do significantly better than through testing q_f of the $|\mathcal{D}_{pw}|$ passwords where q_f is the number of queries made to the $\mathcal{O}_{\text{TestPW}}$ oracle.

Note that proving a concrete scheme to satisfy this property inherently requires some idealized assumption such as the random oracle, which needs to get invoked on the user's password – otherwise we could simply not count the offline password guesses.

Definition 5 (Offline Unforgeability). *A* mkPBC *scheme is offline unforgeable, if for all PPT adversaries $\mathcal{A}$ it holds that* $\Pr[\text{Exp}_{\mathcal{A},\text{mkPBC}}^{\text{offlineUNF}}(\lambda) = 1] \leq \frac{q_f}{|\mathcal{D}_{pw}|} + \text{negl}(\lambda)$, *where q_f is the number of queries to the oracle $\mathcal{O}_{\text{TestPW}}$.*

PW-Hiding. This property guarantees that a malicious server learns nothing about the user's password, or rather that a user-specific key *avk* – despite being derived from a user password *pw* – does not leak any information about *pw*.

To model this property, we follow the classic indistinguishability approach. The adversary chooses two passwords pw_0 and pw_1 for a user *uid*. The challenger randomly chooses a bit b and runs the registration protocol for user *uid* and pw_b, yielding *ask* and *avk*. It hands *avk* to the adversary, whose goal is to output the correct bit b better than through guessing. To model any possible leakage through other parts of the PBC system, we also grant the adversary access to an $\mathcal{O}_{\text{Sign}}$ oracle which is keyed with *ask* and pw_b.

Definition 6 (Pw-Hiding). *A* mkPBC *scheme is pw-hiding, if for all PPT adversaries* $\mathcal{A}$ *it holds that* $\Pr[\mathsf{Exp}_{\mathcal{A},\mathsf{mkPBC}}^{\mathsf{PW-Hiding}}(\lambda) = 1] \leq 1/2 + \mathsf{negl}(\lambda)$.

4 Our Instantiation: Sign-Then-Encrypt Based Scheme

In this section, we describe $\mathsf{PBC_{StE}}$ which securely realizes all security guarantees described in Sect. 3. Our scheme is conceptually entirely different from the one proposed by Zhang et al. [26], which essentially relied on a DL-based algebraic MAC. Our scheme is generic and soley relies on basic building blocks: a signature scheme, encryption scheme and a pseudorandom function. In order to prove security, we need two less common properties from the signature scheme in addition to unforgeability: *complete robustness* and *randomness injectivity*. We stress that both are natural assumptions and argue that they are satisfied by standard signatures schemes such as Schnorr, DSA and BLS. We start by defining the main building blocks and their required security properties before describing our provably secure construction.

4.1 Building Blocks

We now introduce the building blocks needed for our construction, focusing on the lesser known properties that we will require from the signature scheme.

Notation. Since our construction depends on a signature scheme with deterministic key generation algorithm using explicit randomness, we write "$y := A(x; r)$" to highlight that the output y is derived deterministically by algorithm A on input x with randomness r. Conversely, when we write "$y \leftarrow A(x)$", the output y may be derived either deterministically or probabilistically by algorithm A from input x. We utilize "$s \xleftarrow{r} S$" to denote the uniformly random sampling of a value s from the set S.

Pseudorandom Function. We require a secure PRF $F : \{0,1\}^\lambda \times \mathcal{X} \to \mathcal{Y}$. In some of our security experiments, the adversary will be in possession of the PRF key, and we still want unpredictability of outputs – we then resort to assuming F to be a random oracle for the combined input domain of $\{0,1\}^\lambda \times \mathcal{X}$.

Public-Key Encryption. A public-key encryption (PKE) scheme $\Pi_{Enc} :=$ ($\mathsf{KGen}_E, \mathsf{Enc}, \mathsf{Dec}$) consisting of key generation $(pk_{\mathsf{Enc}}, sk_{\mathsf{Enc}}) \leftarrow \mathsf{KGen}_E(1^\lambda)$, an encryption $c \leftarrow \mathsf{Enc}(pk_{\mathsf{Enc}}, m)$ and decryption algorithm $m \leftarrow \mathsf{Dec}(sk_{\mathsf{Enc}}, c)$. We require Π_{Enc} to be indistinguishable against chosen-ciphertext attacks (IND-CCA).

Signature Scheme. A signature scheme $\Pi_{Sign} :=$ ($\mathsf{Setup}_S, \mathsf{KGen}_S, \mathsf{Sign}_S, \mathsf{Vf}_S$) with setup $pp \leftarrow \mathsf{Setup}(1^\lambda)$, key generation $(pk_{\mathsf{Sig}}, sk_{\mathsf{Sig}}) := \mathsf{KGen}(pp; r)$ for randomness r, sign algorithm $\sigma \leftarrow \mathsf{Sign}_S(sk_{\mathsf{Sig}}, m)$, and verify algorithm $b \leftarrow \mathsf{Vf}_S(pk_{\mathsf{Sig}}, m, \sigma)$. Note that we make the randomness used in key generation explicit and assume KGen to be a deterministic function when given randomness $r \in \mathcal{R}_\lambda$ as input. $\mathcal{R}_\lambda$ is part of the public parameters pp and denotes the randomness space. We require the scheme to be existentially unforgeable under chosen-message attacks (EUF-CMA): It must be infeasible for an adversary given pk_{Sig} from $(sk_{\text{Sig}}, pk_{\text{Sig}}) := \text{KGen}(pp; r)$ for random $r \xleftarrow{r} \mathcal{R}_\lambda$ and access to a sign oracle to produce a valid signature on a fresh message. Our construction requires two additional properties: *complete robustness* and *randomness injectivity*.

Complete Robustness. Géraud and Naccache [12] formalized the notion of complete robustness which requires that it should be hard for an adversary to find a message-signature-pair which verifies under two different public keys.

Definition 7 (Complete Robustness). *A signature scheme* $\Pi_{Sign} :=$ (Setup, KGen, Sign, Vf) *achieves* complete robustness (CROB) *or is* CROB-*secure if for* $pp \leftarrow \text{Setup}(1^\lambda)$ *it holds that for every PPT* $\mathcal{A}$, *the probability* $\Pr[(pk, pk', m, \sigma) \leftarrow \mathcal{A}(pp) : pk \neq pk' \wedge \text{Vf}(pk, m, \sigma) = \text{Vf}(pk', m, \sigma) = 1]$ *is negligible in* λ.

Randomness Injectivity. The second property we need is randomness injectivity which requires that the KGen algorithm is injective on the randomness space. We call a signature scheme randomness injective if it is hard for an adversary to find two distinct values $r, r' \in \mathcal{R}$, which, when given to KGen, map to the same sk or pk. This also implies that for every public key there exists only one secret key. In Appendix C, we give a formal definition of randomness injectivity.

4.2   Our PBC$_{\text{StE}}$ Protocol

The idea of our protocol – referred to as PBC$_{\text{StE}}$ – is surprisingly simple and turns classic signature-based authentication into a secure mkPBC. In the following, we describe the intuition and give the full description in Fig. 3.

Upon registration, the user generates a signature key pair $(pk_{\text{Sig}}, sk_{\text{Sig}})$ and sends the public key pk_{Sig} to the server. Such a key pair enables strong authentication through signing (uid, m), but all security will be lost when an attacker gets access to the user's signing key. We therefore do not store (or even generate) the key normally, but derive it *deterministically* as $(pk_{\text{Sig}}, sk_{\text{Sig}}) :=$ KGen$_S(pp; F(k, pw))$ from a PRF key k and the user's password pw. The user now only stores the PRF key k and re-derives the signature key pair when she wants to generate an authentication token.

This solution already satisfies strong and offline unforgeability as well as password hiding. The challenge is to also guarantee online unforgeability, i.e., ensuring that the knowledge of the user's key and an authentication token does not allow to brute-force the password. So far, this isn't achieved as an attacker who knows k and a valid signature σ can mount an offline password test by computing possible key-pairs $(pk'_{\text{Sig}}, sk'_{\text{Sig}})$ from password guesses pw' until he has found the correct pw' under which σ verifies.

Preventing Offline Attacks. We prevent this offline attack by hiding the actual signature σ in the token. Therefore, we let the user encrypt σ under an encryption public-key pk_{Enc} to which the server knows the corresponding secret key sk_{Enc}. More precisely, $(pk_{\mathsf{Enc}}, sk_{\mathsf{Enc}})$ is a key pair that the user normally generated upon registration, where she keeps pk_{Enc} as part of her credential, i.e., $ask = (k, pk_{\mathsf{Enc}})$ and sends the secret decryption key to the server, i.e., $avk = (sk_{\mathsf{Enc}}, pk_{\mathsf{Sig}})$. Now, only the server knowing sk_{Enc} can recover the signature from the authentication token and verify its validity. Thus, this encryption finally turns the verification into a secret-key operation, which is essential for the desired online unforgeability. We stress that this additional and explicit encryption layer is essential for our security and cannot be achieved from assuming secure channels between the user and server: honest user's can be subject to phishing attacks, and accidentally send authentication tokens to a malicious server.

The Challenge of Proving Online Unforgeability. While the additional encryption immediately removes the obvious offline attack, proving that this is sufficient to achieve online unforgeability is not straightforward.

The challenge is that the adversary knows the PRF key k and can offline attack the password and thereby recover the secret signing key $(pk_{\mathsf{Sig}}, sk_{\mathsf{Sig}}) := \mathsf{KGen}_S(pp; F(k, pw))$. Once he knows the correct secret key there is no security left. And indeed, we cannot rely on any unforgeability guarantees of the signature for this proof. The reason why our scheme is still secure stems from the fact that the adversary does not know which key is the *correct* one: he does not know pk_{Sig} (this is part of the server's secret key) nor any signature value (they are encrypted under the server's key). The only way for $\mathcal{A}$ to learn whether a recovered key is correct, is to compute a signature and send it for validation to the server. The crucial part in our proof is to show that every interaction with the honest server for such a verification is bound to a single password guess only, ensuring the desired online unforgeability.

To illustrate how the signature scheme could allow multiple password tests in one interaction, consider a signature σ on m which verifies under two different public keys pk_1 and pk_2 constructed from passwords pw_1 and pw_2. If the adversary sends (m, σ) to the server and learns that the signature is not valid, he concludes that the server's public key is neither pk_1 nor pk_2 and has ruled out the two passwords pw_1 and pw_2 with one interaction. Hence, we require that every signature verifies under at most one public key which is achieved through complete robustness. Another way how the signature scheme could allow multiple password tests is if the public key pk_1 can be constructed from multiple passwords pw_1 and pw_2. Therefore, we require that every password maps to a unique secret key and unique public key. This is achieved if F is injective, and if the signature scheme has randomness injectivity.

4.3   Security Analysis

In this section, we provide the main security theorems for our $\mathsf{PBC_{StE}}$ scheme and sketch their proofs. The detailed proofs are given in the full version of the paper [9]. Table 1 provides an overview of the different security properties and the necessary assumptions on the building blocks of PBC$_{StE}$.

Let $\Pi_{Sign} := (\mathsf{Setup}_S, \mathsf{KGen}_S, \mathsf{Sign}_S, \mathsf{Vf}_S)$ be a signature scheme with explicit randomness for randomness space $\mathcal{R}$, $F : \{0,1\}^\lambda \times \mathcal{D}_{pw} \to \mathcal{R}$ be a pseudorandom function, and $\Pi_{Enc} := (\mathsf{KGen}_E, \mathsf{Enc}, \mathsf{Dec})$ be a public-key encryption scheme.

$\underline{\mathsf{Setup}(1^\lambda)}$: Output $pp \leftarrow \mathsf{Setup}_S(1^\lambda)$.

$\underline{\mathsf{RegU}(uid, pw) \rightleftharpoons \mathsf{RegS}(uid)}$:
User $\mathcal{U}$: $k \xleftarrow{r} \{0,1\}^\lambda$, $(pk_{Sig}, sk_{Sig}) := \mathsf{KGen}_S(pp; F(k, pw))$, $(pk_{Enc}, sk_{Enc}) \leftarrow \mathsf{KGen}_E(1^\lambda)$.
She sends $(uid, avk := (pk_{Sig}, sk_{Enc}))$ to the server and outputs $ask := (k, pk_{Enc})$.

Server $\mathcal{S}$: upon receiving (uid, avk) outputs avk (we assume that (uid, avk) are stored together on the application level).

$\underline{\mathsf{Sign}(uid, ask, pw, m)}$:
Parse $ask := (k, pk_{Enc})$. Compute $(pk_{Sig}, sk_{Sig}) := \mathsf{KGen}_S(pp; F(k, pw))$,
$\sigma \leftarrow \mathsf{Sign}_S(sk_{Sig}, (uid, m))$, $\tau \leftarrow \mathsf{Enc}(pk_{Enc}, \sigma)$ and output τ.

$\underline{\mathsf{Vf}(uid, avk, m, \tau)}$:
Parse $avk := (pk_{Sig}, sk_{Enc})$. Compute $\sigma \leftarrow \mathsf{Dec}(sk_{Enc}, \tau)$ and output $\mathsf{Vf}_S(pk_{Sig}, (uid, m), \sigma)$

Fig. 3. Our PBC$_{StE}$ scheme.

Theorem 1. *If F is a secure PRF and Π_{Sign} is an EUF-CMA secure signature scheme, then* PBC$_{StE}$ *is strongly unforgeable.*

Proof (Sketch). In the strong unforgeability game, the adversary knows the verification key $avk = (pk_{Sig}, sk_{Enc})$ and password pw of a user uid, but not the user credential $ask = (k, pk_{Enc})$. He does have access to a sign oracle $\mathcal{O}_{Sign}$ that creates tokens for ask, and $\mathcal{A}$ wins if he can create an authentication token τ^* which verifies under avk on a fresh message m^*. In this proof, we can ignore the encryption, as the adversary knows sk_{Enc}, i.e., for all tokens returned by $\mathcal{O}_{Sign}$, he can recover the contained signature derived from $(pk_{Sig}, sk_{Sig}) := \mathsf{KGen}_S(pp; F(k, pw))$. Thus, the task of the adversary boils down to forging a standard signature under the unknown sk_{Sig}. This is infeasible if the signature scheme is unforgeable (EUF-CMA) under the assumption that the PRF-derived secret key is indistinguishable from a randomly chosen one. The latter follows from the pseudorandomness of F which concludes our proof.

Theorem 2. *If F is a random oracle, Π_{Sign} is completely robust and randomness injective, and Π_{Enc} is CCA-secure, then* PBC$_{StE}$ *is online unforgeable.*

Proof (Sketch). Here, the adversary knows the high-entropy credential $ask = (k, pk_{Enc})$ of a user uid, but neither her password pw nor the corresponding verification key $avk = (pk_{Sig}, sk_{Enc})$. Both are accessible through the $\mathcal{O}_{Sign}$ and $\mathcal{O}_{Vf}$ oracle though. We must show that if $\mathcal{A}$ outputs a valid token τ^* for a fresh message m^* for uid, he must have conducted a successful online-attack on the password. In this proof, we first show that, due to the CCA-security of encryption, the $\mathcal{O}_{\text{Sign}}$ oracle does not give the adversary any information about the underlying signature. Then, we argue that the adversary knows the PRF key k and may offline guess passwords to create possible key pairs $(pk'_{\text{Sig}}, sk'_{\text{Sig}}) := \text{KGen}_S(pp; F(k, pw'))$ and forge signatures under sk'_{Sig}. However, in order to create a valid authentication token, he needs to use the *correct* secret key sk_{Sig}. As the correct pk_{Sig} is part of the secret avk and $\mathcal{A}$ never sees any signature σ_i, his only chance of learning which key is correct, is by using the verify oracle $\mathcal{O}_{\text{Vf}}$. Complete robustness of the signature ensures that every interaction with $\mathcal{O}_{\text{Vf}}$ only leaks whether $pk_{\text{Sig}} = pk'_{\text{Sig}}$, allowing a single public-key guess per query. The injectivity of F and the randomness injectivity of Π_{Sign} ensure that this pk'_{Sig} maps to a single password guess, thus the adversary can only guess one password per interaction with $\mathcal{O}_{\text{Vf}}$. This concludes our proof.

Theorem 3. *If F is a random oracle and if Π_{Sign} is EUF-CMA secure and randomness injective, then* PBC_{StE} *is offline unforgeable.*

Proof (Sketch). In the offline unforgeability game, the adversary now knows all keys, i.e., $ask = (k, pk_{\text{Enc}})$ and $avk = (pk_{\text{Sig}}, sk_{\text{Enc}})$ of a user uid. The only secret left is her password pw, and we must show that forging a fresh token m^*, τ^* for uid requires to (at least) offline-attack the password. Note that the adversary is given k here, but not the actual signature key $(pk_{\text{Sig}}, sk_{\text{Sig}}) :=$ $\text{KGen}_S(pp; F(k, pw))$, which still depends on the password. Thus the task of $\mathcal{A}$ again boils down to forging a valid signature under pk_{Sig}. He could either aim at forging the signature directly, i.e., without trying to recover the secret key, or brute-force the password to compute sk_{Sig}, as then creating a signature is trivial. The former is infeasible if the signature is unforgeable, and the latter is bounded by the number of password guesses if the signature is randomness injective (RI) and F a random oracle. RI guarantees that there is only one value $r = F(k, pw)$ such that $(pk_{\text{Sig}}, sk_{\text{Sig}}) = \text{KGen}_S(pp; r)$, i.e., there is only a single password that leads to the correct key. Since the password pw was chosen uniformly at random from $\mathcal{D}_{\text{pw}}$, the adversary needs to query the random oracle F for each password guess, and after q_F queries his success probability is bounded by $q_F / |\mathcal{D}_{\text{pw}}|$.

Theorem 4. *If F is a secure PRF, then* PBC_{StE} *is pw-hiding.*

Proof (Sketch). Recall that in the pw-hiding game the adversary receives a verification key $avk = (pk_{\text{Sig}}, sk_{\text{Enc}})$ that is either derived for pw_0 or pw_1, and his task is to determine the underlying password. In our scheme, the only password-dependent information is $(pk_{\text{Sig}}, sk_{\text{Sig}}) := \text{KGen}_S(pp; F(k, pw_b))$. The adversary knows pk_{Sig}, but not the PRF key k, and has access to the key through the sign oracle for $ask = (k, pk_{\text{Enc}})$. As k is chosen at random from $\{0, 1\}^\lambda$, it immediately follows from the PRF property that the adversary cannot distinguish whether pk_{Sig} was created from $r = F(k, pw_b)$ or r chosen at random from $\mathcal{R}_\lambda$. Since in the latter case, the avk is independent of the password, the pw-hiding property follows. Note that we do not require any property from the signature scheme here, as the pw-hiding concerns confidentiality of the password instead of unforgeability as the other three properties.

Concrete Instantiation of Building Blocks. The requirements for both the PRF and PKE are standard, so we only focus on how randomness injectivity and complete robustness can be achieved by a signature scheme. In Appendix D, we show that the DL-based standard signature schemes DSA [16], Schnorr [21] and BLS [5] all achieve both properties (apart from being (EUF-CMA) unforgeable).

Notable signature schemes which are not completely robust include RSA, GHR and Rabin signatures (see [17]). Nevertheless, Géraud and Naccache [12] show a generic method to transform any signature scheme into a completely robust scheme by appending a hash of the public key to the signature. This transformation also preserves the unforgeability property of the scheme.

5   Related Work

While our work builds upon the novel PBC work by Zhang et al. [26], we also put it in a bigger context of password-based authentication schemes.

Works Without Online Unforgeability. Isler and Küpcü [14] give an overview of existing schemes where a user authenticates with the combination of a password and a password-based credential. As in PBCs, the password-based credential is not directly the user's secret key but only a password-protected version of it. They analyzed several existing works [2–4,13,15] and argued that most are not resistant against server-compromise and proposed a new scheme. The main drawback of all schemes (except DE-PAKE [15], discussed below) is that they do not achieve the same strong online unforgeability as [26] and our work. Roughly, when the password-based credential got compromised, their model only guarantees security when the adversary never sees any authentication token from the honest user, thus excluding phishing attacks from their model. Our work provides online unforgeability without assuming full secrecy of tokens.

DE-PAKE. Device Enhanced PAKE by Jarecki et al. [15] is a variant of password-authenticated key exchange where a user and a server derive a shared key based on the user's knowledge of a strong key (stored on an auxiliary device) and a password. Jarecki et al. show a generic solution which uses the Ford-Kaliski method [11] to strengthen her password into a strong key using a PRF and uses this strong key in an asymmetric PAKE protocol to derive a shared key with the server. Our work uses the same PRF-based method to strengthen a password into a key. Similarly to the work of Jarecki et al., we aim to achieve optimal protection against online and offline attacks, albeit in the context of pure user authentication instead of key exchange. Our PBC_{StE} scheme uses simpler building blocks than the solution presented in [15]. As our scheme allows for non-interactive generation of challenge messages (e.g., by hashing the user id with a current timestamp), we can even achieve the optimal solution of user authentication with one message.

6   Conclusion

We revisited the existing framework of password-based credentials from Zhang et al. [26] and found that an important security property was missing – the resistance to server compromise. We showed that achieving this level of security is impossible in their single-key framework. While the attack is simple, it is of practical relevance considering that data breaches happen frequently. This motivated us to propose a new framework called multi-key password-based credentials which remain secure in the presence of server compromise. We established formal definitions for the optimal security levels and proposed a solution that utilizes generic building blocks and satisfies all desirable security properties.

Given the simplicity of our construction, an immediate question is whether our multi-key setting is somehow weakening the overall security guarantees, when compared with the single-key ZWV version. We argue in Appendix B that the opposite is true by showing how a secure mkPBC can be transformed into a secure skPBC scheme.

A   The ZWY Framework

In order to improve the clarity and the consistency with our framework of mkPBC we made some minor changes to the syntax and security definitions of Zhang et al. [26]. We explain the changes and why this does not affect the technical result. Further, we highlight one of the shortcomings of the ZWY framework: It does not consider the registration of corrupt users.

Changes to the Syntax. We made the following minor changes to the syntax of ZWY [26]: (1) We do not explicitly describe the behaviour of the registration protocol if a party aborts. (2) We do not enforce the registration protocol to keep a registry Reg with uid's but assume this happens on the application level.

Changes to the Security Experiments. The ZWY framework models password compromise through an oracle which reveals honest users' passwords. Since in the weak and strong unforgeability definition, the win condition of the adversary is independent of his knowledge of pw, we did not model this oracle but instead hand the adversary all user passwords directly.

Furthermore, the ZWY framework considers the forgery of a user who has not registered with the server a valid attack, while we removed this condition from the security experiment. We argue that this type of forgery is not a concern as it will be caught on the application level. This change was made to focus on attacks that are relevant to the security of the system.

No Registration Oracle. We note that the ZWY security model [26] has another weakness: it does not allow corrupt users to register, which allows to prove entirely insecure schemes secure (e.g. the server sends his secret key ssk

to the user during registration). We stress that this is primarily an oversight in the security model, and can be easily fixed by granting the adversary such registration access. We do not see any issue in the concrete skPBC scheme proposed in [26] and conjecture that it can be proven secure in this adjusted security model.

B   Comparison of mkPBC and skPBC

Given the simplicity of our construction, an immediate question is whether our multi-key setting is somehow weakening the overall security guarantees, when compared with the single-key ZWV version. We show that the opposite is true by showing how a secure mkPBC can be transformed into a secure skPBC scheme. Our transformation additionally requires symmetric authenticated encryption (AE) scheme, thus can only be seen as a relativized comparison.

Table 1. Overview of the different security properties and the security assumptions needed for the building blocks of our PBC$_{StE}$ scheme. CROB stands for complete robustness and RI is randomness injectivity.

Security Property	Leaked Values			Assumptions		
	User		Server			
	$ask = (k, pk_{Enc})$	pw	$avk = (pk_{Sig}, sk_{Enc})$	F	Signature	Encryption
Strong Unforgeability	✗	✓	✓	Secure PRF	Unf	✗
Online Unforgeability	✓	✗	✗	RO	CROB & RI	CCA
Offline Unforgeability	✓	✗	✓	RO	Unf & RI	✗
Pw-Hiding	✗	✗	✓	Secure PRF	✗	✗

The high-level idea of the transformation is as follows: In order to transform the mkPBC to have only one key, the server outsources storage of the user-specific verification keys avk to the users. In the transformation, the server in the skPBC scheme has a single long-term key ssk which is the secret key k_{AE} of an AE scheme. In the registration phase, the server and user run the mkPBC registration, but instead of letting the server store the obtained avk it returns its encryption $c \leftarrow$ AE.Enc($k_{AE}, (uid, avk)$) to the user. During authentication, the user passes c back to the server by appending it to the authentication token τ which is computed via the mkPBC process. The server can decrypt c to obtain the verification key avk and verify the user's token. For the security of the scheme, it is crucial that the user does not learn avk from c otherwise she could run offline attacks. Furthermore, it is important that users cannot pass the valid ciphertext of a different verification key avk' to the server as this would allow forgeries. Both, confidentiality and integrity, is achieved by using a secure *authenticated* encryption scheme.

In the full version, we prove that his transforms yields an online and weakly unforgeable skPBC, if mkPBC is online and strongly unforgeable and AE is a secure authenticated encryption scheme.

C   Formal Definitions

In this section, we give formal definitions for the correctness of a mkPBC scheme, and for the randomness injectivity of a signature scheme.

Definition 8 (Correctness of mkPBC). *A* mkPBC *scheme is correct, if for all* $pp \leftarrow$ Setup(1^λ), $(uid, pw) \in \mathcal{D}_{\text{uid}} \times \mathcal{D}_{\text{pw}}$, $m \in \mathcal{M}$ *it holds that:* Vf$(uid, avk, m,$ Sign$(uid, ask, pw, m)) = 1$ *where* $(ask; avk) \leftarrow \langle$RegU$(uid, pw),$ RegS$(uid)\rangle$.

Definition 9 (Randomness Injectivity). *A signature scheme* $\Pi :=$ (Setup, KGen, Sign, Vf) *is called* randomness injective *if for* $pp \leftarrow$ Setup(1^λ) *with* $\mathcal{R}_\lambda \in pp$, *it holds that for every PPT* $\mathcal{A}$, *the following probability is negligible in* λ:

$$\Pr[(r, r') \leftarrow \mathcal{A}(pp) : r, r' \in \mathcal{R}_\lambda \wedge r \neq r' \wedge (sk = sk' \vee pk = pk')$$
$$\text{for } (pk, sk) \leftarrow \text{KGen}(pp; r), (pk', sk') \leftarrow \text{KGen}(pp; r')]$$

D   Signatures with Complete Robustness

In this section, we show that DSA [16], Schnorr [21] and BLS [5] signatures achieve complete robustness and randomness injectivity.

Theorem 5. *The DSA, Schnorr and BLS signature scheme all achieve randomness injectivity information-theoretically. DSA and Schnorr are CROB-secure assuming a collision-resistant hash function, and BLS is information-theoretically CROB-secure.*

Proof. For the randomness injectivity, observe that DL-based signature schemes where it holds that $pk = g^{sk}$ for $sk \xleftarrow{r} \mathbb{Z}_q$ achieve randomness injectivity by setting $\mathcal{R}_\lambda = \mathbb{Z}_q$ and $(g^r, r) := $ KGen$(pp; r)$.

Since the complete robustness only considers the verification algorithm we can ignore the key generation and signing algorithms. We argue about complete robustness for each of the signatures individually:

DSA: In DSA, a signature $\sigma := (r, s)$ verifies for m under pk if $F(g^{H(m) \cdot s^{-1}} \cdot pk^{r \cdot s^{-1}}) = r$ for two hash functions F and H. Thus, σ verifies under a second public key pk' only if $F(g^{H(m) \cdot s^{-1}} \cdot pk^{r \cdot s^{-1}}) = F(g^{H(m) \cdot s^{-1}} \cdot (pk')^{r \cdot s^{-1}})$ which happens only with negligible probability if F is collision resistant.

Schnorr: In Schnorr signatures, a signature $\sigma = (r, s)$ verifies under pk for message m if $H(g^s \cdot pk^{-r}, m) = r$ for a hash function H. Thus, σ verifies under a second public key pk' only if $H(g^s \cdot pk^{-r}, m) = H(g^s \cdot (pk')^{-r}, m)$ which happens only with negligible probability if the hash function H is collision resistant.

BLS: In BLS signatures, a signature σ verifies under pk for message m if $e(\sigma, g) = e(H(m), pk)$. Thus, it verifies under a second public key pk' only if $e(H(m), pk) = e(H(m), pk')$. But this means that $pk = pk'$ and the signature only verifies under a single public key $pk = pk'$.

References

1. 2012 Linkedin Breach had 117 Million Emails and Passwords Stolen, Not 6.5M (2016). https://www.trendmicro.com/vinfo/us/security/news/cyber-attacks/2012-linkedin-breach-117-million-emails-and-passwords-stolen-not-6-5m
2. Acar, T., Belenkiy, M., Küpçü, A.: Single password authentication. Comput. Netw. **57**, 2597–2614 (2013)
3. Belenkiy, M., Acar, T., Jerez Morales, H.N., Küpcü, A.: Securing passwords against dictionary attacks. US Patent 9015489B2 (2011)
4. Bicakci, K., Atalay, N.B., Yuceel, M., van Oorschot, P.C.: Exploration and field study of a password manager using icon-based passwords. In: Danezis, G., Dietrich, S., Sako, K. (eds.) FC 2011. LNCS, vol. 7126, pp. 104–118. Springer, Heidelberg (2012). https://doi.org/10.1007/978-3-642-29889-9_9
5. Boneh, D., Lynn, B., Shacham, H.: Short signatures from the weil pairing. In: Boyd, C. (ed.) ASIACRYPT 2001. LNCS, vol. 2248, pp. 514–532. Springer, Heidelberg (2001). https://doi.org/10.1007/3-540-45682-1_30
6. Miyaji, A., Rahman, M.S., Soshi, M.: Hidden credential retrieval without random oracles. In: Chung, Y., Yung, M. (eds.) WISA 2010. LNCS, vol. 6513, pp. 160–174. Springer, Heidelberg (2011). https://doi.org/10.1007/978-3-642-17955-6_12
7. Camenisch, J., Lehmann, A., Neven, G.: Optimal distributed password verification. In: CCS 2015 (2015)
8. Das, P., Hesse, J., Lehmann, A.: DPaSE: distributed password-authenticated symmetric encryption. In: ASIACCS 2022 (2022)
9. Dayanikli, D., Lehmann, A.: Password-based credentials with security against server compromise. Cryptology ePrint Archive (2023)
10. Dobran, B.: 1.6 million PayPal customer details stolen in Major Data Breach (2022). https://phoenixnap.com/blog/paypal-customer-details-stolen
11. Ford, W., Kaliski, B.S.: Server-assisted generation of a strong secret from a password. In: WET ICE 2000 (2000)
12. Géraud, R., Naccache, D., Roşie, R.: Robust encryption, extended. In: Matsui, M. (ed.) CT-RSA 2019. LNCS, vol. 11405, pp. 149–168. Springer, Cham (2019). https://doi.org/10.1007/978-3-030-12612-4_8
13. İşler, D., Küpçü, A.: Distributed single password protocol framework. Cryptology ePrint Archive, Report 2018/976 (2018). https://eprint.iacr.org/2018/976
14. İşler, D., Küpçü, A.: Threshold single password authentication. Cryptology ePrint Archive, Report 2018/977 (2018). https://eprint.iacr.org/2018/977
15. Jarecki, S., Krawczyk, H., Shirvanian, M., Saxena, N.: Device-enhanced password protocols with optimal online-offline protection. In: ASIACCS 2016 (2016)
16. Kerry, C.F., Gallagher, P.D.: Digital signature standard (DSS). FIPS PUB, pp. 186–192 (2013)
17. Koblitz, N., Menezes, A.: Another look at security definitions. Cryptology ePrint Archive, Report 2011/343 (2011). https://eprint.iacr.org/2011/343
18. Lindemann, R., Tiffany, E.: FIDO UAF protocol specification (2017)
19. Reynolds, J., Smith, T., Reese, K., Dickinson, L., Ruoti, S., Seamons, K.: A tale of two studies: the best and worst of YubiKey usability. In: S&P 2018 (2018)
20. Roman, J., Ross, R.: Blizzard entertainment reports breach (2012). https://www.databreachtoday.asia/blizzard-entertainment-reports-breach-a-5034
21. Schnorr, C.P.: Efficient identification and signatures for smart cards. In: Brassard, G. (ed.) CRYPTO 1989. LNCS, vol. 435, pp. 239–252. Springer, New York (1990). https://doi.org/10.1007/0-387-34805-0_22

22. Toubba, K.: Notice of recent security incident (2022). https://blog.lastpass.com/2022/12/notice-of-recent-security-incident/
23. W3C Web Authentication Working Group: Web authentication: An API for accessing public key credentials Level 2 (2021). https://www.w3.org/TR/webauthn/
24. Williams, M.: Inside the Russian hack of Yahoo: how they did it (2017). https://www.csoonline.com/article/3180762/inside-the-russian-hack-of-yahoo-how-they-did-it.html
25. Yubico: Net Yubikey SDK: User's Manual. https://docs.yubico.com/yesdk/users-manual/intro.html
26. Zhang, Z., Wang, Y., Yang, K.: Strong authentication without temper-resistant hardware and application to federated identities. In: NDSS 2020 (2020)

Making an Asymmetric PAKE Quantum-Annoying by Hiding Group Elements

Marcel Tiepelt[1] , Edward Eaton[2(✉)] , and Douglas Stebila[3]

[1] KASTEL, Karlsruhe, Germany
marcel.tiepelt@kit.edu
[2] National Research Council Canada, Ottawa, ON, Canada
edwardweaton@gmail.com
[3] University of Waterloo, Waterloo, ON, Canada
dstebila@uwaterloo.ca

Abstract. The KHAPE-HMQV protocol is a state-of-the-art highly efficient asymmetric password-authenticated key exchange protocol that provides several desirable security properties, but has the drawback of being vulnerable to quantum adversaries due to its reliance on discrete logarithm-based building blocks: solving a single discrete logarithm allows the attacker to perform an offline dictionary attack and recover the password. We show how to modify KHAPE-HMQV to make the protocol *quantum-annoying*: a classical adversary who has the additional ability to solve discrete logarithms can only break the protocol by solving a discrete logarithm for each guess of the password. While not fully resistant to attacks by quantum computers, a quantum-annoying protocol could offer some resistance to quantum adversaries for whom discrete logarithms are relatively expensive. Our modification to the protocol is small: encryption (using an ideal cipher) is added to one message. Our analysis uses the same ideal cipher model assumption as the original analysis of KHAPE, and quantum annoyingness is modelled using an extension of the generic group model which gives a classical adversary a discrete logarithm oracle.

Keywords: password-authenticated key exchange ·
quantum-resistant · quantum-annoying · generic group model

1 Introduction

A wide-spread method for authentication in client-server situations involves a key exchange where the server is authenticated through a public key infrastructure, while the client authenticates themselves with a password by transmitting the password directly over the encrypted channel. This method is suboptimal since the user's password is exposed to the server.

A *password authenticated key exchange* (PAKE) protocol enables two parties to perform a key exchange, authenticated using mutual knowledge of a shared

G. Tsudik et al. (Eds.): ESORICS 2023, LNCS 14344, pp. 168–188, 2024.
https://doi.org/10.1007/978-3-031-50594-2_9

password, without revealing the password to the network or to each other. The setting of PAKEs allows two kinds of attacks: online attacks (the adversary interacting with either party), and offline attacks (the adversary operating locally based on what is has observed from previous online interactions). Password-based protocols are always vulnerable to online dictionary attacks, where the adversary can rule out one password guess with each online interaction with a party. The goal of a PAKE is to ensure that offline dictionary attacks are infeasible, for example because of an intractability assumption. While PAKEs have been known for decades, there was little progress in adoption for many years, but there is renewed interest in adoption of PAKEs via a variety of recent and ongoing standardization efforts [1,2,6,18,19].

This paper focuses on KHAPE [10], a compiler that turns a *key hiding* authenticated key exchange (KH-AKE) and a PAKE into an *asymmetric* PAKE (aPAKE). Asymmetric PAKEs improve upon regular PAKEs by forcing an attacker to perform an exhaustive search on the password even after server compromise, since the value stored by the server cannot be used to impersonate the client. The OPAQUE framework [13] introduced the notion of *strong* asymmetric PAKEs (saPAKE), which further guarantees that no pre-computation can be performed to aid in the exhaustive search for the password in the case of server compromise. This is achieved by combining an oblivious pseudo-random function (OPRF) and a PAKE.

Most PAKEs are based on the hardness of solving the discrete logarithm problem (see [11] for an overview), making them vulnerable to attacks by quantum computers, thus motivating the question of building PAKEs that are quantum-resistant. The obvious answer is to build new PAKEs that rely on post-quantum intractability assumptions, and post-quantum PAKEs are starting to emerge in the literature. These new PAKEs (*e.g.*, see [4]) are based on key encapsulation mechanisms to match the standardized quantum-secure encryption [15]. However, there may be other interim options requiring fewer modifications by augmenting existing protocols.

Quantum-Annoying PAKEs. During the CFRG PAKE standardization process in 2019, it was observed [20] for one of the Diffie–Hellman-based candidates that even if an attacker could solve discrete logarithms, they could not immediately recover the password. Instead, an attacker seemed to have to do a discrete logarithm for each guess of the password even during an offline dictionary attack: this property was named "quantum-annoying". If solving such a problem remains reasonably expensive, then a moderate level of security can still be achieved.

Eaton and Stebila [7] developed a formalization of the quantum-annoying property for PAKEs by considering a classical adversary working in the generic group model who is given the additional power of a discrete logarithm oracle. They showed that the base version of the symmetric PAKE protocol CPace [3] was quantum-annoying in the generic group model. One main characteristic of CPace that lead to it being quantum-annoying is that the password π shared by the client and server is used to derive a generator g_π of the group, and then a Diffie–Hellman key exchange is performed using that generator (g_π^{xy}). But from the perspective of an adversary who only sees Diffie–Hellman public keys (g_π^x and g_π^y), no information is gained about the password π since for each π' there is an x' such that $g_{\pi'}^{x'} = g_\pi^x$.

Our Contributions. Whereas CPace is a symmetric PAKE, the KHAPE-HMQV protocol constructed by the KHAPE compiler [10] is an asymmetric PAKE, so compromise of a server using KHAPE-HMQV does not enable the adversary to impersonate a user without first performing an offline dictionary attack. However, the protocol is not quantum-annoying: after seeing just a single transcript, a single discrete logarithm computation suffices to enable an offline dictionary attack to recover the user's password. We address this vulnerability by presenting the QA-KHAPE protocol, a quantum-annoying variant of KHAPE-HMQV. As shown in Fig. 1, our modifications entail encapsulating an additional key into the server-stored credentials, which is later used by the principals to encrypt their Diffie–Hellman key-pairs prior to exchanging messages. This effectively means that each guess of the password causes the transcript to decrypt (under a symmetric key dependent on the password) to a different pair of Diffie–Hellman public keys, so a new discrete logarithm must be performed each time.

The changes to the protocol require only minimal computational and communication overhead, with the same number of rounds as KHAPE-HMQV and only a single additional ideal cipher ciphertext (increasing the server-client ciphertext from three to four elements). The client-server communication remains unchanged, and the protocol requires two additional ideal cipher computations, one encryption, and one decryption.

We show that QA-KHAPE is quantum-annoying following the methodology of [7]: the adversary is a classical adversary in the generic group model with the addition of a discrete logarithm oracle. In Sect. 3.1, we define a security game in the generic group model tailored to capturing the core quantum annoying property of the QA-KHAPE protocol. In Sect. 4, we apply this to show that QA-KHAPE is secure in a quantum-annoying variant of the standard Bellare–Pointcheval–Rogaway (BPR) security model for asymmetric password authenticated key exchange.

Limitations. Just as in the original security proof of KHAPE by [10], our analysis also relies on the ideal cipher assumption. Care must be taken for an instantiation of the IC, which is discussed in [10, Section 8].

Further, we wish to highlight for the reader that the "quantum annoying" security notion is an intermediate notion below fully quantum-resistant. One limitation of the quantum annoying security notion is that it has a narrow view of quantum capabilities: by using a formalism in the generic group model with a discrete logarithm oracle, we are effectively assuming that the only quantum operation an adversary will do is run Shor's algorithm, which is certainly less than the full power available to a polynomial time quantum computer.

Even just considering security against quantum computers running Shor's algorithm, a protocol "secure" in the quantum-annoying model is still vulnerable to attacks by quantum computers, it is just that the attack scales in the size of the password space. This leads to the question of the cost of computing a discrete logarithm on a quantum computer. While it is impossible to predict the efficiency of quantum computers in the far future, current research suggests that the first generations of quantum computers capable of solving cryptographically relevant discrete logarithm problems will require significant resources in order to do so [8,9,16,17]. These estimates are undoubtedly coarse and may be off by several orders of magnitude, but it is plausible that even for early cryptographically relevant quantum computers, computing a single discrete logarithm will not be cheap, and that computing millions of discrete logarithms to find the password in a quantum-annoying PAKE may be prohibitively expensive.

More recently, a preprint has examined the "multiple discrete logarithm" problem induced by the quantum annoying model [12]. In this work, the authors show that it is possible to (asymptotically) solve m discrete logarithm problems (in a generic group) with a quantum computer more efficiently than m times the cost of a single Shor's instance. In particular, their algorithm solves m discrete logarithms with around $\log m$ times fewer quantum group operations (if $m = \Omega(\log p)$, where p is the size of the group). This comes at the expense of requiring large quantum memory to compute everything simultaneously. Whether this represents a concrete improvement to the ability of an adversary to break quantum annoying security (and if so, how large the grouping m should be) is an interesting open question. Our proofs bound the adversary's success probability in terms of the number of discrete logarithm oracle queries made. If it is a practical improvement to group such queries, this does not affect our proofs, only how the induced bounds translate to real-world estimates of adversary cost.

2 Preliminaries

2.1 Quantum Annoying-ness in the Generic Group Model

In the normal generic group model there is a multiplicative public representation of group elements taken uniformly from $\{0,1\}^\kappa$, and an additive secret representation in $\mathbb{Z}_p$. The public representations have no intrinsic structure, and so any information about the group is obtained through the group operation oracle. Let $\langle g \rangle = \mathbb{G}$ be a generic group of size p with group operation $\circ$. When $g_w \circ g_v$ is queried, for example $(g^v, g^w) \mapsto g^{v+w}$, a table T_{ggm} is used to retrieve the secret representations of g_v and g_w, $v, w \in \mathbb{Z}_p$. Then $v + w \pmod{p}$ is the secret representation of g^{v+w}. If g^{v+w} has already been given a public representation, that is returned. Otherwise, a uniformly random string is sampled from $\{0,1\}^\kappa$, assigned as a new public representation to g^{v+w} in the table T_{ggm}, and provided back to the querier. Similarly, the discrete logarithm oracle $\text{DLOG} : \mathbb{G} \times \mathbb{G} \to \mathbb{Z}_p$ takes as input two group elements and outputs the discrete logarithm. The query $\text{DLOG}(g_v, g_w)$ can be responded to by looking up g_v and g_w in T_{ggm} and returning $w \cdot v^{-1} \pmod{p}$.

The generic group model is a powerful tool, but limited in its ability to reason about whether the adversary's interactions with the discrete logarithm oracle are sufficient to determine $\mathrm{DLOG}(g, g_t)$ for a specific group element g_t. Naturally, if they have made exactly this query, the discrete logarithm is known. But other queries, such as $\mathrm{DLOG}(g, g_t^2)$, are also sufficient to make $\mathrm{DLOG}(g, g_t)$ knowable.

The framework of [7] simulates the generic group model in such a way that such specific statements can be made. Let $G_1, G_2, \ldots G_\mu$ be a collection of (public representations of) group elements whose discrete logarithm (with respect to the group generator g) are of potential interest to the adversary. When we maintain the group, rather than imbuing these group elements with specific secret representations in $\mathbb{Z}_p$, we instead denote each as a formal independent variable $\chi_1, \ldots, \chi_\mu$. Group operations now correspond to addition over a *vector space* of dimension $\mu+1$. For example, in computing $(G_1 \circ G_1) \circ G_2$ we would calculate the secret representation as $2\chi_1 + \chi_2$ and give this a unique public representation in $\{0, 1\}^\kappa$. Thus, secret representations can now be written as a linear combination of the χ_i variables, *i.e.*, $\alpha_0 + \sum_i \alpha_i \chi_i$.

Thinking about how these secret representations interact with the DLOG oracle is how we can start to reason about what discrete logarithms are. Say the adversary queries $\mathrm{DLOG}(A, B)$, and the secret representation of A is $\alpha_0 + \sum \alpha_i \chi_i$ (respectively with β for B). If the adversary is given the response δ (so that $A^\delta = B$), this imposes a constraint on our variables. Specifically, it says that $\delta (\alpha_0 + \sum \alpha_i \chi_i) = \beta_0 + \sum \beta_i \chi_i$, which we can rewrite as

$$\sum_{i=1}^\mu (\delta \alpha_i - \beta_i) \chi_i = \beta_0 - \delta \alpha_0. \tag{1}$$

This linear constraint lets us define an equivalence relation: if two secret representations are the same 'modulo' the linear constraints imposed by responses to DLOG, they should have the same public representation. Consequently, if, modulo these constraints, a secret representation χ_i is equivalent to some $a \in \mathbb{Z}_p$, then $\mathrm{DLOG}(g, G_i)$ has taken on a definite value a, whether or not it was actually queried. Otherwise, it can still take on any possible value.

By taking the coefficients of the χ_i variables in Eq. 1 we can construct a matrix D and a vector $\vec{r}$ (we write vectors as column vectors), so that the set of constraints is easily summarized as $D\vec{\chi} = \vec{r}$. Similarly, a secret representation $a_0 + \sum a_i \chi_i$ can be written as the pair $(a_0, \vec{a})$. In more detail, the equivalence relation can be defined as follows:

Definition 1. *For group elements g_a, g_b with secret representation $(a_0, \vec{a})$ and $(b_0, \vec{b})$, we say that g_a is $(D, \vec{r})$-equivalent to g_b if there exists an $\vec{\omega} \in \mathbb{Z}_p^{q_D}$ such that $\vec{\omega}^T D = \vec{a}^T - \vec{b}^T$ and $\vec{\omega}^T \vec{r} = b_0 - a_0$.*

Note that this is indeed an equivalence relation (reflexivity is proven by taking $\vec{\omega} = \vec{0}$, symmetry is proven by taking $-\vec{\omega}$, and transitivity is proven by taking $\vec{\omega}_1 + \vec{\omega}_2$). The reason that this definition gives us what we want is that when it is satisfied, we have that $b_0 - a_0 = \vec{\omega}^T \vec{r} = \vec{\omega}^T D\vec{\chi} = (\vec{a}^T - \vec{b}^T)\vec{\chi} = \vec{a}^T \vec{\chi} - \vec{b}^T \vec{\chi}$, telling us that $a_0 + \sum a_i \chi_i = b_0 + \sum b_i \chi_i$, as we expect. We can now describe how the $\mathbb{G}$ and the DLOG oracle are simulated in full detail. Note that the simulation is not *efficient* [7, Sec. 4], since the simulation requires to search through all previous queries to check if a linear relationship exists. However, the purpose of the framework is to give an information-theoretic bound (in the generic group model) relative to the number of discrete logarithm queries to define a specific discrete logarithm, thus the exact efficiency is not relevant.

$\mathrm{DLOG}(g_V, g_W)$: If g_V or g_W do not exist in T_{ggm}, then abort. Otherwise, let $(v_0, \vec{v}), (w_0, \vec{w})$ be secret representations of g_V, g_W respectively. Sample a random vector $\vec{s}$ such that $D\vec{s} = r$ and compute $\delta = (w_0 + \langle \vec{w}, \vec{s} \rangle)/(v_0 + \langle \vec{v}, \vec{s} \rangle)$. Add the row $\delta \vec{v}^T - \vec{w}^T$ to D, and value $w_0 - \delta v_0$ to vector $\vec{r}$. Then δ is the discrete logarithm that is returned. This corresponds to [7, Alg. 2].

$\circ(g_V, g_W)$: If g_V or g_W do not exist in T_{ggm}, then abort. Otherwise, for the secret representations $(v_0, \vec{v}), (w_0, \vec{w})$, let $(z_0, \vec{z}) = (v_0 + w_0, \vec{v} + \vec{w})$. If z appears in T_{ggm}, return the corresponding public representation. Otherwise, check if there exists an entry $(f_0, \vec{f})$ of T_{ggm} that is $(D, \vec{r})$-equivalent to $(z_0, \vec{z})$. If so, return the public representation of that entry. If no such $(D, \vec{r})$-equivalent entry exists, sample a new public representation, add the entry $T_{\mathrm{ggm}}[g_Z] = (z_0, \vec{z})$ and return g_Z. This corresponds to [7, Alg. 5].

With this setup, we can prove Lemma 1, which is a generalization of [7, Lemma 1] and an instantiation of which is used in a game hop in Sect. 3.2.

Lemma 1 (Unique Solutions). *Let g_a and g_b be public representations of group elements, with corresponding secret representations $(a_0, \vec{a}), (b_0, \vec{b})$. Let $(D, \vec{r})$ be the current set of constraints on discrete logarithms. Then the discrete logarithm of g_b with respect to g_a is defined if and only if $[\vec{b}^T | b_0]$ is in the rowspace of the matrix $\begin{bmatrix} -D & \vec{r} \\ \hline \vec{a}^T & a_0 \end{bmatrix}$.*

Proof. The discrete logarithm is defined if and only if there exists an α such that g_a^α is $(D, \vec{r})$-equivalent to g_b. By definition, this is the same as the existence of $\alpha, \vec{\omega}$ such that $\vec{\omega}^T D = \alpha \vec{a}^T - \vec{b}^T$, and $\vec{\omega}^T \vec{r} = b_0 - \alpha a_0$. We can rewrite this relation as $\left[\vec{b}^T \mid b_0 \right] = \left[-\vec{\omega}^T D + \alpha \vec{a}^T \mid \vec{\omega}^T \vec{r} + \alpha a_0 \right] = \left[\begin{smallmatrix} \vec{\omega} \\ \alpha \end{smallmatrix} \right]^T \begin{bmatrix} -D & \vec{r} \\ \hline \vec{a}^T & a_0 \end{bmatrix}$.

This establishes that if the discrete logarithm is defined, $[\vec{b} \mid b_0]$ is indeed in the rowspace, and if it is in the rowspace that the discrete logarithm is defined (and equal to the α value that is the scalar for the 'a' row). □

Corollary 1. *Let g_b be the public representation of a group element and $(b_0, \vec{b})$ the corresponding secret representation. Let g be the generator of the group, which has secret representation $(1, \vec{0})$. Then the discrete logarithm of g_b with respect to g is defined if and only if $\vec{b}$ is in the row span of D.*

Proof. We apply Lemma 1 with $\vec{a} = \vec{0}$. Since the zero vector cannot affect the row span, we can conclude that $\vec{b}^T$ must be in the row span of D.

For the other direction we know that there exists some $\vec{\omega}$ such that $\vec{\omega}^T D = \vec{b}^T$. Then we claim that the discrete logarithm between g and g_b is $b_0 + \vec{\omega}^T \vec{r}$. This is because we want $(b_0 + \vec{\omega}^T \vec{r}, \vec{0})$ to be $(D, \vec{r})$-equivalent to g_b, and indeed we can see that $-\vec{\omega}$ satisfies $-\vec{\omega}^T D = -\vec{b}^T$ and $-\vec{\omega}^T \vec{r} = b_0 - (b_0 + \vec{\omega}^T \vec{r})$ as desired. □

2.2   Security Model for Asymmetric PAKE

The BPR00 model [5] for security of an asymmetric password-authenticated key exchange protocol is defined by the interaction of a set of instances Π_P^i of principals P, which are either a client C or server S, and i denotes the i-th such instance. Each principal takes as input a long-lived (LL) secret. The client's LL secret is a password π; the server's secrets are the credentials $creds[C]$ that are established during a *Registration* phase. The model further defines a set of oracles that correspond to an adversary's interaction with principals that run the protocol in question. The adversary may receive a passive transcript (EXECUTE queries), or actively engage (SEND queries) in the communication. They may further request the session key (REVEAL queries) or corrupt instances (CORRUPT queries) which effectively returns the principal's long-lived keys (weak corruption). The security is defined by the adversary's probability to decide if they received a session key or a random string after submitting a TEST query to a *fresh* instance. In the setting of quantum-annoying-ness, *fresh* means that neither the instance nor any partnered instance may be corrupted. A challenge bit that is sampled uniformly random before any interaction takes place decides which of the two (*i.e.*, real-or-random) is the case. In the generic group model, the adversary additionally gets access to the group operation and discrete logarithm oracle (cf. Sect. 2.1). A protocol is quantum-annoying in the BPR00 model, if the adversary's advantage to output the challenge bit is bounded by the number of SEND queries (q_{SEND}) and discrete logarithm queries (q_{DLOG}),

$$\text{Adv}_{\text{PROTOCOL}}^{\text{QA-BPR}}(\mathcal{A}) = \left| \Pr\left[\mathcal{A} \text{ guesses challenge bit}\right] - \frac{1}{2} \right| \leq \frac{q_{\text{SEND}} + q_{\text{DLOG}}}{N} + \epsilon, \quad (2)$$

with a password space of size N and ϵ negligible in the security parameter κ.

2.3   KHAPE-HMQV

The KHAPE compiler [10] transforms a key-hiding authenticated key exchange, a PAKE, a random oracle, and an ideal cipher into an asymmetric PAKE which provides key establishment with key integrity and confirmation, mutual authentication and forward secrecy. A highly efficient instantiation [10, Fig. 14] uses the HMQV [14] protocol, the security of which is based on the computational Diffie–Hellman problem.

KHAPE is split into a *registration* and an *aPAKE* phase. During registration the server generates the KH-AKE key-pairs $(a, A := g^a)$, $(b, B := g^b)$, partially encrypts them using the password as a key, $e \leftarrow \text{IC}.E(\pi, a, B)$, and stores the ciphertext along with (A, b). All other values are discarded. In the *aPAKE* phase the server generates a key-pair (y, Y) and sends (Y, e) to the client. The client decrypts e using their password and generates a key pair (x, X). A Diffie–Hellman session is computed from (a, x, B, Y) which is used to derive a key-confirmation value τ, and later the session key. The key confirmation is sent along with the value X to the server, who computes the equivalent Diffie–Hellman session from (b, y, A, X), verifies the key confirmation, and either

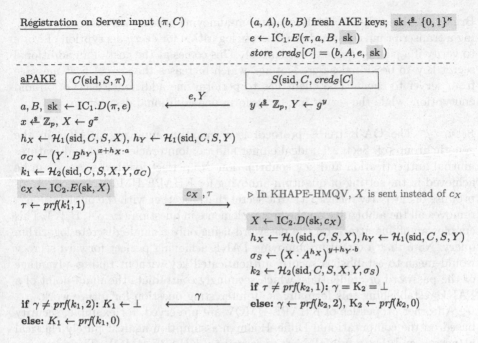

Fig. 1. QA-KHAPE: quantum-annoying variant of KHAPE-HMQV [10, Fig 14], with our changes compared to KHAPE-HMQV highlighted.

computes a session key and a new key confirmation (which is send to the client), or sets both to $\perp$. The client checks the key confirmation and computes the session key, or sets it to $\perp$.

In the quantum-annoying setting, KHAPE-HMQV is susceptible to an offline attack on the password using a single discrete logarithm query. Given a transcript (e, Y, X, τ) an adversary can determine a list of possible values for KH-AKE key-pairs: each password guess π_i gives a pair of candidate values $(a_i, B_i) \leftarrow \mathrm{IC}.D(\pi_i, e)$. Additionally, they can query the discrete logarithm oracle once on the value X, receiving x. Then for each password guess (*i.e.*, for each a_i, B_i), they can verify if the Diffie–Hellman completion results in the key-confirmation value τ from the transcript, effectively providing an offline method to check passwords.

2.4 Quantum-Annoying KHAPE-HMQV

Our QA-KHAPE protocol, presented in Fig. 1, is a quantum-annoying aPAKE. The construction is based on KHAPE-HMQV and requires only minimal changes, which are highlighted in the figure. During the *registration* phase the server generates an additional secret key sk which is then encrypted using the π and stored as part of the credentials. Correspondingly, during the *aPAKE* phase the client decrypts e obtaining this key sk, which they use to encrypt the ephemeral value X, resulting in the ciphertext c, which is then sent to the server.

Briefly speaking, QA-KHAPE is quantum-annoying because an adversary receiving a transcript must now solve a discrete logarithm for *every* decryption of c or e to verify if a password guess was correct. This comes at the cost of an additional secret key to be stored as credentials, which increases the size of first message from server to client. The client has to perform one additional decryption and encryption, while the server has to perform one additional decryption.

Security. The QA-KHAPE protocol is a quantum-annoying aPAKE in the generic group (cf. Sect. 2.1), ideal cipher and random oracle model and features mutual authentication and key confirmation. No perfect forward secrecy can be achieved in the setting of quantum-annoying for KHAPE-HMQV, because compromise of any party releases a static secret that, together with the public value e, removes all the ambiguity on the group elements in question (*i.e.*, A, B, X). This enables an offline attack on the password using only a single discrete logarithm query. Note that a quantum-annoying PAKE achieving perfect forward secrecy would mean to establish a secure, authenticated key without taking advantage of the password or credentials, which seemingly contradicts the main point of a PAKE; establishing this formally is an interesting question for future work.

All other properties of KHAPE-HMQV are preserved, for example, security based on the computational Diffie–Hellman assumption against purely classical attackers, and thus a full fall back to security of KHAPE-HMQV. The quantum-annoying security is summarized in our main contribution, Theorem 1.

Theorem 1. *Let $\mathbb{G}$ be a cyclic group of size p, $\mathcal{H}_1, \mathcal{H}_2$ be random oracles and IC_1, IC_2 ideal ciphers with ciphertext space $\{0,1\}^{n_1}$, $\{0,1\}^{n_2}$ respectively. Let $q_{\text{SEND}}, q_{\text{EXEC}}, q_{\mathcal{H}_i}, q_{IC_i}, q_o, q_{\text{DLOG}}$ be the number of queries to the QA-BPR oracles, and let ϵ_{prf} an adversary's chance to distinguish prf from a random function. Let N be the size of the password space for π. Then the advantage of an adversary to win the QA-BPR game for the QA-KHAPE protocol in Fig. 1 is bounded by*

$$Adv_{QA\text{-}BPR}^{QA\text{-}KHAPE} \leq \frac{q_{\text{DLOG}} + q_{\text{SEND}}}{N} + \epsilon \tag{3}$$

$$\epsilon := \frac{q_{\text{EXEC}} + q_{\text{SEND}}}{\epsilon_{prf}^{-1}} + \frac{(q_{IC_1} + q_{IC_2} + q_o)^2 + (q_{\text{DLOG}}q_o^2)}{p} + \frac{q_{\text{EXEC}}}{2^{n_1}} + \frac{q_{\text{EXEC}} + q_{\text{SEND}}}{2^{n_2}}$$

$$+ \frac{q_{\text{SEND}} \cdot (q_o + 1)}{p} + \frac{(2q_{IC_1} + q_{IC_2})}{p} + \frac{(q_{IC_1})}{2^\kappa} + \frac{(2q_{IC_1}^2 + q_{IC_2}^2)}{p} + \frac{(q_{IC_1}^2)}{2^\kappa} + \frac{q_{\mathcal{H}_2}}{p}$$

We prove Theorem 1 in two steps: first, in Sect. 3.1, we introduce the KHAPE$_{\text{CORE}}$-game that captures the quantum-annoying property of QA-KHAPE in the generic group model. Briefly speaking, the game models the aPAKE without key-confirmation values and is defined such that any adversary can only win if they query the *correct* Diffie–Hellman completion to the random oracle. This allows us to quantify the number of discrete logarithm queries required, and to prove that every password guess requires either an online interaction, or a respective discrete logarithm query. Formally, this is captured in

Theorem 2 which we prove in Sect. 3.2. Second, we reduce the QA-BPR-security of the QA-KHAPE protocol to the $\text{KHAPE}_{\text{CORE}}$-game, which is represented by Theorem 1 and which we prove in Sect. 4. Together, these yield the proof of the quantum-annoying property.

3   Generic Group Security: $\text{KHAPE}_{\text{CORE}}$

We define a game $\text{KHAPE}_{\text{CORE}}$ that captures the quantum annoying property of the protocol in Fig. 1, namely the indistinguishability of the keys k_1, k_2 from random, which translates the approach of [7, Sec 3] into the setting of an aPAKE.

3.1   Security Game

The game is defined over a set $[L]$ registrants; each $l \in [L]$ is associated with static, secret variables $\pi_l, \text{sk}_l, a_l, B_l$ and a static, public variable e_l. The variables are set on initialization of the $\text{KHAPE}_{\text{CORE}}$-game via the REGISTRATION oracle, along with uniformly random sampled challenge bit s. Additionally, each registrant l is associated with a counter ctr_l initialized to 0 corresponding to the interaction with the lth set of static variables. Each interaction is called an instance. The adversary may interact with an arbitrary number of registrants and instances through a set of oracles, eventually allowing the adversary to obtain the keys k_1, k_2. The challenge bit determines if these keys are real (if $s = 0$), in which case they are computed from Diffie-Hellman session, or random (if $s = 1$).

Interface. The oracles take as input a value l matching a set of static variables which are used by the game to respond to a query. Ephemeral variables for an instance (l, ctr_l) are stored for consistent use by the other oracles. The PASSIVE-EXEC oracle (cf. Algorithm 2) corresponds to a passive execution of the protocol in Fig. 1, excluding the key confirmation values. The ACTIVE_C or ACTIVE_S oracles (cf. Algorithms 4 and 5), correspond to interacting with, or impersonating, either party in the QA-KHAPE protocol, and thus at most one of the two may be queried for each instance. The ACTIVE oracles compute, depending on the value of the challenge bit s, either a key value $k_{l,ctr_l,i}$ from the input and the static variables or output a uniformly random string. The GETSTATIC oracle mimics the corruption of parties, which causes the game to reprogram the outputs of the ACTIVE oracles into the respective positions before it returns the secret static variables. Finally, the adversary is given access to the random oracles $\mathcal{H}_1, \mathcal{H}_2$, the block-ciphers IC_1, IC_2 modeled by ideal ciphers and access to an interface of the generic group model.

Output. The $\text{KHAPE}_{\text{CORE}}$-game outputs 1 if the adversary's output matches the challenge bit s or if they if they query $\mathcal{H}_2(l, m, X, Y, \sigma_{l,C})$ (respectively $\mathcal{H}_2(l, m, X, Y, \sigma_{l,S})$) after submitting a query $\text{ACTIVE}_C(l, e, Y)$ (respectively $\text{ACTIVE}_S(l, c)$), but before querying GETSTATIC(l) on the instance. The adversary is then said to *win* the game. The restriction on the GETSTATIC oracle mimics the fact that forward secrecy cannot be achieved in the quantum annoying model. The conditions under which the game outputs 1 are analogous to the winning conditions of [7, Sec. 3.1].

Algorithm 1 REGISTRATION(l)

1: $\pi_l \xleftarrow{\$} [N]$, $\mathrm{sk}_l \xleftarrow{\$} \{0,1\}^\kappa$
2: $a_l, b_l \xleftarrow{\$} \mathbb{Z}_p$
3: $B_l \leftarrow g^{b_l}$, $A_l \leftarrow g^{a_l}$
4: $e_l \leftarrow \mathrm{IC}_1.E(\pi_l, a_l, B_l, \mathrm{sk}_l)$
5: Store $\pi_l, \mathrm{sk}_l, e_l, A_l, b_l$

Algorithm 2 PASSIVEEXEC(l)

Require: $l \leq L$
1: Get stored $\pi_l, \mathrm{sk}_l, e_l, A_l, b_l$
2: Increment ctr_l
3: $x_{l,ctr_l}, y_{l,ctr_l} \xleftarrow{\$} \mathbb{Z}_p$
4: $X_{l,ctr_l} \leftarrow g^{x_{l,ctr_l}}$, $Y_{l,ctr_l} \leftarrow g^{y_{l,ctr_l}}$
5: $c_{l,ctr_l} \leftarrow \mathrm{IC}_2.E(\pi_l, X_{l,ctr_l})$
6: Store $Y_{l,ctr_l}, ctxt_{l,ctr_l}$
7: **return** $e_l, Y_{l,ctr_l}, c_{l,ctr_l}$

Algorithm 3 GETSTATIC(l)

Require: $l \leq L$
1: Mark l corrupted; Get stored π_l, sk_l
2: **for** $m = 0, \ldots, ctr_l$ **do**
3:     **for** $k_{l,m}, c_{l,m} \leftarrow$ ACTIVE$_C(l, e, Y)$
4:     $a, B, \mathrm{sk} \leftarrow \mathrm{IC}_1.D(\pi_l, e)$
5:     $h_X = \mathcal{H}_1(l, m, X_{l,m})$, $h_Y = \mathcal{H}_1(l, m, Y)$
6:     $\sigma_C \leftarrow (Y \circ B^{h_Y})^{x_{l,m} + h_X \cdot a}$
7:     $\mathcal{H}_2(l, m, X_{l,m}, Y, \sigma_C) := k_{l,m,1}$
8:     **for** $k_{l,2} \leftarrow$ ACTIVE$_S(l, c)$
9:     Get stored $Y_{l,m}$
10:     $X \leftarrow \mathrm{IC}_2.D(\mathrm{sk}_l, c)$
11:     $h_X = \mathcal{H}_1(l, m, X)$, $h_Y = \mathcal{H}_1(l, m, Y_{l,m})$
12:     $\sigma_S \leftarrow (X \circ A_{l,m}^{h_X})^{y_{l,m} + h_Y \cdot b_{l,m}}$
13:     $\mathcal{H}_2(l, m, X, Y_{l,m}, \sigma_S) := k_{l,m,2}$
14: **return** (π_l, sk_l)

Theorem 2 (Security of KHAPE$_{\mathrm{CORE}}$). *Let q_{AE_C}, q_{AE_S} be the number of queries to the* ACTIVE *and q_{PE} the number of queries to the* PASSIVEEXEC *oracle. Let $q_{IC_i}, q_{\mathcal{H}_i}, q_\circ, q_{\mathrm{DLOG}}$ be the number of queries to the ideal cipher, random oracle, group operation and discrete logarithm oracles respectively. Then $\mathcal{A}$'s probability to win the KHAPE$_{\mathrm{CORE}}$-game is bounded by*

$$\Pr\left[KHAPE_{CORE} \Rightarrow 1\right] \leq \frac{1}{2} + \frac{q_{\mathrm{AE}_C} + q_{\mathrm{AE}_S} + q_{\mathrm{DLOG}}}{N} + \epsilon_{CORE} \tag{4}$$

$$\epsilon_{CORE} := \overbrace{\frac{(q_{IC_1} + q_{IC_2} + q_\circ)^2 + (q_{\mathrm{DLOG}} q_\circ^2)}{p}}^{// \, G_0 \rightsquigarrow G_1} + \overbrace{\frac{(q_{\mathrm{AE}_C} + q_{\mathrm{AE}_S}) \cdot (q_\circ + 1)}{p}}^{// \, G_3 \rightsquigarrow G_4}$$

$$+ \underbrace{\frac{q_{\mathrm{PE}}}{2^{n_1}} + \frac{q_{\mathrm{PE}} + q_{\mathrm{AE}}}{2^{n_2}}}_{// \, G_2 \rightsquigarrow G_3} + \underbrace{\frac{(2q_{IC_1} + q_{IC_2})}{p} + \frac{(q_{IC_1})}{2^\kappa} + \frac{(2q_{IC_1}^2 + q_{IC_2}^2)}{p} + \frac{(q_{IC_1}^2)}{2^\kappa}}_{// \, G_1 \rightsquigarrow G_2} . \tag{5}$$

3.2 Proof of Theorem 2

The proof of Theorem 2 shows, informally, that the adversary's chance to win the KHAPE$_{\mathrm{CORE}}$-game is limited by their ability to query the DLOG oracle on the *correct* group element, or any of the ACTIVE oracles on a ciphertext encoding a group element the discrete logarithm of which is known to them. In the KHAPE$_{\text{CORE}}$-game, the group elements in question are computed as

Algorithm 4 ACTIVE$_C(l, e, Y)$	**Algorithm 5** ACTIVE$_S(l, c)$
Require: $l \le L$	**Require:** $l \le L$
1: Increment ctr_l; Get stored π_l	1: Increment ctr_l; Get stored sk_l
2: $a, B, \text{sk} \leftarrow \text{IC}_1.D(\pi_l, e)$	2: **if** challenge $s = 0$ or l corrupted :
3: $x_{l,ctr_l} \xleftarrow{\$} \mathbb{Z}_p$, $X_{l,ctr_l} \leftarrow g^{x_{l,ctr_l}}$	3: $\quad X \leftarrow \text{IC}_2.D(\text{sk}_l, c)$
4: $c_{l,ctr_l} \leftarrow \text{IC}_2.E(\text{sk}, X_{l,ctr_l})$	4: $\quad h_X = \mathcal{H}_1(l, ctr_l, X)$, $h_Y =$
5: **if** challenge $s = 0$ or l corrupted :	$\quad \mathcal{H}_1(l, ctr_l, Y_{l,ctr_l})$
6: $\quad h_X = \mathcal{H}_1(l, ctr_l, X_{l,ctr_l})$, $h_Y =$	5: $\quad \sigma_C \leftarrow (X \circ A_l^{h_X})^{y_{l,ctr_l} + h_Y \cdot b_{l,ctr_l}}$
$\quad \mathcal{H}_1(l, ctr_l, Y)$	6: $\quad k_{l,ctr_l,2} = \mathcal{H}_2(l, ctr_l, X, Y_{l,ctr_l}, \sigma_{l,C})$
7: $\quad \sigma_C \leftarrow (Y \circ B^{h_Y})^{x_{l,ctr_l} + h_X \cdot a}$	7: **else** $k_{l,ctr_l,2} \leftarrow \{0,1\}^n$
8: $\quad k_{l,ctr_l,1} = \mathcal{H}_2(l, ctr_l, X_{l,ctr_l}, Y, \sigma_C)$	8: **return** $k_{l,ctr_l,2}$
9: **else** $k_{l,ctr_l,1} \leftarrow \{0,1\}^n$	
10: **return** $k_{l,ctr_l,1}, c_{l,ctr_l}$	

$$\sigma_C = \left(Y \cdot B^{h_Y}\right)^{x + h_X \cdot a} = \left(X \cdot A^{h_X}\right)^{y + h_Y \cdot b} = \sigma_S, \tag{6}$$

where computing σ_C, σ_S depends on either the knowledge of $\text{DLOG}(g, B)$ or $\text{DLOG}(g, X)$. The framework presented in Sect. 2.1, allows us to quantify if these element are knowable based on the number of discrete logarithm queries. This is possible, because the relevant group elements X, B are encrypted under the ideal cipher. On a decryption query the ideal cipher can return a public representations that does not admit a relation to a previously received group element known by the adversary. To learn any such relation, the adversary then has to query the DLOG oracle. Specifically, the *relevant* group elements $\{B_{l,i}, X_{l,i}\}_{i \in [N]}$ correspond to decryptions of (e, c) using a password guess π_i and sk_i as keys respectively. In the KHAPE$_{\text{CORE}}$-game, the *correct* pair $B_{l,i}, X_{l,i}$ is chosen during the *Registration* phase and in the ACTIVE oracles. Due to the values being encrypted by the ideal ciphers, the simulation does not need to commit to any actual pair B_i, X_i.

We prove this by presenting a sequence of game hops where the initial game G_0 is the KHAPE$_{\text{CORE}}$-game as defined in Sect. 3.1, and G_4 is modified such that the keys k_1, k_2 are chosen uniformly random for every instance, and where the discrete logarithm of g and the group elements B, X remain undefined unless sufficiently constrained by queries to the DLOG and ACTIVE oracles. They are undefined because the ciphertexts (e, c) are indistinguishable from random strings, and the key pair (π, sk) is no longer defined from the PASSIVEEXEC or ACTIVE oracles. That means that the *correct* values for (B, X) may correspond to any of the N possible pairs. As long as there is a degree of freedom left for these representations, the discrete logarithm relative to g is also not defined, and the random oracle cannot be queried on the respective Diffie–Hellman completion. These are only defined either if an instance is corrupted, or if sufficiently many discrete logarithms have been queried, allowing to quantify the adversary's probability to win relative to the number of DLOG queries.

G_0 *(KHAPE$_{CORE}$-game).* This is the KHAPE$_{CORE}$ as described in Sect. 3.1.

G_1 *(GGM).* We modify the responses to the group operation $\circ$ and DLOG oracle by simulating the generic group as described in Sect. 2.1. The generator initially given to the adversary is $g_1 = g$, which corresponds to the secret representation 1. The secret representation of the neutral element is 0. Recall that the password space is of size N. The secret variables are represented as a set $\{\chi_{l,i}, X_{l,i}\}_{i \in [N]}$ corresponding to the pairs $B_{l,i}, X_{l,i}$ that can be obtained when querying the ideal ciphers on possible values for π_l or sk_l. The ideal cipher IC_i is maintained via a table T_{IC_i}. On query $\mathrm{IC}_1.D(\pi, e)$, if $T_{\mathrm{IC}_1}[\pi, e]$ is defined, return $T_{\mathrm{IC}_1}[\pi, e]$. Otherwise, sample a random index $j \overset{\$}{\leftarrow} [N]$ for the secret representation and a public representation $g_V \overset{\$}{\leftarrow} \{0,1\}^n$, both of which are added the table $T_{\mathrm{ggm}}[\chi_{i,j}] := g_V$; Then return g_V. The simulation of IC_2 is analog.

The modification changes the distribution of the group elements: public representations returned from the ideal ciphers (on new inputs) in the simulation are unique, whereas the adversary would expect a collision after $\sqrt{p}$ new queries. Additionally, the adversary would expect to see collisions between random public representations, and the elements returned from (sufficiently many) group operations. This happens with probability $(q_{\mathrm{IC}_1} + q_{\mathrm{IC}_2} + q_\circ)^2/p$.

Further, a group element may be assigned two distinct public representations, if first computed from group operations and then returned from an IC query (or vice versa). For example, if the public representation g_x was returned from an IC query, and the representation $g_{\bar{x}} = g^x$ was assigned from group operations, then the adversary may detect the modification by computing $\mathrm{DLOG}(g_1, g_x) = x$. The probability that this happens for group elements randomly assigned by the ideal cipher and for all DLOG queries is $q_{\mathrm{DLOG}} q_\circ^2 / p$. Overall, the adversary can distinguish the two games with probability at most $((q_{\mathrm{IC}_1} + q_{\mathrm{IC}_2} + q_\circ)^2 + q_{\mathrm{DLOG}} q_\circ^2)/p$.

G_2 *(Ideal Ciphers Output).* We change the ideal ciphers to output unique, random values when queried on a new input. On query $\mathrm{IC}_1.D(\pi, e)$, if $T_{\mathrm{IC}_1}[\pi, e]$ is not defined, the ideal cipher IC_1 samples key pairs $a, b \overset{\$}{\leftarrow} \mathbb{Z}_p$ and $\mathrm{sk} \leftarrow \{0,1\}^\kappa$, generates public keys $A = g^a$, $B = g^b$ and a key $\mathrm{sk} \leftarrow \{0,1\}^\kappa$, and programs $T_{\mathrm{IC}_1}[\pi, e] := a, B, \mathrm{sk}$. In the case of a collision, *i.e.*, if (a, B, sk) has been assigned to a value in the map $T_{\mathrm{IC}_1}[\pi, \cdot]$ for any value $\cdot$, G_2 aborts. Since (a, B, sk) are independent random variables, the probability for an abort is bounded by $2q_{\mathrm{IC}_1}/p + q_{\mathrm{IC}_1}/2^\kappa$, neglecting the a deduction for a simultaneous collision of all variables. Since the values a, B, sk are *unique*, two different queries will never output the same values, whereas the adversary would eventually expect a collision in G_1. The same argument applies to IC_2. In total, the divergence is bounded by $(2q_{\mathrm{IC}_1} + q_{\mathrm{IC}_2})/p + (q_{\mathrm{IC}_1})/2^\kappa + (2q_{\mathrm{IC}_1}^2 + q_{\mathrm{IC}_2}^2)/p + (q_{\mathrm{IC}_1}^2)/2^\kappa$.

G_3 *(Random Ciphertexts).* We modify the game to not sample any keys π and sk and to output random strings $e \overset{\$}{\leftarrow} \{0,1\}^{n_1}$, $c \overset{\$}{\leftarrow} \{0,1\}^{n_2}$ in the PASSIVE-EXEC and ACTIVE$_C$ oracles, which removes the game's commitment to any value stored in (e, c). Analogous to the modification in G_2, the game aborts if the values were previously assigned. At the same time the GETSTATIC oracle is changed to reflect the modification: the simulation first decrypts the ciphertext using freshly sampled keys π and sk. The DLOG oracle provides the values necessary to compute the Diffie–Hellman session such that the output of the ACTIVE oracles can be programmed into the correct position of the ideal cipher. For a detailed algorithm of the modified (and "final") PASSIVEEXEC and GETSTATIC oracle we refer the reader to Appendix A1. The distribution of (e, c) returned by PASSIVEEXEC and ACTIVE$_C$ is the same as in G_2 unless it aborts. Since (e, c) are sampled uniformly random from the ciphertext space, the probability for this to happen is bounded by $q_{\text{PE}}/2^{n_1} + (q_{\text{PE}} + q_{\text{AE}_C})/2^{n_2}$.

G_4 *(Embed Random Keys).* The ACTIVE oracles are modified to always return random strings $k \xleftarrow{\$} \{0,1\}^\kappa$ for non-corrupted instances. To notice this change, the adversary must query $\mathcal{H}_2(\mathit{ctr}, X, Y, \sigma_i)$, where the Diffie–Hellman completion σ_i depends on either the knowledge of $\text{DLOG}(g, X)$ and B, or the knowledge of $\text{DLOG}(g, B)$ and X, both of which are not defined by the game unless GETSTATIC has been queried, in which case the adversary cannot win the game anymore.

The probability that $\text{DLOG}(g, X)$ or $\text{DLOG}(g, B)$ are knowable to the adversary is bounded by Corollary 1, which tells us that the discrete logarithms are defined if an only if $\vec{b}, \vec{x}$ are in the row span of D. Both, $\vec{b}$ and $\vec{x}$, are basis vectors with a 1 at the position of the random index associated with the respective secret variable. The number of basis vectors that can appear in the row span are upper bounded by the rank of the matrix D, which is increased by 1 for each DLOG query. Therefore, the probability that the adversary can force the definition for any one value out of N many of these is bounded by q_{DLOG}/N.

Remark: Only public representations returned from the ideal ciphers, and possibly group elements that come from group operation applied to these group elements, provide *useful* input to the DLOG oracle, since the discrete logarithm relation for group elements originating purely from g is already known to the adversary. Therefore, the probability is $\min(q_{\text{IC}_1} + q_{\text{IC}_2}, q_{\text{DLOG}})/N \leq q_{\text{DLOG}}/N$.

Additionally, the adversary may submit a query with a group element, the discrete logarithm of which is known to them. The input $\hat{e}$ to the ACTIVE$_C$ oracle is either a value formerly returned from a previous query to PASSIVEEXEC, in which case the adversary must also query the ideal cipher and the DLOG oracle and there is a chance of $(q_\circ + 1)/p$ that the discrete logarithm of the group element decrypted by ACTIVE$_C$ is known to them. If $\hat{e}$ was crafted by the adversary, *i.e.*, if they queried the ideal cipher on values $\hat{a}, \hat{B}, \hat{sk}$ such that the discrete logarithm of $\hat{B}$ is known to them, then they expect an $1/N$ chance that there choice of $\hat{pw}$ was correct, and that ACTIVE$_C$ used $\hat{b}$ to compute the Diffie–Hellman session.

In total, this result in a divergence for ACTIVE$_C$ queries bounded by $q_{\text{AE}_C} \cdot (q_\circ + 1)/p + q_{\text{AE}_C}/N$. For ACTIVE$_S$, the adversary may submit a value $\hat{c}_x$ for which the same arguments hold, resulting in a total probability for either of both occurring of $(q_{\text{AE}_C} + q_{\text{AE}_S}) \cdot (q_\circ + 1)/p + (q_{\text{AE}_C} + q_{\text{AE}_S})/N$.

Finally, the adversary's advantage to distinguish the simulation from the real game based on DLOG queries depends on the knowledge of at least one key from a ACTIVE oracle, resulting in a factor of $\min(q_{\text{AE}_C} +$

$q_{\text{AE}_S}, 1)$, thus bounding the overall divergence by $\min(q_{\text{AE}_C} + q_{\text{AE}_S}, 1) \cdot \left((q_{\text{AE}_C} + q_{\text{AE}_S}) \cdot (q_\circ + 1)/p + (q_{\text{AE}_C} + q_{\text{AE}_S} + \min(q_{\text{IC}_1}, q_{\text{IC}_2}, q_{\text{DLOG}}))/N \right)$, which is less or equal to $(q_{\text{AE}_C} + q_{\text{AE}_S}) \cdot (q_\circ + 1)/p + (q_{\text{AE}_C} + q_{\text{AE}_S} + q_{\text{DLOG}})/N$.

After G_4, the PASSIVEEXEC and ACTIVE$_C$ oracle output random values as ciphertexts e, c that do not commit to any values a, B, π or X. Particularly, the values $\text{DLOG}(g, X), \text{DLOG}(g, B)$ are defined only upon corruption or after a number of ACTIVE and DLOG queries relative to the password space N. The ACTIVE$_*$ oracles further output a random key independent of the challenge bit $s = 0$. The adversary is left with either guessing the challenge bit, or querying values to $\mathcal{H}_2$. This concludes the proof of Theorem 2. $\qquad\square$

4   aPAKE Security: Sketch of Proof of Theorem 1

The security of the QA-KHAPE protocol (cf. Fig. 1) is proven in the QA-BPR (cf. Sect. 2.2) model. Recall that the adversary may interact through the EXECUTE, SEND, REVEAL, CORRUPT and TEST oracles after the *Registration* phase, where the protocol defines how the principals respond. Additionally, the adversary has access to the group operation, DLOG and random oracle, ideal cipher and pseudo-random function *prf*, as described in Sect. 2.1, and is bounded by Theorem 1. In this section we offer a summary of the proof's main ideas and provide a complete description in Appendix A2.

We consider a sequence of games starting with G_0, which corresponds to the QA-KHAPE protocol illustrated in Fig. 1. As we progress to G_3, the sessions keys are chosen independent and uniformly at random, ensuring that the adversary $\mathcal{A}$ is reduced to a simple guessing attack. Throughout this reduction process, we present a an adversary $\mathcal{B}$ on the KHAPE$_{\text{CORE}}$-game, which maintains a mapping between instances of the KHAPE$_{\text{CORE}}$-game and instances of principals in the QA-BPR-model. To achieve this, we utilize a procedure called *CoreMap*, which bears resemblance to the GETUV procedure described in [7, App. B.2] (cf. Appendix A1 for further details). Intuitively, two counters $ctr_{C,S}$ and $ctr_{C,S,\text{sid}}$, are employed to either map to a set of static variables indexed by l or to an instance ctr_l in the KHAPE$_{\text{CORE}}$-game. The oracles provided by the KHAPE$_{\text{CORE}}$ challenger are referred to as KHAPE$_{\text{CORE}}$.Oracle.

In the sequence of games, the first modification occurs in G_1, where we replace the keys k_1, k_2 in the EXECUTE oracle with random strings. This change is reflected in the CORRUPT oracle, which now programs the random string instead of the actual keys into the random oracle. The distinction between G_0 and G_1 can be reduced to an attacker on the KHAPE$_{\text{CORE}}$-game. To differentiate between these two games, we can provide an extractor for a winning query: utilizing the *CoreMap*, the calls to the EXECUTE and SEND oracles can be forwarded to the KHAPE$_{\text{CORE}}$.PASSIVEEXEC, which returns $(e_{C,S,\text{sid}}, Y_{C,S,\text{sid}}, c_{C,S,\text{sid}})$, These outputs can be queries to KHAPE$_{\text{CORE}}$.ACTIVE$_*$, which provides $(c_{C,S,\text{sid}}, k_{C,S,1})$ or $k_{C,S,2}$. Using from these keys, the confirmation values (τ, γ) that genuinely follow the protocol are computed.

In the modified game, all calls to the ideal cipher are simulated perfectly by forwarding queries to, and responses from, the KHAPE$_{\text{CORE}}$-game. However, queries to the random oracle are not simulated perfectly, because the adversary can submit a query not associated with an instance in the KHAPE$_{\text{CORE}}$, and that gets mapped to different value in the KHAPE$_{\text{CORE}}$-game later on. Nonetheless, in every call to $\mathcal{H}_2$ in the KHAPE$_{\text{CORE}}$, either the group element X or Y is chosen uniformly at random from the group, ensuring that the adversary's probability of querying the same group element beforehand is at most $q_{\mathcal{H}_2}/p$.

The TEST queries in G_1 are simulated perfectly, since the keys are chosen uniformly at random, ensuring that the key confirmation values follow the expected distribution. In the non-TEST queries, as the KHAPE$_{\text{CORE}}$ instances are real-or-random based on the respective challenge bit. Specifically, the keys (k_1, k_2) are real-or-random values. However, the adversary can only detect this if they can query the random oracle $\mathcal{H}_2$ for the position of the programmed random keys. Such a query would immediately be a winning query in the KHAPE$_{\text{CORE}}$-game. Therefore, the adversary's ability to distinguish between the two games can be limited by their capability to win the KHAPE$_{\text{CORE}}$-game, which can be quantified relative to the number of DLOG queries they submit.

In game G_2, the modification is extended to the active queries (*i.e.*, SEND). The extractor for the KHAPE$_{\text{CORE}}$-game acts nearly identical. The only difference is that the quantification of KHAPE$_{\text{CORE}}$ advantage is now also impacted by the adversary's ability to query ciphertexts (e, c), the discrete logarithm of the decryption of which is knowable to them. This adds an additional term for the number of SEND queries. The probability to detect the modifications from the non-TEST queries in game G_1 and G_2 result in the term $(q_{\text{DLOG}} + q_{\text{SEND}})/N + \epsilon_{\text{CORE}}$.

The last modification occurs in game G_3, where we exchange the sessions keys with random values. Since the keys (k_1, k_2) are already random strings, and the session key is the output of the *prf*, this can be reduced to the adversary's ability to distinguish *prf* from a random function, *i.e.*, ϵ_{prf}. This adds an additional divergence of $(q_{\text{EXECUTE}} + q_{\text{SEND}})\epsilon_{prf}$ and concludes the proof.

Acknowledgements. M.T. was supported by funding from the topic Engineering Secure Systems of the Helmholtz Association (HGF) and by KASTEL Security Research Labs. D.S. was supported by Natural Sciences and Engineering Research Council of Canada (NSERC) Discovery grant RGPIN-2022-03187 and NSERC Alliance grant ALLRP 578463-22.

A1   Oracles for Proof of Theorem 2

Algorithms 6 to 8 are detailed oracles for the proof of Theorem 2 in Sect. 3.2.

Algorithm 6 Sim. of REGIS-TRATION(l)

1: $e_l \xleftarrow{\$} \{0,1\}^{n_1}$
2: Store e_l

Algorithm 7 Sim. of PASSIVEEXEC(l)

1: Get stored e_l; Increment ctr_l
2: $c_{ctr,X} \xleftarrow{\$} \{0,1\}^{n_2}$
3: $y_{ctr} \leftarrow \mathbb{Z}_p, Y_{ctr} \leftarrow g^{y_{ctr}}$
4: **return** $(Y_{ctr}, e_{ctr}), (c_{ctr,X})$

Algorithm 8 Sim. of GETSTATIC(l)

Require: $l \in \mathbb{Z}$
1: Mark l corrupted; $\pi_l \leftarrow [N], sk_l \leftarrow \{0,1\}^\kappa$
2: **for** $m = 0, \dots, ctr_l$ **do**
3:     **for** $k_{l,m}, c_{l,m} \leftarrow \text{ACTIVE}_C(l, e, Y)$
4:     $a, B, sk \leftarrow \text{IC}_1.D(\pi_l, e)$
5:     $X \leftarrow \text{IC}_2.D(sk, c_{l,m}); x \leftarrow \text{DLOG}(g, X)$
6:     $h_X = \mathcal{H}_1(l, m, X), h_Y = \mathcal{H}_1(l, m, Y)$
7:     $\sigma_{l,m,C} \leftarrow (Y \circ B^{h_Y})^{x + h_X \cdot a}$
8:     $\mathcal{H}_2(l, m, X, Y, \sigma_{l,m,C}) := k_{l,m,1}$
9:     **for** $k_{l,2} \leftarrow \text{ACTIVE}_S(l, c)$
10:     $X \leftarrow \text{IC}_2.D(sk_l, c)$
11:     $a, B, sk_2 \leftarrow \text{IC}_1.D(\pi_l, e_l); b \leftarrow \text{DLOG}(g, B)$
12:     $h_X = \mathcal{H}_1(m, l, X), h_Y = \mathcal{H}_1(m, l, Y_{m,l})$
13:     $\sigma_{m,l,C} \leftarrow (X \circ A^{h_X})^{y_l + h_Y \cdot b}$
14:     $\mathcal{H}_2(m, l, X, Y_{m,l}, \sigma_{m,l,S}) := k_{m,l,2}$
15: **return** (π_l, sk_l)

A2   Full Proof of Theorem 1

We offer the complete proof of Theorem 1 as a sequence of game hops. First, the function $CoreMap(C, S, sid)$ uses the counter $\bar{l}$ mapping to the static variables indexed with l, and $ctr_{\bar{l}}$, $ctr_{C,S}$, $ctr_{C,S,sid}$ corresponding to the instances using these static variables. All variables are initialized to *zero*. The $CoreMap$ works as follows: if the $ctr_{C,S,sid} > 0$, the respective transcript $e_{ctr_{C,S}}, Y_{ctr_{C,S}, ctr_{C,S,sid}}, c_{ctr_{C,S}, ctr_{C,S,sid}}$ has been generated before and is returned. Otherwise, if $ctr_{C,S} = 0$, then this is the first interaction with registrant l. The reduction sets $ctr_{C,S} \leftarrow \bar{l}$, $ctr_{\bar{l}} \leftarrow 1$, increments $\bar{l}$, corresponding to ctr_l in the $\text{KHAPE}_{\text{CORE}}$, and sets $ctr_{C,S,sid} \leftarrow 1$. The oracle $\text{KHAPE}_{\text{CORE}}.\text{PASSIVEEXEC}(ctr_{C,S})$ is queried; the output stored and returned. If $ctr_{C,S} > 0$, The reduction sets $ctr_{C,S,sid} \leftarrow ctr_{\bar{l}}$, increments $ctr_{\bar{l}}$ and queries $\text{KHAPE}_{\text{CORE}}.\text{PASSIVEEXEC}(ctr_{C,S})$. The output is stored in $e_{ctr_{C,S}}, Y_{ctr_{C,S}, ctr_{C,S,sid}}, c_{ctr_{C,S}, ctr_{C,S,sid}}$ and returned.

G_0 *(Figure 1)*. This is the real protocol.

G_1 *(Passive Sessions)*. On input $\text{EXECUTE}(C, S, sid)$, we set $k_1 = k_2 \leftarrow \{0,1\}^\kappa$ and compute the key confirmation values τ, γ and sessions keys using the *prf*. The adversaries oracle calls to all instances l for which EXECUTE has been called are simulated as follows: First, the simulation invokes $CoreMap(C, S, sid)$ to obtain k_1, c'_X from $\text{KHAPE}_{\text{CORE}}.\text{ACTIVE}_C(ctr_{C,S,sid}, e, Y)$, is used to compute the confirmation values τ, γ. On a $\text{CORRUPT}(C, S)$ query, the extraction calls $\text{KHAPE}_{\text{CORE}}.\text{GETSTATIC}(ctr_{C,S})$ returning π_l, sk_l, which programs the key k_1 returned by a $\text{KHAPE}_{\text{CORE}}.\text{ACTIVE}$ oracle into the *correct* position of the random oracle $\mathcal{H}_2$. The extraction receives a, B, sk from the ideal cipher on query $\text{IC}_1.D(sk_1, e)$ as well as the discrete logarithm b from $\text{KHAPE}_{\text{CORE}}.\text{DLOG}(B)$.

It then computes $A \leftarrow g^a$. Let $\mathcal{P}$ be a table corresponding to all N passwords. The extraction sets $\pi \leftarrow \mathcal{P}[\text{sk}_1]$, *i.e.*, the sk_1'th entry of the table and returns $\pi, (e, A, b, \text{sk})$, which is a perfect simulation. For the queries $\mathcal{H}_1(\text{sid}, C, S, *)$, if the entry $ctr_{C,S,\text{sid}}$ is defined, the query is forwarded to the KHAPE$_\text{CORE}$-challenger, and the result is returned. Otherwise, a random value is sampled uniformly at random from the range of $\mathcal{H}_1$, and a table is maintained for consistent responses. $\mathcal{H}_2(\text{sid}, C, S, *)$ is simulated analogous to $\mathcal{H}_1$. All queries to IC_1 and IC_2 are forwarded to the KHAPE$_\text{CORE}$-challenger. In Sect. 4 the divergence $q_{\mathcal{H}_2}/p$ from this simulation, *i.e.*, the random oracle and ideal cipher queries, has already been discussed.

Finally, the adversary may query a TEST or REVEAL query, receiving the session key from the KHAPE$_\text{CORE}$ is returned. In the first case, In the second case, extraction either simulates either G_0, if the KHAPE$_\text{CORE}$ challenge bit is *zero*, or G_1, if the KHAPE$_\text{CORE}$ challenge bit s is *one*. When $s = 0$, the values of e, c_X as well as τ, γ are distributed as expected (*i.e.*, as in G_0), since the keys $k_1 = k_2$ are identical and thus γ can also be computed from k_1. On the other hand, if $s = 1$, the key k_1 is chosen uniformly random as expected, and thus the key confirmation values also have the expected distribution.

In the second case, key k_1 returned from the simulation is real-or-random, but would be expected to always be real. However, from an adversary detecting this change an extraction of a winning query to the KHAPE$_\text{CORE}$ can be provided: In order to notice the change, the adversary $\mathcal{A}$ has to query the random oracle on $\mathcal{H}_2(\text{sid}, C, S, X, Y, \sigma_C)$ or $\mathcal{H}_2(\text{sid}, C, S, X, Y, \sigma_S)$, both of which allow to instantly win the KHAPE$_\text{CORE}$-game. Note that the key confirmation values returned by the aPAKE impact the advantage to win the KHAPE$_\text{CORE}$, since even a passive execution allows to verify if a derived session key is correct. Therefore, the term $\min(q_{\text{AE}_C} + q_{\text{AE}_S}, 1)$ is 1. Further, the inputs to *CoreMap*.ACTIVE$_*$ are sampled in KHAPE$_\text{CORE}$.PASSIVEEXEC such that no *new* group elements, the discrete logarithm of which is knowable to the adversary, have to be considered in the probability to win the KHAPE$_\text{CORE}$-game. Consequently, the number of these queries is exactly the number of EXECUTE queries. The probability to detect the difference between game G_0 and G_1 is then bounded by $q_{\text{DLOG}}/N + \epsilon_{passiv} + q_{\mathcal{H}_2}/p$ with $\epsilon_{passiv} := (q_{\text{IC}_1} + q_{\text{IC}_2} + q_o)^2 + (q_{\text{DLOG}} q_o^2)/p + q_{\text{IC}_1}^2 + q_{\text{EXECUTE}}/2^{n_1} + q_{\text{IC}_2}^2 + q_{\text{EXECUTE}}/2^{n_2}$.

G_2 *(Active Sessions).* In G_2, the modifications are extended to active sessions: On input SEND$(C, l, M = (S, \text{sid}))$ the simulation responds with the values e, Y retrieved from KHAPE$_\text{CORE}$.PASSIVEEXEC. On input SEND$(C, l, M = (S, \text{sid}, c_X, \tau))$ we sample the $k_2 \leftarrow \{0, 1\}^\kappa$ uniformly at random and computes $\tau' \leftarrow prf(k_2, 1)$. The session key and the key confirmation value are generated from k_1, k_2 based on $\tau = \tau'$ as in an genuine execution of the protocol. On input SEND$(C, l, M = (S, \text{sid}, e, Y))$ the simulation samples a uniformly random value for $k_1 \leftarrow \{0, 1\}^\kappa$ and computes the key confirmation value τ using the *prf*. On input SEND$(C, l, M = (S, \text{sid}, \gamma))$ we compute $\gamma' \leftarrow prf(k_1, 2)$ and set the session key conditionally on the outcome of $\gamma = \gamma'$ (*i.e.*, as in the *real* protocol). On queries to the random oracle, ideal cipher, REVEAL and CORRUPT the reduction behaves identical to G_1, and thus the divergence is identical.

Eventually, the adversary may query a TEST or REVEAL query receiving a session key from the KHAPE$_{\text{CORE}}$. To bound the adversaries chance to detect the modification, a similar extractor of a winning query to the KHAPE$_{\text{CORE}}$-game is provided. Similarly to Appendix A2, the reduction calls *CoreMap* to map instances of the QA-BPR-game to instances of the KHAPE$_{\text{CORE}}$-game.

Impersonation of Clients: On SEND($C, l, M = (S, \text{sid})$) the extraction calls *CoreMap*(C, S, sid), which causes $ctr_{C,S}$ to become defined if it previously was not, and the retrieved values e, Y are returned. On SEND($C, i, M = (S, \text{sid}, c_X, \tau)$) the reduction calls *CoreMap*(C, S, sid) to subsequently obtain $k_2 \leftarrow$ KHAPE$_{\text{CORE}}$.ACTIVE($ctr_{C,S}, c_X$). The key confirmation value τ' is computed from the obtained key using the *prf*. The session key and key confirmation value are set conditioned on $\tau = \tau'$ as in the real protocol.

Impersonation of Server: On SEND($S, i, M = (C, \text{sid}, j, e, Y)$), the reduction calls *CoreMap*(C, S, sid), which causes $ctr_{C,S}$ to become defined it it previously was not. Then the reduction calls $k_1 \leftarrow$ KHAPE$_{\text{CORE}}$.ACTIVE($ctr_{C,S}, e, Y$) and computes the key confirmation value τ genuinely using the *prf*, and returns c_X, τ. On SEND($S, i, M = (C, j, \gamma, \text{sid})$), the reduction computes γ' from the key k_2 using the *prf* and compares this to γ. If they match, the session key is set to $K_1 \leftarrow prf(k_1, 0)$, and otherwise, to $\perp$.

For SEND the arguments are analogous to G_1: If TEST was queried, the reduction simulates G_1 (and thus G_0) perfectly if the KHAPE$_{\text{CORE}}$ challenge bit $s = 0$, and simulates G_2 if $s = 1$. Otherwise, the adversary can detect the change only by querying the random oracle on either of the two inputs $\mathcal{H}_2(\text{sid}, C, S, X, Y, \sigma_C)$ or $\mathcal{H}_2(\text{sid}, C, S, X, Y, \sigma_S)$, both of which are winning queries for the reduction in KHAPE$_{\text{CORE}}$. The number of ACTIVE queries for which the adversary may choose the input is bounded by the number of SEND queries, bounding the difference between game G_1 and G_2 by $(q_{\text{DLOG}} + q_{\text{SEND}})/N + \epsilon_{activ} + q_{\mathcal{H}_2}/p$ with $\epsilon_{activ} := (q_{\text{IC}_1} + q_{\text{IC}_2} + q_{\text{o}})^2 + (q_{\text{DLOG}}q_{\text{o}}^2)/p + q_{\text{IC}_1}^2 + q_{\text{SEND}}/2^{n_1} + q_{\text{IC}_2}^2 + q_{\text{SEND}}/2^{n_2}$.

G_3 *(Random Sessions Keys)*. The final modification in G_3 was discussed in Sect. 4, resulting in the term $(q_{\text{EXEC}} + q_{\text{SEND}})\epsilon_{prf}$. The sessions keys are now uniformly random and independent of the password and credentials leaving adversary to a guessing attack. The probability that the adversary can distinguish G_0 from G_3 is bounded by $(q_{\text{DLOG}} + q_{\text{SEND}})/N + q_{\mathcal{H}_2}/p + (q_{\text{EXEC}} + q_{\text{SEND}})\epsilon_{prf} + \epsilon$, with $\epsilon \leq (q_{\text{IC}_1} + q_{\text{IC}_2} + q_{\text{o}})^2 + (q_{\text{DLOG}}q_{\text{o}}^2)/p + (q_{\text{IC}_1}^2 + q_{\text{SEND}} + q_{\text{EXEC}})/2^{n_1} + (q_{\text{IC}_2}^2 + q_{\text{SEND}} + q_{\text{EXEC}})/2^{n_2}$. This conclude the proof. □

References

1. IEEE standard specification for password-based public-key cryptographic techniques. IEEE Std 1363.2-2008 (2009). https://doi.org/10.1109/IEEESTD.2009.4773330
2. Information technology - personal identification - ISO-compliant driving licence. ISO/IEC 18013–3:2027 (2017)

3. Abdalla, M., Haase, B., Hesse, J.: Security analysis of CPace. In: Tibouchi, M., Wang, H. (eds.) ASIACRYPT 2021. LNCS, vol. 13093, pp. 711–741. Springer, Cham (2021). https://doi.org/10.1007/978-3-030-92068-5_24

4. Beguinet, H., Chevalier, C., Pointcheval, D., Ricosset, T., Rossi, M.: Get a CAKE: generic transformations from key encapsulation mechanisms to password authenticated key exchanges. In: Tibouchi, M., Wang, X. (eds.) Applied Cryptography and Network Security. ACNS 2023. LNCS, vol. 13906, pp. 516–538. Springer, Cham (2023). https://doi.org/10.1007/978-3-031-33491-7_19

5. Bellare, M., Pointcheval, D., Rogaway, P.: Authenticated key exchange secure against dictionary attacks. In: Preneel, B. (ed.) EUROCRYPT 2000. LNCS, vol. 1807, pp. 139–155. Springer, Heidelberg (2000). https://doi.org/10.1007/3-540-45539-6_11

6. Bourdrez, D., Krawczyk, D.H., Lewi, K., Wood, C.A.: The OPAQUE Asymmetric PAKE Protocol. Internet-Draft draft-irtf-cfrg-opaque-10, Internet Engineering Task Force, MarCH 2023. https://datatracker.ietf.org/doc/draft-irtf-cfrg-opaque/10/

7. Eaton, E., Stebila, D.: The quantum annoying property of password-authenticated key exchange protocols. In: Cheon, J.H., Tillich, J.-P. (eds.) PQCrypto 2021 2021. LNCS, vol. 12841, pp. 154–173. Springer, Cham (2021). https://doi.org/10.1007/978-3-030-81293-5_9

8. Gheorghiu, V., Mosca, M.: Benchmarking the quantum cryptanalysis of symmetric, public-key and hash-based cryptographic schemes. arXiv:1902.02332 (2019)

9. Gidney, C., Ekerå, M.: How to factor 2048 bit RSA integers in 8 hours using 20 million noisy qubits. Quantum 5, 433 (2021). https://doi.org/10.22331/q-2021-04-15-433

10. Gu, Y., Jarecki, S., Krawczyk, H.: KHAPE: asymmetric PAKE from key-hiding key exchange. In: Malkin, T., Peikert, C. (eds.) CRYPTO 2021. LNCS, vol. 12828, pp. 701–730. Springer, Cham (2021). https://doi.org/10.1007/978-3-030-84259-8_24

11. Hao, F., van Oorschot, P.C.: SoK: password-authenticated key exchange - theory, practice, standardization and real-world lessons. In: Proceedings of the 2022 ACM on Asia Conference on Computer and Communications Security, pp. 697–711. ASIA CCS '22, Association for Computing Machinery, New York, NY, USA (2022). https://doi.org/10.1145/3488932.3523256

12. Hhan, M., Yamakawa, T., Yun, A.: Quantum complexity for discrete logarithms and related problems. Cryptology ePrint Archive, Paper 2023/1054 (2023). https://eprint.iacr.org/2023/1054

13. Jarecki, S., Krawczyk, H., Xu, J.: OPAQUE: an asymmetric PAKE protocol secure against pre-computation attacks. In: Nielsen, J.B., Rijmen, V. (eds.) EUROCRYPT 2018. LNCS, vol. 10822, pp. 456–486. Springer, Cham (2018). https://doi.org/10.1007/978-3-319-78372-7_15

14. Krawczyk, H.: HMQV: a high-performance secure Diffie-Hellman protocol. In: Shoup, V. (ed.) CRYPTO 2005. LNCS, vol. 3621, pp. 546–566. Springer, Heidelberg (2005). https://doi.org/10.1007/11535218_33

15. NIST: Nist: Selected algorithm 2022 (2022). https://csrc.nist.gov/Projects/post-quantum-cryptography/selected-algorithms-2022

16. Parker, E., Vermeer, M.J.D.: Estimating the energy requirements to operate a cryptanalytically relevant quantum computer. arXiv:2304.14344 (2023)

17. Roetteler, M., Naehrig, M., Svore, K.M., Lauter, K.: Quantum resource estimates for computing elliptic curve discrete logarithms. In: Takagi, T., Peyrin, T. (eds.) ASIACRYPT 2017. LNCS, vol. 10625, pp. 241–270. Springer, Cham (2017). https://doi.org/10.1007/978-3-319-70697-9_9

18. Schmidt, J.M.: Requirements for Password-Authenticated Key Agreement (PAKE) Schemes. RFC 8125, April 2017. https://doi.org/10.17487/RFC8125, https://www.rfc-editor.org/info/rfc8125

19. Taubert, T., Wood, C.A.: SPAKE2+, an Augmented PAKE. Internet-Draft draft-bar-cfrg-spake2plus-08, Internet Engineering Task Force, May 2022. https://datatracker.ietf.org/doc/draft-bar-cfrg-spake2plus/08/, work in Progress

20. Thomas, S.: Re: [CFRG] proposed PAKE selection process. CFRG Mailing List, June 2019. https://mailarchive.ietf.org/arch/msg/cfrg/dtf91cmavpzT47U3AVxrVGNB5UM/#

Commitments with Efficient Zero-Knowledge Arguments from Subset Sum Problems

Jules Maire$^{(\boxtimes)}$ and Damien Vergnaud

Sorbonne Université, CNRS, LIP6, 75005 Paris, France
Jules.maire@lip6.fr

Abstract. We present a cryptographic string commitment scheme that is computationally hiding and binding based on (modular) subset sum problems. It is believed that these NP-complete problems provide post-quantum security contrary to the number theory assumptions currently used in cryptography. Using techniques recently introduced by Feneuil, Maire, Rivain and Vergnaud, this simple commitment scheme enables an efficient zero-knowledge proof of knowledge for committed values as well as proofs showing Boolean relations amongst the committed bits. In particular, one can prove that committed bits $m_0, m_1, ..., m_\ell$ satisfy $m_0 = C(m_1, ..., m_\ell)$ for any Boolean circuit C (without revealing any information on those bits). The proof system achieves good communication and computational complexity since for a security parameter λ, the protocol's communication complexity is $\tilde{O}(|C|\lambda + \lambda^2)$ (compared to $\tilde{O}(|C|\lambda^2)$ for the best code-based protocol due to Jain, Krenn, Pietrzak and Tentes).

1 Introduction

A commitment scheme [7] is a cryptographic protocol that enables one party to commit to a value (or set of values) without revealing it, while ensuring that this value cannot be modified. In constructing sophisticated cryptographic protocols, it can be necessary to prove some property of a committed message without revealing anything more than the property itself. This is usually achieved through the use of zero-knowledge proofs of knowledge [14]. This *commit-and-prove* paradigm [11,20] is used in many areas of applied cryptography (anonymous credentials, blockchains, electronic voting, . . .).

In 1994, Shor [26] introduced a quantum algorithm that could break cryptosystems based on the hardness of factoring large integers or solving discrete logarithm problems. This has emphasized the need for new cryptographic systems, leading to the emergence of a new field, known as *post-quantum cryptography*, which focuses on creating cryptographic algorithms that are secure against quantum (and classical) computers.

The (modular) subset sum problem is to find, given integers t and q, a subset of given integers $\gamma_1, \ldots, \gamma_n$, whose sum is t modulo q. This NP-complete problem was used in the 1980s, following [22], for the construction of several public-key

G. Tsudik et al. (Eds.): ESORICS 2023, LNCS 14344, pp. 189–208, 2024.
https://doi.org/10.1007/978-3-031-50594-2_10

encryption schemes. The majority of those schemes were broken using lattice-based techniques (see [23]), but the problem itself remains unsolvable for specific parameters and is even thought to be intractable for quantum computers. A plethora of cryptographic constructions have been proposed whose security is based on the difficulty of the subset sum problem [1,15,21]. In a celebrated paper, Impagliazzo and Naor [15] presented in particular a pseudo-random generator and an elegant bit commitment scheme. We extend the latter to a simple string commitment scheme and provide efficient zero-knowledge proofs for any relation amongst committed values using the recent zero-knowledge proof system proposed by Feneuil, Maire, Rivain, and Vergnaud and based on the *MPC-in-the-head* paradigm.

Contributions of the Paper

Commitment scheme. We first present a modified version of the bit-commitment based on the subset sum problem proposed in [15]. This new scheme enables commitments to bit-strings and is related to the one from [15] in a similar manner to how the well-known Pedersen commitment scheme [24] is related to preliminary discrete-logarithm based bit-commitments from [9,10].

The design principle is simple but seems to have been overlooked for more than 30 years (even if similar ideas have been used in lattice-based cryptography). For a security level $\lambda \in \mathbb{N}$ (*i.e.* against an adversary making 2^λ bit-operations using a $2^{\lambda/2}$-bits memory), it enables to commit to bit-strings of length $\ell \leq 2\lambda$ using a 2λ-bits modulus q and $(\ell + 2\lambda)$ integers smaller than q. The setup thus requires $O(\lambda^2)$ random or pseudo-random bits that can be generated easily using a so-called *extendable-output function* (XOF). A commitment is a sum of a (randomized) subset of these integers modulo q; therefore, it is of optimal bit-length 2λ and can be computed in $O(\lambda^2)$ binary operations. The *hiding* property (*i.e.* one cannot learn anything about the committed message from the commitment) relies on the hardness of the subset-sum problem, while its *binding* property (*i.e.* one cannot open a commitment to two different messages) relies on the hardness of the related *weighted knapsack problem*. With the proposed parameters, both problems are believed to be resistant to a quantum adversary that makes at most $2^{\lambda/2}$ qubits operations.

Zero-Knowledge Protocols. Very recently, Feneuil, Maire, Rivain, and Vergnaud [13] proposed zero-knowledge arguments for the subset sum problem. They introduced the idea of *artificial abort* to the so-called *MPC-in-the-head paradigm* [16] and achieved an asymptotic improvement by producing arguments of size $O(\lambda^2)$. Their protocol readily gives a way to prove knowledge of the committed bit-string without revealing anything about it.

We extend their work to prove that a committed triple $(b_1, b_2, b_3) \in \{0,1\}^3$ satisfy a Boolean relation (*e.g.* $b_1 \wedge b_2 = b_3$ or $b_1 \oplus b_2 = b_3$) without revealing any additional information about them. The bits can be in arbitrary positions in the same or in different commitments and the proof of the Boolean relation does not add any overhead compared to the basic opening proof. This flexibility allows proving that committed bits $m_0, m_1, ..., m_\ell$ satisfy $m_0 = C(m_1, ..., m_\ell)$ for any Boolean circuit C with good communication and computational complexity. Indeed, by packing the commitments of bits on the circuit wires, we obtain a protocol with communication complexity $\tilde{O}(|C|\lambda + \lambda^2)$ where $|C|$ denotes the number of AND/XOR gates of C. This has to be compared with the code-based protocol due to Jain, Krenn, Pietrzak, and Tentes [17]. They provide a commitment scheme with zero-knowledge proofs from the LPN-assumption (or hardness of decoding a random linear code). This scheme has $\tilde{O}(|C|\lambda^2)$ communication complexity and allows only proving Boolean relations bit-wise on binary strings (which may result in a large overhead depending on the circuit considered). There also exist lattice-based constructions of commitment schemes with zero-knowledge proofs [2,3,6] but the messages committed are small integers. They can be used to prove the satisfiability of arithmetic circuits but proving the satisfiability of a Boolean circuit with these schemes results in an important overhead in communication and computation.

2 Preliminaries

2.1 Notations

All logarithms are in base 2. We denote the security parameter by λ, which is given to all algorithms in the unary form 1^λ. Unless otherwise stated, algorithms are randomized, and "PPT" stands for "probabilistic polynomial-time" in the security parameter. Random sampling from a finite set X according to the uniform distribution is denoted by $x \xleftarrow{\$} X$. The symbol $\xleftarrow{\$}$ is also used for assignments from randomized algorithms, and the symbol $\leftarrow$ is used for assignments from deterministic algorithms and calculations. For the sake of simplicity, we denote the set of integers $\{1, ..., N\}$ by $[1, N]$.

We denote integer vectors in bold print. A vector composed only of 1's or 0's is denoted as $\mathbf{1}$ or $\mathbf{0}$ respectively (its length will be clear within the context). Given two integer vectors of the same length $\boldsymbol{\gamma}$ and $\boldsymbol{x}$, $\langle \boldsymbol{\gamma}, \boldsymbol{x} \rangle$ denotes their inner-product. For two bit-strings $\boldsymbol{x} \in \{0,1\}^n$ and $\boldsymbol{y} \in \{0,1\}^m$, $(\boldsymbol{x}\|\boldsymbol{y}) \in \{0,1\}^{n+m}$ denotes the concatenation of $\boldsymbol{x}$ and $\boldsymbol{y}$, and $\boldsymbol{x} \cdot \boldsymbol{y}$ denotes the component-wise product.

Two distributions $\{D_\lambda\}_\lambda$ and $\{\tilde{D}_\lambda\}_\lambda$ are deemed (t, ϵ)-indistinguishable if, for any algorithm $\mathcal{A}$ running in time at most $t(\lambda)$, we have

$$|\Pr[\mathcal{A}(1^\lambda, x) = 1 \mid x \xleftarrow{\$} D_\lambda] - \Pr[\mathcal{A}(1^\lambda, x) = 1 \mid x \xleftarrow{\$} \tilde{D}_\lambda]| \leq \epsilon(\lambda).$$

A (ℓ, t, ϵ)-*pseudo-random generator* (PRG) is a deterministic algorithm G that, for all $\lambda \in \mathbb{N}$, on input a bit-string $\boldsymbol{x} \in \{0,1\}^\lambda$ outputs $G(\boldsymbol{x}) \in \{0,1\}^{\ell(\lambda)}$ with $\ell(\lambda) > \lambda$ such that the distributions $\{G(\boldsymbol{x}) \mid \boldsymbol{x} \xleftarrow{\$} \{0,1\}^\lambda\}_\lambda$ and $\{\boldsymbol{r} \mid \boldsymbol{r} \xleftarrow{\$} \{0,1\}^{\ell(\lambda)}\}_\lambda$ are (t, ϵ)-indistinguishable. From such a generator, with $\ell(\lambda) = 2\lambda$, it is possible to construct a *tree PRG* [19], which takes a root $\boldsymbol{x} \in \{0,1\}^\lambda$ as input and generates $N = 2^t$ pseudo-random λ-bit strings in a structured fashion as follows: $\boldsymbol{x}$ is the label of the root of a depth-t complete binary tree in which the right/left child of each node is labeled with the λ most/least significant bits of the output of the PRG applied to the root label. This structure allows revealing $N - 1$ pseudo-random values of the leaves by revealing only $\log(N)$ labels of the tree (by revealing the labels on the siblings of the paths from the root to this leaf).

2.2 Commitments

Definition 1. *(Commitment scheme). A commitment scheme is a triple of PPT algorithms* (Setup, Com, Ver) *such that:*

- Setup$(1^\lambda) \to$ pp. *On input* λ, *the* setup *algorithm outputs the public parameters* pp *containing a description of the message space* $\mathcal{M}$.
- Com$($pp$, m) \to (c,$ aux$)$. *On input* pp *and* $m \in \mathcal{M}$, *the* commit *algorithm outputs a commitment-opening pair* $(c,$ aux$)$.
- Ver$($pp$, m, c,$ aux$) \to b \in \{0,1\}$. *On input* pp, $m \in \mathcal{M}$ *and* $(c,$ aux$)$, *the* verifying *(or opening) algorithm outputs a bit* $b \in \{0,1\}$.

Moreover, it satisfies the following correctness property: we have for all $\lambda \in \mathbb{N}$,

$$\Pr[\mathsf{Ver}(\mathsf{pp}, m, c, \mathsf{aux}) = 1 \mid \mathsf{pp} \xleftarrow{\$} \mathsf{Setup}(1^\lambda), m \xleftarrow{\$} \mathcal{M}, (c, \mathsf{aux}) \xleftarrow{\$} \mathsf{Com}(\mathsf{pp}, m)] = 1.$$

There are two security notions underlying a commitment scheme.

Definition 2. *Let* $t : \mathbb{N} \to \mathbb{N}$ *and* $\epsilon : \mathbb{N} \to [0,1]$. *A commitment scheme* (Setup, Com, Ver) *is said:*

- (t, ϵ)-*computationally hiding if for all two-phases algorithm* $\mathcal{A} = (\mathcal{A}_1, \mathcal{A}_2)$, *we have for all* $\lambda \in \mathbb{N}$:

$$\Pr\left[b = b' \,\middle|\, \begin{array}{l} \mathsf{pp} \xleftarrow{\$} \mathsf{Setup}(1^\lambda), (m_0, m_1, s) \xleftarrow{\$} \mathcal{A}_1(\mathsf{pp}), b \xleftarrow{\$} \{0,1\} \\ (c, \mathsf{aux}) \xleftarrow{\$} \mathsf{Com}(\mathsf{pp}, m_b), b' \xleftarrow{\$} \mathcal{A}_2(c, s) \end{array}\right] \leq \frac{1}{2} + \epsilon(\lambda)$$

when $\mathcal{A}$ *runs in time at most* $t(\lambda)$ *in this probabilistic computational game.*
- (t, ϵ)-*computationally binding if for all algorithm* $\mathcal{A}$, *we have for all* $\lambda \in \mathbb{N}$:

$$\Pr\left[\begin{array}{l} m_1 \neq m_2 \\ \mathsf{Ver}(\mathsf{pp}, m_1, c, aux_1) = 1 \\ \mathsf{Ver}(\mathsf{pp}, m_2, c, aux_2) = 1 \end{array} \,\middle|\, \begin{array}{l} \mathsf{pp} \xleftarrow{\$} \mathsf{Setup}(1^\lambda), \\ (m_1, m_2, \mathsf{aux}_1, \mathsf{aux}_2, c) \xleftarrow{\$} \mathcal{A}(1^\lambda, \mathsf{pp})\} \end{array}\right] \leq \epsilon(\lambda)$$

when $\mathcal{A}$ *runs in time at most* $t(\lambda)$ *in this probabilistic computational game.*

2.3 Zero-Knowledge Arguments

A zero-knowledge protocol for a polynomial-time decidable binary relation $\mathcal{R}$ is defined by two interactive algorithms, a prover $\mathcal{P}$ and a verifier $\mathcal{V}$. Both algorithms are given a common input x, and $\mathcal{P}$ is given an additional *witness* w such that $(x, w) \in \mathcal{R}$. The two algorithms then exchange messages until $\mathcal{V}$ outputs a bit b, with $b = 1$ meaning $\mathcal{V}$ accepts $\mathcal{P}$'s claim and $b = 0$ meaning $\mathcal{V}$ rejects it. This sequence of messages and the answer b is referred to as a *transcript* and denoted $\text{View}(\mathcal{P}(x, w), \tilde{\mathcal{V}}(x))$. In this paper, we consider *zero-knowledge argument of knowledge* which are protocols that allow a PPT prover to convince a PPT verifier that they *knows* a witness w. There are three security notions underlying a zero-knowledge argument of knowledge.

Definition 3. *Let* $t : \mathbb{N} \to \mathbb{N}$, $\epsilon, \alpha, \zeta : \mathbb{N} \to [0, 1]$, *and* $\mathcal{R}$ *be a polynomial-time decidable binary relation. A zero-knowledge argument* $(\mathcal{P}, \mathcal{V})$ *for* $\mathcal{R}$ *achieves:*

- α-*completeness, if for all* $\lambda \in \mathbb{N}$ *and all* $(x, w) \in \mathcal{R}$, *with* $x \in \{0, 1\}^\lambda$, $\Pr[\text{View}(\mathcal{P}(x, w), \mathcal{V}(x)) = 1] \geq 1 - \alpha(\lambda)$ *(i.e.* $\mathcal{P}$ *succeeds in convincing* $\mathcal{V}$, *except with probability* α*).*
- ϵ-*(special) soundness, if for all PPT algorithm* $\tilde{\mathcal{P}}$ *such that for all* $\lambda \in \mathbb{N}$ *and all* $x \in \{0, 1\}^\lambda$, $\tilde{\epsilon}(\lambda) := \Pr[\text{View}(\tilde{\mathcal{P}}(x), \mathcal{V}(x)) = 1] > \epsilon(\lambda)$, *there exists a PPT algorithm* $\mathcal{E}$ *(called the* extractor*) which, given rewindable black-box access to* $\tilde{\mathcal{P}}$ *outputs a witness* w *such that* $(x, w) \in \mathcal{R}$ *in time* $\mathsf{poly}(\lambda, (\tilde{\epsilon} - \epsilon)^{-1})$ *with probability at least* $1/2$.
- (t, ζ)-*zero-knowledge, if for every PPT algorithm* $\tilde{\mathcal{V}}$, *there exists a PPT algorithm* $\mathcal{S}$ *(called the* simulator*) which, given the input statement* $x \in \{0, 1\}^\lambda$ *and rewindable black-box access to* $\mathcal{V}$, *outputs a simulated transcript whose distribution is* (t, ζ)-*indistinguishable from* $\text{View}(\mathcal{P}(x, w), \tilde{\mathcal{V}}(x))$.

2.4   Subset Sum Problems

We define hereafter two variants of the subset sum problem on which the security of our commitment scheme relies. The first one is the standard subset sum problem mentioned in the introduction, while the second one is a slightly stronger assumption that has already been used in cryptography (see, *e.g.* [5,27]).

Definition 4. *Let* $t : \mathbb{N} \to \mathbb{N}$ *and* $\epsilon : \mathbb{N} \to [0, 1]$. *Let* $\ell, m : \mathbb{N} \to \mathbb{N}$ *and* modulus *be an algorithm which given* $\lambda \in \mathbb{N}$ *outputs an integer* q *of bit-length* $m(\lambda)$. *We consider the two following assumptions:*

- (t, ϵ)-*(decision) subset-sum assumption for* $(\ell, m, \mathsf{modulus})$*: for every algorithm* $\mathcal{A}$, *we have for all* $\lambda \in \mathbb{N}$:

$$\Pr\left[b = b' \left| \begin{array}{l} q \xleftarrow{\$} \mathsf{modulus}(1^\lambda), \gamma \xleftarrow{\$} [0, q-1]^{\ell(\lambda)}, x \xleftarrow{\$} \{0, 1\}^{\ell(\lambda)}, \\ t_0 = \langle \gamma, x \rangle \bmod q, t_1 \xleftarrow{\$} [0, q-1], b \xleftarrow{\$} \{0, 1\}, \\ b' \xleftarrow{\$} \mathcal{A}(1^\lambda, q, \gamma, t_b) \end{array} \right. \right] \leq \frac{1}{2} + \epsilon(\lambda)$$

  when $\mathcal{A}$ *runs in time at most* $t(\lambda)$ *in this probabilistic computational game.*
- (t, ϵ)-*weighted knapsack assumption for* $(\ell, m, \mathsf{modulus})$*: for every algorithm* $\mathcal{A}$, *we have for all* $\lambda \in \mathbb{N}$:

$$\Pr\left[\begin{array}{l} \langle \gamma, y \rangle = 0 \bmod q \\ y \neq \mathbf{0} \in \{-1, 0, 1\}^{\ell(\lambda)} \end{array} \left| \begin{array}{l} q \xleftarrow{\$} \mathsf{modulus}(1^\lambda), \gamma \xleftarrow{\$} [0, q-1]^{\ell(\lambda)}, \\ y \xleftarrow{\$} \mathcal{A}(1^\lambda, q, \gamma) \end{array} \right. \right] \leq \epsilon(\lambda)$$

when $\mathcal{A}$ runs in time at most $t(\lambda)$ in this probabilistic computational game.

The search version of the subset sum assumption is polynomial-time equivalent to the decision version stated above. The hardness of these problems depends greatly on the *density* defined as $d(\lambda) = \ell(\lambda)/m(\lambda)$. If the density is too small (e.g. $d(\lambda) < 1/\ell(\lambda)$) or too large (e.g. $d(\lambda) > \ell(\lambda)$) then both problems can be solved in polynomial time (see e.g. [12] and references therein). Coster, Joux, LaMacchia, Odlyzko, Schnorr, and Stern [12] proved that the subset sum problem can be solved in polynomial-time with a single call to an oracle that can find the shortest vector in a special lattice of dimension $\ell(\lambda) + 1$ if $d(\lambda) < 0.9408$ and Li and Ma proved a similar result for the weighted knapsack problem if $d(\lambda) < 0.488$. It is worth mentioning that these results do not break the assumptions in polynomial time since the best algorithm for finding the shortest vector in these lattices has computational complexity $2^{\Theta(\ell(\lambda))}$ (and cryptographic protocols relying on these problems with much smaller densities have been proposed, e.g. [21]).

In our construction, we will consider instances of these problems with density $d(\lambda) \simeq 1$ (i.e. $q \simeq 2^{\ell(\lambda)}$) for the subset sum problem since they are arguably the hardest ones [15]. This will result in instances for the weighted knapsack problem with density $d(\lambda) > 1$ and for conservative security, we will restrict ourselves to $d(\lambda) \leq 2$. In this case, lattice-based algorithms do not work and the best-known algorithms use very clever time-memory tradeoffs with the best algorithm due to Bonnetain, Bricout, Schrottenloher, and Shen [8] having time and memory complexities $\tilde{O}(2^{0.283\ell(\lambda)})$. These algorithms neglect the cost to access an exponential memory but even with this optimistic assumption, for $\ell(\lambda) = 256$, all known algorithms require at least a time complexity lower-bounded by 2^{128} operations or a memory of size at least 2^{64} bits. There also exists a vast literature on quantum algorithms for solving these problems (see [8] and references therein) and for $\ell(\lambda) = 256$, the best quantum algorithm requires about 2^{64} quantum operations and quantum memory.

3   String Commitments from Subset Sum Problems

3.1   Design Principle

In this section, we present our modified version of the bit-commitment based on the subset sum problem proposed in [15]. This new scheme enables commitments to bit-strings.

In [10], Brassard, Chaum, and Crépeau introduced the notion of *blob*, which is very similar to bit commitment, and presented an elegant construction based on the discrete-logarithm problem in groups of known prime order q (see also [9]). The commitment of a single bit consists of a group element (see Fig. 1 (a) for an equivalent form of their commitment). Shortly afterward, Pedersen [24] introduced his celebrated commitment scheme that enables committing to an integer in $\mathbb{Z}_q$ with a single group element (see Fig. 1 (c)). Impagliazzo and Naor [15] proposed a bit-commitment whose hiding and binding security properties rely on the subset sum problem. It has many similarities with the discrete-logarithm-based blob from [9,10] (see Fig. 1 (b)).

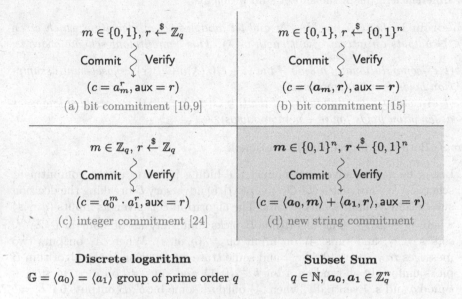

$$m \in \{0,1\}, r \overset{\$}{\leftarrow} \mathbb{Z}_q$$

Commit $\gtrless$ Verify

$$(c = a_m^r, \mathsf{aux} = r)$$

(a) bit commitment [10,9]

$$m \in \{0,1\}, r \overset{\$}{\leftarrow} \{0,1\}^n$$

Commit $\gtrless$ Verify

$$(c = \langle a_m, r \rangle, \mathsf{aux} = r)$$

(b) bit commitment [15]

$$m \in \mathbb{Z}_q, r \overset{\$}{\leftarrow} \mathbb{Z}_q$$

Commit $\gtrless$ Verify

$$(c = a_0^m \cdot a_1^r, \mathsf{aux} = r)$$

(c) integer commitment [24]

$$\boldsymbol{m} \in \{0,1\}^n, r \overset{\$}{\leftarrow} \{0,1\}^n$$

Commit $\gtrless$ Verify

$$(c = \langle \boldsymbol{a_0}, \boldsymbol{m} \rangle + \langle \boldsymbol{a_1}, r \rangle, \mathsf{aux} = r)$$

(d) new string commitment

Discrete logarithm
$\mathbb{G} = \langle a_0 \rangle = \langle a_1 \rangle$ group of prime order q

Subset Sum
$q \in \mathbb{N}, \boldsymbol{a_0}, \boldsymbol{a_1} \in \mathbb{Z}_q^n$

Fig. 1. Illustration of the Similarities between Commitment Schemes

To build our string commitment scheme, we push this analogy and propose a variant of Pedersen's protocol based on the subset sum (see Fig. 1 (d)). The design principle is simple and maybe folklore but does not seem to have been published in this form (even if similar ideas have been used in lattice-based cryptography).

3.2   Formal Description and Security Analysis

Let $\ell, n, m : \mathbb{N} \to \mathbb{N}$ and let modulus be an algorithm which given $\lambda \in \mathbb{N}$ outputs an integer q of bit-length $m(\lambda)$. Typically, modulus outputs a random $m(\lambda)$-bit prime number or the unique integer $q = 2^{m(\lambda)-1}$. The function ℓ defines the message length while the function n defines the randomness length.

Setup(1^λ) $\to$ pp. On input λ, the setup algorithm generates a modulus q by running modulus(1^λ) and picks uniformly at random $\boldsymbol{w} \in \mathbb{Z}_q^{\ell(\lambda)}$ and $\boldsymbol{s} \in \mathbb{Z}_q^{n(\lambda)}$. It outputs the public parameters pp $= (q, \boldsymbol{w}, \boldsymbol{s})$ and the message space is $\mathcal{M} = \{0,1\}^{\ell(\lambda)}$.

Com(pp, m) $\to$ (c, aux). On input pp and $\boldsymbol{m} \in \mathcal{M}$, the commit algorithm picks aux $= r \in \{0,1\}^{n(\lambda)}$ uniformly at random, computes $c = \langle \boldsymbol{w}, \boldsymbol{m} \rangle + \langle \boldsymbol{s}, r \rangle \bmod q$ and outputs (c, aux).

Ver(pp, m, c, aux) $\to b \in \{0,1\}$. On input pp, $\boldsymbol{m} \in \mathcal{M}$ and (c, aux), the verifier outputs 1 if $c = \langle \boldsymbol{w}, \boldsymbol{m} \rangle + \langle \boldsymbol{s}, r \rangle \bmod q$ where $r =$ aux $\in \{0,1\}^{n(\lambda)}$, and 0 otherwise.

We prove that our commitment scheme is hiding and binding assuming the hardness of the subset sum and the weighted knapsack problems (respectively) for different lengths in the subset sum problems.

Theorem 1. *Let $\ell, n, m : \mathbb{N} \to \mathbb{N}$ and let* **modulus** *be an algorithm which given $\lambda \in \mathbb{N}$ outputs an integer of bit-length $m(\lambda)$. This commitment scheme above is:*

1. *(t, ϵ)-computationally hiding if the $(t + O(\ell(\lambda)m(\lambda)), \epsilon)$- subset-sum assumption holds for $(\ell, m, \text{modulus})$;*
2. *(t, ϵ)-computationally binding if the $(t + O(\ell(\lambda) + n(\lambda)), \epsilon)$-weighted knapsack assumption holds for $(\ell + n, m, \text{modulus})$.*

Proof. Both security reductions are simple.

1. Let $\mathcal{A}$ be a (t, ϵ)-adversary against the hiding property of the commitment scheme. We construct a $(t + O(\ell(\lambda)m(\lambda)), \epsilon)$ adversary $\mathcal{B}$ breaking the decision subset sum assumption as follows. The algorithm $\mathcal{B}$ is given as inputs $(q, \boldsymbol{\gamma}, t)$ where $\boldsymbol{\gamma} \in \mathbb{Z}_q^{n(\lambda)}$. The algorithm $\mathcal{B}$ picks uniformly at random $\boldsymbol{w} \in \mathbb{Z}_q^{\ell(\lambda)}$, sets $\boldsymbol{s} = \boldsymbol{\gamma}$, and runs $\mathcal{A}_1$ on input $\mathsf{pp} = (q, \boldsymbol{w}, \boldsymbol{s})$. When $\mathcal{A}_1$ outputs two messages $\boldsymbol{m_0}, \boldsymbol{m_1} \in \{0,1\}^{\ell(\lambda)}$ and some state information s, the algorithm $\mathcal{B}$ picks uniformly at random a bit $b \in \{0,1\}$ and runs $\mathcal{A}_2$ on $c = \langle \boldsymbol{w}, \boldsymbol{m_b} \rangle + t \bmod q$ and s. Eventually, when $\mathcal{A}_2$ outputs some bit b', $\mathcal{B}$ outputs 0 if $b' = b$ and 1 otherwise. A routine argument shows that the advantage of $\mathcal{B}$ for the decision subset sum problem is identical to the one of $\mathcal{A}$ for breaking the hiding property.
2. Let $\mathcal{A}$ be a (t, ϵ)-adversary against the binding property of the commitment scheme. We construct a $(t + O(\ell(\lambda) + n(\lambda)), \epsilon)$ adversary $\mathcal{B}$ breaking the weighted knapsack assumption as follows. The algorithm $\mathcal{B}$ is given as inputs $(q, \boldsymbol{\gamma})$ where $\boldsymbol{\gamma} \in \mathbb{Z}_q^{\ell(\lambda) + n(\lambda)}$. It sets $\boldsymbol{w} = (\gamma_1, \ldots, \gamma_{\ell(\lambda)}) \in \mathbb{Z}_q^{\ell(\lambda)}$ and $\boldsymbol{s} = (\gamma_{\ell(\lambda)+1}, \ldots, \gamma_{\ell(\lambda)+n(\lambda)}) \in \mathbb{Z}_q^{n(\lambda)}$ and runs $\mathcal{A}$ on input $\mathsf{pp} = (q, \boldsymbol{w}, \boldsymbol{s})$. When $\mathcal{A}$ outputs $(\boldsymbol{m_1}, \boldsymbol{m_2}, \mathsf{aux_1}, \mathsf{aux_2}, c)$, we have $\boldsymbol{m_1} \neq \boldsymbol{m_2}$ and $\mathsf{Ver}(pp, m_1, c, aux_1) = \mathsf{Ver}(pp, m_2, c, aux_2) = 1$ with probability $\epsilon(\lambda)$. In this case, since $\boldsymbol{m_1} \neq \boldsymbol{m_2}$ and $(\boldsymbol{m_1}, \mathsf{aux_1}), (\boldsymbol{m_2}, \mathsf{aux_2}), \in \{0,1\}^{\ell(\lambda)+n(\lambda)}$, if $\mathcal{B}$ outputs the vector $\boldsymbol{y} = (\boldsymbol{m_1}, \mathsf{aux_1}) - (\boldsymbol{m_2}, \mathsf{aux_2})$ (where the substraction is done coordinate-wise), it belongs to $\{-1, 0, 1\}^{\ell(\lambda)+n(\lambda)}$, is non-zero and satisfies $\langle \boldsymbol{\gamma}, \boldsymbol{y} \rangle = 0 \bmod q$ (and is thus a solution to the weighted knapsack problem $(q, \boldsymbol{\gamma})$).

$\square$

The hiding property thus relies on the hardness of the subset sum problem with density $n(\lambda)/m(\lambda)$ while its binding property on the hardness of the weighted knapsack problem with density $(\ell(\lambda) + n(\lambda))/m(\lambda)$. In the following, to simplify the protocols, we consider the case where $n(\lambda) = m(\lambda)$ (*i.e.* density 1 subset sum) and $\ell(\lambda) = n(\lambda)$ (*i.e.* density 2 weighted knapsack). To lighten the notations, we henceforth denote $n = n(\lambda) = \ell(\lambda)$.

3.3 Zero-Knowledge Arguments for Our Commitment

In this section, we present a zero-knowledge argument of knowledge for our string commitment. We apply readily the protocol recently proposed by Feneuil *et al.* [13] for the subset sum problem. It is based on the MPC-in-the-Head paradigm and is described in Protocol 1. We provide an explicit description of the protocol as we use it in the following sections but refer to [13] for details and precise security analysis.

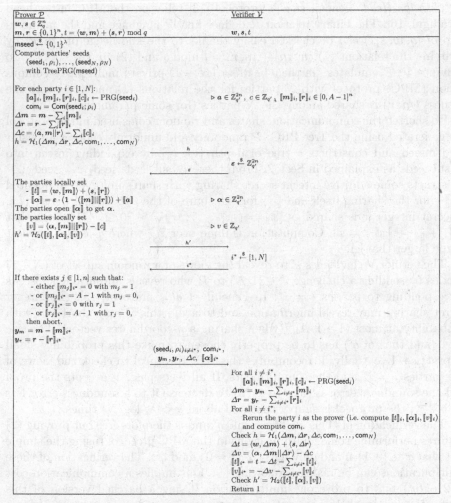

Protocol 1: Zero-knowledge argument for string-commitment using batch product verification to prove binarity.

Context. We consider the binary relation $\mathcal{R} = \{(q, \boldsymbol{w}, \boldsymbol{s}, t), (\boldsymbol{m}, \boldsymbol{r})) \mid \langle \boldsymbol{w}, \boldsymbol{m} \rangle + \langle \boldsymbol{s}, \boldsymbol{r} \rangle = t \bmod q\}$ where $q \in \mathbb{N}$, $\boldsymbol{w}, \boldsymbol{s} \in \mathbb{Z}_q^n$, $t \in \mathbb{Z}_q$, and $\boldsymbol{m}, \boldsymbol{r} \in \{0,1\}^n$. Both the prover $\mathcal{P}$ and the verifier $\mathcal{V}$ know $(q, \boldsymbol{w}, \boldsymbol{s}, t)$ and $\mathcal{P}$ knows $(\boldsymbol{m}, \boldsymbol{r})$ and wants to convince the verifier of this fact. The protocol makes use of a PRG, a tree PRG [19], a commitment scheme (Setup, Com, Ver) (the one proposed in the previous section or any other efficient scheme) and two collision-resistant hash functions $\mathcal{H}_1$ and $\mathcal{H}_2$. The protocol involves two integer parameters A and a prime q' (that depends on n) that are known by $\mathcal{P}$ and $\mathcal{V}$.

MPC-in-the-Head. Feneuil *et al.*'s protocol [13] relies on the MPC-in-the-head paradigm [16]. The binary relation $\mathcal{R}$ defines an NP language and the membership of $(q, \boldsymbol{w}, \boldsymbol{s}, t)$ can be checked easily thanks to the knowledge of $(\boldsymbol{m}, \boldsymbol{r})$ by verifying the relations (1) $\langle \boldsymbol{w}, \boldsymbol{m} \rangle + \langle \boldsymbol{s}, \boldsymbol{r} \rangle = t \bmod q$ and (2) $\boldsymbol{m}, \boldsymbol{r} \in \{0,1\}^n$. To convince $\mathcal{V}$, $\mathcal{P}$ emulates "in their head" a $(N-1)$-private multi-party computation (MPC) protocol with N parties for the relations (1) and (2) where the witness $(\boldsymbol{m}, \boldsymbol{r})$ is shared among the N parties (for some parameter $N \in \mathbb{N}$).

To shorten the communication, shares and random coins used in the protocol are generated using the Tree PRG: $\mathcal{P}$ randomly and uniformly chooses a master seed mseed and constructs a tree of depth $\lceil \log N \rceil$ by expanding mseed into N subseeds as explained in Sect. 2. From these N subseeds $\mathsf{seed}_1, \ldots, \mathsf{seed}_N$, $\mathcal{P}$ constructs some additive integer secret sharing with shares in $[0, A-1]$ denoted as $[\![\cdot]\!]$ for the sharing itself and $[\![\cdot]\!]_i$ for the share of the i-th virtual player (*i.e.* a secret integer x is shared as $[\![x]\!] = ([\![x]\!]_1, \ldots, [\![x]\!]_N) \in [0, A-1]^N$ such that $[\![x]\!]_1 + \cdots + [\![x]\!]_N = x$). Computation is done over $\mathbb{Z}_{q'}$ where q' is the smallest prime larger than A.

The verifier $\mathcal{V}$ challenges $\mathcal{P}$ to reveal the views of a random subset of $(N-1)$ parties by sending a challenge $i^* \in [1, N]$ to $\mathcal{P}$ who reveals all-but-one subseeds corresponding to parties $i \neq i^*$. In Feneuil *et al.*'s protocol [13], the integer secret sharing may reveal information and to avoid this $\mathcal{P}$ may abort but with probability at most $(1 - 1/A)^n$ (when sharing a n-coordinates vector). The size of A (and thus of q') has to be properly chosen to make this probability small in practice. Eventually, $\mathcal{V}$ recomputes the MPC protocol to check the views of the parties $i \neq i^*$ and the commitments. If all tests pass, $\mathcal{V}$ accepts the proof and the soundness error is close to $1/N$. To decrease it to a soundness error less than $2^{-\lambda}$, the protocol is simply repeated about $\tau \approx \lambda/\log(N)$ times.

The verification of (1) is linear modulo q' and is therefore free but proving (2) requires performing some multiplications in the MPC protocol (using the simple fact that $x \in \{0,1\}$ if and only if $x(1-x) = 0 \bmod q'$). The verification of these multiplications can be realized following [4]. This implies a communication cost of $2\log(q')$ bits to prove one multiplication. Using a batched version of this verification protocol [18], one gets a communication cost of $(n+1)\log_2 q'$ for n multiplications. The soundness error of this protocol follows from the Schwartz-Zippel Lemma [25,28].

Security analysis. The following theorem from [13] states the completeness, soundness and zero-knowledge of Protocol 1.

Theorem 2 (Protocol 1). *Let the PRG used in Protocol 1 be (t, ε_{PRG})-secure and the commitment scheme* Com *be (t, ε_{Com})-hiding. Protocol 1 is a zero-knowledge proof of knowledge for the relation $\mathcal{R}$ with $(1 - 1/A)^{2n}$-completeness, $1/q' + 1/N - 1/Nq'$ soundness and $(t, \varepsilon_{PRG} + \varepsilon_{Com})$-zero-knowledge.*

Communication complexity. The communication cost (in bits) of the Protocol 1 with τ repetitions is

$$4\lambda + \tau \left[2n(\log_2(A-1) + \log_2(q')) + \log_2(q') + \lambda \log_2 N + 2\lambda \right].$$

Since the rejection rate after τ repetitions (i.e. that any of the τ repetition aborts) is given by $1 - (1 - 1/A)^{2n\tau} \simeq 2n\tau/A$ where the approximation is tight when A is sufficiently large. Thus by taking $A = \Theta(n\tau)$, we get a (small) constant rejection probability.

Remark 1. Feneuil *et al.*'s [13] proposed a second approach to prove (2) using "*cut-and-choose*". It can be used to prove the knowledge of a commitment opening but does not adapt well for proving Boolean relations of committed values.

Remark 2. It is worth mentioning that our commitment and argument of knowledge of opening can be easily generalized to a proof of partial opening by revealing bits of the committed message, modifying the value of the commitment accordingly and proving the knowledge of the remaining hidden bits. This enables to provide a range proof of the committed message at no additional cost.

4   Zero-Knowledge Arguments for Boolean Relations

Using a batched version of the verification protocol [4,18] for multiplications of the form $xy = c$ with $x, y, c \in \mathbb{Z}_{q'}$ and c a public value, one gets a communication cost of $(n + 1) \log_2 q'$ bits for n multiplications. In the following, we deal with multiplications of the form $xy = z$, where z is a linear combination of shared elements, and the communication cost remains $(n + 1) \log_2 q'$ bits for n multiplications.

4.1   AND Gate

Coordinate-wise AND Gates. We first consider the case where three n-bits vectors $\boldsymbol{m^1}, \boldsymbol{m^2}, \boldsymbol{m^3}$ are committed and $\mathcal{P}$ wants to prove that $\boldsymbol{m^1} \cdot \boldsymbol{m^2} = \boldsymbol{m^3}$. Note that proving that $\boldsymbol{m^1}$ and $\boldsymbol{m^2}$ are binary and that $\boldsymbol{m^1} \cdot \boldsymbol{m^2} = \boldsymbol{m^3} \mod q'$ implies that $\boldsymbol{m^3}$ is binary and $\boldsymbol{m^1} \cdot \boldsymbol{m^2} = \boldsymbol{m^3}$. In addition, $\mathcal{P}$ has to prove that the three random vectors $\boldsymbol{r^1}, \boldsymbol{r^2}, \boldsymbol{r^3}$ used in the commitment are all binary (since no relation is proved between them). Using this approach, $\mathcal{P}$ has to prove $6n$ multiplications and therefore the argument requires sending $6n + 1$ integers in $\mathbb{Z}_{q'}$ via [4,18].

Actually, it is possible to batch some verification equations and reduce this number from $6n + 1$ to $5n + 1$. Indeed, checking $\boldsymbol{m^1} \cdot \boldsymbol{m^2} = \boldsymbol{m^3} \mod q'$ and (for instance) the binarity of m^2 is equivalent (with a small soundness error coming from the Schwartz-Zippel Lemma) to check that

$$\lambda_1 m^2 \cdot (1 - m^2) + \lambda_2 m^1 \cdot m^2 = \lambda_2 m^3 \mod q' \tag{1}$$

for $\lambda_1, \lambda_2 \in \mathbb{Z}_{q'}$ random elements chosen by $\mathcal{V}$. Hence, we can batch all the multiplications checking by verifying the component-wise product

$$(m^1||r^1||r^2||r^3||m^2) \cdot ((1-(m^1||r^1||r^2||r^3))||\lambda_1(1-m^2)+\lambda_2 m^1) = (0||\lambda_2 m^3)$$

and obtain Protocol 2.

Arbitrary AND Gates. Protocol 2 is similar to the protocols from [2,3,6,17] since it can be used only to prove multiplication coordinate-wise. We generalize it to obtain a more flexible protocol able to prove relations such as $m_i^1 \wedge m_j^2 = m_k^3$ for arbitrary coordinates $i, j, k \in [1, n]$.

Assume $\mathcal{P}$ has to prove the satisfiability of $K \geq 1$ AND gates with components belonging to $L \geq 1$ committed vectors $\{m^\ell\}_{1 \leq \ell \leq L} \in \{0,1\}^n$. Suppose that there are $M \leq K$ AND gates such that each of them has at least one coordinate of a fixed committed vector m^ℓ as input (for some $\ell \in [1, L]$). Assume these M gates are of the form $m_{x_k}^{\ell_k} \wedge m_{y_k}^{\ell_k} = m_{z_k}^{\ell'_k}$ for $k \in [1, M], \ell_k, \ell'_k \in [1, L], x_k, y_k, z_k \in [1, n]$ (again, we fix the vector m^ℓ). Moreover, as seen previously to check that m^ℓ is binary, $\mathcal{V}$ can verify $m^\ell \circ (1 - m^\ell) = 0 \mod q'$. Then we can batch these verifications as

$$m^\ell \cdot [-\lambda_0 m^\ell + \sum_{k=1}^{M} \lambda_k m_{y_k}^{\ell_k} e_{x_k}] = -\lambda_0 m^\ell + \sum_{k=1}^{M} \lambda_k m_{z_k}^{\ell'_k} e_{x_k} \mod q' \tag{2}$$

where e_i is the i-th vector of the canonical basis of $\mathbb{Z}_{q'}^n$ and $\{\lambda_k\}_{0 \leq k \leq M} \in \mathbb{Z}_{q'}$ are random elements chosen by $\mathcal{V}$. Thus, $\mathcal{P}$ can batch all the gates' evaluation checking satisfying that at least one input for each of these gates belongs to the same committed vector. This batching can include the binary verification of this specific vector. In other words, the number of equations does not depend anymore on the number of gates (i.e. is independent of the distribution of AND gates over the committed bits). We obtain the generalized Protocol 3 as a direct extension of Protocol 2 (essentially the batching part is slightly different) which can be found in Appendix A.

Security analysis. The following theorems state the completeness, soundness, and zero-knowledge of Protocol 2 and Protocol 3. The proofs are similar to those in [13] and are omitted due to lack of space.

Theorem 3 (Protocol 2). *Let the PRG used in Protocol 1 be (t, ε_{PRG})-secure and the commitment scheme Com be (t, ε_{Com})-hiding. Protocol 2 is a zero-knowledge proof of knowledge for the relation $\mathcal{R}$ with $(1 - 1/A)^{6n}$-completeness, $1/q' + 1/N - 1/Nq'$ soundness and $(t, \varepsilon_{PRG} + \varepsilon_{Com})$-zero-knowledge.*

Prover $\mathcal{P}$	Verifier $\mathcal{V}$
$w, s \in \mathbb{Z}_q^n, m^k, r^k \in \{0,1\}^n$ for $1 \le k \le 3$	w, s, t^k
$m^1 \cdot m^2 = m^3, t^k = \langle w, m^k \rangle + \langle s, r^k \rangle$	

$\mathsf{mseed} \xleftarrow{\$} \{0,1\}^\lambda$	
Compute parties' seeds	
$\quad (\mathsf{seed}_1, \rho_1), \ldots, (\mathsf{seed}_N, \rho_N)$	
$\quad$ with $\mathsf{TreePRG}(\mathsf{mseed})$	
For each party $i \in [1, N]$:	
$\quad [\![a]\!]_i, [\![c]\!]_i, \{[\![m^k]\!]_i, [\![r^k]\!]_i\}_{1 \le k \le 3}$	
$\quad \leftarrow \mathsf{PRG}(\mathsf{seed}_i)$	$\triangleright\, a \in \mathbb{Z}_{q'}^{5n}, c \in \mathbb{Z}_{q'}, [\![m^k]\!]_i, [\![r^k]\!]_i \in [0, A-1]^n$
$\quad \mathsf{com}_i = \mathsf{Com}(\mathsf{seed}_i; \rho_i)$	
For $1 \le k \le 3$:	
$\quad \Delta m^k = m^k - \sum_i [\![m^k]\!]_i$	
$\quad \Delta r^k = r^k - \sum_i [\![r^k]\!]_i$	
$\Delta c = -\langle a, m^1 \| r^1 \| r^2 \| r^3 \| m^2 \rangle - \sum_i [\![c]\!]_i$	
$h = \mathcal{H}_1(\{\Delta m^k, \Delta r^k\}_{1 \le k \le 3}, \Delta c,$	
$\mathsf{com}_1, \ldots, \mathsf{com}_N)$	

$$\xrightarrow{\qquad h \qquad}$$

$$\xleftarrow{\qquad \varepsilon \qquad} \quad \varepsilon \xleftarrow{\$} \mathbb{Z}_{q'}^{5n}, \lambda_1, \lambda_2 \xleftarrow{\$} \mathbb{Z}_{q'}$$

The parties locally set	
$\quad - [\![t^k]\!] = \langle w, [\![m^k]\!] \rangle + \langle s, [\![r^k]\!] \rangle$ for $1 \le k \le 3$	
$\quad - [\![\alpha]\!] = \varepsilon \cdot ((1 - [\![m^1]\!] \| r^1 \| r^2 \| r^3]\!]) \|$	
$\quad \lambda_1 (1 - [\![m^2]\!]) + \lambda_2 [\![m^1]\!]) + [\![a]\!]$	$\triangleright\, \alpha \in \mathbb{Z}_{q'}^{5n}$ (computation in $\mathbb{Z}_{q'}$)
The parties open $[\![\alpha]\!]$ to get α.	
The parties locally set	
$\quad [\![v]\!] = \langle \alpha, [\![m^1]\!] \| r^1 \| r^2 \| r^3 \| m^3]\!] \rangle - [\![c]\!] -$	
$\quad \langle \varepsilon, 0 \| \lambda_2 [\![m^3]\!] \rangle$	$\triangleright\, v \in \mathbb{Z}_{q'}$ (computation in $\mathbb{Z}_{q'}$)
$h' = \mathcal{H}_2(\{[\![t^k]\!]\}_{1 \le k \le 3}, [\![\alpha]\!], [\![v]\!])$	

$$\xrightarrow{\qquad h' \qquad}$$

$$\xleftarrow{\qquad i^* \qquad} \quad i^* \xleftarrow{\$} [1, N]$$

If there exists $k \in [1, 3]$ and $j \in [1, n]$ such that:	
$\quad - $ either $[\![m_j^k]\!]_{i^*} = 0$ with $m_j^k = 1$	
$\quad - $ or $[\![m_j^k]\!]_{i^*} = A - 1$ with $m_j^k = 0$,	
$\quad - $ or $[\![r_j^k]\!]_{i^*} = 0$ with $r_j^k = 1$	
$\quad - $ or $[\![r_j^k]\!]_{i^*} = A - 1$ with $r_j^k = 0$,	
$\quad$ then abort.	
$y_{m^k} = m^k - [\![m^k]\!]_{i^*}$ and	
$y_{r^k} = r^k - [\![r^k]\!]_{i^*}$ for $k \in [1, 3]$	

$$\xrightarrow{\substack{(\mathsf{seed}_i, \rho_i)_{i \ne i^*}, \ \mathsf{com}_{i^*}, \\ \{y_{m^k}, y_{r^k}\}_{1 \le k \le 3}, \ \Delta c, \ [\![\alpha]\!]_{i^*}}}$$

	For all $i \ne i^*$,
	$\quad [\![a]\!]_i, [\![c]\!]_i, \{[\![m^k]\!]_i, [\![r^k]\!]_i\}_{1 \le k \le 3}$
	$\quad \leftarrow \mathsf{PRG}(\mathsf{seed}_i)$
	For all $i \ne i^*$,
	$\quad$ Rerun the party i as the prover
	$\quad$ and compute the commitment com_i.
	For $1 \le k \le 3$,
	$\quad \Delta m^k = y_{m^k} - \sum_{i \ne i^*} [\![m^k]\!]_i$
	$\quad \Delta r^k = y_{r^k} - \sum_{i \ne i^*} [\![r^k]\!]_i$
	$\quad \Delta t^k = \langle w, \Delta m^k \rangle + \langle s, \Delta r^k \rangle$
	$\quad [\![t^k]\!]_{i^*} = t^k - \Delta t^k - \sum_{i \ne i^*} [\![t^k]\!]_i$
	$\Delta v = \langle \alpha, \Delta m^1 \| \Delta r^1 \| \Delta r^2 \| \Delta r^3 \| \Delta m^2 \rangle$
	$\quad - \Delta c - \langle \varepsilon, 0 \| \lambda_2 \Delta m^3; \rangle$
	$[\![v]\!]_{i^*} = -\Delta v - \sum_{i \ne i^*} [\![v]\!]_i$
	Check $h = \mathcal{H}_1(\{\Delta m^k, \Delta r^k\}_{1 \le k \le 3}, \Delta c,$
	$\mathsf{com}_1, \ldots, \mathsf{com}_N)$
	Check $h' = \mathcal{H}_2(\{[\![t^k]\!]\}_{1 \le k \le 3}, [\![\alpha]\!], [\![v]\!])$
	Return 1

Protocol 2: Zero-knowledge argument for AND.

Theorem 4 (Protocol 3). *Let the PRG used in Protocol 1 be* (t, ε_{PRG})*-secure and the commitment scheme* Com *be* (t, ε_{Com})*-hiding. Protocol 3 is a zero-knowledge proof of knowledge for the relation* $\mathcal{R}$ *with* $(1 - 1/A)^{2Ln}$*-completeness,* $1/q' + 1/N - 1/Nq'$ *soundness and* $(t, \varepsilon_{PRG} + \varepsilon_{Com})$*-zero-knowledge.*

Remark 3. Note that Protocol 2 and 3 have the same soundness as Protocol 1. This follows from the Schwartz-Zippel Lemma, since the underlying multinomial still has the same degree after batching, and so it does not impact the soundness error.

The communication cost (in bits) of Protocols 2 and 3 are respectively:

$$4\lambda + \tau \left[n(6\log_2(A-1) + 5\log_2(q')) + \log_2(q') + \lambda \log_2 N + 2\lambda \right],$$

$$4\lambda + \tau \left[2Ln(\log_2(A-1) + \log_2(q')) + \log_2(q') + \lambda \log_2 N + 2\lambda \right].$$

We notice that it does not depend on the number K of AND gates to prove.

4.2 XOR Gate

Coordinate-wise XOR Gates. We first consider, as above, the case where three n-bits vectors $\boldsymbol{m^1}, \boldsymbol{m^2}, \boldsymbol{m^3}$ are committed and $\mathcal{P}$ wants to prove that $\boldsymbol{m^1} \oplus \boldsymbol{m^2} = \boldsymbol{m^3}$ (coordinate-wise).

Let f be the polynomial $f(x) = 2x - x^2$ defined over $\mathbb{Z}_{q'}$ with $q' \geq 3$ a prime number. One can easily check that if $\boldsymbol{m^1}$ and $\boldsymbol{m^2}$ are binary vectors, then $f(\boldsymbol{m^1} + \boldsymbol{m^2}) \bmod q' = \boldsymbol{m^1} \oplus \boldsymbol{m^2} \in \{0, 1\}$. Thus, proving that $f(\boldsymbol{m^1} + \boldsymbol{m^2}) = \boldsymbol{m^3} \bmod q'$ in conjunction with the argument of knowledge of opening of the corresponding commitments, implies $\boldsymbol{m^1} \oplus \boldsymbol{m^2} = \boldsymbol{m^3}$.

Arbitrary XOR Gates. Again, this protocol is not enough flexible and can not be used to prove relations such as $m_i^1 \oplus m_j^2 = m_k^3$ for arbitrary $i, j, k \in [1, n]$, but we outline how to generalize it.

Assume that $\mathcal{P}$ has to prove the satisfiability of K XOR gates with inputs/output belonging to L committed vectors $\{\boldsymbol{m^\ell}\}_{1 \leq \ell \leq L} \in \{0, 1\}^n$. As for the AND gates, suppose that there are $M \leq K$ gates of the form $m_{x_k}^{\ell_k} \oplus m_{y_k}^{\ell_k} = m_{z_k}^{\ell_k'}$ for $k \in [1, M]$, $\ell_k, \ell_k' \in [1, L], x_k, y_k, z_k \in [1, n]$. We assume the binarity of each committed vector is checked during the protocol, so that

$$f(m_{x_k}^\ell + m_{y_k}^{\ell_k}) = 2(m_{x_k}^\ell + m_{y_k}^{\ell_k}) - (m_{x_k}^\ell + m_{y_k}^{\ell_k})^2 = m_{x_k}^\ell \oplus m_{y_k}^{\ell_k} = m_{z_k}^{\ell_k'} \mod q'.$$

Moreover, as seen previously, to check that $\boldsymbol{m^\ell}$ is binary, $\mathcal{V}$ can verify $\boldsymbol{m^\ell} \cdot (1 - \boldsymbol{m^\ell}) = 0 \mod q'$. If the binarity of $\boldsymbol{m^{\ell_k}}$ and $\boldsymbol{m^\ell}$ is proven elsewhere, $\mathcal{V}$ is convinced that $m_{y_k}^{\ell_k} m_{y_k}^{\ell_k} = m_{y_k}^{\ell_k} \bmod q'$ and $m_{x_k}^\ell m_{x_k}^\ell = m_{x_k}^\ell \bmod q'$. Hence, the batching equation becomes

$$\boldsymbol{m^\ell} \cdot [-\lambda_0 \boldsymbol{m^\ell} - 2\sum_{k=1}^{M} \lambda_k m_{y_k}^{\ell_k} \boldsymbol{e_{x_k}}]$$

$$= -\lambda_0 \boldsymbol{m^\ell} + \sum_{k=1}^{M} \lambda_k \left(m_{z_k}^{\ell_k'} - m_{y_k}^{\ell_k} - m_{x_k}^\ell \right) \boldsymbol{e_{x_k}} \mod q', \quad (3)$$

where e_i is the i-th vector of the canonical basis of $\mathbb{Z}_{q'}^n$ and $\{\lambda_k\}_{0 \leq k \leq M} \in \mathbb{Z}_{q'}$ are random elements chosen by $\mathcal{V}$.

Security analysis. The theorems stating the completeness, soundness and zero-knowledge of the protocol for the bit-wise XOR and its generalization are the same as Theorems 3 and 4 (respectively). This follows directly from Remark 3.

The communication complexity (in bits) of the protocol for arbitrary XOR gates with τ repetitions is:

$$4\lambda + \tau \left[2Ln(\log_2(A-1) + \log_2(q')) + \log_2(q') + \lambda \log_2 N + 2\lambda \right],$$

while the one for the bit-wise XOR is a subcase when $L = 3$. We notice that the size is the same as Protocol 3 and is independent of K.

4.3   Instantiation and Performances

We present sets of parameters for an instantiation of our commitment scheme with $m(\lambda) = \ell(\lambda) = n(\lambda) = 256$ (*i.e.* with security based on density 1 subset-sum and density 2 weighted knapsack). We present performances for the component-wise protocols for AND and XOR gates. To decrease the rejection rate, we use a strategy introduced in [13] that consists in allowing $\mathcal{P}$ to abort in $0 \leq \eta < \tau$ out of the τ iterations and $\mathcal{V}$ accepts the proof if the prover can answer to $\tau - \eta$ challenges among the τ iterations. This relaxed proof has a significantly lower rejection rate (at the cost of a small increase of the soundness error) (Table 1).

Table 1. Comparison of performances with $n = 256$ and $q \approx 2^{256}$.

Protocol	Parameters				Proof size	Rej. rate	Soundness err.
	τ	η	N	A			
Protocol 1 (Opening)	21	3	256	2^{13}	35.4 KB	0.035	133 bits
Protocol 1 (Opening)	19	2	256	2^{13}	33.3 KB	0.104	128 bits
Protocol 2 (AND)	21	3	256	2^{15}	98.9 KB	0.014	133 bits
Protocol 2 (AND)	19	2	256	2^{15}	93.4 KB	0.054	128 bits
Protocol XOR	21	3	256	2^{15}	107.4 KB	0.014	133 bits
Protocol XOR	19	2	256	2^{15}	101.3 KB	0.054	128 bits

5   Verification of Circuit Evaluation

Let C be a Boolean circuit with $|C|$ gates (AND or XOR) and T input bits. Let $m \in \{0,1\}^T$ and $v_1, \ldots, v_{|C|} \in \{0,1\}$ be committed elements such that m is an input that satisfy C and the v's are the outputs of each gates of C when evaluated on m, *i.e.* $C(m_1, \ldots, m_T) = v_{|C|} = 1$. The prover $\mathcal{P}$ wants to prove that m indeed satisfies C. For this purpose, we will use protocols that have been presented in the previous sections. For simplicity, we assume without loss of generality that $T \leq n$. Since n bits can be committed via the same commitment (n is the size of the subset-sum instance), we need $|C|/n + 1$ string commitments. We introduce the following notation to simplify the batching equation: for $k \in [0, |C|/n]$, $v^0 = (m||v_1||\ldots||v_{n-T}), \ldots, v^{|C|/n} = (v_{|C|-T+1}||\ldots||v_{|C|}||\mathbf{0})$. Following the batching from Equation (2) and Equation (3), we can set x, y, z as follows so that the circuit satisfiability verification consists in checking that $x \cdot y = z$:

$$y = (v^0||\ldots||v^{|C|/n}||r^0||\ldots||r^{|C|/n}),$$

$$x = \left(-\lambda_0 v^0 + \sum_{i=1}^{n} \sum_{j=0}^{|C|/n} \sum_{k=1}^{n} \lambda_{v_k^j} \left(\delta_{0,i,j,k} v_k^j - 2\zeta_{0,i,j,k} v_k^j \right) e_i || \ldots \right.$$

$$|| -\lambda_{|C|/n} v^{|C|/n} + \sum_{i=1}^{n} \sum_{j=0}^{|C|/n} \sum_{k=1}^{n} \lambda_{v_k^j} \left(\delta_{|C|/n,i,j,k} v_k^j - 2\zeta_{|C|/n,i,j,k} v_k^j \right) e_i$$

$$\left. ||1 - r^1||\ldots||1 - r^{|C|/n} \right)$$

where $r^0, \ldots, r^{|C|/n}$ is the randomness used in the commitment and the vector z can be computed as a linear combination of $v^0, \ldots, v^{|C|/n}$. As above, e_i is the i-th vector of the canonical basis of $\mathbb{Z}_{q'}^n$, λ's are random public values chosen by the verifier $\mathcal{V}$, and the binary elements ζ and δ depend on the circuit structure, i.e. $\delta_{\ell,i,j,k} = 1$ if and only if $v_i^\ell \wedge v_k^j = v_p^u$ for some $u \in [0, |C|/n]$ and $v \in [1, n]$ (and $\zeta_{\ell,i,j,k} = 1$ if and only if $v_i^\ell \oplus v_k^j = v_p^u$). Hence, $\mathcal{V}$ has to check $x \cdot y = z$ to be convinced of the binarity of the vectors, and of the satisfiability of the circuit. The full protocol is given as Protocol 4 in Appendix A.

Theorem 5 (Protocol 4). *Let the PRG used in Protocol 4 be (t, ε_{PRG})-secure and the commitment scheme* Com *be (t, ε_{Com})-hiding. The protocol 4 is a zero-knowledge proof of knowledge for the relation $\mathcal{R}$ with $(1 - 1/A)^{2(|C|+n)}$-completeness, $1/q' + 1/N - 1/Nq'$ soundness and $(t, \varepsilon_{PRG} + \varepsilon_{Com})$-zero-knowledge.*

The communication cost (in bits) of Protocol 4 with τ repetitions is:

$$4\lambda + \tau \left[2(|C| + n)(\log(A-1) + \log(q')) + \log(q') + \lambda \log N + 2\lambda \right].$$

With $n = 2\lambda$ and $A = \Theta((|C|+n)\tau)$ (for a small constant rejection probability), its asymptotic complexity is $\Theta\left(\frac{\lambda(|C|+\lambda)}{\log N} \log\left(\frac{\lambda(|C|+\lambda)}{\log N} \right) + \lambda^2 \right)$. With $N = \Theta(\lambda)$ to minimize, we get asymptotic complexity $\tilde{\Theta}(\lambda|C| + \lambda^2)$ to be compared with $\tilde{\Theta}(|C|\lambda^2)$ in [17] (which can only prove Boolean relations bit-wise on binary strings and may result in a large overhead depending on the circuit considered).

A   Description of Protocols 3 and 4

In order to describe the circuit during Protocol 3, we set $S \leftarrow \emptyset$. Then construct S as follows: if $m_{x_k}^\ell \wedge m_{y_k}^{\ell_k} = m_{z_k}^{\ell'_k}$ for $k \in [1, M], \{\ell, \ell_k, \ell'_k\} \in [1, L]^3, \{x_k, y_k, z_k\} \in [1, n]^3$, then $S = S \cup \{(\ell, x_k; \ell_k, y_k; \ell'_k, z_k)\}$.

Prover $\mathcal{P}$	Verifier $\mathcal{V}$
$\boldsymbol{w}, \boldsymbol{s} \in \mathbb{Z}_q^n, S$	
For $1 \leq \ell \leq L$,	
$\quad \boldsymbol{m}^\ell, \boldsymbol{r}^\ell \in \{0,1\}^n$	
$\quad t^\ell = \langle \boldsymbol{w}, \boldsymbol{m}^\ell \rangle + \langle \boldsymbol{s}, \boldsymbol{r}^\ell \rangle \in \mathbb{Z}_q$	t^ℓ for $1 \leq \ell \leq L$
$\boldsymbol{x} \cdot \boldsymbol{y} = \boldsymbol{z}$ as described in Section 4	$S, \boldsymbol{w}, \boldsymbol{s}$

$\mathsf{mseed} \xleftarrow{\$} \{0,1\}^\lambda$	
Compute parties' seeds	
$\quad (\mathsf{seed}_1, \rho_1), \ldots, (\mathsf{seed}_N, \rho_N)$	
$\quad$ with $\mathsf{TreePRG}(\mathsf{mseed})$	
For each party $i \in [1, N]$:	
$\quad [\![\boldsymbol{a}]\!]_i, [\![\boldsymbol{c}]\!]_i, \{[\![\boldsymbol{m}^\ell]\!]_i, [\![\boldsymbol{r}^\ell]\!]_i\}_{1 \leq \ell \leq L}$	
$\quad \leftarrow \mathsf{PRG}(\mathsf{seed}_i)$	$\triangleright \boldsymbol{a} \in \mathbb{Z}_{q'}^{2Ln}$, $c \in \mathbb{Z}_{q'}$, $[\![\boldsymbol{m}^\ell]\!]_i, [\![\boldsymbol{r}^\ell]\!]_i \in [0, A-1]^n$
$\quad \mathsf{com}_i = \mathsf{Com}(\mathsf{seed}_i; \rho_i)$	
For $1 \leq \ell \leq L$:	
$\quad \varDelta \boldsymbol{m}^\ell = \boldsymbol{m}^\ell - \sum_i [\![\boldsymbol{m}^\ell]\!]_i$	
$\quad \varDelta \boldsymbol{r}^\ell = \boldsymbol{r}^\ell - \sum_i [\![\boldsymbol{r}^\ell]\!]_i$	
$\varDelta c = -\langle \boldsymbol{a}, \boldsymbol{y} \rangle - \sum_i [\![\boldsymbol{c}]\!]_i$	
$h = \mathcal{H}_1(\{\varDelta \boldsymbol{m}^\ell, \varDelta \boldsymbol{r}^\ell\}_{1 \leq \ell \leq L}, \varDelta c, \mathsf{com}_1, \ldots, \mathsf{com}_N)$	
$\xrightarrow{\quad\quad\quad h \quad\quad\quad}$	
	$\varepsilon \xleftarrow{\$} \mathbb{Z}_{q'}^{2Ln}, \{\lambda_i\}_{1 \leq i \leq L+K} \xleftarrow{\$} \mathbb{Z}_{q'}$
$\xleftarrow{\quad\quad\quad \varepsilon \quad\quad\quad}$	
The parties locally set	
$\quad$ - $[\![t^\ell]\!] = \langle \boldsymbol{w}, [\![\boldsymbol{m}^\ell]\!] \rangle + \langle \boldsymbol{s}, [\![\boldsymbol{r}^\ell]\!] \rangle$ for $\ell \in [1, L]$	
$\quad$ - $[\![\boldsymbol{\alpha}]\!] = \varepsilon \cdot [\![\boldsymbol{x}]\!] + [\![\boldsymbol{a}]\!]$	$\triangleright \boldsymbol{\alpha} \in \mathbb{Z}_{q'}^{2Ln}$
The parties open $[\![\boldsymbol{\alpha}]\!]$ to get $\boldsymbol{\alpha}$.	
The parties locally set	
$\quad [\![v]\!] = \langle \boldsymbol{\alpha}, [\![\boldsymbol{y}]\!] \rangle - [\![c]\!] - \langle \varepsilon, \boldsymbol{z} \rangle$	$\triangleright v \in \mathbb{Z}_{q'}$
$h' = \mathcal{H}_2(\{[\![t^\ell]\!]\}_{1 \leq \ell \leq L}, [\![\boldsymbol{\alpha}]\!], [\![v]\!])$	
$\xrightarrow{\quad\quad\quad h' \quad\quad\quad}$	
	$i^* \xleftarrow{\$} [1, N]$
$\xleftarrow{\quad\quad\quad i^* \quad\quad\quad}$	
If $\exists \ell \in [1, L]$ and $j \in [1, n]$ such that:	
$\quad$ - either $[\![m_j^\ell]\!]_{i^*} = 0$ with $m_j^\ell = 1$	
$\quad$ - or $[\![m_j^\ell]\!]_{i^*} = A - 1$ with $m_j^\ell = 0$,	
$\quad$ - or $[\![r_j^\ell]\!]_{i^*} = 0$ with $r_j^\ell = 1$	
$\quad$ - or $[\![r_j^\ell]\!]_{i^*} = A - 1$ with $r_j^\ell = 0$,	
$\quad$ then abort.	
$\boldsymbol{y}_{m^\ell} = \boldsymbol{m}^\ell - [\![\boldsymbol{m}^\ell]\!]_{i^*}$ and $\boldsymbol{y}_{r^\ell} = \boldsymbol{r}^\ell - [\![\boldsymbol{r}^\ell]\!]_{i^*}$ for $\ell \in [1, L]$	
$\xrightarrow[\quad\quad\quad]{(\mathsf{seed}_i, \rho_i)_{i \neq i^*}, \ \mathsf{com}_{i^*},}$	
$\xrightarrow[\quad\quad\quad]{\{\boldsymbol{y}_{m^\ell}, \boldsymbol{y}_{r^\ell}\}_{1 \leq \ell \leq L}, \ \varDelta c, \ [\![\boldsymbol{\alpha}]\!]_{i^*}}$	
	For all $i \neq i^*$:
	$\quad [\![\boldsymbol{a}]\!]_i, [\![\boldsymbol{c}]\!]_i, \{[\![\boldsymbol{m}^\ell]\!]_i, [\![\boldsymbol{r}^\ell]\!]_i\}_{1 \leq \ell \leq L} \leftarrow \mathsf{PRG}(\mathsf{seed}_i)$
	$\quad$ Rerun the party i as the prover and compute com_i.
	For $\ell \in [1, L]$:
	$\quad \varDelta \boldsymbol{m}^\ell = \boldsymbol{y}_{m^\ell} - \sum_{i \neq i^*} [\![\boldsymbol{m}^\ell]\!]_i$
	$\quad \varDelta \boldsymbol{r}^\ell = \boldsymbol{y}_{r^\ell} - \sum_{i \neq i^*} [\![\boldsymbol{r}^\ell]\!]_i$
	$\quad \varDelta t^k = \langle \boldsymbol{w}, \varDelta \boldsymbol{m}^\ell \rangle + \langle \boldsymbol{s}, \varDelta \boldsymbol{r}^\ell \rangle$
	$\quad [\![t^\ell]\!]_{i^*} = t^\ell - \varDelta t^\ell - \sum_{i \neq i^*} [\![t^\ell]\!]_i$
	$\varDelta v = \langle \boldsymbol{\alpha}, \varDelta \boldsymbol{x} \rangle - \varDelta c - \langle \varepsilon, \varDelta \boldsymbol{z} \rangle$
	$[\![v]\!]_{i^*} = -\varDelta v - \sum_{i \neq i^*} [\![v]\!]_i$
	Check $h = \mathcal{H}_1(\{\varDelta \boldsymbol{m}^\ell, \varDelta \boldsymbol{r}^\ell\}_{1 \leq \ell \leq L},$
	$\varDelta c, \mathsf{com}_1, \ldots, \mathsf{com}_N)$
	Check $h' = \mathcal{H}_2(\{[\![t^\ell]\!]\}_{1 \leq \ell \leq L}, [\![\boldsymbol{\alpha}]\!], [\![v]\!])$
	Return 1

Protocol 3: Zero-knowledge argument for arbitrary AND gates.

Prover $\mathcal{P}$	Verifier $\mathcal{V}$

$C, \boldsymbol{w}, \boldsymbol{s} \in \mathbb{Z}_{q'}^n$
For $0 \leq \ell \leq |C|/n$
$\quad \boldsymbol{v}^\ell, \boldsymbol{r}^\ell \in \{0,1\}^n$
$\quad t^\ell = \langle \boldsymbol{w}, \boldsymbol{v}^\ell \rangle + \langle \boldsymbol{s}, \boldsymbol{r}^\ell \rangle$
$\boldsymbol{x} \cdot \boldsymbol{y} = \boldsymbol{z}$ as described in Section 5

$\qquad\qquad\qquad\qquad\qquad\qquad\qquad\qquad C, \boldsymbol{w}, \boldsymbol{s}, t^\ell$ for $0 \leq \ell \leq |C|/n$

$\mathsf{mseed} \xleftarrow{\$} \{0,1\}^\lambda$
Compute parties' seeds
$\quad (\mathsf{seed}_1, \rho_1), \ldots, (\mathsf{seed}_N, \rho_N)$
$\quad$ with $\mathsf{TreePRG}(\mathsf{mseed})$

For each party $i \in [1, N]$:
$\quad [\![\boldsymbol{a}]\!]_i, [\![\boldsymbol{c}]\!]_i, \{[\![\boldsymbol{v}^\ell]\!]_i, [\![\boldsymbol{r}^\ell]\!]_i\}_{0 \leq \ell \leq |C|/n}$
$\quad \leftarrow \mathsf{PRG}(\mathsf{seed}_i)$ $\triangleright\, \boldsymbol{a} \in \mathbb{Z}_{q'}^{2(|C|+n)}\,,\; \boldsymbol{c} \in \mathbb{Z}_{q'}\,,\; [\![\boldsymbol{r}^\ell]\!]_i, [\![\boldsymbol{v}^\ell]\!]_i \in [0, A-1]^n$
$\quad \mathsf{com}_i = \mathsf{Com}(\mathsf{seed}_i; \rho_i)$
For $0 \leq \ell \leq |C|/n$:
$\quad \Delta \boldsymbol{r}^\ell = \boldsymbol{r}^\ell - \sum_i [\![\boldsymbol{r}^\ell]\!]_i$
$\quad \Delta \boldsymbol{v}^\ell = \boldsymbol{v}^\ell - \sum_i [\![\boldsymbol{v}^\ell]\!]_i$
$\Delta c = -\langle \boldsymbol{a}, \boldsymbol{y} \rangle - \sum_i [\![\boldsymbol{c}]\!]_i$
$h = \mathcal{H}_1(\{\Delta \boldsymbol{r}^\ell, \Delta \boldsymbol{v}^\ell\}_{0 \leq \ell \leq |C|/n}, \Delta c, \mathsf{com}_1, \ldots, \mathsf{com}_N)$

$\qquad\qquad\qquad\qquad\qquad \xrightarrow{\qquad\qquad h \qquad\qquad}$

$\qquad\qquad\qquad\qquad\qquad\qquad\qquad\qquad \boldsymbol{\varepsilon} \xleftarrow{\$} \mathbb{Z}_{q'}^{2(|C|+n)}$
$\qquad\qquad\qquad\qquad\qquad\qquad\qquad\qquad \{\lambda_i\}_{0 \leq i \leq |C|(1+1/n)} \xleftarrow{\$} \mathbb{Z}_{q'}$

$\qquad\qquad\qquad\qquad\qquad \xleftarrow{\qquad\qquad \boldsymbol{\varepsilon} \qquad\qquad}$

The parties locally set
$\quad$ - $[\![t^\ell]\!] = \langle \boldsymbol{w}, [\![\boldsymbol{v}^\ell]\!] \rangle + \langle \boldsymbol{s}, [\![\boldsymbol{r}^\ell]\!] \rangle$ for $\ell \in [0, |C|/n]$
$\quad$ - $[\![\boldsymbol{\alpha}]\!] = \boldsymbol{\varepsilon} \cdot [\![\boldsymbol{x}]\!] + [\![\boldsymbol{a}]\!]$ $\triangleright\, \boldsymbol{\alpha} \in \mathbb{Z}_{q'}^{2(|C|+n)}$
The parties open $[\![\boldsymbol{\alpha}]\!]$ to get $\boldsymbol{\alpha}$.
The parties locally set $[\![v]\!] = \langle \boldsymbol{\alpha}, [\![\boldsymbol{y}]\!] \rangle - [\![\boldsymbol{c}]\!] - \langle \boldsymbol{\varepsilon}, [\![\boldsymbol{z}]\!] \rangle$ $\triangleright\, v \in \mathbb{Z}_{q'}$
$h' = \mathcal{H}_2(\{[\![t^\ell]\!]\}_{0 \leq \ell \leq |C|/n}, [\![\boldsymbol{\alpha}]\!], [\![v]\!])$

$\qquad\qquad\qquad\qquad\qquad \xrightarrow{\qquad\qquad h' \qquad\qquad}$

$\qquad\qquad\qquad\qquad\qquad\qquad\qquad\qquad i^* \xleftarrow{\$} [1, N]$

$\qquad\qquad\qquad\qquad\qquad \xleftarrow{\qquad\qquad i^* \qquad\qquad}$

If $\exists \ell \in [0, |C|/n], j \in [1, n]$ such that:
$\quad$ - either $[\![v_j^\ell]\!]_{i^*} = 0$ with $v_j^\ell = 1$
$\quad$ - or $[\![v_j^\ell]\!]_{i^*} = A - 1$ with $v_j^\ell = 0$,
$\quad$ - or $[\![r_j^\ell]\!]_{i^*} = 0$ with $r_j^\ell = 1$
$\quad$ - or $[\![r_j^\ell]\!]_{i^*} = A - 1$ with $r_j^\ell = 0$,
$\quad$ then abort.
$\boldsymbol{y}_{v^\ell} = \boldsymbol{v}^\ell - [\![\boldsymbol{v}^\ell]\!]_{i^*}$ and $\boldsymbol{y}_{r^\ell} = \boldsymbol{r}^\ell - [\![\boldsymbol{r}^\ell]\!]_{i^*}$

$\qquad\qquad\qquad\qquad (\mathsf{seed}_i, \rho_i)_{i \neq i^*},\; \mathsf{com}_{i^*},$
$\qquad\qquad\qquad \{\boldsymbol{y}_{v^\ell}, \boldsymbol{y}_{r^\ell}\}_{0 \leq \ell \leq |C|/n},\; \Delta c,\; [\![\boldsymbol{\alpha}]\!]_{i^*}$
$\qquad\qquad\qquad\qquad \xrightarrow{\hspace{5cm}}$

$\qquad\qquad\qquad\qquad$ For all $i \neq i^*$,
$\qquad\qquad\qquad\qquad\quad [\![\boldsymbol{a}]\!]_i, [\![\boldsymbol{c}]\!]_i, \{[\![\boldsymbol{v}^\ell]\!]_i, [\![\boldsymbol{r}^\ell]\!]_i\}_{0 \leq \ell \leq |C|/n} \leftarrow \mathsf{PRG}(\mathsf{seed}_i)$
$\qquad\qquad\qquad\qquad\quad$ Rerun the party i as the prover and compute com_i.
$\qquad\qquad\qquad\qquad$ For $0 \leq \ell \leq |C|/n$,
$\qquad\qquad\qquad\qquad\quad \Delta \boldsymbol{v}^\ell = \boldsymbol{y}_{v^\ell} - \sum_{i \neq i^*} [\![\boldsymbol{v}^\ell]\!]_i,\; \Delta \boldsymbol{r}^\ell = \boldsymbol{y}_{r^\ell} - \sum_{i \neq i^*} [\![\boldsymbol{r}^\ell]\!]_i$
$\qquad\qquad\qquad\qquad\quad \Delta t^\ell = \langle \boldsymbol{w}, \Delta \boldsymbol{v}^\ell \rangle + \langle \boldsymbol{s}, \Delta \boldsymbol{r}^\ell \rangle$
$\qquad\qquad\qquad\qquad\quad [\![t^\ell]\!]_{i^*} = t^\ell - \Delta t^\ell - \sum_{i \neq i^*} [\![t^\ell]\!]_i$
$\qquad\qquad\qquad\qquad \Delta v = \langle \boldsymbol{\alpha}, \Delta \boldsymbol{x} \rangle - \Delta c - \langle \boldsymbol{\varepsilon}, \Delta \boldsymbol{z} \rangle,\; [\![v]\!]_{i^*} = -\Delta v - \sum_{i \neq i^*} [\![v]\!]_i$
$\qquad\qquad\qquad\qquad$ Check $h = \mathcal{H}_1(\{\Delta \boldsymbol{v}^\ell, \Delta \boldsymbol{r}^\ell\}_{0 \leq \ell \leq |C|/n}, \Delta c, \mathsf{com}_1, \ldots, \mathsf{com}_N)$
$\qquad\qquad\qquad\qquad$ Check $h' = \mathcal{H}_2(\{[\![t^\ell]\!]\}_\ell, [\![v]\!])$
$\qquad\qquad\qquad\qquad$ Return 1

Protocol 4: Zero-knowledge argument for Circuit Satisfiability.

References

1. Ajtai, M., Dwork, C.: A public-key cryptosystem with worst-case/average-case equivalence. In: 29th ACM STOC, El Paso, TX, USA, May 4–6, pp. 284–293. ACM Press (1997)
2. Attema, T., Lyubashevsky, V., Seiler, G.: Practical product proofs for lattice commitments. In: Micciancio, D., Ristenpart, T. (eds.) CRYPTO 2020. LNCS, vol. 12171, pp. 470–499. Springer, Cham (2020). https://doi.org/10.1007/978-3-030-56880-1_17
3. Baum, C., Damgård, I., Lyubashevsky, V., Oechsner, S., Peikert, C.: More efficient commitments from structured lattice assumptions. In: Catalano, D., De Prisco, R. (eds.) SCN 2018. LNCS, vol. 11035, pp. 368–385. Springer, Cham (2018). https://doi.org/10.1007/978-3-319-98113-0_20
4. Baum, C., Nof, A.: Concretely-efficient zero-knowledge arguments for arithmetic circuits and their application to lattice-based cryptography. In: Kiayias, A., Kohlweiss, M., Wallden, P., Zikas, V. (eds.) PKC 2020. LNCS, vol. 12110, pp. 495–526. Springer, Cham (2020). https://doi.org/10.1007/978-3-030-45374-9_17
5. Bellare, M., Micciancio, D.: A new paradigm for collision-free hashing: incrementality at reduced cost. In: Fumy, W. (ed.) EUROCRYPT 1997. LNCS, vol. 1233, pp. 163–192. Springer, Heidelberg (1997). https://doi.org/10.1007/3-540-69053-0_13
6. Benhamouda, F., Krenn, S., Lyubashevsky, V., Pietrzak, K.: Efficient zero-knowledge proofs for commitments from learning with errors over rings. In: Pernul, G., Ryan, P.Y.A., Weippl, E. (eds.) ESORICS 2015. LNCS, vol. 9326, pp. 305–325. Springer, Cham (2015). https://doi.org/10.1007/978-3-319-24174-6_16
7. Blum, M.: Coin flipping by telephone - a protocol for solving impossible problems. In: COMPCON 1982, Digest of Papers, Twenty-Fourth IEEE Computer Society International Conference, San Francisco, California, USA, February 22–25, 1982, pp. 133–137. IEEE Computer Society (1982)
8. Bonnetain, X., Bricout, R., Schrottenloher, A., Shen, Y.: Improved classical and quantum algorithms for subset-sum. In: Moriai, S., Wang, H. (eds.) ASIACRYPT 2020. LNCS, vol. 12492, pp. 633–666. Springer, Cham (2020). https://doi.org/10.1007/978-3-030-64834-3_22
9. Boyar, J., Kurtz, S.A., Krentel, M.W.: A discrete logarithm implementation of perfect zero-knowledge blobs. J. Cryptol. 2(2), 63–76 (1990)
10. Brassard, G., Chaum, D., Crépeau, C.: Minimum disclosure proofs of knowledge. J. Comput. Syst. Sci. 37(2), 156–189 (1988)
11. Canetti, R., Lindell, Y., Ostrovsky, R., Sahai, A.: Universally composable two-party and multi-party secure computation. In: 34th ACM STOC, Montréal, Québec, Canada, May 19–21, pp. 494–503. ACM Press (2002)
12. Coster, M.J., Joux, A., LaMacchia, B.A., Odlyzko, A.M., Schnorr, C., Stern, J.: Improved low-density subset sum algorithms. Comput. Complex. 2, 111–128 (1992)
13. Feneuil, T., Maire, J., Rivain, M., Vergnaud, D.: Zero-knowledge protocols for the subset sum problem from MPC-in-the-head with rejection. Cryptology ePrint Archive, Report 2022/223 (2022). https://eprint.iacr.org/2022/223
14. Goldwasser, S., Micali, S., Rackoff, C.: The knowledge complexity of interactive proof systems. SIAM J. Comput. 18(1), 186–208 (1989)
15. Impagliazzo, R., Naor, M.: Efficient cryptographic schemes provably as secure as subset sum. J. Cryptol. 9(4), 199–216 (1996)
16. Ishai, Y., Kushilevitz, E., Ostrovsky, R., Sahai, A.: Zero-knowledge proofs from secure multiparty computation. SIAM J. Comput. 39(3), 1121–1152 (2009)

17. Jain, A., Krenn, S., Pietrzak, K., Tentes, A.: Commitments and efficient zero-knowledge proofs from learning parity with noise. In: Wang, X., Sako, K. (eds.) ASIACRYPT 2012. LNCS, vol. 7658, pp. 663–680. Springer, Heidelberg (2012). https://doi.org/10.1007/978-3-642-34961-4_40

18. Kales, D., Zaverucha, G.: Efficient lifting for shorter zero-knowledge proofs and post-quantum signatures. Cryptology ePrint Archive, Paper 2022/588 (2022). https://eprint.iacr.org/2022/588

19. Katz, J., Kolesnikov, V., Wang, X.: Improved non-interactive zero knowledge with applications to post-quantum signatures. In: Lie, D., Mannan, M., Backes, M., Wang, X., (eds.) ACM CCS 2018, Toronto, ON, Canada, October 15–19, pp. 525–537. ACM Press (2018)

20. Kilian, J.: Uses of randomness in algorithms and protocols, Ph. D. thesis, Massachusetts Institute of Technology (1989)

21. Lyubashevsky, V., Palacio, A., Segev, G.: Public-key cryptographic primitives provably as secure as subset sum. In: Micciancio, D. (ed.) TCC 2010. LNCS, vol. 5978, pp. 382–400. Springer, Heidelberg (2010). https://doi.org/10.1007/978-3-642-11799-2_23

22. Merkle, R.C., Hellman, M.E.: Hiding information and signatures in trapdoor knapsacks. IEEE Trans. Inf. Theory 24(5), 525–530 (1978)

23. Odlyzko, A.M.: The rise and fall of knapsack cryptosystems. Cryptology Comput. Number Theory 42, 75–88 (1990)

24. Pedersen, T.P.: Non-interactive and information-theoretic secure verifiable secret sharing. In: Feigenbaum, J. (ed.) CRYPTO 1991. LNCS, vol. 576, pp. 129–140. Springer, Heidelberg (1992). https://doi.org/10.1007/3-540-46766-1_9

25. Schwartz, J.T.: Fast probabilistic algorithms for verification of polynomial identities. J. ACM 27(4), 701–717 (1980)

26. Shor, P.W.: Algorithms for quantum computation: discrete logarithms and factoring. In: 35th FOCS, Santa Fe, NM, USA, November 20–22, pp. 124–134. IEEE Computer Society Press (1994)

27. Steinfeld, R., Pieprzyk, J., Wang, H.: On the provable security of an efficient RSA-based pseudorandom generator. In: Lai, X., Chen, K. (eds.) ASIACRYPT 2006. LNCS, vol. 4284, pp. 194–209. Springer, Heidelberg (2006). https://doi.org/10.1007/11935230_13

28. Zippel, R.: Probabilistic algorithms for sparse polynomials. In: Ng, E.W. (ed.) Symbolic and Algebraic Computation. LNCS, vol. 72, pp. 216–226. Springer, Heidelberg (1979). https://doi.org/10.1007/3-540-09519-5_73

Fully Tally-Hiding Verifiable E-Voting for Real-World Elections with Seat-Allocations

Carmen Wabartha, Julian Liedtke[ID], Nicolas Huber[✉][ID], Daniel Rausch[ID], and Ralf Küsters[ID]

University of Stuttgart, Stuttgart, Germany
st161329@stud.uni-stuttgart.de,
{julian.liedtke,nicolas.huber,daniel.rausch,
ralf.kusters}@sec.uni-stuttgart.de

Abstract. Modern e-voting systems provide what is called verifiability, i.e., voters are able to check that their votes have actually been counted despite potentially malicious servers and voting authorities. Some of these systems, called tally-hiding systems, provide increased privacy by revealing only the actual election result, e.g., the winner of the election, but no further information that is supposed to be kept secret. However, due to these very strong privacy guarantees, supporting complex voting methods at a real-world scale has proven to be very challenging for tally-hiding systems.

A widespread class of elections, and at the same time, one of the most involved ones is parliamentary election with party-based seat-allocation. These elections are performed for millions of voters, dozens of parties, and hundreds of individual candidates competing for seats; they also use very sophisticated multi-step algorithms to compute the final assignment of seats to candidates based on, e.g., party lists, hundreds of electoral constituencies, possibly additional votes for individual candidates, overhang seats, and special exceptions for minorities. So far, it has not been investigated whether and in how far such elections can be performed in a verifiable tally-hiding manner.

In this work, we design and implement the first verifiable (fully) tally-hiding e-voting system for an election from this class, namely, for the German parliament (Bundestag). As part of this effort, we propose several new tally-hiding building blocks that are of independent interest. We perform benchmarks based on actual election data, which show, perhaps surprisingly, that our proposed system is practical even at a real-world scale. Our work thus serves as a foundational feasibility study for this class of elections.

1 Introduction

E-voting is of rising interest. In order to ensure secure and correct elections, modern e-voting systems are designed to be (end-to-end) verifiable [1–3,6–8,16–18,20,24], that is, voters should be able to check that their votes/ballots were

G. Tsudik et al. (Eds.): ESORICS 2023, LNCS 14344, pp. 209–228, 2024.
https://doi.org/10.1007/978-3-031-50594-2_11

submitted correctly, and voters, election officials, and even external observers should be able to check that the election result corresponds to the votes that were cast. A stronger notion of verifiability is accountability, which states that, if the result turns out to be incorrect, then a misbehaving party causing this mistake can be identified and be held accountable. A very common method for election systems to achieve verifiability is by publishing the full tally, which consists of all (potentially aggregated) individual votes, along with additional evidence, such as zero-knowledge proofs (ZKPs), which proves that the tally was computed correctly. With the knowledge of the full tally, everyone is able to compute the actual election result, e.g., the winner of the election, and check whether this corresponds to the claimed election result.

More recently, verifiable tally-hiding e-voting systems (e.g. [4,5,9,12,14,15, 19,23,27]), have been proposed that defer from revealing the full tally. They are rather designed to only publish the actual election result, e.g., the winning candidate(s) of an election, and as little further information as possible (ideally none), while the correctness of the election result can still be verified. Following the terminology of [15], tally-hiding systems can be divided into three classes: Fully tally-hiding systems (e.g., [5,9,14,19]) are the strongest ones as they reveal only the election result. Publicly or partially tally-hiding systems (see, e.g., [15,23]) are more relaxed in that they reveal some information beyond the election result, possibly only to certain parties. As discussed for example in [9,14,15,19], tally-hiding systems offer several attractive features such as improved ballot privacy for voters, avoiding embarrassment or weakening of candidates, protection against a specific class of coercion attacks called Italian attacks [4,13], and preventing Gerrymandering. So far, it has been shown that simple election schemes can be performed at a large scale, even in a fully tally-hiding manner. However, due to the strong privacy requirements, more complex voting methods have proven to be a challenge for all types of tally-hiding systems, with some types of elections even turning out to be practical only for very few candidates and/or voters (cf. Sect. 6).

A very important class of elections in practice is *parliamentary election with party-based seat allocation* as carried out by many countries around the world. These are among the most complex types of elections: They usually involve millions of voters, dozens of parties, hundreds of individual candidates, and hundreds of electoral constituencies. In some cases, voters have not just one but multiple votes that they can distribute among parties and possibly also individual candidates. Sophisticated multi-step algorithms are used to compute the election result, i.e., the assignment of seats to individual candidates. An important component for this process is a so-called *seat allocation method*, which takes as input a number of available seats and a set of parties with their total number of votes and then computes the number of seats assigned to each party. While a crucial part this seat allocation method is only a small step in the computation of the actual election result. Additional steps are taken, e.g., to combine the results of different constituencies to distribute seats that are directly allocated to individual candidates instead of just parties, to take into account minimum vote counts for parties before they are assigned any seats, and to include special exceptions for minorities. Furthermore, the seats assigned to each party need to be mapped to individual candidates, typically according to party candidate lists for each constituency and weighted by how many votes a party has obtained in the respective constituency. In some cases, even the size of the parliament is modified while computing the election result, possibly only after the seat allocation method has already been computed to more closely reflect the vote distribution.

Perhaps due to this intimidating complexity, so far, it has not been investigated *whether and in how far this class of elections can be performed in a tally-hiding manner, and whether this is possible even at the same scale in terms of voters, parties, candidates, and constituencies as needed in real-world elections*. There are only a few existing works that propose tally-hiding algorithms for computing certain seat allocation methods, namely, the d'Hondt method [9] and the Hare-Niemeyer method [14]. As explained above, while seat allocation methods are important components, they constitute just a small portion of the entire election scheme, and hence, these prior works do not answer the above question. In this work, we therefore, for the first time, investigate this open research question.

Contributions. More specifically, we design, implement, and benchmark the *first verifiable (and even accountable) fully tally-hiding e-voting system for a major real-world party-based parliamentary election*, namely, the election of the German parliament (Bundestag). Perhaps surprisingly, and as our main insight, with this system, we are able to *show that such a parliamentary election scheme with party-based seat allocation can actually be performed in a verifiable, fully tally-hiding manner at a real-world scale*. Our system supports the strongest level of tally-hiding, namely full tally-hiding. That is, if desired, one can reveal only the allocation of individual candidates to seats and the number of voters who cast a vote and nothing else to anybody. But one can also easily relax the kind of information that is revealed, e.g., by additionally publishing the winners of individual constituencies.

On a technical level, to obtain our voting system, we follow and slightly modify a generic approach for constructing verifiable fully tally-hiding systems, namely the Ordinos framework [19]. The Ordinos framework provides a general blueprint for the structure of such systems. Some components in this blueprint are unspecified and have to be filled in by protocol designers on a case-by-case basis to obtain a concrete instantiation of Ordinos that can perform an election for a specific voting method. It has been shown in [19] that, as long as those components meet specific requirements, the overall system/instantiation is a secure verifiable, fully tally-hiding e-voting system. The main challenge lies in constructing those components for a specific voting method in such a way that they provide all expected security properties while achieving practical performance.

The most important and also most difficult to design component is a publicly verifiable secure multi-party computation (MPC) protocol that computes the election result for the German parliament from the set of (encrypted) ballots. Due to the inherent complexity and scale of this election, this requires special care to obtain not just a theoretically secure but also a practically efficient system. Specifically, we first propose several MPC building blocks, including the first MPC subroutine for computing the Sainte-Laguë seat allocation method used for parliamentary elections, not just in Germany but also in, e.g., Indonesia, New Zealand, Nepal, Sweden, Norway, and Kosovo. Based on these building blocks, we then construct an efficient MPC protocol that performs the entire election evaluation for the German parliament. Along the way, we evaluate different options for designing our algorithms and propose several novel optimizations to improve the overall efficiency. We note that many of our ideas and building blocks, such as our MPC protocol for the Sainte-Laguë method, are of interest also for other parliamentary election schemes since such elections often use similar concepts and components.

The overall practicality of e-voting systems following the Ordinos approach is determined essentially only by the performance of the MPC component. Hence, to evaluate the performance and identify potential limitations of our system, we have implemented our full MPC protocol for electing the German parliament and performed extensive benchmarks based on actual real-world election data consisting of the votes of all respective constituencies. Our solution needs about a day to compute the election result, which is within the usual time frame expected for this election, thus demonstrating that our MPC protocol is practical even for such a complex large-scale political election.

Altogether, our results serve as a foundational feasibility study for (fully) tally-hiding elections for the important class of parliamentary elections with party-based seat allocation. Of course, as can be seen in countries already using or aiming at online elections, establishing and actually deploying a full-fledged ready-to-use system in the real world requires a huge effort beyond studying feasibility. Future deployments can build on our results by considering further aspects of parliamentary elections that are out of scope of this work, such as deciding which parties run the election in a distributed fashion, tackling the risk of voter coercion, establishing procedures for handling voter complaints, etc.

Structure. We recall the Ordinos framework in Sect. 2. In Sect. 3, we present novel building blocks that we have constructed to realize the voting methods in this work. In Sect. 4, we present the Sainte-Laguë method, including a novel variant to compute the Sainte-Laguë seat allocation and different tally-hiding algorithms to compute the Sainte-Laguë method. We present our voting system for the German Bundestag in Sect. 5. We discuss related work and conclude in Sect. 6. Our implementation is available at [26]. A full version of this paper with complete details for all of our results is available at [25].

2   Preliminaries

Notation. We write $[n]$ to denote the set $\{0, \ldots, n-1\}$. Let n_{cand} be the number of candidates/parties/choices, and let n_{votes} be the (maximal) number of votes. We will use n_{seats} to denote the number of seats that are being distributed among n_{parties} parties. With n_{votes}^{j} we denote the number of votes, and with

n_{seats}^j the number of seats that party j has received. The format of a plain, i.e., unencrypted, ballot is defined via a finite *choice space* $C \subseteq \mathbb{N}^{n_{\text{cand}}}$, i.e., a ballot assigns each candidate a number subject to constraints defined by C. For example, a single vote election where a plain ballot contains one vote for a single candidate/party/choice can be modeled via the choice space $C_{\text{single}} := \{(b_0, \ldots, b_{n_{\text{cand}}-1}) \in \{0,1\}^{n_{\text{cand}}} \mid \sum_i b_i = 1\}$. For voter j we denote her plain ballot by $v^j := (v_i^j)_{i \in [n_{\text{cand}}]} \in C$.

The Ordinos Framework. The Ordinos framework was introduced in [19] as a general blueprint for constructing verifiable, fully tally-hiding e-voting systems. Systems following the Ordinos approach use a voting authority, an arbitrary number of voters, n_t trustees, an authentication server, and an append-only bulletin board (B) and roughly work as follows. In an initial *setup phase*, parameters of the election are generated and published on B, including a public key and corresponding secret key shares for an additively homomorphic t-out-of-n_t threshold public key encryption scheme $\mathcal{E} = (E, D)$. Each trustee has one secret key share and publishes a non-interactive zero-knowledge proof of knowledge (NIZKP) $\pi^{\text{KeyShareGen}}$ to prove knowledge of their key share. The choice space C and the result function f_{res} of the election are published on B as well, where f_{res} takes as input a tally and outputs the corresponding election result, e.g., the candidate with the most votes. In the following *voting phase*, the voters first encrypt their ballots and then publish them on B, authenticating themselves as eligible voters with the help of the authentication server and the authentication server adds a signature to the ballot. An encrypted ballot of voter j has the form $(E_{\text{pk}}(v_i^j))_{i \in [n_{\text{cand}}]}$, i.e., each component of the plain ballot is encrypted separately. The encrypted ballot comes with a NIZKP π^{Enc} that proves validity of the plain ballot, i.e., $v^j = (v_i^j)_{i \in [n_{\text{cand}}]} \in C$. The published encrypted ballots can be homomorphically (and publicly) aggregated to obtain an encryption of the aggregated full tally, i.e., one obtains one ciphertext on each $v_i := \sum_{j \in [n_{\text{votes}}]} v_i^j$, where v_i is the total number of votes/points that candidate/choice i obtained in the election. In the *tallying phase*, the trustees run a publicly verifiable MPC protocol P_{MPC} to compute f_{res}. This protocol takes as (secret) inputs the secret key shares of the trustees and the (public) encrypted aggregated tally and outputs the election result $res = f_{\text{res}}(v_0, \ldots, v_{n_{\text{cand}}-1})$. This result, along with any material that is needed to allow external parties to verify the MPC computation, is published by the trustees on B. Finally, in the *verification phase*, voters can check that their ballots appear on B, and everyone can verify that the election result res was computed correctly from the encrypted ballots by re-computing the homomorphic aggregation, checking all NIZKPs, and checking the MPC computation (which typically involves additional NIZKP verifications).

Many of the above components are not fixed by the Ordinos framework because they strongly depend on the specific election method that is to be implemented. Specifically, the following parameters and components have to be specified or constructed by a protocol designer to create an instantiation of Ordinos for a concrete election method: *(i)* the choice space C and election result function f_{res}, *(ii)* a threshold encryption scheme $\mathcal{E}$, *(iii)* NIZKPs $\pi^{\text{KeyShareGen}}$ and π^{Enc}, *(iv)* a EUF-CMA-secure signature scheme $\mathcal{S}$, and *(v)* an MPC protocol P_{MPC} for computing the election result function f_{res}.

Voting systems following the Ordinos approach are intended to provide verifiability and full tally-hiding. As already mentioned, verifiability intuitively means that everyone can check whether the election result returned by the voting system corresponds to the actual votes. Full tally-hiding intuitively means that no one, including attackers, learns anything besides the number of submitted ballots and the final election result; this property, therefore, also implies the security notion of ballot privacy. We refer interested readers to [19] for formal definitions of both verifiability and full tally-hiding. Küsters et al. [19] have shown that if the above components defined by protocol designers meet certain properties, then the resulting Ordinos instance, indeed achieves both security notions:

Theorem 1 (Verifiability and Full Tally Hiding [19]**, informal).** *Let $\mathcal{E}$ be an additively homomorphic threshold public-key encryption scheme $\mathcal{E}$, $\pi^{KeyShareGen}$ and π^{Enc} be secure NIZKPs for $\mathcal{E}$, $\mathcal{S}$ be an EUF-CMA-secure signature scheme, and P_{MPC} be a publicly verifiable secure MPC protocol for computing f_{res}, i.e., if the result does not correspond to the input, then this can be detected, and at least one misbehaving trustee can be identified; this must hold even if all trustees running the MPC protocol are malicious. Then, the resulting instance of Ordinos is verifiable and fully tally-hiding.*[1]

Existing Building Blocks. In this work, we will use a threshold variant of the Paillier encryption scheme [10] to implement $\mathcal{E}$. Given a public key pk for this encryption scheme, there exist publicly verifiable MPC building blocks [10,14,22] that allow the owners of the corresponding secret key shares to compute the following basic operations for $a, b, c \in \mathbb{Z}_n$ (all operations are mod n where n is determined by pk):

- $E_{pk}(c) = f_{add}(E_{pk}(a), E_{pk}(b))$ s.t. $c = a + b$; for brevity, we denote this operation by $\oplus$.
- $E_{pk}(c) = f_{mul}(E_{pk}(a), E_{pk}(b))$ s.t. $c = a \cdot b$, for brevity, we denote this operation by $\odot$.
- $E_{pk}(c) = f_{gt}(E_{pk}(a), E_{pk}(b))$ s.t. $c = 1$ iff $a \geq b$ and 0 otherwise.
- $E_{pk}(c) = f_{eq}(E_{pk}(a), E_{pk}(b))$ s.t. $c = 1$ iff $a = b$ and 0 otherwise.
- $(E_{pk}(s_i))_{i=1}^n = f_{max}((E_{pk}(v_i))_{i=1}^n)$ s.t. $s_i \in \{0, 1\}$ and $s_i = 1$ means that $v_i = \max_{j \in \{1,...,n\}} v_j \wedge \forall j \in \{i+1, ..., n\} : v_j < v_i$.
- $c = f_{dec}(E_{pk}(c))$ s.t. $E_{pk}(c)$ is an encryption of c.

The MPC building blocks for computing the above operations have a useful property, namely, encrypted outputs from one building block can be used as inputs for another building block such that the resulting combined protocol is still a secure, publicly verifiable MPC protocol [22]. In other words, they allow

---

[1] Full tally-hiding requires that at most $t - 1$ trustees are malicious, verifiability does not require any honest trustees at all. This theorem uses further standard e-voting assumptions, such as honesty of B. We refer interested readers to [19] for full details.

for building more complex protocols such as $\mathsf{P_{MPC}}$ for Ordinos that meet the requirements of Theorem 1. We further note that the MPC building blocks for computing $f_{\mathsf{gt}}()$ and $f_{\mathsf{eq}}()$ proposed by [22] offer sublinear runtime as long as an upper bound $< n$ for both input values a and b is known; hence, performance drastically increases as long as a, b are known to remain small. This, in turn, also improves performance of MPC protocols based on these two building blocks, including the MPC building block for computing $f_{\mathsf{max}}()$ [14].

3   New MPC Building Blocks

In this section, based on the primitives introduced in Sect. 2, we describe several new publicly verifiable MPC building blocks that we need for constructing our $\mathsf{P_{MPC}}$, with full details provided in [25]. We note that these building blocks are of independent interest.

Election methods for parliamentary elections often make use of divisions that produce fractions, which is an issue for encryption schemes and MPC protocols which operate on natural numbers, such as those from Sect. 2. One common approach [9,14] to deal with this is to multiply all values by the least common multiple of all divisors used in a computation such that divisions are guaranteed to always produce natural numbers. This can drastically increase the size of numbers, which in turn severely reduces the efficiency gain of the sublinear comparisons protocols $f_{\mathsf{gt}}()$, $f_{\mathsf{eq}}()$ from Sect. 2. Therefore, we instead take an alternative approach to deal with fractions by representing our values, where needed, as rational numbers consisting of a numerator n and denominator d. Encrypted rational numbers are denoted as $E_{\mathsf{pk}}^{\mathsf{frac}}(a) := (E_{\mathsf{pk}}(a.n), E_{\mathsf{pk}}(a.d))$ where $a.n$ is the numerator and $a.d$ the denominator of a. We denote by $\mathrm{FRACTION}(n, d)$ the operation that creates an encrypted rational number with numerator n and denominator d (if the inputs n and/or d are not already encrypted, then they are first encrypted with public constant randomness). Based on this representation, we design and implement MPC components for basic arithmetic computations on encrypted rational numbers, including addition, multiplication, and comparisons.

Based on $f_{\mathsf{max}}()$ (see Sect. 2), we propose the method `getMaxFraction` that takes a list of k encrypted fractions and returns another list of the same length with $E_{\mathsf{pk}}(1)$ at the index of the maximal fraction and $E_{\mathsf{pk}}(0)$ everywhere else, where if there are multiple maxima, only the last one in the list is marked $E_{\mathsf{pk}}(1)$.

Election methods often need to deal with breaking ties. For this purpose, Cortier et al. [9] proposed an algorithm that finds the maximum in a list and additionally takes care of tie-breaking by scaling values and adding small tie-breaking values. While this scaling idea is conceptually simple, care must be taken to obtain a correct implementation. As we discuss in the full version [25], we found cases where directly applying the tie-breaking mechanism described in [9] in our setting, where fractions are represented by their numerator and denominator, which leads to an incorrect output. We address this problem in our implementation `getMaxFractionByRank` shown in Fig. 1. This algorithm additionally takes encrypted ranks $r = (E_{\mathsf{pk}}(r_i))_{i=1}^{k}$ as input, where the $(r_1, \ldots, r_k)$

procedure GETMAXFRACTIONBYRANK($l = (E_{pk}^{frac}(v_i))_{i=1}^{k}, k, r = (E_{pk}(r_i))_{i=1}^{k}$)
    $E_{pk}^{frac}(c\_max\_val) = E_{pk}^{frac}(v_1)$
    $E_{pk}(c\_max\_idx) = E_{pk}(1)$
    $E_{pk}(c\_max\_r) = E_{pk}(r_1)$
    for $i = 2, \ldots, k$ **do**
        $E_{pk}(m_{max}) = E_{pk}^{frac}(c\_max\_val) \odot E_{pk}(c\_max\_val.d) \odot E_{pk}(v_i.d) \odot k \oplus E_{pk}(c\_max\_r)$
        $E_{pk}(m_i) = E_{pk}^{frac}(v_i) \odot E_{pk}(v_i.d) \odot E_{pk}(c\_max\_val.d) \odot k \oplus E_{pk}(r_i)$
        $E_{pk}(set) = f_{gt}(E_{pk}(m_i), E_{pk}(m_{max}))$
        $E_{pk}(c\_max\_val) = E_{pk}(set) \odot E_{pk}(v_i) \oplus (1 - E_{pk}(set)) \odot E_{pk}(c\_max\_val)$
        $E_{pk}(c\_max\_idx) = E_{pk}(set) \odot E_{pk}(i) \oplus (1 - E_{pk}(set)) \odot E_{pk}(c\_max\_idx)$
        $E_{pk}(c\_max\_r) = E_{pk}(set) \odot E_{pk}(r_i) \oplus (1 - E_{pk}(set)) \odot E_{pk}(c\_max\_r)$
    $result = (f_{eq}(E_{pk}(i), E_{pk}(c\_max\_idx)))_{i=1}^{k}$
    return result

Fig. 1. Algorithm to find a maximum in a list of fractions, including tie breaking by rank.

procedure FLOORDIVISION($E_{pk}(a)$, $E_{pk}(b)$, u)
    $length = $ BITLENGTH(u)
    $E_{pk}(lower) = E_{pk}(0)$
    for $i = 1, \ldots, length$ **do**
        $E_{pk}(j) = E_{pk}(lower) \oplus E_{pk}(2^{length-i})$
        $E_{pk}(gt) = f_{gt}(E_{pk}(a), E_{pk}(j) \odot E_{pk}(b))$
        $E_{pk}(lower) = E_{pk}(lower) \oplus (2^{length-i} \odot E_{pk}(gt))$
    return $E_{pk}(lower)$

Fig. 2. Floor Division to calculate $E_{pk}(\lfloor \frac{a}{b} \rfloor)$ where u is a known upper bound.

form a permutation of $0, \ldots, k-1$, and first scales all ciphertexts q_i by a certain value, adds the encrypted ranking r_i to the scaled q_i, and then continues just as getMaxFraction. By the scaling the addition of r_i does not change the output if the q_i are not tied. But, if any of the inputs q_i are equal, then the party with the highest rank r_i will have the greater (encrypted) value after the addition.

Finally, in Fig. 2 we introduce a new MPC algorithm for computing the floor division $E_{pk}(\lfloor \frac{a}{b} \rfloor)$ from two encrypted natural numbers $E_{pk}(a), E_{pk}(b)$ and a publicly known upper bound $u \geq \lfloor \frac{a}{b} \rfloor$ of the result. Compared to the floor division MPC algorithm presented in [14], we require u but can be much more efficient by performing a binary search instead of iterating over a full set of values.

4   MPC Protocol for the Sainte-Laguë Method

The Sainte-Laguë method (also called Webster method) is a seat allocation method, i.e., a procedure that describes how a given number of seats is allocated to a set of parties depending on the number of votes each party has received. The Sainte-Laguë method is used by parliamentary elections in many countries, for example, Indonesia, New Zealand, Nepal, Sweden, Norway, Germany, and Kosovo. As part of computing the election result, these elections run the Sainte-Laguë method multiple times on different inputs. For example, the official evaluation of the final seat distribution of the German Bundestag of the election in 2021 required running the Sainte-Laguë method 23 times (in addition to several other steps, as explained in Sect. 1). Hence, in order to obtain an efficient tally-hiding voting system for these elections, it is crucial to design a heavily optimized MPC component for computing the Sainte-Laguë method. In this section, we first give both a general overview of the Sainte-Laguë method and then present our efficient tally-hiding MPC algorithm, including several optimizations and variations.

4.1 Computing a Sainte-Laguë Distribution

There are essentially two distinct (but provably equivalent [21]) algorithms for computing the seat allocation following the Sainte-Laguë method, one based on highest quotients and one on finding suitable denominators. Both algorithms take as input the number of seats n_{seats} to be distributed and, for each party $j \in [n_{\text{parties}}]$, the total number of votes n_{votes}^j that party j has received. They return the number of seats assigned to each party.

- **Highest-Quotients.** For $i \in [n_{\text{seats}}], j \in [n_{\text{parties}}]$ compute the quotients $q_i^j := \frac{n_{\text{votes}}^j}{2i+1}$. Let M be the list of the n_{seats} highest quotients. Then party j is assigned k seats, where k is the number of quotients in M that belong to j, i.e., quotients of the form $q_i^j, i \in [n_{\text{seats}}]$.

- **Suitable-Denominator.** Given a *suitable denominator* d, the number n_{seats}^j of seats assigned to party j is computed as $n_{\text{seats}}^j = \lfloor \frac{n_{\text{votes}}^j}{d} \rceil$, where $\lfloor \cdot \rceil$ denotes rounding to the closest integer (rounding of .5 can be chosen to be either up or down and can be chosen differently for each j). A denominator d is *suitable* if the result of this computation leads to the number of desired total seats, i.e., if $\sum_j n_{\text{seats}}^j = n_{\text{seats}}$. To find a suitable denominator, one generally starts with an arbitrary denominator d, e.g., $d = \left\lfloor \frac{\sum_j n_{\text{votes}}^j}{n_{\text{seats}}} \right\rceil$, checks the corresponding number of seats that would be assigned, and then tweaks d until a suitable value has been found.

For both algorithms, there might be ties that would need to be resolved. E.g., in the highest-quotients algorithm, there might be two equal quotients while there is only enough space left in M for one of them. In the suitable-denominator algorithm, it can happen that all suitable denominators are such that the quotients of multiple parties end on .5 and some of which need to be rounded up while others need to be rounded down to achieve an overall sum of n_{seats}. The Sainte-Laguë method does not define any specific tie-breaking mechanism. Instead, elections using this method additionally need to specify how they handle ties.

```
1: procedure AddSeatBasic((q = E_pk^frac(q_current^j))_{j=0}^{n_parties−1}, s = (E_pk(n_seats^j))_{j=0}^{n_parties−1})
2:    t = (E_pk(m_j))_{j=0}^{n_parties−1} = GETMAXFRACTION(q)
3:    for j ∈ [n_parties] do
4:        d = E_pk(q_j.d) ⊕ 2 ⊙ t_j
5:        q_j = FRACTION(E_pk(q_j.n), d)                    ▷ Update q
6:        s_j = s_j ⊕ t_j                                    ▷ Update seats (s)
7:    return q, s
```

Fig. 3. One iteration step of SLQBasic.

4.2 Tally-Hiding MPC Realization of Sainte-Laguë

We want to construct a tally-hiding MPC component that takes as inputs $E_{pk}(n_{votes}^j)$ for each party as well as publicly known values $n_{parties}$ and n_{seats}[2], and computes the encrypted Sainte-Laguë seat distribution $E_{pk}(n_{seats}^j)$. As an initial insight, we observe that basing the MPC protocol on the suitable-denominator algorithm is generally very inefficient: This algorithm has to iterate over several potential denominators d until a suitable one is found. Since the number of iterations required to find d would reveal non-trivial information about the secret inputs, the MPC protocol would rather have to be constructed such that it always uses an apriori fixed number m of iterations (some of which will discard their results if a suitable divisor has already been found by a previous iteration) where m must be chosen sufficiently large such that, for all possible input sequences, a suitable divisor d is guaranteed to always be found. This worst case approximation introduces a lot of additional overhead.

Therefore, we have constructed a basic tally-hiding MPC realization SLQBasic of the Sainte-Laguë method following the highest-quotients approach: each party j is assigned its current quotient $q_{current}$ (see the description of the highest-quotients algorithm) and seats n_{seats}^j thus far. Figure 3 shows this excerpt of a single iteration step. Note that this SLQBasic uses the fast getMaxFraction algorithm in all iterations, and hence, breaks ties via a fixed mechanism that always assigns the seat to the party with the highest index j.

Support for Breaking Ties by Lot. Many elections use more involved tie-breaking algorithms than the default one implemented by SLQBasic. For example, for many parliamentary elections, e.g., elections in Indonesia, Sweden, and Germany, whenever several parties are tied for a seat, then a new lot is drawn to resolve the tie. A more general tally-hiding MPC implementation SLQCustomTiebreaking for this election does not only have to support this tie-breaking mechanism but also has to keep secret whether any lots were drawn and what the result was. In particular, to build such a SLQCustomTiebreaking we need to first extend/modify the iteration step AddSeatBasic shown in Fig. 3, obtaining a new subroutine AddSeatTieBreaking which takes as additional input

---

[2] As we explain in our full version [25], all MPC algorithms presented in this and the next section can be extended to run with a secret number of seats n_{seats}, as long as an upper limit of seats is known.

an encrypted ranking of parties $r = (E_{\mathsf{pk}}(r_0), \ldots, E_{\mathsf{pk}}(r_{n_{\mathsf{parties}}-1}))$ where r is a uniformly chosen permutation of $0, \ldots, n_{\mathsf{parties}} - 1$, and then resolves ties based on that ranking.

We construct AddSeatTieBreaking by making use of getMaxFractionByRank as presented in Sect. 3. That is, we replace the call to getMaxFraction in Line 2 of AddSeatBasic by our algorithm getMaxFractionByRank which takes as additional input the ranking r. Based on this AddSeatTieBreaking, we have constructed two versions of a SLQCustomTiebreaking MPC component which implement Sainte-Laguë. In essence, these MPC components first compute, in each iteration, an encrypted ranking r that encodes the result of tie-breaking and then use AddSeatTieBreaking with that r. There are two main optimizations that we introduce in both cases: First, for tie-breaking by lot, we run a distributed randomness generation protocol [22] for each iteration to then compute r based on the results. Since this step is input/vote independent, it can be pre-computed even before the election. Secondly, observe that if a tie occurs between m parties in one iteration of the quotient approach while there are at least m seats to be distributed, then all parties in the tie will obtain a seat in the next m iterations, i.e., it does not actually matter how this tie is broken. Hence, only ties during the last $n_{\mathsf{parties}} - 1$ iterations need to be handled by AddSeatTieBreaking, while otherwise we use the faster AddSeatBasic algorithm.

4.3 Sainte-Laguë Based on Floor Division

While our MPC algorithms SLQBasic and SLQCustomTiebreaking based on the highest-quotients approach are already practical in terms of efficiency, they always use n_{seats} iterations to assign all seats and thus do not scale overly well for elections where a high number of seats n_{seats} needs to be allocated. To improve performance in such cases, we propose a new algorithm for computing the Sainte-Laguë method which we call *floor division method*. Our floor division method is different from the highest-quotient and the suitable-denominator methods and allows us to construct an MPC component, called SLQFloorDiv, that requires n_{parties} instead of n_{seats} many iterations, and thus, is more efficient in the common case that the number of seats exceeds the number of parties. In what follows, we first present the floor division method and then describe our MPC component SLQFloorDiv.

Description of Our Method. Intuitively, the main idea of our floor division method is to replace the initial iterations and hence seat assignments of the quotient method by computing an under- and an overestimation of the final seat allocation, and then run only the final (at most n_{parties} many) iterations of the quotient method to add/remove a seat from both of these initial estimations until exactly n_{seats} many seats are assigned. As we prove one of the resulting final seat distributions will be the correct Sainte-Laguë distribution, and it can be determined efficiently which one is correct.

Concretely, for each party j compute $m_j := \lfloor \frac{n_{\mathsf{votes}}^j \cdot n_{\mathsf{seats}}}{n_{\mathsf{votes}}} \rfloor$. For the underestimation case, we start by assigning m_j seats to party j. Note that $s_{\mathsf{initial}}^{\mathsf{min}} :=$

$\sum_{j \in [n_{\text{parties}}]} m_j$ might be smaller than n_{seats}, but not smaller than $n_{\text{seats}} - n_{\text{parties}}$. Hence, in order to distribute exactly n_{seats} seats in total, we distribute the remaining $n_{\text{seats}} - s_{\text{initial}}^{\min}$ ($\le n_{\text{parties}}$) seats to the parties by executing the final iterations of the highest-quotients method (and the desired tie-breaking mechanism). That is, starting from the intermediate quotients $q_{m_j}^j := \frac{n_{\text{votes}}^j}{2m_j + 1}$ instead of starting from the initial q_0^j for each party j. For the overestimation case, we start by assigning $m_j + 1$ seats to party j, which might result in at most n_{parties} additional seats being assigned beyond the desired total of n_{seats}. To remove those seats, we use a reverse variant of the highest-quotients algorithm. For this purpose, we again initialize the quotients as $q_{m_j}^j$ and then, in each iteration step, determine the minimal current quotient and remove a seat from the corresponding party (using the desired tie-breaking mechanism). Then, we update the quotient of that party by reducing the denominator by 2.[3] This continues until only a total of n_{seats} seats is distributed.

Finally, to figure out which result is the correct Sainte-Laguë distribution, we evaluate the underestimation case an additional time to compute the next seat that would be assigned. If the corresponding quotient is less than all the initial quotients $q_{m_j}^j$ of the underestimation, then the result computed based on the underestimation is the correct seat distribution. Otherwise, the result computed based on the overestimation is the correct seat distribution. In the full version [25], we show the following result for our algorithm:

Lemma 1 (Correctness of SLQFloorDiv). *The algorithm SLQFloorDiv as presented above is correct, i.e., always outputs the seat allocation according to the Sainte-Laguë method with the desired tie-breaking.*

Tally-Hiding MPC Component. Using our building blocks described in Sect. 3 and the other building blocks from Sect. 2, most of our tally-hiding MPC protocol for computing the above algorithm for Sainte-Laguë is straightforward. The main issue left to be solved is that the number of iterations that our algorithm needs to add/subtract seats from the MPC protocol reveals initial seat assignment (this would reveal non-trivial information about the inputs/votes). We solve this by always using n_{parties} iterations in our MPC protocol, which is an upper bound on the number of iterations that are needed.

Our benchmarks of single runs of the Sainte-Laguë algorithms show that this variant of the Sainte-Laguë method is indeed faster than SLQCustomTiebreaking for larger numbers of seats and smaller numbers of parties. For example, we have the following runtime for ten parties: To distribute 60 resp. 100 seats using SLQCustomTiebreaking, the runtime is 6.7 h resp. 12.6 h while SLQFloorDiv only needs 4.7 h resp. 5 h. However, for smaller numbers of, say, 20 seats, SLQCustomTiebreaking is faster with 1.6 h instead of SLQFloorDiv, which

---

[3] It might happen that all $m_j + 1$ seats are removed from a party j. In that case, this party is ignored in the following iterations. Note that this special case is non-trivial to implement in our SLQFloorDiv MPC component since we cannot reveal the values m_j or the quotients.

needs 4.6 h. We compare benchmarks for further values of n_{seats} and n_{parties} in Appendix A.2.

5   Election of the German Parliament (Bundestag)

The election of the German federal parliament, the *Bundestag*, which consists of at least 598 seats is a combination of proportional representation and first-past-the-post voting. Each voter has two votes: a constituency vote (called *first vote*) given towards an individual candidate, who is typically but not necessarily also a member of a party, and a vote for state-specific party lists (called *second vote*) which determines the proportions of parties in the parliament. The first votes are evaluated for each of the 299 constituencies individually: The candidate with the most votes wins the constituency and is guaranteed a seat in the parliament, called a *direct mandate*.[4] Each constituency belongs to exactly one of the 16 German states, say state $l \in L$ where L is the set of all states. We denote by $s_{j,l}^{\text{d}}$ the total number of direct mandates that candidates of party j win in state l.

Let $v_{j,l}$ be the number of second votes for party j in state l and $v_j := \sum_{l \in L} v_{j,l}$ the total number of second votes for party j. In the next step, the baseline of 598 seats of the parliament are assigned to the states in proportion to their number of inhabitants; we call this the *first top distribution* and refer to these seats as *state seats*. A party j can obtain state seats if v_j is at least 5% of all second votes, j has obtained at least $\sum_{l \in L} s_{j,l}^{\text{d}} \geq 3$ direct mandates, or j represents a special minority. Let $\mathfrak{S}$ be the set of parties that are allowed to obtain state seats. Then, for each state l, the state seats are assigned to parties $j \in \mathfrak{S}$ following the Sainte-Laguë method based on $v_{j,l}$. The resulting seats are called *quota seats*, denoted by $s_{j,l}^{\text{q}}$ for party j and state l. We call this distribution the *first low distribution*. It usually happens in several states l that a party $j \in \mathfrak{S}$ wins more direct mandates and hence guaranteed seats for their candidates than the party actually receives in terms of quota seats, i.e., $s_{j,l}^{\text{d}} > s_{j,l}^{\text{q}}$. In such cases, the overall size of the parliament is increased, and the seat assignment to parties is updated such that *(i)* parties have enough seats for all their candidates with direct mandates and *(ii)* the number of seats given to party j in the final parliament is "close" to the Sainte-Laguë seat distribution based on v_j (up to 3 additional seats, called *overhang seats*, are tolerated). This is computed via the following procedure.

Let $s_j^{\min} := \sum_{l \in L} \left(\max(\lceil \frac{s_{j,l}^{\text{d}} + s_{j,l}^{\text{q}}}{2} \rceil, s_{j,l}^{\text{d}}) \right)$ be a lower bound for the seats that party $j \in \mathfrak{S}$ will receive. Compute $d_{\text{no}} := \min_{j \in \mathfrak{S}} \left(\frac{v_j}{s_j^{\min} - 0.5} \right)$. Then, for each party $j \in \mathfrak{S}$, it is determined whether there is a state $l \in L$ such that $t(j,l) := s_{j,l}^{\text{d}} - s_{j,l}^{\text{q}} > 0$. This value is also called the *threatening overhang* of party j in state l. Based on these values, one computes a set of divisors: $D_{\text{overh}} =$

---

[4] Ties for the first place and hence the direct mandate are resolved by lot. Ties in any of the following iterations of the Sainte-Laguë method are also resolved by lot with one exception discussed below.

$\{\frac{v_j}{s_j^{\min}-i} \mid i \in \{0.5, 1.5, 2.5, 3.5\}, j \in \mathfrak{S}$ and $\exists l : \ t(j,l) > 0, t(j,l) + 1 > i\}$. Let d_{overh} be the fourth smallest element of D_{overh} and set $d := \min(d_{\text{no}}, d_{\text{overh}})$.

Then, as in the suitable-denominator algorithm (c.f. Sect. 4), party $j \in \mathfrak{S}$ receives $n_{\text{seats}}^j := \lfloor \frac{n_{\text{votes}}^j}{d} \rceil$ seats, where .5 is always rounded up, i.e., in this step, ties are resolved by giving every tied party a seat. The resulting distribution is called the *second top distribution*. Next, for each party $j \in \mathfrak{S}$, these n_{seats}^j are assigned to individual states following the Sainte-Laguë method weighted by $v_{j,l}$, resulting in the *second low distribution*.

In addition to those n_{seats}^j seats, (some) parties further receive $\alpha_j := s_j^{\min} - n_{\text{seats}}^j (\leq 3)$ overhang seats to cover a possibly remaining surplus of direct mandates. These overhang seats are then also distributed to states according to the smallest α_j many values from the following set: $O_{\text{overh}}^j = \{\frac{v_{j,l}}{s_{j,l}^{\min}-i} \mid i \in \{0.5, 1.5, 2.5\}, l \in L, i < \alpha_j\}$.

All seats assigned to party $j \in \mathfrak{S}$ in state l are then assigned to candidates as follows. First, candidates of party j that won a direct mandate in a constituency of state l obtain a seat. The remaining seats, if any, are assigned to the party candidate list for that state, starting with the first one and skipping any candidates that have already obtained a direct mandate. Finally, if there are any direct mandates for candidates that do not belong to a party from $\mathfrak{S}$, then each of these candidates receives a seat that is added to the parliament. The resulting set of seats defines the updated size of the parliament.

Our Tally-Hiding Realization. We construct our e-voting system by following the general Ordinos approach, except for one difference. The original Ordinos framework proposed in [19] was designed for elections without electoral constituencies or with just a single constituency where all votes are treated equally. We capture the existence of several constituencies in the German parliamentary elections, where the result also depends on the constituency that a vote was submitted in, via the following small changes: The list of eligible voters that is published during the setup phase now additionally assigns each voter to a constituency. Ballots are extended to additionally contain (in plain) the identifier of the constituency they were cast in such that everyone can check whether ballots were cast for the correct constituency. Encrypted ballots are aggregated per constituency and then evaluated via (the MPC component for) f_{res}. We note that this difference in settings also slightly changes the meaning of full tally-hiding: For elections without electoral constituencies, only the number of submitted votes (since this is public on B) and the final result become known. In the setting with electoral constituencies, only the number of submitted votes *per constituency* and the final result becomes known. As part of our security proof (cf. Theorem 2), we define full tally-hiding for our setting and verify that the original proofs of Theorem 1 carry over in a natural way to our setting using the same preconditions.

We hence instantiate the (modified) Ordinos approach for the German election by using the threshold Paillier encryption scheme $\mathcal{E}$, choice space $C_{\text{single}} \times C_{\text{single}}$, standard NIZKPs $\pi^{\text{KeyShareGen}}$ and π^{Enc} [10] and any standard

EUF-CMA-secure signature scheme from the literature, result function $f_{\text{res-Ger}}$ for the German parliamentary election as described above, and importantly our new MPC protocol $\mathsf{P}_{\text{MPC-Ger}}$ for $f_{\text{res-Ger}}$ described next.

Constructing $\mathsf{P}_{\text{MPC-Ger}}$. We have constructed $\mathsf{P}_{\text{MPC-Ger}}$ using the components from Sects. 2 and 3 to compute the full evaluation procedure for German parliament, as described above. This includes all small details and special cases, e.g., computing and changing the final parliament size, determining and distributing up to 3 overhang seats per party, and exempting parties from obtaining state seats iff they did not win 5% of the total second votes, won less than 3 direct mandates, and are not representing a special minority.

Of course, capturing the full complexity of the election evaluation of the German parliament in an MPC protocol $\mathsf{P}_{\text{MPC-Ger}}$ comes at a hefty cost in terms of performance and hence runs the risk of becoming impractical. We have therefore spent considerable effort into carefully optimizing $\mathsf{P}_{\text{MPC-Ger}}$ by, among others, the following: *(i)* Computing the election result requires multiple iterations of Sainte-Laguë. We use both SLQCustomTiebreaking and SLQFloorDiv, depending on the number of seats and candidates that has to be processed in the current iteration. *(ii)* We have constructed $\mathsf{P}_{\text{MPC-Ger}}$ in such a way that, as far as possible, substeps such as repeated state-wise operations can be computed in parallel. We have performed benchmarks for various numbers of threads, which demonstrate that this is a major factor in improving performance, see Table 1. *(iii)* We first compute and reveal the set of parties that will obtain at least one seat in the parliament. This allows us to tailor the following computations to this specific set of parties and thus save time by not having to perform the same operations for (dozens of) parties that will not obtain a seat. As part of Theorem 2, we argue that this construction is still a secure MPC protocol as, intuitively, the intermediate output can be computed from/is part of the final result. *(iv)* By proposing a different algorithm for computing the final number of seats for each party in the German parliament based on an encrypted divisor $d = \min(d_{\text{no}}, d_{\text{overh}})$, we can use an efficient binary search on encrypted data to obtain this value.

We provide full details of $\mathsf{P}_{\text{MPC-Ger}}$, including all of our optimizations in the full version [25]. We have the following:

Theorem 2 (Security). *Let $\mathsf{P}_{\text{MPC-Ger}}$ be our MPC protocol from above. Then, the Ordinos instance using the components mentioned above is a verifiable[5] and fully tally-hiding e-voting system for the election of the German parliament.*

We prove this theorem in the full version [25]. As part of this, we define full tally-hiding for elections with constituencies, re-verify the original proofs of the Ordinos framework for our setting, and show that our $\mathsf{P}_{\text{MPC-Ger}}$ is a secure, publicly verifiable MPC protocol for $f_{\text{res-Ger}}$.

Benchmarks: We have benchmarked our system using the election data for the German parliament in 2021 available at [11]. This election had $61,181,072$

---

[5] We actually show that our voting system achieves the stronger notion of accountability as well. That is, if the result turns out to be incorrect, then a misbehaving party causing this mistake can be identified and be held accountable.

eligible voters, $46,854,508$ valid submitted ballots, and 47 parties with 6211 candidates running in 299 constituencies. With each trustee running on an ESP-RIMO Q957 (64 bit, i5-7500T CPU @ 2.70 GHz, 16 GB RAM) using 8 cores, we can evaluate (and verify, as explained in Appendix A.4) the German parliamentary elections based on this real-world data in about a day. For more details on our setup and further benchmarks, see Appendix A and our full version [25].

6   Related Work and Conclusion

Various tally-hiding e-voting systems for a wide variety of election types have been proposed so far, e.g., [4,5,9,12,14,15,19,23,27]. For simple types of elections such as single vote (every voter submits a single vote for the candidate of their choice with the winner(s) being the candidate(s) with the most votes), it has been demonstrated that they can be performed in a verifiable tally-hiding manner, even at a large scale (see, e.g., [9,14,15,19]). However, many real-world elections, notably political ones, are much more complex and have proven to be a challenge for tally-hiding systems.

Preferential Elections: An important class of complex real-world elections are preferential ones. Tally hiding has already been studied for several voting methods from this class, with such systems typically being viable at a small to medium scale but often being impractical for large-scale applications. For example: (i) Recent advances in tally-hiding e-voting have managed to support instant-runoff voting (IRV) for small numbers of candidates [15,23]. However, none of these systems remain practical for more than 6 candidates. (ii) Cortier et. al [9] have proposed the first MPC component that can be used to construct a fully tally-hiding voting system for single transferable vote (STV), a preferential voting method somewhat similar to IRV. However, they state that the computational cost of the resulting system would be too high for large-scale elections. (iii) For the Condorcet Schulze election scheme, Hertel et.al. [14] proposed an Ordinos instantiation that can handle small numbers of candidates, however, already needs about 9 days to compute an election result for 20 candidates (and essentially arbitrary numbers of voters). Cortier et. al [9] proposed an alternative tally-hiding MPC component for computing Condorcet Schulze, which is faster for small numbers of voters but can be extrapolated to also require 9 days for 20 candidates as soon as there are $\sim$32.000 voters.

Parliamentary Elections With Party-Based Seat Allocations: As already explained in the introduction, prior to our work, it had not been investigated for any election from this class, whether and in how far, it can be performed in a tally-hiding manner. In this work, we have proposed several new tally-hiding building blocks, as well as the first verifiable tally-hiding voting system for an election from this class, namely, the German parliament. Our results serve as an important foundational feasibility study, which, perhaps surprisingly and for the first time, demonstrates that even such a complex and large-scale real-world election can, in principle be performed in a verifiable fully tally-hiding manner.

It is interesting future work to use our building blocks and ideas to construct tally-hiding voting systems for further elections from this class.

Acknowledgements. This research was supported by the DFG through grant KU 1434/11-1, by the Carl Zeiss Foundation, and by the Centre for Integrated Quantum Science and Technology (IQST).

A Appendix

A.1 Details of the Setup for Our Benchmarks

We use a Paillier key of size 2048 bits. The setup for our benchmarks consists of three trustees communicating over a local network. Each trustee ran on an ESPRIMO Q957 (64 bit, i5-7500T CPU @ 2.70 GHz, 16 GB RAM). As in [19], the benchmarks of our MPC protocols start with an already aggregated tally. Küsters et al. [19] showed for the MPC protocols in their Ordinos instances that the number of trustees does not influence the benchmarks in a noticeable way and that, due to the sublinear communication complexity of the comparison protocols, there is no significant difference between a local network and the Internet. Since our MPC protocols are based on the same primitives and basic building blocks as used by [19], the same is also true for our MPC protocols. Our benchmarks therefore focus mostly on the number of candidates/parties which is the main factor for the performance of our protocols.

A.2 Comparison of **SLQCustomTiebreaking** and **SLQFloorDiv**

We present benchmarks for both SLQFloorDiv and SLQCustomTiebreaking (cf. Sect. 4) in Fig. 4. As the figure shows, SLQCustomTiebreaking is linear in the number of seats. While SLQFloorDiv has a larger overhead depending on the number of parties, it is nearly constant in the number of seats.

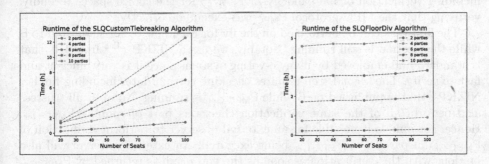

Fig. 4. Benchmarks for one execution of SLQFloorDiv and SLQCustomTiebreaking from Sect. 4.

A.3 Benchmarks of the Evaluation of the Elections for the German Bundestag in 2021

In Table 1 we present our benchmarks of the evaluation of the elections for the German Bundestag in 2021 using real-world data available at [11]. Each row in the table represents one main step of the algorithm, where each of these main steps is executed in sequence. Within each individual step, it is possible to leverage parallelism. We show the resulting runtime for various numbers of threads/cpu cores. Further benchmarks are presented in the full version [25].

Table 1. Benchmarks of the election for the German Bundestag in 2021 using real-world data available at [11] with different numbers of available parallel threads for each trustee.

# Threads per Trustee	1	2	4	8	16	32
Single-member constituency seats	40.03 h	20.04 h	10.06 h	5.06 h	2.56 h	1.32 h
Determine which parties enter the Bundestag	71 min	36 min	18 min	9 min	5 min	3 min
First low distribution	23.38 h	11.77 h	6.07 h	3.25 h	1.82 h	1.1 h
Minimal number of seats per party	11.68 h	5.84 h	2.93 h	1.46 h	0.74 h	0.36 h
Second top distribution	2.81 h	2.0 h	1.42 h	1.19 h	1.19 h	1.19 h
Second low distribution	77.06 h	38.53 h	19.4 h	12.34 h	6.3 h	5.93 h
Assigning overhang seats	6.67 h	3.33 h	2.2 h	1.14 h	1.14 h	1.14 h
Computing the final result	4 min	2 min	1 min	1 min	0 min	0 min
Total Runtime	163 h	82 h	42 h	24.3 h	13.8 h	11.1 h

A.4 Verification of the Election

Verification of an election following the Ordinos approach essentially consists of two main tasks: Firstly, checking the correctness of the ballots submitted to B including verification of the ballot NIZKPs π^{Enc} for the choice space. Secondly, verifying that the MPC protocol $\mathsf{P_{MPC}}$ was executed correctly.

The first task can be performed on the fly for each new ballot submitted to B while the election is still running. Notably, we use a NIZKP π^{Enc} from [10] that is standard and employed by many e-voting systems since it is very efficient and fast to verify. The second step requires checking certain data, including further NIZKPs, that is published on B while $\mathsf{P_{MPC\text{-}Ger}}$ is running. Notably, all trustees also perform all of the same verification checks as part of running $\mathsf{P_{MPC\text{-}Ger}}$. Hence, not only is it possible for an external observer to perform verification of $\mathsf{P_{MPC\text{-}Ger}}$ in parallel to $\mathsf{P_{MPC\text{-}Ger}}$ being executed. An external observer will also be done with this verification as soon as the end result is returned by $\mathsf{P_{MPC\text{-}Ger}}$ because he has to perform strictly less work than the trustees running $\mathsf{P_{MPC\text{-}Ger}}$. We therefore only had to benchmark the runtime of $\mathsf{P_{MPC\text{-}Ger}}$ to obtain the overall time for *both computing and verifying* the election result of our system proposed in Sect. 5.

References

1. Adida, B.: Helios: web-based Open-Audit Voting. In: Proceedings of the 17th USENIX Security Symposium, pp. 335–348. USENIX Association (2008)
2. Benaloh, J.: Verifiable secret ballot elections. Ph.D. thesis, Yale University (1987)
3. Benaloh, J., et al.: Star-vote: a secure, transparent, auditable, and reliable voting system. In: 2013 Electronic Voting Technology Workshop/Workshop on Trustworthy Elections, EVT/WOTE '13. USENIX Association (2013)
4. Benaloh, J., Moran, T., Naish, L., Ramchen, K., Teague, V.: Shuffle-sum: coercion-resistant verifiable tallying for STV voting. IEEE Trans. Inf. Forensics Secur. $4(4)$, 685–698 (2009). https://doi.org/10.1109/TIFS.2009.2033757
5. Canard, S., Pointcheval, D., Santos, Q., Traoré, J.: Practical strategy-resistant privacy-preserving elections. In: Lopez, J., Zhou, J., Soriano, M. (eds.) ESORICS 2018. LNCS, vol. 11099, pp. 331–349. Springer, Cham (2018). https://doi.org/10.1007/978-3-319-98989-1_17
6. Chaum, D., Carback, R., Clark, J., Essex, A., Popoveniuc, S., Rivest, R.L., Ryan, P.Y.A., Shen, E., Sherman, A.T.: Scantegrity II: end-to-end verifiability for optical scan election systems using invisible ink confirmation codes. In: 2008 USENIX/ACCURATE Electronic Voting Workshop, EVT 2008, Proceedings. USENIX Association (2008)
7. Clarkson, M.R., Chong, S., Myers, A.C.: Civitas: toward a secure voting system. In: 2008 IEEE Symposium on Security and Privacy (S&P 2008), pp. 354–368. IEEE Computer Society (2008). https://doi.org/10.1109/SP.2008.32
8. Cortier, V., Galindo, D., Glondu, S., Izabachène, M.: Election verifiability for Helios under weaker trust assumptions. In: Kutyłowski, M., Vaidya, J. (eds.) ESORICS 2014. LNCS, vol. 8713, pp. 327–344. Springer, Cham (2014). https://doi.org/10.1007/978-3-319-11212-1_19
9. Cortier, V., Gaudry, P., Yang, Q.: A toolbox for verifiable tally-hiding e-voting systems. In: Atluri, V., Di Pietro, R., Jensen, C.D., Meng, W. (eds.) ESORICS 2022. LNCS, vol. 13555, pp. 631–652. Springer, Cham (2022)
10. Damgård, I., Jurik, M., Nielsen, J.B.: A generalization of Paillier's public-key system with applications to electronic voting. Int. J. Inf. Secur. $9(6)$, 371–385 (2010). https://doi.org/10.1007/s10207-010-0119-9
11. Der Bundeswahlleiter: Wahl zum 20. Deutschen Bundestag am 26. September 2021: Heft 3 Endgültige Ergebnisse nach Wahlkreisen (2021). https://bundeswahlleiter.de/dam/jcr/cbceef6c-19ec-437b-a894-3611be8ae886/btw21_heft3.pdf, https://www.bundeswahlleiter.de/bundestagswahlen/2021/ergebnisse/opendata/csv/
12. Haines, T., Pattinson, D., Tiwari, M.: Verifiable homomorphic tallying for the Schulze vote counting scheme. In: Chakraborty, S., Navas, J.A. (eds.) VSTTE 2019. LNCS, vol. 12031, pp. 36–53. Springer, Cham (2020). https://doi.org/10.1007/978-3-030-41600-3_4
13. Heather, J.: Implementing STV securely in Prêt à voter. In: IEEE 20th Computer Security Foundations Symposium (CSF 2007), pp. 157–169. IEEE Computer Society (2007). https://doi.org/10.1109/CSF.2007.22
14. Hertel, F., Huber, N., Kittelberger, J., Küsters, R., Liedtke, J., Rausch, D.: Extending the tally-hiding ordinos system: implementations for Borda, Hare-Niemeyer, condorcet, and instant-runoff voting. In: Electronic Voting - 6th International Joint Conference, E-Vote-ID 2021, Proceedings, pp. 269–284. University of Tartu Press (2021)

15. Huber, N., et al.: Kryvos: publicly tally-hiding verifiable e-voting. In: CCS 2022, pp. 1443–1457. ACM (2022). https://doi.org/10.1145/3548606.3560701
16. Juels, A., Catalano, D., Jakobsson, M.: Coercion-resistant electronic elections. In: Proceedings of the 2005 ACM Workshop on Privacy in the Electronic Society, WPES 2005, pp. 61–70. ACM (2005). https://doi.org/10.1145/1102199.1102213
17. Kiayias, A., Zacharias, T., Zhang, B.: DEMOS-2: scalable E2E verifiable elections without random oracles. In: CCS 2015, pp. 352–363. ACM (2015). https://doi.org/10.1145/2810103.2813727
18. Kiayias, A., Zacharias, T., Zhang, B.: End-to-end verifiable elections in the standard model. In: Oswald, E., Fischlin, M. (eds.) EUROCRYPT 2015. LNCS, vol. 9057, pp. 468–498. Springer, Heidelberg (2015). https://doi.org/10.1007/978-3-662-46803-6_16
19. Küsters, R., Liedtke, J., Müller, J., Rausch, D., Vogt, A.: Ordinos: a verifiable tally-hiding e-voting system. In: 2020 IEEE European Symposium on Security and Privacy (EuroS&P 2020), pp. 216–235. IEEE Computer Society (2020). https://doi.org/10.1109/EuroSP48549.2020.00022
20. Küsters, R., Müller, J., Scapin, E., Truderung, T.: sElect: a lightweight verifiable remote voting system. In: IEEE 29th Computer Security Foundations Symposium (CSF 2016), pp. 341–354. IEEE Computer Society (2016). https://doi.org/10.1109/CSF.2016.31
21. Lijphart, A.: Degrees of proportionality of proportional representation formulas. Rivista Italiana Di Scienza Politica 13(2), 295–305 (1983)
22. Lipmaa, H., Toft, T.: Secure equality and greater-than tests with sublinear online complexity. In: Fomin, F.V., Freivalds, R., Kwiatkowska, M., Peleg, D. (eds.) ICALP 2013. LNCS, vol. 7966, pp. 645–656. Springer, Heidelberg (2013). https://doi.org/10.1007/978-3-642-39212-2_56
23. Ramchen, K., Culnane, C., Pereira, O., Teague, V.: Universally verifiable MPC and IRV ballot counting. In: Goldberg, I., Moore, T. (eds.) FC 2019. LNCS, vol. 11598, pp. 301–319. Springer, Cham (2019). https://doi.org/10.1007/978-3-030-32101-7_19
24. Ryan, P.Y.A., Rønne, P.B., Iovino, V.: Selene: voting with transparent verifiability and coercion-mitigation. In: Clark, J., Meiklejohn, S., Ryan, P.Y.A., Wallach, D., Brenner, M., Rohloff, K. (eds.) FC 2016. LNCS, vol. 9604, pp. 176–192. Springer, Heidelberg (2016). https://doi.org/10.1007/978-3-662-53357-4_12
25. Wabartha, C., Liedtke, J., Huber, N., Rausch, D., Küsters, R.: Fully tally-hiding verifiable e-voting for real-world elections with seat-allocations. Cryptology ePrint Archive, Paper 2023/1289 (2023). https://eprint.iacr.org/2023/1289, Full Version of this Paper
26. Wabartha, C., Liedtke, J., Huber, N., Rausch, D., Küsters, R.: Implementation of our System. (2023). https://github.com/JulianLiedtke/ordinos-bundestag
27. Wen, R., Buckland, R.: Minimum disclosure counting for the alternative vote. In: Ryan, P.Y.A., Schoenmakers, B. (eds.) Vote-ID 2009. LNCS, vol. 5767, pp. 122–140. Springer, Heidelberg (2009). https://doi.org/10.1007/978-3-642-04135-8_8

An Ultra-High Throughput AES-Based Authenticated Encryption Scheme for 6G: Design and Implementation

Ravi Anand[1](✉), Subhadeep Banik[2], Andrea Caforio[3], Kazuhide Fukushima[4], Takanori Isobe[1](✉), Shisaku Kiyomoto[4], Fukang Liu[1], Yuto Nakano[4], Kosei Sakamoto[1], and Nobuyuki Takeuchi[1]

[1] University of Hyogo, Kobe, Japan
ravianandsps@gmail.com, takanori.isobe@ai.u-hyogo.ac.jp
[2] Universita della Svizzera Italiana, Lugano, Switzerland
[3] École Polytechnique Fédérale de Lausanne, Lausanne, Switzerland
[4] KDDI Research, Inc., Saitama, Japan

Abstract. In this paper, we propose Rocca-S, an authenticated encryption scheme with a 256-bit key and a 256-bit tag targeting 6G applications bootstrapped from AES. Rocca-S achieves an encryption/decryption speed of more than 200 Gbps in the latest software environments. In hardware implementation, Rocca-S is the first cryptographic algorithm to achieve speeds more than 2 Tbps without sacrificing other metrics such as occupied silicon area or power/energy consumption making Rocca-S a competitive choice satisfying the requirements of a wide spectrum of environments for 6G applications.

Keywords: Authenticated Encryption · High Throughput · Quantum Security · 6G

1 Introduction

The imminent global standardization of 5G telecommunication networks marks an important turning point for the involved research community whose gaze should hereafter be directed beyond the 5G era. The 6Genesis project kickstarted this endeavour with a white paper [9] in which 6G channels are projected to provide throughput rates upwards of 100 Gbps in software eclipsing their 5G counterparts by more than an order of magnitude. Concerning peak throughput, the paper further illuminates potential avenues that would allow for rates in the Terabit range and states: *"6G research should look at the problem of transmitting up to 1 Tbps per user."*

Naturally, performance only covers half of the requirements for a prospective 6G standard with the other one being security as discussed by the 3GPP standardization organization which examined the possible impacts of quantum computing in the coming years especially due to Grover's algorithm. The motivation is to design a cipher that provides 256-bit classical security and 128-bit

G. Tsudik et al. (Eds.): ESORICS 2023, LNCS 14344, pp. 229–248, 2024.
https://doi.org/10.1007/978-3-031-50594-2_12

quantum security for key recovery. Apart from the 256-bit key size, proposing an AEAD scheme with a suitable tag length is also important to ensure the security against the state-recovery attack. Specially, if the tag size is smaller than 256 bits, it is possible to use the decryption oracle to mount a fast state-recovery attack with time complexity smaller than 2^{256} [6,22], especially when each message block is absorbed by a weak permutation as in AEGIS-256 [22] and Rocca [19]. By using a keyed permutation for the initialization phase as in AEGIS-256 and the revised version of Rocca [20], while the key-recovery attack can be prevented even if the state-recovery attack succeeds, it may be still a potential threat to the AEAD scheme since attackers can extract more information from the full secret state with this state-recovery attack. In this sense, we believe it is meaningful to design an AEAD scheme with a 256-bit tag.

Motivation. To the best of our knowledge, none of the existing algorithms dedicated to 5G and beyond provide throughput rates of more than 1 Tbps, more than 100 Gbps in software, and support 256-bit tags, including the AEGIS [22], Tiaoxin-346 [17], and Rocca [19,20] as well as 5G ciphers such as ZUC-256 [21] and SNOW-V [3]. This fact motivates a search for new algorithms which meets all three of these requirements for 6G applications.

Contributions and Organization

In this paper, we propose Rocca-S, which is an AES-based authenticated encryption scheme with a 256-bit key and a 256-bit tag, which provides 256- and 128-bit security for key recovery attacks against classical and quantum adversary, respectively. One of the main contribution is to design new round functions supporting 256-bit tags, without sacrificing performance. Rocca-S achieves more than 200 Gbps in latest software environments and more than 1 Tbps in hardware. Rocca-S is the first algorithm that achieves both requirements for 6G, namely a 256-bit tag and throughput rates beyond 1 Terabit. The specification of Rocca-S is given in Sect. 2.

- The design rationale is explained in Sect. 3. The most difficult challenge is to design round functions supporting 256-bit tag without sacrificing performance. To accomplish it, we take advantage of an interesting insight that while increasing the number of aesenc from 4 (Rocca's case) to 6 in the round function, the overhead in software performance can be made negligible by reducing state size from 8 to 7. From a hardware point of view, as these are executed in parallel, there is no overhead regarding throughput, and small state size rather reduces the circuit area. This allows us to add more nonlinear operations into each round and open up new design space to increase the security against forgery attacks while keeping the performance. Our comprehensive large-scale search with MILP-aided tools enables finding a very small class of round functions that guarantee the sufficient level of security against forgery attacks and competitive performance in software and hardware.

- We discuss the security analysis of Rocca-S in Sect. 4. We show that Rocca-S is secure against several classes of attacks by classic and quantum adversaries.
- The software performance is discussed in Sect. 5. We show that Rocca-S outperforms existing algorithms and achieves a throughput of 205 Gbps in AEAD mode on a machine equipped with an Intel(R) Core(TM) i9 12900K.
- Ultimately, we meticulously explore the design space of ASIC implementations by proposing several constructions ranging from round-based circuits to unrolled variants in Sect. 6. In particular, the round-based and unrolled circuits achieve throughput rates that exceed 1 Terabit per second (even crossing the 2 Tbps barrier for some instances) and thus eclipse related AEAD circuits by at least 50% without sacrificing other metrics such as occupied silicon area or power/energy consumption making Rocca-S a competitive choice satisfying the requirements of a wide spectrum of environments.

2 Specification

Throughout this paper, a block denotes a 16-byte value. S is the state of Rocca-S, which is composed of 7 blocks of the form $S = (S[0], S[1], \ldots, S[6])$, where $S[i]$ $(0 \leq i \leq 6)$ are blocks and $S[0]$ is the first block. $\mathsf{AES}(X, Y)$ is defined as:

$$\mathsf{AES}(X, Y) = (\text{MixColumns} \circ \text{ShiftRows} \circ \text{SubBytes}(X)) \oplus Y,$$

where MixColumns, ShiftRows, and SubBytes are the same operations as that of AES. $A(X)$ is $A(X) = \text{MixColumns} \circ \text{ShiftRows} \circ \text{SubBytes}(X)$. $R(S, X_0, X_1)$ is the round function used to update the state S. We utilize the same constants as in Tiaoxin-346 [17], namely $Z_0 = $ 428a2f98d728ae227137449123ef65cd and $Z_1 = $ b5c0fbcfec4d3b2fe9b5dba58189dbbc.

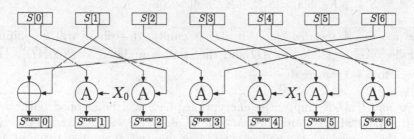

Fig. 1. Round function of Rocca-S (RF-1)

2.1 The Round Update Function

The input of the round function $R(S, X_0, X_1)$ of Rocca-S consists of the state S and two blocks (X_0, X_1). $S^{new} \leftarrow R(S, X_0, X_1)$ is illustrated as Fig. 1 and defined as:

$$S^{new}[0] = S[6] \oplus S[1], \qquad S^{new}[1] = \mathsf{AES}(S[0], X_0), S^{new}[2] = \mathsf{AES}(S[1], S[0]),$$
$$S^{new}[3] = \mathsf{AES}(S[2], S[6]), \quad S^{new}[4] = \mathsf{AES}(S[3], X_1), S^{new}[5] = \mathsf{AES}(S[4], S[3]),$$
$$S^{new}[6] = \mathsf{AES}(S[5], S[4]).$$

2.2 Specification of Rocca-S

Rocca-S is an authenticated-encryption with associated-data scheme composed of four phases: *initialization, processing the associated data, encryption* and *finalization*. The input consists of a 256-bit key $K_0 \| K_1 \in \mathbb{F}_2^{128} \times \mathbb{F}_2^{128}$, a 128-bit nonce N, the associated data AD and the message M, where $X \| Y$ is the concatenation of X and Y. The output is the corresponding ciphertext C and a 256-bit tag T. $|X|$ is the length of X in bits. Define $\overline{X} = X \| 0^l$ where 0^l is a zero string of length l bits, and l is the minimal non-negative integer such that $|\overline{X}|$ is a multiple of 256. In addition, write X as $X = X_0 \| X_1 \| \ldots \| X_{\frac{|X|}{256}-1}$ with $|X_i| = 256$. Further, X_i is written as $X_i = X_i^0 \| X_i^1$ with $|X_i^0| = |X_i^1| = 128$.

Initialization. First, (N, K_0, K_1) is loaded into the state S in the following way:

$$S[0] = K_1, S[1] = N, S[2] = Z_0, S[3] = K_0, S[4] = Z_1, S[5] = N \oplus K_1, S[6] = 0$$

Here, two 128-bit constants Z_0 and Z_1 are encoded as 16-byte little endian words and loaded into $S[2]$ and $S[3]$ respectively. Then, 16 iterations of the round function $R(S, Z_0, Z_1)$ is applied to the state S. After 16 iterations of the round function, two 128-bit keys are XORed with the state S in the following way;

$$S[0] = S[0] \oplus K_0, S[1] = S[1] \oplus K_0, S[2] = S[2] \oplus K_1, S[3] = S[3] \oplus K_0,$$
$$S[4] = S[4] \oplus K_0, S[5] = S[5] \oplus K_1, S[6] = S[6] \oplus K_1.$$

Processing the Associated Data. If AD is empty, this phase will be skipped. Otherwise, AD is padded to $\overline{AD}$ and the state is updated as $R(S, \overline{AD}_i^0, \overline{AD}_i^1)$ for $i = 0$ to $d - 1$, where $d = \frac{|\overline{AD}|}{256}$.

Encryption. If M is empty, the encryption phase will be skipped. Otherwise, M is first padded to $\overline{M}$ and then $\overline{M}$ will be absorbed with the round function. During this procedure, the ciphertext C is generated. If the last block of M is incomplete and its length is b bits, i.e., $0 < b < 256$, the last block of C will be truncated to the first b bits. Each encryption round unfolds as follows:

$$C_i^0 = \mathsf{AES}(S[3] \oplus S[5], S[0]) \oplus \overline{M}_i^0, C_i^1 = \mathsf{AES}(S[4] \oplus S[6], S[2]) \oplus \overline{M}_i^1, R(S, \overline{M}_i^0, \overline{M}_i^1),$$

where $i = 0$ to $m - 1$, and $m = \frac{|\overline{M}|}{256}$.

Finalization. The state S will again pass through 16 iterations of the round function $R(S, |AD|, |M|)$ and then the 256-bit tag is computed:

$$T = \bigoplus_{i=0}^{3} S[i] \| \bigoplus_{i=4}^{6} S[i].$$

The length of associated data and message is encoded as a 16-byte little endian word and stored into $|AD|$ and $|M|$, respectively. A illustration corresponding to the presented procedures is shown in Fig. 2

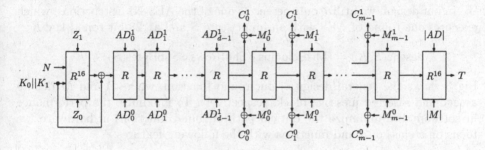

Fig. 2. Overview of Rocca-S

A Raw Encryption Scheme. If the phases of processing the associated data and finalization are removed, a raw encryption scheme is obtained.

A Keystream Generation Scheme. If the phases of processing the associated data and finalization are removed and there is no message injection into round function such that $R(S, 0, 0)$, a keystream generation scheme is obtained.

2.3 Security Claims

Classical Setting. Rocca-S provides 256-bit security against key-recovery and 192-bit security against forgery attacks in the nonce-respecting setting. Rocca-S does not claim security against nonce-misuse setting. We do not claim its security in the related-key and known-key settings. The message length for a fixed key and the number of different messages that are produced for a fixed key are limited to at most 2^{128}. The length of associated data of a fixed key is up to 2^{64}.

Quantum Setting. Rocca-S provides 128-bit key-recovery and forgery security against quantum adversaries with classical online queries. Rocca-S does not claim security against online superposition attacks.

3   Design Rationale

3.1   General Design

The general design of Rocca-S follows the key features of AEGIS family [22], Tiaoxin-346 [17] and Rocca [19,20], i.e., SIMD-friendly round function and efficient permutation-based structure. To further increase the resistance against several attacks on AEGIS and Tiaoxin-346 [11,15] while keeping the performance, we carefully design the nonce and key loading scheme at the initial state and output function. Furthermore, we add key-forward operations in the initialization phase as similar to the suggestion by the recent attacks on Rocca [6],

In our design, we utilize only aesenc as one of the AES-NI instructions, which executes one round of AES with an input state S and a 128-bit round key K:

$$\text{aesenc}(S, K) = (\text{MixColumns} \circ \text{ShiftRows} \circ \text{SubBytes}(S)) \oplus K.$$

Fig. 3 shows the general design of our round function, where A and M denote aesenc and inserted message block, respectively. To maximize the performance in software and minimize the critical path of round functions in hardware, we focus on a class of round functions with the following features.

– Applying only either aesenc or XOR to each block in one round.
– Applying a state-wise permutation before operations of aesenc or XOR.

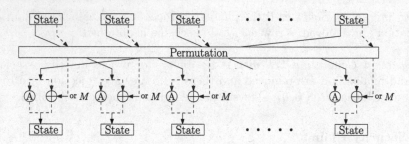

Fig. 3. General Design for the Round Function of Rocca-S.

In hardware, since a state-wise permutation does not cause any delay, the critical path of this round function is the execution of a single aesenc module. This delay is the lower bound for AES-based round functions, meaning that the delay of the round function cannot be reduced any further.

Design Challenge. The existing round functions of AEGIS [22], Tiaoxin-346 [17], Rocca [19,20] and all of Jean and Nikolić's ones [7] can be categorized into this type of class, however, these support only 128-bit tags, i.e., they ensure only 128-bit security against forgery attacks in the classic setting. We should also note here that the bound of forgery attack of Rocca is 2^{-144}, meaning the security margin is only 16 bits [19,20]. Therefore, our main challenge in this paper is to support a 256-bit tag while maintaining high performance in both software and hardware. To be more specific, the number of active S-boxes for forgery attacks should be much more than that of Rocca [19,20] without sacrificing performance.

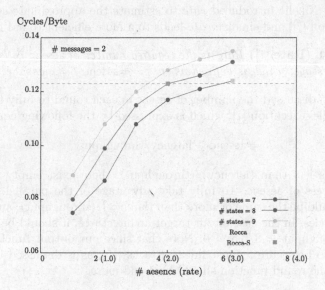

Fig. 4. Relationship between the number of AES-NI and performance.

Our Solution. Our core insights to accomplish this challenge is as follows: (1) smaller state is more efficient and (2) even if increasing #aesenc from 4 to 6, the overhead is marginal in software, as shown in Fig. 4. This allows us to add more nonlinear operations into each round, and then open up new design space of AES-based round functions while keeping the software's performance. Interestingly, the speed of Rocca parameters (#aesenc = 4 and #state size = 8) is almost same as those of Rocca-S (#aesenc = 6 and #state size = 7).

From a hardware point of view, as these are executed in parallel, there is no overhead regarding throughput. Beside, smaller #*state* leads to be smaller circuit scale and low energy consumption in hardware.

3.2 Requirements of Round Function for Performance and Security

This section clarifies the requirements for finding optimal parameters of AES-based round functions for our purpose.

Performance. The performance of AES-NI can be measured d by latency and throughput. Latency means the number of clock cycles that are required for the execution of an instruction. Throughput means the number of clock cycles required to wait before the responsible ports can accept the same instruction again. Dispa These depend on the CPU architectures [18]. This paper focuses on the latest architectures after Intel Ice-lake series CPU where latency and throughput of aesenc are 3 and 0.5, respectively. Let #*state*, #aesenc, and #*message* be the number of states, aesencs, and inserted message blocks in a single round, respectively.

Jean and Nikolić introduced *rate* to estimate the approximate speed of the round function [7], and smaller *rate* leads to a more efficient round function.

Definition 1 (Rate [7]) *Rate is the required number of* aesenc *calls to encrypt a 128-bit message, which is defined as rate =* #aesenc / #*message*.

They also discussed the number of aesenc in each round to fully take advantage of parallel execution [7], which is expressed by the following equation:

$$\#\text{aesenc} \geq \text{latency/throughput}.$$

If #aesenc is less than (latency)/(throughput), there exist empty cycles in a parallel process of aesenc. To fully take advantage of the parallel processing, #aesenc should be the same or more than (latency)/(throughput), and there are no empty cycles. In the case of our target architectures, it should be #aesenc $\geq$ latency/throughput = 3/0.5 = 6. Note that since our output function utilizes two aesenc to be secure against linear attacks [15], as is discussed in Sect. 3.4, #aesenc in the round function should be 4 and more.

Security. We estimate the security against forgery by the lower bound for the number of differentially active S-boxes. Since the maximum differential probability of an S-box is 2^{-6}, we aim at finding round functions in which the lower bound for the number of active S-boxes in the forgery setting is at least 43 so that the differential probability is less than 2^{-256}.

Summary of Requirements. Taking these issues into consideration, we clarify requirements for the AES-based round function for our purposes as follows:

Req 1. *Rate* (= #aesenc/#*message*) is as small as possible.
Req 2. #aesenc is 4 or more in each round function.
Req 3. #*state* is as small as possible.
Req 4. The lower bound for the number of active S-boxes is $\geq$ 43.

3.3 Finding Optimal Parameters of Round Functions

In this section, we search for optimal parameters that satisfy the requirements. Let s, a, and m be #*state*, #aesenc, and #*message*, respectively.

Search Method. Once we select *rate* and s according to Req 1 and 3, then we can properly choose pairs of a and m by Req 2. Specifically, we search for all 15 candidates with parameters such that *rate* = 2 to 3 and $s = 6, 7, 8$ as shown in Table 1. For each parameter, we try to search for candidates that satisfy

Req 4 for all patterns of block permutations and the combinations of positions of inserted messages and aesenc/XOR in the target class of Fig. 3 by MILP-aided evaluation. Sakamoto *et al.* estimated the total number of search space as $s! \times \binom{s}{a} \times \binom{s}{m}$ [19]. However, this search space includes equivalent class of round functions. Considering such equivalent classes, we can reduce it by the formula of $\frac{s!}{m!} \times \binom{s}{m} \times \binom{s}{a}$. For example, the candidates of the class of $s = 7$, $a = 4$, and $m = 2$ can be reduced from $2^{21.82}$ in Sakamoto *et al.* [19], to $2^{20.82}$. In our evaluation, if the total number of candidates in the class exceeds 2^{23}, we randomly choose 2^{20} candidates and evaluate these due to the limitations of the computational power.

Table 1. Candidate of round functions for each class.

#state	#aesenc	#message	rate	Total	# of searched	# of found
6	4	2	2.0	$2^{16.31}$	All	0
6	6	3	2.0	$2^{11.29}$	All	0
6	5	2	2.5	$2^{16.98}$	All	0
6	6	2	3.0	$2^{12.40}$	All	0
7	4	2	2.0	$2^{20.82}$	All	0
7	6	3	2.0	$2^{17.65}$	All	0
7	7	3	2.33	$2^{14.84}$	All	0
7	5	2	2.5	$2^{20.08}$	All	0
7	6	2	3.0	$2^{18.50}$	All	14
8	4	2	2.0	$2^{25.24}$	2^{20}	0
8	6	3	2.0	$2^{23.33}$	2^{20}	0
8	7	3	2.33	$2^{21.52}$	All	0
8	5	2	2.5	$2^{24.91}$	2^{20}	0
8	8	3	2.67	$2^{18.52}$	All	0
8	6	2	3.0	$2^{23.91}$	2^{20}	784

Table 2. Lower bound of differentially active S-boxes, maximum rounds of the integral distinguisher, and speeds.

Target	# of active S-boxes					Integral distinguisher	Speed (cycles / Byte)
	6R	7R	8R	9R	10R		
AEGIS-128L	85	86	94	111	120	6R	0.188985
Tiaoxin-346	53	93	99	123	134	15R	0.200404
Rocca	54	62	82	85	93	7R	0.123258
RF-1 (Rocca-S)	94	113	122	134	152	5R	0.122219
RF-2	76	88	103	115	131	6R	0.129443
RF-3	96	101	114	129	136	6R	0.118518
RF-4	80	100	108	120	145	5R	0.122185
RF-5	81	86	95	121	141	5R	0.122286
RF-6	97	113	122	139	151	6R	0.129258
RF-7	97	110	128	132	137	6R	0.129523

Table 3. The lower bound of differentially active S-boxes and # rounds for full diffusion

# of active S-boxes	# rounds for full diffusion	# of candidates
44	6	7
46	5	7

Results. Table 1 shows the summary of our search. We found 14 candidates in $s = 7$, $a = 6$, and $m = 2$ and 784 candidates in $s = 8$, $a = 6$, and $m = 2$ which satisfy Req 4. Due to Req 3, we choose 14 candidates of the class of $s = 7$, $a = 6$, and $m = 2$. This evaluation requires about 45 d on three computers equipped with AMD Ryzen Threadripper 3990X (64-Core) and 256 GB RAMs.

Selecting Best Round Function for Rocca-S. To determine one round function from 14 candidates of $s = 7$, $a = 6$, and $m = 2$, we evaluate the security and performance of these.

- Table 3 shows the required number of rounds for full diffusion and the lower bound for the number of active S-boxes for forgery setting. We choose seven candidates which attain 46 active S-boxes and achieve the full diffusion after 5 rounds named as RF-1, 2, 3, ..., 7.

– Table 2 shows the security of the initialization phase of these candidates against differential attacks and integral attacks by a byte-based MILP, assuming that the adversary can control only nonce. In addition, Table 2 compares the speed of the round function of 7 candidates and Rocca, where the speed is measured as the average of the round function executed $2^{23.25}$ times with 64 kB messages on Intel(R) Core(TM) i7-1068NG7 CPU @ 2.30GHz.

Considering results of Table 2, we finally adopt RF-1 as shown in Fig. 1.

3.4   On the Loading Scheme and Output Functions

For the loading scheme of the nonce and key, we mainly want to avoid the case occurring in Tiaoxin-346. Specifically, we expect that after some number of rounds, the whole state words cannot be expressed only in terms of $A(N)$ and (K_0, K_1). If this happens, there will be a useless round and it opens a door for more powerful attacks [11]. By setting $S[5] = N \oplus K_1$, such a case is avoided.

To resist the linear attacks on output function, that has been successfully applied to AEGIS [15], we use the MILP model [2] to search for secure ones. For efficiency and security, we choose the output functions of the following form:

$$C_i^0 = \mathsf{AES}(S[j_0] \oplus S[j_1], S[j_2]) \oplus \overline{M}_i^0,$$
$$C_i^1 = \mathsf{AES}(S[j_3] \oplus S[j_4], S[j_5]) \oplus \overline{M}_i^1,$$

where $j_{u_1} \neq j_{u_2}$ for $u_1 \neq u_2$ and $0 \leq j_0, j_1, j_2, j_3, j_4, j_5 \leq 6$.

Then, with the truncated MILP model [2], for each choice of the tuple $(j_0, j_1, j_2, j_3, j_4, j_5)$, we can compute the lower bound of the number of active S-boxes for a exploitable linear trail that can be used for attacks. For our choice, the lower bound of the number of active S-boxes is 45. Hence, the time complexity of the linear attack will be higher than $2^{45 \times 6} = 2^{270}$. Note that there is a big gap between the truncated model and the bit-wise model and the actual linear trail that can be used for attacks may be of much lower bias and the time complexity may be much higher than 2^{270}.

3.5   The Key Feed-Forward Operation

It has been observed by the designers of AEGIS-256 that the internal state can be fully recovered by using the decryption oracle for about 2^t times, where t is the tag size in bits. Specifically, after making 2^t calls to the decryption oracle, the attacker can expect to find another plaintext-ciphertext pair under the same (N, K). Then, a trivial state-recovery attack can be launched since only 1 round of AES is used to update the state at the keystream phase. In Rocca-S, $t = 256$ ensures that the time complexity of this attack is bounded by 2^{256}. Moreover, even if the state is recovered with some other methods, we expect that the key cannot be recovered. In AEGIS-256, this is ensured by using a keyed permutation for the initialization phase. In Rocca-S, we adopt the similar idea, also mentioned in [6]. Specifically, we simply use a key feed-forward operation to prevent the further key-recovery attack because the attackers cannot invert the initialization phase without knowing the key even if the state after this phase is fully known.

4   Security Evaluation

4.1   Differential/Linear Attack

In order to evaluate the security against differential and linear attacks, we compute the lower bound for the number of active S-boxes in the initialization phase by a MILP-aided method [16]. Since the maximal differential/linear probability of the S-box of AES is 2^{-6}, it is sufficient to guarantee the security against differential/linear attacks if there are 43 active S-boxes, as it gives $2^{(-6 \times 43)} < 2^{-256}$ as an estimate of the differential/linear probability. Our evaluation shows that there are 68 active S-boxes over 5 rounds in the single-key setting and 53 active S-boxes over 8 rounds in the related-key setting in the initialization phase.

4.2   State-Recovery Attack

At the keystream phase, with the knowledge of plaintexts and ciphertexts, it is possible to recover the internal state with some guess-and-determine (GnD) strategies. To recover the whole internal state, we need to consider at least 4 consecutive rounds at the keystream phase. Specifically, we need to solve the following nonlinear equation system in terms of $S[i]$ ($0 \leq i \leq 6$) where α_j ($0 \leq j \leq 7$) are known values:

$$\alpha_0 = A(S[3] \oplus S[5]) \oplus S[0], \quad \alpha_1 = A(S[4] \oplus S[6]) \oplus S[2],$$

$$\alpha_2 = A(A(S[2]) \oplus S[6] \oplus A(S[4]) \oplus S[3]) \oplus S[1] \oplus S[6],$$

$$\alpha_3 = A(A(S[3]) \oplus A(S[5]) \oplus S[4]) \oplus A(S[1]) \oplus S[0],$$

$$\alpha_4 = A(A(A(S[1]) \oplus S[0]) \oplus A(S[5]) \oplus S[4] \oplus A(A(S[3])) \oplus A(S[2]) \oplus S[6])$$
$$\oplus A(S[0]) \oplus A(S[5]) \oplus S[4],$$

$$\alpha_5 = A(A(A(S[2]) \oplus S[6]) \oplus A(A(S[4]) \oplus S[2]) \oplus A(S[3]))$$
$$\oplus A(A(S[0])) \oplus S[1] \oplus S[6],$$

$$\alpha_6 = A(A(A(A(S[0])) \oplus S[1] \oplus S[6]) \oplus A(A(S[4]) \oplus S[3]) \oplus A(S[3]))$$
$$\oplus A(A(A(S[2]) \oplus S[6])) \oplus A(A(S[1]) \oplus S[0]) \oplus A(S[5]) \oplus S[4])$$
$$\oplus A(s[1] \oplus S[6]) \oplus A(A(S[4]) \oplus S[3]) \oplus A(S[3]),$$

$$\alpha_7 = A(A(A(A(S[1]) \oplus S[0]) \oplus A(S[5]) \oplus S[4])$$
$$\oplus A(A(A(S[3])) \oplus A(S[1]) \oplus S[0]) \oplus A(A(S[2]) \oplus S[6]))$$
$$\oplus A(A(S[1] \oplus S[6])) \oplus A(S[0]) \oplus A(S[5]) \oplus S[4].$$

It can be found that for (α_2, α_3) 2 rounds of AES, for (α_4, α_5), 3 rounds of AES and for (α_6, α_7), 4 rounds of AES are involved. Indeed, for the state-recovery attack on Rocca discussed in [19], the attacker also needs to consider 4 consecutive rounds and similar 8 equations in 8 variables. However, for all those 8 equations, at most 2 rounds of AES are involved and Rocca still has a strong resistance against this attack. This implies that recovering the state of Rocca-S becomes much more difficult. As 2 rounds of AES can achieve the full diffusion, it soon implies the GnD attack is not a threat and Rocca-S has a strong resistance against this type of state-recovery attack.

4.3   The Linear Bias of the Keystream

It has been discussed in Sect. 3 that the used output functions are chosen in such a way that it can resist the linear attack proposed in [15]. Specifically, by computing the lower bound of the active S-boxes, we expect that the time complexity of the linear attack [15] is higher than 2^{256}.

4.4   Forgery Attack

It has been shown in [17] that the forgery attack is a main threat to the constructions like Tiaoxin-346 and AEGIS as only one-round update is used to absorb each block of associated data and message. Such a concern has been taken into account in our design phase, as reported in Sect. 3. Specifically, in the forgery attack, the aim is to find a differential trail where the attackers can arbitrarily choose differences at the associated data and expect that such a choice of difference can lead to a collision in the internal state after several number of rounds. The resistance against this attack can be efficiently evaluated with an automatic method [16]. As Rocca-S is based on the AES round function, it suffices to prove that the number of active S-boxes in such a trail is larger than 43 as the length of the tag is 256 bits. With the MILP-based method, it is found that the lower bound is 46. However, these estimates do not take into consideration additional constant factors of improvements and optimizations, e.g. using clustering effect, which is why we reduce our security claims. Consequently, Rocca-S can provide 192-bit security against the forgery attack.

4.5   Security Against Quantum Attacks

A quantum adversary has the ability to leverage Grover's algorithm [5] to perform an exhaustive key search given a limited number of plaintext-ciphertext pairs. In the case of Rocca-S, this would require $2^{256/2} = 2^{128}$ iterations, with each iteration involving the evaluation of the quantum implementation of Rocca-S (similar to AES as described in [4]). According to [8], if there exists a classical distinguisher (such as a differential or linear distinguisher) with a probability of 2^{-p}, a quantum adversary can utilize this to mount a distinguishing attack with a time and data complexity of $2^{p/2}$.

However, as demonstrated in the previous sections, the probability p for the distinguishers (differential or linear) of Rocca-S exceeds 256. Therefore, a quantum distinguishing attack would require a time and data complexity of at least 2^{128}. Hence, Rocca-S claims to provide 128-bit quantum security against key recovery and forgery when the adversary is restricted to classical online queries only. It is important to note that Rocca-S *does not* claim security against quantum adversaries with access to online superposition queries.

5   Software Implementation

In this section, we evaluate the performance of Rocca-S and show that modifications only incur small overhead to the performance, despite the increase of number of AES round functions in one round of state update. For the comparison to existing algorithms, we included Rocca-S as well as AEGIS, SNOW-V, and Tiaoxin to OpenSSL 3.1.0-dev and measured their performances with speed command. The implementation of SNOW-V is published in [3], and implementations of Tiaoxin-346 and AEGIS are publicly available.[1]. As shown in Table 4, Rocca-S exhibits the highest performance and achieves a throughput of 205 Gbps, which is the fastest in our comparison even compared to 128-bit key and tag algorithms.

Table 4. Software performance evaluation.

Algorithms	Key length	Tag length	Size of input (bytes)				
			16384	8192	1024	256	64
AEAD (Gbps)							
AEGIS-128	128-bit	128-bit	46.76	45.42	32.42	16.32	5.38
AEGIS-128L			151.53	137.49	60.37	20.68	5.40
Tiaoxin-346 v2			176.94	159.51	68.13	22.90	5.92
AEGIS-256	256-bit		47.96	46.50	33.29	16.72	5.52
AES-256-GCM			60.29	57.67	36.23	15.86	5.06
ChaCha20-Poly1305			22.40	21.71	15.25	6.15	2.15
SNOW-V-GCM			37.87	36.60	25.15	12.15	3.97
Rocca *			199.88	177.41	68.98	22.33	6.01
Rocca-S		256-bit	**205.68**	**183.22**	**74.33**	**24.78**	**6.65**

*: Updated version of Rocca [20], which is secure against the attack [6]

6   Hardware Implementation

The design of Rocca S lends itself well to hardware implementations as, apart from the state registers and the AES modules of the round and encryption functions, little additional circuitry is required. In this section, we commence by investigating two separate round-based implementations of the Rocca-S specification and compare them to related AES-based AEAD constructions that also feature a key size of 256 bits. Our approach follows a similar structure to what was established in the work by Caforio et al. [1] for the SNOW-V stream cipher In particular, the authors investigated several micro-architectural directions to implement the AES round function components.

- S-Box. The substitution table can be synthesized in a straightforward fashion by providing the look-up table specification (LUT) to the circuit compiler and letting the tool choose the actual implementation in terms of logic gates. The Decode-Switch-Encode (DSE) architecture mitigates the power overhead of the S-box look-up table by encoding and decoding the inputs and outputs

---

[1] https://github.com/floodyberry/supercop

to the look-up table in order to reduce the switching activity of each wire. The combinatorial optimization space of the S-box was explored in a work by Maximov and Ekdahl [13] in which the currently smallest description of the S-box in terms of logic gates was proposed S alongside a low-depth variant F and a trade-off alternative T between the former two.

- *MixColumns.* We can similarly distinguish several ways to implement the linear layer. The currently smallest circuit comprised of 92 two-input XOR gates is due to Maximov [12]. In a separate work, Li *et al.* [10] demonstrated a low-depth implementation consisting of 103 XOR gates. For the sake of conciseness we will limit ourselves to the low-depth circuit of [10].
- *T-Table.* The T-table approach is particularly efficient in software implementations but can also be emulated in hardware similarly to the approach of synthesizing the S-box look-up table mentioned beforehand. Henceforth, the T-table configuration will be denoted by the abbreviation TT.

Simulation Environment. All presented designs were synthesized using the Synopsys Design Compiler (version 2017.09) using two standard cell libraries, i.e., NanGate 15 nm process and the more industry-grade TSMC 28 nm process. The power and energy consumption was then extracted in post-synthesis using the Synopsys Power Compiler via back-annotation.

6.1   Circuits

A round-based implementation of Rocca-S computes one invocation of the round update function R in one clock cycle, hence sixteen cycles are required to execute both the initialization and finalization routines and, in the same vein, the circuit absorbs 256-bit data blocks and outputs 256-bit ciphertext blocks per clock cycle. The approach we follow for the round-based implementation is relatively elementary and can be deduced from the original schematic in Fig. 1. Six AES modules, whose plaintext inputs are directly fed from the state registers, are placed in parallel. Their computed outputs are wired back to the corresponding register inputs thus taking care of the permutation without additional circuitry.

Unrolled Round Function. The round update function of Rocca-S can easily be replicated and chained together in order to compute multiple invocation in a single clock cycle. Although the area increase quickly reaches prohibitive regions, the length of the critical path usually rises at slower pace thus yielding designs that admit the highest throughput.

6.2   Synthesis Results

Our round-based Rocca-S hardware implementations are compared against other AEAD schemes with a key size of 256 bits, namely AEGIS-256, AES-256-GCM and SNOW-V-GCM [3,14,22]. Note that actual published ASIC implementations of said algorithms are hard to come by, hence we chose to devise them for this comparison section. AEGIS-256 is reminiscent of Rocca-S in design and thus can be adapted accordingly, on the other hand, AES-256-GCM and SNOW-V-GCM require a Galois field multiplication module over 128 bits for which we opted for a straightforward Karatsuba architecture which is then attached to a AES-256 module extracted and extended from the Rocca-S round function and a SNOW-V stream cipher core whose implementation is available in [1].

Circuit Area. The lion's share of gate area in Rocca-S is due to the eight AES round function cores that compose its round function and ciphertext generation function. This induces a significant overhead in comparison to the other schemes. AEGIS-256 requires only six cores whereas AES-256-GCM and SNOW-V-GCM are equipped with only and two core respectively. The Galois field multiplication module, a notoriously difficult function to map to hardware, found in the latter two has an area footprint of roughly 30000 GE across cell libraries and thus constitutes a sizeable percentage of their overall area. Across all implementation choices the area of our round-based Rocca-S circuit remains competitive.

Throughput. The premise of Rocca-S is a high-speed construction that improves on other known schemes in terms of throughput i.e., how many bits per second can be processed. In hardware, this figure is inextricably tied to the length of the critical path which specifies the maximum clock frequency at which a design can be run. In both Rocca-S and AEGIS-256 the critical path is due to the AES modules, thus it is highly variable regarding the choice of round function implementation, whereas in AES-256-GCM and SNOW-V-GCM it is imposed by the field multiplication thus constant across implementation choices. This means that for both AES-256-GCM and SNOW-V-GCM unrolling the round function exerts only marginal effects on the overall throughput. Excluding the initialization and finalization phases, Rocca-S processes 256 bits of data with each clock cycle. Similarly AEGIS-256 and SNOW-V-GCM are able to process one 128-bit data block in one clock cycle whereas AES-256-GCM requires a full AES-256 encryption for each 128-bit plaintext block hence asymptotically for large plaintexts AES-256-GCM only processes roughly 8 bits per clock cycle. Consequently, the ability to accept larger data blocks paired with a competitive critical path allows Rocca-S to reach a throughput well beyond 1 Terabit per second for the NanGate 15 nm cell library regardless of the choice of round function implementation, outperforming the other schemes by at least 50%. Also, a throughput rate beyond 2 Terabits is reached for 2-round unrolled circuits, marking Rocca-S as the first cryptographic algorithm that crosses this barrier as shown in Table 5.

Table 5. Maximum throughput (Tbps) comparison using a TT AES module for round-based and 2-round unrolled circuits.

	Rocca-S	AEGIS-256	AES-256-GCM	SNOW-V-GCM
NanGate 15 nm	**1.653/2.019**	0.970/1.028	0.023/0.024	0.365/0.442
TSMC 28 nm	**0.373/0.409**	0.188/0.190	0.007/0.007	0.088/0.106

Power/Energy Consumption. Our power/energy experiments were conducted on two workloads. A short workload describes the processing of 1024 bits of associated data and 2048 bits of plaintext whereas a long workload consists of 1024 bits of associated data and 1.28 Megabits of plaintext. Again, the round-based Rocca-S circuit stands as competitive choice regarding its power and energy consumption. A list of all obtained power/energy measurements is given in Table 7.

7   Conclusion

In this paper, we proposed the AES-based authenticated encryption scheme Rocca-S with a 256-bit key and a 256-bit tag. Rocca-S achieves a speed of more than 200 Gbps in software. In hardware implementation, Rocca-S is the first cryptographic algorithm to achieve speeds consistently between 1 and 2 Terabits per second without sacrificing other metrics.

Acknowledgments. Takanori Isobe is supported by JST, PRESTO Grant Number JPMJPR2031. This research was in part conducted under a contract of "Research and development on new generation cryptography for secure wireless communication services" among "Research and Development for Expansion of Radio Wave Resources (JPJ000254)", which was supported by the Ministry of Internal Affairs and Communications, Japan. We thank Akinori Hosoyamada, Akiko Inoue, Ryoma Ito, Tetsu Iwata, Kazuhiko Mimematsu, Ferdinand Sibleyras, Yosuke Todo, Patrick Derbez, Pierre-Alain Fouque, André Schrottenloher, Santanu Sarkar, Satyam Kumar, Chandan Dey and anonymous reviewers for their valuable comments.

Appendix

See Fig. 5.

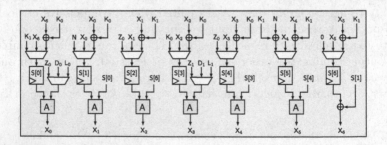

Fig. 5. Rocca-S round function circuit.

Table 6. Circuit area (GE) and Throughput (Critical Path and Max TP) comparison of the investigated AEAD scheme for two cell libraries and several round function implementations. Note that the T-table approach of implementing the round function offers the overall best choice for both Rocca-S and AEGIS-256. This phenomenon was already observed in [1].

(a) Rocca-S

	LUT	DSE	S	F	T	TT
Round-Based						
NanGate 15 nm						
GE	116130	116638	56889	61918	56728	145364
Critical Path (ns)	0.179	0.177	0.232	0.208	0.207	0.154
Max TP (Tbps)	1.431	1.451	1.102	1.229	1.234	1.653
TSMC 28 nm						
GE	100689	110273	58688	63681	57452	134220
Critical Path (ns)	0.95	0.81	1.00	0.83	0.93	0.71
Max TP (Tbps)	0.269	0.316	0.256	0.308	0.275	0.373
2-Round Unrolled						
NanGate 15 nm						
GE	218629	220428	100814	110802	99728	277691
Critical Path (ns)	0.321	0.322	0.412	0.383	0.388	0.253
Max TP (Tbps)	1.590	1.589	1.241	1.333	1.319	2.019
TSMC 28 nm						
GE	188199	208045	104876	114861	102402	255938
Critical Path (ns)	1.78	1.48	1.84	1.53	1.73	1.25
Max TP (Tbps)	0.287	0.348	0.279	0.334	0.294	0.409

(b) AEGIS-256

	LUT	DSE	S	F	T	TT
Round-Based						
NanGate 15 nm						
GE	88521	89116	44266	48009	43854	110591
Critical Path (ns)	0.167	0.165	0.21	0.196	0.198	0.132
Max TP (Tbps)	0.766	0.776	0.610	0.653	0.646	0.970
TSMC 28 nm						
GE	75608	83081	44392	48137	43465	101043
Critical Path (ns)	0.88	0.73	0.92	0.76	0.86	0.68
Max TP (Tbps)	0.145	0.175	0.139	0.168	0.149	0.188
2-Round Unrolled						
NanGate 15 nm						
GE	167333	168650	78939	86426	78125	211599
Critical Path (ns)	0.321	0.318	0.409	0.381	0.384	0.249
Max TP (Tbps)	0.798	0.805	0.626	0.672	0.667	1.028
TSMC 28 nm						
GE	143435	158156	80779	88269	78925	194077
Critical Path (ns)	1.72	1.46	1.79	1.49	1.69	1.35
Max TP (Tbps)	0.149	0.175	0.143	0.172	0.151	0.190

(c) AES-256-GCM

	LUT	DSE	S	F	T	TT
Round-Based						
NanGate 15 nm						
GE	50080	51381	42038	42816	41951	64082
Critical Path (ns)	0.349	0.349	0.349	0.349	0.349	0.349
Max TP (Tbps)	0.023	0.023	0.023	0.023	0.023	0.023
TSMC 28 nm						
GE	50908	52447	44384	45166	44192	62450
Critical Path (ns)	1.23	1.23	1.23	1.23	1.23	1.23
Max TP (Tbps)	0.007	0.007	0.007	0.007	0.007	0.007
2-Round Unrolled						
NanGate 15 nm						
GE	98058	98307	79615	81177	79447	123739
Critical Path (ns)	0.673	0.673	0.674	0.674	0.674	0.674
Max TP (Tbps)	0.024	0.024	0.024	0.024	0.024	0.024
TSMC 28 nm						
GE	98398	101517	85394	86957	85010	121520
Critical Path (ns)	2.14	2.15	2.15	2.13	2.13	2.16
Max TP (Tbps)	0.007	0.007	0.007	0.007	0.007	0.007

(d) SNOW-V-GCM

	LUT	DSE	S	F	T	TT
Round-Based						
NanGate 15 nm						
GE	75729	75912	60964	62205	60827	83074
Critical Path (ns)	0.351	0.351	0.351	0.351	0.351	0.351
Max TP (Tbps)	0.365	0.365	0.365	0.365	0.365	0.365
TSMC 28 nm						
GE	71396	73860	60966	62214	60656	79846
Critical Path (ns)	1.45	1.45	1.45	1.45	1.45	1.45
Max TP (Tbps)	0.088	0.088	0.088	0.088	0.088	0.088
2-Round Unrolled						
NanGate 15 nm						
GE	136139	136622	106715	109212	106445	150935
Critical Path (ns)	0.579	0.577	0.579	0.577	0.579	0.579
Max TP (Tbps)	0.442	0.444	0.442	0.444	0.442	0.442
TSMC 28 nm						
GE	131342	136269	110477	112974	109857	148241
Critical Path (ns)	2.41	2.41	2.41	2.41	2.41	2.41
Max TP (Tbps)	0.106	0.106	0.106	0.106	0.106	0.106

Table 7. Power/energy consumption comparison of the investigated AEAD scheme for two cell libraries and several round function implementations. All figures were obtained by clocking the designs at constant frequency of 10 MHz.

(a) Rocca-S

	LUT	DSE	S	F	T	TT
Round-Based						
Lat. Short (Cycles)	44	44	44	44	44	44
Lat. Long (Cycles)	5036	5036	5036	5036	5036	5036
NanGate 15 nm						
Power (mW)	1.401	0.765	1.255	1.314	1.134	0.881
Energy Short (nJ)	6.165	3.368	5.522	5.780	4.985	3.876
Energy Long (nJ)	705.6	385.5	632.1	661.6	570.5	443.7
TSMC 28 nm						
Power (mW)	0.830	0.389	0.754	0.709	0.690	0.373
Energy Short (nJ)	3.650	1.709	3.316	3.119	3.034	1.642
Energy Long (nJ)	417.8	195.6	379.5	357.0	347.2	187.9
2-Round Unrolled						
Lat. Short (Cycles)	22	22	22	22	22	22
Lat. Long (Cycles)	2518	2518	2518	2518	2518	2518
NanGate 15 nm						
Power (mW)	6.254	2.140	5.631	5.824	5.248	2.202
Energy Short (nJ)	13.76	4.70	12.39	12.81	11.55	4.85
Energy Long (nJ)	1574.1	538.8	1417.8	1466.5	1321.5	554.6
TSMC 28 nm						
Power (mW)	3.963	1.345	3.293	2.985	2.922	1.074
Energy Short (nJ)	8.720	2.959	7.244	6.568	6.429	2.364
Energy Long (nJ)	998.1	338.7	829.1	751.7	735.9	270.5

(b) AEGIS-256

	LUT	DSE	S	F	T	TT
Round-Based						
Lat. Short (Cycles)	48	48	48	48	48	48
Lat. Long (Cycles)	10032	10032	10032	10032	10032	10032
NanGate 15 nm						
Power (mW)	1.106	0.613	1.014	1.081	0.954	0.691
Energy Short (nJ)	5.309	2.945	4.868	5.184	4.579	3.317
Energy Long (nJ)	1109	615.6	1017	1083	956.9	693.3
TSMC 28 nm						
Power (mW)	0.619	0.297	0.564	0.531	0.518	0.288
Energy Short (nJ)	2.975	1.426	2.707	2.549	2.488	1.380
Energy Long (nJ)	621.8	298.1	565.8	532.8	520.1	288.4
2-Round Unrolled						
Lat. Short (Cycles)	24	24	24	24	24	24
Lat. Long (Cycles)	5016	5016	5016	5016	5016	5016
NanGate 15 nm						
Power (mW)	4.147	1.674	3.779	3.887	3.539	1.670
Energy Short (nJ)	9.953	4.018	9.069	9.328	8.494	4.008
Energy Long (nJ)	2080.1	839.7	1895.3	1949.5	1775.3	837.8
TSMC 28 nm						
Power (mW)	2.483	0.918	2.115	1.925	1.901	0.915
Energy Short (nJ)	5.958	2.202	5.077	4.621	4.562	2.196
Energy Long (nJ)	1245.3	460.22	1061.0	965.78	953.49	459.06

(c) AES-256-GCM

	LUT	DSE	S	F	T	TT
Round-Based						
Lat. Short (Cycles)	266	266	266	266	266	266
Lat. Long (Cycles)	160010	160010	160010	160010	160010	160010
NanGate 15 nm						
Power (mW)	0.521	0.417	0.502	0.515	0.490	0.577
Energy Short (nJ)	13.85	11.09	13.36	13.69	13.04	15.33
Energy Long (nJ)	8328	6674	8035	8235	7843	9224
TSMC 28 nm						
Power (mW)	0.326	0.249	0.312	0.303	0.304	0.329
Energy Short (nJ)	8.661	6.645	8.291	8.070	8.076	8.759
Energy Long (nJ)	5209	3997	4987	4854	4857	5269
2-Round Unrolled						
Lat. Short (Cycles)	133	133	133	133	133	133
Lat. Long (Cycles)	80005	80005	80005	80005	80005	80005
NanGate 15 nm						
Power (mW)	1.356	1.145	1.313	1.339	1.287	1.461
Energy Short (nJ)	18.03	15.23	17.46	17.80	17.11	19.43
Energy Long (nJ)	10845	9159.8	10505	10710	10293	11689
TSMC 28 nm						
Power (mW)	0.825	0.671	0.795	0.778	0.777	0.831
Energy Short (nJ)	10.97	8.930	10.58	10.35	10.34	11.05
Energy Long (nJ)	6599.6	5369.9	6362.8	6226.8	6219.6	6645.2

(d) SNOW-V-GCM

	LUT	DSE	S	F	T	TT
Round-Based						
Lat. Short (Cycles)	42	42	42	42	42	42
Lat. Long (Cycles)	10026	10026	10026	10026	10026	10026
NanGate 15 nm						
Power (mW)	0.726	0.602	0.689	0.704	0.676	0.634
Energy Short (nJ)	3.047	2.528	2.895	2.958	2.840	2.662
Energy Long (nJ)	727.4	603.5	691.2	706.0	678.1	635.3
TSMC 28 nm						
Power (mW)	0.408	0.333	0.396	0.389	0.386	0.334
Energy Short (nJ)	1.714	1.399	1.663	1.634	1.619	1.402
Energy Long (nJ)	409.2	333.9	397.1	390.2	386.5	334.8
2-Round Unrolled						
Lat. Short (Cycles)	21	21	21	21	21	21
Lat. Long (Cycles)	5013	5013	5013	5013	5013	5013
NanGate 15 nm						
Power (mW)	1.947	1.520	1.862	1.902	1.820	1.551
Energy Short (nJ)	4.089	3.192	3.910	3.994	3.822	3.257
Energy Long (nJ)	976.13	761.73	933.57	953.62	912.57	777.62
TSMC 28 nm						
Power (mW)	1.090	0.827	1.029	0.996	0.992	0.805
Energy Short (nJ)	2.289	1.736	2.161	2.091	2.082	1.691
Energy Long (nJ)	546.32	414.32	515.89	499.24	497.04	403.65

References

1. Caforio, A., Balli, F., Banik, S.: Melting SNOW-V: improved lightweight architectures. J. Cryptogr. Eng. **12**(1), 53–73 (2022)
2. Eichlseder, M., Nageler, M., Primas, R.: Analyzing the linear keystream biases in AEGIS. IACR Trans. Symmetric Cryptol. **2019**(4), 348–368 (2019)
3. Ekdahl, P., Johansson, T., Maximov, A., Yang, J.: A new SNOW stream cipher called SNOW-V. IACR Trans. Symmetric Cryptol. **2019**(3), 1–42 (2019)
4. Grassl, M., Langenberg, B., Roetteler, M., Steinwandt, R.: Applying Grover's algorithm to AES: quantum resource estimates. In: Takagi, T. (ed.) PQCrypto 2016.

LNCS, vol. 9606, pp. 29–43. Springer, Cham (2016). https://doi.org/10.1007/978-3-319-29360-8_3

5. Grover, L.K.: A fast quantum mechanical algorithm for database search. In: Proceedings of the Twenty-Eighth Annual ACM Symposium on Theory of Computing, pp. 212–219 (1996)

6. Hosoyamada, A., et al.: Cryptanalysis of Rocca and feasibility of its security claim. IACR Trans. Symmetric Cryptol. **2022**(3), 123–151 (2022)

7. Jean, J., Nikolić, I.: Efficient design strategies based on the AES round function. In: Peyrin, T. (ed.) FSE 2016. LNCS, vol. 9783, pp. 334–353. Springer, Heidelberg (2016). https://doi.org/10.1007/978-3-662-52993-5_17

8. Kaplan, M., Leurent, G., Leverrier, A., Naya-Plasencia, M.: Quantum differential and linear cryptanalysis. IACR Trans. Symmetric Cryptol. **2016**(1), 71–94 (2016)

9. Latva-aho, M., Leppänen, K.: Key drivers and research challenges for 6G ubiquitous wireless intelligence (2019)

10. Li, S., Sun, S., Li, C., Wei, Z., Lei, H.: Constructing low-latency involutory MDS matrices with lightweight circuits. IACR Trans. Symm. Cryptol. **2019**(1), 84–117 (2019)

11. Liu, F., Isobe, T., Meier, W., Sakamoto, K.: Weak keys in reduced aegis and Tiaoxin. Cryptology ePrint Archive, Report 2021/187 (2021). https://eprint.iacr.org/2021/187

12. Maximov, A.: AES MixColumn with 92 XOR gates. Cryptology ePrint Archive, Report 2019/833 (2019). https://eprint.iacr.org/2019/833

13. Maximov, A., Ekdahl, P.: New circuit minimization techniques for smaller and faster AES SBoxes. IACR TCHES **2019**(4), 91–125 (2019). https://tches.iacr.org/index.php/TCHES/article/view/8346

14. David, A.: McGrew and John Viega. The security and performance of the Galois/counter mode (GCM) of operation. In: Canteaut, A., Viswanathan, K. (eds.) INDOCRYPT 2004. LNCS, vol. 3348, pp. 343–355. Springer, Heidelberg (2004). https://doi.org/10.1007/978-3-540-30556-9_27

15. Minaud, B.: Linear biases in AEGIS keystream. In: Joux, A., Youssef, A.M., editors, Selected Areas in Cryptography - SAC 2014–21st International Conference, Montreal, QC, Canada, August 14–15, 2014, Revised Selected Papers, volume 8781 of Lecture Notes in Computer Science, pp. 290–305. Springer (2014)

16. Mouha, N., Wang, Q., Gu, D., Preneel, B.: Differential and linear cryptanalysis using mixed-integer linear programming. In: Wu, C.-K., Yung, M., Lin, D. (eds.) Inscrypt 2011. LNCS, vol. 7537, pp. 57–76. Springer, Heidelberg (2012). https://doi.org/10.1007/978-3-642-34704-7_5

17. Nikolić, I.: Tiaoxin-346: version 2.0. CAESAR Competition (2014)

18. Real-Time and Embedded Sys Lab. uops.info. Official webpage. https://www.uops.info/

19. Sakamoto, K., Liu, F., Nakano, Y., Kiyomoto, S., Isobe, T.: Rocca: an efficient AES-based encryption scheme for beyond 5G. IACR Trans. Symmetric Cryptol. **2021**(2), 1–30 (2021)

20. Sakamoto, K., Liu, F., Nakano, Y., Kiyomoto, S., Isobe, T.: Rocca: an efficient AES-based encryption scheme for beyond 5G (full version). IACR Cryptol. ePrint Arch., 116 (2022)

21. The ZUC design team. The ZUC-256 Stream Cipher. http://www.is.cas.cn/ztzl2016/zouchongzhi/201801/W020180126529970733243.pdf (2018)

22. Wu, Hongjun, Preneel, Bart: AEGIS: a fast authenticated encryption algorithm. In: Lange, Tanja, Lauter, Kristin, Lisoněk, Petr (eds.) SAC 2013. LNCS, vol. 8282, pp. 185–201. Springer, Heidelberg (2014). https://doi.org/10.1007/978-3-662-43414-7_10

Secure Outsourced Matrix Multiplication with Fully Homomorphic Encryption

Lin Zhu, Qiang-sheng Hua[✉], Yi Chen, and Hai Jin

National Engineering Research Center for Big Data Technology and System,
Services Computing Technology and System Lab, School of Computer Science
and Technology, Huazhong University of Science and Technology,
Wuhan 430074, People's Republic of China
qshua@hust.edu.cn

Abstract. Fully Homomorphic Encryption (FHE) is a powerful cryptographic tool that enables the handling of sensitive encrypted data in untrusted computing environments. This capability allows for the outsourcing of computational tasks, effectively addressing security and privacy concerns. This paper studies the secure matrix multiplication problem, a fundamental operation used in various outsourced computing applications such as statistical analysis and machine learning. We propose a novel method to solve the secure matrix multiplication $A_{m \times l} \times B_{l \times n}$ with arbitrary dimensions, which requires only $O(l)$ rotations and $\min(m, l, n)$ homomorphic multiplications. In comparison to the state-of-the-art method [14], our approach stands out by achieving a remarkable reduction in the number of rotations by a factor of $O(\log \max(l, n))$, as well as a reduction in the number of homomorphic multiplications by a factor of $O(l / \min(m, l, n))$. We implemented [14,21], and our method using the BGV scheme supported by the HElib library. Experimental results show that our scheme has the best performance for matrix multiplication of any dimension. For example, for $A_{16 \times 128} \times B_{128 \times 4} = C_{16 \times 4}$, the runtime of our method is 32 s, while both [14,21] take 569 seconds.

Keywords: Secure outsourced computation · Fully homomorphic encryption · Matrix multiplication

1 Introduction

In the era of cloud computing, accessing storage and computing resources through network-based services has become an economical alternative to construct and maintain costly IT systems. However, the protection of data privacy poses a significant challenge, particularly when dealing with sensitive information in domains such as economics and medicine. Fully Homomorphic Encryption (FHE) offers a natural solution by enabling computations to be performed on encrypted data, thereby ensuring data privacy guarantees for outsourced computing tasks in cloud-based applications.

G. Tsudik et al. (Eds.): ESORICS 2023, LNCS 14344, pp. 249–269, 2024.
https://doi.org/10.1007/978-3-031-50594-2_13

FHE has emerged as a promising post-quantum cryptography, primarily due to the security assumptions it relies on, such as the Learning with Errors (LWE) problem. In contrast, other privacy-preserved computing technologies like traditional secure multi-party computation depend on additional security assumptions and offer relatively weaker data protection. Gentry [8] introduced the groundbreaking FHE scheme, which theoretically allows for the evaluation of any function on ciphertexts. Since then, extensive research efforts have been devoted to enhancing the efficiency of FHE schemes both in theory and practice (e.g., [1–4, 15, 23, 26]). Second-generation FHE schemes, including BFV [6], BGV [1], and CKKS [3], have gained widespread support from mainstream FHE libraries(e.g., SEAL [18], HElib [13]), owing to their support for SIMD (Single Instruction Multiple Data) batch processing.

Matrix multiplication is a fundamental operation extensively utilized in scientific, engineering, and machine learning applications, and often demands substantial computational resources. However, outsourcing matrix computations to untrusted servers raises concerns about data confidentiality. Consequently, the development of an efficient and highly secure matrix multiplication scheme becomes imperative for secure outsourced data processing. Based on FHE, this paper investigates this problem, and an efficient matrix multiplication scheme that can adapt to any matrix dimension is proposed.

1.1   System Model

To perform matrix multiplication, a client with limited computational resources first encrypts the two input matrices with a public key and sends the ciphertexts with evaluation keys to the computationally powerful cloud server. Then, the cloud server computes the secure matrix multiplication by performing a series of homomorphic operations on the ciphertexts. Finally, the client receives the computation result from the cloud server, and decrypts it by the private key. In this paper, we adopt a semi-honest model [10], where the server executes the protocol correctly but tries to obtain additional information from the client data.

1.2   Fully Homomorphic Encryption and Hypercube Structure

In this paper, we specifically study the Ring-LWE variant [9] of the BGV scheme [1], which is worked over a polynomial ring modulo a cyclotomic polynomial $\mathbb{A} = \mathbb{Z}[X]/\phi_M(X)$, where $\phi_M(X)$ is the M-th cyclotomic polynomial. Given a plaintext space $\mathcal{M}$ and a ciphertext space $\mathcal{C}$, an FHE scheme is specified by five algorithms: KeyGen, Enc, Dec, Add and Mult, which represent key generation, encryption, decryption, homomorphic addition and multiplication, respectively. We use $\text{Add}(ct_1, ct_2) = ct_1 \oplus ct_2$ and $\text{Mult}(ct_1, ct_2) = ct_1 \odot ct_2$ to denote the homomorphic addition and multiplication, respectively, where $ct_1, ct_2 \in \mathcal{C}$. In addition, the symbol $\odot$ is also used to represent scalar multiplication between ct and U, denoted as $\text{CMult}(ct, U)$, where $ct \in \mathcal{C}$ and $U \in \mathcal{M}$ is scalar.

An important property of RLWE-based FHE schemes is the *packing* technique [24], which enables SIMD homomorphic operations. Using this method, every homomorphic operation over ciphertexts implies element-wise operations over plaintext slots. The packing technique also supports a basic data movement operation called rotation. Utilizing these operations can reduce space and time complexity while avoiding the need to repack plaintext data. The BGV scheme incorporates the hypercube structure for organizing plaintext and its associated rotation operation [11]. This operation rotates hypercolumns in specific dimension within a multi-dimensional hypercube structure. This paper uses a two-dimensional hypercube structure to represent the plaintext matrix. $\text{Rotate1D}(ct, 0, k)$ denotes each column of the matrix rotated down by k positions, and $\text{Rotate1D}(ct, 1, k)$ denotes each row of the matrix rotated right by k positions. Note that k can also be negative, resulting in the plaintext slots' upward or leftward rotation. Figure 1 describes the operations mentioned above. Among these operations, Mult and Rotate1D are the most expensive. Therefore, to design efficient algorithms, our priority is to reduce the number of Mult and Rotate1D.

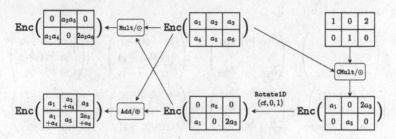

Fig. 1. Typical operations on plaintext slot data in the hypercube structure

1.3 Related Works

For secure matrix multiplication $A_{m \times l} \times B_{l \times n} = C_{m \times n}$, a straightforward approach is to encrypt each matrix element into a ciphertext. However, this method requires a significant number of element-wise multiplication operations, totaling mln. Recognizing that each element of C is the inner product of a row of A and a column of B, [25] encrypts each row/column of the matrix into a ciphertext in the SIMD environment. The number of rotations and homomorphic multiplications required are $mn \log l$ and mn, respectively.

By applying the encoding methods [20, 27] to an RLWE-based FHE scheme, [5] proposed a scheme that encodes a matrix into a constant polynomial in the plaintext space. This method requires only a single homomorphic multiplication operation. Subsequently, [19] proposed an improved scheme built upon this work. However, this approach results in meaningless terms in the resulting ciphertext. When performing more computations, decryption, and re-encoding procedure are required to remove these terms, resulting in limited performance in practical applications.

[16] proposed an efficient square matrix multiplication scheme, which exploits a row ordering encoding map to transform an $l \times l$ matrix as a vector of dimension l^2. This method requires $O(l)$ rotations and homomorphic multiplication operations. Although [16] extends the square matrix multiplication to rectangular matrix multiplication $A_{m \times l} \times B_{l \times n} = C_{m \times n}$, it considers only the case where $m \mid l$ and $l = n$. By exploiting the idle slots of the ciphertext, [22] reduces the number of homomorphic multiplications of [16] to $O(1)$. However, a disadvantage of this method is that it only works with very few available matrix entries.

The most relevant works [14,17,21], which are based on the Fox Matrix multiplication method [7], can be regarded as an extension of the diagonal-order method for solving matrix-vector multiplication [11]. Specifically, given two $l \times l$ square matrices A and B and a hypercube structure, the method first extracts the i-th diagonal of A, i.e., $A_i = \{a_{0,i}, a_{1,i+1}, ..., a_{l-1,i+l-1}\}$, where $i = \{0, 1, ..., l-1\}$. Then, A_i is replicated along the row to get $\hat{A}_i$, and each column of B is rotated upward by i positions to get B_i, i.e., $B_i = \mathsf{Rotate1D}(B, 0, -i)$. The multiplication of A and B is obtained by $A \cdot B = \sum_{i=0}^{l-1} \hat{A}_i \odot B_i$. Below we give an example with $l = 3$.

$$\begin{pmatrix} a_{00} & a_{01} & a_{02} \\ a_{10} & a_{11} & a_{12} \\ a_{20} & a_{21} & a_{22} \end{pmatrix} \cdot \begin{pmatrix} b_{00} & b_{01} & b_{02} \\ b_{10} & b_{11} & b_{12} \\ b_{20} & b_{21} & b_{22} \end{pmatrix} = \begin{pmatrix} a_{00} & a_{00} & a_{00} \\ a_{11} & a_{11} & a_{11} \\ a_{22} & a_{22} & a_{22} \end{pmatrix} \odot \begin{pmatrix} b_{00} & b_{01} & b_{02} \\ b_{10} & b_{11} & b_{12} \\ b_{20} & b_{21} & b_{22} \end{pmatrix}$$

$$\oplus \begin{pmatrix} a_{01} & a_{01} & a_{01} \\ a_{12} & a_{12} & a_{12} \\ a_{20} & a_{20} & a_{20} \end{pmatrix} \odot \begin{pmatrix} b_{10} & b_{11} & b_{12} \\ b_{20} & b_{21} & b_{22} \\ b_{00} & b_{01} & b_{02} \end{pmatrix} \oplus \begin{pmatrix} a_{02} & a_{02} & a_{02} \\ a_{10} & a_{10} & a_{10} \\ a_{21} & a_{21} & a_{21} \end{pmatrix} \odot \begin{pmatrix} b_{20} & b_{21} & b_{22} \\ b_{00} & b_{01} & b_{02} \\ b_{10} & b_{11} & b_{12} \end{pmatrix}.$$

[17,21] use the above method to compute the secure square matrix multiplication, with the difference that the former packs each row of each matrix into a ciphertext with a linear array structure, while the latter packs the entire matrix into a ciphertext with a two-dimension hypercube structure. [14] extends the method to rectangular matrix multiplication. Although the replication procedure for calculating $\hat{A}_i$ can be implemented by CMult, $\mathsf{Rotate1D}$ and Add, this procedure requires high rotations and space complexities. Motivated by this, we revisit the secure matrix multiplication problem in this paper.

1.4　Our Contribution

We propose a novel scheme for square matrix multiplication of dimension l using the hypercube structure based on FHE. Compared to existing methods [14,21], our scheme asymptotically reduces the number of rotations from $O(l \log l)$ to $O(l)$. Moreover, we extend the square matrix multiplication to rectangular matrix multiplication. For matrix multiplication $A_{m \times l} \times B_{l \times n} = C_{m \times n}$ of arbitrary dimensions, our scheme requires only $O(l)$ rotations and $\min(m, l, n)$ homomorphic multiplications, while [14] requires $O(l \log \max(l, n))$ rotations and l homomorphic multiplications. The experimental results also demonstrate the superiority of our algorithms.

2   Secure Matrix Multiplication Scheme with FHE

For general matrix multiplication $A_{m \times l} \times B_{l \times n} = C_{m \times n}$, we discuss the following four cases and give different strategies for each: (1) $m = l = n$; (2) $l = \min\{m, l, n\}$; (3) $l = \text{median}\{m, l, n\}$; (4) $l = \max\{m, l, n\}$.

2.1   Square Matrix Multiplication

Suppose the input matrices are $A_{l \times l}$ and $B_{l \times l}$, we let the hypercube structure be an $l \times l$ matrix, then A and B can be put exactly into their hypercube structures. Based on the most efficient scheme [16], the following equality describes the square matrix multiplication using the hypercube structure for the case of $l = 3$.

$$
\begin{pmatrix} a_{00} \, a_{01} \, a_{02} \\ a_{10} \, a_{11} \, a_{12} \\ a_{20} \, a_{21} \, a_{22} \end{pmatrix} \cdot \begin{pmatrix} b_{00} \, b_{01} \, b_{02} \\ b_{10} \, b_{11} \, b_{12} \\ b_{20} \, b_{21} \, b_{22} \end{pmatrix} = \begin{pmatrix} a_{00} \, a_{01} \, a_{02} \\ a_{11} \, a_{12} \, a_{10} \\ a_{22} \, a_{20} \, a_{21} \end{pmatrix} \odot \begin{pmatrix} b_{00} \, b_{11} \, b_{22} \\ b_{10} \, b_{21} \, b_{02} \\ b_{20} \, b_{01} \, b_{12} \end{pmatrix}
$$
$$
\oplus \begin{pmatrix} a_{01} \, a_{02} \, a_{00} \\ a_{12} \, a_{10} \, a_{11} \\ a_{20} \, a_{21} \, a_{22} \end{pmatrix} \odot \begin{pmatrix} b_{10} \, b_{21} \, b_{02} \\ b_{20} \, b_{01} \, b_{12} \\ b_{00} \, b_{11} \, b_{22} \end{pmatrix} \oplus \begin{pmatrix} a_{02} \, a_{00} \, a_{01} \\ a_{10} \, a_{11} \, a_{12} \\ a_{21} \, a_{22} \, a_{20} \end{pmatrix} \odot \begin{pmatrix} b_{20} \, b_{01} \, b_{12} \\ b_{00} \, b_{11} \, b_{22} \\ b_{10} \, b_{21} \, b_{02} \end{pmatrix} . \tag{1}
$$

The homomorphic scheme is described as follows.

Step 1: Denote by $ct.A$ and $ct.B$ the two ciphertexts of input matrices A and B after being encrypted, respectively. This step obtains $ct.A_0$ by rotating the k-th row of $ct.A$ by k positions, and obtains $ct.B_0$ by rotating the k-th column of $ct.B$ by k positions ($k = \{0, 1, ..., l - 1\}$).

Taking the calculation of $ct.A_0$ as an example, in round k, we first extract the k-th row of $ct.A$ using the multiplication mask operation to get $ct.d_k$, and then rotate $ct.d_k$ by k positions per row. Finally, all $ct.d_k$ are summed by homomorphic addition to get $ct.A_0$. The calculation of $ct.A_0$ can be represented as

$$
ct.A_0 = \sum_k ct.d_k = \sum_k \mathsf{Rotate1D}(U_k \odot ct.A, 1, -k),
$$

where $k = \{0, 1, ..., l - 1\}$, U_k is an $l \times l$ plaintext matrix and is defined by

$$
U_k[I][J] = \begin{cases} 1 & \text{If } I = k; \\ 0 & \text{otherwise.} \end{cases}
$$

For the convenience of later discussion, we propose a general algorithm in Algorithm 1. We denote by $\mathsf{RotateAlign}(ct.X, 1, l)$ the rotation of the k-th row of $ct.X$ by $k \bmod l$ positions, which can be achieved by Algorithm 1. Similarly, we use $\mathsf{RotateAlign}(ct.X, 0, l)$ to denote the rotation of the k-th column of $ct.X$ by $k \bmod l$ positions. The complexity of this step is about $2l$ additions, $2l$ constant multiplications, and $2l$ rotations.

For step 1, here is an example when $l = 3$. Let

$$
ct.A = \begin{pmatrix} a_{00} \, a_{01} \, a_{02} \\ a_{10} \, a_{11} \, a_{12} \\ a_{20} \, a_{21} \, a_{22} \end{pmatrix}, ct.B = \begin{pmatrix} b_{00} \, b_{01} \, b_{02} \\ b_{10} \, b_{11} \, b_{12} \\ b_{20} \, b_{21} \, b_{22} \end{pmatrix} .
$$

Algorithm 1: Rotate k-th row(column) of $ct.X$ by k mod l positions

1 **procedure** RotateAlign($ct.X, dim, l$)
   Input: $ct.X$: a ciphertext with $D_0 \times D_1$ hypercube structure
   Input: $ct.X_0$: ciphertext with $D_0 \times D_1$ hypercube structure padded by zeros
   Output: $ct.X_0$: Rotate the k-th row(column) of $ct.X$ by k mod l positions
2 **for** $k = 0$ **to** $l - 1$ **do**
3     $U[I][J] \leftarrow \begin{cases} 1 & \text{if } dim = 1 \text{ and } I = k \pmod l \\ 1 & \text{if } dim = 0 \text{ and } J = k \pmod l \\ 0 & \text{otherwise} \end{cases}$
4     $ct.d = U \odot ct.X$ ▷ U: a $D_0 \times D_1$ plaintext matrix
5     $ct.d =$ Rotate1D($ct.d, dim, -k$)
6     $ct.X_0 = ct.X_0 \oplus ct.d$
7 **end**
8 **return** $ct.X_0$

then

$$ct.d_0 = \begin{pmatrix} a_{00} & a_{01} & a_{02} \\ 0 & 0 & 0 \\ 0 & 0 & 0 \end{pmatrix}, ct.d_1 = \begin{pmatrix} 0 & 0 & 0 \\ a_{11} & a_{12} & a_{10} \\ 0 & 0 & 0 \end{pmatrix}, ct.d_2 = \begin{pmatrix} 0 & 0 & 0 \\ 0 & 0 & 0 \\ a_{22} & a_{20} & a_{21} \end{pmatrix}.$$

By performing homomorphic addition on all $ct.d_k$, we get

$$ct.A_0 = \begin{pmatrix} a_{00} & a_{01} & a_{02} \\ a_{11} & a_{12} & a_{10} \\ a_{22} & a_{20} & a_{21} \end{pmatrix}, \text{ similarly, } ct.B_0 = \begin{pmatrix} b_{00} & b_{11} & b_{22} \\ b_{10} & b_{21} & b_{02} \\ b_{20} & b_{01} & b_{12} \end{pmatrix}.$$

In fact, RotateAlign requires only $O(\sqrt{l})$ rotations by utilizing the baby-step/giant-step approach (BSGS) [12]. If we select the *good* dimensions for the hypercube structure, Rotate1D(ct, d, k) applies one automorphism denoted by $\rho_{g_d}^k$. RotateAlign can be rewritten as $\sum_{k=0}^{l-1} U_k \rho_{g_d}^k(ct) = \sum_{i=0}^{h-1} \rho_{g_d}^{fi} \left[\sum_{j=0}^{f-1} U'_{j+fi} \cdot \rho_{g_d}^j(ct) \right]$, where $h, f \approx \sqrt{l}$ and $U'_{j+fi} = \rho_{g_d}^{-fi}(U_{j+fi}) = U_{j+fi}$. Then we compute $\rho_{g_d}^j(ct)$ only once during the inner loop for baby steps.

Step 2: There are l rounds in this step. In round i, where $i = \{0, 1, ..., l - 1\}$, two rotations and a homomorphic multiplication operation are performed to calculate Rotate1D($ct.A_0, 1, -i$) $\odot$ Rotate1D($ct.B_1, 0, -i$). Then the results of these l rounds are summed by the homomorphic addition operation, i.e.,

$$ct.A \cdot ct.B = \sum_i \text{Rotate1D}(ct.A_0, 1, -i) \odot \text{Rotate1D}(ct.B_0, 0, -i). \quad (2)$$

The complexity of this step is about l homomorphic multiplications, l additions, and $2l$ rotations. An example of step 2 is Eq. (1).

Actually, the above two steps with slight adjustments are also used heavily in the case of rectangular matrix multiplication. Therefore, for simplicity, we call the above two steps the fully homomorphic encryption matrix multiplication main procedure. Assuming that the input matrices are $A_{m \times l}$ and $B_{l \times n}$ and the hypercube structure is $D_0 \times D_1$, we present FHE-MatMultMain $(ct.A, ct.B, m, l, n, D_0, D_1)$ in Algorithm 2, which implements step 1 and step 2. Table 1 summarizes the time complexity and depth of each step in Algorithm 2. When $m = l = n = D_0 = D_1$, Algorithm 2 is the secure square matrix multiplication algorithm.

Table 1. Time Complexity and Depth of Algorithm 2

Step	Add	CMult	Rot	Mult	Depth
1	$2l$	$2l$	$2l$	-	1Cmult
2	$\min(m, l, n)$	-	$2\min(m, l, n)$	$\min(m, l, n)$	1Mult
Total	$2l + \min(m, l, n)$	$2l$	$2l + 2\min(m, l, n)$	$\min(m, l, n)$	1CMult+1Mult

* When $m = l = n$, Algorithm 2 is the secure square matrix multiplication algorithm.

Algorithm 2: FHE matrix multiplication main procedure

---

1 **procedure:** FHE-MatMultMain $(ct.A, ct.B, m, l, n, D_0, D_1)$
 Input: $ct.A, ct.B$: two ciphertexts of the input matrices $A_{m \times l}$ and $B_{l \times n}$
 Input: $ct.C$: ciphertext with $D_0 \times D_1$ hypercube structure and padded by zeros
 Output: $ct.C$
2 **[Step 1:]**
3 $ct.A_0$=RotateAlign$(ct.A, 1, l)$ ▷ computing $ct.A_0$
4 $ct.B_0$=RotateAlign$(ct.B, 0, l)$ ▷ computing $ct.B_0$
5 **[Step 2:]**
6 **for** $i = 0$ **to** $\min(m, l, n)$ **do**
7 $\quad ct.C = ct.C \oplus ct.A_0 \odot ct.B_0$ ▷ computing $ct.C$
8 $\quad ct.A_0 = $ Rotate1D$(ct.A_0, 1, -1)$
9 $\quad ct.B_0 = $ Rotate1D$(ct.B_0, 0, -1)$
10 **end**
11 **return** $ct.C$

2.2 Rectangular Matrix Multiplication

Suppose the input matrices are $A_{m \times l}$ and $B_{l \times n}$, for different matrix dimensions we divide into three cases and give efficient schemes for each. Consider that for any matrix, we can transform it into a matrix whose two dimensions are both to the power of 2 by zero padding. The matrix size increases by up to 4 times after zero-padding. For the sake of simplicity, we assume that the dimensions m, l, and n are all to the power of 2.

Rectangular Matrix Multiplication with $l = \min\{m, l, n\}$. Let the hypercube structure be $m \times n$ in this case. Let $A_{m \times l}$ be put into the $m \times n$ hypercube structure by padding the right of A with zeros, and let the $B_{l \times n}$ be put into the $m \times n$ hypercube structure by padding the bottom of B with zeros. The homomorphic scheme is described as follows.

Step 1: This step replicates $ct.A$ along the rows to get $ct.A_0$ and $ct.B$ along the columns to get $ct.B_0$. Specifically, let the hypercube structure of a ciphertext $ct.A$ be $D_0 \times D_1$ and its dim-th dimension has d_{dim} non-zero elements, where $dim = \{0, 1\}$ and $d_{dim} \leq D_{dim}$. We denote by $\mathsf{Replicate1D}(ct, dim, d_{dim})$ the replicating of d_{dim} non-zero elements to the whole hypercube structure along the dim-th dimension. We give a scheme description in Algorithm 3, which uses a "repeated doubling" method. Note that in line 3, $\log(D_{dim}/d_{dim})$ is an integer since D_i and d_i are all to the power of 2. Since there are l non-zero elements in each row of $ct.A$, this step takes about $\log \frac{n}{l}$ rotations and additions to get $ct.A_0$. Similarly, this step takes about $\log \frac{m}{l}$ rotations and additions to get $ct.B_0$.

Algorithm 3: Replicate a ciphertext along the row/column

---

1 **procedure:** $\mathsf{Replicate1D}(ct.X, dim, d_{dim})$
  Input: $ct.X$: ciphertext with $D_0 \times D_1$ hypercube structure and the number of non-zero elements is $d_0 \times d_1$
  Output: $ct.X_0$: ciphertext got by replicating $ct.X$ along the dimension dim
2 $ct.X_0 = ct.X$
3 **for** $k = 1$ **to** $\log(D_{dim}/d_{dim})$ **do**
4 $\quad | \quad ct.X_0 = ct.X_0 \oplus \mathsf{Rotate1D}(ct.X_0, dim, k \cdot d_{dim})$
5 **end**
6 **return** $ct.X_0$

For step 1, here is an example when $m = 4$, $l = 2$, and $n = 8$. Let A be a 4×2 matrix and B be a 2×8 matrix, then the hypercube structure is 4×8, and

$$
ct.A = \begin{pmatrix} a_{00} & a_{01} & 0 & 0 & 0 & 0 & 0 & 0 \\ a_{10} & a_{11} & 0 & 0 & 0 & 0 & 0 & 0 \\ a_{20} & a_{21} & 0 & 0 & 0 & 0 & 0 & 0 \\ a_{30} & a_{31} & 0 & 0 & 0 & 0 & 0 & 0 \end{pmatrix}, ct.B = \begin{pmatrix} b_{00} & b_{01} & b_{02} & b_{03} & b_{04} & b_{05} & b_{06} & b_{07} \\ b_{10} & b_{11} & b_{12} & b_{13} & b_{14} & b_{15} & b_{16} & b_{17} \\ 0 & 0 & 0 & 0 & 0 & 0 & 0 & 0 \\ 0 & 0 & 0 & 0 & 0 & 0 & 0 & 0 \end{pmatrix}. \tag{3}
$$

Given $ct.A$ and $ct.B$ in Eq. (3), $ct.A_0$ and $ct.B_0$ are

$$
ct.A_0 = \begin{pmatrix} a_{00} & a_{01} & a_{00} & a_{01} & a_{00} & a_{01} & a_{00} & a_{01} \\ a_{10} & a_{11} & a_{10} & a_{11} & a_{10} & a_{11} & a_{10} & a_{11} \\ a_{20} & a_{21} & a_{20} & a_{21} & a_{20} & a_{21} & a_{20} & a_{21} \\ a_{30} & a_{31} & a_{30} & a_{31} & a_{30} & a_{31} & a_{30} & a_{31} \end{pmatrix}, ct.B_0 = \begin{pmatrix} b_{00} & b_{01} & b_{02} & b_{03} & b_{04} & b_{05} & b_{06} & b_{07} \\ b_{10} & b_{11} & b_{12} & b_{13} & b_{14} & b_{15} & b_{16} & b_{17} \\ b_{00} & b_{01} & b_{02} & b_{03} & b_{04} & b_{05} & b_{06} & b_{07} \\ b_{10} & b_{11} & b_{12} & b_{13} & b_{14} & b_{15} & b_{16} & b_{17} \end{pmatrix}. \tag{4}
$$

Step 2: This step performs the FHE matrix multiplication main procedure with $ct.A_0$ and $ct.B_0$ as input, i.e., $ct.C \leftarrow \mathsf{FHE\text{-}MatMultMain}(ct.A_0, ct.B_0, m, l, n, m, n)$. The complexity of this step is about l homomorphic multiplications, $3l$ additions, $2l$ constant multiplications, and $2l$ rotations (see Table 1). For example, given $ct.A_0$ and $ct.B_0$ in Eq. (4), $ct.C$ is obtained as

Table 2. Time Complexity and Depth of Algorithm 4 ($l = \min\{m, l, n\}$)

Step	Add	CMult	Rot	Mult	Depth
1	$\log \frac{mn}{l^2}$	-	$\log \frac{mn}{l^2}$	-	-
2	$3l$	$2l$	$4l$	l	1CMult
Total	$3l + \log \frac{mn}{l^2}$	$2l$	$4l + \log \frac{mn}{l^2}$	l	1CMult+1Mult

$$
\begin{pmatrix}
a_{00} & a_{01} & a_{00} & a_{01} & a_{00} & a_{01} & a_{00} & a_{01} \\
a_{11} & a_{10} & a_{11} & a_{10} & a_{11} & a_{10} & a_{11} & a_{10} \\
a_{20} & a_{21} & a_{20} & a_{21} & a_{20} & a_{21} & a_{20} & a_{21} \\
a_{31} & a_{30} & a_{31} & a_{30} & a_{31} & a_{30} & a_{31} & a_{30}
\end{pmatrix}
\odot
\begin{pmatrix}
b_{00} & b_{11} & b_{02} & b_{13} & b_{04} & b_{15} & b_{06} & b_{17} \\
b_{10} & b_{01} & b_{12} & b_{03} & b_{14} & b_{05} & b_{16} & b_{07} \\
b_{00} & b_{11} & b_{02} & b_{13} & b_{04} & b_{15} & b_{06} & b_{17} \\
b_{10} & b_{01} & b_{12} & b_{03} & b_{14} & b_{05} & b_{16} & b_{07}
\end{pmatrix}
$$

$$\oplus$$

$$
\begin{pmatrix}
a_{01} & a_{00} & a_{01} & a_{00} & a_{01} & a_{00} & a_{01} & a_{00} \\
a_{10} & a_{11} & a_{10} & a_{11} & a_{10} & a_{11} & a_{10} & a_{11} \\
a_{21} & a_{20} & a_{21} & a_{20} & a_{21} & a_{20} & a_{21} & a_{20} \\
a_{30} & a_{31} & a_{30} & a_{31} & a_{30} & a_{31} & a_{30} & a_{31}
\end{pmatrix}
\odot
\begin{pmatrix}
b_{10} & b_{01} & b_{12} & b_{03} & b_{14} & b_{05} & b_{16} & b_{07} \\
b_{00} & b_{11} & b_{02} & b_{13} & b_{04} & b_{15} & b_{06} & b_{17} \\
b_{10} & b_{01} & b_{12} & b_{03} & b_{14} & b_{05} & b_{16} & b_{07} \\
b_{00} & b_{11} & b_{02} & b_{13} & b_{04} & b_{15} & b_{06} & b_{17}
\end{pmatrix}.
$$

We describe the homomorphic matrix multiplication scheme with $l = \min\{m, l, n\}$ in Algorithm 4. Table 2 summarizes the time complexity and depth of each step in Algorithm 4.

Algorithm 4: Homomorphic matrix multiplication ($l = \min\{m, l, n\}$)

1 **procedure:** FHE-RecMatMult$^{l=\min\{m,l,n\}}$ $(ct.A \cdot ct.B)$
   Input: $ct.A, ct.B$: two ciphertexts of the input matrices $A_{m \times l}$ and $B_{l \times n}$
   Input: $ct.C$: ciphertext with $m \times n$ hypercube structure and padded by zeros
   Output: $ct.C$: $ct.A \cdot ct.B$
2 **[step 1:]**
3 $ct.A_0 = \mathsf{Replicate1D}(ct.A, 1, l)$ ▷ computing $ct.A_0$
4 $ct.B_0 = \mathsf{Replicate1D}(ct.B, 0, l)$ ▷ computing $ct.B_0$
5 **[step 2:]**
6 $ct.C \leftarrow$ FHE-MatMultMain $(ct.A_0, ct.B_0, m, l, n, m, n)$
7 **return** $ct.C$

Rectangular Matrix Multiplication with $l = \operatorname{median}\{m, l, n\}$. In this case, if $m \geq l \geq n$, we let the hypercube structure be $m \times l$. Otherwise, if $n \geq l \geq m$, we let the hypercube structure be $l \times n$. For simplicity, we discuss the case of $m \geq l \geq n$ in detail, and the case of $n \geq l \geq m$ is similar.

For $m \geq l \geq n$, let $A_{m \times l}$ be put into the $m \times l$ hypercube structure, and let $B_{l \times n}$ be put into the $m \times l$ hypercube structure by padding the right and bottom of B with zeros. The homomorphic scheme is described as follows.

Step 1: This step first replicates $ct.B$ along the rows to get $ct.d_0$, and then replicates $ct.d_0$ along the columns to get $ct.d_1$. The generation of $ct.d_0$ and $ct.d_1$ can be achieved by Algorithm 3. Since there are n non-zero elements in each row of $ct.B$, this step takes about $\log \frac{l}{n}$ additions and rotations to get $ct.d_0$.

Similarly, this step takes about $\log \frac{m}{l}$ additions and rotations to get $ct.d_1$. For step 1, here is an example when $m = 4$, $l = 4$, and $n = 2$. Let A be an 8×4 matrix and B be a 4×2 matrix, then the hypercube structure is 8×4, and

$$
ct.A = \begin{pmatrix} a_{00} & a_{01} & a_{02} & a_{03} \\ a_{10} & a_{11} & a_{12} & a_{13} \\ a_{20} & a_{21} & a_{22} & a_{23} \\ a_{30} & a_{31} & a_{32} & a_{33} \\ a_{40} & a_{41} & a_{42} & a_{43} \\ a_{50} & a_{51} & a_{52} & a_{53} \\ a_{60} & a_{61} & a_{62} & a_{63} \\ a_{70} & a_{71} & a_{72} & a_{73} \end{pmatrix}, ct.B = \begin{pmatrix} b_{00} & b_{01} & 0 & 0 \\ b_{10} & b_{11} & 0 & 0 \\ b_{20} & b_{21} & 0 & 0 \\ b_{30} & b_{31} & 0 & 0 \\ 0 & 0 & 0 & 0 \\ 0 & 0 & 0 & 0 \\ 0 & 0 & 0 & 0 \\ 0 & 0 & 0 & 0 \end{pmatrix} .ct.d_0 = \begin{pmatrix} b_{00} & b_{01} & b_{00} & b_{01} \\ b_{10} & b_{11} & b_{10} & b_{11} \\ b_{20} & b_{21} & b_{20} & b_{21} \\ b_{30} & b_{31} & b_{30} & b_{31} \\ 0 & 0 & 0 & 0 \\ 0 & 0 & 0 & 0 \\ 0 & 0 & 0 & 0 \\ 0 & 0 & 0 & 0 \end{pmatrix}, ct.d_1 = \begin{pmatrix} b_{00} & b_{01} & b_{00} & b_{01} \\ b_{10} & b_{11} & b_{10} & b_{11} \\ b_{20} & b_{21} & b_{20} & b_{21} \\ b_{30} & b_{31} & b_{30} & b_{31} \\ b_{00} & b_{01} & b_{00} & b_{01} \\ b_{10} & b_{11} & b_{10} & b_{11} \\ b_{20} & b_{21} & b_{20} & b_{21} \\ b_{30} & b_{31} & b_{30} & b_{31} \end{pmatrix}.
\tag{5}
$$

Step 2: This step performs the FHE matrix multiplication main procedure with $ct.A$ and $ct.d_1$ as input, i.e., $ct.C_0 \leftarrow$ FHE-MatMultMain $(ct.A, ct.d_1, m, l, n, m, l)$. The complexity of this step is about n homomorphic multiplications, $2l + n$ additions, $2l$ constant multiplications, and $2l + 2n$ rotations (see Table 1). For example, given $ct.A$ and $ct.d_1$ in Equation (5), $ct.C_0$ is obtained as

$$
\begin{pmatrix} a_{00} & a_{01} & a_{02} & a_{03} \\ a_{11} & a_{12} & a_{13} & a_{10} \\ a_{22} & a_{23} & a_{20} & a_{21} \\ a_{33} & a_{30} & a_{31} & a_{32} \\ a_{40} & a_{41} & a_{42} & a_{43} \\ a_{51} & a_{52} & a_{53} & a_{50} \\ a_{62} & a_{63} & a_{64} & a_{60} \\ a_{73} & a_{70} & a_{71} & a_{72} \end{pmatrix} \otimes \begin{pmatrix} b_{00} & b_{11} & b_{20} & b_{31} \\ b_{10} & b_{21} & b_{30} & b_{01} \\ b_{20} & b_{31} & b_{00} & b_{11} \\ b_{30} & b_{01} & b_{10} & b_{21} \\ b_{00} & b_{11} & b_{20} & b_{31} \\ b_{10} & b_{21} & b_{30} & b_{01} \\ b_{20} & b_{31} & b_{00} & b_{11} \\ b_{30} & b_{01} & b_{10} & b_{21} \end{pmatrix} \oplus \begin{pmatrix} a_{01} & a_{02} & a_{03} & a_{00} \\ a_{12} & a_{13} & a_{10} & a_{11} \\ a_{23} & a_{20} & a_{21} & a_{22} \\ a_{30} & a_{31} & a_{32} & a_{33} \\ a_{41} & a_{42} & a_{43} & a_{40} \\ a_{52} & a_{53} & a_{50} & a_{51} \\ a_{63} & a_{64} & a_{60} & a_{62} \\ a_{70} & a_{71} & a_{72} & a_{73} \end{pmatrix} \otimes \begin{pmatrix} b_{10} & b_{21} & b_{30} & b_{01} \\ b_{20} & b_{31} & b_{00} & b_{11} \\ b_{30} & b_{01} & b_{10} & b_{21} \\ b_{00} & b_{11} & b_{20} & b_{31} \\ b_{10} & b_{21} & b_{30} & b_{01} \\ b_{20} & b_{31} & b_{00} & b_{11} \\ b_{30} & b_{01} & b_{10} & b_{21} \\ b_{00} & b_{11} & b_{20} & b_{31} \end{pmatrix}
$$

$$
= \begin{pmatrix} a_{00}b_{00} + a_{01}b_{10} & a_{01}b_{11} + a_{02}b_{21} & a_{02}b_{20} + a_{03}b_{30} & a_{03}b_{31} + a_{00}b_{01} \\ a_{11}b_{10} + a_{12}b_{20} & a_{12}b_{21} + a_{13}b_{31} & a_{13}b_{30} + a_{10}b_{00} & a_{10}b_{01} + a_{11}b_{11} \\ a_{22}b_{20} + a_{23}b_{30} & a_{23}b_{31} + a_{20}b_{01} & a_{20}b_{00} + a_{21}b_{10} & a_{21}b_{11} + a_{22}b_{21} \\ a_{33}b_{30} + a_{30}b_{00} & a_{30}b_{01} + a_{31}b_{11} & a_{31}b_{10} + a_{32}b_{20} & a_{32}b_{21} + a_{33}b_{31} \\ a_{40}b_{00} + a_{41}b_{10} & a_{41}b_{11} + a_{42}b_{21} & a_{42}b_{20} + a_{43}b_{30} & a_{43}b_{31} + a_{40}b_{01} \\ a_{51}b_{10} + a_{52}b_{20} & a_{52}b_{21} + a_{53}b_{31} & a_{53}b_{30} + a_{50}b_{00} & a_{50}b_{01} + a_{51}b_{11} \\ a_{62}b_{20} + a_{63}b_{30} & a_{63}b_{31} + a_{60}b_{01} & a_{60}b_{00} + a_{61}b_{10} & a_{61}b_{11} + a_{62}b_{21} \\ a_{73}b_{30} + a_{70}b_{00} & a_{70}b_{01} + a_{71}b_{11} & a_{71}b_{10} + a_{72}b_{20} & a_{72}b_{21} + a_{73}b_{31} \end{pmatrix}
\tag{6}
$$

Step 3: The $m \times l$ ciphertext $ct.C_0$ can be divided into $\frac{l}{n}$ column blocks, where each block has size $m \times n$. By rotation and homomorphic addition operations, this step adds all other column blocks to a column block by exploiting the "repeated doubling" method, and gets a ciphertext $ct.C$ that encrypts the $m \times n$ matrix $C = AB$ in each column block. This step talks about $\log \frac{l}{n}$ rotations and $\log \frac{l}{n}$ additions to get $ct.C$. For example, given $ct.C_0$ in Eq. (6), $ct.C$ is obtained as

$$
\overset{C}{\begin{pmatrix} \sum_{k=0}^{3} a_{0k}b_{k0} & \sum_{k=0}^{3} a_{0k}b_{k1} & \sum_{k=0}^{3} a_{0k}b_{k0} & \sum_{k=0}^{3} a_{0k}b_{k1} \\ \sum_{k=0}^{3} a_{1k}b_{k0} & \sum_{k=0}^{3} a_{1k}b_{k1} & \sum_{k=0}^{3} a_{1k}b_{k0} & \sum_{k=0}^{3} a_{1k}b_{k1} \\ \sum_{k=0}^{3} a_{2k}b_{k0} & \sum_{k=0}^{3} a_{2k}b_{k1} & \sum_{k=0}^{3} a_{2k}b_{k0} & \sum_{k=0}^{3} a_{2k}b_{k1} \\ \sum_{k=0}^{3} a_{3k}b_{k0} & \sum_{k=0}^{3} a_{3k}b_{k1} & \sum_{k=0}^{3} a_{3k}b_{k0} & \sum_{k=0}^{3} a_{3k}b_{k1} \\ \sum_{k=0}^{3} a_{4k}b_{k0} & \sum_{k=0}^{3} a_{4k}b_{k1} & \sum_{k=0}^{3} a_{4k}b_{k0} & \sum_{k=0}^{3} a_{4k}b_{k1} \\ \sum_{k=0}^{3} a_{5k}b_{k0} & \sum_{k=0}^{3} a_{5k}b_{k1} & \sum_{k=0}^{3} a_{5k}b_{k0} & \sum_{k=0}^{3} a_{5k}b_{k1} \\ \sum_{k=0}^{3} a_{6k}b_{k0} & \sum_{k=0}^{3} a_{6k}b_{k1} & \sum_{k=0}^{3} a_{6k}b_{k0} & \sum_{k=0}^{3} a_{6k}b_{k1} \\ \sum_{k=0}^{3} a_{7k}b_{k0} & \sum_{k=0}^{3} a_{7k}b_{k1} & \sum_{k=0}^{3} a_{7k}b_{k0} & \sum_{k=0}^{3} a_{7k}b_{k1} \end{pmatrix}}
$$

Algorithm 5: Summing a ciphertext along the row(column)

---

1 **procedure:** Sum1D(ct, dim, d_{dim})
   Input: ct: ciphertext with $D_0 \times D_1$ hypercube structure
   Input: $\bar{ct}$: ciphertext with $D_0 \times D_1$ hypercube structure and padded by zeros
   Output: $\bar{ct}$: the ciphertext obtained by summing every $d_0(d_1)$ rows(columns)
       of ct along the columns(rows)
2 **for** $k = \log(D_{dim}/d_{dim})$ **to** 1 **do**
3 | $\bar{ct} = \bar{ct} \oplus$ Rotate1D($\bar{ct}, dim, k \cdot d_{dim}$)
4 **end**
5 **return** $\bar{ct}$

---

which encrypts the 8×2 matrix $C = AB$ in its first two columns.

For the convenience of later discussion, we give a general algorithm in Algorithm 5. Let the hypercube structure of a ciphertext ct be $D_0 \times D_1$, which can be viewed as $\frac{D_1}{d_1}$ matrice blocks of size $D_0 \times \frac{D_1}{d_1}$ ($D_1 \geq d_1$ and $d_1 \mid D_1$). We denote by Sum1D($ct, 1, d_1$) the summation of these $\frac{D_1}{d_1}$ matrices along the rows. Similarly, we denote by Sum1D($ct, 0, d_0$) the summation of $\frac{D_0}{d_0}$ matrices with size $\frac{D_0}{d_0} \times D_1$ along the columns. The summation can be achieved by Algorithm 5

Table 3. Time Complexity and Depth of Algorithm 6 ($m \geq l \geq n$)

Step	Add	CMult	Rot	Mult	Depth
1	$\log \frac{m}{n}$	-	$\log \frac{m}{n}$	-	-
2	$2l + n$	$2l$	$2l + 2n$	n	1CMult+1Mult
3	$\log \frac{l}{n}$	-	$\log \frac{l}{n}$	-	1CMult
Total	$3l + \log \frac{ml}{n^2}$	$2l$	$4l + \log \frac{ml}{n^2}$	n	1CMult+1Mult

From the above description, we give the homomorphic matrix multiplication algorithm with $m \geq l \geq n$ in Algorithm 6. Table 3 summarizes the time complexity and depth of each step in Algorithm 6.

Rectangular Matrix Multiplication with $l = \max\{m, l, n\}$. In this case, let the hypercube structure be $l \times l$, a natural scheme is to transform it into a square matrix multiplication by zero padding, and then call Algorithm 2. From Table 1, the homomorphic multiplication of this scheme is $l = \max\{m, l, n\}$.

We give an improved scheme, which requires only $\min\{m, l, n\}$ homomorphic multiplications. We discuss in detail the case of $l \geq m \geq n$ below, and the case of $l \geq n \geq m$ is similar.

Step 1: This step replicates $ct.A$ along the columns to get $ct.A_0$, and replicates $ct.B$ along the rows to get $ct.B_0$. Since there are m non-zero elements in each column of $ct.A$, this step takes about $\log \frac{l}{m}$ rotations and additions to get $ct.A_0$. Similarly, this step takes about $\log \frac{l}{n}$ rotations and additions to get $ct.B_0$.

Algorithm 6: Homomorphic matrix multiplication $(m \geq l \geq n)$

---

1 **procedure:** FHE-RecMatMult$^{m \geq l \geq n}$ $(ct.A \cdot ct.B)$

   Input: $ct.A, ct.B$: two ciphertexts of the input matrices $A_{m \times l}$ and $B_{l \times n}$

   Input: $ct.C_0, ct.C$: two ciphertexts with $m \times l$ hypercube structure and padded by zeros

   Output: $ct.C$: $ct.A \cdot ct.B$

2 [step 1:]

3 $ct.d_0 = \mathsf{Replicate1D}(ct.B, 1, n)$ ▷ computing $ct.d_0$

4 $ct.d_1 = \mathsf{Replicate1D}(ct.d_0, 0, l)$ ▷ computing $ct.d_1$

5 [step 2:]

6 $ct.C_0 \leftarrow \mathsf{FHE\text{-}MatMultMain}\ (ct.A, ct.d_1, m, l, n, m, l)$

7 [step 3:]

8 $ct.C = \mathsf{Sum1D}(ct.C_0, 1, n)$ ▷ computing $ct.C$

9 **return** $ct.C$

For step 1, here is an example when $m = 2$, $l = 4$, and $n = 1$. Let A be a 2×4 matrix and B be a 4×1 matrix, then the hypercube structure is 4×4, and

$$ct.A = \begin{pmatrix} a_{00}\ a_{01}\ a_{02}\ a_{03} \\ a_{10}\ a_{11}\ a_{12}\ a_{13} \\ 0\ \ \ 0\ \ \ 0\ \ \ 0 \\ 0\ \ \ 0\ \ \ 0\ \ \ 0 \end{pmatrix}, ct.B = \begin{pmatrix} b_{00}\ 0\ 0\ 0 \\ b_{10}\ 0\ 0\ 0 \\ b_{20}\ 0\ 0\ 0 \\ b_{30}\ 0\ 0\ 0 \end{pmatrix}, ct.A_0 = \begin{pmatrix} a_{00}\ a_{01}\ a_{02}\ a_{03} \\ a_{10}\ a_{11}\ a_{12}\ a_{13} \\ a_{00}\ a_{01}\ a_{02}\ a_{03} \\ a_{10}\ a_{11}\ a_{12}\ a_{13} \end{pmatrix}, ct.B_0 = \begin{pmatrix} b_{00}|b_{00}|b_{00}|b_{00} \\ b_{10}|b_{10}|b_{10}|b_{10} \\ b_{20}|b_{20}|b_{20}|b_{20} \\ b_{30}|b_{30}|b_{30}|b_{30} \end{pmatrix}. \tag{7}$$

Step 2: This step performs the FHE matrix multiplication main procedure with $ct.A_0$ and $ct.B_0$ as input, i.e., $ct.C_0 \leftarrow$ FHE-MatMultMain $(ct.A_0, ct.B_0, m, l, n, l, l)$. The complexity of this step is about n homomorphic multiplications, $2l+n$ additions, $2l$ constant multiplications, and $2l+2n$ rotations (see Table 1). For example, given $ct.A_0$ and $ct.B_0$ in Eq. (7), $ct.C_0$ is obtained as

$$\begin{pmatrix} a_{00}\ a_{01}\ a_{02}\ a_{03} \\ a_{11}\ a_{12}\ a_{13}\ a_{10} \\ a_{02}\ a_{03}\ a_{00}\ a_{01} \\ a_{13}\ a_{10}\ a_{11}\ a_{12} \end{pmatrix} \otimes \begin{pmatrix} b_{00}\ b_{10}\ b_{20}\ b_{30} \\ b_{10}\ b_{20}\ b_{30}\ b_{00} \\ b_{20}\ b_{30}\ b_{00}\ b_{10} \\ b_{30}\ b_{00}\ b_{10}\ b_{20} \end{pmatrix} = \begin{pmatrix} a_{00}b_{00}\ a_{01}b_{10}\ a_{02}b_{20}\ a_{03}b_{30} \\ a_{11}b_{10}\ a_{12}b_{20}\ a_{13}b_{30}\ a_{10}b_{00} \\ a_{02}b_{20}\ a_{03}b_{30}\ a_{00}b_{00}\ a_{01}b_{10} \\ a_{13}b_{30}\ a_{10}b_{00}\ a_{11}b_{10}\ a_{12}b_{20} \end{pmatrix}. \tag{8}$$

Table 4. Time Complexity and Depth of Algorithm 7 $(l \geq m \geq n)$

Step	Add	CMult	Rot	Mult	Depth
1	$\log \frac{l^2}{mn}$	-	$\log \frac{l^2}{mn}$	-	-
2	$2l + n$	$2l$	$2l + 2n$	n	1CMult+1Mult
3	$\log \frac{l}{n}$	-	$\log \frac{l}{n}$	-	1CMult
Total	$3l + \log \frac{l^3}{mn^2}$	$2l$	$4l + \log \frac{l^3}{mn^2}$	n	1CMult+1Mult

Step 3: The $l \times l$ ciphertext $ct.C_0$ is divided into $\frac{l}{n}$ matrices by column where each matrix has size $l \times n$. This step gets $ct.C$ by summing these $\frac{l}{n}$ blocks along the rows, which can be achieved by Algorithm 5. The complexity of this step is

about $\log \frac{l}{n}$ additions and $\log \frac{l}{n}$ rotations. For example, given $ct.C_0$ in Eq. (8), by Algorithm 5,

$$
ct.C = \overset{C}{\begin{pmatrix} \sum_{k=0}^{3} a_{0k}b_{k0} & \sum_{k=0}^{3} a_{0k}b_{k0} & \sum_{k=0}^{3} a_{0k}b_{k0} & \sum_{k=0}^{3} a_{0k}b_{k0} \\ \sum_{k=0}^{3} a_{1k}b_{k0} & \sum_{k=0}^{3} a_{1k}b_{k0} & \sum_{k=0}^{3} a_{1k}b_{k0} & \sum_{k=0}^{3} a_{1k}b_{k0} \\ \sum_{k=0}^{3} a_{0k}b_{k0} & \sum_{k=0}^{3} a_{0k}b_{k0} & \sum_{k=0}^{3} a_{0k}b_{k0} & \sum_{k=0}^{3} a_{0k}b_{k0} \\ \sum_{k=0}^{3} a_{1k}b_{k0} & \sum_{k=0}^{3} a_{1k}b_{k0} & \sum_{k=0}^{3} a_{1k}b_{k0} & \sum_{k=0}^{3} a_{1k}b_{k0} \end{pmatrix}},
$$

which encrypts the 2×1 matrix $C = AB$ in its first two rows and first column.

We describe the scheme in Algorithm 7. Table 4 summarizes the time complexity and depth of each step in Algorithm 7.

Algorithm 7: Homomorphic matrix multiplication $(l \geq m \geq n)$

---

1 **procedure: FHE-RecMatMult**$^{l \geq m \geq n}$ $(ct.A \cdot ct.B)$
   Input: $ct.A, ct.B$: two ciphertexts of the input matrices $A_{m \times l}$ and $B_{l \times n}$
   Input: $ct.C_0$: ciphertext with $l \times l$ hypercube structure and padded by zeros
   Output: $ct.C$: $ct.A \cdot ct.B$
2 **[step 1:]**
3 $ct.A_0 = \mathsf{Replicate1D}(ct.A, 0, m)$ ▷ computing $ct.A_0$
4 $ct.B_0 = \mathsf{Replicate1D}(ct.B, 1, n)$ ▷ computing $ct.B_0$
5 **[step 2:]**
6 $ct.C_0 \leftarrow \mathsf{FHE\text{-}MatMultMain}\ (ct.A_0, ct.B_0, m, l, n, l, l)$
7 **[step 3:]**
8 $ct.C = \mathsf{Sum1D}(ct.C_0, 1, n)$ ▷ computing $ct.C$
9 **return** $ct.C$

---

3   Complexity Analysis

In this section, we give a comparison of the complexity between our algorithm and the state-of-the-art algorithms [14,16,21]. Note that [16,21] deal mainly with secure square matrix multiplication. For rectangular matrix multiplication, a trivial method is to transform rectangular matrices into square matrices by zero padding and then solve the problem using the existing method. Suppose the input matrices are $A_{m \times l}$ and $B_{l \times n}$, we denote by $k_1 = \max\{m, l, n\}$, $k_2 = \mathrm{median}\{m, l, n\}$, $k_3 = \min\{m, l, n\}$, and $t = \max\{l, n\}$. Table 5 summarizes the complexities of existing methods and our scheme. It can be found that in all cases, the number of Mult of our method is the lowest, as $k_3 = \min\{m, l, n\}$. Compared to [14,21], the Rot of our method is asymptotically reduced by $\frac{k_1 \log k_1}{l}$ and $\log t$ times, respectively.

4   Experimental Evaluation

4.1   Experimental Setup

Our experiments were conducted on a machine equipped with an Intel(R) Xeon(R) Platinum 8475B@2.5 GHz(16 Cores), accompanied by 128 GB of

Table 5. Complexity comparison between our method and existing methods

Method	Add	CMult	Rot	Mult	Depth
[16]	$6k_1$	$4k_1$	$3k_1 + 5\sqrt{k_1}$	k_1	2CMult+1Mult
[21]	$k_1 \log k_1 + k_1$	k_1	$k_1 \log k_1 + k_1$	k_1	1CMult+1Mult
[14]	$l \log t + l$	l	$l \log t + l$	l	1CMult+1Mult
Ours (square)	$3l$	$2l$	$4l$	k_3	1CMult+1Mult
Ours (rectangular)	$3l + \log \frac{k_1^3}{k_2 k_3^2}$	$2l$	$4l + \log \frac{k_1^3}{k_2 k_3^2}$	k_3	1CMult+1Mult

memory. The machine is operated on Ubuntu 22.04.2. Our implementation of secure matrix computation was built upon the foundation provided by the BGV scheme in HElib, and the code was compiled using g++ version 11.3.0. We utilized the openMP library to implement a multi-threaded version, and the number of threads in the implementation is up to 32.

For any given matrix dimensions, we compare the running time of our method with [14,21]. Both methods are implemented using HElib and perform better than [16]. Since [21] is a secure square matrix multiplication method, we adopt the zero padding strategy utilized in [14] for rectangular matrices. For the choice of parameters p, M and (m_0, m_1), we follow the method of [21], where p is the plaintext modulus, M defines the M-th cyclotomic polynomial, (m_0, m_1) is the actual dimensions of the hypercube structure. Based on the conditions specified in [21]: (1) $M = k \cdot m_0 \cdot m_1 + 1$; (2) k, m_0 and m_1 are pairwise coprime; (3) $\mathrm{ord}(p) = k$. We can find two generators g_1 and g_2 with orders m_0 and m_1 in $\mathbb{Z}_M^*$ such that $\mathbb{Z}_M^*/\langle p \rangle = \langle g_0, g_1 \rangle$. Thus we achieve a hypercube with two *good* dimensions m_0 and m_1. More details can be found in [21]. The Appendix A.1 contains a discussion of implementation challenges and their corresponding solutions arising from choosing *good* dimensions.

The selection of other parameters in HElib maintains the default, except for setting bits $= 600$ for the minimal bit length of the ciphertext modulus and $H = 120$ for the Hamming weight of the secret key. The value of H differs from the experiments of other work(i.e., 64) in order to meet the minimum requirements of the latest HElib version. For all the experiments, these settings ensure a minimum security level of 80 bits. (We remark that the assessment of the security level in HElib is more stringent and distinct from the homomorphic encryption standard. It encompasses not only considerations related to polynomial degrees and ciphertext modulus.)

4.2 Results and Analysis

We compare the performance of our method with existing methods in Fig. 2. It can be found that for all cases, the execution time (MatMult) of our algorithm is the lowest. In the case of square matrix multiplication, [14,21] have equal MatMult time, and our method has the best performance because it requires $O(\log l)$ times fewer rotations (see Table 5). For the same reason, we have a

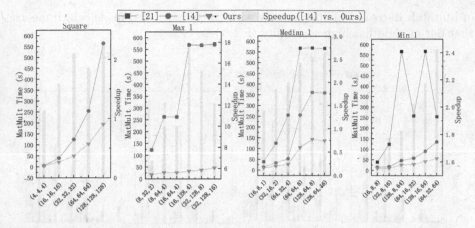

Fig. 2. The running time (s) of [14,21], our method and speedup ([14] vs. our method).

higher speedup as the matrix dimension increases. In the case of rectangular matrix multiplication, the MatMult time of [14,21] and our method are positively correlated with $\max(m,l,n)$, l and $\min(m,l,n)$, respectively. This is because different methods require different numbers of Mult (see Table 5). Since our method requires $l/\min(m,l,n)$ times fewer homomorphic multiplications, when $l/\min(m,l,n)$ is maximum $((m,l,n)=(16,128,4))$, we can achieve the highest speedup, up to 18X.

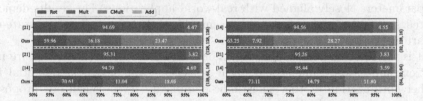

Fig. 3. Operating-level runtime breakdown (%).

Figure 3 shows the runtime breakdown at the operational level. The analysis reveals that a significant portion of the runtime in [14,21] is dedicated to rotation operations. Due to 2 times more CMult operations than the other methods, the percentage of CMult runtime is greater in our method. We also provide noise testing and analysis, interested readers can refer to Appendix A.3.

In addition to the single-threaded implementation shown in Fig. 2, we also utilize multi-threaded (MT) to implement our method in parallel. We mainly parallelize the most time-consuming rotations in RotateAlign, and the degree of parallelism is at most l. Therefore, when the number of threads is greater than l, the increase in the number of threads does not further reduce the running time of MatMult. When the number of threads is less than l, the running time of MatMult decreases almost linearly with the number of threads, which means that our method has high scalability (Fig. 4).

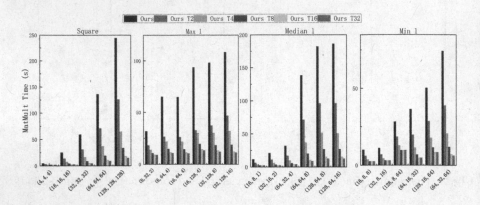

Fig. 4. Multi-threaded runtime of our method.

5   Conclusion

In this work, we propose an efficient secure matrix multiplication of arbitrary dimensions based on BGV fully homomorphic encryption scheme. This method leverages the plaintext slots of the hypercube structure and special homomorphic operations on them. We conducted extensive microbenchmark tests, employing parameters closely aligned with real-world applications. The results demonstrated significant performance enhancements when compared to the state-of-the-art methods.

It is worth noting that applications built upon the hypercube structure not only encompass one-dimensional linear structures but also hold potential for further optimization at the algorithmic complexity level. When our proposed algorithm serves as a building block in a larger secure computation, temporarily adjusting parameters is infeasible. It demonstrates scalability on par with one-dimensional linear structures, coupled with additional options. For instance, in situations where there are many non-data dependent matrix multiplications, and the parameters allow encoding multiple matrices at once, the algorithm can be easily adapted to enable single-ciphertext multi-matrix computations. In situations where only one single small matrix multiplication is involved, the extended version can be used to achieve slight performance improvements. Furthermore, due to the characteristics of hypercube encoding, such an adaptation simplifies the implementation of general homomorphic linear transformation with fewer homomorphic operations, leading to asymptotic reductions in computationally expensive homomorphic operations such as homomorphic multiplication and rotation throughout the entire application. Consequently, we posit that this work can serve as a valuable source of inspiration for subsequent work utilizing hypercube structure packing techniques.

In our future work, we aim to expand the algorithm's capabilities to handle considerably large matrices, thereby facilitating its utility in big data privacy applications that involve massive datasets as inputs.

Acknowledgements. This work was supported in part by National Key Research and Development Program of China (Grant No. 2022YFB4501500 and 2022YFB4501502).

A   Appendix

A.1   Practical Implementation Issues and Solutions

Choosing the *good* dimensions in the hypercube can minimize the overhead of a Rotation1D. Therefore, for performance reasons, the implementation always prioritizes the hypercube with *good* dimensions. However, to meet this requirement, the actual hypercube size chosen is usually larger than the expected minimum size. For example, when using Algorithm 2 to calculate a 3×3 square matrix multiplication, the expected hypercube size is 3×3, while the actual size that fulfills the requirement is 3×4 (refer to the first matrix in Fig. 5a). Calling RotateAlign directly becomes incorrect due to the presence of redundant columns. By observing the terminal error state(i.e., the second matrix in Fig. 5a), it becomes apparent that the correction can be performed in a single step, utilizing 2 CMult, 1 Rotate1D, and 1 Add(see the changes brought by the first arrow in Fig. 5b). Subsequent operations of Rotate1D can also be corrected by employing an additional CMult and Add, as illustrated in Fig. 5b. These corrections only introduce a few constant operations.

One alternative is to expand the dimensions of the hypercube, although this may not always be feasible. Specifically, we can set the expected value of m_1 to $3m_1^* - 2(m_1^*$ denotes the minimum number of columns required in the aforementioned algorithm), thereby ensuring the correctness of all subsequent steps without requiring the correction steps shown in Fig. 5b. Figure 6 depicts the state

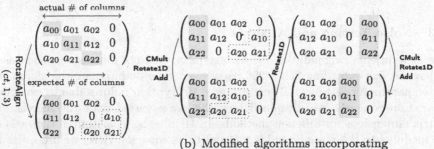

(a) Illustration of the error in Step 2 after RotateAlign.

(b) Modified algorithms incorporating corrections for Step 2 and subsequent Step 3.

Fig. 5. An overview of the error in raw RotateAlign and the modified algorithms addressing the issue in subsequent steps.

of the extended version after performing a raw RotateAlign. All the columns required for subsequent steps have been prepared. This extension may seem to degrade performance due to an increase in M. However, the constraints of k, m_0, and m_1 as mentioned in Sect. 4.1, allow for generating similar values of M when the expected size is selected as $(m_0^*, 3m_1^* - 2)$ or (m_0^*, m_1^*). More details and suggestions for leveraging the extended version can be found in Appendix A.2.

$$
\begin{pmatrix}
a_{00} & a_{01} & a_{02} & a_{00} & a_{01} & a_{02} & a_{00} & 0 \\
a_{10} & a_{11} & a_{12} & a_{10} & a_{11} & a_{12} & a_{10} & 0 \\
a_{20} & a_{21} & a_{22} & a_{20} & a_{21} & a_{22} & a_{20} & 0
\end{pmatrix}
\xrightarrow[\ (ct,1,3)\ ]{\text{RotateAlign}}
\begin{pmatrix}
a_{00} & a_{01} & a_{02} & a_{00} & a_{01} & a_{02} & a_{00} & 0 \\
a_{11} & a_{12} & a_{10} & a_{11} & a_{12} & a_{10} & 0 & a_{10} \\
a_{22} & a_{20} & a_{21} & a_{22} & a_{20} & 0 & a_{20} & a_{21}
\end{pmatrix}
$$

$\underleftrightarrow{\qquad\text{necessity:} \geq (3m-2)\text{columns}\qquad}$ $\underbrace{\qquad\qquad}_{\text{actually used}}$

Fig. 6. Modified algorithm in the extended version.

A.2 Speedup of Extended and Non-extended Versions

In practical implementations, a minimum value for M is typically set to meet security requirements. This leads to selecting p of ord(p) is large when the matrix dimension is small. When ord$(p) \geq 3$, switching to an extended version provides the opportunity to fully utilize the potential of generating a larger hypercube structure with a large M, thereby achieving a certain degree of performance improvement. The performance comparison results and parameter sets $\mathcal{P}_1$ and $\mathcal{P}_2$ for the two scenarios are shown in Table 6. The extended version achieved $3.1\times$ speedup compared to [21] when the dimension is 64. The slight improvement over the non-extended version indicates that the correction steps have a limited impact. Considering the potential performance improvement, it is applicable in real-world applications to generate parameters using two different expected hypercube sizes: (m_0^*, m_1^*) and $(m_0^*, 3m_1^* - 2)$. If the value of M generated by the extended version parameter setting is similar to that of the non-extended version, the extended version can offer performance benefits.

A.3 Noise Testing and Analysis

The experiments originally aimed to test larger matrix dimensions, such as a hypercube size exceeding 256×256. However, when maintaining the aforementioned parameter settings, [21] encountered decryption failures due to excessive noise. Consequently, we examined how the noise varied with the increase in matrix dimensions for different methods. In HElib, the logarithm of the ratio of the modulus to the noise bound is referred to as *capacity*. Here, we use *noise* to represent the difference between the initial capacity and the remaining capacity. The breakdown of the initial capacity is illustrated in Fig. 7, with the shaded part representing the noise generated by evaluation and the light part representing the remaining capacity. While [11] asserts that Rot introduces less noise than Mult and CMult, the depth of Rot also significantly contributes to noise growth,

Table 6. Performance(seconds) of homomorphic square matrix multiplication and speedup $\mathcal{S}($ [21] and non-extended version vs. extended version). The parameter sets $\mathcal{P}_1$ and $\mathcal{P}_2$ correspond to $(m_0, m_1, \mathrm{ord}(p))$ and M for the non-extended and extended versions, respectively.

dimension	4		8		16		32		64		
$(m_0, m_1, \mathrm{ord}(p))$	$(4, 5, 1001)$		$(8, 9, 281)$		$(16, 17, 95)$		$(32, 35, 27)$		$(64, 71, 5)$		$\Big\}\mathcal{P}_1$
M	20021		20233		25841		30241		22721		
$(m_0, m_1, \mathrm{ord}(p))$	$(4, 11, 455)$		$(8, 23, 117)$		$(16, 47, 35)$		$(32, 95, 9)$		$(64, 315, 1)$		$\Big\}\mathcal{P}_2$
M	20021		21529		26321		27361		20161		
Method	T(s)	$\mathcal{S}$	T(s)	$\mathcal{S}$	T(s)	$\mathcal{S}$	T(s)	$\mathcal{S}$	T(s)	$\mathcal{S}$	
[21]	4.469	1.32	11.704	1.54	35.895	1.86	109.140	2.19	219.199	3.11	$\Big\}$Non-Ext
Ours	4.253	1.25	8.784	1.16	23.170	1.20	49.882	1.04	115.616	1.64	
Extend	3.394	-	7.593	-	19.279	-	49.882	-	70.381	-	

particularly in the case of the prominently dominant Rot illustrated in Fig. 3. Compared to [21], our method increases Add but heavily decreases Rot, resulting in slower growth of noise with increasing matrix dimension.

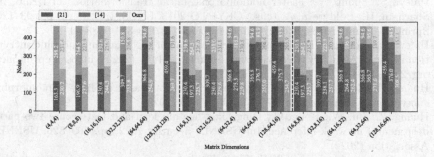

Fig. 7. Noise generation volume. The bottom (shaded) part represents generated noise, while the top (light) part represents the remaining capacity.

References

1. Brakerski, Z., Gentry, C., Vaikuntanathan, V.: (leveled) fully homomorphic encryption without bootstrapping. In: Innovations in Theoretical Computer Science 2012, pp. 309–325. ACM (2012)
2. Brakerski, Z., Vaikuntanathan, V.: Fully homomorphic encryption from ring-LWE and security for key dependent messages. In: Rogaway, P. (ed.) CRYPTO 2011. LNCS, vol. 6841, pp. 505–524. Springer, Heidelberg (2011). https://doi.org/10.1007/978-3-642-22792-9_29
3. Cheon, J.H., Kim, A., Kim, M., Song, Y.: Homomorphic encryption for arithmetic of approximate numbers. In: Takagi, T., Peyrin, T. (eds.) ASIACRYPT 2017. LNCS, vol. 10624, pp. 409–437. Springer, Cham (2017). https://doi.org/10.1007/978-3-319-70694-8_15

4. Coron, J.-S., Mandal, A., Naccache, D., Tibouchi, M.: Fully homomorphic encryption over the integers with shorter public keys. In: Rogaway, P. (ed.) CRYPTO 2011. LNCS, vol. 6841, pp. 487–504. Springer, Heidelberg (2011). https://doi.org/10.1007/978-3-642-22792-9_28
5. Duong, D.H., Mishra, P.K., Yasuda, M.: Efficient secure matrix multiplication over LWE-based homomorphic encryption. Tatra Mount. Math. Publ. **67**(1), 69–83 (2016)
6. Fan, J., Vercauteren, F.: Somewhat practical fully homomorphic encryption. IACR Cryptolog ePrint Archive, p. 144 (2012). http://eprint.iacr.org/2012/144
7. Fox, G.C., Otto, S.W., Hey, A.J.G.: Matrix algorithms on a hypercube I: matrix multiplication. Parallel Comput. **4**(1), 17–31 (1987). https://doi.org/10.1016/0167-8191(87)90060-3
8. Gentry, C.: Fully homomorphic encryption using ideal lattices. In: Mitzenmacher, M. (ed.) STOC 2009, pp. 169–178. ACM (2009)
9. Gentry, C., Halevi, S., Smart, N.P.: Homomorphic evaluation of the AES circuit. In: Safavi-Naini, R., Canetti, R. (eds.) CRYPTO 2012. LNCS, vol. 7417, pp. 850–867. Springer, Heidelberg (2012). https://doi.org/10.1007/978-3-642-32009-5_49
10. Goldreich, O.: The Foundations of Cryptography - Volume 2: Basic Applications. Cambridge University Press (2004)
11. Halevi, S., Shoup, V.: Algorithms in HElib. In: Garay, J.A., Gennaro, R. (eds.) CRYPTO 2014. LNCS, vol. 8616, pp. 554–571. Springer, Heidelberg (2014). https://doi.org/10.1007/978-3-662-44371-2_31
12. Halevi, S., Shoup, V.: Faster homomorphic linear transformations in HElib. In: Shacham, H., Boldyreva, A. (eds.) CRYPTO 2018. LNCS, vol. 10991, pp. 93–120. Springer, Cham (2018). https://doi.org/10.1007/978-3-319-96884-1_4
13. Halevi, S., Shoup, V.: Design and implementation of HElib: a homomorphic encryption library. IACR Cryptology ePrint Archive, p. 1481 (2020). https://eprint.iacr.org/2020/1481
14. Huang, H., Zong, H.: Secure matrix multiplication based on fully homomorphic encryption. J. Supercomput. **79**(5), 5064–5085 (2023)
15. Huang, Z., Lu, W., Hong, C., Ding, J.: Cheetah: lean and fast secure two-party deep neural network inference. In: USENIX Security 2022, pp. 809–826. USENIX Association (2022)
16. Jiang, X., Kim, M., Lauter, K.E., Song, Y.: Secure outsourced matrix computation and application to neural networks. In: CCS 2018, pp. 1209–1222. ACM (2018)
17. Lu, W., Kawasaki, S., Sakuma, J.: Using fully homomorphic encryption for statistical analysis of categorical, ordinal and numerical data. In: NDSS 2017. The Internet Society (2017)
18. Microsoft: Microsoft seal library (2021). https://github.com/microsoft/SEAL
19. Mishra, P.K., Duong, D.H., Yasuda, M.: Enhancement for Secure Multiple Matrix Multiplications over Ring-LWE Homomorphic Encryption. In: Liu, J.K., Samarati, P. (eds.) ISPEC 2017. LNCS, vol. 10701, pp. 320–330. Springer, Cham (2017). https://doi.org/10.1007/978-3-319-72359-4_18
20. Naehrig, M., Lauter, K.E., Vaikuntanathan, V.: Can homomorphic encryption be practical? In: Cachin, C., Ristenpart, T. (eds.) CCSW 2011, pp. 113–124. ACM (2011)
21. Rathee, D., Mishra, P.K., Yasuda, M.: Faster PCA and linear regression through hypercubes in HElib. In: Proceedings of the 2018 Workshop on Privacy in the Electronic Society, WPES@CCS 2018, pp. 42–53. ACM (2018)
22. Rizomiliotis, P., Triakosia, A.: On matrix multiplication with homomorphic encryption. In: Regazzoni, F., van Dijk, M. (eds.) CCSW 2022, pp. 53–61. ACM (2022)

23. Smart, N.P., Vercauteren, F.: Fully homomorphic encryption with relatively small key and ciphertext sizes. In: Nguyen, P.Q., Pointcheval, D. (eds.) PKC 2010. LNCS, vol. 6056, pp. 420–443. Springer, Heidelberg (2010). https://doi.org/10.1007/978-3-642-13013-7_25
24. Smart, N.P., Vercauteren, F.: Fully homomorphic SIMD operations. Des. Codes Cryptogr. **71**(1), 57–81 (2014)
25. Wu, D., Haven, J.: Using homomorphic encryption for large scale statistical analysis. FHE-SI-Report, Univ. Stanford, Tech. Rep. TR-dwu4 (2012)
26. Yang, Y., Zhang, H., Fan, S., Lu, H., Zhang, M., Li, X.: Poseidon: practical homomorphic encryption accelerator. In: HPCA 2023, pp. 870–881. IEEE (2023)
27. Yasuda, M., Shimoyama, T., Kogure, J., Yokoyama, K., Koshiba, T.: New packing method in somewhat homomorphic encryption and its applications. Secur. Commun. Networks **8**(13), 2194–2213 (2015)

Sequential Half-Aggregation
of Lattice-Based Signatures

Katharina Boudgoust[1] and Akira Takahashi[2(✉)]

[1] Aarhus University, Aarhus, Denmark
katharina.boudgoust@cs.au.dk
[2] University of Edinburgh, Edinburgh, UK
takahashi.akira.58s@gmail.com

Abstract. With Dilithium and Falcon, NIST selected two lattice-based
signature schemes during their post-quantum standardization project.
Whereas Dilithium follows the Fiat-Shamir with Aborts (Lyubashevsky,
Asiacrypt'09) blueprint, Falcon can be seen as an optimized version of
the GPV-paradigm (Gentry et al., STOC'06). An important question
now is whether those signatures allow additional features such as the
aggregation of distinct signatures. One example are sequential aggregate signature (SAS) schemes (Boneh et al., Eurocrypt'04) which allow
a group of signers to sequentially combine signatures on distinct messages in a compressed manner. The present work first reviews the state
of the art of (sequentially) aggregating lattice-based signatures, points
out the insecurity of one of the existing Falcon-based SAS (Wang and
Wu, PROVSEC'19), and proposes a fix for it. We then construct the
first Fiat-Shamir with Aborts based SAS by generalizing existing techniques from the discrete-log setting (Chen and Zhao, ESORICS'22) to
the lattice framework. Going from the pre-quantum to the post-quantum
world, however, does most often come with efficiency penalties. In our
work, we also meet obstacles that seem inherent to lattice-based signatures, making the resulting scheme less efficient than what one would
hope for. As a result, we only achieve quite small compression rates.
We compare our construction with existing lattice-based SAS which all
follow the GPV-paradigm. The bottom line is that none of the schemes
achieves a good compression rate so far.

1 Introduction

Aggregate signature (AS) schemes, introduced by [7], allow N signers to individually produce signatures $\sigma_1, \ldots, \sigma_N$ on distinct messages $m_1, \ldots, m_N$, and
later combine them into a single, compact signature σ_{AS}. Such σ_{AS} can be verified with respect to the participants' verification keys $pk_1, \ldots, pk_N$. Classical
applications of aggregate signatures include certificate chains: in a public key
infrastructure one has to include their certificate in every sent message, which
itself comes from a chain of certificates issued by different authorities. Since the
naive concatenation of single-user signatures significantly adds to the certificate

G. Tsudik et al. (Eds.): ESORICS 2023, LNCS 14344, pp. 270–289, 2024.
https://doi.org/10.1007/978-3-031-50594-2_14

chain (e.g., [7] reports 15% of a typical X.509 certificate length is occupied by the signature), it is paramount to replace them with a compact, aggregated signature to save bandwidth. In the literature, essentially two different paradigms of fully compact aggregate signatures have been proposed: (1) dedicated constructions based on bilinear pairings [3,7], and (2) generic solutions exploiting iO [30] or non-interactive arguments [2,17,46], where a signature aggregator produces a succinct proof of knowledge of N valid signatures.

There also exists the slightly restricted notion of *sequential aggregate signatures* (SAS) [34]. In this setting, signing and aggregation are carried out altogether: signer i associated with pk_i receives from signer $i-1$ *aggregate so-far* σ_{i-1} with a key-message list $L_{i-1} = (\mathsf{pk}_1, m_1, \ldots, \mathsf{pk}_{i-1}, m_{i-1})$, adds a signature on the message m_i of their own choice to produce σ_i, and then passes along σ_i and $L_i = L_{i-1} \| (\mathsf{pk}_i, m_i)$ to the next signer $i + 1$. Unlike general aggregate signatures, SAS require round-robin communication among signers, which however fits well in typical application scenarios such as a certificate chain. A plethora of work proposed highly efficient, constant-size SAS using pairings [3,6,23,33] or assuming the existence of trapdoor permutations [12,26,34,41].

Half-Aggregation of Fiat-Shamir Signatures. Perhaps unsurprisingly, not many aggregation methods tailored to *Fiat-Shamir signatures* [22] such as Schnorr [44] are known.[1] Fiat-Shamir signatures are typically constructed from three-round Σ-protocols [15]: the signer invokes the underlying Σ-protocol prover to generate the first-round *commit* value u, samples random *challenge* c by hashing u together with the message m to be signed, creates *response* z, and outputs $\sigma = (c, z)$ as a signature. The verifier then reconstructs u from (pk, c, z) through certain algebraic operations and checks the recomputed hash against c. Equivalently, the signer can set $\sigma = (u, z)$ and the verifier recomputes the hash c, while checking if a certain relation between c and (pk, u, z) holds. The difficulty of aggregating Fiat-Shamir mainly lies in the challenge hash function: since its typical instantiation such as SHA-256 has no algebraic structure, it does not blend well with nice homomorphic properties of the underlying Σ-protocol transcript. This is why the existing approaches (e.g., [4,19,42]) require (at least) two rounds of interaction so that all signers can first agree on a combined u that leads to the same challenge c, from which they compute shares of z.

To avoid interaction, recent papers proposed *half-aggregation* of Schnorr/EdDSA [13,14,31]. These are middle ground solutions where only the u or the z component gets aggregated, and the other part consists of a concatenation of N partial signatures. Although it is asymptotically no better than the trivial concatenation of N signatures, reducing the signature size by a constant factor has meaningful implications in practice, e.g., in certain cases the entire certificate chain of size $O(N)$ needs to be transmitted anyway.

---

[1] It is well known that *interactive* multi-signatures can be generically converted to interactive aggregate signatures by asking all participants to sign a concatenation of N messages and public keys [4,19,42]. However, this requires the signers to agree on all N messages and who they co-sign with in advance, and does not fit in the typical use cases of aggregate signatures such as a certificate chain.

Another possible approach would be adapting one of the aforementioned generic solutions and having an aggregator node to prove the knowledge of N tuples of the form (u, c, z) satisfying the verification conditions descried as a circuit. However, the prover's complexity likely hinges on mixture of algebraic operations and non-algebraic hash computation in verification. Another issue with such a generic solution applied to typical Fiat-Shamir signatures is that the security proof would likely rely on heuristics. Since an aggregator of the generic method requires a concrete description of the hash function, its security is only guaranteed assuming the security of the underlying signature scheme in the standard model, whereas the majority of existing Fiat-Shamir signatures are only proven in the random oracle model.

Aggregate Signatures from Lattices. Given that NIST has announced in their post-quantum cryptography standardization project two signature finalists, Falcon [43] and Dilithium [37], based on (structured) lattice assumptions, a natural question is whether tailor-made aggregate signatures can be instantiated using lattices (instead of generic solutions such as [2,17]). Both finalists represent the two major design principles to build lattice-based signatures: Dilithium follows Lyubashevsky's Fiat-Shamir with Aborts (FSwA) paradigm [35,36] and Falcon is a GPV-type signature using preimage sampleable trapdoor functions [27].

There are a limited number of proposals within the FSwA paradigm. Boneh and Kim [8] presented a lattice-based instantiation of [4] but it requires three rounds of interactions. Boudgoust and Roux-Langlois [10] are the first to securely instantiate non-interactive half-aggregation of FSwA. From a high level perspective, they adapt the half-aggregation of Schnorr [13] to the lattice-setting. Whereas in Schnorr, it does not really matter whether we output $\sigma = (u, z)$ or $\sigma = (c, z)$, it makes a big difference in the lattice setting. The signature size significantly decreases in the second case. During the half-aggregation of [10], only the z-parts are aggregated, but all the u-parts are transmitted. Note that it is not sufficient to transmit all the c-parts, as we cannot recover the different commitments anymore from an aggregated response. However, we need every single commitment in order to verify an aggregate signature. In consequence, the provably secure version of their construction outputs a signature $\sigma_{AS} = (u_1, \ldots, u_N, z)$ which is *always* larger than the naive concatenation of N signatures $\sigma_{con} = (c_1, z_1, \ldots, c_N, z_N)$. The MMSAT scheme [18] is a candidate half-aggregate signature scheme based on a non-standard lattice problem, called the Partial Fourier Recovery problem. However, it turned out that the security proof is flawed and even simple forgery attacks exist [10]. Regarding sequential aggregation, the only known lattice-based solutions we are aware of follow the GPV-paradigm [20,45], of which the latter turns out to be insecure as we sketch below. Given all this, we are motivated to ask the following question in this paper:

Can we construct a non-interactive sequential half-aggregate FSwA signature scheme (1) with a signature size smaller than the naive concatenation, and (2) without invoking expensive generic solutions?

1.1   Our Contributions

In this work, we positively answer this question. In Sect. 3, we present a sequential half-aggregate signature based on the Fiat-Shamir with Aborts framework. The aggregation paradigm closely follows recent Schnorr-based SAS due to Chen and Zhao [14]. As elaborated before, the main obstacle in previous works is that without interaction it is difficult to aggregate the commitments $u_1, \ldots, u_N$ that are responsible for the large aggregate signature size in [10]. If, however, we place ourselves in the *sequential* aggregate model, we can aggregate over the u-parts by letting the parties sign one after each other. A sequential aggregate signature of our construction now is of the form $\sigma_{\mathsf{SAS}} = (u, z_1, \ldots, z_N)$. Once the size of $(c_1, \ldots, c_N)$ is larger than the size of u, our SAS produces signatures that are indeed smaller than the trivial concatenation σ_{con}. Unfortunately, when looking at the ratio between σ_{SAS} and σ_{con}, it is the $(z_1, \ldots, z_N)$-part (that both have in common) that makes up for most of the signature size and hence the compression rate is close to 1. Although our concrete parameter estimates in Sect. 4 indicate the output signature is only $\sim 1\%$ smaller than the naive concatenation, we believe ours to be an important step towards better understanding the possibilities and limits of lattice-based aggregate signatures.

The security of our scheme tightly reduces to the existential unforgeability of the standard single-user FSwA scheme instantiated with structured lattices. We prove security in the so-called *full history* setting of SAS. In the full version of this paper [11, App. A], we also discuss its security in a new model that has been introduced in [14], which we call the *partial-signature history-free* security model. Although our construction closely follows the one of [14], our security proof is more involved because of subtleties that arise in the lattice setting. We have to consider several bad events that might happen and bound their probability. In Sect. 4, we also compare our scheme with the two existing lattice-based SAS [20,45] following the GPV-paradigm. As in the lattice setting we only have so-called preimage sampleable trapdoor functions (and no trapdoor permutation), they cannot achieve constant-size SAS either. The upshot is that neither of them saves more than 4% of signature size if a fair comparison is made against the naive concatenation and taking recent advances [21] into account.

As a separate contribution, we point out the insecurity of one of the existing Falcon-based SAS [45]. We show in Sect. 5 that their construction does not guarantee the claimed security property due to the existence of a forgery attack. As an independent contribution, we provide another attack on the Dilithium-based interactive multi-signature of [25] (which can be generically turned into an aggregate signature using [4]'s trick). The description of the attack can be found in the full version of this paper [11, Sec. 5.2]. The latter attack highlights that, even after knowing how to aggregate signatures that follow a general paradigm, it is not trivial to make the aggregation work for optimized instantiations.

Given the above attacks on existing solutions and the concrete parameter estimates of our construction, we conclude that concretely efficient aggregation of the lattice-based NIST finalists is still an unexplored area and mark it as an interesting direction for future work.

1.2 Other Related Work

Imposing a sequential way of signing is not the only way how to restrict the model of aggregate signatures. Other works look for instance at a synchronous model [1,28], where signatures are aggregated together if they have been issued at the same time interval. One recent result studies lattice-based aggregate signatures in the synchronous model [24]. As already mentioned before, a related concept are multi-signatures [5,39], where we allow the parties to interact with each other. There are several recent results on lattice-based multi-signatures [9,16] and we refer to the references therein.

2 Preliminaries

Notations. For any positive integer N, we denote by $[N]$ the set $\{1,\dots,N\}$. For a finite set S, we denote its cardinality by $|S|$ and the uniform distribution over S by $U(S)$. We simply write $s \xleftarrow{\$} S$ to indicate sampling s from $U(S)$. For a probability distribution $\mathscr{D}$, we write $s \leftarrow \mathscr{D}$ to indicate sampling s from $\mathscr{D}$; for a randomized (resp. deterministic) algorithm $\mathcal{A}$ we write $s \leftarrow \mathcal{A}$ (resp. $s := \mathcal{A}$) to indicate assigning an output from $\mathcal{A}$ to s. Throughout, the security parameter is denoted by λ. The abbreviation PPT stands for probabilistic polynomial-time.

Throughout the paper, we work over the ring $R =: \mathbb{Z}[X]/\langle X^n + 1\rangle$, where n is a power of 2. For any ring element $r \in R$, we define $\|r\|_2$, $\|r\|_1$ and $\|r\|_\infty$ to be the respective norms of its coefficient vector. For some prime q, we define $R_q := R/(qR)$ and for some positive integer γ, we set $S_\gamma := \{r \in R: \|r\|_\infty \leq \gamma\}$.

2.1 Fiat-Shamir with Aborts Signatures

In this paper, we build a sequential aggregate signature FSwA-SAS starting from a well-studied signature scheme FSwA-S = (Setup, Gen, Sign, Ver) whose definition we recall in Algorithm 1. It follows the so-called *Fiat-Shamir with Aborts* paradigm [35,36] and can be seen as the module variant of [29] or the 'vanilla' flavor of Dilithium.

Modification. A difference to the standard design is that instead of outputting $\sigma = (c, \mathbf{z})$, we output $\sigma = (\mathbf{u}, \mathbf{z})$. For a single signature, both cases are equivalent, as $\mathbf{u}$ defines c via the hash function H (and the public key $\mathbf{t}$ and the message m) and c defines $\mathbf{u}$ via the equation $\mathbf{u} = \bar{\mathbf{A}}\mathbf{z} - c \cdot \mathbf{t}$. However, this is not the case for a (sequential) aggregate signature scheme and we thus need to transmit the information $\mathbf{u}$.

Distribution $\mathscr{D}$. During the signing algorithm Sign, the FSwA-S scheme uses a distribution $\mathscr{D}$ to sample a vector of ring elements of short norm over R. In the literature, mainly two different ways of instantiating $\mathscr{D}$ are studied. The first uses discrete Gaussian distributions (as for instance in [36]) and the second uses the uniform distribution over a bounded set, i.e., $\mathscr{D} = U(S_\gamma)$ for some $\gamma \ll q$ (as for instance in [29]). The concrete instantiation of $\mathscr{D}$ then influences the choice

---

Algorithm 1: Description of the FSwA-S Signature

The challenge space is $\mathsf{Ch} := \big\{ c \in R : \|c\|_\infty = 1 \,\wedge\, \|c\|_1 = \kappa \big\}$ and the message space is $M = \{0,1\}^l$. The random oracle is $\mathsf{H} : \{0,1\}^* \to \mathsf{Ch}$.

$\mathsf{Setup}(1^\lambda)$
1: $\mathbf{A} \xleftarrow{\$} R_q^{k\times\ell}$
2: $\bar{\mathbf{A}} := [\mathbf{A}|\mathbf{I}_k]$
3: **return** $\bar{\mathbf{A}}$

$\mathsf{Sign}(\mathsf{sk}, m)$
1: $\mathbf{s} := \mathsf{sk}$
2: $\mathbf{t} := \bar{\mathbf{A}}\mathbf{s} \bmod q$
3: $\mathbf{z} := \bot$
4: **while** $\mathbf{z} := \bot$ **do**
5:     $\mathbf{y} \leftarrow \mathscr{D}^{\ell+k}$
6:     $\mathbf{u} := \bar{\mathbf{A}}\mathbf{y} \bmod q$
7:     $c := \mathsf{H}(\mathbf{u}, \mathbf{t}, m)$
8:     $\mathbf{z} := c \cdot \mathbf{s} + \mathbf{y}$
9:     $\mathbf{z} := \mathsf{RejSamp}(\mathbf{z}, c \cdot \mathbf{s})$
10: $\sigma := (\mathbf{u}, \mathbf{z})$
11: **return** σ

$\mathsf{Gen}(\bar{\mathbf{A}})$
1: $\mathbf{s} \xleftarrow{\$} S_\eta^{\ell+k}$
2: $\mathbf{t} := \bar{\mathbf{A}}\mathbf{s} \bmod q$
3: $\mathsf{sk} := \mathbf{s}$
4: $\mathsf{pk} := \mathbf{t}$
5: **return** $(\mathsf{sk}, \mathsf{pk})$

$\mathsf{Ver}(\mathsf{pk}, \sigma, m)$
1: $(\mathbf{u}, \mathbf{z}) := \sigma$
2: $\mathbf{t} := \mathsf{pk}$
3: $c := \mathsf{H}(\mathbf{u}, \mathbf{t}, m)$
4: **if** $\|\mathbf{z}\|_\infty \leq B \wedge \bar{\mathbf{A}}\mathbf{z} = c \cdot \mathbf{t} + \mathbf{u}$ **then**
5:     **return** 1
6: **else**
7:     **return** 0

---

of the rejection algorithm $\mathsf{RejSamp}$ during signing and of the bound B during verification. In this paper, we focus on the latter as this is the choice commonly used in practice, as for instance in $\mathsf{Dilithium}$. In this case, the algorithm $\mathsf{RejSamp}$ outputs $\bot$ if $\|\mathbf{z}\|_\infty > \gamma - \kappa \cdot \eta =: B$, else it outputs $\mathbf{z}$.

Security. Overall, the UF-CMA security of the scheme FSwA-S as specified in Algorithm 1 is based on the hardness of M-LWE and M-SIS [32]. Definitions of both hardness assumptions can be found in the full version [11, Sec. 2.2]. For the reason of space limits, we refer the interested reader to the original security proofs in [29,36] in the random oracle model.

2.2 Sequential Aggregate Signatures

Sequential aggregate signatures (SAS) were first introduced in [34]. We recall now the syntax of a (full-history) SAS scheme, together with the definitions of correctness and security following the notations of Gentry et al. [26].

Definition 2.1 (SAS). *A* sequential aggregate signature *scheme* (SAS) *for a message space M consists of a tuple of* PPT *algorithms* SAS = (Setup, Gen, SeqSign, SeqVerify) *defined as follows:*

$\mathsf{Setup}(1^\lambda) \to \mathsf{pp}$: *On input the security parameter λ, the setup algorithm outputs the public parameters* pp.

Game 1: Description of the $\mathsf{FH\text{-}UF\text{-}CMA}_{\mathsf{SAS}}(\mathcal{A}, \lambda)$ Security Game

1: $\mathsf{pp} \leftarrow \mathsf{Setup}(1^\lambda)$
2: $(\mathsf{pk}, \mathsf{sk}) \leftarrow \mathsf{Gen}(\mathsf{pp})$
3: $\mathcal{Q} := \varnothing$
4: $(L_N^*, \sigma_N^*) \leftarrow \mathcal{A}^{\mathsf{OSeqSign}}(\mathsf{pp}, \mathsf{pk})$
5: **if** $\mathsf{SeqVerify}(L_N^*, \sigma_N^*) \ \wedge \ \exists i^* \in$ $[N]: (\mathsf{pk}_{i^*} = \mathsf{pk} \wedge (m_{i^*}, L_{i^*-1}) \notin \mathcal{Q})$
   then
6:      **return** 1
7: **else**
8:      **return** 0

$\mathsf{OSeqSign}(m_i, \sigma_{i-1}, L_{i-1})$
1: $\sigma_i \leftarrow \mathsf{SeqSign}(\mathsf{sk}, m_i, L_{i-1}, \sigma_{i-1})$
2: $\mathcal{Q} := \mathcal{Q} \cup \{(m_i, L_{i-1})\}$
3: **return** σ_i

$\mathsf{Gen}(\mathsf{pp}) \to (\mathsf{sk}, \mathsf{pk})$: *On input the public parameters* pp, *the key generation algorithm outputs a pair of secret key* sk *and public key* pk.

$\mathsf{SeqSign}(\mathsf{sk}_i, m_i, L_{i-1}, \sigma_{i-1}) \to \sigma_i$: *On input a secret key* sk_i, *a message* $m_i \in M$, *a list* L_{i-1} *with* $L_{i-1} := (\mathsf{pk}_1, m_1)\|\ldots\|(\mathsf{pk}_{i-1}, m_{i-1})$, *and a so-far signature* σ_{i-1}, *the sequential signing algorithm outputs a new so-far signature* σ_i.

$\mathsf{SeqVerify}(L_N, \sigma_N) \to \{0, 1\}$: *On input a list* L_N *of* N *message-public-key pairs and a sequential aggregate signature* σ_N, *the sequential verification algorithm either outputs* 1 *(accept) or* 0 *(reject)*.

For convenience, given a list $L_j = (\mathsf{pk}_1, m_1)\|\ldots\|(\mathsf{pk}_j, m_j)$, we denote by L_i its ith prefix $L_i := (\mathsf{pk}_1, m_1)\|\ldots\|(\mathsf{pk}_i, m_i)$ for $1 \leq i < j$.

Definition 2.2 (Correctness). *Let* $\mathsf{SAS} = (\mathsf{Setup}, \mathsf{Gen}, \mathsf{SeqSign}, \mathsf{SeqVerify})$ *be a sequential aggregate signature scheme for a message space* M. *It is called correct if for all* $\lambda, N \in \mathbb{N}$ *it yields where* $m_i \in M$, $\mathsf{pp} \leftarrow \mathsf{Setup}(1^\lambda)$, $(\mathsf{sk}_i, \mathsf{pk}_i) \leftarrow \mathsf{Gen}(\mathsf{pp})$, $L_i = (\mathsf{pk}_1, m_1)\|\ldots\|(\mathsf{pk}_i, m_i)$ *and* $\sigma_i \leftarrow \mathsf{SeqSign}(\mathsf{sk}_i, m_i, L_{i-1}, \sigma_{i-1})$ *for all* $i \in [N]$. *Let* $L_0 = \varnothing$ *and* $\sigma_0 = (\mathbf{0}, \mathbf{0})$.

Informally, full history unforgeability against chosen message attacks captures the following security notion. An adversary is given a challenge public key and has access to a sequential signing oracle that, on input a message, a so-far signature and a list of public keys and messages (called 'history') provides the next so-far signature using the secret key corresponding to the challenge key. A forgery is composed of an sequentially aggregate signature together with a history (i.e., a list of message-key pairs). The forgery is successful if it passes verification, if one of the public keys is the challenge key and if the signing oracle has not yet been queried on the same message *and* history.

Definition 2.3 (FH-UF-CMA Security). *A* SAS *scheme satisfies* <u>f</u>ull <u>h</u>istory <u>unf</u>orgeabilty against <u>c</u>hosen <u>m</u>essage <u>a</u>ttacks, *if for all* PPT *adversaries* $\mathcal{A}$,

$$\mathsf{Adv}_{\mathsf{SAS}}^{\mathsf{FH\text{-}UF\text{-}CMA}}(\mathcal{A}) := \Pr\left[\mathsf{FH\text{-}UF\text{-}CMA}_{\mathsf{SAS}}(\mathcal{A}, \lambda) = 1\right] = \mathsf{negl}(\lambda),$$

where the $\mathsf{FH\text{-}UF\text{-}CMA}_{\mathsf{SAS}}$ *game is described in Game 1*.

3 Sequential Half-Aggregation of FSwA Signatures

3.1 Definition and Correctness of the Scheme

Our scheme is described in Algorithm 2. The overall structure closely follows the one by Chen and Zhao [14]. We remark that, for the sake of security proof, the key generation algorithm slightly differs from the original one in Algorithm 1. It keeps regenerating a key pair until the public key $\mathbf{t}$ contains at least one invertible element. This terminates relatively quickly in practice. Let p_{inv} be the probability that $\mathbf{t} = \bar{\mathbf{A}}\mathbf{s}$ has at least one invertible coefficient over R_q, where $\mathbf{s}$ is uniformly sampled from $S_\eta^{\ell+k}$. Then the expected running time of Gen is $1/p_{\mathsf{inv}}$. One can experimentally find p_{inv} for each parameter set.

Remark 3.1. Whereas it seems to be hard to give unconditionally provable lower bounds for p_{inv} (at least in our parameter setting), it is possible to bound it assuming the hardness of M-LWE (which is also used in the security proof of FSwA-S). Let p_{R_q} denote the probability that an element of R_q sampled uniformly at random is invertible. There exist exact formulas to express this number, depending on the splitting behavior of the ideal generated by q in the ring R. For the fully splitting case, i.e., $q = 1 \bmod 2n$, it yields $p_{R_q} = (1 - 1/q)^n$, see for instance [38, Claim 2.25]. Assuming the hardness of M-LWE, it yields $p_{\mathsf{inv}} = p_{R_q} + \mathsf{negl}(\lambda)$. If not, an adversary against M-LWE could simply test a given instance for invertibility.

Remark 3.2. In its current presentation, all secret-public key pairs are using the same matrix $\mathbf{A}$. However, this is not required in our construction, and actually every party could use their own matrix. In that case, the public key would need to contain not only $\mathbf{t}$, but also $\mathbf{A}$, requiring larger storage. This, in turn, could be reduced by computing the matrix via some small seed and a pseudorandom function (as done in Dilithium). We highlight that using different matrices for different parties is not possible in all other proposed (non-interactive or interactive) aggregate signature schemes following the Fiat-Shamir with aborts paradigm. As they compute a linear combination of (parts of) the single signatures, every party must use the same $\mathbf{A}$. Using the same matrix $\mathbf{A}$ for every party leads to an instance of *multi-secret* M-LWE and its security is implied by standard M-LWE via some simple hybrid argument [40, Lemma 8].

Lemma 3.3 (Correctness). *The scheme* FSwA-SAS $=$ (Setup, Gen, SeqSign, SeqVerify) *as specified in Algorithm 2 is correct.*

Proof. We inductively show that, if an i-th so-far signature $\sigma_i = (\tilde{\mathbf{u}}_i, \mathbf{z}_1, \dots, \mathbf{z}_i)$ with $1 \le i < N$ is correct, the $(i+1)$-th signature $\sigma_{i+1} = (\tilde{\mathbf{u}}_{i+1}, \mathbf{z}_1, \dots, \mathbf{z}_{i+1})$ is also correct. As $\mathbf{z}_{i+1}$ has been correctly computed by the $(i+1)$-th signer, it yields $\bar{\mathbf{A}} \cdot \mathbf{z}_{i+1} - \mathbf{t}_{i+1} \cdot c_{i+1} = \mathbf{u}_{i+1}$. Hence, $\tilde{\mathbf{u}}_i$ can be recovered via $\tilde{\mathbf{u}}_{i+1} - \mathbf{u}_{i+1}$ and thus $\sigma_i = (\tilde{\mathbf{u}}_i, \mathbf{z}_1, \dots, \mathbf{z}_i)$ verifies by the induction hypothesis. Now, let's consider the base case $i = 1$. It yields $\|\mathbf{z}_1\|_\infty \le B$ and $\bar{\mathbf{A}} \cdot \mathbf{z}_1 = \mathbf{t}_1 \cdot c_1 + \tilde{\mathbf{u}}_1$ because of the linearity of matrix-vector multiplication over R_q. $\square$

Algorithm 2: Description of the FSwA-SAS Sequential Aggregate Signature

The challenge space is $\mathsf{Ch} := \{c \in R : \|c\|_\infty = 1 \wedge \|c\|_1 = \kappa\}$ and the message space is $M' = \{0,1\}^l$. The random oracle is $\mathsf{H} : \{0,1\}^* \to \mathsf{Ch}$. The starting point is $i = 1$. Let $L_0 = \varnothing$ and $\sigma_0 = (\mathbf{0}, \mathbf{0})$. Setup is as in Algorithm 1.

$\mathsf{Gen}(\bar{\mathbf{A}})$
1: $\mathbf{t} := \mathbf{0}$
2: **while** $\mathbf{t}$ has no invertible coefficient **do**
3:    $\mathbf{s} \xleftarrow{\$} S_\eta^{\ell+k}$
4:    $\mathbf{t} := \bar{\mathbf{A}}\mathbf{s} \bmod q$
5: $\mathsf{sk} := \mathbf{s}$
6: $\mathsf{pk} := \mathbf{t}$
7: **return** $(\mathsf{sk}, \mathsf{pk})$

$\mathsf{SeqSign}(\mathsf{sk}_i, m_i, L_{i-1}, \sigma_{i-1})$
1: $(\tilde{\mathbf{u}}_{i-1}, \mathbf{z}_1, \ldots, \mathbf{z}_{i-1}) := \sigma_{i-1}$
2: $\mathbf{s}_i := \mathsf{sk}_i$
3: $\mathbf{t}_i := \bar{\mathbf{A}}\mathbf{s}_i \bmod q$
4: $L_i := L_{i-1}\|(\mathbf{t}_i, m_i)$
5: $\mathbf{z}_i := \bot$
6: **while** $\mathbf{z}_i := \bot$ **do**
7:    $\mathbf{y}_i \leftarrow \mathscr{D}^{\ell+k}$
8:    $\mathbf{u}_i := \bar{\mathbf{A}}\mathbf{y}_i \bmod q$
9:    $\tilde{\mathbf{u}}_i := \tilde{\mathbf{u}}_{i-1} + \mathbf{u}_i \bmod q$
10:   $c_i := \mathsf{H}(\tilde{\mathbf{u}}_i, L_i, \mathbf{z}_{i-1})$
11:   $\mathbf{z}_i := c_i \cdot \mathbf{s}_i + \mathbf{y}_i$
12:   $\mathbf{z}_i := \mathsf{RejSamp}(\mathbf{z}_i, c_i \cdot \mathbf{s}_i)$
13: $\sigma_i := (\tilde{\mathbf{u}}_i, \mathbf{z}_1, \ldots, \mathbf{z}_i)$
14: **return** σ_i

$\mathsf{SeqVerify}(L_N, \sigma_N)$
1: $(\mathbf{t}_1, m_1)\|\ldots\|(\mathbf{t}_N, m_N) := L_N$
2: $(\tilde{\mathbf{u}}_N, \mathbf{z}_1, \ldots, \mathbf{z}_N) := \sigma_N$
3: $\mathbf{z}_0 := 1$
4: **if** $\exists i$ such that $\mathbf{t}_i$ has no invertible element **then**
5:    **return** 0
6: **for** $i = N, \ldots, 1$ **do**
7:    **if** $\|\mathbf{z}_i\|_2 > B$ **then**
8:       **return** 0
9:    $L_i := (\mathbf{t}_1, m_1)\|\ldots\|(\mathbf{t}_i, m_i)$
10:   $c_i := \mathsf{H}(\tilde{\mathbf{u}}_i, L_i, \mathbf{z}_{i-1})$
11:   $\mathbf{u}_i := \bar{\mathbf{A}}\mathbf{z}_i - c_i \mathbf{t}_i \bmod q$
12:   $\tilde{\mathbf{u}}_{i-1} := \tilde{\mathbf{u}}_i - \mathbf{u}_i \bmod q$
13: **if** $\tilde{\mathbf{u}}_1 = \mathbf{u}_1$ **then return** 1

3.2 Security Proof

We now prove the FH-UF-CMA security (as in Definition 2.3) of Algorithm 2. For completeness, we also sketch in the full version of this paper [11, App. A] the security of our scheme in a new model that has been introduced in [14], which we call the *partial-signature history-free* security model.

Theorem 3.4 (FH-UF-CMA security). *Let $k, \ell, n, q, \eta, \gamma, l \in \mathbb{N}$ such that n is a power of 2, q is prime and $\ell \geq k \cdot \frac{\log_2 q}{\log_2(2\gamma+1)} + O\left(\frac{\log_2 q}{\log_2(2\gamma+1)}\right)$. Let p_{inv} be the probability that $\bar{\mathbf{A}}\mathbf{s}$ has at least one invertible coefficient over R_q, where $\mathbf{s}$ is uniformly sampled from $S_\eta^{\ell+k}$ and $\bar{\mathbf{A}} = [\mathbf{A}|\mathbf{I}_k]$ with $\mathbf{A}$ is uniformly sampled from $R_q^{k \times \ell}$, respectively. If the signature scheme FSwA-S with message space $M = \{0,1\}^l$, as described in Algorithm 1, is UF-CMA secure, then is the sequential aggregate signature FSwA-SAS, as described in Algorithm 2, FH-UF-CMA secure. Concretely, for any adversary $\mathcal{A}$ against FH-UF-CMA security that makes at* *most Q_h queries to the random oracle H, Q_s queries to the OSeqSign oracle and outputs a forgery with a history of length N, there exists an adversary $\mathcal{B}$ against* UF-CMA *security such that*

$$\mathbf{Adv}_{\mathsf{FSwA\text{-}SAS}}^{\mathsf{FH\text{-}UF\text{-}CMA}}(\mathcal{A}) \leq \frac{\mathbf{Adv}_{\mathsf{FSwA\text{-}S}}^{\mathsf{UF\text{-}CMA}}(\mathcal{B})}{p_{\mathsf{inv}}} + O\left(\frac{Q_s(Q_h + Q_s)}{q^{nk/2}}\right)$$
$$+ \frac{(Q_h + Q_s + 1)^2}{|\mathsf{Ch}|} + \frac{Q_s(2Q_h + 1)}{2^l},$$

and $\mathrm{Time}(\mathcal{B}) = \mathrm{Time}(\mathcal{A}) + O((N + Q_h)k\ell t_{\mathsf{pmul}})$, *where* t_{pmul} *is the time of polynomial multiplication in* R_q.

Proof Sketch. Due to space limitations, definitions of technical lemmas, hardness assumptions, and the complete security proof are deferred to the full version [11]. We sketch the high level ideas of the reduction $\mathcal{B}$.

The random oracle and the signing oracle in the FH-UF-CMA game (resp. UF-CMA game) are denoted by H and OSeqSign (resp. H' and OSign). On receiving the public parameter $\mathbf{A}$ and the challenge public key $\mathbf{t}^*$, $\mathcal{B}$ checks that $\mathbf{t}^* \in R_q^k$ contains at least one invertible element. If so, $\mathcal{B}$ forwards $(\mathbf{A}, \mathbf{t}^*)$ to $\mathcal{A}$. OSeqSign replies to queries by asking OSign for a signature on uniformly chosen m and programs H such that it outputs c returned by the outer random oracle H'. Here we cannot just forward m_i to OSign, because it might be that a forgery submitted by $\mathcal{A}$ later reuses the same m_i. Then submitting a forgery w.r.t. m_i is not valid in the UF-CMA game, causing $\mathcal{B}$ to lose.

At the core of reduction is simulation of responses to H queries (obtained through a sequence of hybrid games). Suppose the message-key list L_N as part of the forgery tuple contains $(\mathbf{t}_i, m_i)$ such that $\mathbf{t}_i = \mathbf{t}^*$. Then $\mathcal{B}$ must have extracted the corresponding $\mathbf{u}_i$ and forwarded $\mathbf{u}_i$ to H' together with a random message m (Step 8 in [11, Alg. 3]), so that $(m, (\mathbf{u}_i, \mathbf{z}_i))$ qualifies as a valid forgery in the UF-CMA game. This extraction operation crucially makes use of $\mathbf{z}_{i-1}$ when $(\tilde{\mathbf{u}}_i, L_i, \mathbf{z}_{i-1})$ is queried to H. Intuitively, $\mathbf{z}_{i-1}$ serves as a look-up key to obtain the previous aggregated $\tilde{\mathbf{u}}_{i-1}$, which allows $\mathcal{B}$ to extract $\mathbf{u}_i - \tilde{\mathbf{u}}_i - \tilde{\mathbf{u}}_{i-1}$.

4   Performance Estimates and Comparison

4.1   Performance Estimates

In the following, we provide some concrete sample parameters and performance estimates for the FSwA-SAS from Sect. 3. We provide a formula for the compression rate τ and a lower bound for N, from which on our SAS signature σ_N is smaller than the trivial solution of concatenating N independent single signatures σ_{con}. The compression rate is defined as $\tau(N) = \frac{\mathsf{len}(\sigma_N)}{\mathsf{len}(\sigma_{\mathsf{con}})}$, where $\mathsf{len}(\cdot)$ denotes the bit size of an element.

A FSwA-SAS signature after N steps is given by $\sigma_N = (\tilde{\mathbf{u}}_N, \mathbf{z}_1, \ldots, \mathbf{z}_N)$ and the concatenation of N single FSwA-S signatures by $\sigma_{\mathsf{con}} = $

Table 1. Tipping point N_0 (where aggregate signatures start to be smaller than trivial concatenations) and some τ values of our FSwA-SAS (Algorithm 2) for the three different parameter sets of Dilithium.

Parameter	Level 2	Level 3	Level 5
q	8380417	8380417	8380417
n	256	256	256
(k,ℓ)	$(4,4)$	$(6,5)$	$(8,7)$
$B = \gamma - \kappa \cdot \eta$	130994	524092	524168
N_0	92	138	184
$\tau(200)$	0.9961	0.9985	0.9997
$\tau(250)$	0.9954	0.9979	0.9991
$\tau(500)$	0.9941	0.9966	0.9978
$\tau(1000)$	0.9934	0.9959	0.9971
$\tau(1,000,000)$	0.9927	0.9952	0.9965

$(c_1, \ldots, c_N, \mathbf{z}_1, \ldots, \mathbf{z}_N)$. Here, we have applied the standard trick to shorten FSwA-S signatures by replacing the commitment $\mathbf{u}$ by the challenge c. Thus, its compression rate is

$$\tau(N) = \frac{\mathsf{len}(\mathbf{u}) + N \cdot \mathsf{len}(\mathbf{z})}{N \cdot \mathsf{len}(c) + N \cdot \mathsf{len}(\mathbf{z})} = \frac{kn\lceil \log_2 q\rceil + N(k+\ell)n\lceil \log_2 B\rceil}{Nn + N(k+\ell)n\lceil \log_2 B\rceil} \qquad (1)$$

$$= 1 - \frac{1}{1 + (k+\ell)\lceil \log_2 B\rceil} + \frac{k\lceil \log_2 q\rceil}{N + N(k+\ell)\lceil \log_2 B\rceil}, \qquad (2)$$

where $\mathbf{u} \in R_q^k$, $\mathbf{z} \in S_B^{\ell+k}$ and $c \in \mathsf{Ch} := \{c \in R : \|c\|_\infty = 1 \wedge \|c\|_1 = \kappa\}$. An element $c \in \mathsf{Ch}$ can be represented by n bits [37, Sec. 5.3].

The SAS signature starts to be smaller than the concatenation as soon as $\mathsf{len}(\mathbf{u}) < N \cdot \mathsf{len}(c)$, hence, the tipping point is $N_0 > \frac{kn\lceil \log_2 q\rceil}{n} = k\lceil \log_2 q\rceil$.

In Table 1, we provide concrete numbers for N_0 and τ for different parameter sets. More precisely, we take the same parameters as the ones provided for different security levels of Dilithium, denoted by Level 2, Level 3 and Level 5. We can clearly see that in Eq. 2 the compression rate asymptotically goes towards $1 - 1/(1 + (k+\ell)\lceil \log_2 B\rceil)$ and for example for the Level 2 parameters of Dilithium this is exactly the rate 0.9927 that we observe at $N = 1,000,000$.

Unlike other proposals to aggregate lattice-based signatures (either interactive [9,16] or non-interactive [10]), the modulus q doesn't need to be increased in our construction. This is due to the fact that we aggregate over the $\mathbf{u}$-parts of the signature (which are uniform modulo q), and not over the $\mathbf{z}$-parts (which are small and hence the size of their sum increases).

We remark that the needed time to sequentially aggregate N signatures is linear in N. This is unavoidable when sequentially aggregating, as signing cannot be parallelized. As mentioned before, our sequential aggregate signature scheme FSwA-SAS can be seen as the vanilla version of Dilithium, ignoring several optimizations of the latter to further improve efficiency. Hence, the given numbers in Table 1 are only valid for our scheme and do not directly apply to Dilithium.

4.2   Comparison with SAS Using Trapdoors

In this part, we compare our lattice-based SAS scheme with existing proposals of lattice-based SAS schemes [20,45]. As summarized in the introduction, they can be seen as sequential aggregate versions of GPV-signatures. In the following, we take Falcon as a concrete instantiation for such a signature.

As for the FSwA-S signature, the size of a single GPV-signature can be significantly reduced by applying a small trick. More precisely, a Falcon signature of a message m is defined as $\sigma = (s_1, s_2, r)$, where $(s_1, s_2) \in R \times R$ is a pair of short polynomials such that $s_1 h + s_2 = H(m, r)$, where H is a random oracle, r is some randomness salt and $h \in R_q$ defines the public basis of the underlying NTRU lattice. Here, R is again the ring $\mathbb{Z}[X]/\langle X^n + 1 \rangle$ for n a power of 2 and q some prime integer. As s_2 is determined by m and s_1 (given the public key h and the salt r), one can omit s_2 in the signature and only set $\sigma = (s_1, r)$. Intuitively, this (roughly) halves the signature size.

Unfortunately, this trick can't be used in the (sequential) aggregate signature setting. Thus, when assessing the compactness of an aggregate signature, one has to compare it with the trivial concatenation of all single signatures, where each is only composed of the second polynomial. This fair comparison has been done in [20], but not in [45].

Recently, Espitau et al. [21] used exactly this trick to make Falcon signatures even shorter. By using elliptical instead of spherical Gaussians, the norm of s_1 can be made smaller. At the same time, the norm of s_2 gets larger, accordingly. Again, this trick does not apply to (sequential) aggregate signatures, as the total size of (s_1, s_2) stays the same.

In the existing SAS schemes that aggregate GPV-style signatures, the main bottleneck is that in the lattice setting there are no known trapdoor permutations. To circumvent this, they replace the trapdoor permutations from the RSA setting by so-called preimage sampleable trapdoor functions [27]. However, those functions have different domain Do and range Ra spaces. In the case of Falcon, the domain is given by R_q, i.e., any element $x \in$ Ra is of bit length $\mathsf{len}(x) = n\lceil \log_2 q \rceil$. The range, however, is given by pairs of polynomials of degree less than n with coefficients that come from a discrete Gaussian distribution. Naively, one could apply the Gaussian tail bound to argue that the coefficient's absolute values are bounded by some parameter β, and hence any element $y \in$ Do can be represented by a bit string of length $\mathsf{len}(y) = 2n\lceil \log_2 \beta \rceil$.[2] The specifications of Falcon [43, Sec. 3.11.2] propose a more intelligent representation of elements in the domain by using the Huffman encoding. Note that in both cases it yields $\mathsf{len}(\mathsf{Ra}) > \mathsf{len}(\mathsf{Do})$. As the output of one preimage sampleable function serves as the input for the next preimage sampleable function (of the same domain as before), existing constructions [20] pack as many bits

---

[2] This analysis has been done by [20].

of the so-far signature as they can into a vector that serves as the new input. The remaining bits ($b := \text{len}(\text{Ra}) - \text{len}(\text{Do})$) are stored in some vector α and appended (at every step) to the so-far signature and appear at the end in the final sequential aggregate signature. Clearly, they can't achieve a constant-size aggregate signature.

For concreteness, take the sample parameters of Falcon-512, i.e., $q = 12289$ and $n = 512$. It yields $\text{len}(\text{Do}) = n\lceil \log_2 q \rceil = 7168$ and $\text{len}(\text{Ra}) = 2 \cdot 5000$, and hence $b = 2832$.[3] The final sequential aggregate signature after N steps is given by $\sigma_N = (s_{N,1}, s_{N,2}, \alpha_1, \ldots, \alpha_{N-1}, r_1, \ldots, r_N)$, where $(s_{N,1}, s_{N,2}) \in$ Ra, $\text{len}(\alpha_i) = b$ and $\text{len}(r_i) = 328$ for $i \in [N]$. On the other side, the concatenation of N single Falcon signatures is given by $\sigma_{\text{con}} = (s_{1,1}, \ldots, s_{N,1}, r_1, \ldots, r_N)$, where we applied the 'omit the second polynomial' trick. Thus, its compression rate is given by

$$\tau(N) = \frac{\text{len}(s_1) + \text{len}(s_2) + (N-1) \cdot \text{len}(\alpha) + N \cdot \text{len}(r)}{N \cdot \text{len}(s_1) + N \cdot \text{len}(r)}$$

$$= \frac{2 \cdot 5000 + (N-1)b + N \cdot 328}{N \cdot 5000 + N \cdot 328} = 1 - \frac{5000 - b}{5000 + 328} + \frac{10000 - b}{N(5000 + 328)},$$

where $(s_1, s_2) \in$ Ra, α is the carry-over information and r the salt.

We provide the number N_0 and some τ values for the two different security parameters of Falcon in Table 2. From the equations above, we can clearly see that the compression rate asymptotically goes towards $1 - (5000 - b)/5328$, which is exactly the rate 0.5931 that we observe at $N = 1,000,000$.

In the following, we explain how the recent results of Espitau et al. [21] extremely leverage the benefit of GPV-style SAS. Overall, they significantly reduce the size of the trivial concatenation by replacing spherical Gaussians by elliptical Gaussians. The main idea is that there are now two different lengths, $\text{len}(s_1)$ and $\text{len}(s_2)$, where the first holds for s_1 and the latter for s_2 for every pair $(s_1, s_2) \in$ Ra. Whereas before both s_1 and s_2 followed a Gaussian distribution of width σ, they now introduce a distortion factor γ and set $\sigma_1 = \sigma/\gamma$ and $\sigma_2 = \sigma\gamma$. One can see that the total size of (s_1, s_2) is preserved as it yields $2\log_2 \sigma = \log_2 \sigma_1 + \log_2 \sigma_2$. If one takes $\gamma = 8$ (as suggested by Espitau et al. [21, Table 1]), one can see that $\text{len}(s_1) = 2952$, by again using the formulas of the Falcon specifications.

The compression rate in the elliptical Gaussian case is

$$\tau(N) = \frac{\text{len}(s_1) + \text{len}(s_2) + (N-1) \cdot \text{len}(\alpha) + N \cdot \text{len}(r)}{N \cdot \text{len}(s_1) + N \cdot \text{len}(r)}$$

$$= \frac{2 \cdot 5000 + (N-1)b + N \cdot 328}{N \cdot 2952 + N \cdot 328} = 1 - \frac{2952 - b}{2952 + 328} + \frac{10000 - b}{N(2952 + 328)},$$

where $(s_1, s_2) \in$ Ra, α is the carry-over information and r the salt. Here, we can clearly see that the compression rate asymptotically goes towards $1 - (2952 - b)/(2952 + 328)$, which is exactly the rate 0.9634 that we observe at $N = 1,000,000$.

---

[3] We compute $\text{len}(\text{Ra})$ as $2 \cdot (8 \cdot \text{sbytelen} - 328)$ with sbytelen taken from [43, Table 3.3].

Table 2. Tipping point N_0 (where aggregate signatures start to be smaller than trivial concatenations) and some τ values for SAS based on Falcon-512, for spherical and elliptical Gaussians (distortion factor $\gamma = 8$).

Parameter	Falcon-512 (spherical)	Falcon-512 (elliptical)
q	12289	12289
n	512	512
len(Do)	7168	7168
len(s_1)	5000	2952
len(s_2)	5000	7048
b	2832	2832
len(r)	328	328
N_0	4	60
$\tau(150)$	0.6021	0.9780
$\tau(200)$	0.5998	0.9743
$\tau(250)$	0.5985	0.9722
$\tau(500)$	0.5958	0.9678
$\tau(1000)$	0.5944	0.9656
$\tau(1,000,000)$	0.5931	0.9634

5 Attack on [45]

In the following, we identify an insecurity of the history-free sequential aggregate signature from Wang and Wu [45], published in the proceedings of the PROVSEC conference from 2019. More precisely, Lemma 5.1 gives an attack that breaks its security in the *history-free* setting. Intuitively, a history-free SAS does not require each signer i to take a so-far message-key pair list L_{i-1} as input. The winning condition in the HF-UF-CMA game (formally recalled in the full version [11, App. A.1]) is adjusted such that they win as long as the forged message associated with a challenge public key pk has never been queried to the signing oracle. From a high level perspective, the signing procedure of [45] closely follows SAS$_2$ of [26] in the so-called *ideal cipher model*, except one crucial optimization that reduces the signature size: it deterministically derives ephemeral randomness from the message to be signed and an aggregate so-far, whereas the original SAS$_2$ requires each signer to append fresh randomness to an aggregate signature. We observe this small change does not sufficiently randomize the scheme and leads to a variant of simple forgery attacks in the history-free setting, which were already pointed out by Brogle et al. [12, App. A] and Gentry et al. [26, Sec. 4.3]. Recall that their construction focuses on lattice signatures that follow the GPV-paradigm. For simplicity, we adapt in the rest of the section the syntax of Falcon, as in Sect. 5 of [45].

Let us (again) briefly recap how Falcon works. As before, we are working over the ring $R_q = \mathbb{Z}_q[X]/\langle X^n + 1\rangle$ for some power-of-two integer n and some prime

---

Algorithm 3: Description of History-Free SAS' [45]

The message space is $M = \{0,1\}^l$. The two random oracles are $\mathsf{H}_1, \mathsf{H}_2 \colon \{0,1\}^* \to \{0,1\}^\lambda$ and the ideal cipher is $\pi \colon \{0,1\}^* \times R_q \to R_q$ with inverse $\pi^{-1} \colon \{0,1\}^* \times R_q \to R_q$. Let $\sigma_0 = ((0,0),0)$.

$\mathsf{Gen}(1^\lambda)$

  1: $(h, T_h) \leftarrow \mathsf{TrapGen}(1^\lambda)$
  2: $\mathsf{pk} := h$
  3: $\mathsf{sk} := (h, T_h)$
  4: **return** $(\mathsf{pk}, \mathsf{sk})$

$\mathsf{SeqSign}(\mathsf{sk}_i, m_i, \sigma_{i-1})$

  1: $(x_{i-1}, \alpha_{i-1}) := \sigma_{i-1}$
  2: $(h_i, T_{h_i}) := \mathsf{sk}_i$
  3: $K_i := h_i \| \mathsf{H}_1(m_i) \| \mathsf{H}_2(\alpha_{i-1})$
  4: $(s_{i-1}, s'_{i-1}) := x_{i-1}$
  5: $\alpha_i := \alpha_{i-1} \| s'_{i-1}$
  6: $y_i := \pi^{-1}(K_i, s_{i-1}) \in R_q$
  7: $x_i \leftarrow \mathsf{SamplePre}(T_{h_i}, y_i) \in \mathsf{Do}$
  8: **return** $\sigma_i := (x_i, \alpha_i)$

$\mathsf{SeqVerify}(L_N, \sigma_N)$

  1: $\{(h_1, m1), \dots, (h_N, m_N)\} := L_N$
  2: $(x_N, \alpha_N) := \sigma_N$
  3: $(s'_1, \dots, s'_N) := \alpha_N$
  4: **for** $i = N, \dots, 1$ **do**
  5:      $\alpha_i = (s'_1, \dots, s'_i)$
  6:      $K_i = h_i \| \mathsf{H}_1(m_i) \| \mathsf{H}_2(\alpha_i)$
  7:      $s_{i-1} = \pi(K_i, f_{h_i}(x_i))$
  8:      $x_{i-1} = (s_{i-1}, s'_{i-1})$
  9:      **if** $x_{i-1} \notin \mathsf{Do}$ **then**
 10:          **return** 0
 11: **if** $x_0 = (0,0)$ **then**
 12:      **return** 1
 13: **else**
 14:      **return** 0

---

modulus q. The key generation algorithm invokes a function $\mathsf{TrapGen}$ which outputs a ring element $h \in R_q$, together with an associated trapdoor T_h. This trapdoor is needed to invert the function $f_h \colon \mathsf{Do} \subset R_q \times R_q \to R_q = \mathsf{Ra}$, where $f_h(s, s') = hs + s'$, with the help of a pre-image sampleable function $\mathsf{SamplePre}(T_h, \cdot)$. Without specifying the domain Do precisely, we remark that it only contains pairs of *short* ring elements. The trapdoor defines the secret key, whereas the element h defines the public key. In order to sign a message m, a random oracle $\mathsf{H} \colon \{0,1\}^* \to R_q$ is invoked on m which outputs a ring element in R_q. Then, the function $\mathsf{SamplePre}$ is used to compute $(s, s') \in \mathsf{Do}$ such that $f_h(s, s') = hs + s' = \mathsf{H}(m)$. The signature is defined as $x = (s, s')$. In order to verify a signature $x = (s, s')$ for a message m, one simply checks if $(s, s') \in \mathsf{Do}$ and if the equation $hs + s' = \mathsf{H}(m)$ holds in R_q.

The main idea of the history-free sequential aggregate signature SAS' by Wang and Wu [45] is to adapt the framework for trapdoor-permutation-based sequential aggregate signatures by Gentry et al. [26] to the lattice setting. As in [26], the scheme is making use of an ideal cipher. Additionally, and in contrast to [26], the scheme in [45] also uses two random oracles. As the domain $\mathsf{Do} \subset R_q \times R_q$ is larger than the range $\mathsf{Ra} = R_q$, we don't have trapdoor permutations in the case of lattice signatures, but only pre-image sampleable functions [27]. This is why a so-far signature σ_{i-1} has to be split into a first part (denoted by x_{i-1}) that contains the output of a previous call on $\mathsf{SamplePre}$, and a second part (denoted by α_{i-1}) which stores the information of the previous signatures that didn't fit into the sequential signing process. This part grows linearly in the number of signed messages.

We summarize the SAS' scheme of [45] in Algorithm 3 (assuming **enc** and **dec** are instantiated with simple split and merge functions as in [45, §5]) and present the attack in Lemma 5.1. The key idea of the attack is that an adversary can *predict* the one-time key K_i for a message m_i and public key h_i, even though K_i is randomized due to random oracles.

Lemma 5.1. *The history-free* SAS' *described in Algorithm 3 is not* HF-UF-CMA.

Proof. Let $\mathcal{A}$ be a PPT adversary. Their goal is to generate an aggregate signature σ^* for a list L^* claiming that signer i signed message m_i (where the public key h_i of signer i is the challenge public key pk given to $\mathcal{A}$) without having queried the signing oracle OSeqSign on input m_i. $\mathcal{A}$ proceeds as follows.

1 Compute $\sigma_{i-1} = (x_{i-1}, \alpha_{i-1})$ for arbitrary and self-chosen key pairs and messages, defining L_i. Let $(s_{i-1}, s'_{i-1}) := x_{i-1}$.
2 Choose some $m_i \neq \widetilde{m}_i$ and let $K_i := h_i||\mathsf{H}_1(m_i)||\mathsf{H}_2(\alpha_{i-1})$ and $\widetilde{K}_i := h_i||\mathsf{H}_1(\widetilde{m}_i)||\mathsf{H}_2(\alpha_{i-1})$.
3 Compute $\widetilde{s_{i-1}} := \pi(\widetilde{K}_i, \pi^{-1}(K_i, s_{i-1}))$.
4 Let $\widetilde{x_{i-1}} := (\widetilde{s_{i-1}}, s'_{i-1})$. Query OSeqSign with input $\widetilde{\sigma_{i-1}} := (\widetilde{x_{i-1}}, \alpha_{i-1})$ and $\widetilde{m}_i$.

The oracle responds with $\widetilde{\sigma}_i = (x_i, \alpha_i)$, such that (1) $\alpha_i = \alpha_{i-1}||s'_{i-1}$ and (2) $\pi(\widetilde{K}_i, f_{h_i}(x_i)) = \widetilde{s_{i-1}}$. The adversary outputs $\sigma^* := \widetilde{\sigma}_i$ and $L^* := L_i \cup \{(h_i, m_i)\}$. Recall from Step 3 that $\pi^{-1}(\widetilde{K}_i, \widetilde{s_{i-1}}) = \pi^{-1}(K_i, s_{i-1})$ while m_i has never been queried to OSeqSign. This is a valid forgery as $\pi(K_i, f_{h_i}(x_i)) = s_{i-1}$. □

Remark 5.2. An easy fix against this attack, at the expense of larger sequential aggregate signatures, is to make the key for the ideal cipher *unpredictable* for the adversary. One possible strategy is to freshly sample a truly random string $r \in \{0,1\}^\lambda$ and append it to the public key h and the message m to obtain the ideal cipher key $K := h||m||r$. Besides, this makes the use of the random oracles H_1 and H_2 superfluous. However, the randomness r has to be carried over throughout the sequential signing process, increasing the size of the final signature by $\lambda \cdot N$ bits, where N is the number of involved signatures. This strategy has already been formalized in the second construction of Gentry et al. [26, Sec. 4.2]. One may think that the scheme instantiated with Falcon can be patched by having each signer reject s_{i-1} with too large norm, since maliciously crafted $\widetilde{s_{i-1}}$ in the above attack is uniform in the range R_q of the ideal cipher π. This ad-hoc countermeasure however does not make the scheme provably secure: since the ideal cipher key $K_i = h_i||\mathsf{H}_1(m_i)||\mathsf{H}_2(\alpha_{i-1})$ can still be predicted by querying the random oracle, the ideal cipher table can be determined before any signing query is made, whereas the abort probability analysis in the simulation of aggregate signing oracle in the proof of [45, Theorem 1] crucially requires the input of the ideal cipher to be unpredictable. In fact, Gentry et al. instead suggest using *tag-based* trapdoor permutations [26, Sec. 4.3] as a provable secure way to maintain deterministic signing. It would be interesting to study whether this approach can be adapted to pre-image sampleable functions.

Acknowledgment. Katharina Boudgoust is supported by the Danish Independent Research Council under project number 0165-00107B (C3PO) as well as by the Protocol Labs Research Grant Program RFP-013. Akira Takahashi is supported by the Protocol Labs Research Grant Program PL-RGP1-2021-064. The authors are grateful for Claudio Orlandi for discussions in the earlier stages of this work. We thank our anonymous referees for their thorough proof reading and constructive feedback.

References

1. Ahn, J.H., Green, M., Hohenberger, S.: Synchronized aggregate signatures: new definitions, constructions and applications. In: Al-Shaer, E., Keromytis, A.D., Shmatikov, V. (eds.) ACM CCS 2010, pp. 473–484. ACM Press, October 2010. https://doi.org/10.1145/1866307.1866360
2. Albrecht, M.R., Cini, V., Lai, R.W.F., Malavolta, G., Thyagarajan, S.A.: Lattice-based SNARKs: publicly verifiable, preprocessing, and recursively composable. Cryptology ePrint Archive, Report 2022/941 (2022). https://eprint.iacr.org/2022/941
3. Bellare, M., Namprempre, C., Neven, G.: Unrestricted aggregate signatures. In: Arge, L., Cachin, C., Jurdziński, T., Tarlecki, A. (eds.) ICALP 2007. LNCS, vol. 4596, pp. 411–422. Springer, Heidelberg (2007). https://doi.org/10.1007/978-3-540-73420-8_37
4. Bellare, M., Neven, G.: Multi-signatures in the plain public-key model and a general forking lemma. In: Juels, A., Wright, R.N., De Capitani di Vimercati, S. (eds.) ACM CCS 2006, pp. 390–399. ACM Press, Oct/Nov 2006. https://doi.org/10.1145/1180405.1180453
5. Boldyreva, A.: Threshold signatures, multisignatures and blind signatures based on the gap-Diffie-Hellman-group signature scheme. In: Desmedt, Y.G. (ed.) PKC 2003. LNCS, vol. 2567, pp. 31–46. Springer, Heidelberg (2003). https://doi.org/10.1007/3-540-36288-6_3
6. Boldyreva, A., Gentry, C., O'Neill, A., Yum, D.H.: Ordered multisignatures and identity-based sequential aggregate signatures, with applications to secure routing. In: Ning, P., De Capitani di Vimercati, S., Syverson, P.F. (eds.) ACM CCS 2007, pp. 276–285. ACM Press, October 2007. https://doi.org/10.1145/1315245.1315280
7. Boneh, D., Gentry, C., Lynn, B., Shacham, H.: Aggregate and verifiably encrypted signatures from bilinear maps. In: Biham, E. (ed.) EUROCRYPT 2003. LNCS, vol. 2656, pp. 416–432. Springer, Heidelberg (2003). https://doi.org/10.1007/3-540-39200-9_26
8. Boneh, D., Kim, S.: One-time and interactive aggregate signatures from lattices. Preprint (2020). https://crypto.stanford.edu/~skim13/agg_ots.pdf
9. Boschini, C., Takahashi, A., Tibouchi, M.: MuSig-L: lattice-based multi-signature with single-round online phase. IACR Cryptol. ePrint Arch. 1036 (2022). Accepted at Crypto 22
10. Boudgoust, K., Roux-Langlois, A.: Compressed linear aggregate signatures based on module lattices. Cryptology ePrint Archive, Report 2021/263 (2021). https://eprint.iacr.org/2021/263
11. Boudgoust, K., Takahashi, A.: Sequential half-aggregation of lattice-based signatures. Cryptology ePrint Archive, Report 2023/159 (2023). https://eprint.iacr.org/2023/159

12. Brogle, K., Goldberg, S., Reyzin, L.: Sequential aggregate signatures with lazy verification from trapdoor permutations. In: Wang, X., Sako, K. (eds.) ASIACRYPT 2012. LNCS, vol. 7658, pp. 644–662. Springer, Heidelberg (2012). https://doi.org/10.1007/978-3-642-34961-4_39

13. Chalkias, K., Garillot, F., Kondi, Y., Nikolaenko, V.: Non-interactive half-aggregation of EdDSA and variants of Schnorr signatures. In: Paterson, K.G. (ed.) CT-RSA 2021. LNCS, vol. 12704, pp. 577–608. Springer, Cham (2021). https://doi.org/10.1007/978-3-030-75539-3_24

14. Chen, Y., Zhao, Y.: Half-aggregation of Schnorr signatures with tight reductions. In: Atluri, V., Di Pietro, R., Jensen, C.D., Meng, W. (eds.) ESORICS 2022, Part II. LNCS, vol. 13555, pp. 385–404. Springer, Heidelberg (2022). https://doi.org/10.1007/978-3-031-17146-8_19

15. Cramer, R.: Modular design of secure yet practical cryptographic protocols. Ph.D. thesis, CWI, Amsterdam, November 1996. https://ir.cwi.nl/pub/21438

16. Damgård, I., Orlandi, C., Takahashi, A., Tibouchi, M.: Two-round n-out-of-n and multi-signatures and trapdoor commitment from lattices. In: Garay, J.A. (ed.) PKC 2021. LNCS, vol. 12710, pp. 99–130. Springer, Cham (2021). https://doi.org/10.1007/978-3-030-75245-3_5

17. Devadas, L., Goyal, R., Kalai, Y., Vaikuntanathan, V.: Rate-1 non-interactive arguments for batch-NP and applications. Cryptology ePrint Archive, Paper 2022/1236 (2022). https://eprint.iacr.org/2022/1236

18. Doröz, Y., Hoffstein, J., Silverman, J.H., Sunar, B.: MMSAT: a scheme for multimessage multiuser signature aggregation. Cryptology ePrint Archive, Report 2020/520 (2020). https://eprint.iacr.org/2020/520

19. Drijvers, M., Edalatnejad, K., Ford, B., Kiltz, E., Loss, J., Neven, G., Stepanovs, I.: On the security of two-round multi-signatures. In: 2019 IEEE Symposium on Security and Privacy, pp. 1084–1101. IEEE Computer Society Press, May 2019. https://doi.org/10.1109/SP.2019.00050

20. El Bansarkhani, R., Buchmann, J.: Towards lattice based aggregate signatures. In: Pointcheval, D., Vergnaud, D. (eds.) AFRICACRYPT 2014. LNCS, vol. 8469, pp. 336–355. Springer, Cham (2014). https://doi.org/10.1007/978-3-319-06734-6_21

21. Espitau, T., Tibouchi, M., Wallet, A., Yu, Y.: Shorter hash-and-sign lattice-based signatures. IACR Cryptol. ePrint Arch. 785 (2022). Accepted at Crypto 22

22. Fiat, A., Shamir, A.: How to prove yourself: practical solutions to identification and signature problems. In: Odlyzko, A.M. (ed.) CRYPTO 1986. LNCS, vol. 263, pp. 186–194. Springer, Heidelberg (1987). https://doi.org/10.1007/3-540-47721-7_12

23. Fischlin, M., Lehmann, A., Schröder, D.: History-free sequential aggregate signatures. In: Visconti, I., De Prisco, R. (eds.) SCN 2012. LNCS, vol. 7485, pp. 113–130. Springer, Heidelberg (2012). https://doi.org/10.1007/978-3-642-32928-9_7

24. Fleischhacker, N., Simkin, M., Zhang, Z.: Squirrel: efficient synchronized multisignatures from lattices. IACR Cryptol. ePrint Arch. 694 (2022)

25. Fukumitsu, M., Hasegawa, S.: A lattice-based provably secure multisignature scheme in quantum random oracle model. In: Nguyen, K., Wu, W., Lam, K.Y., Wang, H. (eds.) ProvSec 2020. LNCS, vol. 12505, pp. 45–64. Springer, Cham (2020). https://doi.org/10.1007/978-3-030-62576-4_3

26. Gentry, C., O'Neill, A., Reyzin, L.: A unified framework for trapdoor-permutation-based sequential aggregate signatures. In: Abdalla, M., Dahab, R. (eds.) PKC 2018. LNCS, vol. 10770, pp. 34–57. Springer, Cham (2018). https://doi.org/10.1007/978-3-319-76581-5_2

27. Gentry, C., Peikert, C., Vaikuntanathan, V.: Trapdoors for hard lattices and new cryptographic constructions. In: Ladner, R.E., Dwork, C. (eds.) 40th ACM STOC, pp. 197–206. ACM Press, May 2008. https://doi.org/10.1145/1374376.1374407

28. Gentry, C., Ramzan, Z.: Identity-based aggregate signatures. In: Yung, M., Dodis, Y., Kiayias, A., Malkin, T. (eds.) PKC 2006. LNCS, vol. 3958, pp. 257–273. Springer, Heidelberg (2006). https://doi.org/10.1007/11745853_17

29. Güneysu, T., Lyubashevsky, V., Pöppelmann, T.: Practical lattice-based cryptography: a signature scheme for embedded systems. In: Prouff, E., Schaumont, P. (eds.) CHES 2012. LNCS, vol. 7428, pp. 530–547. Springer, Heidelberg (2012). https://doi.org/10.1007/978-3-642-33027-8_31

30. Hohenberger, S., Koppula, V., Waters, B.: Universal signature aggregators. In: Oswald, E., Fischlin, M. (eds.) EUROCRYPT 2015. LNCS, vol. 9057, pp. 3–34. Springer, Heidelberg (2015). https://doi.org/10.1007/978-3-662-46803-6_1

31. Kondi, Y., Shelat, A.: Improved straight-line extraction in the random oracle model with applications to signature aggregation. Cryptology ePrint Archive, Paper 2022/393 (2022). https://eprint.iacr.org/2022/393

32. Langlois, A., Stehlé, D.: Worst-case to average-case reductions for module lattices. Des. Codes Cryptogr. **75**(3), 565–599 (2015). https://doi.org/10.1007/s10623-014-9938-4

33. Lu, S., Ostrovsky, R., Sahai, A., Shacham, H., Waters, B.: Sequential aggregate signatures and multisignatures without random oracles. In: Vaudenay, S. (ed.) EUROCRYPT 2006. LNCS, vol. 4004, pp. 465–485. Springer, Heidelberg (2006). https://doi.org/10.1007/11761679_28

34. Lysyanskaya, A., Micali, S., Reyzin, L., Shacham, H.: Sequential aggregate signatures from trapdoor permutations. In: Cachin, C., Camenisch, J.L. (eds.) EUROCRYPT 2004. LNCS, vol. 3027, pp. 74–90. Springer, Heidelberg (2004). https://doi.org/10.1007/978-3-540-24676-3_5

35. Lyubashevsky, V.: Fiat-Shamir with aborts: applications to lattice and factoring-based signatures. In: Matsui, M. (ed.) ASIACRYPT 2009. LNCS, vol. 5912, pp. 598–616. Springer, Heidelberg (2009). https://doi.org/10.1007/978-3-642-10366-7_35

36. Lyubashevsky, V.: Lattice signatures without trapdoors. In: Pointcheval, D., Johansson, T. (eds.) EUROCRYPT 2012. LNCS, vol. 7237, pp. 738–755. Springer, Heidelberg (2012). https://doi.org/10.1007/978-3-642-29011-4_43

37. Lyubashevsky, V., et al.: Crystals-dilithium. Technical report, National Institute of Standards and Technology (2020). https://csrc.nist.gov/projects/post-quantum-cryptography/post-quantum-cryptography-standardization/round-3-submissions

38. Lyubashevsky, V., Peikert, C., Regev, O.: A toolkit for ring-LWE cryptography. In: Johansson, T., Nguyen, P.Q. (eds.) EUROCRYPT 2013. LNCS, vol. 7881, pp. 35–54. Springer, Heidelberg (2013). https://doi.org/10.1007/978-3-642-38348-9_3

39. Micali, S., Ohta, K., Reyzin, L.: Accountable-subgroup multisignatures: extended abstract. In: Reiter, M.K., Samarati, P. (eds.) ACM CCS 2001, pp. 245–254. ACM Press, November 2001. https://doi.org/10.1145/501983.502017

40. Micciancio, D.: On the hardness of learning with errors with binary secrets. Theory Comput. **14**(1), 1–17 (2018). https://doi.org/10.4086/toc.2018.v014a013

41. Neven, G.: Efficient sequential aggregate signed data. In: Smart, N. (ed.) EUROCRYPT 2008. LNCS, vol. 4965, pp. 52–69. Springer, Heidelberg (2008). https://doi.org/10.1007/978-3-540-78967-3_4

42. Nick, J., Ruffing, T., Seurin, Y.: MuSig2: simple two-round Schnorr multisignatures. In: Malkin, T., Peikert, C. (eds.) CRYPTO 2021. LNCS, vol. 12825, pp. 189–221. Springer, Cham (2021). https://doi.org/10.1007/978-3-030-84242-0_8

43. Prest, T., et al.: FALCON. Technical report, National Institute of Standards and Technology (2020). https://csrc.nist.gov/projects/post-quantum-cryptography/post-quantum-cryptography-standardization/round-3-submissions

44. Schnorr, C.P.: Efficient signature generation by smart cards. J. Cryptol. **4**(3), 161–174 (1991). https://doi.org/10.1007/BF00196725

45. Wang, Z., Wu, Q.: A practical lattice-based sequential aggregate signature. In: Steinfeld, R., Yuen, T.H. (eds.) ProvSec 2019. LNCS, vol. 11821, pp. 94–109. Springer, Cham (2019). https://doi.org/10.1007/978-3-030-31919-9_6

46. Waters, B., Wu, D.J.: Batch arguments for NP and more from standard bilinear group assumptions. In: Dodis, Y., Shrimpton, T. (eds.) CRYPTO 2022, Part II. LNCS, vol. 13508, pp. 433–463. Springer, Heidelberg (2022). https://doi.org/10.1007/978-3-031-15979-4_15

Oblivious Extractors and Improved Security in Biometric-Based Authentication Systems

Ivan De Oliveira Nunes[1]([⊠]), Peter Rindal[2], and Maliheh Shirvanian[3]

[1] Rochester Institute of Technology, Rochester, USA
ivanoliv@mail.rit.edu
[2] Visa Research, Palo Alto, USA
[3] Netflix Inc., Los Gatos, USA

Abstract. We study the problem of biometric-based authentication with template privacy. Typical schemes addressing this problem, such as Fuzzy Vaults (FV) and Fuzzy Extractors (FE), allow a server, *aka* Authenticator, to store "random looking" Helper Data (HD) instead of biometric templates in clear. HD hides information about the corresponding biometric while still enabling secure biometric-based authentication. Even though these schemes reduce the risk of storing biometric data, their correspondent authentication procedures typically require sending the HD (stored by the Authenticator) to a client who claims a given identity. The premise here is that only the identity owner – i.e., the person whose biometric was sampled to originally generate the HD– is able to provide the same biometric to reconstruct the proper cryptographic key from HD. As a side effect, the ability to freely retrieve HD, by simply claiming a given identity, allows invested adversaries to perform offline statistical attacks (a biometric analog for dictionary attacks on hashed passwords) or re-usability attacks (if the FE scheme is not reusable) on the HD to eventually recover the user's biometric template.

In this work, we develop Oblivious Extractors: a new construction that allows an Authenticator to authenticate a user requiring neither the user to send a biometric to the Authenticator, nor the server to send the HD to the client. Oblivious Extractors provide concrete security advantages for biometric-based authentication systems. From the perspective of secure storage, an oblivious extractor is as secure as its non-oblivious fuzzy extractor counterpart. In addition, it enhances security against aforementioned statistical and re-usability attacks. To demonstrate the construction's practicality, we implement and evaluate a biometric-based authentication prototype using Oblivious Extractors.

1 Introduction

Biometric-based authentication systems have grown in popularity especially due to their ease of use and potential for increased security. In contrast with other traditional modes/factors of authentication, such as passwords/PINs ("something you know") and physical authentication tokens ("something you have"),

© The Author(s), under exclusive license to Springer Nature Switzerland AG 2024
G. Tsudik et al. (Eds.): ESORICS 2023, LNCS 14344, pp. 290–312, 2024.
https://doi.org/10.1007/978-3-031-50594-2_15

biometrics do not require additional burden (e.g., to memorize a password or carry an authentication token around) on the users. Biometrics are a reasonably unique part of the user ("something you are") and therefore their usage for authentication is convenient.

Despite its tangible advantages, the use of biometrics for authentication also introduces unique security challenges. The storage of stable biometrics (stable refers to not changing much through the life-span of an individual – e.g., fingerprints, iris scans) also represents a privacy and security risk. In contrast with passwords/PINs or authentication tokens, stable biometrics cannot be changed. Therefore, leakage of biometric templates is a serious threat which unfortunately has already happened in large scale [1]. In addition, typical measures used to protect the confidentiality of passwords/PINs, such as salted hashing, are not applicable to biometrics. This is because all biometric samples are always slightly different from each other, due to noise and imperfections in the biometric sensor hardware and sensing process. Consequently, even with small noises, cryptographic hashes applied to biometrics result is completely different digests, making the matching of hashed templates infeasible.

Fuzzy Extractors (FE) [2] are cryptographic constructions that allow provably secure biometric storage and matching of noisy samples, thus enabling secure biometric-based authentication with biometric template confidentiality (we overview a concrete construction for a Fuzzy Extractor in Sect. 2.2). In a nutshell, an FE embeds a reference Biometric Template (BT) and a cryptographic key $(\mathcal{K})$ into random looking helper data (HD). Given that BT has sufficient entropy, then computation of $\mathcal{K}$ from HD is intractable. However, during authentication, if one is able to provide BT' such that BT' is "close enough" (within some configurable distance function and threshold) to BT, BT' can be used in conjunction with HD to reconstruct $\mathcal{K}$, i.e., the same cryptographic key chosen during HD's generation. This property, in turn, allows a client and a server to agree upon a common secret if and only if the client is able to provide the same biometric registered to the server during user enrollment. Figure 1 depicts a typical user authentication procedure utilizing FE-generated HD.

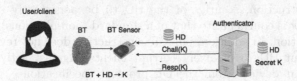

Fig. 1. Typical authentication using FE

As shown in Fig. 1, a user who wishes to authenticate starts by claiming an identity (e.g., a user ID). Authenticator then sends back to the user the HD corresponding to this identity. To reconstruct the authentication key $(\mathcal{K})$ from HD, the user provides a new sample of its own biometric. If the matching succeeds, $\mathcal{K}$ is reconstructed and can be used in a standard challenge-response authentication protocol. By authenticating in this way, the user's BT is never visible to the Authenticator.

We argue that this authentication approach has an intrinsic problem: anyone is able to retrieve HD by simply claiming an identity. The ability to retrieve HD allows invested attackers to perform offline attacks on HD to recover $\mathcal{K}$ and/or BT, e.g., [3,4]. These attacks are analogous to a password-server sending the hashed password to a client which in turn would allow them to mount an offline dictionary attack.

Another possible attack is based on the lack re-usability of several practical FE schemes [5–8]. If an FE is not reusable, anyone able to obtain two (or more) instances of the scheme, i.e, HD_1 and HD_2, generated using the same template BT, is able to reconstruct BT in clear. In this case, an attacker could claim the user's identity at two different service providers, $Authenticator_1$ and $Authenticator_2$, to learn BT.

Considering these problems, this work proposes a construction for Oblivious Extractors (OEs). OEs enjoy the same security guarantees as typical fuzzy extractors with respect to secure storage of biometric templates. However, the HD generation algorithm is constructed such that the corresponding authentication phase does not require the Authenticator to send the HD to the client nor the client to send the BT to the Authenticator. In such a setting, offline statistical attacks are not possible and online attacks can be throttled by having Authenticator to limit the maximum number of authentication attempts per user per time interval. Conversely, re-usability attacks are only possible if two or more enterprise databases (that store two or more HD for the same user) are simultaneously breached, given that the HD is no longer revealed during authentication. As it will become clear in Sect. 2.2, generic secure 2-party computation techniques (e.g., garbled circuits) are too heavyweight for authentication using FE. Instead, we propose a protocol, specific to FE-based authentication, based on cheaper and widely used primitives, namely oblivious programmable PRFs [9] and polynomial secret-sharing [10]. In summary we make the following contributions:

- We define a primitive called Oblivious Extractor (OE) along with a corresponding definition for its ideal functionality $\mathcal{F}_{OE}$.
- We present an OE construction and analyze it, showing that it fulfills $\mathcal{F}_{OE}$. In our construction, security of the HD to be persistently stored by the Authenticator is equivalent to that of a standard (non-oblivious) fuzzy extractor construction. In addition, our OE construction does not reveal any information about HD to passively corrupt clients. Against actively malicious clients – that deviate from the OE protocol specification – we show that leakage about HD is minimal and, whenever it happens, adversarial behavior on the client's part is detected by the Authenticator with high probability. We stress that even in these cases no information is leaked about BT itself, but only about HD. Upon detection, Authenticator can take further measures, e.g., reporting and blacklisting the malicious client.
- We implement an OE-based biometric authentication system using human fingerprints. We evaluate our prototype considering computation and communication requirements. Furthermore, we show that our scheme does not affect the accuracy of the underlying biometric matching.

1.1 Design Principles

In addition to the principal goal of providing better security via oblivious evaluation of the authentication function, our construction and system are designed with a set of secondary goals in mind. We believe that, by attaining this goals, our construction will have better usability and deployability, in addition to increased security:

(1) Biometric Agnostic: While some FE constructions work for specific distance functions (that are used to compare the features extracted from specific biometrics), our scheme can be used with any distance function. Compatibility with any distance function makes the scheme flexible and applicable to different types of biometrics, as long as the their features can be encoded into a metric space. This encoding has been demonstrated for several popular types of biometric [11–13] with high matching accuracy.

(2) No Trusted Hardware Requirements: Several commercial biometric-based authentication systems, especially those deployed on smart-phones (e.g. FIDO [14]), rely on trusted hardware to perform the biometric matching. In these systems, the reference BT is stored in clear by the trusted hardware module and the matching is performed also in clear during authentication. The assumption is that the trusted hardware can not be breached and that its manufacturer can be trusted not to violate the user's privacy. We emphasize that, in a setting where this assumption is acceptable, our scheme can be used seamlessly as an additional layer of security. Furthermore, hardware-based approaches do not scale to settings with multiple users and multiple authentication entry points, such as enterprise settings (see below). In these settings our construction might be especially applicable.

(3) Stateless Authentication Terminals: Ideally, the system should not require that users always use the same (or a restricted set of) device(s) to authenticate. Consider, for example, the setting where Authenticator is a company that uses biometric-based authentication to grant physical access to its buildings and the users are the employees. Users must be able to authenticate from different physical entry points. This requires authentication terminals (i.e, the sensor devices that sample the biometric during authentication) to be stateless. Otherwise, only terminals persistently storing the authentication meta-data would be able to authenticate the corresponding user.

2 Preliminaries

2.1 Biometric Template Matching

A Biometric Template (BT) is composed of features identifying the individual. In biometric matching applications (e.g., biometric-based authentication), first a BT is sampled and stored. This initial process is referred to as *enrollment*. Later, when a matching is required, the same feature extraction procedure is applied to collect a second BT'. This new BT' is compared to the one stored and, if their similarity exceeds a pre-defined threshold, the matching succeeds. We represent a BT corresponding to a user as a vector:

$$BT = (b_1, ..., b_m) \in \mathbb{D}^m \tag{1}$$

where $b_1, ..., b_m \in \mathbb{D}$ are data points in some set $\mathbb{D}$ representing details of U's biometric. For instance, in fingerprints, each $b_i \in BT$ typically represents the location and orientation of one of the fingerprint's *minutiae*. *Minutiae*, in turn, are regions in the fingerprint image in which fingerprint lines merge and/or split. In turn, each *minutiae* point is encoded as:

$$b_i = (x_i, y_i, \theta_i), \tag{2}$$

where, $\mathbb{D} = \mathbb{Z}^3$, $x_i, y_i \in \mathbb{Z}$ are Cartesian coordinates and $\theta_i \in \mathbb{Z}$ is the angle representing the orientation of the minutiae b_i. Similar encoding techniques can be used for other biometric modalities [11–13], such as iris scans and faces. We note that other representations are possible, for example, BT could be an embedding output by an appropriately trained neural network.

Fuzzy Vaults (FV) and more generally Fuzzy Extractors (FE) are cryptographic schemes that use an input BT to generate Helper Data (HD). HD encodes a secret k. It is hard to recover the secret k or BT from HD, unless prompted with BT' close/similar enough to the original BT used to generate the HD. It then follows that even if the HD is leaked or made public, the BT is also hard to recover. Section 2.2 overviews a concrete example of such a construction and discusses its shortcoming against offline attacks.

2.2   Fuzzy Vault Scheme

A Fuzzy Vault (FV) [15] is a practical construction designed to work with BTs that are represented as unordered sets of data points as shown earlier, in Eq. 1. The scheme has two components:

1. the points $BT = (b_1, ..., b_m)$ are obfuscated by shuffling them with n random points, $r_1, ..., r_n \in \mathbb{D}$. The security of the scheme relies on the difficulty of identify the b_i points given the set $\{b_1, ..., b_m, r_1, ..., r_n\}$ (in random order). For this to hold it is critical that the r_i values are sampled from the same distribution as the b_i values.
2. a mechanism to recover a hidden key k if the user can identify exactly $d + 1$ of b_i points (see the definition of parameter d below).

In more detail, the FV scheme consists of two algorithms, (FV_{GEN}, FV_{OPEN}). The former is defined as a randomized algorithm

$$FV_{GEN}(BT, k) : \mathbb{D}^m \times \mathbb{F}_p \to \mathcal{H} \tag{3}$$

which takes U's biometric template BT as input, along with a key k sampled from large prime field $\mathbb{F}_p$. It outputs an instance of the helper data HD $\in \mathcal{H}$.

The scheme is further parameterized by some public parameters $m, n, d, w, p \in \mathbb{Z}$ and requires that $\forall_{i,j} : \text{dist}(b_i, b_j) > w$ for distinct $i, j \in [m]$ where dist is some distance function (i.e., some metric). This is because points within distance w are in some sense considered to be the same across different impressions of the same biometric.

The generation algorithm samples n so called "chaff points" $r_1, ..., r_n \in \mathbb{D}$ from the same distribution as $b_i \in \text{BT}$. Let $\widetilde{\text{BT}} = (\tilde{b}_1, ..., \tilde{b}_{m+n}) \in \mathbb{D}^{m+n}$ consist of the b_i, r_i points in a random order. As with the b_i values, the r_i values are sampled such that $\forall i, j : \text{dist}(\tilde{b}_i, \tilde{b}_j) > w$ for distinct i, j.

The algorithm then samples a random polynomial $P \in \mathbb{F}[x]$ of degree $d < m$ such that $P(0) = k$, similar to the polynomial in a Shamir secret sharing scheme, where k is the secret being shared. For $\tilde{b}_i \in \widetilde{\text{BT}}$, if $\tilde{b}_i \in \text{BT}$ then let[1] $v_i = P(\tilde{b}_i)$ and otherwise uniformly sample $v_i \leftarrow \mathbb{F}$. Finally, the algorithm outputs the helper data as $\text{HD} = ((\tilde{b}_1, v_1), ..., (\tilde{b}_{m+n}, v_{m+n}), H(k)) \in \mathcal{H}$ where $\mathcal{H} = (\mathbb{D} \times \mathbb{F})^{m+n} \times \{0,1\}^{\kappa}$ and $H : \{0,1\}^* \to \{0,1\}^{\kappa}$ is a random oracle.

The FV_{OPEN} algorithm can then recover the key $k \in \mathbb{F}_p$ given a close enough biometric BT' and HD:

$$\text{FV}_{OPEN}(\text{BT}', \text{HD}) : \mathbb{F}_p \tag{4}$$

Close enough here means that more than d points (where d is the polynomial degree) in BT's are less than w apart from points in the original BT, i.e.:

$$|\{b_i' \in \text{BT}', s.t. \exists [b_j \in \text{BT} \wedge \text{dist}(b_i', b_j) \leq w]\}| > d. \tag{5}$$

As such, the parameters w, d control how similar the two biometrics must be for it to be considered a match and therefore also control the trade-off between false positive/negative rates during authentication.

In FV_{OPEN}, first the set $S = \{(b_i', v_i) \in \text{HD s.t. } \exists [b_j \in \text{BT}' \wedge \text{dist}(b_i', b_j) \leq w]\}$ is computed. Then for each subset S' of S s.t. $|S'| = d + 1$, the algorithm interpolates the points $(\tilde{b}_i, v_i) \in S'$ to obtain the polynomial $P(x)$. If $H(P(0)) = H(k)$, then the algorithm will output $P(0)$. If no such subset S' exists, then the algorithm outputs $\perp$.

If we apply this scheme in the traditional manner, the overall protocol then consists of:

1. **Enrollment** – the user U enrolls by interacting with a trusted enrollment device. The enrollment device generates fresh $k \leftarrow \mathbb{F}_p$ and HD from U's BT and sends $k \leftarrow \mathbb{F}_p$ and $\text{HD} \leftarrow \text{FV}_{GEN}(\text{BT}, k)$ to the Authenticator. Authenticator persistently stores this data associated with the newly created user identity.

2. **Authentication** – Later, when a client wishes to authenticate as U, the Authenticator will send the associated HD back to the client. The authentication will succeed if the client can successfully answer a challenge which requires knowledge of the key k, e.g., standard challenge-response protocols based on the encryption of nonces.

---

[1] Here, we assume that $\tilde{b}_i \in \mathbb{D}$ can be interpreted as an element of $\mathbb{F}$. This can be achieved by defining an injective or random function $\phi : \mathbb{D} \to \mathbb{F}$ and defining $v_i = P(\phi(\tilde{b}_i))$.

Ideally, this protocol would achieve the following security guarantees. When the user U enrolls, the helper data HD reveals no information about BT to Authenticator (nor any other entities aside from the trusted enrollment device itself – e.g., a biometric sensor). Similarly, the online authentication procedure would not reveal information about the newly supplied biometric BT' to Authenticator, apart from whether it matched or not.

One method of formalizing this is with an indistinguishably based security definition. For example, given two distinct biometrics (BT_1, BT_2), the adversary should not be able to distinguish the distribution of $HD_1 \leftarrow FV_{GEN}(BT_1, k)$ from $HD_2 \leftarrow FV_{GEN}(BT_2, k)$. However, these two are trivial to distinguish since the FV_{OPEN} algorithm must be efficient. Moreover, BT_1, BT_2 are directly contained in HD_1, HD_2 respectively. And yet, given that there are sufficiently many chaff points, HD does to some extent obfuscate the original biometric BT. In particular, this allows a weaker security notion. Let us assume that all $BT = (b_1, ..., b_m)$ are generated such that each b_i is sampled iid from some distribution $\mathcal{D}$ over $\mathbb{D}$. Then it follows that the adversary has a negligible in k probability of outputting k given HD alone. To see why, recall that $HD = ((\tilde{b}_1, v_1), ..., (\tilde{b}_{m+n}, v_{m+n}), H(k))$ and since all b_i, r_j are iid (by assumption), so are all of the $\tilde{b}_i$ values. As such, the adversary is tasked with identifying a set of m-out-of-$(m+n)$ points $(\tilde{b}_i, v_i)$ which lay on a degree-d polynomial where each $\tilde{b}_i \leftarrow \mathcal{D}$ and all but $m-d$ v_i values are uniform in $\mathbb{F}$. For appropriately set parameters, this problem is conjectured to be intractable [15].

We note however that, in practical deployments, biometrics might have significantly less entropy than the computational security parameter k [3,4]. As such, statistical guessing of the biometric template BT could allow for an adversary to recover k from HD with noticeable probability. Moreover, since HD contains a hash of the k (and $m > d+1$ points that lie in the polynomial), the adversary can perform such an attack in an offline setting (after receiving HD in clear) and check whether or not the correct k (or the correct polynomial) was obtained.

Definition 1 (Fuzzy Vault (FV) Syntax)
A Fuzzy Vault is defined as $FV = (FV_{GEN}, FV_{OPEN}, \Phi)$, *where* Φ *is a set of parameters*
$\Phi = (m, n, d, \mathbb{F}, M, dist, w)$:
- *m is the number of biometric features, referred to as* **minutiae** *points.*
- *n is the number of randomizing features, referred to as* **chaff** *points.*
- *d is a polynomial degree;*
- *$\mathbb{F}_p$ is a prime field with size $p - 1$;*
- *M is a metric space;*
- *$dist$ is some distance function defined over M;*
- *w is a distance threshold;*
FV_{GEN} *and* FV_{OPEN} *are algorithms:*

- FV_{GEN}:
  - *Inputs: k and BT, s.t., $k \in \mathbb{F}_p$.*
  - *Output: HD*
- FV_{OPEN}:
  - *Inputs: HD and BT'_U*
  - *Output: $k' \in \mathbb{F}_p$.*

Definition 2 (FV-Completeness)
FV $= (\text{FV}_{GEN}, \text{FV}_{OPEN}, \Phi)$ *is complete with* (w, d)-*fuzziness if for every possible* k *and every pair* BT, BT$'$ *such that,*

$$|\{b_i' \in \text{BT}', s.t. \exists [b_j \in \text{BT} \wedge dist(b_i', b_j) \leq w]\}| > d, \tag{6}$$

it holds that:
$$\text{FV}_{OPEN}(\text{FV}_{GEN}(k, \text{BT}), \text{BT}') = k \tag{7}$$

with overwhelming probability.

Definition 3 (FV-Security)
FV $= (\text{FV}_{GEN}, \text{FV}_{OPEN}, \Phi)$ *is* p-*secure if a Probabilistic Polynomial Time (P.P.T.) adversary with access to* HD, *where:*
$$\text{HD} = \text{FV}_{GEN}(k, \text{BT}) \tag{8}$$

is able to guess either, BT *or* k, *with success probability of at most* p.

Looking forward, we will mitigate this attack by not sending the helper data HD to the each user U' that claims an identity and requests to authenticate. This limits the exposure of HD to only the Authenticator. Since in many cases we can assume the Authenticator is honest, they will not perform such brute force attacks (this assumption is equivalent to that in current password-based authentication servers storing salted hashes). However, in the unlikely event that they do become corrupted, e.g. hacked, then the adversary is still tasked with performing a potentially expensive offline attack in order to recover the underlying biometric BT and key k. This can give the organization the crucial amount of time to mitigate the potential fallout.

The syntax for the FV construction and respective notation are summarized in Definition 1. Definitions 2 and 3 state FV's completeness and security guarantees.

2.3 Oblivious Programmable PRF

An Oblivious Programmable PRF (OPPRF) is a two party functionality consisting of a sender and receiver. The functionality is shown in Fig. 2. The sender has a set of input pairs $(y_1, z_1), ..., (y_n, z_n)$ with distinct y_i. The functionality samples a key k such that $F_k(y_i) = z_i$ and at all other input points it outputs a random value. The receiver on input points $x_1, ..., x_n$ then obtains $F_k(x_i)$ for all i.

Parameters: There are two parties, a sender with input $L = \{(y_1, \tilde{y}_1), ..., (y_{n_y}, \tilde{y}_{n_y})\}$ where $y_i \in \mathbb{F}, \tilde{y} \in \{0,1\}^{\text{out}}$ and a receiver with a set $X \subseteq \mathbb{F}$ where $|X| = n_x$.

Functionality: Upon input (sender, sid, L) from the sender and (receiver, sid, X) from the receiver, the functionality samples a random function $F : \mathbb{F} \rightarrow \{0,1\}^{\text{out}}$ such that $F_k(y) = \tilde{y}$ for each $(y, \tilde{y}) \in L$ and sends $X' := \{F_k(x) \mid x \in X\}$ to the receiver.
Subsequently, upon input (sender, sid, y) from the sender, the functionality returns $F(y)$ to the sender.

Fig. 2. Ideal functionality $\mathcal{F}_{\text{opprf}}$ of Oblivious Programmable PRF.

This functionality can be realized from a standard OPRF along with polynomial interpolation or a similar encoding method. Loosely speaking, the sender samples a normal OPRF key k and sends the minimum degree polynomial P such that $P(y_i) = z_i - F_k(y_i)$. The parities compute the final output as $F_k(x) + P(x)$ where F_k is evaluated via the OPRF protocol. See [9] for efficient constructions.

As we explain in Sect. 3, our OE construction leverages OPPRFs to enable efficient oblivious computation of FV_{OPEN} while keeping input BT' private to the Client and input HD private to Authenticator.

3   Oblivious Extractor: Intuition

Our Oblivious Extractor (OE) construction is based on a few simple observations that we discuss through the rest of this section. This section omits some protocol details in order to convey the general idea. Detailed specifications are presented in Sect. 4.

First, we note that *checking if two points are within a certain distance threshold from each other* is equivalent to *generating the set of all points that are within a certain threshold from the first point and checking for existence of the second point in the generated set*. More formally, for any distance function dist and two elements a and b in $\mathbb{F}$:

$$\text{dist}(a,b) < w \equiv |\{b\} \cap A| = 1 \quad \text{where} \quad A = \{a_i \mid \text{dist}(a,a_i) < w\} \tag{9}$$

This is because set A contains all points in $\mathbb{F}$ that are sufficiently close (given threshold w and metric dist) to a, therefore, b must exist in set A if it is within this proximity. We note that this approach works because $\mathbb{F}$ is discrete (as opposed continuous spaces such as real numbers in $\mathbb{R}$), and $|A| = O(\text{poly}(k))$ is reasonably small for our application.

This observation allows us to use an oblivious set membership operation to obliviously perform distance-based matching of each $b'_1, ..., b'_m$ in BT' to each $\tilde{b}_1, ..., \tilde{b}_{m+n}$ in HD. This matching is equivalent to the one performed in clear by the regular FV. More importantly, Eq. 9 is independent of the particular dist used for the feature matching. Thus, distance matching based on oblivious set membership testing can in principle be used to match biometric features of multiple biometric modalities, e.g., iris scans, faces, etc.

In addition to minutiae-to-minutiae matching, the regular FV also verifies if at least d minutiae are matched correctly, where d is the threshold defined by the polynomial degree (see Sect. 2 for details). To achieve the same property, our scheme relies on Shamir's secret sharing.

In a nutshell, the modified HD is generated by $OE_{GEN}(BT, k)$ via the following process:

1. OE_{GEN} generates $\widetilde{BT} = (\tilde{b}_1, ..., \tilde{b}_{n+m})$ where a random subset of $\widetilde{BT}$ is in BT while the remainder are random chaff points. As such, it obfuscates the original BT in the exact same way as in the original FV scheme.
2. For each chaff point, uniformly sample an associated random pair $(x_i, y_i) \leftarrow \mathbb{F}^2$. For each $\tilde{b}_j \in \widetilde{BT}$ that is a real *minutiae* in BT, sample a random point

that lies on a $d-1$ degree polynomial P (i.e., $P(x_j) = y_j$ for all j such that $\tilde{b}_j \in$ BT) and require that $P(0) = k$.

That is, every pair (x_j, y_j) that is associated with a real biometric point from BT forms one Shamir secret share of k.

3. Output HD $= (\widetilde{\mathsf{BT}}, X, Y, H(k))$ as the helper data, where $\widetilde{\mathsf{BT}} = (\tilde{b}_1, ..., \tilde{b}_{n+m})$, $X = [x_1, ..., x_{n+m}]$ and $Y = [y_1, ..., y_{n+m}]$. By construction, it holds that for all $j \in [n+m]$ such that $\tilde{b}_j \in$ BT, $y_j = P(x_j)$. In other words, every position j that is associated with a real *minutiae* is also associated with a secret share of k. On the other hand, positions that contain chaff points are associated to random (x', y') pairs that do not lie in the polynomial P.

Given HD and a sufficiently similar biometric BT$' = \{b'_1, ..., b'_m\}$, k can be recovered by interpolating the correct (x_j, y_j) pairs which are identified based on the condition that $\mathsf{dist}(b'_j, \tilde{b}_i) < w$ for some $b'_j \in$ BT$'$. Given that there may be several degree at most $d-1$ polynomials which fit this criteria, the correct one can be identified by requiring $H(P(0)) = H(k)$.

We note, however, that there are several challenges when converting this basic idea into an oblivious protocol. First is how to evaluate the distance function. A *naïve* method would be for all $O(m^2)$ possible i, j to check if $\mathsf{dist}(b'_j, \tilde{b}_i) < w$ either using a generic 2PC scheme or via the idea of directly turning $\tilde{b}_i$ into a set A and performing a set membership test (e.g., using off-the-shelf protocols for private set operations). Though possible, this would be very inefficient.

Secondly, it is critical that the Client does not learn if the binary result of $\mathsf{dist}(b'_j, \tilde{b}_i) < w$ since this would leak if some information about each $\tilde{b}_i$ in HD. For example, a Client could query the Authenticator many times and enumerate all elements in $A = \{a_j \mid \mathsf{dist}(a_j, \tilde{b}_i) < w\}$ and therefore learn a $\tilde{b}_i$ exactly.

We address both of these issues simultaneously with the use of an OPPRF. The idea is that, during authentication, Authenticator will sample an OPPRF key k' such that for all $i \in [n+m]$ and $a_j \in \{a_j \mid \mathsf{dist}(a_j, \tilde{b}_i) < w\}$, the OPPRF outputs $F_{k'}(a_j) = (x_i, y_i)$. Recall that when the Client evaluates the OPPRF, they will receive either the programmed (x_i, y_i) value if they input one of the corresponding a_j values or they will receive a uniformly random (x', y') pair.

Let us assume that BT, BT$'$ are not similar. Therefore the Client learns at most d pairs (x_i, y_i) which correspond to the actual biometric BT. These (x_i, y_i) pairs lay on the degree d polynomial P while all others are uniformly random. Recall that it takes $d+1$ pairs to reconstruct P and therefore the key $k = P(0)$ remains uniformly distributed in the view of the Client, since they are lacking at least one pair. Moreover, the Client can not distinguish if they obtained a programmed point (x_i, y_i) or a uniformly random point (x', y') since both are distributed uniformly random. Critically, we require that the Client only inputs $b'_j \in$ BT$'$ values which are at least distance $2w$ apart to ensure that no two b'_j fall into the same set $A = \{a_j \mid \mathsf{dist}(a_j, \tilde{b}_i) < w\}$.

Now consider the case in which BT, BT$'$ are similar. From the OPPRF evaluation, the Client will learn at least $d+1$ pairs (x_i, y_i) which indeed lay on the degree d polynomial P (in addition to possibly some points that do not lay in P, because there might a small number of chaff points that are coincidentally close to some of the points in BT′). As such, the client can use the obtained set of points to try to interpolate all subsets of $d + 1$ points, resulting in a degree d polynomial P' at each attempt. For each interpolation, the client checks if $H(P'(0)) = H(k)$. If so, it learns that $P = P'$ and outputs $k = P'(0)$.

4 Oblivious Extractor in Detail

4.1 Definitions

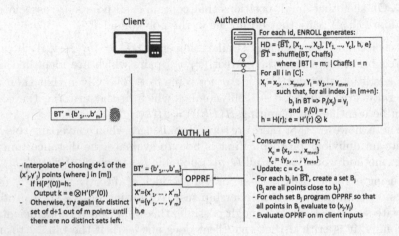

Fig. 3. OE authentication combining HD, OPPRF-based set membership test, and secret sharing.

OE consists of two sub-protocols: ENROLL and AUTH. Each sub-protocol instance involves a Client and an Authenticator. Figure 4 presents OE ideal functionality $\mathcal{F}_{OE}$. It answers to two queries, modeling the ideal behavior of sub-protocols ENROLL and AUTH.

A query to ENROLL is accompanied by a reference biometric template BT (obtained securely during initial user enrollment) and parameter c, determining the maximum number of authentication attempts possible within the life-time of the particular HD to be generated. It outputs a user ID i to Client and generates a user credential in the system, represented by the Client's ID i, an associated HD and c, to be stored by Authenticator. The ideal functionality records BT, and HD and k, computed using FV′.Gen(BT).

A query to AUTH is initiated by Client and must contain a claimed user ID i and corresponding input biometric template BT′. The functionality verifies if there exists a registered user with ID i and if the limit c' of authentication attempts for that particular user has not been exceeded. If these checks succeed, the query returns k if BT' is sufficiently close to the reference BT and $\perp$ otherwise. k and BT used in this step are the same recorded during ENROLL for ID i. Every AUTH query decrements associated c to record the authentication attempt. Figure 3 shows illustrates the OE authentication protocol, with a detailed construction in Fig. 5.

Parameters: An Authenticator and one or more clients, each generically denoted as Client. A FV scheme described in Section 2.2.

Functionality: Initialize id := 0. The functionality answers the following queries.

1. Upon receiving $(\text{ENROLL}, \text{BT}, \text{HD}, k, c)$ from Client, where $(\text{HD}, k) \leftarrow \text{FV}'.\text{Gen}(\text{BT}, k, c)$, record the tuple $(id, c, \text{BT}, \text{HD}, k)$. FV$'$ is defined as the procedure which computes HD in Figure 5 (step f of Enroll). Output (i) to Client and (i, c, HD) to Authenticator. Update id as id := id $+ 1$.

2. Upon receiving $(\text{AUTH}, i, \text{BT}')$ from Client and (AUTH, i) from Authenticator, if there exists a tuple $(i, c, \text{BT}, \text{HD}, k)$ for i such that

$$c > 0 \wedge |\{b'_i \in \text{BT}', s.t. \exists [b_j \in \text{BT} \wedge \text{dist}(b'_i, b_j) \leq w]\}| > d,$$

where d is the polynomial degree of HD, then output (k, BT^*) to Client where BT^* are these d' points in BT$'$ which are similar to BT. Otherwise output $\bot$ to Client. Update $c = c - 1$.

Fig. 4. Ideal oblivious extractor functionality $\mathcal{F}_{\text{OE}}$.

4.2   Construction

This section presents an OE construction fulfilling $\mathcal{F}_{\text{OE}}$ (Fig. 4) in the honest-but-curious model. The protocol is specified in Fig. 5.

Public parameters include two random oracles H and H' and the FV scheme described in Sect. 2.2, including the FV parameters themselves (e.g., a metric dist, a distance threshold w, polynomial degree d, etc.). Before any sub-protocol interactions, Authenticator initializes a monotonically increasing counter $id := 0$ representing unique IDs assigned to users upon successful enrollment.

ENROLL:

The first part of the enrollment protocol (up to the generation of $\widetilde{\text{BT}}$) remains similar to the regular FV scheme, discussed in Sect. 2.2. BT is sampled from the user yielding m biometric data points, sufficiently distant from each other by threshold $2w$ for chosen metric dist. A set of n chaff points are randomly sampled following the same distribution as real biometric points and also obeying the sparsity restriction (for threshold $2w$ and dist). The set of real biometric data points and chaffs are shuffled according to permutation π selected uniformly at random. The resulting shuffled list of pairs is denoted $\widetilde{\text{BT}}$.

Following generation of $\widetilde{\text{BT}}$, ENROLL will sample randomness $r \leftarrow_\$ \mathbb{F}$ and c random polynomials defined over $\mathbb{F}$. The independent/constant term in all c random polynomials is set to r (i.e., for $j \in [c]$, $P_j(0) = r$). Each P_j is used as an independent instance of a Shamir secret sharing scheme to sample m shares of r (in the form $(x \leftarrow_\$ \mathbb{F}, P_j(x))$). For each P_j, two lists X_j and Y_j are created using the m shares. X_j and Y_j are constructed such that if index i of $\widetilde{\text{BT}}$ (after shuffling) contains a real biometric data point (i.e., $\tilde{b}_i \in \text{BT}$), then $Y_{j,i} = P_j(X_{j,i})$ – where $X_{j,i}$ and $Y_{j,i}$ are used to denote the i-th element of X_j and Y_j, respectively. For all other indices, elements of X_j and Y_j are selected independently, uniformly at random. The HD is then given to (and persistently stored by) Authenticator composed of $\widetilde{\text{BT}}$, $X := (X_1, ..., X_c)$, $Y := (Y_1, ..., Y_c)$, $h := \text{H}(r), e := \text{H}'(r) \oplus k$. As it will become clear, a pair of lists $X_{c'}, Y_{c'}$ is consumed on each AUTH interaction.

Parameters: An Authenticator and one or more clients, each generically denoted as Client. An FV scheme described in Section 2.2 (and associated parameters, e.g., dist, m, n, w, d, etc). Two random oracles $H : \mathbb{F} \to \{0,1\}^\kappa$, $H' : \mathbb{F} \to \{0,1\}^\kappa$.
Protocol: Authenticator will initialize id := 0.

[**Enroll**] Upon the command (ENROLL, BT, k, c) from Client, the Client performs

(a) [**Parse**] Parse $(b_1, ..., b_m) = $ BT where $b_i \in \mathbb{D}$. Abort if for distinct $i, i' \in [m]$, $\text{dist}(b_i, b_{i'}) > w$.

(b) [**Add Chaff**] Sample $b_{m+1}, ..., b_{m+n} \leftarrow \mathcal{D}$ s.t. for all distinct $i, i' \in [m+n]$, $\text{dist}(b_i, b_{i'}) > w$.

(c) [**Shuffle**] Sample a random permutation $\pi : [m+n] \to [m+n]$ and define $\widetilde{BT} := (\tilde{b}_1, ..., \tilde{b}_{m+n})$ where $\tilde{b}_i := b_{\pi(i)}$.

(d) [**Secret Share**] Sample $r \leftarrow \mathbb{F}$. For $j \in [c]$, sample a random degree d polynomial $P_j \in \mathbb{F}[x]$ such that $P_j(0) = r$.

(e) [**Shares**] Sample $X_j \leftarrow \mathbb{F}^{n+m}$ and define $(x_{j,1}, ..., x_{j,m+n}) := X_j$. For $j \in [c]$, $i \in [n+m]$, if $\tilde{b}_i \in $ BT then define $y_{j,i} := P_j(x_{j,i})$. Otherwise define $y_{j,i} \leftarrow \mathbb{F}$. Let $Y_j := (y_{j,1}, ..., y_{j,m+n})$. Define $X := (X_1, ..., X_c)$ and $Y := (Y_1, ..., Y_c)$.

(f) [**Output**] Send HD := $(\widetilde{BT}, X, Y, h, e)$ to Authenticator where $h := H(r)$, $e := H'(r) \oplus k$.

Authenticator receives HD and sends id back. Authenticator records the tuple (id, c, HD) and increments id as id := id + 1.

[**Auth**] Upon the command (AUTH, id', BT') from Client, Authenticator looks up the tuple (id', c', HD). If none exists, Authenticator sends back $\bot$. Otherwise let $(\widetilde{BT}, X, Y, h, e) := $ HD and $X, Y \in \mathbb{F}^{c' \times (m+n)}$. If $c' = 0$, send $\bot$ to Client and abort. Otherwise:

(a) [**Program OPPRF**] Let $(\tilde{b}_1, ..., \tilde{b}_{m+n}) := \widetilde{BT}$. Define $L \in (\mathbb{F} \times \mathbb{F}^2)$ where for each $i \in [m+n]$ and $b \in \{b \in \mathbb{D} \mid \text{dist}(\tilde{b}_i, b) < w\}$, it holds that $(b, (X_{c',i}, Y_{c',i})) \in L$.

(b) [**Invoke OPPRF**] Authenticator and Client invoke $\mathcal{F}_{OPPRF}$ where Authenticator is the sender with input L. The Client inputs BT' = $(b'_1, ..., b'_m)$, restricted that for distinct $i, i' \in [m]$, $\text{dist}(b'_i, b'_{i'}) > w$, and receives $(x'_i, y'_i) = F(b'_i) \in \mathbb{F}^2$ for $i \in [m]$.

(c) [**Remove Row**] Authenticator updates X, Y by removing rows $X_{c'}$, $Y_{c'}$ and $c' := c' - 1$.

(d) [**Interpolate**] Authenticator sends h and e to Client. For each $S_j \subset [m]$ of size $d + 1$, Client defines the degree d polynomial $P_{S_j} \in \mathbb{F}_p[x]$ s.t. $P_S(x'_i) = y'_i$ for all $i \in S_j$.

(e) [**Output**] If there exists a S_j s.t. $H(P_{S_j}(0)) = h$, then Client outputs $k := H'(P_{S_j}(0)) \oplus e$. Otherwise Client outputs $\bot$.

Fig. 5. Oblivious extractor protocol Π_{OE}.

Given random shuffling of $\widetilde{BT}$, sufficiently large number of chaff points, and indistinguishability between Shamir secret shares and random elements in $\mathbb{F} \times \mathbb{F}$ (present in X and Y), HD produced by OE hides BT and k from Authenticator. More formally, FV security can be reduced to OE security.

AUTH:

To authenticate, a user initiates an interaction with Authenticator by claiming an identity id' and locally sampling BT' := $(b'_1, ..., b'_m)$ at the Client machine. Authenticator looks up HD based on claimed id'. Authenticator also checks if the maximum number of authentication attempts allowed for the lifetime of the associated HD has not been exceeded, aborting otherwise. In practical systems that employ throttling to prevent online guessing, an additional check should occur to determine if the maximum number of attempts within a pre-defined time-window (e.g., 10 attempts per day) has been exceeded. This step is omitted from the protocol for simplicity. If the aforementioned checks succeed, Authenticator will initiate an instance of the oblivious biometric matching phase, based on BT' (in possession of Client) and $HD_{id'} = (\widetilde{BT}, X, Y, h, e)$ (stored by Authenticator associated to id').

The c'-th instance of AUTH consumes list $X'_c \in X$ and list $Y'_c \in Y$. To prevent information leakage across multiple executions of AUTH, each X'_c and Y'_c pair is only used once, hence the cap c on the number of AUTH interactions per HD. For each element $\tilde{b}_i \in \widetilde{\mathsf{BT}}$ – including both chaff and real biometric points (recall that Authenticator cannot distinguish between them) – Authenticator generates the set of all points in $\mathbb{F}$ that are sufficiently close to $\tilde{b}_i$, i.e., all $b \in \mathbb{F}$ such that $\mathrm{dist}(b, \tilde{b}_i) < w$. All such b close to $\tilde{b}_i$ are associated to the same pair $(X_{c',i}, Y_{c',i})$ and added to a list L, where each $l \in L$ is in the form $(b, (X_{c',i}, Y_{c',i}))$, i.e., $l \in (\mathbb{F}, \mathbb{F}^2)$. As a result, L contains all points b in $\mathbb{F}$ that are sufficiently close to any $\tilde{b}_i \in \widetilde{\mathsf{BT}}$. By construction (recall ENROLL sub-protocol), all $\tilde{b}_i \in \mathsf{BT}$ and close enough points appear in L associated to a secret share of randomness r. On the other hand, all $\tilde{b}_i \notin \mathsf{BT}$ (i.e., chaff points) and close enough points are associated to random pairs in $(\mathbb{F} \times \mathbb{F})$.

To perform oblivious authentication, Client and Authenticator invoke $\mathcal{F}_{\mathsf{OPPRF}}$ on their respective inputs: $\mathsf{BT}' = (b'_1, ..., b'_m)$ and L. For each $b'_u \in \mathsf{BT}'$, if b'_u is sufficiently close to any point in $\widetilde{\mathsf{BT}}$ (real or chaff), it also exists in L, thus Client receives an associated pair $(X_{c',v}, Y_{c',v})$, for some index $v \in [m+n]$. If b'_u is in fact close to a real biometric data point from BT (the reference template used to construct HD in ENROLL), it is also the case that $Y_{c',v} = P'_c(X_{c',v})$, i.e., Client receives a secret share of randomness r (recall from ENROLL that $P'_c(0) = r$). If b'_u does not exist in L (b'_u is close neither to real biometric data points nor chaff points), $\mathcal{F}_{\mathsf{OPPRF}}$ returns a random element from $(\mathbb{F} \times \mathbb{F})$.

Given the degree d of P'_c, if at least $d+1$ points in BT' are sufficiently close to points in BT, Client retrieves enough shares of r to reconstruct k. Most importantly, if less than $d+1$ points are sufficiently close to points in the original BT, Client cannot distinguish any of the received elements from random in $(\mathbb{F} \times \mathbb{F})$, irrespective of whether each element was generated as a share of r, as random pair during construction of $X_{c'}$ and $Y_{c'}$) (see ENROLL), or as a result of $\mathcal{F}_{\mathsf{OPPRF}}$ evaluation on an element that does not exist in L and thus has not been programmed by the OPPRF. It follows that, if Client fails to authenticate, nothing is learned by Client about BT or HD. At the same time, BT and BT' are hidden from Authenticator.

Upon completion of AUTH, Authenticator decrements c'. This assures that fresh $X_{c'}$ and $Y_{c'}$ are used in different AUTH sessions even with the same HD, preventing leakage/linkability across multiple/successive authentication attempts.

4.3 OE Security Analysis and Actively Malicious Cases

OE security analysis and the discussion on how to handle actively malicious Client and Authenticator are deferred to Appendix A due to space constraints.

5 Implementation and Evaluation

5.1 Fingerprint Pre-processing and Parameters

Pre-processing and extraction procedures generate a biometric template BT from a fingerprint image. As discussed in Sect. 2, each data point in BT is the position and orientation (x_i, y_i, θ) of a fingerprint minutiae. To extract the BT we use NIST Biometric Image Software (NBIS) [16]. NBIS returns a set of identified minutiae points with corresponding confidence levels. From NBIS output, we select 20 points with the highest confidence and encode them as data points in $\mathbb{F}$. Following the FV implementation guidelines from [17] and [18], in our prototype, we implement OE using the following set of public parameters $\Phi = (m, n, d, \mathbb{F}, \mathbb{M}, \mathbb{w})$:

– Number of minutiae $m = 20$; Number of chaff points $n = 200$; Polynomial degree $d = 9$; $\mathbb{F}$ is a prime field with prime of at least 128 bits; Distance threshold $w = 20$.

In addition, the distance function (dist) used to compare fingerprint features (based on the empirical characterization from [18]) and generate the sets is given by:

$$D(b_i, b_j) = \sqrt{(x_i - x_j)^2 + (y_i - y_j)^2} \quad + \quad 0.2 \times min(|\theta_i - \theta_j|, 360 - |\theta_i - \theta_j|) \tag{10}$$

The OE polynomial degree is set to 9 (also based on [18]). Finite field polynomial operations were implemented using the Number Theory Library (NTL) [19].

In **Auth**, points are matched from HD based on their distance to minutiae points in the new template BT$'$ sampled from the user. Similar to [18], we the distance function between $p_i \in$ HD and $p_j' \in$ BT$'$ defined as in Eq. 10. These parameters must be empirically calibrated to yield the best accuracy results. We rely on these parameters based the work by Nandakumar et al. [18], that focuses on biometric matching accuracy with FVs. To improve accuracy results for noisy fingerprint readings before extracting the template, during the biometric sampling,

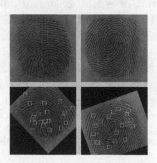

Fig. 6. Fingerprint pre-processing and identified minutiae

we also run the fingerprint pre-alignment algorithm from [20]. Figure 6 illustrates the result of the template extraction for two pre-aligned fingerprint images. White squares highlight the $n = 20$ minutiae points detected in these fingerprints.

Remark: *We implement our own* BT *extraction to have a fully working prototype and report on its accuracy. We stress that there is no difference in the accuracy of oblivious versus regular* FVs*, which is determined by the underlying biometric pre-processing techniques. These techniques are orthogonal and not affected by our work.*

5.2   Performance Analysis

Setup: Results presented in this section reflect measurements performed on an Intel Core i7-3770 octa-core CPU @3.40 GHz, with 16 GB of RAM, running Linux (Ubuntu 18.04LTS). Client and Authenticator were implemented as independent processes communicating though TCP sockets. An artificial delay of 10 milliseconds is introduced in order to simulate a typical communication delay for a local area network (LAN).

Protocol	Avg. Time	Std. Dev.
OE_{GEN} (User Enrollment)	945.9 ms	24.1 ms
OE_{OPEN} (User Authentication)	1.2 s	0.1 s

(a) Total execution times for OE protocols

Operation	Avg. Time	Std. Dev.
OPPRF (Authenticator)	340 ms	71 ms
Network delay (2 LAN RTTs)	20 ms	none
Poly. Interpolations (Client)	876 ms	26.2 ms

(b) Break-down of operations in OE_{OPEN}

Polynomial Degree (d)	GAR	FAR
5	97.70%	21.93%
6	93.96%	11.48%
7	89.65%	4.84%
8	86.20%	2.04%
9	80.17%	0
10	70.68%	0

(c) OE_{OPEN} accuracy results

Fig. 7. OE evaluation results: computational cost and prototype accuracy

Figure 7 presents the evaluation results. Our protocol has two main costs, the OPPRF and the Client performing interpolation. We implement the OPPRF based on the protocol of [21] with optimizations provided by [22,23]. The resulting overhead is that a OPPRF with n programmed points has communication overhead of $32 \times 1.3 \times n$ bytes plus a small setup cost of [23]. Using the parameter specified above this results in programming approximately $n = 154000$ points with an overhead 5.6 MB per authentication and requires 0.34 s. The successive interpolation operations to reconstruct k take on average 876 ms for the selected parameters.

Accuracy of the underlying biometric matching is not affected by our use-case. Improving its accuracy is an orthogonal effort. Nonetheless, for completeness, we report on the accuracy considering the implementation used in our prototype. Similar accuracy analysis for biometric matching using fuzzy vaults (also considering other biometrics modalities) can be found in [11,17,18]. We report on our prototype's accuracy considering metrics for:

- **Genuine Acceptance Rate (GAR):** Percentage of biometric samples correctly matched to other samples acquired from the same biometric.
- **False Acceptance Rate (FAR):** Percentage of biometric samples incorrectly matched to any sample not acquired from the same biometric.

We conducted accuracy experiments using FVC2000 publicly available[2] fingerprint database. FVC2000 includes multiple fingerprint images (10 different noisy images of each fingerprint) acquired using 4 types of low-cost biometric sensors. As discussed in Sect. 2.2, the polynomial degree allows configuring the number of matching data points in two biometric samples necessary to consider that the samples belong to the same user. Therefore, accuracy results are presented as a function of FV polynomial degree in Table 7c. Per Table 7c, an ideal choice would be degree 9 with zero false acceptances. The same degree results in GAR of 80%, meaning that 1 out of 5 times a genuine user would be rejected and required to attempt authentication again.

6   Related Work

Fuzzy Vaults (FVs) [15] were developed (and implemented in [18]) to ensure privacy of reference biometric templates (BTs). An FV generates random looking data from BTs, only storing such data (HD) in the back-ends, and is still able to authenticate users from HD. Subsequently, the notion of Fuzzy Extractors (FE) was formalized, and derived from secure sketches [24], and also applied to biometrics [25]. Most FV/FE provide statistical security. Computational FE schemes were only recently introduced [26]. These computational FE schemes rely on hardness of the Learning With Errors (LWE) problem. FE re-usability was identified as an important issue to ensure security for repeated usage with the same biometric. Re-usability enables one to extract multiple HD from the same biometric without leaking any additional information. Not every FE/FV can be reused and still ensure security (illustrated in [7,8]). In fact, from the two Helper Data HD-1 and HD-2, created with two instances of the scheme on the same biometric, an attacker can learn the original biometric inputs. New (indistinguishability based) definitions for re-usability were presented [5] and theoretical analysis demonstrated that the computational FE scheme in [26] is not (weakly or strongly) reusable.

Secure two/multi-party computation (2PC/MPC) protocols enable mutually distrusting parties to compute functions of their private inputs, while guaranteeing output correctness and input privacy, against misbehaving parties. Prior work [27–29] used 2PC/MPC to verify whether a biometric exists in a database, a problem commonly referred to as "identification". We target the related yet different problem of oblivious authentication with template privacy "vis-a-vis" Authenticator, which demands not only oblivious fuzzy matching of templates, but also subsequent key agreement for cryptographic operations (e.g., challenge-response protocols, decryption).

---

[2] Database available at: http://bias.csr.unibo.it/fvc2000/.

The problem of strengthening password-based user authentication has also been well-studied under the common umbrella of Password-Authenticated Key Agreement (PAKE) protocols [30,31]. Since they work with passwords, PAKE protocols typically rely on Client and Authenticator sharing and storing the exact same secret (either in clear or hashed form). Therefore, they are not appropriate for authentication using biometrics, in which Authenticator and Client inputs are always slightly different. The notion of fuzzy PAKE (fPAKE) was introduced in [32]. However, fPAKE protocols do not handle the case where the reference secret (e.g., the biometric) must also be cryptographically protected when stored at the Authenticator. OE bridges this gap by enabling oblivious biometric-based authentication from HD, instead of requiring a reference BT to be stored in clear by Authenticator.

7 Conclusion

In this work we defined a new primitive called Oblivious Extractor (OE). We argued that OEs could be used to enhance the security of existing biometric-based authentication systems and provide examples of such applications. Finally, we implemented and evaluated a concrete construction for OEs to demonstrate its practicality.

Acknowledgments. We thank ESORICS 2023 reviewers for valuable feedback. Part of this work was performed while the first and third authors were at Visa Research.

Appendix

A   OE Security Analysis

Our OE construction does not affect the FV-Completeness and FV-Security guarantees provided by the original FV scheme. For completeness, this follows from the equivalence in Eq. 9 (implying that the accuracy of the distance-based matching of individual elements in BT and BT$'$ is not affected) and the fact that secret shares used in our scheme are generated with the same polynomial degree (therefore, the number of individual matches required to reconstruct k is the same). For security, we note that the only difference in the HD stored by Authenticator in OEs versus that stored by Authenticator in FVs is that the polynomial is evaluated on additional randomly generated points during enrollment. The obfuscation of BT, by shuffling minutiae and chaff points, which yields FV security notion (per analysis in [15]) is still performed in the exact same way as in the original scheme.

Therefore, in the remainder of this section, we stress to prove that our Π_{OE} protocol securely realizes the $\mathcal{F}_{\mathsf{OE}}$ functionality of Fig. 4 in the semi-honest UC model [33]. In practical terms this means that the messages received during the protocol can be simulated given only the input of that party and the output of the ideal functionality $\mathcal{F}_{\mathsf{OE}}$.

Proof. **Corrupt** Authenticator.

First, we consider a semi-honest Authenticator. When interacting with the ideal functionality, Authenticator receives (i, c, HD) each time a Client enrolls. By definition this is effectively the same information that Authenticator receives from the Client in the real interaction, i.e. the simulator outputs HD to Authenticator.

As discussed in Sect. 2.2, it is the case that HD reveals some information about BT. However, the functionality explicitly allows Authenticator to learn this information. Moreover, this leakage is inherently required for this type of functionality due to the possibility of Authenticator running the Auth protocol with themselves and thereby learn information about BT.

In the ideal world Authenticator participates in the Auth protocol by sending (AUTH, i) to the ideal functionality. They receive no output from the functionality. In the real protocol the view of Authenticator consists of the $\mathcal{F}_{\mathsf{OPPRF}}$ query, which they also receive no output from. Therefore the simulation follows directly.

Proof. **Corrupt** Client.

For a corrupt Client, the view of the Enroll protocol is trivial to simulate. Effectively, it consists of the Client receiving their identifier id. This is also provided by the ideal functionality which the simulator can forward to the Client.

For proving the security of the Auth protocol we consider two cases. The first is the corrupt Client is authenticating on a id which they registered or one which an honest party registered. In the former, the simulation is to simply run the real protocol. Observe that this is secure due to the adversary already knowing the underlying HD value.

The most interesting case is the latter, when a corrupt Client requests to authenticate on an id which was registered by an honest user. The view of the Client in the ideal worlds is either k if their biometric BT' matches and otherwise $\perp$.

Let us assume that the biometric does not match and therefore the simulator obtained $\perp$ from $\mathcal{F}_{\mathsf{OE}}$. In the real protocol recall that $X_{c'}, Y_{c'}$ consists of $m + n$ values in F. Out of these a random set of m lay on a degree $d - 1$ polynomial. Since the functionality would have output $\perp$, the Client would have received at most $d - 1$ of the points which lay on the degree $d - 1$ polynomial. Critically, the distribution of these points (and all others) are uniformly random. Therefore, the simulator will simply sample a uniformly random set of points and use these in place of $X_{c'}, Y_{c'}$. The view of the Client is identical when modeled in the $\mathcal{F}_{\mathsf{OPPRF}}$-hybrid.

In the case that there is a match, the simulator learns the key k and the $d' \geq d$ biometric points BT^* which matched from the functionality. With this the simulator can identify which of the $X_{c'}, Y_{c'}$ points should lay on a degree $d - 1$ polynomial. Since there was a match there are $d' \geq d$ such points. The simulator samples $X_{c'}, Y_{c'}$ such that these points lay on a random degree $d - 1$ polynomial P which has $P(0) = k$ while all other points are uniform. The Client will then reconstruct k as described by the protocol.

A.1 Active Malicious Authenticator

We argue that an actively malicious Authenticator does not gain any advantage. To see why, note that no message sent by Client depends on Authenticator behavior. Hence, an actively malicious Authenticator does not learn Client's inputs that an honest-but-curious Authenticator would not.

The remaining possibility is to deviate from the protocol to tamper with Client's output (i.e., k). At best, this case prevents Client from authenticating itself to Authenticator, hence causing Authenticator to refuse access/service to Client. However, a malicious Authenticator can always refuse service to a Client, irrespective of the OE scheme (e.g., by simply ignoring Client's request to authenticate).

A.2 Active Malicious Client

Leakage in the case where Client may deviate from the protocol is due to the fact that a malicious Client may not respect the restriction that, for a new biometric sample provided for authentication $(b'_1, ..., b'_m) = \mathsf{BT}'$, it must hold that for distinct $i, i' \in [m]$, $\mathsf{dist}(b'_i, b'_{i'}) > w$. As a consequence, different instance of the OPPRF for different b'_i and $b'_{i'}$ in the same BT' may yield the same result if both points lie close enough to the same point in $\widetilde{\mathsf{BT}}$. In turn, this allows Client to learn whether or not a point close to b'_i and b'_j (either real biometric point or chaff point) exists in $\widetilde{\mathsf{BT}}$. Though strictly better than sending HD as a whole to Client, this still reveals some small amount of information about HD's structure, which may be undesirable.

To prevent this, the Client should always be required to prove to Authenticator usage of sufficiently distant b'_i and $b'_{i'}$ for all distinct i, i'. Importantly, this proof should not reveal anything about b'_i and $b'_{i'}$ to Authenticator, which can be hard and expensive to achieve in practice and may significantly complicate the protocol.

Instead, we suggest a simpler approach based on a slightly modified version of the protocol presented in Sect. 4.2. Instead of preventing, it allows Authenticator to detect Client's malicious behavior whenever a Client learns that small piece of information about HD. Upon detection, a malicious Client device can be blacklisted and banned from the system. This modified version of the protocol works as follows:

1. Let S be the set of all points that are not sufficiently close to any point in $\widetilde{\mathsf{BT}}$, i.e., if $(b, (X, Y)) \notin L$ for some X and Y (see L in [**Program OPPRF**] step in Fig. 5), then $b \in \mathsf{S}$.
2. Before the start of the protocol Authenticator generates an additional key K_m and produces $|\mathsf{S}| + m + n$ shares of K_m in an m out of $(|\mathsf{S}| + m + n)$ Shamir secret sharing scheme.
3. L in [**Program OPPRF**] step of Fig. 5 is augmented to also include every element in S. Each $b \in \mathsf{S}$ is programmed with a distinct random pair $(X, Y) \in \mathbb{F}^2$.

4. All elements in the new augmented L are also programmed with a secret share of K_m restricted that: for all $(b_i, (X_i, Y_i))$ and $(b_{i'}, (X_{i'}, Y_{i'}))$ in L, if $(X_i, Y_i) = (X_{i'}, Y_{i'})$, then b_i and $b_{i'}$ are programmed to yield <u>the same share</u> of K_m.
5. Conversely, for all $(b_i, (X_i, Y_i))$ and $(b_{i'}, (X_{i'}, Y_{i'}))$ in L, if $(X_i, Y_i) \neq (X_{i'}, Y_{i'})$, then b_i and $b_{i'}$ are programmed to yield <u>different shares</u> of K_m.

The basic idea behind this approach is that any honest Client authentication terminal that follows the protocol will always receive m secret shares $[K_m]$ and will be able to reconstruct it and prove knowledge of K_m to Authenticator irrespective of whether the user succeeded in authenticating herself using the biometric.

On the other hand, a Client authentication terminal that cheats by selecting b_i' and b_j' close to each other and learns that in fact a corresponding point exists in $\widetilde{BT}$ (because both of them return the same (X, Y) pair) will also be unable to reconstruct K_m. This client will obtain at most $m - 1$ shares of K_m, because at least one of the shares will be repeated. Hence, the Client will fail to prove knowledge of K_m. Therefore, Authenticator is able to detect this malicious behavior and block/ban the malicious Client authentication terminal accordingly.

References

1. CNN. Alleged breach of India's biometric database could put 1.2bn users at risk. https://www.cnn.com/2018/01/11/asia/india-security-breach-biometric-database-intl/index.html. Accessed 03 Dec 2018
2. Dodis, Y., Reyzin, L., Smith, A.: Fuzzy extractors: how to generate strong keys from biometrics and other noisy data. In: Cachin, C., Camenisch, J.L. (eds.) EUROCRYPT 2004. LNCS, vol. 3027, pp. 523–540. Springer, Heidelberg (2004). https://doi.org/10.1007/978-3-540-24676-3_31
3. Rathgeb, C., Uhl, A.: Statistical attack against iris-biometric fuzzy commitment schemes. In: CVPR 2011 WORKSHOPS, pp. 23–30. IEEE (2011)
4. Tams, B., et al.: Security considerations in minutiae-based fuzzy vaults. IEEE TIFS **10**(5), 985–998 (2015)
5. Apon, D., Cho, C., Eldefrawy, K., Katz, J.: Efficient, reusable fuzzy extractors from LWE. In: Dolev, S., Lodha, S. (eds.) CSCML 2017. LNCS, vol. 10332, pp. 1–18. Springer, Cham (2017). https://doi.org/10.1007/978-3-319-60080-2_1
6. Boyen, X.: Reusable cryptographic fuzzy extractors. In: CCS (2004)
7. Blanton, M., Aliasgari, M.: On the (non-)reusability of fuzzy sketches and extractors and security in the computational setting. In: SECRYPT (2011)
8. Blanton, M., Aliasgari, M.: Analysis of reusability of secure sketches and fuzzy extractors. IEEE TIFS **8**(9), 1433–1445 (2013)
9. Kolesnikov, V., et al.: Practical multi-party private set intersection from symmetric-key techniques. In: CCS (2017)
10. Shamir, A.: How to share a secret. Commun. ACM **22**(11), 612–613 (1979)
11. Lee, Y.J., Bae, K., Lee, S.J., Park, K.R., Kim, J.: Biometric key binding: fuzzy vault based on iris images. In: Lee, S.-W., Li, S.Z. (eds.) ICB 2007. LNCS, vol. 4642, pp. 800–808. Springer, Heidelberg (2007). https://doi.org/10.1007/978-3-540-74549-5_84

12. Kumar, A., Kumar, A.: Development of a new cryptographic construct using palmprint-based fuzzy vault. EURASIP J Adv. Sig. Process. **2009**, 1–11 (2009)
13. Wang, Y., Plataniotis, K.N.: Fuzzy vault for face based cryptographic key generation. In: 2007 Biometrics Symposium, pp. 1–6. IEEE (2007)
14. https://fidoalliance.org/ . Accessed 10 Jan 2020
15. Juels, A., Sudan, M.: A fuzzy vault scheme. Des. Codes Cryptography **38**, 237–257 (2006)
16. Ko, K.: User's guide to NIST biometric image software (NBIS). NIST Interagency/Internal Report (NISTIR)-7392 (2007)
17. De Oliveira Nunes, I., et al.: SNUSE: a secure computation approach for large-scale user re-enrollment in biometric authentication system. In: FGCS (2019)
18. Nandakumar, K., et al.: Fingerprint-based fuzzy vault: implementation and performance. IEEE TIFS **2**(4), 744–757 (2007)
19. Shoup, V.: NTL: a library for doing number theory (2001). https://www.shoup.net/ntl/
20. Tams, B.: Absolute fingerprint pre-alignment in minutiae-based cryptosystems. In: BIOSIG, pp. 1–12 (2013)
21. Rindal, P., Schoppmann, P.: VOLE-PSI: fast OPRF and circuit-psi from vector-ole. In: Eurocrypt (2021)
22. Garimella, G., Pinkas, B., Rosulek, M., Trieu, N., Yanai, A.: Oblivious key-value stores and amplification for private set intersection. In: Malkin, T., Peikert, C. (eds.) CRYPTO 2021. LNCS, vol. 12826, pp. 395–425. Springer, Cham (2021). https://doi.org/10.1007/978-3-030-84245-1_14
23. Couteau, G., Rindal, P., Raghuraman, S.: Silver: silent VOLE and oblivious transfer from hardness of decoding structured LDPC codes. In: Malkin, T., Peikert, C. (eds.) CRYPTO 2021. LNCS, vol. 12827, pp. 502–534. Springer, Cham (2021). https://doi.org/10.1007/978-3-030-84252-9_17
24. Dodis, Y., et al.: Fuzzy extractors: how to generate strong keys from biometrics and other noisy data. SIAM J. Comput. **38**(1), 97–139 (2008)
25. Boyen, X., Dodis, Y., Katz, J., Ostrovsky, R., Smith, A.: Secure remote authentication using biometric data. In: Cramer, R. (ed.) EUROCRYPT 2005. LNCS, vol. 3494, pp. 147–163. Springer, Heidelberg (2005). https://doi.org/10.1007/11426639_9
26. Fuller, B., Meng, X., Reyzin, L.: Computational fuzzy extractors. In: Sako, K., Sarkar, P. (eds.) ASIACRYPT 2013. LNCS, vol. 8269, pp. 174–193. Springer, Heidelberg (2013). https://doi.org/10.1007/978-3-642-42033-7_10
27. Erkin, Z., Franz, M., Guajardo, J., Katzenbeisser, S., Lagendijk, I., Toft, T.: Privacy-preserving face recognition. In: Goldberg, I., Atallah, M.J. (eds.) PETS 2009. LNCS, vol. 5672, pp. 235–253. Springer, Heidelberg (2009). https://doi.org/10.1007/978-3-642-03168-7_14
28. Sadeghi, A.-R., Schneider, T., Wehrenberg, I.: Efficient privacy-preserving face recognition. In: Lee, D., Hong, S. (eds.) ICISC 2009. LNCS, vol. 5984, pp. 229–244. Springer, Heidelberg (2010). https://doi.org/10.1007/978-3-642-14423-3_16
29. Osadchy, M., et al.: SCIFI-a system for secure face identification. In: IEEE Symposium on Security and Privacy (2010)
30. Bellare, M., Pointcheval, D., Rogaway, P.: Authenticated key exchange secure against dictionary attacks. In: Preneel, B. (ed.) EUROCRYPT 2000. LNCS, vol. 1807, pp. 139–155. Springer, Heidelberg (2000). https://doi.org/10.1007/3-540-45539-6_11

31. Gennaro, R.: Faster and shorter password-authenticated key exchange. In: Canetti, R. (ed.) TCC 2008. LNCS, vol. 4948, pp. 589–606. Springer, Heidelberg (2008). https://doi.org/10.1007/978-3-540-78524-8_32

32. Dupont, P.-A., Hesse, J., Pointcheval, D., Reyzin, L., Yakoubov, S.: Fuzzy password-authenticated key exchange. In: Nielsen, J.B., Rijmen, V. (eds.) EURO-CRYPT 2018. LNCS, vol. 10822, pp. 393–424. Springer, Cham (2018). https://doi.org/10.1007/978-3-319-78372-7_13

33. Lindell, Y.: How to simulate it-a tutorial on the simulation proof technique. In: Tutorials on the Foundations of Cryptography, pp. 277–346 (2017)

Optimally-Fair Multi-party Exchange Without Trusted Parties

Ivo Maffei[(✉)] [iD] and A. W. Roscoe [iD]

Department of Computer Science, University of Oxford, Oxford, UK
{ivo.maffei,bill.roscoe}@cs.ox.ac.uk

Abstract. We present a multi-party exchange protocol that achieves optimal partial fairness even in the presence of a dishonest majority. We demonstrate how this protocol can be applied to any type of multi-party exchange scenario where the network topology is complete. When combined with standard secure multi-party computation techniques, our protocol enables SMPC with partial fairness when a dishonest majority is involved. Fairness optimality is proven in an abstract model which applies to all protocols based on the concept of concealing the point when the secrets are exchanged. Our protocol improves known results via the use of timed-release encryption and commutative blinding.

Keywords: Multi-party fair exchange · Timed-release encryption · Commutative encryption · Secure multi-party computation · Fair exchange · Partial fairness

1 Introduction

A multi-party fair exchange protocol allows any number of parties to exchange items in an arbitrary way while guaranteeing fairness: either everyone receives all the items they expected or nobody obtains anything. The problem of fair exchange has primarily been studied in the two-party setting where it was already known to be impossible in 1986 thanks to Cleve [8] and later to Pagnia and Gärtner [21]. Fair exchange is often solved with the aid of a trusted party either being present (e.g. [13]) or acting only as a judge in case of misbehaviour (e.g. [3,12]). The protocols following the latter approach are called optimistic since they assume that most of the time the parties involved will all be honest. Among these, a recent approach involves the use of crypto currencies as collateral for failed exchanges (e.g. [2]). Alternative solutions require stronger assumptions such as similarity in general or sequential computing power [6,11]. A more satisfactory approach is the weakening of the fairness requirement to allow a small but not negligible chance of failure [5,9,24]. Other approaches to multi-party fair exchange without introducing trust are based on rationality assumptions [1]. A related research field is the

This research was funded in whole, or in part, by UKRI 2421791 and Crypto.com. For the purpose of Open Access, the author has applied a CC BY public copyright licence to any Author Accepted Manuscript (AAM) version arising from this submission.

G. Tsudik et al. (Eds.): ESORICS 2023, LNCS 14344, pp. 313–333, 2024.
https://doi.org/10.1007/978-3-031-50594-2_16

study of Secure Multi-Party Computation (SMPC). The problem tackled by this branch of computer science is how a group of parties, each with a private input, can compute a function on these inputs without revealing them. This problem appears to be more general than the simple fair exchange, yet SMPC do not always require fairness, instead it mainly focuses on ensuring that the outputs are correct. In particular, in the presence of a dishonest majority, SMPC protocols allow the computation of an arbitrary functionality guaranteeing privacy, correctness but not fairness [15]. That is, the private inputs are kept private, the outputs are guaranteed to be correct, but the dishonest parties can choose not to let the honest parties receive the outputs. This is clearly unsatisfactory in the context of fair exchange, yet the theory of SMPC proves that fairness cannot be achieved in this scenario. In a brief summary, SMPC can be achieved with "standard assumptions" under the following circumstances [15, 22]:

- in the presence of any number of passive adversaries;
- in the presence of an active adversary controlling only a minority of the parties;
- in the presence of an active adversary controlling a majority of the parties if early abortion is not a security violation.

The above results show that the fair exchange problem can be solved in the presence of an honest majority (e.g. via the use of secret sharing), but it is not possible otherwise. To escape this impossibility result, we follow the approach of partial fairness set out by Gordon and Katz [16] and applied in the multi-party setting by Beimel et al. [4].

1.1 Our Contribution

In this paper, we propose a protocol that achieves optimal partial fairness[1] in the presence of a dishonest majority. In particular, we design a protocol where the fairness requirement is weakened so that there is a small probability that the exchange is not fair. This protocol follows the blueprint of other protocols (e.g. [4, 9, 16, 24]) where the secrets are hidden among other dummy messages so that no party knows when the secrets are truly exchanged. By hiding the secrets among other items, the parties can exchange messages without anyone knowing whether they have received or sent any secret. This lack of information leads to the guarantee of partial fairness, i.e. only a lucky guess will break fairness. Moreover, the specific way in which the secrets are distributed leads to the optimality result. We vastly improve the round complexity of [4] as well as escape their impossibility results via the use of Timed-Release Encryption [23]. In particular, Beimel et al.'s protocols that are fair with probability $1 - \frac{1}{p}$ against an arbitrary number m of malicious entities require at least $O(mp^{2^m})$ rounds, while ours is roughly mp. The impossibility result presented in [4] states that, for some parameter depending on the number of malicious entities and the functionality

---

[1] See Appendix A and [16] for a formal definition of partial fairness and Sect. 3 for an intuitive description.

to compute, fairness cannot be guaranteed with probability higher than $\frac{1}{2} +$ negl(λ). By assuming the existence of Timed-Release Encryption, our protocol can achieve fairness with any user-defined probability regardless of the context in which it is used. In particular, our protocol can be rendered fair against malicious adversaries with standard zero-knowledge proofs techniques [14, 15, 22] and fair exchange can be used to achieve fairness in SMPC [18, 19].

We also present a general model to easily describe the exchange protocols based on hiding and, within this model, prove an upper bound on partial fairness as well as a protocol that can achieve this bound. Our impossibility result has no assumptions on the cryptographic primitives used, and therefore it is much stronger than the previous ones we circumvent in this paper. Therefore, our contribution to the body of knowledge is a twofold:

1. An abstract and theoretical analysis of multi-party protocols based on hiding the actual exchange of secrets;
2. An efficient protocol that achieves optimal fairness.

In the next section, we describe the setting of a multi-party fair exchange as well as the adversarial model we consider. Section 3 is dedicated to the security definitions and requirements of the cryptographic primitives used in our protocol, which is described in Sect. 4. The security of the protocol is sketched in the Appendix A. The paper concludes with an extensive abstract analysis of the multi-party protocols based on hiding, which also proves the optimality of our protocol.

2   Multi-party Fair Exchange

In this section, we describe the context of our study as well as the adversarial model. We follow the most general definition of Asokan et al. [3]. We assume the presence of K parties $\mathbf{P_1}, \ldots, \mathbf{P_K}$, and we define a matrix Σ to describe an arbitrary exchange. In particular, $\Sigma_{i,j}$ is the secret that $\mathbf{P_i}$ is meant to send to $\mathbf{P_j}$. In this model, we set no restriction on the type of exchange, but we do assume that the network is a complete graph, i.e. any party can communicate with any other party. Intuitively, we say that an exchange is fair if and only if either all parties receive all the items they expect or nobody receives anything. Even if the exchange Σ is built from two separate sub-exchanges, by requiring that the whole of Σ is fair, the completion of one sub-exchange requires the completion of the other sub-exchange. Although this constraint might seem unreasonable in the abstract model, it is quite common in the real world, e.g. when moving to new house the two separate transactions of buying the new place and selling the old one typically depend on each other. In Sect. 4, we will show that this complex model for fair exchange can be reduced to a much simpler one. In particular, each of the K parties is given a secret s_i, and the aim of the exchange is for all parties to know all secrets. We assume that knowing all but one secret is of no use. This is justified by thinking about these secrets as shares of some larger secret (often the case in SMPC). In this simpler model, the exchange is fair if and only if whenever a party discloses their secret, they receive all the other secrets.

2.1 Adversarial Model

We assume that the network topology is complete, but communication channels do not need to be secure. However, we require them to guarantee confidentiality; stronger properties are not needed since adversaries are passive. Delivery is not guaranteed, and we assume the use of agreed-upon timeouts to universally establish if the protocol is aborted. We are only interested in the case where at least one honest party is involved in the protocol, and we assume that corruptions are static (non-adaptive adversary), i.e. the coalitions of malicious parties do not change after the protocol starts. In our discussions, we talk about a group of malicious parties which coordinate and share knowledge as a coalition. Alternatively, the reader can think of a coalition of parties as a group of entities controlled by a single malicious actor. Crucially, we allow the presence of a dishonest majority, but adversaries are passive, i.e. they will follow the protocol, but can abort communication at any point in time without detection.

3 Preliminaries

In this section, we introduce all the cryptographic primitives used in our protocol as well as the security requirements they need to satisfy.

3.1 Notation

We write an n-length vector (or array) from a set X as $\boldsymbol{v} \in X^n$, and we denote its ith element by $\boldsymbol{v}[i]$ where $1 \leq i \leq n$. If we have a function $f : X \to Y$ and a vector $\boldsymbol{v} \in X^n$, then we write $f^*(\boldsymbol{v})$ to mean the vector $\langle f(\boldsymbol{v}[i]) \mid 1 \leq i \leq n \rangle$ where f is applied to each element. We use S_n for the group of permutations over the set $\{1, \ldots, n\}$, but for $\sigma \in S_n$ and $\boldsymbol{v} \in X^n$, we will write $\sigma(\boldsymbol{v})$ to mean the vector $\boldsymbol{w} = \langle \boldsymbol{v}[\sigma^{-1}(i)] \mid 1 \leq i \leq n \rangle$. That is, if $\sigma(a) = b$, then $\boldsymbol{w}[b] = \boldsymbol{v}[a]$. We write R_n for the subset of rotations in S_n: $\{\tau \in S_n \mid \forall i \; \tau(i+1) = (\tau(i) + 1 \bmod n)\}$. If $\boldsymbol{\sigma} \in S_n^K$ and M is a $K \times n$ matrix, then $\boldsymbol{\sigma}(M)$ is the result of applying $\boldsymbol{\sigma}[i]$ to the ith row of M. We use $a\|b$ for the concatenation of a and b where these are interpreted as bitstrings.

3.2 Partial Fairness

We define fairness in the usual idea vs real world setting. Assume an ideal world where we have an incorruptible trusted party which acts as an intermediary collecting and delivering the secrets. We say that our protocol is $\frac{1}{p}$-fair if for any adversary to our protocol there is a simulator in the ideal world so that the two runs are computationally indistinguishable with probability $1 - \frac{1}{p} - \mathsf{negl}(\lambda)$ (where $\mathsf{negl}(\lambda)$ is a negligible function of the security parameter λ). The above means that our $\frac{1}{p}$-fair protocol can be unfair with probability at most $\frac{1}{p} + \mathsf{negl}(\lambda)$. See Appendix A for a formal definition.

3.3 Symmetric Encryption

Our protocol will take advantage of a symmetric encryption scheme (KGen, Enc, Dec) which we only require to be COA (Ciphertext Only Attack) secure, and each key will only be used once. However, in order to formally prove the security of our protocol, we require the encryption scheme to be non-committing [10]. This means that we require the additional property that for any message-message-key (m_1, m_2, k_1) triple there is another key k_2 so that $\mathsf{Dec}_{k_2}(\mathsf{Enc}_{k_1}(m_1)) = m_2$. For simplicity, the reader can assume that the scheme used is the one-time-pad.

3.4 Delay Encryption

Delay encryption (sometimes called Timed-Release Encryption [23]) is an unusual cryptographic primitive whose aim is not to provide confidentiality of a message from other parties, but to hide the message from anyone for some pre-defined amount of time. For the reader accustomed to timed-release encryption, what we use and define is a "delay" time-lock-puzzle-based encryption scheme rather than time-specific schemes using trusted parties. This is justified because we don't want to introduce trust in the fair exchange context.

More formally, a delay encryption scheme is a triple of algorithms (Pgen, Delay, Open) with associated sets $\mathcal{M}, \mathcal{C}, \mathcal{P}$ such that

$$\text{Pgen: } \{1\}^* \times \mathbb{N} \to \mathcal{P} \qquad \text{Delay: } \mathcal{M} \times \mathcal{P} \to \mathcal{C} \qquad \text{Open: } \mathcal{C} \times \mathcal{P} \to \mathcal{M}$$

Intuitively, $\mathsf{Pgen}(1^\lambda, T)$ generates public parameters *params* that are used to delay a message for time T. We omit *params* and write $\mathsf{Delay}_T(m)$ for the ciphertext delaying m for elapsed time T. Similarly, we omit *params* and write $\mathsf{Open}(c)$. Practically speaking, $\mathsf{Delay}_T(m)$ will create a puzzle c so that $\mathsf{Open}(c)$ can solve the puzzle and obtain m only after at least T (sequential) time. Thus, Open will most likely not be a PPT algorithm. However, an honest party with moderate computational power should be able to run $\mathsf{Open}(c)$ in sequential time not much longer than T. This might be μT for a small integer μ such as 10 or 20.

In order for our scheme to make sense, we set the following requirement

$$\forall m \in M \; \forall T \in \mathbb{N} \quad \mathsf{Open}(\mathsf{Delay}_T(m)) = m$$

We say that a delay encryption is COA-secure if for any family of circuits $\mathcal{A}$ of conceivable size and depth at most $\mu(\lambda)T$, we have

$$\Pr_{\substack{m \leftarrow_\$ \mathcal{M} \\ T \leftarrow_\$ \mathbb{N}}} \left[m \leftarrow \mathcal{A}(c, T, params) \mid c \leftarrow \mathsf{Delay}_T(m) \wedge params \leftarrow \mathsf{Pgen}(1^\lambda, T) \right]$$

$$< \frac{1}{|\mathcal{M}|} + \mathsf{negl}(\lambda)$$

Intuitively, a COA-secure delay encryption scheme correctly hides encrypted messages for the expected amount of time. We remark that the size of such circuits will depend on the current state of technology. As noted in [20], allowing all polynomially-sized circuits could lead to misleading results with circuits much larger than what is feasible at the time of writing.

3.5   Commutative Blinding

A feature of our protocol is the use of commutative blinding (a.k.a. commutative encryption) to efficiently shuffle the secrets. The need for commutativity arises because the first party blinding the message cannot ever reveal their blinding key. Therefore, they need to unblind such message *after* it has been blinded by the other parties. We firstly present a definition that is easy to understand, but it is stricter than what is needed by the protocol. We use this definition for ease of presentation, but discuss the more general one in this section since it will be used in the formal proof of security.

Definition 1. *We call a pair of PPT algorithms* (Blind, Unblind) *a commutative blinding scheme if*

$$\text{Blind} : \mathcal{M} \times \mathcal{K} \to \mathcal{C} \qquad \qquad \text{Unblind} : \mathcal{C} \times \mathcal{K} \to \mathcal{M}$$

$$\forall m \in \mathcal{M} \; \forall k \in \mathcal{K} \; \text{Unblind}(\text{Blind}(m, k), k) = m$$

Moreover the commutativity property is given by

$$\forall m \in \mathcal{M} \; \forall k_1, k_2 \in \mathcal{K} \; \text{Blind}(\text{Blind}(m, k_1), k_2) = \text{Blind}(\text{Blind}(m, k_2), k_1)$$

In its fully generality, to run a protocol with K parties, we only require $K + 1$ pairs $(\text{Blind}_0, \text{Unblind}_0), \dots, (\text{Blind}_K, \text{Unblind}_K)$, such that

$$\text{Unblind}_K(\dots \text{Unblind}_0(\text{Blind}_K(\dots \text{Blind}_0(m, k_0) \dots, k_K), k_0), \dots, k_K) \; = \; m$$

Writing the protocol and security requirements using the above will result in a hardly readable script. Therefore, we use the stronger commutativity property and simplify the exposition of the protocol. In terms of security requirements, we need the blinding to satisfy the usual IND-CPA definition. In particular, we require each Blind_i to be IND-CPA secure. As an example, this primitive could be instantiated using ElGamal and the re-encryption procedure often used in voting schemes (e.g. [17]). A proof the above, together with a more precise and slightly more relaxed security definition, is given in the full version of the paper.

4   The Protocol

Firstly, we show a reduction from the general fair exchange we described before to a simpler context that we will consider in the rest of this paper. Recall that we consider K parties $\{\mathbf{P_1}, \dots, \mathbf{P_K}\}$ and that all items exchanged are encoded in the matrix Σ so that $\Sigma_{i,j}$ is what $\mathbf{P_i}$ sends to $\mathbf{P_j}$. Recall from Sect. 2.1 that we assume the communication channels provide privacy. We now go one step further and assume that privacy is implemented using some (symmetric or asymmetric) encryption scheme. In our exchange protocol, $\mathbf{P_i}$ holds only one secret $s_i = \langle \mathsf{Enc}_{k_{i,j}}(\Sigma_{i,j}) \mid j \neq i \rangle$ where $k_{i,j}$ is the key $\mathbf{P_i}$ uses to communicate confidentially with $\mathbf{P_j}$. Therefore, in the rest of this script, we assume that each party holds only one compound secret, and that this should be revealed to all the other participants.

Our protocol follows the idea of concealing from all the point where the secrets are exchanged. Therefore, the protocol can be split into two phases: a setup phase where the shuffling of the secrets occurs, and an exchange phase where the secrets (and dummy values) are exchanged.

In this scenario, we assume the K parties have agreed on a number N of exchange messages as well as a number L which represents the size of the coalition the protocol should be optimal against. We expect that in most cases $L = K - 1$, but some contexts may wish to lower such value. As we will see in Sect. 6, the secrets might *not* be uniformly distributed, instead there are only a few "configurations" or "states" where those should be. We define $\langle \pi_1, \ldots, \pi_\delta \rangle$ to be the permutations that send the lists of secrets and dummies to those valid configurations. Formulae for those permutations and the value δ are described in Sect. 6. For ease of notation, we assume that all parties send n exchange messages (i.e. $N = nK$).

4.1   Protocol Overview

A crucial aspect of our protocol is that the parties involved will not exchange the secrets directly as in [4,16], instead they will encrypt the secrets and exchange keys for the used encryption scheme. Since the ciphertext is delayed to the end of the protocol using Timed-Release Encryption, any auxiliary information about the secrets is rendered useless. The parties will only be able to test the exchanged keys when the delayed message opens *after* the protocol is terminated. This is what allows us to escape the impossibility results of [4,16] as well as drastically improving the efficiency of the protocol. Before analysing what should be included in the delayed messages, we describe how the keys are shuffled.

Initially, all parties will construct a list of n random keys where the first element is the one used to encrypt the secret. All those lists are blinded and sent to $\mathbf{P_1}$ who will collate them in a matrix so that the xth row is the list sent by $\mathbf{P_x}$. It is worth remarking that $\mathbf{P_1}$ is not a trusted party, but one of parties involved in the exchange. Since this matrix will need to end up in one of the δ valid configurations (as defined in Sect. 6), $\mathbf{P_1}$ creates δ pairs $(M_1, f_1), \ldots, (M_\delta, f_\delta)$ so that $\{f_i(M_i) \mid 1 \leq i \leq \delta\}$ is the set of all the valid configurations. This decoupling allows us to shuffle the pairs uniformly. Hence, starting from $\mathbf{P_1}$, each party will randomly rotate the list of these δ pairs and pass it to the next participant. In order to keep those rotations secret, each party will need to mask all the pairs. Masking (M, f) will be done in the following way: each element of M is blinded using a commutative blinding scheme, while f is masked by computing $f \circ g^{-1}$ for

---

Multi-party Fair Exchange

Define $F(M, f, b, g) = (g(\mathsf{Blind}^*(M, b)), f \circ g^{-1})$

$\mathbf{P_i}$

$k_i \leftarrow_\$ \mathcal{K}^n; \; b_i \leftarrow_\$ \mathcal{B}^2; \; \sigma_i \leftarrow_\$ (S_n^K)^\delta; \tau_i \leftarrow_\$ R_\delta$

$L_i \leftarrow \langle \mathsf{Blind}(k_i[i], b_i[1]) \mid 1 \leq i \leq n \rangle$

$D_i \leftarrow \mathsf{Delay}(\mathsf{Enc}_{k_i[1]}(s_i) \| \tau_i \| b_i[2])$

$$\xrightarrow{\hspace{3cm} L_i, D_i \hspace{2cm}} \mathbf{P_1}$$

$\mathbf{P_1}$

$E \leftarrow \langle L_1, \ldots, L_K \rangle$

$S^1 \leftarrow \tau_1(\langle F(E, \pi_i, b_1[2], \sigma_1[i]) \mid 1 \leq i \leq \delta \rangle)$

$$\xrightarrow{\hspace{4cm} S^1 \hspace{3cm}} \mathbf{P_2}$$

$\mathbf{P_j}$ after receiving S^{j-1}

let $S^{j-1} = \langle (M_1, o_1), \ldots, (M_\delta, o_\delta) \rangle$

$S^j \leftarrow \tau_j(\langle F(M_i, o_i, b_j[2], \sigma_j[i]) \mid 1 \leq i \leq \delta \rangle)$

$$\xrightarrow{\hspace{4cm} S^j \hspace{3cm}} \mathbf{P_{j+1}}$$

$\mathbf{P_K}$ after receiving S^{K-1}

let $S^{K-1} = \langle (M_1, o_1), \ldots, (M_\delta, o_\delta) \rangle$

$S^K \leftarrow \tau_j(\langle F(M_i, o_i, b_K[2], \sigma_K[i]) \mid 1 \leq i \leq \delta \rangle)$

$E^K \leftarrow o_f(M_f)$ where $(M_f, o_f) \leftarrow S^K[1]$

$$\xrightarrow{\hspace{3cm} E^K[i] \hspace{2cm}} \mathbf{P_i}$$

$\mathbf{P_i}$ after receiving $E^K[i]$

$M^i \leftarrow \mathsf{Unblind}^*(E^K[i], b_i[1])$

$\ldots\ldots\ldots\ldots\ldots\ldots\ldots\ldots\ldots\ldots\ldots\ldots$ Exchange phase $\ldots\ldots\ldots\ldots\ldots\ldots\ldots\ldots\ldots\ldots\ldots\ldots\ldots$

during round r for $1 \leq r \leq n$

in order from $\mathbf{P_1}$ to $\mathbf{P_K}$

$\mathbf{P_i}$

$$\xrightarrow{\hspace{3cm} M^i[r] \hspace{2cm}} \mathbf{Group}$$

Fig. 1. Fair exchange protocol.

some randomly picked permutation g. The resulting pair $(\mathsf{Blind}^*(M, b), f \circ g^{-1})$ might not satisfy the property that $(f \circ g^{-1})(\mathsf{Blind}^*(M, b))$ is a valid configuration, therefore, we apply g to the matrix M as well. Hence, (M, f) is transformed into $(g(\mathsf{Blind}^*(M, b)), f \circ g^{-1})$ for some random permutation g and blinding key b. For security reasons, g will need to be different for each pair. In Fig. 1, the above transformation is encoded in the function F and S^x indicates the list of pairs after being rotated x times. The random permutations g are called $\sigma_j[i]$ where j indicates which party picked it and i indicates which of the δ matrices the permutation should be applied to.

The last party $\mathbf{P_K}$ will receive the list of pairs rotated by all the other parties. Therefore, they will simply rotate and blind one last time as well as pick the first element (M, f) of the list. By computing $f(M)$, $\mathbf{P_K}$ obtains a random valid configuration, called E^K in Fig. 1. The resulting matrix will have its elements blinded by all the parties, moreover, each xth row is blinded by $\mathbf{P_x}$ twice.[2] All that is left to do is for $\mathbf{P_K}$ to send back to each party $\mathbf{P_x}$ their list (the xth row of E^K). Now all parties can remove their first blinding and proceed to exchange the items in the list one by one.

In order to retrieve the secret, one needs to unblind the exchanged messages and identify which keys were used to encrypt the secrets. Therefore, the delayed message must include the rotation used by each party as well as all of the keys used for the blindings that are not removed. In particular, the setup messages are blinded with keys which are never revealed $\{b_1[1], \ldots, b_K[1]\}$. This prevents any malicious adversary from extracting the secrets by looking only at the setup phase. After the setup phase, the parties will exchange the items of their list one at a time.

4.2 Protocol Analysis

In this brief subsection, we analyse the setup phase to understand its result. We note the following (ignoring blinding)

$$E^K = \pi_{(\tau_1^{-1} \circ \ldots \circ \tau_K^{-1})(1)}(E)$$

If there is at least one honest party, then there is at least one truly random τ_i meaning that the permutation π_i picked is uniformly distributed. If during the exchange phase no further information is leaked[3], then the coalition of corrupted parties has no knowledge on when the $k_i[1]$ are exchanged. Hence, the corrupted coalition can attack the protocol only by aborting the exchange phase at an arbitrary point. Their strategy is successful only if they stop after having received all the honest parties' secret keys but without having revealed all of theirs. In Sect. 6, we will prove that the permutations π_i's can be picked so that this strategy has the smallest possible success rate.

---

[2] This is why we need $K + 1$ blinding functions in the general definition of Sect. 3.5.
[3] See Appendix A for a proof of this fact.

We note that the round complexity of the setup phase is $K + 2$ with $3K$ messages sent overall. The exchange phase is run in N rounds with NK messages overall. These numbers are a large improvement over the protocol by Beimel et al. [4].

5   Security Proof

We only have space to give a brief overview the security proof of our protocol. More details are in Appendix A.

Let $\mathcal{F}_{ex}$ be the ideal functionality where all K parties perform the fair exchange by handling their secrets to a central trusted party which redistributes them.

Definition 2. *Let* $\mathsf{IDEAL}_{\mathcal{F}_{ex},\mathcal{S}(\mathsf{aux})}(\Sigma, 1^\lambda)$ *be the random variable consisting of the output of the* K *parties involved in an ideal-world run of the functionality* $\mathcal{F}_{ex}$, *where* Σ *represents the matrix of secrets to exchange and* $\mathcal{S}(\mathsf{aux})$ *is a non-uniform PPT adversary with auxiliary information* aux.

Definition 3. *Let* $\mathsf{REAL}_{\Pi,\mathcal{A}(\mathsf{aux})}(\Sigma, 1^\lambda)$ *be the random variable consisting of the output of the* K *parties involved in a real-world run of the protocol* Π, *where* Σ *represents the matrix of secrets to exchange and* $\mathcal{A}(\mathsf{aux})$ *is a non-uniform PPT adversary with auxiliary information* aux.

Definition 4. *We say that a protocol* Π *implements the ideal functionality* $\mathcal{F}_{ex}$ *with* $\frac{1}{p}$-*partial fairness, if for every non-uniform PPT adversary* $\mathcal{A}$ *there exists a non-uniform PPT simulator* $\mathcal{S}$ *such that*

$$\left\{ \mathsf{IDEAL}_{\mathcal{F}_{ex},\mathcal{S}(\mathsf{aux})}(\Sigma, 1^\lambda) \right\} \overset{\frac{1}{p}}{\approx} \left\{ \mathsf{REAL}_{\Pi,\mathcal{A}(\mathsf{aux})}(\Sigma, 1^\lambda) \right\}$$

i.e. the two probability ensembles are computationally indistinguishable with probability $1 - \frac{1}{p} - \mathsf{negl}(\lambda)$ *for some negligible function* $\mathsf{negl}(\lambda)$.

For ease of presentation, we only consider the scenario where the adversary controls all but one honest party $\mathbf{P}_{\mathcal{H}}$. Furthermore, we assume that $1 \neq \mathcal{H} \neq K$.[4]

We prove the security of the protocol in a 3-step process. Firstly, we prove that retrieving the secret $s_{\mathcal{H}}$ is the equivalent to obtaining $k_{\mathcal{H}}[1]$ (Theorem 1).

Theorem 1. *If* Delay *is COA secure,* Enc *is COA secure and* Blind *is IND-CPA, then no non-uniform PPT adversary* $\mathcal{A}$ *can obtain* $s_{\mathcal{H}}$ *unless* $D_{\mathcal{H}}$ *is opened, and they have received the message containing* $k_{\mathcal{H}}[1]$ *during the exchange phase.*

Working in the hybrid model [7], we assume the existence of an ideal functionality $\mathcal{F}_{\mathsf{setup}}$ where each party submits their secret s and receives back the shuffled and blinded list $E^K[i]$ together with the delayed messages D_i of all the other parties. The configuration picked by $\mathcal{F}_{\mathsf{setup}}$ is chosen uniformly among the δ possibilities. We assume that this functionality is secure-with-abort, i.e. the

---

[4] The other cases are a simplification of what presented here, hence omitted for brevity.

corrupted parties can stop the honest parties from receiving their outputs, but not alter the output. In this context, we prove that our protocol achieves partial fairness (Theorem 2).

Theorem 2. *Let Π^{hyb} be the protocol of Fig. 1 where the setup phase has been replaced by an ideal functionality $\mathcal{F}_{setup}$. Assume that the delay encryption scheme is COA secure and that the symmetric encryption scheme is non-committing and COA secure, then Π^{hyb} implements the fair exchange ideal functionality $\mathcal{F}_{ex}$ with $\frac{K-1}{N+1-K}$-partial fairness.*

To complete the security proof, we show that the setup phase described in Fig. 1 implements the ideal functionality. In Sect. 4.2, we have already shown that our protocol already computes the setup phase correctly, so we only need to show that it does so privately (Theorem 3).

Theorem 3. *If* Blind *is* IND-CPA *and* Delay *is* COA *secure, then the setup phase of Fig. 1 does not reveal any information about $\tau_\mathcal{H}$ while $D_\mathcal{H}$ is not opened.*

6 Fairness Optimality

We represent a protocol of N messages and $K = \{p_1, \dots, p_K\}$ parties by a pair $\Pi = (\mathcal{M}, \mathcal{P})$, where

- $\mathcal{M} : \mathbb{N} \to \{1, \dots, K\}$ is a map indicating in which order the parties are sending messages, i.e. $\mathcal{M}(i) = j$ means that message i is sent by party p_j.
- a "configuration" $t : \{1, \dots, K\} \to \mathbb{N}$ is a function such that $t(i) = j$ means that p_i's secret is in the jth message.
- $\mathcal{P}$ is a function which associates to each configuration its probability of happening.

We set the constraint: $t(i) = j \implies \mathcal{M}(j) = i$. That is, if p_i's secret is disclosed at the jth message, then such message must be sent by p_i. This is due to the principle that if a secret is disclosed to someone, it is disclosed to everyone. When we say "p_i's secret is in the jth message" or "p_i's secret is disclosed at the jth message" we do not mean that the jth message gives immediate knowledge of p_i's secret, but that knowledge is guaranteed to happen. Looking at the exchange protocol of Sect. 4, s_i is "disclosed" when the blinded $k_i[1]$ is sent by P_i during the exchange phase. However, the other parties will have knowledge of s_i only after the delay message D_i is opened.

Given a protocol $\Pi = (\mathcal{M}, \mathcal{P})$, we define the probability that a coalition of parties I "wins" by stopping at $S \in \mathbb{N}$ to be

$$\Pr_\Pi[I, S] = \sum_{t \in \mathcal{T}(\Pi, I, S)} \mathcal{P}(t)$$

where $\mathcal{T}(\Pi, I, S) = \{t \mid \exists i \in I \ t(i) > S \land \forall j \notin I \ t(j) \le S\}$

Intuitively, I wins by stopping at S if someone in I has not released their secret after the Sth message but all parties not in I have already sent their secrets. For ease of presentation we write $t < S$ if for $1 \le i \le K$ $t(i) < S$ and similarly for $t > S$.

In our search for an optimal protocol, we assume that no party sends consecutive messages.

We measure the unfairness of a protocol Π against coalitions of size L by computing

$$\max_{\substack{I,S \\ |I|=L}} \Pr_\Pi[I,S]$$

Lemma 1. *Let $\Pi_b = (\mathcal{M}_b, \mathcal{P}_b)$ be a protocol with a configuration t_b. Let t_g be a configuration such that $\max t_g = \max t_b$ and $\forall i$ $t_g(i) \ge t_b(i)$. Define $\Pi_g = (\mathcal{M}_b, \mathcal{P}_g)$ where $\mathcal{P}_g(t_b) = 0$, $\mathcal{P}_g(t_g) = \mathcal{P}_b(t_g) + \mathcal{P}_b(t_b)$ and $\mathcal{P}_g(t) = \mathcal{P}_b(t)$ for any other t. Then for any L*

$$\max_{\substack{I,S \\ |I|=L}} \Pr_{\Pi_b}[I,S] \ge \max_{\substack{I,S \\ |I|=L}} \Pr_{\Pi_g}[I,S]$$

Proof. We prove the statement by showing that for all I,S we have

$$\Pr_{\Pi_b}[I,S] \ge \Pr_{\Pi_g}[I,S] \tag{1}$$

Note that $\mathcal{T}(\Pi_g,I,S) = \mathcal{T}(\Pi_b,I,S)$. Hence, the inequality above becomes:

$$\sum_{t\in\mathcal{T}(\Pi_b,I,S)} \mathcal{P}_b(t) \ge \sum_{t\in\mathcal{T}(\Pi_b,I,S)} \mathcal{P}_g(t)$$

Therefore, it is enough to show that $t_g \in \mathcal{T}(\Pi_b,I,S) \implies t_b \in \mathcal{T}(\Pi_b,I,S)$, i.e. if I wins by stopping at S when t_g happens, then I wins by stopping at S also when t_b happen. Assume that $t_g \in \mathcal{T}(\Pi_b,I,S)$, then $\forall i \notin I$ $t_g(i) \le S$. Therefore, $\forall i \notin I$ $t_b(i) \le t_g(i) \le S$. Moreover, $j = \arg\max t_g \in I \wedge t_g(j) > S$. Since $\max t_b = \max t_g$, we have that $t_b(j) > S$. Hence $t_b \in \mathcal{T}(\Pi_b,I,S)$. □

For every x such that there is a configuration t with $\max t = x$, there is exactly one configuration t_x such that for all other configurations t' $\forall i$ $t_x(i) \ge t'(i)$. Such t_x is constructed by setting $t_x(i)$ to be the largest (valid) integer up to x. The above lemma proves that we only need to consider those "short" configurations because longer ones are always worse.

Let $\Pi_g^L = (\mathcal{M}_g, \mathcal{P}_g)$ be a protocol where

- $\mathcal{M}_g(i) = (i - 1 \bmod K) + 1$
- $\mathcal{P}_g(t_i) = \alpha_i$
- $\mathcal{P}_g(t) = 0$ for other configurations
- the α_i's are picked to minimise: $\max_{\substack{I,S \\ |I|=L}} \Pr_{\Pi_g^L}[I,S]$

Lemma 2. *Consider a protocol Π_g^x as described above for some x and pick $L < K$, then*

$$\max_{\substack{I,S \\ |I|=L}} \Pr_{\Pi_g^x}[I,S] = \max\{\alpha_i + \cdots + \alpha_{i+L-1} \mid K \leq i \leq N+1-L\}$$

Proof. The short configurations t_i can be described as the map $y \mapsto i - ((\mathcal{M}(i) - y) \bmod K)$. That is, the secrets are sent in messages $\{i - K + 1, i - K + 2, \ldots, i\}$. All the short configurations of the protocol Π_g^x are exactly the t_i configurations described above where $K \leq i \leq N$. Note that

$$\max_{\substack{I,S \\ |I|=L}} \Pr_{\Pi_g^x}[I,S] = \max\{\max_{I;|I|=L} \Pr_{\Pi_g^x}[I,S] \mid 1 \leq S \leq N\}$$

Fix an S. Consider the configurations $T = \{t_{S+1}, t_{S+2}, \ldots, t_{S+L}\}$.[5] Pick any other configuration t_i, one of two scenarios can happen

1. $i \leq S$, i.e. all secrets are exchanged up to (including) the Sth message
2. $i > S + L$, i.e. more than L secrets are exchanged after S^{th} message

In both scenarios, there is no coalition of size L that can win by stopping at S in those configurations. Pick any configuration $t \in T$, then any coalition containing $\{p_j \mid t(j) > S\}$ can win in t by stopping at S. In particular, only the coalition $J = \{p_j \mid j = M(i), \; S+1 \leq i \leq S+L\}$ wins in all such configurations. Therefore, $\max_{I;|I|=L} \Pr_{\Pi_g^x}[I,S] = \Pr_{\Pi_g^x}[J,S] = \alpha_{S+1} + \cdots + \alpha_{S+L}$.[6] By iterating over the possible S, we obtain the following set of sums:

$$\{\alpha_K, \alpha_K + \alpha_{K+1}, \alpha_K + \alpha_{K+1} + \alpha_{K+2}, \ldots, \alpha_K + \cdots + \alpha_{K+L-1}\}$$
$$\cup \{\alpha_i + \cdots + \alpha_{i+L-1} \mid K \leq i \leq N+1-L\}$$
$$\cup \{\alpha_{N+1-L} + \cdots + \alpha_N, \alpha_{N+2-L} + \cdots + \alpha_N, \ldots, \alpha_N\}$$

Note that the sums in the first and third set are all "sub-sums" of sums in the second set. Therefore, the maximum over the above three sets is the same as the maximum over the second set. The lemma follows. □

Theorem 4. *Let $\Pi = (\mathcal{M}, \mathcal{P})$ be any protocol, then*

$$\max_{\substack{I,S \\ |I|=L}} \Pr_\Pi[I,S] \geq \max_{\substack{I,S \\ |I|=L}} \Pr_{\Pi_g^L}[I,S]$$

Proof. First, we construct an intermediate protocol $\Pi_b = (\mathcal{M}_b, \mathcal{P}_b)$ such that

- $\mathcal{M}_b = \mathcal{M}$
- $\mathcal{P}_b(t_i) = \beta_i$, where t_i are the "short" configurations in $\mathcal{M}_b$

---

[5] Some of these configurations may not exist if $S + L > N$, so they can be removed from the set.

[6] Once again, some of this α might refer to non-existing configurations, in such scenario those values can be considered to be zero.

- $\mathcal{P}_b(t) = 0$ for other t's
- the β's minimise: $\max_{\substack{I,S \\ |I|=L}} \mathrm{Pr}_{\Pi_b}[I,S]$

We first point out that $\max_{\substack{I,S \\ |I|=L}} \mathrm{Pr}_{\Pi}[I,S] \geq \max_{\substack{I,S \\ |I|=L}} \mathrm{Pr}_{\Pi_b}[I,S]$ due to Lemma 1 and the definition of $\mathcal{P}_b$. Therefore, we can prove the theorem by showing the same inequality between Π_b and Π_g^L.

By the previous lemmas, we have that the α's minimise

$$\max\{\alpha_i + \cdots + \alpha_{i+L-1} \mid K \leq i \leq N+1-L\} \left(= \max_{\substack{I,S \\ |I|=L}} \mathrm{Pr}_{\Pi_g^L}[I,S] \right)$$

Recall that β_i is the probability of the configuration t_i which is the unique shortest one with $\max t_i = i$.[7] We have constructed the set $\{\beta_K, \ldots, \beta_N\}$. We prove the result by showing that:

$$\max_{\substack{I,S \\ |I|=L}} \mathrm{Pr}_{\Pi_b}[I,S] \geq \max\{\beta_i + \cdots + \beta_{i+L-1} \mid K \leq i \leq N+1-L\}$$

$$\geq \max\{\alpha_i + \cdots + \alpha_{i+L-1} \mid K \leq i \leq N+1-L\}$$

The second inequality comes straight from the definition of the α's and Lemma 2. Fix any i and consider the configurations $T = \{t_i, t_{i+1}, \ldots, t_{i+L-1}\}$ and the coalition $I = \{p_j \mid \mathcal{M}_b(\max t) = j \text{ for } t \in T\}$ of the parties sending the messages from i to $i+L-1$.[8] Set $S = i-1$. By the definition of I, all messages sent after S up to (including) $i+L-1$ are sent by parties in I. Therefore, I wins in all the coalitions in T by stopping at S. Hence $\mathrm{Pr}_{\Pi_b}[I,S] \geq \beta_i + \cdots + \beta_{i+L-1}$. Since i was arbitrary, we have

$$\max_{\substack{I,S \\ |I|=L}} \mathrm{Pr}_{\Pi_b}[I,S] \geq \max\{\beta_i + \cdots + \beta_{i+L-1} \mid K \leq i \leq N+1-L\}$$

and the theorem follows.   □

As a result of the above theorem, we know that Π_g^L is optimal against coalitions of size L. We now analyse Π_g^L to find out exactly the values of the α's.

Lemma 3. *Given n non-negative numbers $\alpha_1, \ldots, \alpha_n$ whose sum is 1 and any $l \leq n$, set $\lambda = \lceil \frac{n}{l} \rceil$, then*

$$\max\{\alpha_i + \cdots + \alpha_{i+l-1} \mid 1 \leq i \leq n+1-l\} \geq \frac{1}{\lambda} \qquad (2)$$

---

[7] It might be the case that for all small i up to some x, t_i does not exist. For instance, say that the first K messages are all sent by two parties, then "earliest" configuration t will have $\max t \geq 2K-2$ and therefore $t = t_K$ doesn't exist. If t_i as described above doesn't exist, we let it be one of the many configurations where $\max t_i$ is minimal (dropping the constraint of it being short).

[8] T might contain configurations t_i, t_j with $\mathcal{M}_b(i) = \mathcal{M}_b(j)$, then I will not have size L. If this is the case, I can be extended to a coalition of size L arbitrarily, therefore we assume $|I| = L$.

Proof. Assume for a contradiction that Eq. 2 doesn't hold. Let $v_i = \{\alpha_{l(i-1)+1}, \alpha_{i+1}, \ldots, \alpha_{li}\}$ for $1 \leq i \leq \lfloor \frac{n}{l} \rfloor$. If $n \bmod l \neq 0$, then set $v_\lambda = \{\alpha_{n+1-l}, \ldots, \alpha_n\}$. Since Eq. 2 doesn't hold, we have that for all $1 \leq i \leq \lambda$, the inequality $\sum_{\alpha \in v_i} \alpha < \frac{1}{\lambda}$ holds. However,

$$1 = \sum_{i=1}^{n} \alpha_i \leq \sum_{i=1}^{\lambda} \sum_{\alpha \in v_i} \alpha < \sum_{i=1}^{\lambda} \frac{1}{\lambda} = 1$$

□

Theorem 5. *Given n non-negative numbers $\alpha_1, \ldots, \alpha_n$ whose sum is 1 and any $l \leq n$, set $\lambda = \lceil \frac{n}{l} \rceil$, then*

$$\min_{\alpha} \max\{\alpha_i + \cdots + \alpha_{i+l-1} \mid 1 \leq i \leq n+1-l\} = \frac{1}{\lambda} \qquad (3)$$

Proof. By the previous Lemma 3, it is enough to exhibit a set of α's so that

$$\max\{\alpha_i + \cdots + \alpha_{i+l-1} \mid 1 \leq i \leq n+1-l\} = \frac{1}{\lambda}$$

For $1 \leq i < \lambda$, set $\alpha_{l(i-1)+1} = \frac{1}{\lambda}$ and let $\alpha_n = \frac{1}{\lambda}$. Every other α is zero. Note that these values are picked so that non-zero values have at least $l - 1$ zero values between each other. Therefore, any sum $\alpha_i + \cdots + \alpha_{i+l-1}$ will contain at most 1 non-zero value and all the non-zero sums will be $\frac{1}{\lambda}$. The theorem follows immediately. □

This last theorem tells us that the optimal fairness is $\frac{1}{\lambda}$ and also how this can be achieved. It is easy to see that there are other values of α's for which this optimal fairness can be achieved, so what we have proved so far is not enough for a complete classification. Nevertheless, it contains enough information to obtain an optimally-fair protocol.

Corollary 1. *Let $N + 1 - K$ be a multiple of $\operatorname{lcm}\{2, 3, \ldots, K-1\}$. Then Π_g^1 is optimally fair against coalitions of any size.*

Proof. By our definition of $\Pi_g^1 = (\mathcal{M}_1, \mathcal{P}_1)$ and Lemma 2, we have that the α_i's minimise

$$\max\{\alpha_i \mid K \leq i \leq N\}$$

Hence, $\alpha_i = \frac{1}{N+1-K}$ for all i. In particular, all the $N + 1 - K$ shortest configurations are equally likely.

Pick any $L < K$. We already know from Theorem 4, that $\Pi_g^L = (\mathcal{M}_L, \mathcal{P}_L)$ is optimally fair against coalitions of size L. Let $\mathcal{P}_L(t_i) = \beta_i$. Note that the shortest configurations in Π_g^1 and Π_g^L are the same, therefore β_i and α_i refer to the same configuration t_i. We know from Lemma 2 that these β's minimise

$$\max_{\substack{I,S \\ |I|=L}} \operatorname{Pr}_{\Pi_g^L}[I, S] = \max\{\beta_i + \cdots + \beta_{i+L-1} \mid K \leq i \leq N+1-L\}$$

By Theorem 5, we know that the above has value $\frac{1}{\left\lceil \frac{N+1-K}{L} \right\rceil} = \frac{L}{N+1-K}$ since L divides $N + 1 - K$. Finally, by Lemma 2 the theorem follows:

$$\max_{\substack{I,S \\ |I|=L}} \Pr_{\Pi_g^1}[I, S] = \max\{\alpha_i + \cdots + \alpha_{i+L-1} \mid K \leq i \leq N + 1 - L\} = \frac{L}{N + 1 - K}$$

$\square$

With this corollary we show how to construct a protocol which is optimally fair against any coalition size. The protocol we described in Sect. 4 can be used to achieve this fairness. In particular, using the notation of Fig. 1 and assuming the parties agreed on an N for which Corollary 1 applies, $\mathbf{P_1}$ needs to construct a permutation π_i for each of the $N + 1 - K$ "shortest" configurations. Hence, $\pi_i[x] = i - 1 + ((x - i) \mod K)$, i.e. π_i rotates the xth row forward by $\pi_i[x]$. We also note that the protocol of Fig. 1 can be used to achieve the distribution of Π_g^L for any L. Thus, for large values of K, since using values of N suitable for Corollary 1 is prohibitive, the protocol of Fig. 1 can be tuned to be optimal against specific values of L (rather than all).

7   Conclusions and Future Developments

In this paper, we have proposed an efficient exchange protocol which achieves optimal partial fairness even in the presence of a dishonest majority. This is achieved by concealing when the exchange actually happens among a linear amount of dummy messages. Our concrete instantiation of the protocol takes advantage of delay encryption and commutative blinding and provides security against passive adversaries. Using our protocol in conjunction with other SMPC protocols improves the known bounds of partial fairness in the presence of a dishonest majority. In this regard, we provide a large improvement over the current state of the art [4, 9, 16]. We also provide a deep and abstract analysis of the protocols achieving partial fairness by concealing the point where the secrets are exchanged. Since our analysis does not involve any assumption on the cryptographic primitives used, it proves a very general impossibility result and shows the optimality of our protocol. However, our research leaves a couple of unanswered questions. Our abstract analysis does not provide a complete classification of the optimally-fair protocols. Therefore, could a protocol be designed to achieve optimal fairness without the use of delay encryption? Moreover, the protocols of [4] achieves complete fairness if an honest majority is present. This leaves open the question of whether our method could be modify to obtain the same feature.

Appendix A   Formal security proof

In this section, we provide some proof sketches for the theorems presented in Sect. 5. More details are available in the full version of the paper. We assume the setting described in Sect. 3 as well as only considering the exchange in its simplest form after the reduction of Sect. 4.

Proof (Theorem 1 proof). Consider the function described in Fig. 2. It computes the view of the protocol of an adversary $\mathcal{A}$ controlling all parties but $\mathbf{P}_{\mathcal{H}}$. For brevity, Fig. 2 only shows how the messages that depends on $\mathbf{P}_{\mathcal{H}}$ are computed. If Delay is COA secure and $D_{\mathcal{H}}$ is not opened yet, then $\mathcal{A}$ has no access to $s_{\mathcal{H}}$. So assume that the content of $D_{\mathcal{H}}$ are known to $\mathcal{A}$, then $\mathcal{A}$ must obtain $k_{\mathcal{H}}[1]$. By using the commutativity property of Blind, we can remove the appearance of $b_{\mathcal{H}}[1]$ from the computation of $M^{\mathcal{H}}$. Now modify ColView into ColView$_2$ which only outputs the messages of $M^{\mathcal{H}}$ up to (excluding) the message containing $k_{\mathcal{H}}[1]$. Since Blind is IND-CPA and $b_{\mathcal{H}}[1]$ only appears in $L_{\mathcal{H}}$, ColView$_2$ is computationally indistinguishable from ColView$_3$ which behaves the same but constructs $L_{\mathcal{H}}$ using some random (and known by $\mathcal{A}$) key ε instead of $k_{\mathcal{H}}[1]$. In ColView$_3$, $\mathcal{A}$ cannot obtain $s_{\mathcal{H}}$. Thus, $\mathcal{A}$ can obtain $s_{\mathcal{H}}$ only if $D_{\mathcal{H}}$ is opened and the part of $M^{\mathcal{H}}$ containing $k_{\mathcal{H}}[1]$ is exchanged. $\qquad\square$

Max coalition view

ColView$(k_i, b_i, \sigma_i, \tau_i, \quad$ for $i \neq \mathcal{H}) :=$

$k_{\mathcal{H}}, b_{\mathcal{H}}, \sigma_{\mathcal{H}}, \tau_{\mathcal{H}} \leftarrow\!\!\$\ \mathbf{P}_{\mathcal{H}}$'s input

$D_{\mathcal{H}} \leftarrow \mathsf{Delay}(\mathsf{Enc}_{k_{\mathcal{H}}[1]}(s_{\mathcal{H}}) \| \tau_{\mathcal{H}} \| b_{\mathcal{H}}[2])$

$L_{\mathcal{H}} \leftarrow \langle \mathsf{Blind}(k_{\mathcal{H}}[i], b_{\mathcal{H}}[1]) \mid 1 \leq i \leq n \rangle$

let $S^{\mathcal{H}-1} = \langle (M_1, o_1), \ldots, (M_\delta, o_\delta) \rangle$

$S^{\mathcal{H}} \leftarrow \tau_{\mathcal{H}}(\langle F(M_i, o_i, b_{\mathcal{H}}[2], \sigma_{\mathcal{H}}[i]) \mid 1 \leq i \leq \delta \rangle)$

$M^{\mathcal{H}} \leftarrow \mathsf{Unblind}^*(E^K[i], b_{\mathcal{H}}[1])$

return D_i, L_i, S^i, E^K, M^i for $\forall i$

Fig. 2. View of a maximal malicious coalition.

Proof (Theorem 2 proof). To prove the statement we need to construct a simulator $\mathcal{S}$ in the ideal world for any non-uniform PPT adversary $\mathcal{A}$ in the hybrid model. So, fix an adversary $\mathcal{A}$, the simulator $\mathcal{S}$ will work as follows:

- $\mathcal{S}$ runs a local instance of $\mathcal{A}$ to which passes the secrets of the corrupted parties as well as the auxiliary information;
- whenever $\mathcal{A}$ aborts, so does $\mathcal{S}$;
- when $\mathcal{A}$ interacts with the functionality performing the setup phase, $\mathcal{S}$ picks a random input $s'_{\mathcal{H}}$ and carries out the functionality $\mathcal{F}_{\text{setup}}$;
- during the exchange phase $\mathcal{S}$ acts as $\mathbf{P}_{\mathcal{H}}$ and behaves accordingly to the output they produced when simulating the functionality $\mathcal{F}_{\text{setup}}$;
- when $\mathcal{S}$ should send the exchange message containing $k_{\mathcal{H}}[1]$, $\mathcal{S}$ will interact with $\mathcal{F}_{\text{ex}}$ to carry out the exchange in the ideal world and obtain the real secret $s_{\mathcal{H}}$. Using the non-committing property of the encryption scheme, $\mathcal{S}$ can compute a key which will decrypt the ciphertext $\mathsf{Enc}_{k_{\mathcal{H}}[1]}(s'_{\mathcal{H}})$ that $\mathcal{A}$ holds into the real secret $s_{\mathcal{H}}$. $\mathcal{S}$ will use this key in the exchange message;

– when $\mathcal{A}$ returns, $\mathcal{S}$ will output the same result.

Firstly, the view of $\mathcal{A}$ in its interaction with $\mathcal{S}$ is the same as it would be in the real world. This follows from Theorem 1 and the non-committing property of the encryption scheme. Hence, the output of $\mathcal{S}$ in the ideal world is the same as the output of $\mathcal{A}$ in the real world. However, the output of $\mathbf{P}_{\mathcal{H}}$ might differ. If $\mathcal{A}$ aborts the communication when one of the corrupted party would have sent a message that reveals their secret, then such secret is kept confidential in the real world, while it is not in the ideal world. Thanks to Sects. 4.2 and 6, and the use of ideal functionality $\mathcal{F}_{\text{setup}}$, we know that $\mathcal{A}$ will abort at such a point with probability at most $\frac{K-1}{N+1-K}$. □

Before proving the correctness of our setup phase, we show that the helper function F defined in Fig. 1 is an IND-CPA encryption scheme.

Lemma 4. *If* Blind *is IND-CPA, then function* $F(M, f, b, g)$ *defined in Fig. 1 is an* IND-CPA *encryption scheme of* (M, f) *provided that* g *is not fixed.*[9]

Proof (sketch) Consider the Impossible game of Fig. 3. Intuitively, $\mathcal{A}$ wins the impossible game if they can pick a permutation τ so that they can tell if a list of unknown values has been permuted with τ or not. We rely on the fact that k is kept confidential, so $\text{Blind}^*(\varepsilon, k)$ is an unpredictable $n \times K$ matrix of values for $\mathcal{A}$ (note that if Blind is deterministic, then the impossibility of the game is glaring). Now assume that $\mathcal{B}$ is a PPT adversary so that $\text{IND-CPA}_F^{\mathcal{B}}(1^\lambda) = 1$ with probability greater than $\frac{1}{2} + \text{negl}(\lambda)$ for all negligible functions $\text{negl}(\lambda)$. We then argue that $\text{Reduction}^{\mathcal{B}}(1^\lambda) = 1$ with the same probability. In particular, note that $\text{R}(M_0, M_1, f_1, f_0) = \text{O}(M_0, M_1, f_1, f_0)$. However, solving the Reduction games means solving the Impossible game since, in $\text{Reduction}^{\mathcal{B}}(1^\lambda)$, the bit b is used (implicitly) only in the call to shuffle. Therefore, no such $\mathcal{B}$ can exist. □

$\text{IND-CPA}_F^{\mathcal{A}}(1^\lambda)$	$\text{Impossible}^{\mathcal{A}}(1^\lambda)$	$\text{Reduction}^{\mathcal{A}}(1^\lambda)$
$b \leftarrow_\$ \{0,1\}$; $k \leftarrow_\$ \mathcal{K}$	$b \leftarrow_\$ \{0,1\}$; $k \leftarrow_\$ \mathcal{K}$;	$b \leftarrow_\$ \{0,1\}$; $k \leftarrow_\$ \mathcal{K}$;
$\text{O}(M_0, M_1, f_0, f_1) := \{$	$\varepsilon \leftarrow_\$ \mathcal{M}^{n \times K}$; $\sigma \leftarrow_\$ S_n^K$	$\varepsilon \leftarrow_\$ \mathcal{M}^{n \times K}$; $\sigma \leftarrow_\$ S_n^K$
$\sigma \leftarrow_\$ S_n^K$	$\text{shuffle}(\tau) := \{$	$\text{R}(M_0, M_1, f_0, f_1) := \{$
$\textbf{return } F(M_b, f_b, k, \sigma)\}$	$\textbf{return } (\sigma \circ \tau^b)(\text{Blind}^*(\varepsilon, k))$	$\tau \leftarrow f_0^{-1} \circ f_1$
$b' \leftarrow \mathcal{A}^{\text{O}}(1^\lambda)$	$\}$	$c \leftarrow \text{shuffle}(\tau)$
$\textbf{return } b' = b$	$b' \leftarrow \mathcal{A}^{\text{shuffle}}(1^\lambda, \varepsilon, \sigma)$	$\textbf{return } (c, f_0 \circ \sigma^{-1})\}$
	$\textbf{return } b' = b$	$b' \leftarrow \mathcal{A}^{\text{R}}(1^\lambda)$
		$\textbf{return } b = b'$

Fig. 3. Proof that F is IND-CPA.

---

[9] See Fig. 3 for a precise definition of the IND-CPA game for F.

Proof (Theorem 3 proof). Consider Fig. 2, the function ColView returns the view of the dishonest entity $\mathcal{A}$ controlling all parties but $\mathbf{P}_{\mathcal{H}}$. For brevity, Fig. 2 only shows how the messages that depends on $\mathbf{P}_{\mathcal{H}}$ are computed. Firstly, since we assume the security of the time-release encryption, we ignore the delayed messages. By using the fact that F is IND-CPA, we note that ColView is computationally indistinguishable from $\mathsf{ColView}_2$ which behaves the same but $S^{\mathcal{H}}$ is replaced by $\langle F(M_\varepsilon, o_\varepsilon, b_{\mathcal{H}}[2], \sigma'_{\mathcal{H}}[i] \mid 1 \leq i \leq \delta \rangle$ for some fixed (and known by $\mathcal{A}$) $M_\varepsilon, o_\varepsilon$ and fresh $\sigma'_{\mathcal{H}}[i]$. This is enough to show that the setup phase doesn't leak any information about $\tau_{\mathcal{H}}$ (since $\tau_{\mathcal{H}}$ doesn't appear at all in $\mathsf{ColView}_2$). $\square$

References

1. Alcaide, A., Estevez-Tapiador, J.M., Hernandez-Castro, J.C., Ribagorda, A.: A multi-party rational exchange protocol. In: Meersman, R., Tari, Z., Herrero, P. (eds.) OTM 2007. LNCS, vol. 4805, pp. 42–43. Springer, Heidelberg (2007). https://doi.org/10.1007/978-3-540-76888-3_21

2. Andrychowicz, M., Dziembowski, S., Malinowski, D., Mazurek, L: Fair two-party computations via bitcoin deposits. In: Böhme, R., Brenner, M., Moore, T., Smith, M. (eds.) FC 2014. LNCS, vol. 8438, pp. 105–121. Springer, Heidelberg (2014). https://doi.org/10.1007/978-3-662-44774-1_8

3. Asokan, N., Schunter, M., Waidner, M.: Optimistic protocols for multi-party fair exchange. IBM Research Division (1996)

4. Beimel, A., Lindell, Y., Omri, E., Orlov, I.: $\frac{1}{p}$-secure multiparty computation without an honest majority and the best of both worlds. J. Cryptol. **33**(4), 1659–1731 (2020). https://doi.org/10.1007/s00145-020-09354-z

5. Ben-Or, M., Goldreich, O., Micali, S., Rivest, R.L.: A fair protocol for signing contracts. IEEE Trans. Inf. Theor. **36**(1), 40–46 (1990). https://doi.org/10.1109/18.50372

6. Boneh, D., Naor, M.: Timed commitments. In: Bellare, M. (ed.) CRYPTO 2000. LNCS, vol. 1880, pp. 236–254. Springer, Heidelberg (2000). https://doi.org/10.1007/3-540-44598-6_15

7. Canetti, R.: Security and composition of multiparty cryptographic protocols. J. Cryptol. **13**(1), 143–202 (2000). https://doi.org/10.1007/s001459910006

8. Cleve, R.: Limits on the security of coin flips when half the processors are faulty. In: Proceedings of the Eighteenth Annual ACM Symposium on Theory of Computing, STOC 1986, pp. 364–369. Association for Computing Machinery, New York, NY, USA (1986). https://doi.org/10.1145/12130.12168

9. Couteau, G., Roscoe, A.W., Ryan, P.Y.A.: Partially-fair computation from timed-release encryption and oblivious transfer. In: Baek, J., Ruj, S. (eds.) ACISP 2021. LNCS, vol. 13083, pp. 330–349. Springer, Cham (2021). https://doi.org/10.1007/978-3-030-90567-5_17

10. Damgård, I., Nielsen, J.B.: Improved non-committing encryption schemes based on a general complexity assumption. In: Bellare, M. (ed.) CRYPTO 2000. LNCS, vol. 1880, pp. 432–450. Springer, Heidelberg (2000). https://doi.org/10.1007/3-540-44598-6_27

11. Damgård, I.B.: Practical and provably secure release of a secret and exchange of signatures. J. Cryptol. **8**(4), 201–222 (1995). https://doi.org/10.1007/BF00191356

12. Feng, B., Deng, R., Nguyen, K.Q., Varadharajan, V.: Multi-party fair exchange with an off-line trusted neutral party. In: Proceedings of the Tenth International Workshop on Database and Expert Systems Applications, DEXA 1999, pp. 858–862 (1999). https://doi.org/10.1109/DEXA.1999.795294

13. Franklin, M., Tsudik, G.: Secure group barter: multi-party fair exchange with semi-trusted neutral parties. In: Hirchfeld, R. (ed.) FC 1998. LNCS, vol. 1465, pp. 90–102. Springer, Heidelberg (1998). https://doi.org/10.1007/BFb0055475

14. Goldreich, O., Micali, S., Wigderson, A.: How to play any mental game. In: Proceedings of the Nineteenth Annual ACM Symposium on Theory of Computing, STOC 1987, pp. 218–229. Association for Computing Machinery, New York, NY, USA (1987). https://doi.org/10.1145/28395.28420

15. Goldreich, O.: Foundations of Cryptography, vol. 2. Cambridge University Press (2004). https://doi.org/10.1017/CBO9780511721656

16. Gordon, S.D., Katz, J.: Partial fairness in secure two-party computation. In: Gilbert, H. (ed.) EUROCRYPT 2010. LNCS, vol. 6110, pp. 157–176. Springer, Heidelberg (2010). https://doi.org/10.1007/978-3-642-13190-5_8

17. Jakobsson, M.: Flash mixing. In: Proceedings of the Eighteenth Annual ACM Symposium on Principles of Distributed Computing, PODC 1999, pp. 83–89. Association for Computing Machinery, New York, NY, USA (1999). https://doi.org/10.1145/301308.301333

18. Kılınç, H., Küpçü, A.: Efficiently making secure two-party computation fair. In: Grossklags, J., Preneel, B. (eds.) FC 2016. LNCS, vol. 9603, pp. 188–207. Springer, Heidelberg (2017). https://doi.org/10.1007/978-3-662-54970-4_11

19. Küpçü, A., Mohassel, P.: Fast optimistically fair cut-and-choose 2PC. In: Grossklags, J., Preneel, B. (eds.) FC 2016. LNCS, vol. 9603, pp. 208–228. Springer, Heidelberg (2017). https://doi.org/10.1007/978-3-662-54970-4_12

20. Maffei, I., Roscoe, A.W.: Delay encryption by cubing (2022). https://doi.org/10.48550/ARXIV.2205.05594

21. Pagnia, H., Gärtner, F.C.: On the impossibility of fair exchange without a trusted third party. Technical report, Darmstadt University of Technology (1999). https://www.cs.utexas.edu/~shmat/courses/cs395t_fall04/pagnia.pdf

22. Prabhakaran, M.M., Sahai, A.: Secure Multi-Party Computation. IOS Press (2013). https://ebookcentral.proquest.com/lib/oxford/detail.action?docID=1137458

23. Rivest, R.L., Shamir, A., Wagner, D.A.: Time-lock Puzzles and Timed-release Crypto. Report, Massachusetts Institute of Technology (1996)

24. Roscoe, A.W., Ryan, P.Y.A.: Auditable PAKEs: approaching fair exchange without a TTP. In: Stajano, F., Anderson, J., Christianson, B., Matyáš, V. (eds.) Security Protocols 2017. LNCS, vol. 10476, pp. 278–297. Springer, Cham (2017). https://doi.org/10.1007/978-3-319-71075-4_31

Cheap and Fast Iterative Matrix Inverse in Encrypted Domain

Tae Min Ahn, Kang Hoon Lee, Joon Soo Yoo, and Ji Won Yoon[✉]

School of Cybersecurity, Korea University, Seoul 02841, Korea
{xoals3563,hoot55,sandiegojs,jiwon_yoon}@korea.ac.kr

Abstract. Homomorphic encryption (HE) is a promising technique for preserving the privacy of sensitive data by enabling computations to be performed on encrypted data. However, due to the limitations of arithmetic HE schemes, which typically only support addition and multiplication, many nonlinear operations must be approximated using these basic operations. As a result, some nonlinear operations cannot be executed in the same manner as they would be in the plain domain. For instance, the matrix inverse can be calculated using the Gaussian elimination method in the plain domain, which is not possible using only the usual arithmetic. Therefore, much literature has turned to iterative matrix inverse algorithms such as the Newton method, which can be implemented using only additions and multiplications. In this paper, we propose a new matrix inversion method with better performance and prove that the new method outperforms the existing method; the number of depths of the new method is fewer than that of the existing method. Thus, we can evaluate more operations and design the algorithm efficiently since the number of operations is limited in HE. We experiment on ML algorithms such as linear regression and LDA to show that our matrix inverse operation is more efficient than Newton's in HE. Our approach exhibits approximately twice the performance improvement compared to the Newton's method.

Keywords: inverse matrix · homomorphic encryption · machine learning

1 Introduction

Privacy-preserving data mining (PPDM) is becoming significantly vital as more and more data is collected, analyzed, and shared. In addition to this trend, privacy regulations such as the General Data Protection Regulation (GDPR) and the California Consumer Privacy Act (CCPA) have boosted the significance of privacy-preserving techniques by necessitating organizations to protect sensitive and personal information. In this regard, various techniques such as differential privacy and homomorphic encryption (HE) are proposed to protect sensitive information. Among these techniques, homomorphic encryption, which is based

© The Author(s), under exclusive license to Springer Nature Switzerland AG 2024
G. Tsudik et al. (Eds.): ESORICS 2023, LNCS 14344, pp. 334–352, 2024.
https://doi.org/10.1007/978-3-031-50594-2_17

on lattice-based cryptography, is considered a post-quantum resistant encryption algorithm and one of the most promising solutions to attacks from quantum computers. The technique is often referred to as the "holy grail" of cryptography, as it allows for computation on encrypted data. Hence, much literature [3–5] has focused on the execution of privacy-preserving data analysis using homomorphic encryption.

However, homomorphic encryption is often considered impractical due to its poor time performance, albeit with its promising properties. Specifically, the computation of HE circuits typically requires more time at least by the several order of magnitude compared to the construction of plain circuits. In [3], the evaluation of a logistic regression model on the Edinburgh Myocardial Infarction dataset, which consists of 1,253 observations and 10 features, has been reported to require 116 min when implemented within the HE scheme. In contrast, the same process in the plain domain, utilizing a personal computer, can be completed in a matter of seconds. In light of this limitation, much of the recent research has focused on algorithmically [14,15] improving the time performance of HE, as well as on the use of parallel structures [6] in the hardware construction of HE schemes, in an effort to make the technique practical for deployment.

The most efficient and practical implementation of a fully homomorphic encryption scheme based on the Learning with Errors (LWE) problem is the CKKS scheme with leveled homomorphic encryption (LHE) setting. While the CKKS scheme offers the ability to perform arbitrary computations through the use of bootstrapping techniques, its practical deployment is limited to the LHE setting. In this context, the depth of the circuit must be pre-determined, with the number of multiplications per ciphertext serving as the determining factor. Furthermore, as the scheme is based on arithmetic homomorphic encryption, the majority of algorithms must be approximated using only the basic operations of addition and multiplication.

The primary concern when executing privacy-preserving data mining algorithms in HE is the low latency of matrix operations. Among these operations, the most challenging and time-consuming task to construct within HE is the inverse operation. In the plain domain, the inverse of a matrix can be easily obtained through the use of Gaussian elimination. However, in the encrypted domain, all HE circuits must be designed for the worst-case scenario. Additionally, the encrypted elements in a matrix necessitate comparison operations for all elementary row (or column) operations and time-consuming divisions.

In order to overcome this problem, there are several attempts at designing matrix inverse operations in the context of HE. However, they have been met with limited success due to their naïve implementation, resulting in a significant increase in computational time and multiplicative depth. Cheon et al. [7] use a matrix version of Goldschmidt's algorithm described in [8] since it can only be operated using additions and multiplications. However, it is not practical to use as it requires knowledge of a threshold value in advance, which is infeasible in the encrypted domain. Therefore, much literature generally uses Newton's method [9] for matrix inversion in HE [11,12] because it obtains an approximate matrix inverse using only additions and multiplications in an iterative manner. However, it also has a drawback as it requires many iterations and multiplications.

The issue of multiplicative depth is also crucial when designing homomorphic circuits, as most algorithms in practice use leveled homomorphic encryption (LHE), in which the multiplicative depth is predetermined. In the encrypted domain, the matrix inverse must be approximated using a sequence of matrix multiplications, which significantly increases the multiplicative depth of the circuit. For example, the Newton method requires a multiplicative depth of 43 to approximate the inverse matrix, taking up most of the circuit's depth and preventing further operations. Although a technique called bootstrapping can increase the multiplicative depth of the ciphertext, it requires a much greater amount of time and is therefore avoided in practical circuit construction.

Therefore, it is crucial to design an efficient matrix inverse operation with fewer depths in leveled homomorphic encryption (LHE). By reducing the number of multiplications per ciphertext in the matrix inverse algorithm, one can design an HE circuit with a shallower multiplicative depth. Additionally, with the same security parameter set, more operations can be added for further computations within a leveled homomorphic encryption scheme or smaller parameters can be chosen for more efficient computation of the circuit.

In short, our contributions are summarized as the following:

- We present a novel iterative matrix inverse operation. Our technique can reduce the number of depths by nearly a half compared to the Newton's method, mostly used algorithms in the current literature.
- We provide mathematical proofs and experimental result comparing two approaches—ours and Newton's method. Specifically, we demonstrate the convergence speed and required depths of both approaches in theory and implementation.
- Our matrix inverse algorithm seamlessly integrates with the inverse matrix in HE. We substantiate our claim by presenting experimental results.

2   Background

2.1   Homomorphic Encryption

Homomorphic encryption (HE) is a technique that allows for computations to be performed on the encrypted data without the need for decryption, utilizing a one-to-one model between the client and the server. This is achieved by designing the encryption scheme based on the Learning with Errors (LWE) problem [10], which uses noise as a means of ensuring security. However, as computations are performed on the encrypted data, the noise in the ciphertext accumulates, and if this noise exceeds a certain threshold, the correctness of the decryption process can no longer be guaranteed.

Let $\mathcal{M}$ and $\mathcal{C}$ denote the spaces of plaintexts and ciphertexts, respectively. The process of HE is typically composed of four algorithms: key generation, encryption, decryption, and evaluation.

1. **Key generation**: Given the security parameter λ, this algorithm outputs a public key pk, a public evaluation key evk and a secret key sk.
2. **Encryption**: Using the public key pk, the encryption algorithm encrypts a plaintext $m \in \mathcal{M}$ into a ciphertext $ct \in \mathcal{C}$.
3. **Decryption**: For the secret key sk and a ciphertext ct, the decryption algorithm outputs a plaintext $m \in \mathcal{M}$.
4. **Evaluation**: Suppose a function $f : \mathcal{M}^k \rightarrow \mathcal{M}$ is performed over the plaintexts $m_1, \cdots, m_k$. Then, the evaluation algorithm takes in ciphertext $c_1, \cdots, c_k$ corresponding to $m_1, \cdots, m_k$ and the evaluation key evk to output c^* such that $\mathsf{Dec}(c^*) = f(m_1, \cdots, m_k)$.

In the field of homomorphic encryption, there are two primary categories of encryption schemes: fully homomorphic encryption (FHE) and leveled homomorphic encryption (LHE). FHE permits any computation to be executed on the encrypted data, while LHE is more restricted in the types of computations that can be performed. These distinctions are due to the various methods used to handle the accumulation of noise in the ciphertext.

FHE utilizes a specialized technique known as *bootstrapping* to reduce the noise in the ciphertext and increase the multiplicative level of the ciphertext, allowing for further computations to be performed on the encrypted data. However, the use of bootstrapping is a computationally expensive technique and can be time-consuming. In practical applications, LHE is often preferred for its faster performance when working with limited depth circuits. This is because LHE does not rely on the use of bootstrapping and thus is less computationally intensive.

Homomorphic encryption can be categorized in terms of evaluation based on the type of computations that can be performed on the encrypted data. Arithmetic homomorphic encryption allows for basic arithmetic operations such as addition and multiplication to be performed on the encrypted data. Two popular examples are CKKS encryption [1] and BFV [13] encryption schemes, where the CKKS encryption scheme is the latest and the most practical HE solution providing real number arithmetics. Boolean-based homomorphic encryption allows for Boolean operations, such as AND, OR, and NOT, to be performed on the encrypted data. TFHE [15] and FHEW [14] are two examples. The choice of the homomorphic encryption scheme depends on the specific application and the type of computations that need to be performed on the data.

2.2   Arithmetic HE

Arithmetic HE generally uses the usual arithmetic such as addition and multiplication within the limited multiplicative depth which is pre-defined by the encryption parameters. Therefore, one needs to consider the depth of the circuit in advance for the optimal performance since the more depth of the circuit requires larger parameter set resulting in the performance degradation. In the BFV and CKKS schemes, the depth of the circuit is mostly determined by the number of multiplications per chiphertext required for the HE circuit.

Moreover, the multiplication operation is more complex designed than the addition in HE. In BFV and CKKS, the multiplication between two ciphertexts entails auxiliary procedures such as relinearization and modulus switching. Therefore, the time gap between such operations differs in a significant amount. As an illustration, within the CKKS scheme, the computational time required for multiplication exceeds that of addition by a factor greater than 46 (time for mult. : $649\,ms$, add: $14\,ms$)[1]. Hence, it is important to note that reducing number of multiplication is crucial in HE circuit design.

One of the key features of the CKKS scheme is the use of the Single Instruction Multiple Data (SIMD) structure. SIMD [17] is a structure that enables the packing of vector plaintexts into a single ciphertext, and operations are performed in vector units. Another feature is additional functionalities such as slot rotation. Rotations enable us to interact with values located in different ciphertext slots. These features allow for efficient operations on vectors and matrices. Halevi et al. [16] introduce a matrix encoding method based on diagonal decomposition, where the matrix is arranged in diagonal order. This method requires $O(n)$ ciphertexts to represent the matrix, and the matrix multiplication can be computed using $O(n^2)$ rotations and multiplications and two circuit depths given the multiplication of two square matrices of size n.

Additionally, Jiang et al. [18] propose the matrix multiplication method that reduces the complexity of multiplications and rotations to $O(n)$ by employing three levels of computational depth. These approaches are beneficial in terms of computational efficiency. Nevertheless, within the scope of this paper, we employ a naive matrix multiplication approach that necessitates $O(n^3)$ multiplicative operations for the computation of the inverse matrix. The evaluation of an inverse matrix typically entails substantial computational depth. Utilizing a naive matrix multiplication method is advantageous in this regard, as it necessitates only a single depth.

2.3   Circuit Depth

In leveled homomorphic encryption, the total count of multiplication evaluations for a single ciphertext is predetermined by the initial depth parameter of the HE system. For example, when a ciphertext is assigned a depth level denoted as L, it is intrinsically constrained to execute a maximum of L multiplicative operations. Beyond this specified threshold of L multiplications, the ciphertext ceases to support further multiplication operations.

The design of HE circuits can significantly influence the multiplicative depths, making it a crucial consideration. To illustrate this point, consider four distinct ciphertexts denoted as $x, y, z,$ and w, each initially possessing a depth level of L. When these ciphertexts are multiplied sequentially, it consumes 3 depth levels, resulting in a ciphertext denoted as $xyzw$ with a reduced depth of $L - 3$.

Alternatively, we can initially perform a multiplication between x and y, yielding xy with a depth decrement of 1; likewise, we can evaluate a multipli-

---

[1] $\lambda = 128,\ N = 2^{16},\ \Delta = 2^{50},\ L = 50$.

cation on z and w. Finally, the multiplication of xy and zw results in a cipher-text $xyzw$ with a reduced depth of $L - 2$. Importantly, both approaches yield equivalent results and require an identical count of 3 multiplication operations. However, the depth level of the resulting ciphertext differs by a factor of 1.

Note that when multiplying ciphertexts with different levels, the multiplication operations are executed based on the lowest level among them.

2.4 Conventional Iterative Matrix Inverse

There are mainly two approaches in implementing the iterative matrix inverse operation: Goldschmidt's method [8] and Newton's method.

Goldschmidt Algorithm. (See the details in Algorithm 3) Let $\mathbf{A}$ be an invertible square matrix that satisfies $\|\bar{\mathbf{A}}\| \leq \epsilon < 1$ for $\bar{\mathbf{A}} = \mathbf{I} - \frac{1}{2^t}\mathbf{A}$ for some non-negative integer t. It follows that

$$\frac{1}{2^t}\mathbf{A}(\mathbf{I} + \bar{\mathbf{A}})(\mathbf{I} + \bar{\mathbf{A}}^2)\cdots(\mathbf{I} + \bar{\mathbf{A}}^{2^{r-1}}) = \mathbf{I} - \bar{\mathbf{A}}^{2^r}$$

where $\mathbf{I}$ is the identity matrix. Additionally, we note that $\|\bar{\mathbf{A}}^{2^r}\| \leq \|\bar{\mathbf{A}}\|^{2^r} \leq \epsilon^{2^r}$, which implies that $\frac{1}{2^t}\prod_{i=0}^{r-1}(\mathbf{I} + \bar{\mathbf{A}}^{2^i}) = \mathbf{A}^{-1}(\mathbf{I} - \bar{\mathbf{A}}^{2^r})$ is an approximate inverse of $\mathbf{A}$ when $\epsilon^{2^r} \ll 1$.

The algorithm is able to correctly output the approximate matrix inverse for some sufficiently large $r \in \mathbb{N}$. Using the Goldschmidt algorithm, Cheon et al. propose a matrix inverse method over HE schemes [7].

Newton's Method. (See the details in Algorithm 4) Likewise, let $\mathbf{A} \in \mathbb{R}^{n \times n}$ be any invertible square matrix, and let α be the reciprocal of the dominant eigenvalue of $\mathbf{A}\mathbf{A}^T$. Newton's method computes the following sequence of matrices $\{X_k\}_{k \geq 0}$ as:

$$\mathbf{X}_0 = \alpha\mathbf{A}^T \quad \text{and} \quad \mathbf{X}_{k+1} = \mathbf{X}_k(2\mathbf{I} - \mathbf{A}\mathbf{X}_k),$$

until $\mathbf{X}_k$ converges to $\mathbf{A}^{-1}$. We will dive into the details including the proof for convergence in Theorem 1.

Newton's method for obtaining an approximate inverse matrix consists of three steps: (1) computing $\mathbf{A}\mathbf{A}^T$, (2) computing the dominant eigenvalue of $\mathbf{A}\mathbf{A}^T$, and (3) calculating a sequence of $\mathbf{X}_n$ to approximate the inverse of $\mathbf{A}$. It is worth noting that α is the reciprocal of a dominant eigenvalue of $\mathbf{A}\mathbf{A}^T$ which can be approximated using the Goldschmidt's algorithm through a combination of addition and multiplication operations.

In fact, it is difficult to directly obtain the dominant eigenvalue from homomorphic encryption. However, in this paper, we demonstrate that convergence can be proven even when a larger value is used rather than the exact value of the dominant eigenvalue. Therefore, some literature uses a trace instead of a dominant eigenvalue when obtaining the inverse matrix in homomorphic encryption by Newton's method [12]. The trace of a square matrix is the sum of its main diagonal elements. Thus, the trace of $\mathbf{AA}^T$ is always greater than the dominant eigenvalue of $\mathbf{AA}^T$ since the trace is the sum of eigenvalues and $\mathbf{AA}^T$ is positive-definite.

3   Problems in Two Popular Methods

In this section, we will delve into the details and challenges associated with the implementation of the iterative matrix inverse operation in HE using two distinct approaches: Goldschmidt's method and Newton's method.

First, a major limitation of Goldschmidt's method is that the value of $\bar{\mathbf{A}}$ must be known in advance in order to satisfy the condition where $\|\bar{\mathbf{A}}\|$ is less than 1. This is infeasible, as all values—including input, intermediate, and output—are processed in an encrypted state. In other words, it is not possible to find t such that $\|\bar{\mathbf{A}}\| = \|\mathbf{I} - \frac{1}{2^t}\mathbf{A}\| < 1$. As a result, the algorithm cannot be initiated at all. It may be suggested to raise the value of t sufficiently large to match the condition of $\|\bar{\mathbf{A}}\| < 1$, however, this would highly likely zero out the elements of $\bar{\mathbf{A}} = \mathbf{I} - \frac{1}{2^t}\mathbf{A}$, thus the approach cannot provide the approximate matrix inverse for all $\mathbf{A}$.

Next, a drawback of Newton's method is the significant computational complexity in terms of overall time consumption. Upon examination of Newton's method, the sequence of $\mathbf{X}_n$ requires two matrix multiplications in one iteration; assuming that the process converges in r iterations, the time complexity of step (3) in Sect. 2.4 is $O(n^2 r)$. Additionally, step (3) consumes $2r$ circuit-depth. As a result, the time complexity of Newton's method and its depth-consumption are significant. To provide an intuitive example, for a small matrix of size $n = 10$ and iteration number $r = 15$, the total number of multiplications in a HE setting is 4,500. If we assume that each multiplication takes 649 ms, the expected time for the inverse matrix operation would be at least 2,920 s.

4   Proposed Approach

We propose a novel matrix inverse method by combining elements from both Goldschmidt's method and Newton's method.

4.1   Motivation

Goldschmidt's approach requires the value of t for the convergence of $\bar{\mathbf{A}} = \mathbf{I} - \frac{1}{2^t}\mathbf{A}$, however, as previously mentioned, finding this value in the encrypted domain is infeasible.

In contrast, Newton's method relates the dominant eigenvalue of $\mathbf{AA}^T$ to the scaling of $\mathbf{AA}^T$, where the scaling by α ensures that the norm of $\mathbf{AA}^T$ is less than 1.

4.2 Efficient Matrix Inverse

Based on this observation, we posit that the dominant eigenvalue λ_1 is correlated with the role of t in Goldschmidt's method. To address this issue, (1) we first find the dominant eigenvalue of $\mathbf{A}\mathbf{A}^T$, and (2) scale $\mathbf{A}\mathbf{A}^T$ by its dominant eigenvalue. (3) We then use the normalized $\mathbf{A}\mathbf{A}^T$ to iteratively approximate the matrix inverse using the Goldschmidt's sequence for $\mathbf{Y}_i$, as detailed in Algorithm 1.

Algorithm 1. Our Approach

1: **Input:** $n \times n$ invertible matrix $\mathbf{A}$, iteration number r
2: **Output:** approximate inverse matrix $\mathbf{Y}_r$
3: $\lambda_1 \leftarrow$ a dominant eigenvalue or trace of $\mathbf{A}\mathbf{A}^T$
4: $\mathbf{Y}_0 \leftarrow \frac{1}{\lambda_1}\mathbf{A}^T$
5: $\bar{\mathbf{A}}_0 \leftarrow \mathbf{I}_{n \times n} - \frac{1}{\lambda_1}\mathbf{A}\mathbf{A}^T$
6: **for** $i = 1$ **to** r **do**
7: $\quad \mathbf{Y}_i \leftarrow \mathbf{Y}_{i-1}(\mathbf{I}_{n \times n} + \bar{\mathbf{A}}_{i-1})$
8: $\quad \bar{\mathbf{A}}_i \leftarrow \bar{\mathbf{A}}_{i-1}^2$
9: **end for**

In summary, our approach diverges from Newton's method in two fundamental ways: (1) we employ the Goldschmidt algorithm to approximate the inverse of matrix $\mathbf{A}$, and (2) our technique incurs a multiplicative depth of only 1 per iteration, while Newton's method entails a depth of 2 per iteration.

It is worth emphasizing that both methods involve the same number of multiplications per iteration, namely, 2. However, the discrepancy in depth utilization per iteration between the two methods arises from the fact that our approach permits the computation of multiplications independently, incurring a depth cost of 1 for each operation. In contrast, Newton's method conducts matrix multiplications sequentially, incurring a depth cost of 2 per iteration.

Furthermore, it is crucial to note that both Newton's method and our approach require an equivalent number of iterations to achieve convergence. Consequently, given that Newton's method necessitates a depth of 2 per iteration, our approach ultimately requires only half the depth cost to achieve convergence compared to Newton's method. Further details regarding this matter will be addressed in the subsequent proof section.

The reason for finding the dominant eigenvalue of $\mathbf{A}\mathbf{A}^T$, instead of $\mathbf{A}$ itself, is because not all eigenvalues of the input matrix $\mathbf{A}$ are necessarily positive. For convergence, it is essential that the norm of $\bar{\mathbf{A}}_0$ (the matrix used in the Algorithm 1) be less than 1. $\mathbf{A}\mathbf{A}^T$ has the property that all of its eigenvalues are positive. By using the dominant eigenvalue of $\mathbf{A}\mathbf{A}^T$, we ensure that the norm of $\bar{\mathbf{A}}_0$ remains less than 1 for any invertible matrix $\mathbf{A}$. In the case that the input matrix $\mathbf{A}$ is positive definite, it is unnecessary to calculate $\mathbf{A}\mathbf{A}^T$. Under such circumstances, we can directly evaluate the inverse matrix using the following approach.

Algorithm 2. Our Approach

1: **Input:** $n \times n$ positive-definite invertible matrix $\mathbf{A}$, iteration number r
2: **Output:** approximate inverse matrix $\mathbf{Y}_r$
3: $\lambda_1 \leftarrow$ a dominant eigenvalue or trace of $\mathbf{A}$
4: $\mathbf{Y}_0 \leftarrow \frac{1}{\lambda_1} \mathbf{I}_{n \times n}$
5: $\bar{\mathbf{A}}_0 \leftarrow \mathbf{I}_{n \times n} - \frac{1}{\lambda_1} \mathbf{A}$
6: **for** $i = 1$ to r **do**
7:     $\mathbf{Y}_i \leftarrow \mathbf{Y}_{i-1}(\mathbf{I}_{n \times n} + \bar{\mathbf{A}}_{i-1})$
8:     $\bar{\mathbf{A}}_i \leftarrow \bar{\mathbf{A}}_{i-1}^2$
9: **end for**

5   Convergence and Depth Analysis

In this work, we demonstrate that our proposed method converges to the inverse matrix, and it does so at the same rate as Newton's method. To support our claim, we provide the following lemma, which establishes the convergence of a matrix $\mathbf{A}$ under a specific condition.

Lemma 1. *Suppose $\mathbf{A}$ is an $n \times n$ complex matrix with spectral radius $\rho(\mathbf{A})$. Then,* $\lim\limits_{k \to \infty} \mathbf{A}^k = 0$ *if $\rho(\mathbf{A}) < 1$.*

5.1   Proof of Convergence

Suppose that the eigenvalues of an $n \times n$ matrix $\mathbf{A}$ by $\lambda_i(\mathbf{A}), i = 1, \ldots, n$. When $\mathbf{A}$ is positive-definite, we can order its eigenvalues in a non-decreasing order as follows:

$$\lambda_1(\mathbf{A}) \geq \lambda_2(\mathbf{A}) \geq \cdots \geq \lambda_n(\mathbf{A}) > 0.$$

It is worth noting that the eigenvalues of a positive definite matrix are real and positive.

We first state the convergence of Newton's iterative algorithm. We provide details of the proof of Theorem 1 in Appendix B.1 since it is used in other theorems.

Theorem 1. *Let $\mathbf{A} \in \mathbb{R}^{n \times n}$ be an invertible matrix and define the sequence $\{\mathbf{X}_k\}_{k \geq 0}$ of matrices as follows:*

$$\begin{cases} \mathbf{X}_0 = \alpha \mathbf{A}^T, \\ \mathbf{X}_{k+1} = \mathbf{X}_k(2\mathbf{I} - \mathbf{A}\mathbf{X}_k). \end{cases}$$

where $\alpha = \frac{1}{\lambda_1(\mathbf{A}\mathbf{A}^T)}$. Then, $\mathbf{X}_k \to \mathbf{A}^{-1}$ as $k \to \infty$.

Next, we prove that the sequence in our approach (in Algorithm 1) converges to an inverse matrix, i.e., $\mathbf{Y}_i \to \mathbf{A}^{-1}$.

Theorem 2. *Let* $\mathbf{A} \in \mathbb{R}^{n \times n}$ *be an invertible matrix and define the sequence* $\{\mathbf{Y}_k\}_{k \geq 0}$ *of matrices as follows:*

$$\begin{cases} \mathbf{Y}_0 = \alpha \mathbf{A}^T, \ with \ \alpha = \frac{1}{\lambda_1(\mathbf{A}\mathbf{A}^T)}, \\ \bar{\mathbf{A}} = \mathbf{I} - \alpha \mathbf{A}\mathbf{A}^T, \\ \mathbf{Y}_{k+1} = \mathbf{Y}_k(\mathbf{I} + \bar{\mathbf{A}}^{2^k}). \end{cases}$$

Then, $\mathbf{Y}_k \to \mathbf{A}^{-1}$ *as* $k \to \infty$.

Proof. From the definition of Theorem 2, we get

$$\mathbf{Y}_k = \alpha \mathbf{A}^T(\mathbf{I} + \bar{\mathbf{A}})(\mathbf{I} + \bar{\mathbf{A}}^2) \cdots (\mathbf{I} + \bar{\mathbf{A}}^{2^{k-1}}) = \mathbf{A}^{-1}(\mathbf{I} - \bar{\mathbf{A}}^{2^k}). \qquad (1)$$

We show that $\rho(\bar{\mathbf{A}}) = \rho(\mathbf{I} - \alpha \mathbf{A}\mathbf{A}^T) < 1$. We note that the eigenvalues $\lambda_i(\bar{\mathbf{A}})$ are given by, $\lambda_i(\bar{\mathbf{A}}) = 1 - \alpha \lambda_i(\mathbf{A}\mathbf{A}^T)$. Since $\mathbf{A}\mathbf{A}^T$ is positive-definite and $\alpha = \frac{1}{\lambda_1(\mathbf{A}\mathbf{A}^T)}$, we have $|\lambda_i(\bar{\mathbf{A}})| < 1$. Thus, we can get $\rho(\bar{\mathbf{A}}) < 1$. Therefore, by Lemma 1 we have $\lim_{k \to \infty} \bar{\mathbf{A}}^k = 0$. We note that $\mathbf{Y}_k = \alpha \mathbf{A}^T \prod_{i=0}^{k-1}(\mathbf{I} + \bar{\mathbf{A}}^{2^i}) = \mathbf{A}^{-1}(\mathbf{I} - \bar{\mathbf{A}}^{2^k})$ follows from Eq. (1). Therefore,

$$\lim_{k \to \infty} \mathbf{Y}_k = \alpha \mathbf{A}^T \prod_{i=0}^{\infty}(\mathbf{I} + \bar{\mathbf{A}}^{2^i}) = \mathbf{A}^{-1}(\mathbf{I} - \lim_{k \to \infty} \bar{\mathbf{A}}^{2^k}) = \mathbf{A}^{-1}.$$

In the context of our method, we posit the use of the trace of $\mathbf{A}\mathbf{A}^T$ in place of the dominant eigenvalue of $\mathbf{A}\mathbf{A}^T$. Our method still guarantees convergence of the iterative process, as the spectral radius of the modified matrix $\bar{\mathbf{A}}$, denoted as $\rho(\bar{\mathbf{A}})$, remains less than one under this assumption.

5.2 Convergence Comparison

We prove that our method has the same convergence rate as Newton's method.

Theorem 3. *Let* $\mathbf{A} \in \mathbb{R}^{n \times n}$ *be an invertible matrix. Suppose* $\{\mathbf{X}_k\}_{k \geq 0}$ *is the sequence of matrices generated from Newton's method of Theorem 1 and* $\{\mathbf{Y}_k\}_{k \geq 0}$ *generated from Theorem 2 with* $\mathbf{A}$. *Then for any* $0 < \epsilon \ll \|\mathbf{A}^{-1}\|$, *let* $R_1, R_2 \in \mathbb{N}$ *be the smallest integers that satisfy* $\|\mathbf{A}^{-1} - \mathbf{X}_i\| < \epsilon$ *for all* $i > R_1$ *and* $\|\mathbf{A}^{-1} - \mathbf{Y}_j\| < \epsilon$ *for all* $j > R_2$ *respectively. Then we have* $R_1 = R_2$. *That is, the method illustrated in Theorem 2 converges with the same iterations as Newton's method.*

Proof. From the proofs of Theorem 1 and Theorem 2, we have

$$\mathbf{X}_k = \mathbf{A}^{-1}(\mathbf{I} - \mathbf{R}_k) = \mathbf{A}^{-1}\left(\mathbf{I} - \left(\mathbf{I} - \frac{1}{\lambda_1(\mathbf{A}\mathbf{A}^T)}\mathbf{A}\mathbf{A}^T\right)^{2^k}\right),$$

$$\mathbf{Y}_k = \mathbf{A}^{-1}(\mathbf{I} - \bar{\mathbf{A}}^{2^k}).$$

We first prove that R_1 and R_2 always exist for $0 < \epsilon < \|\mathbf{A}^{-1}\|$. Define two sequences $\{x_k\}_{k \geq 0}$ and $\{y_k\}_{k \geq 0}$ with $x_k = \|\mathbf{A}^{-1} - \mathbf{X}_k\|$ and $y_k = \|\mathbf{A}^{-1} - \mathbf{Y}_k\|$.

For simplicity, we denote the greatest eigenvalue of $\mathbf{A}\mathbf{A}^T$ as λ_1, and the smallest eigenvalue as λ_n. Then we have

$$
\begin{aligned}
x_k = \|\mathbf{A}^{-1} - \mathbf{X}_k\| &= \left\| \mathbf{A}^{-1} \left(\mathbf{I} - \frac{1}{\lambda_1} \mathbf{A}\mathbf{A}^T \right)^{2^k} \right\| \\
&\leq \|\mathbf{A}^{-1}\| \cdot \left\| \mathbf{I} - \frac{1}{\lambda_1} \mathbf{A}\mathbf{A}^T \right\|^{2^k} \\
&= \|\mathbf{A}^{-1}\| \cdot \left(\frac{\lambda_1 - \lambda_n}{\lambda_1} \right)^{2^k}.
\end{aligned}
$$

Also for y_k, we have

$$
\begin{aligned}
y_k = \|\mathbf{A}^{-1} - \mathbf{Y}_k\| = \left\| \mathbf{A}^{-1} \mathbf{A} \bar{\mathbf{A}}^{T^{2^k}} \right\| &= \left\| \mathbf{A}^{-1} \left(\mathbf{I} - \frac{1}{\lambda_1} \cdot \mathbf{A}\mathbf{A}^T \right)^{2^k} \right\| \\
&\leq \|\mathbf{A}^{-1}\| \cdot \left\| \mathbf{I} - \frac{1}{\lambda_1} \cdot \mathbf{A}\mathbf{A}^T \right\|^{2^k} \\
&= \|\mathbf{A}^{-1}\| \cdot \left(\frac{\lambda_1 - \lambda_n}{\lambda_1} \right)^{2^k}.
\end{aligned}
$$

Then by the definition of λ_1 and λ_n, we have the inequality

$$
0 < \frac{\lambda_1 - \lambda_n}{\lambda_1} < 1.
$$

From the results, we can observe that both sequences x_n and y_n monotonically decrease and both converge to 0 as $k \to \infty$. Thus, for any $0 < \epsilon \ll \|\mathbf{A}^{-1}\|$, there always exist $R_1, R_2 \in \mathbb{N}$ such that

$$
x_i < \epsilon \text{ for all } i > R_1, \text{ and } y_j < \epsilon \text{ for all } j > R_2.
$$

We further investigate the behavior of x_k and y_k to compare the minimal iteration required, namely R_1 and R_2:

$$
x_{R_1} = \left\| \mathbf{A}^{-1} \left(\mathbf{I} - \frac{1}{\lambda_1} \mathbf{A}\mathbf{A}^T \right)^{2^{R_1}} \right\| < \epsilon,
$$

$$
y_{R_2} = \left\| \mathbf{A}^{-1} \left(\mathbf{I} - \frac{1}{\lambda_1} \mathbf{A}\mathbf{A}^T \right)^{2^{R_2}} \right\| < \epsilon.
$$

It is readily evident that, for a given ϵ value, R_1 is equal to R_2.

Our proposed method, despite relying on the trace instead of the dominant eigenvalue when compared to Newton's method, demonstrates an equivalent convergence rate. The proof for this is similar to Theorem 3.

5.3   Depth Comparison

From Theorem 3, we confirm that our method converges at the same rate as Newton's method. It implies that our method uses less multiplicative depth for matrix inverse operation.

Specifically, let t_{div} denote the iteration number required for the division algorithm method. Moreover, let $\mathbf{X}_k$ and $\mathbf{Y}_k$ represent the previous two algorithms, and assume that $\mathbf{X}_k$ and $\mathbf{Y}_k$ converge at iterations of R_1 and R_2, respectively. Then, the total number of multiplications required for $\mathbf{X}_k$ is $2t_{div} + n^3 + n^2 + 2n^3R_1$ and the total number of multiplications required for $\mathbf{Y}_k$ is $2t_{div} + 2n^2 + 2n^3R_2$. Since the division algorithm requires the same amount of multiplications for both algorithms, we only compare the remaining terms. Hence, $\mathbf{Y}_k$ requires almost the same number of multiplications since $R_1 = R_2$.

For a depth comparison, we analysis the sequence equation $\mathbf{X}_{k+1} = \mathbf{X}_k(2\mathbf{I} - \mathbf{AX}_k)$ in Theorem 1 and the sequence equation $\mathbf{Y}_{k+1} = \mathbf{Y}_k(\mathbf{I} + \bar{\mathbf{A}}^{2^k})$ in Theorem 2. First, assuming the depth level of the input matrix $\mathbf{A}$ is denoted as L, and the level of $\mathbf{X}_0$ is assumed to be $L - 5$, we can observe that $\mathbf{X}_1$ is computed by multiplying $\mathbf{A}$ and $\mathbf{X}_0$, then subtracting it from $2\mathbf{I}$, followed by another multiplication with $\mathbf{X}_0$. Considering only the multiplication operations (since addition and subtraction do not affect the level), the level of $\mathbf{AX}_0$ becomes $L - 6$, and after another multiplication with $\mathbf{X}_0$, the resulting matrix $\mathbf{X}_1$ has a level of $L-7$. Following this pattern, we can see that $\mathbf{X}_2$ has a $L - 9$ level, $\mathbf{X}_3$ has a $L - 11$ level, and so on. Since the level difference between $\mathbf{X}_k$ and $\mathbf{X}_{k+1}$ ($k \geq 0$) is 2, we can conclude that the Newton method consumes 2 depths per iteration.

Next, assuming the level of $\mathbf{Y}_0$ is L, then $\bar{\mathbf{A}}$ has a $L-1$ level. $\mathbf{Y}_1$ is computed by adding $\bar{\mathbf{A}}$ and $\mathbf{I}$ and then multiplying it by $\mathbf{Y}_0$, resulting in a $L - 2$ level. $\bar{\mathbf{A}}^2$ is the square of $\bar{\mathbf{A}}$, which has $L-2$ level. $\mathbf{Y}_2$ is the result of multiplying $\mathbf{Y}_1$ and $\bar{\mathbf{A}}^2$, which makes its level $L - 3$. This pattern continues, and we can observe that $\mathbf{Y}_3$ has a $L - 4$ level, $\mathbf{Y}_4$ has a $L - 5$ level, and so on. The level difference between $\mathbf{Y}_k$ and $\mathbf{Y}_{k+1}$ ($k \geq 1$) is always 1. Therefore, our method consumes 1 depth per iteration.

Based on the observation, the total depths required for $\mathbf{X}_k$ is $t_{div} + 2 + 2R_1$ and the total depths required for $\mathbf{Y}_k$ is $t_{div} + 3 + R_2$. Since $R_1 = R_2$, and assuming that $R_1 = R_2 \geq 2$, our method can achieve the inverse matrix with fewer depths compared to the Newton method.

6   Experiment

In this section, we conduct a comparative analysis to evaluate the performance of the proposed algorithm and Newton's method when applied to invertible matrices in both the plain and encrypted domains. The evaluation focuses on two critical metrics: circuit depth and iteration number. Subsequently, the proposed algorithm is applied to linear regression and LDA in the encrypted domain to validate its computational efficiency.

6.1   Experiment Setting

Environment. In our cryptographic experiments, we employed OpenFHE [2] library for implementing the CKKS scheme. All experiments were evaluated on a system consisting of Intel Core i9-9900K CPU 3.60GHz × 16, 62.7 GiB RAM, Ubuntu 20.04.4 LTS.

CKKS Scheme Setting. We employed a 128-bit security level for all CKKS implementations. The other encryption parameters, including the ring dimension N, scaling factor Δ, and circuit depth D, were pre-determined to perform the inverse matrix operations or machine learning algorithms. Furthermore, we exclusively used a leveled approach and avoided the use of bootstrapping during the evaluation of homomorphic circuits.

6.2   Invertible Matrix and Machine Learning

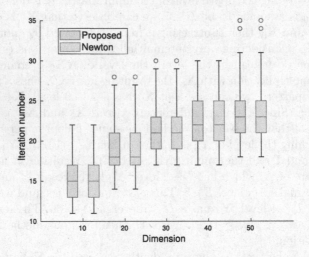

Fig. 1. The distribution of iteration numbers required for convergence to the inverse matrix across various dimensions for two algorithms—ours and Newton method.

Iteration Number Distribution. Figure 1 demonstrates the distributions of the iteration numbers for our proposed algorithm and the Newton's method. We conducted 100 experiments for matrix dimensions of $10, 20, \ldots, 50$ and depicted their distributions using box plots. We randomly generated square invertible matrices of varying sizes, with the smallest eigenvalue greater than 10^{-7} to avoid being recognized as zero. We recorded the iteration numbers at which convergence was achieved, with ϵ set to 0.001 and compared the approaches in the plain domain using Matlab R2022b. The results of our experiments show that our proposed algorithm converges identically to Newton's method regardless of dimension.

Time and Memory w.r.t. Circuit Depth. The reduction in depths has a significant impact on both the multiplication time and the memory size of ciphertext and keys in the encrypted domain. For example, in the CKKS scheme, with the same parameter set (λ, N, Δ), the multiplication time increases proportionally with respect to the depth D of the circuit (see Table 1). Specifically, multiplication time for $D = 1$ is 0.037, while 0.649 for $D = 50$; the latter is approximately 17 times greater.

Table 1. Impact of circuit depth on the multiplication and key generation time in the CKKS encryption scheme with fixed encryption parameters (λ, N, Δ).

λ	N	Δ	Depth	Mult. Time (s)	KeyGen Time (s)
128	2^{16}	2^{50}	1	0.037	0.225
128	2^{16}	2^{50}	10	0.14	0.763
128	2^{16}	2^{50}	20	0.251	1.323
128	2^{16}	2^{50}	30	0.361	1.884
128	2^{16}	2^{50}	40	0.486	2.461
128	2^{16}	2^{50}	50	0.649	3.062

Additionally, in the leveled-CKKS scheme, the size of the ciphertext and key are linearly determined by the circuit depth. This is due to the fact that the CKKS scheme uses rescaling (or similarly modulus-reduction in other schemes) procedure, which reduces the ciphertext size (modulus) after multiplication. Consequently, a larger initial ciphertext size is necessary to accommodate the entire circuit multiplications. Therefore, the depth of the circuit is a crucial factor that determines both the time performance and memory capacity in leveled encryption schemes.

Comparison of Implementation in Encrypted Domain: Time and Depth. We compare our proposed algorithm with the Newton's method for a randomly generated square matrix of size 5 with regards to error at specific iterations, under varying circuit depths (as seen in Table 2) in the encrypted domain. We use the same set of parameters (λ, N, Δ) as in Table 1 and measure the error of the approximated inverse matrix using the spectral norm. For the convergence of the approximated inverse, we set $\epsilon = 0.001$.

The results indicate that our algorithm converges at iteration number 16, which can be efficiently implemented with a circuit depth of $D = 27$. In contrast, the Newton's method converges at the same iteration number 16; however, it requires a circuit depth of $D = 43$.

Therefore, we conclude that our proposed algorithm has the same convergence speed as the Newton's method in the encrypted domain. However, as our algorithm can be implemented with a smaller circuit depth, its total execution

Table 2. Evaluation of our approach and Newton's method in the encrypted domain based on iteration number, circuit depth, and error (both use trace instead of dominant eigenvalue).

Depth	Our Method			Newton Method		
	#Iter	Error	Time(s)	#Iter	Error	Time(s)
20	9	0.4957	242.36	4	2.3868	177.97
25	14	0.0036	442.15	7	1.5761	301.48
27	16	$4.59e^{-6}$	596.62	8	1.0687	409.17
35	16	$4.59e^{-6}$	1054.35	12	0.1296	791.84
40	16	$4.59e^{-6}$	1242.98	14	0.0036	1042.87
43	16	$4.59e^{-6}$	1410.56	16	$4.59e^{-6}$	1256.37

time is about 596 s, whereas the Newton's method's execution time is about 1,256 s, making our method 2.1 times faster.

Table 3. Comparison of our proposed approach and Newton's method in performing ML algorithms—linear regression and LDA (both use trace instead of dominant eigenvalue).

ML. Alg.	Our Method		Newton Method	
	Iter. (Depth)	Time (s)	Iter. (Depth)	Time (s)
Linear	22(58)	14921.42	22(58)	13352.61
Regression	22(37)	7541.7	N/A	N/A
LDA	9(36)	1902.33	9(36)	1884.76
	9(28)	1481.71	N/A	N/A

Application to ML Algorithms. We demonstrate the efficiency of our approach through two popular ML algorithms, linear regression and LDA, that utilize a positive definite matrix as input to evaluate its inverse. We compare the efficiency of our method with the Newton's algorithm in terms of circuit depth and time performance in the encrypted domain; we show that our algorithm significantly enhances the overall performance.

For our evaluation of linear regression in the encrypted domain, we employed 100 samples with 8 features from the well-known public dataset "Diabetes dataset". We used the same encryption parameters λ, N, Δ and set $\epsilon = 0.001$ for the convergence of the matrix inverse operation. The linear regression of the dataset requires an inverse of a 8×8 square matrix. Our method and Newton's method both required 22 iteration number (see Table 3). However, our method requires less depth per iteration than Newton's method. This results in a circuit depth optimization of 37 for our method, compared to 58 for the Newton's method.

Initially, we conducted an experiment using the same circuit depth of 58 for both our method and Newton's method. Our approach closely resembles Newton's method in terms of the number of iterations required for convergence. However, it is noteworthy that as the depth level of the ciphertext decreases, the ciphertext modulus decreases as well, resulting in an increase in multiplication speed. In contrast to our method, which consumes only one depth in a single iteration, Newton's method consumes two depths in a single iteration. Consequently, even when performing the same number of operations, the multiplication of ciphertexts with a relatively lower depth level in Newton's method takes less time than in our approach. This phenomenon results in a decrease in the total execution time of Newton's method, reducing it by 1568.81 s compared to the execution time of our method. However, our method can perform additional 21 multiplications followed by the acquisition of the inverse matrix. Conversely, in the case of the Newton's method, further multiplication was no longer feasible upon obtaining the inverse matrix.

Subsequently, we measured the execution time of our approach with an optimal circuit depth of 37. Our approach demonstrated approximately 1.8 times less execution time compared to the Newton's method. It is important to note that the Newton's method cannot be implemented with a depth of 37; a minimum circuit depth of 58 is required to ensure correctness of the result.

In the evaluation of LDA, we used a subset of 150 samples from Iris flower dataset, which consists of 4 features and 3 species. With the same setting as in the linear regression, the LDA algorithm has to compute over an inverse of 4×4 matrix. Our method and Newton's method both required 9 iterations. Hence, the total depth required for each approach was 28 and 36, respectively, for constructing the optimal circuit. The evaluation time for the optimal circuit for each approach was approximately 1481.71 s for our method and 1884.46 s for the Newton's method, indicating a 1.27 times improvement in time performance of our proposed algorithm.

7   Conclusion

This paper presents a novel iterative matrix inverse algorithm that reduces multiplicative depths compared to the widely used Newton's method in the homomorphic encryption domain. Our algorithm offers significant improvements in computational time efficiency, with about 2 times reduction, and is advantageous in machine learning algorithms requiring the inverse of matrices.

Acknowledgements. This work was supported by an Institute of Information & Communications Technology Planning Evaluation (IITP) grant funded by the Korea government (MSIT) (No. 2021-0-00558-003, Development of National Statistical Analysis System using Homomorphic Encryption Technology).

A   Iterative Matrix Inverse Methods

A.1   Goldschmidt's Matrix Inverse Method

Algorithm 3. Goldschmidt's Matrix Inverse Approach

1: **Input:** $n \times n$ invertible matrix $\mathbf{A}$, iteration number r
2: **Output:** approximate inverse matrix $\mathbf{B}_r$
3: $t \leftarrow 1$
4: **while true do**
5:     $\bar{\mathbf{A}}_0 \leftarrow \mathbf{I}_{n \times n} - \frac{1}{2^t}\mathbf{A}$
6:     **if** $\|\bar{\mathbf{A}}_0\| < 1$ **then**
7:         break;
8:     **end if**
9:     $t \leftarrow t + 1$
10: **end while**
11: $\mathbf{B}_0 \leftarrow \frac{1}{2^t}\mathbf{I}_{n \times n}$
12: **for** $i = 1$ to r **do**
13:     $\mathbf{B}_i \leftarrow \mathbf{B}_{i-1}(\mathbf{I}_{n \times n} + \bar{\mathbf{A}}_{i-1})$
14:     $\bar{\mathbf{A}}_i \leftarrow \bar{\mathbf{A}}_{i-1}^2$
15: **end for**

A.2   Newton's Matrix Inverse Method

Algorithm 4. Newton's Matrix Inverse Approach

1: **Input:** $n \times n$ invertible matrix $\mathbf{A}$, iteration number r
2: **Output:** approximate inverse matrix $\mathbf{B}_r$
3: $\lambda_1 \leftarrow$ a dominant eigenvalue of $\mathbf{AA}^T$
4: $\mathbf{B}_0 \leftarrow \frac{1}{\lambda_1}\mathbf{A}^T$
5: **for** $i = 1$ to r **do**
6:     $\mathbf{B}_i \leftarrow \mathbf{B}_{i-1}(2\mathbf{I}_{n \times n} - \mathbf{AB}_{i-1})$
7: **end for**

B   Detailed Proof

B.1   Proof of Theorem 1

Proof. Let $\mathbf{R}_k = \mathbf{I} - \mathbf{AX}_k$. Then, we note that $\mathbf{X}_{n+1} = \mathbf{X}_k(\mathbf{I} + \mathbf{R}_k)$. We first show that $\rho(\mathbf{R}_0) = \rho(\mathbf{I} - \alpha\mathbf{AA}^T) < 1$. We note that the eigenvalues $\lambda_i(\mathbf{R}_0)$ are given by, $\lambda_i(\mathbf{R}_0) = 1 - \alpha\lambda_i(\mathbf{AA}^T)$. Since $\mathbf{AA}^T$ is positive-definite and $\alpha = \frac{1}{\lambda_1(\mathbf{AA}^T)}$, we have $|\lambda_i(\mathbf{R}_0)| < 1$. Thus, we get $\rho(\mathbf{R}_0) < 1$. Therefore, by Lemma 1, we have

$$\lim_{k \to \infty} \mathbf{R}_0^k = 0. \tag{2}$$

Next, we note that,

$$\begin{aligned}
\mathbf{R}_k = \mathbf{I} - \mathbf{A}\mathbf{X}_k &= \mathbf{I} - \mathbf{A}\mathbf{X}_{k-1}(\mathbf{I} + \mathbf{R}_{k-1}) \\
&= \mathbf{I} - \mathbf{A}\mathbf{X}_{k-1} - \mathbf{A}\mathbf{X}_{k-1}\mathbf{R}_{k-1} \\
&= \mathbf{R}_{k-1} - \mathbf{A}\mathbf{X}_{k-1}\mathbf{R}_{k-1} \\
&= (\mathbf{I} - \mathbf{A}\mathbf{X}_{k-1})\mathbf{R}_{k-1} = (\mathbf{R}_{k-1})^2.
\end{aligned}$$

Therefore, inductively, we have $\mathbf{R}_k = \mathbf{R}_0^{2^k}$. Hence, $\lim_{n\to\infty} \mathbf{R}_k = \lim_{k\to\infty} \mathbf{R}_0^{2^k} = 0$, where the last equality follows from Eq. (2). Finally, from the definition of $\mathbf{R}_k$, we note that $\mathbf{X}_k = \mathbf{A}^{-1}(\mathbf{I} - \mathbf{R}_k)$. Therefore,

$$\lim_{n\to\infty} \mathbf{X}_k = \lim_{n\to\infty} \mathbf{A}^{-1}(\mathbf{I} - \mathbf{R}_k) = \mathbf{A}^{-1}.$$

Consider the scenario in which the trace of the matrix product $\mathbf{A}\mathbf{A}^T$ is utilized in place of the dominant eigenvalue. Despite the replacement of the scalar parameter alpha with the reciprocal of the trace of $\mathbf{A}\mathbf{A}^T$, the spectral radius of the matrix $\mathbf{R}_0$ remains less than one. This ensures that the iterative process converges.

References

1. Cheon, J.H., Kim, A., Kim, M., Song, Y.: Homomorphic encryption for arithmetic of approximate numbers. In: Takagi, T., Peyrin, T. (eds.) ASIACRYPT 2017. LNCS, vol. 10624, pp. 409–437. Springer, Cham (2017). https://doi.org/10.1007/978-3-319-70694-8_15
2. Al Badawi, A., et al.: OpenFHE: open-source fully homomorphic encryption library. In: Proceedings of the 10th Workshop on Encrypted Computing & Applied Homomorphic Cryptography, pp. 53–63 (2022)
3. Kim, A., Song, Y., Kim, M., Lee, K., Cheon, J.H.: Logistic regression model training based on the approximate homomorphic encryption. BMC Med. Genomics 11(4), 23–31 (2018)
4. Sun, X., Zhang, P., Liu, J.K., Yu, J., Xie, W.: Private machine learning classification based on fully homomorphic encryption. IEEE Trans. Emerg. Top. Comput. 8(2), 352–364 (2018)
5. Wood, A., Najarian, K., Kahrobaei, D.: Homomorphic encryption for machine learning in medicine and bioinformatics. ACM Comput. Surv. (CSUR) 53(4), 1–35 (2020)
6. Jung, W., Kim, S., Ahn, J. H., Cheon, J. H., Lee, Y.: Over 100x faster bootstrapping in fully homomorphic encryption through memory-centric optimization with GPUS. ACM Comput. Surv. (CSUR), 114–148 (2021)
7. Cheon, J.H., Kim, A., Yhee, D.: Multi-dimensional packing for HEAAN for approximate matrix Arithmetics. Cryptology ePrint Archive (2018)
8. Cetin, G.S., Doroz, Y., Sunar, B., Martin, W.J.: Arithmetic using word-wise homomorphic encryption. Cryptology ePrint Archive (2015)
9. Guo, C.H., Higham, N.J.: A schur-newton method for the matrix\boldmath p th Root and its Inverse. SIAM J. Matrix Analy. Appl. 28(3), 788–804 (2006)

10. Regev, O.: On lattices, learning with errors, random linear codes, and cryptography. J. ACM (JACM) **56**(6), 1–40 (2009)
11. Mital, N., Ling, C., Gündüz, D.: Secure distributed matrix computation with discrete Fourier transform. IEEE Trans. Inf. Theory **68**(7), 4666–4680 (2022)
12. Cock, M.D., Dowsley, R., Nascimento, A.C., Newman, S.C.:Fast, privacy preserving linear regression over distributed datasets based on pre-distributed data. In: Proceedings of the 8th ACM Workshop on Artificial Intelligence and Security, pp. 3–14 (2015)
13. Fan, J., Vercauteren, F.: Somewhat practical fully homomorphic encryption. Cryptology ePrint Archive (2012)
14. Ducas, L., Micciancio, D.: FHEW: bootstrapping homomorphic encryption in less than a second. In: Oswald, E., Fischlin, M. (eds.) EUROCRYPT 2015. LNCS, vol. 9056, pp. 617–640. Springer, Heidelberg (2015). https://doi.org/10.1007/978-3-662-46800-5_24
15. Chillotti, I., Gama, N., Georgieva, M., Izabachène, M.: TFHE: fast fully homomorphic encryption over the torus. J. Cryptol. **33**(1), 34–91 (2020)
16. Halevi, S., Shoup, V.: Faster homomorphic linear transformations in HElib. In: Shacham, H., Boldyreva, A. (eds.) CRYPTO 2018. LNCS, vol. 10991, pp. 93–120. Springer, Cham (2018). https://doi.org/10.1007/978-3-319-96884-1_4
17. Smart, N.P., Vercauteren, F.: Fully homomorphic SIMD operations. Des. Codes Crypt. **71**, 57–81 (2014)
18. Jiang, X., Kim, M., Lauter, K., Song, Y.: Secure outsourced matrix computation and application to neural networks. In: Proceedings of the 2018 ACM SIGSAC Conference on Computer and Communications Security, pp. 1209–1222 (2018)

Practical Randomized Lattice Gadget Decomposition with Application to FHE

Sohyun Jeon[1] (ID), Hyang-Sook Lee[1] (ID), and Jeongeun Park[2](✉) (ID)

[1] Department of Mathematics, Ewha Womans University, Seoul, Republic of Korea
jeonsh099@ewhain.net, hsl@ewha.ac.kr
[2] imec-COSIC, KU Leuven, Leuven, Belgium
jeongeun.park@esat.kuleuven.be

Abstract. Gadget decomposition is widely used in lattice based cryptography, especially homomorphic encryption (HE) to keep the noise growth slow. If it is randomized following a subgaussian distribution, it is called subgaussian (gadget) decomposition which guarantees that we can bound the noise contained in ciphertexts by its variance. This gives tighter and cleaner noise bound in average case, instead of the use of its norm. Even though there are few attempts to build efficient such algorithms, most of them are still not practical enough to be applied to homomorphic encryption schemes due to somewhat high overhead compared to the deterministic decomposition. Furthermore, there has been no detailed analysis of existing works. Therefore, HE schemes use the deterministic decomposition algorithm and rely on a Heuristic assumption that every output element follows a subgaussian distribution independently.

In this work, we introduce a new practical subgaussian gadget decomposition algorithm which has the least overhead (less than 14%) among existing works for certain parameter sets, by combining two previous works. In other words, we bring an existing technique based on an uniform distribution to a simpler and faster design (PKC' 22) to exploit parallel computation, which allows to skip expensive parts due to precomputation, resulting in even simpler and faster algorithm. When the modulus is large (over 100-bit), our algorithm is not always faster than the other similar work. Therefore, we give a detailed comparison, even for large modulus, with all the competitive algorithms for applications to choose the best algorithm for their choice of parameters.

Keywords: Subgaussian Decomposition · Randomized Gadget Decomposition · Homomorphic Encryption

1 Introduction

Gadget decomposition algorithm is an essential building block for lattice based cryptography which leads to various applications such as identity based encryption (IBE) [8,20], attributed based encryption (ABE) [4,15], homomorphic encryption (HE) [21] and more. A Gadget matrix is defined as $\mathbf{G} = \mathbf{I}_n \otimes \mathbf{g}$, where $\mathbf{g} := (1, b, b^2, \ldots, b^{k-1})$ is called a gadget vector, and $\mathbf{I}_n$ is a n-by-n identity matrix for some positive integer n. A gadget decomposition algorithm was

© The Author(s), under exclusive license to Springer Nature Switzerland AG 2024
G. Tsudik et al. (Eds.): ESORICS 2023, LNCS 14344, pp. 353–371, 2024.
https://doi.org/10.1007/978-3-031-50594-2_18

firstly introduced by Micciancio et al. [24] as preimage sampling for $f_{\mathbf{G}}(\mathbf{x}) = \mathbf{G}\mathbf{x}$ mod q. For an input $\mathbf{u}$, the algorithm samples a point $\mathbf{x}$ in $\Lambda_{\mathbf{u}}^{\perp}(\mathbf{G})$ which is a coset of $\Lambda_{q}^{\perp}(\mathbf{G})$. We consider the case $n = 1$ so that the algorithm samples a point in $\Lambda_{u}^{\perp}(\mathbf{g}^{t})$ for an input $u \in \mathbb{Z}_{q}$. Depending on a distribution which the output follows, applications may differ. Specifically, if the output $\mathbf{x}$ is a subgaussian random variable, we call it a subgaussian gadget decomposition (subgaussian sampling for short, throughout this paper).

The subgaussian distribution has an important role in lattice based cryptosystems due to its Pythagorean additivity. Informally, any distribution of which tails are bounded by tails of a Gaussian distribution is a subgaussian distribution. Therefore, a discrete Gaussian distribution also belongs to a subgaussian distribution. In particular, the property, Pythagorean additivity, enables to tightly analyze the noise growth of average case in many lattice based homomorphic encryption (HE) schemes like [5,7,12,16,17,21]. A ciphertext of HE schemes has the noise term which becomes larger whenever homomorphic evaluation is performed, leading to decryption failure if it is not refreshed at some point. Therefore, Gentry et al. [21] firstly introduce the use of the gadget decomposition to keep the noise growth small, hence, their scheme allows more operations before decryption failure occurs. Towards more practical use, there have been many HE schemes [5,12,16] which basically were built on top of this strategy, and they have been called GSW-like schemes in the related literature. If such schemes use a *randomized* gadget decomposition, there are more advantages for them: 1) one can analyze the noise contained in ciphertexts with cleaner and tighter bound than the use of other measures such as Euclidean/infinite norm [2], and 2) circuit privacy can be achieved almost for free [6]. That is why we need practical randomized gadget decomposition since FHE schemes and their applications are becoming more practical.

Analyzing the noise growth precisely as much as possible in homomorphic encryption is highly important since the noise growth is closely related to choosing the right parameters of applications based on HE schemes to achieve the best performance. Moreover, one can estimate how many homomorphic operations are possible before decryption fails based on the analysis. More importantly, the parameters of HE schemes determine the bit security of the schemes based on well known attacks. Therefore, the noise analysis can be a tool to justify their choice of parameters which makes the schemes safe from the attacks as in [5].

1.1 Subgaussian Sampling in Homomorphic Encryption

GSW-like schemes [5,11,16,21] which implement gate operations consisting of linear operation over ciphertexts can model their noise coefficient as subgaussian random variable due to linearity. Hence, Ducas and Micciancio [16] started to use subgaussian analysis to estimate how much the noise grows after evaluating a complicated circuit on average. Nevertheless, the follow-up schemes heuristically assume that their final noise elements independently follow a subgaussian distribution (called independence Heuristic in [11]), then use a deterministic gadget decomposition in their implementation for the sake of practical performance.[1] The main reason is that 1) subgaussian sampling was studied only in a theoretical way previously so that such work did not receive much attention in practical fields and 2) the only existing algorithm they could employ for their randomized decomposition algorithm was discrete Gaussian sampling [18,24] which might cause huge computational overhead in implementations. Afterwards, all the follow-up works and applications based on HE keep relying on the Heuristic assumption and using the deterministic algorithm in their implementations. Therefore, it had seemed that this was the only solution to achieve both practicality and such tight noise analysis until Genise et al. [19] presented the first efficient randomized digit decomposition, recently. We denote their algorithm by GMP19 in this paper.

They focus on subgaussian sampling itself which can be implemented more efficiently than the discrete Gaussian sampling in practice mainly due to its relaxed probability condition. As a result, they presented the first subgaussian sampling which outperforms existing discrete Gaussian sampling, so that it became closer to practical algorithm for GSW-like schemes [5,11,16,21]. Despite of their efforts, the computational overhead, which is the extra running time after running deterministic decomposition algorithm, is not negligible. Later, Jeon, Lee, and Park [22] observed that the main two subalgorithms of GMP19 were sequential so that they parallelized the two with a uniform distribution and showed that their uniform distribution is subgaussian. With this approach, one algorithm can be considered as a pre-computation, hence, their solution performs over 50% better than GMP19.

Moreover, Zhang and Yu [29] also improved GMP19 when q is not a power of b, introducing a plausible idea by calling the simpler algorithm of [19] for $q = b^k$ for some positive integer k as a subalgorithm. In more detail, Genise et al. presented two different subgaussian samplings depending on the relation between q and b due to different basis structures of the lattice. The algorithm when $q \neq b^k$ has more complicated steps than the other one for $q = b^k$, hence it takes more time than the other. Zhang and Yu focused on the similarity of the two bases. In other words, the two bases look exactly same up to the $(k-1)$-th column, and the last column of them only differs. Therefore, they run the faster algorithm to obtain the result up to the $(k-1)$-th digit of the final result by reducing the modulus q such that $b^{k-1} < q < b^k$ to $q' = b^{k-1}$, then determine the last digit by checking all the previous outcome. Due to the use of simpler and faster algorithm, they could have better computation time than GMP19. However, the algorithm is still not practical enough in terms of the actual computation time. In reality, the main computation overhead of evaluating a homomorphic circuit would be caused by this randomized gadget decomposition algorithm. Furthermore, no detailed comparison between the two different techniques [22,29], both of which outperform [19], has been addressed in any literature. In fact, it is important to compare these existing algorithms to see the trade-offs in different parameter

---

[1] Note that the deterministic gadget decomposition takes a uniform random ciphertext, hence its output follows a uniform random distribution.

settings for those who is interested in HE and its applications. It is because the performance of the gadget decomposition and the noise growth of the output highly depend on the choice of b and k for a fixed q. In detail, the larger k, the lower noise is added to the output ciphertext, but also the slower computation time the algorithm has.

1.2 Our Contribution

In this work, we present a faster randomized gadget decomposition (subgaussian sampling) with the least computation overhead compared to the deterministic decomposition among the existing works. We bring the technique of Zhang-Yu [29] (denoted by ZY22 for short) to the subgaussian sampling of Jeon-Lee-Park [22] (denoted by JLP21) which uses a uniform distribution, so that we can fully exploit the advantage of precomputation of JLP21 in the structure of ZY22. In other words, we replace the call of GMP19 by the call of JLP21 in Zhamg-Yu's structure, so we could already gain a little improvement because JLP21 is faster than GMP19. And the last step of this algorithm, which checks all the previous outcome to determine the last digit, becomes simpler than ZY22 since we can skip this step by checking the only one precomputed value. Consequently, our results range between 5x to 14x faster compared to Zhang-Yu's.

In addition, we give a detailed analysis and comparison among the existing such algorithms [19,22,29], which has not been covered in the previous literature. In more detail, our experimental result shows that our algorithm outperforms ZY22 and slightly faster than JLP21 for small q ($\approx 2^{60}$). We note that the value k increases as b decreases for a fixed q. Our algorithm is 82% faster than ZY22 at most and 35% faster than JLP21 with the large k. JLP21 becomes similar to ours as k gets smaller since one of its subalgorithms which depends on k becomes faster than one of ours which takes constant time. Also, we have the least computational overhead (from 2% to 14% depending on k) among existing works, which means that it takes only a little bit longer time than deterministic algorithm.

For larger q such as $q \approx 2^{102}$, the computation cost of four different algorithms are almost same due to the use of BigInteger type which represents a number over 64-bit in implementation. However, both JLP21 and our algorithm are slightly faster thanks to the uniform distribution. When q is large and k is small, JLP21 outperforms our algorithm due to the same reason as q is small. Hence, it is suitable for applications which require low multiplication depth when the modulus q is large. We note that most of applications of HE which require large q such as [7,10] use CRT/RNS technique to avoid multi-precision as discussed in [19], so that the result with smaller q would be more helpful for such applications.

We also note that the tighter bound of the noise is still preserved when non-centered distribution is used in HE since the extra term is much smaller than the dominant term in the variance (discussed in Sect. 4.2). Therefore, the non-centered case has slightly larger size of output, so does the noise in ciphertexts of HE, but it does not directly influence on the most significant bit of the noise.

1.3   Technical Overview

Let's say that we want to obtain a decomposition of $u \in \mathbb{Z}_q$ where $q \neq b^k$, given a gadget vector $\mathbf{g} = (1, b, b^2, \ldots, b^{k-1})$. JLP21 works as follows: 1) sample a vector $\mathbf{y}$ uniformly at random and 2) compute $(x_0, \ldots, x_{k-1}) =: \mathbf{x} = \mathbf{S}_q \mathbf{y} + \mathbf{u}$, where $\mathbf{u}$ is a deterministic digit decomposition of u. Since sampling $\mathbf{y}$ is totally independent of the input u in their algorithm, this step can be computed previously as a preprocessing. We observed that the last component of $\mathbf{y}$, say y_{k-1}, determines if $\mathbf{x}$ is a decomposition of u or $u - q$ in JLP21 since y_{k-1} is a coefficient of the last column of the basis. Therefore, the algorithm already knows that whether the composed value will be u or $u - q$ by checking the precomputed value y_{k-1}.

Then, we let the algorithm fix a value denoted by u' for depending on y_{k-1}, that is, $u' = u \mod b^{k-1}$ if $y_{k-1} = 0$ and $u' = u - q \mod b^{k-1}$ if $y_{k-1} = -1$. Next, we use the trick of ZY22 to compute from x_0 to x_{k-2} of $\mathbf{x}$ by running the subgaussian sampling of JLP21 for power of b case taking u' and $q' = b^{k-1}$ on input. Now, it is time to decide the last component of $\mathbf{x}$, x_{k-1}. As [29] observed already, the last component x_{k-1} is determined by the value of $\langle \mathbf{x}', \mathbf{g}' \rangle$, where $\mathbf{x} = (\mathbf{x}', x_{k-1})$ and $\mathbf{g} = (\mathbf{g}', b^{k-1})$.

Due to sequential process of ZY22, it is necessary to compute the dot product, however, we can already check the value by checking the second last component of the precomputed vector $\mathbf{y}$, y_{k-2}, by our observation of JLP21 structure. Consequently, we can more quickly determine the last component of $\mathbf{x}$ than the previous work.

2   Preliminaries

Notation: Numbers are denoted as small letters, such as $a \in \mathbb{Z}$, vectors as bold small letters, $\mathbf{a} \in \mathbb{Z}^n$, and matrices as capital bold letters, $\mathbf{A} \in \mathbb{R}^{n \times n}$. We denote the inner product of two vectors $\mathbf{v}, \mathbf{w}$ by $\langle \mathbf{v}, \mathbf{w} \rangle$. We use the ℓ_2 norm as a default norm for a vector $\mathbf{x}$. $[u]_b^k = (u_0, \ldots, u_{k-1})$ denotes a vector, where $u_i \in \{0, \ldots, b-1\}$, which is b-ary decomposition of u such that $\sum_i b^i u_i = u$ for an integer base $b > 0$. A notation $a \xleftarrow{\$} S$ means that a is chosen uniformly from a set S.

2.1   Subgaussian Random Variables

We explain subgaussian random variables and their significant properties in this section. We describe the general definition for a univariate δ-subgaussian random variable for some $\delta \geq 0$ as in [24].

Definition 1. *A random variable V over $\mathbb{R}$ is δ-subgaussian ($\delta \geq 0$) with parameter $s > 0$ if its moment generating function satisfies, for all $t \in \mathbb{R}$,*

$$\mathbb{E}[\exp(2\pi t V)] \leq \exp(\delta) \exp(\pi s^2 t^2).$$

We call the parameter s the standard parameter. It is easy to see that if X is δ-subgaussian with parameter s, then cX is also δ-subgaussian with parameter $|c|s$ for any $c \in \mathbb{R}$. In addition, if a random variable V is centered at 0 and bounded with B, then V is 0-subgaussian with parameter $B\sqrt{2\pi}$ [28]. If there exists a 0-subgaussian random variable, we can make it into a δ-subgaussian random variable for nonzero δ by shifting the variable with some real number as stated in Lemma 1. Therefore, we can deal with δ-subgaussian distribution by considering a shifted centered subgaussian distribution.

Lemma 1 (Lemma 7 in [26]). *If $\overline{V}$ is a 0-subgaussian with parameter $\overline{s}$, then the real-valued shifted random variable $V = \overline{V} + \alpha$ for $\alpha \in \mathbb{R}$ is a δ-subgaussian with parameter s such that $s > \overline{s}$ for some non-negative real-valued δ such that $\delta \geq \alpha^2 \pi / (s^2 - \overline{s}^2)$.*

In other words, a subgaussian distribution centered at nonzero is δ-subgaussian where $\delta > 0$. Informally speaking, a distribution is more centered at 0 if δ is closer to 0.

Lemma 2 says that $\delta(> 0)$-subgaussian random variable with parameter s has variance bounded by s^2. Informally, the tails of V are dominated by a Gaussian function with standard deviation s.

Lemma 2 (Lemma 8 in [26]). *If V is a univariate real-valued δ-subgaussian with parameter $s \geq 0$, then $\mathsf{Var}(V) \leq s^2$, where $\mathsf{Var}(V)$ is the variance of V.*

The sum of independent subgaussian variables is easily seen to be subgaussian. It is also proved that the sum of subgaussian variables is also subgaussian even when random variables are conditioned on the other random variables. And we use this property to prove that our algorithm follows a subgaussian distribution.

Lemma 3 (Claim 2.1 in [23]). *Let $\delta_i, s_i \geq 0$ and X_i be random variables for $i = 1, \ldots, k$. Suppose that for every i, when conditioning on any values of $X_1, \ldots, X_{i-1}$, the random variable X_i is δ_i-subgaussian with parameter s_i. Then $\sum X_i$ is $\sum \delta_i$-subgaussian with parameter $\sqrt{\sum s_i^2}$.*

Using Lemma 3, we can prove that a vector with subgaussian coordinates is also subgaussian, which is a general extension from Lemma 2.2 in [19]. To do this, we use the fact that a random vector $\mathbf{x} \in \mathbb{R}^n$ is δ-subgaussian with parameter $s > 0$ if $\langle \mathbf{x}, \mathbf{u} \rangle$ is δ-subgaussian with parameter s for all unit vectors $\mathbf{u}$, given in [24]. The proof of this lemma is in Appendix A.

Lemma 4 (The general version of Lemma 2.2 in [19]). *Let $\mathbf{x}$ be a discrete random vector over $\mathbb{R}^n$ such that each coordinate x_i is δ_i-subgaussian with parameter s_i given the previous coordinates take any values. Then $\mathbf{x}$ is a $\sum \delta_i$-subgaussian vector with parameter $\max_i \{s_i\}$.*

2.2   Gadget and Lattices

We use the same gadget $\mathbf{g} = (1, b, \ldots, b^{k-1})$ defined in [24] for a positive integer b. A lattice Λ with the rank k and basis $\mathbf{B} = [\mathbf{b}_1, \ldots, \mathbf{b}_k]$ is a set of all linear combinations of the basis vectors with coefficients in $\mathbb{Z}$. A coset of a lattice Λ is a set $\mathbf{c} + \Lambda = \{\mathbf{c} + \mathbf{z} : \mathbf{z} \in \Lambda\}$. In this work, we focus on the gadget lattice $\Lambda_q^{\perp}(\mathbf{g}^t) = \{\mathbf{z} \in \mathbb{Z}_q^k : \langle \mathbf{g}, \mathbf{z} \rangle = 0 \mod q\}$ for $q \leq b^k$. For any $u \in \mathbb{Z}_q$, $\Lambda_u^{\perp}(\mathbf{g}^t) = \{\mathbf{z} \in \mathbb{Z}^k : \langle \mathbf{g}, \mathbf{z} \rangle = u \mod q\}$ is a coset of $\Lambda_q^{\perp}(\mathbf{g}^t)$ since $\Lambda_u^{\perp}(\mathbf{g}^t) = \mathbf{u} + \Lambda_q^{\perp}(\mathbf{g}^t)$ where $\mathbf{u}$ is a vector such that $\langle \mathbf{g}, \mathbf{u} \rangle = u \mod q$. A basis of the gadget lattice $\Lambda_q^{\perp}(\mathbf{g}^t)$ is like the following:

$$
\mathbf{S}_q = \begin{bmatrix} b & & & q_0 \\ -1 & \ddots & & \vdots \\ & & b & q_{k-2} \\ & & -1 & q_{k-1} \end{bmatrix} = \left[\begin{array}{c|c} \mathbf{S}' & \\ \hline & \mathbf{q} \\ -1 & \end{array} \right] = \begin{bmatrix} b & & & \\ -1 & \ddots & & \\ & & b & \\ & & -1 & b \end{bmatrix} \begin{bmatrix} 1 & & & d_0 \\ & \ddots & & \vdots \\ & & 1 & d_{k-2} \\ & & & d_{k-1} \end{bmatrix} = \mathbf{SD},
$$

where $\mathbf{q}$ is a b-decomposition of q, and $\mathbf{S}' \in \mathbb{Z}^{(k-1) \times (k-1)}$ and $\mathbf{S} \in \mathbb{Z}^{k \times k}$ is a basis of the gadget lattice for $q = b^{k-1}$ and $q = b^k$ respectively. The efficiency of the algorithm highly depends on the structure of the basis of the gadget lattice. When $q < b^k$, which is the general case, the basis $\mathbf{S}_q$ looks similar to $\mathbf{S}$, but has additional elements on its last column, hence the sampling algorithm is more complicated than the special case when q is a power of b. Therefore, [19] uses the factorization $\mathbf{S}_q = \mathbf{SD}$ where $\mathbf{S}$ and $\mathbf{D}$ are sparse and triangular matrix. And then the algorithm requires the linear transformation.

3 New Practical Subgaussian Sampling

In this section, we present our new gadget subgaussian decomposition algorithm for the general case when $q < b^k$. We substitute the call of GMP19 in Zhang- Yu's structure by the call of JLP21 when the modulus q is reduced to $q' = b^{k-1}$.

$$
\begin{aligned}
\mathbf{x} = \mathbf{u} + \mathbf{S}_q \mathbf{y} &= \begin{bmatrix} u_0 \\ \vdots \\ u_{k-2} \\ u_{k-1} \end{bmatrix} + \begin{bmatrix} b & & & q_0 \\ -1 & \ddots & & \vdots \\ & \ddots & b & q_{k-2} \\ & & -1 & q_{k-1} \end{bmatrix} \begin{bmatrix} y_0 \\ \vdots \\ y_{k-2} \\ y_{k-1} \end{bmatrix} \\
&= \begin{bmatrix} u_0 \\ \vdots \\ u_{k-2} \\ u_{k-1} \end{bmatrix} + y_{k-1} \begin{bmatrix} q_0 \\ \vdots \\ q_{k-2} \\ q_{k-1} \end{bmatrix} + \begin{bmatrix} b & & & \\ -1 & \ddots & & \\ & \ddots & b & \\ & & & -1 \end{bmatrix} \begin{bmatrix} y_0 \\ \vdots \\ y_{k-2} \end{bmatrix} \\
&= \mathbf{u} + y_{k-1}\mathbf{q} + [\mathbf{S}'\mathbf{y}'| - y_{k-2}]
\end{aligned} \tag{1}
$$

We observed that the last component of $\mathbf{y}$, denoted by y_{k-1} actually determines whether the output is going to be a decomposition of u or $u - q$ in JLP21. Here each component of $\mathbf{y}$ is chosen as either -1 or 0 at uniformly random. If $q = b^k$ and y_{k-1} is -1, the last component of $\mathbf{S}_q\mathbf{y}(= \mathbf{Sy})$ has $-b$ term as seen in Eq. (1) (especially the left red part of $\mathbf{S}_q$). So when it is composed to an integer in $\mathbb{Z}_q$

with the gadget vector $\mathbf{g}$, it contains $-b^k$ which is $-q$. Moreover, when $q < b^k$ and $y_{k-1} = -1$, it influences on every component of $\mathbf{S}_q\mathbf{y}$ due to the structure of $\mathbf{S}_q$ (see the right purple part of the Eq. (1)). In other words, each component of $\mathbf{S}_q\mathbf{y}$ has a decomposition element q, and then it outputs $-q$ after the inner product with $\mathbf{g}$. Therefore, the last column means that a composition value becomes $u - q$.

Algorithm 1. Precompute(b, q)

Input: q, b
Output: $k = \lceil \log_b q \rceil$, $\mathbf{y} \in \{-1, 0\}^k$, $\mathbf{z} = \mathbf{S}\mathbf{y}$
1: $k = \lceil \log_b q \rceil$
2: **for** $i \leftarrow 0, \ldots, k-1$ **do**
3:     $y_i \overset{\$}{\leftarrow} \{-1, 0\}$
4: $\mathbf{z} \leftarrow \mathbf{S}\mathbf{y}$
5: **return** $k, \mathbf{y}, \mathbf{z}$

Now, we use the above observation for our algorithm to improve the efficiency. Our algorithm firstly samples $\mathbf{y}$ by running Algorithm 1 in advance and employ it for online phase as JLP21 does. Like ZY22, we also sample $\mathbf{x}'$ where $\mathbf{x} := (\mathbf{x}', x_{k-1})$ for the reduced modulus $q' = b^{k-1}$. To do this, we first need to fix u' and a, which are an input and the candidate of x_{k-1}, by checking y_{k-1}. In other words, $u' = u \mod b^{k-1}$ and $a = \lfloor \frac{u}{b^{k-1}} \rfloor$ if $y_{k-1} = 0$, $u' = u - q \mod b^{k-1}$ and $a = \lfloor \frac{u-q}{b^{k-1}} \rfloor$ otherwise. It is because the last component of $\mathbf{y}$ determines if the final output $\mathbf{x}$ is going to be a decomposition of u or $u - q$ due to the structure of the base of $\Lambda_q^{\perp}(\mathbf{g}^t)$ as we observed above.

Next it runs Subgaussian' (Algorithm 2), which is JLP21 for a power-of-base modulus, on input (b, q', u') and the first $k - 1$ components of $\mathbf{y}$.

Algorithm 2. Subgaussian'$(b, q, k, \mathbf{y}, u)$: subgaussian sampling for $q = b^k$ of [22]

Input: $u \in \mathbb{Z}_q$, $(k, \mathbf{y}, \mathbf{z}) \leftarrow$ Precompute(b, q)
Output: $\mathbf{x} \in \Lambda_u^{\perp}(\mathbf{g}^t)$ distributed uniformly in a bounded set.
1: Let $\mathbf{u} := [u]_b^k$ ($[u]_b^k$ is u's b-ary decomposition)
2: $\mathbf{x} \leftarrow \mathbf{z} + \mathbf{u}$
3: **return** $\mathbf{x}$

Then we obtain $\mathbf{x}'$ from Subgaussian'. Since the subgaussian sampling is a randomized decomposition, $\mathbf{x}'$ can be such that $\langle \mathbf{g}', \mathbf{x}' \rangle = u'$ or $u' - b^{k-1}$ where $\mathbf{g}' = (1, b, \ldots, b^{k-2})$. It is correct for the reduced modulus b^{k-1} since $u' - b^{k-1} \equiv u' \mod b^{k-1}$. However, what we want to obtain is the vector for the modulus q which is not a power of b. Hence, we should compute the last component with a. To determine the last component of output $\mathbf{x}$, ZY22 verifies whether $\langle \mathbf{g}', \mathbf{x}' \rangle = u'$

or $u' - b^{k-1}$ by computing the dot product. Unlike their approach, we can verify this by only checking y_{k-2} based on the same observation. As a result, we can skip the last step of ZY22 which computes $\langle \mathbf{g}', \mathbf{x}' \rangle$, thus we can quickly determine x_{k-1} based on y_{k-2}.

Algorithm 3. Subgaussian$(b, q, k, \mathbf{y}, u)$: our subgaussian sampling for $q < b^k$

Input: $u \in \mathbb{Z}_q, (k, \mathbf{y}, \mathbf{z}) \leftarrow$ Precompute(b, q)
Output: $\mathbf{x} \in \Lambda_u^\perp(\mathbf{g}^t)$ distributed uniformly in a bounded set.

1: **if** $y_{k-1} = 0$ **then**
2:      $u' \leftarrow u \mod b^{k-1}$
3:      $a \leftarrow \lfloor \frac{u}{b^{k-1}} \rfloor$
4: **else**
5:      $u' \leftarrow u - q \mod b^{k-1}$
6:      $a \leftarrow \lfloor \frac{u-q}{b^{k-1}} \rfloor$
7: $\mathbf{x}' = $ Subgaussian$'(b, b^{k-1}, k-1, \mathbf{y}', u')$ where $\mathbf{y} = (\mathbf{y}', y_{k-1})$
8: **if** $y_{k-2} = 0$ **then**
9:      **return** $\mathbf{x} = (\mathbf{x}', a)$
10: **else**
11:      **return** $\mathbf{x} = (\mathbf{x}', a+1)$

We show that our algorithm outputs a δ-subgaussian vector with a standard parameter which is slightly larger compared to the previous sequential algorithms in Theorem 1.

Theorem 1. *Let* $b, q \in \mathbb{N}$, $k = \lceil \log_b q \rceil$, *and* $u \in \mathbb{Z}_q$. *Then the output vector* $\mathbf{x}$ *of Algorithm 3 is* $\frac{k+3}{6}$-*subgaussian with parameter* $b\sqrt{2\pi}$.

Proof. First, we will show that x_{k-1} is a subgaussian and find the parameter for x_{k-1}. x_{k-1} has four possible value $\{a_0, a_0 + 1, a_1, a_1 + 1\}$. Since we use a uniform distribution, $\mathbb{E}[x_{k-1}] = \frac{1}{4}(a_0 + a_0 + 1 + a_1 + a_1 + 1) - \frac{a_0 + a_1 + 1}{2}$. Let $\alpha = \mathbb{E}[x_{k-1}] = \frac{a_0 + a_1 + 1}{2}$, then $|\alpha| \leq b - \frac{1}{2} \leq b$ since $-b \leq a_0, a_1 < b$. Let $\overline{x} = x_{k-1} - \alpha$, then $\overline{x}$ is a random variable centered at 0 (i.e., $\mathbb{E}[\overline{x}] = 0$) and $|\overline{x}| \leq \frac{b}{2}$. Hence $\overline{x}$ is 0-subgaussian with parameter $\overline{s} = \frac{b}{2}\sqrt{2\pi}$. By Lemma 1, if $s > \overline{s}$ and $\delta \geq \alpha^2 \pi / (s^2 - \overline{s}^2)$, then x_{k-1} is δ-subgaussian with parameter s. Since

$$\frac{\alpha^2 \pi}{s^2 - \overline{s}^2} \leq \frac{b^2 \pi}{b^2 2\pi - (b^2/4)2\pi} = \frac{2}{3},$$

x_{k-1} is $\frac{2}{3}$-subgaussian with parameter $b\sqrt{2\pi}$.

Since $\mathbf{x}'$ is the output of Subgaussian$'(b, b^{k-1}, k-1, \mathbf{y}, u)$, and in proof of Theorem 1 of [22], $x_0, \ldots, x_{k-2}$ are $\frac{1}{6}$-subgaussian with parameter $b\sqrt{2\pi}$. Analogously to the proof of Lemma 4,

$$\mathbb{E}[\exp(2\pi t \langle \mathbf{x}, \mathbf{u} \rangle)] \leq \exp(\frac{k+3}{6}) \exp(\pi t^2 (b\sqrt{2\pi})^2).$$

Therefore, $\mathbf{x} = (\mathbf{x}', x_{k-1})$ is $\frac{k+3}{6}$-subgaussian with parameter $b\sqrt{2\pi}$. $\qquad \square$

4   Comparison with Previous Works

Experimental Setup. All experiments are performed on a laptop with Apple M1 @ 3.2 GHz (8 cores). We used PALISADE Library [1] to implement our algorithm.

4.1   Randomness

GMP19 uses $k \log q = O(k^2 \log b)$ random bits to sample an output with a certain probability. It is better to generate less number of random bits to achieve faster implementation result. ZY22 has improved the number of random bits which is $O(k \log b)$ due to the randomness-efficient subroutine for a modulus b^{k-1}. Since our algorithm follows a uniform distribution over $\{-1, 0\}$, we only generate $k \log 2 = O(k)$ random bits. Therefore, we have faster implementation result than the others. However, in the offline phase when we sample $\mathbf{y}$, we store k random bits for being used in the online phase, hence we have additional small memory overhead.

4.2   Magnitude Comparison

Remark 1. Unlike other previous works employing centered distributions, the output of our algorithm has non-zero mean value. Therefore, we note that the noise analysis with our algorithm in homomorphic encryption is less simple than the one with centered distribution. In more detail, the (average-case) noise analysis of HE (especially GSW-like schemes) highly relies on the variance of the product of two independent polynomials x, y of degree N. The two random variable x and y are δ-subgaussian with parameter s. Then the variance of $x \cdot y$ is bounded as follows: $\mathsf{Var}(x \cdot y) \leq N \cdot \mathsf{Var}(x) \cdot \mathsf{Var}(y) + \mathbb{E}(x)^2 \cdot \mathsf{Var}(y) + \mathbb{E}(y)^2 \cdot \mathsf{Var}(x)$. If x and y have both zero mean, then it has clear and simple bound (the last two terms are eliminated). However, in our case, the mean of x and y are non-zero but less than b (since it is a digit decomposition with the base b). In GSW-like schemes [5, 12], for example, $N \gg b$ and $\mathsf{Var}(x) \cdot \mathsf{Var}(y)$ is the dominant term of the noise after homomorphic operation. After bootstrapping of TFHE, the final noise contained in the output has the variance of the sum of $\sum_{i \in [n]} \mathsf{Var}(x_i \cdot y_i)$, hence the dominant term is still unchanged, where x_i's and y_i's are independent subgaussian variables, where $|\mathbb{E}(x_i)| \leq b$ and $|\mathbb{E}(y_i)| = 0$ for all i. As a result, the bound is still tighter than the bound of worst-case with Euclidean/infinite norm.

As we see from the remark above, the variance of the noise will have slightly larger bound if an FHE scheme uses a δ-subgaussian distribution, than the one using 0-subgaussian distribution, but the tighter bound is still preserved. We show the size of output in each case in the figure above. Figure 1 shows the magnitude of output of each algorithm. We executed the experiment for 10000 runs with the base $b = 2$, and an uniform random input u by increasing the modulus q.

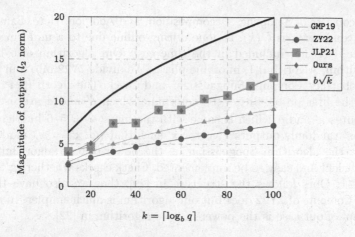

Fig. 1. The magnitude average of 10000 runs with $b = 2$, uniform random input u, and different moduli.

In Sect. 3, we show that our algorithm outputs a δ-subgaussian vector with the parameter $\delta = \frac{k+3}{6}$ and the standard parameter $s = b\sqrt{2\pi}$. Our standard parameter s is similar to other algorithms, and s is the upper bound of the standard deviation of the distribution. The variance of ours is also bounded by standard parameter $2b^2\pi$ by Lemma 2 like other non-uniform algorithms. Since our δ is nonzero unlike other sequential algorithms GMP19 and ZY22, the mean of the distribution is also nonzero. Therefore, ours is expected to have larger size of output than the others since ours has slightly larger mean (still less than b).

The experimental result shows that the magnitude of the output is a little bit larger than them as we expected. But, in practice, we see that the output is much smaller than the least upper bound $b\sqrt{k}$ of Euclidean norm of outputs. Moreover, we have similar magnitude to JLP21 because we have the similar values of δ and s due to the use of the same uniform distribution. As discussed in [29], GMP19 has slightly larger s than ZY22 with the same $\delta = 0$, hence they have smaller magnitude in general.

4.3 Complexity Comparison

In order to analyze the complexity of each subgaussian algorithm in detail, we divide each into its main subalgorithms and compute complexity of each subalgorithm in terms of the number of bit operations (see Table 1).

First, we briefly recall the subalgorithms of each algorithm. GMP19 consists of Decomposition, Transformation, Sampling, and Addition. Decomposition is the deterministic algorithm which outputs b-ary decomposition of u. Transformation computes $\mathbf{t} = \mathbf{S}^{-1}\mathbf{u}$ where $\mathbf{u}$ is the output of Decomposition to use $\mathbf{D}$. Sampling chooses a vector in $\Lambda_q^{\perp}(\mathbf{g}^t)$ with a subgaussian distribution centered at $-\mathbf{u}$. Addition combines the output vectors of Decomposition and Sampling to obtain a vector in $\Lambda_u^{\perp}(\mathbf{g}^t)$.

JLP21 consists of Sampling, Decomposition, and Addition. Here, Sampling, of which the complexity is $O(k)$, is done during offline due to a uniform distribution. Hence, it is not included in the time cost. Our algorithm also have the same algorithm, Algorithm 1, in offline phase. We divide ZY22 into four subalgorithms; Probability, Compute, Subgaussian', and Check. The algorithm Probability computes the first probability $\frac{u}{q}$ to determine which u' and a are used. Compute computes u' and a which is same with the line 2–3 or 5–6 in Algorithm 3. Subgaussian' randomly outputs a vector $\mathbf{x}'$ such that $\langle \mathbf{g}', \mathbf{x}' \rangle = u' \mod b^{k-1}$.

In fact, the algorithm Subgaussian' is the power-of-base algorithm in [19] which is efficient and easy to be implemented. Check checks whether $\langle \mathbf{g}', \mathbf{x}' \rangle = u'$ or $u' - b^{k-1}$. Ours follows the structure in [29], thus we also have the same process as Compute of ZY22 does but our algorithm is much simpler. In addition, Subgaussian' of our case is the power-of-base algorithm in [22].

Table 1. The number of bit operations of the subalgorithms of each sampler for fixed $q \approx b^k$, where $k = \lceil \log_b q \rceil$ and $\ell = \log_2 b$. T is the running time for computing each entry of $\mathbf{t}$. P denotes the computation time of sampling from given distribution. p denotes the computation time of computing the probability of ZY22. c_1, c_2 are for computing u' and a of the modulus reduction sampler. P, p, c_1, c_2 are constants which do not depend on k for given u and q.

	Decomposition	Sampling	Transformation	Addition
GMP19	$O(k^2(\ell^2 + \ell))$	$k \cdot P$	$k \cdot T$	$k(\ell^2 + 3\ell)$
JLP21	$O(k^2(\ell^2 + \ell))$	N/A	N/A	$k(2\ell^2 + 5\ell)$
	Subgaussian'	Probability	Compute	Check
ZY22	$O(k^2(\ell^2 + \ell) + k\ell)$	p	c_1	$O(k\ell)$
Ours	$O(k^2(\ell^2 + \ell) + k\ell)$	N/A	c_2	N/A

Decomposition has the complexity $O(k^2(\ell^2 + \ell))$ in terms of the number of bit operations since they compute each component of a k-dimensional vector using u and q whose the bit length is k times bit lengths of b (i.e., k times computation with $k\ell$ bit lengths numbers). Subgaussian' runs Decomposition up to the $(k-1)$-th component of the output for the modulus b^{k-1}. Additionally, it contains the addition of two vectors of dimension of $k - 1$.

On the other hand, Addition and Check require k times arithmetic operations over $\mathbb{Z}_b$, so that they depend on k and $\log b$. Transformation and Sampling also require computation of each component of k-dimensional vector, but of floating-point operations which consume constant cost. The operations are independent of a fixed q, hence, we denote the complexity of floating-point operations in Transformation and Sampling constant, denoted by T and P respectively, for convenience.

Similarly, the complexity of Probability, Compute of ZY22, and our Compute is denoted by constants p, c_1 and c_2 respectively, since both only compute $\frac{u}{q}, u'$

and a on floating-point numbers. Subgaussian' of ZY22 consists of Decomposition, Sampling, and Addition which adds the output of Decomposition and Sampling of GMP19's power-of-base case, whereas the one of ours consists of Decomposition and Addition of JLP21's power-of-base case.

Overall, the dominant complexity comes from Decomposition , which is highly depends on the choice of parameters ℓ and k. Moreover, ZY22 and ours has constant factor in one of subalgorithms, in practice, the constant time can be a key factor which decides shortest running time in total.

4.4   Computation Cost Comparison

We compare the actual time cost of existing subgaussian decomposition algorithms [22,29] and ours. We do not include the experimental result of GMP19 for small modulus q since the comparison to GMP19 is already covered in [22,29]. For larger modulus $q \geq 2^{100}$, we included GMP19 as well since there has been no analysis about the algorithm with such q. We note that all our experiments consider the case that the modulus q is not a power of the base b (general case).

Table 2. Average runtimes for 10000 runs of subgaussian sampling for $\log_2 q \approx 60$ and uniformly random input $u \in \mathbb{Z}_q$ with the different base b

b	$k = \lceil \log_b q \rceil$	ZY22 $[\mu s]$	JLP21 $[\mu s]$	Ours $[\mu s]$
2^1	60	1.2709	0.5439	0.3539
2^2	30	0.6634	0.1888	0.1547
2^3	20	0.4723	0.1077	0.1008
2^4	15	0.3650	0.0762	0.0692
2^6	10	0.2628	0.0502	0.0477
2^8	8	0.1431	0.0441	0.0412

Table 3. Average runtimes of 10000 runs of each subalgorithm for $\log_2 q \approx 60$ and uniformly random input u with the different b (as a result with the different k)

	(b,k)	$(2,60)$	$(2^2,30)$	$(2^4,15)$	$(2^8,8)$
ZY22 $[\mu s]$	Subgaussian'	1.2163	0.6152	0.3165	0.0959
	Compute	0.0192	0.0170	0.0167	0.0163
	Check	0.0180	0.0156	0.0152	0.0154
	Probability	0.0174	0.0156	0.0167	0.0154
JLP21 $[\mu s]$	Decomposition	0.3355	0.1349	0.0553	0.0263
	Addition	0.2084	0.0540	0.0210	0.0178
Ours $[\mu s]$	Subgaussian'	0.3358	0.1383	0.0529	0.0253
	Compute	0.0181	0.0163	0.0163	0.0159

For Small Modulus q. As we already checked the complexity in Table 1, Decomposition has the dominant complexity, so it takes the dominant time in our experimental result. We can see that Decomposition of JLP21 and Subgaussian' of both ZY22 and Ours takes the dominant time in the detailed time cost of Table 2 and Table 3. Despite of all the plausible tricks of ZY22, the computation time of JLP21 outperforms ZY22 due to the benefit of the precomputation.

Even though Subgaussian' of Ours runs one less iterations of deterministic decomposition algorithm, it includes additional operations (we refer Algorithm 1 of [22]), hence it takes slightly longer than Decomposition of JLP21. However, when k is large, Addition of JLP21 is significantly slower than our other subalgorithm Compute which is independent of k. That is why there is the biggest performance gap between JLP21 and Ours with the largest k, i.e., our algorithm is 35% faster than JLP21. As k decreases, the computation time of Addition becomes small as k decreases, even similar to Compute of Ours. Therefore, there becomes almost no difference between JLP21 and Ours as k significantly decreases. The reason why Ours is faster than ZY22 is that our algorithm makes use of precomputed value as JLP21 does, hence the dominant part, Subgaussian' of Ours, is faster than the one of ZY22. Moreover, Ours has faster Compute, and it does not need additional subalgorithms like Check and Probability. As a result, our algorithm is 77%–82% faster than ZY22.

Many applications of homomorphic encryption [9,14,25,27] use various value of k to achieve both the best performance and correctness. As we explained in Sect. 1, increasing k in subgaussian sampling causes lower noise growth resulting in supporting more homomorphic operations, but also slower performance at the same time. Therefore, the choice of parameter k is highly depends on the application. With our experimental result, we can conclude that for those applications which uses large k for $q \approx 2^{60}$, our algorithm is highly recommended.

Table 4. Average runtimes for 10000 runs of subgaussian sampling for BigInteger q such that $\log_2 q \approx 102$ and uniformly random input u with the different base b

b	$k = \lceil \log_b q \rceil$	GMP19 [μs]	ZY22 [μs]	JLP21 [μs]	Ours [μs]
2^1	102	20.6274	22.3322	19.3688	19.0677
2^2	51	12.1608	13.5447	11.5216	11.3985
2^3	34	9.6771	10.7968	9.1633	9.1606
2^4	26	6.4006	7.2784	6.0475	6.0294
2^6	17	4.9778	5.6145	4.7116	4.7783
2^8	13	3.2420	3.6676	3.0062	3.0776

For Large Modulus q. Zhang and Yu [29] and Jeon et al. [22] compared the running time of their algorithm and GMP19 only when $q \approx 2^{60}$. We provide the experimental result with larger $q \approx 2^{102}$, which shows that ZY22 is not always faster than GMP19 with such larger modulus.

Table 5. Average runtimes of 10000 runs of each subalgorithm for BigInteger q such that $\log_2 q \approx 102$ and uniformly random input u with the different b (as a result with the different k)

	(b, k)	$(2, 102)$	$(2^2, 51)$	$(2^4, 26)$	$(2^8, 13)$
GMP19 [μs]	Decomposition	18.9774	11.3175	5.9694	2.9893
	Sampling	1.1783	0.6206	0.3133	0.1758
	Transformation	0.3864	0.1813	0.0923	0.0568
	Addition	0.0854	0.0413	0.0256	0.0200
ZY22 [μs]	Subgaussian$'$	22.0206	13.2311	6.9424	3.3370
	Compute	0.2743	0.2793	0.3024	0.2970
	Check	0.0161	0.0159	0.0155	0.0154
	Probability	0.0212	0.0184	0.0181	0.0182
JLP21 [μs]	Decomposition	18.9793	11.3154	5.9718	2.9814
	Addition	0.3896	0.2062	0.0757	0.0248
Ours [μs]	Subgaussian$'$	18.7783	11.0823	5.7161	2.7584
	Compute	0.2895	0.3162	0.3132	0.3192

The total running time increases significantly compared to the smaller q case (See Table 4). It is mainly because computation over numbers of BigInteger type, which was used in PALISADE library [1], takes more time than the other smaller bit length setting. Therefore, as you can see Table 5, Decomposition which deals with large bit length has the dominant computation time, so do Subgaussian$'$ of ZY22 and Ours. However, Sampling of GMP19 deals with floating-point numbers which has the length less than 64-bits, so that there is a huge computation gap between Sampling and Decomposition of GMP19. Subgaussian$'$ of ZY22 contains Sampling and Decomposition of GMP19. But Sampling in their implementation is done over larger integer type BigInteger to compute probability, hence it takes longer time than GMP19. Therefore, ZY22 is slower than GMP19 with larger q in total when k is small.

Apart from ZY22, all the algorithms take similar time, it is because Sampling which samples a bit for each element takes negligible time comparing to Decomposition for large q, so the precomputation does not make any difference in this case. Interestingly, Compute of Ours takes more time than the case when q is small since it depends of q. Consequently, as mentioned above, there is a point that Addition of JLP21 becomes faster than Compute when k is small. This small difference makes JLP21 take the shortest time in total.

However, since all implementations of homomorphic encryption we are aware of use RNS technique to use 64-bit machine language for large ciphertext modulus in practice, the result of Table 2 is helpful for such cases.

The gadget decomposition of homomorphic encryption takes n-dimensional vector $\mathbf{u}$ on input and outputs $\mathbf{x}$ such that $\mathbf{Gx} = \mathbf{u}$ for $\mathbf{G} = \mathbf{I}_n \otimes \mathbf{g}^t$. We run the deterministic decomposition, which is same with Decomposition, and sub-

368   S. Jeon et al.

Table 6. Comparison of performance results between the deterministic decomposition and subgaussian samplings. The number of trial: 10000 for a 60-bits modulus q and n-dimensional input where $n = 2048$, with the different base b.

b	k	Decomposition $[\mu s]$	ZY22 $[\mu s]$	JLP21 $[\mu s]$	Ours $[\mu s]$
2^1	60	640.7155	2418.6132	1050.4242	647.5024
2^2	30	311.9202	1346.4805	395.8116	315.4322
2^4	15	145.9810	695.3398	162.1303	148.0831
2^8	8	50.0841	381.8072	73.8022	57.6720

gaussian algorithms for a 60-bits modulus q and a 2048-dimensional input with the different base b (see Table 6). We note that these parameters are commonly used in many HE based applications [3,9,13,14,27] to achieve high security level (larger than 110 bits of security). Obviously, the subgaussian algorithms take more time than the deterministic decomposition since they need more process to sample a random output.

We can check the computational overhead which shows how much the extra step costs than just running deterministic decomposition in order to see which one is suitable for the practical use. As we can see that from the table above, ZY22 has the largest computational overhead, whereas Ours has the least overhead in any choice of k. The overhead varies from 2% to 14% depending on k.

5 Conclusion

We propose a faster subgaussian decomposition by combining ZY22 and JLP21. To incorporate ZY22 and JLP21, we replace the call of GMP19 by the call of JLP21 in the structure of ZY22. And we also prove that a bounded uniform distribution is also subgaussian in the structure of ZY22. Previous works, GMP19, JLP21, and ZY22, also output actual subgaussian vectors so that they can be applied to HE schemes to analyze the noise growth without a Heuristic assumption. However, in the perspective of efficiency, they are too slower than the deterministic decomposition as shown in Table 6. In contrast, our algorithm has the lowest overhead only in the range from 2% to 14% to obtain actual subgaussian outputs. In addition, we give a detailed comparison, even for large modulus, with all the competitive algorithms, allowing applications to choose the best algorithm for their choice of parameters.

Acknowledgement. This work was supported by the National Research Foundation of Korea (NRF) grant funded by the Korea government (MSIT) (No. NRF-2021R1A2C1094821) and partially supported by the Basic Science Research Program through the NRF funded by the Ministry of Education (Grant No. 2019R1A6A1A11051177). The third-listed author (J.Park) has been supported by CyberSecurity Research Flanders with reference number VR20192203.

A Proof of Lemma 4

Lemma (The general version of Lemma 2.2 in [19]**).** *Let* $\mathbf{x}$ *be a discrete random vector over* $\mathbb{R}^n$ *such that each coordinate* x_i *is* δ_i*-subgaussian with parameter* s_i *given the previous coordinates take any values. Then* $\mathbf{x}$ *is a* $\sum \delta_i$*-subgaussian vector with parameter* $\max_i\{s_i\}$.

Proof. The moment generating function of $\langle \mathbf{x}, \mathbf{u} \rangle$ is

$$
\begin{aligned}
\mathbb{E}[\exp(2\pi t\langle \mathbf{x}, \mathbf{u} \rangle)] &= \mathbb{E}[\exp(2\pi t \sum x_i u_i)] \\
&\leq \exp(\sum \delta_i)\exp(\pi t^2 \sum s_i^2 u_i^2)(\because \text{Lemma 3}) \\
&\leq \exp(\sum \delta_i)\exp(\pi t^2 (\max s_i)^2 \sum u_i^2) \\
&= \exp(\sum \delta_i)\exp(\pi t^2 (\max s_i)^2 \|\mathbf{u}\|^2) \\
&= \exp(\sum \delta_i)\exp(\pi t^2 (\max s_i)^2 (\because \text{unit vector } \mathbf{u}).
\end{aligned}
$$

References

1. PALISADE Lattice Cryptography Library (release 1.11.6), January 2022. https://palisade-crypto.org/
2. Alperin-Sheriff, J., Peikert, C.: Faster bootstrapping with polynomial error. In: Garay, J.A., Gennaro, R. (eds.) CRYPTO 2014. LNCS, vol. 8616, pp. 297–314. Springer, Heidelberg (2014). https://doi.org/10.1007/978-3-662-44371-2_17
3. Angel, S., Chen, H., Laine, K., Setty, S.T.V.: PIR with compressed queries and amortized query processing. In: 2018 IEEE Symposium on Security and Privacy, pp. 962–979. IEEE Computer Society Press, May 2018. https://doi.org/10.1109/SP.2018.00062
4. Boneh, D.: Fully key-homomorphic encryption, arithmetic circuit ABE and compact garbled circuits. In: Nguyen, P.Q., Oswald, E. (eds.) EUROCRYPT 2014. LNCS, vol. 8441, pp. 533–556. Springer, Heidelberg (2014). https://doi.org/10.1007/978-3-642-55220-5_30
5. Bonte, C., Iliashenko, I., Park, J., Pereira, H.V.L., Smart, N.P.: FINAL: faster FHE instantiated with NTRU and LWE. Cryptology ePrint Archive, Paper 2022/074 (2022). https://eprint.iacr.org/2022/074
6. Bourse, F., Del Pino, R., Minelli, M., Wee, H.: FHE circuit privacy almost for free. In: Robshaw, M., Katz, J. (eds.) CRYPTO 2016. LNCS, vol. 9815, pp. 62–89. Springer, Heidelberg (2016). https://doi.org/10.1007/978-3-662-53008-5_3
7. Brakerski, Z., Gentry, C., Vaikuntanathan, V.: (leveled) fully homomorphic encryption without bootstrapping. In: Proceedings of the 3rd Innovations in Theoretical Computer Science Conference, ITCS 2012, pp. 309–325. Association for Computing Machinery, New York, NY, USA (2012). https://doi.org/10.1145/2090236.2090262. https://doi-org.kuleuven.e-bronnen.be/10.1145/2090236.2090262
8. Chatterjee, S., Menezes, A.: Type 2 structure-preserving signature schemes revisited. In: Iwata, T., Cheon, J.H. (eds.) ASIACRYPT 2015. LNCS, vol. 9452, pp. 286–310. Springer, Heidelberg (2015). https://doi.org/10.1007/978-3-662-48797-6_13

9. Chen, H., Chillotti, I., Ren, L.: Onion ring ORAM: efficient constant bandwidth oblivious RAM from (leveled) TFHE. In: Cavallaro, L., Kinder, J., Wang, X., Katz, J. (eds.) ACM CCS 2019, pp. 345–360. ACM Press, November 2019. https://doi.org/10.1145/3319535.3354226

10. Cheon, J.H., Kim, A., Kim, M., Song, Y.: Homomorphic encryption for arithmetic of approximate numbers. In: Takagi, T., Peyrin, T. (eds.) ASIACRYPT 2017, Part I. LNCS, vol. 10624, pp. 409–437. Springer, Cham (2017). https://doi.org/10.1007/978-3-319-70694-8_15

11. Chillotti, I., Gama, N., Georgieva, M., Izabachène, M.: Faster fully homomorphic encryption: bootstrapping in less than 0.1 seconds. In: Cheon, J.H., Takagi, T. (eds.) ASIACRYPT 2016. LNCS, vol. 10031, pp. 3–33. Springer, Heidelberg (2016). https://doi.org/10.1007/978-3-662-53887-6_1

12. Chillotti, I., Gama, N., Georgieva, M., Izabachène, M.: TFHE: fast fully homomorphic encryption over the torus. J. Cryptol. 33(1), 34–91 (2020). https://doi.org/10.1007/s00145-019-09319-x

13. Cong, K., Das, D., Nicolas, G., Park, J.: Panacea: non-interactive and stateless oblivious RAM. Cryptology ePrint Archive, Paper 2023/274 (2023). https://eprint.iacr.org/2023/274

14. Cong, K., Das, D., Park, J., Pereira, H.V.: SortingHat: efficient private decision tree evaluation via homomorphic encryption and transciphering. In: Proceedings of the 2022 ACM SIGSAC Conference on Computer and Communications Security, CCS 2022, pp. 563–577. Association for Computing Machinery, New York, NY, USA (2022). https://doi.org/10.1145/3548606.3560702

15. Dai, W., et al.: Implementation and evaluation of a lattice-based key-policy ABE scheme. IEEE Trans. Inf. Forensics Secur. 13(5), 1169–1184 (2018)

16. Ducas, L., Micciancio, D.: FHEW: bootstrapping homomorphic encryption in less than a second. In: Oswald, E., Fischlin, M. (eds.) EUROCRYPT 2015. LNCS, vol. 9056, pp. 617–640. Springer, Heidelberg (2015). https://doi.org/10.1007/978-3-662-46800-5_24

17. Fan, J., Vercauteren, F.: Somewhat practical fully homomorphic encryption. Cryptology ePrint Archive, Report 2012/144 (2012). https://eprint.iacr.org/2012/144

18. Genise, N., Micciancio, D.: Faster Gaussian sampling for trapdoor lattices with arbitrary modulus. In: Nielsen, J.B., Rijmen, V. (eds.) EUROCRYPT 2018. LNCS, vol. 10820, pp. 174–203. Springer, Cham (2018). https://doi.org/10.1007/978-3-319-78381-9_7

19. Genise, N., Micciancio, D., Polyakov, Y.: Building an efficient lattice gadget toolkit: subgaussian sampling and more. In: Ishai, Y., Rijmen, V. (eds.) EUROCRYPT 2019. LNCS, vol. 11477, pp. 655–684. Springer, Cham (2019). https://doi.org/10.1007/978-3-030-17656-3_23

20. Gentry, C., Peikert, C., Vaikuntanathan, V.: Trapdoors for hard lattices and new cryptographic constructions. In: STOC, pp. 197–206 (2008). https://doi.org/10.1145/1374376.1374407

21. Gentry, C., Sahai, A., Waters, B.: Homomorphic encryption from learning with errors: conceptually-simpler, asymptotically-faster, attribute-based. In: Canetti, R., Garay, J.A. (eds.) CRYPTO 2013. LNCS, vol. 8042, pp. 75–92. Springer, Heidelberg (2013). https://doi.org/10.1007/978-3-642-40041-4_5

22. Jeon, S., Lee, H.S., Park, J.: Efficient lattice gadget decomposition algorithm with bounded uniform distribution. IEEE Access 9, 17429–17437 (2021). https://doi.org/10.1109/ACCESS.2021.3053288. https://eprint.iacr.org/2021/048

23. Lyubashevsky, V., Peikert, C., Regev, O.: A toolkit for ring-LWE cryptography. In: Johansson, T., Nguyen, P.Q. (eds.) EUROCRYPT 2013. LNCS, vol. 7881, pp. 35–54. Springer, Heidelberg (2013). https://doi.org/10.1007/978-3-642-38348-9_3

24. Micciancio, D., Peikert, C.: Trapdoors for lattices: simpler, tighter, faster, smaller. In: Pointcheval, D., Johansson, T. (eds.) EUROCRYPT 2012. LNCS, vol. 7237, pp. 700–718. Springer, Heidelberg (2012). https://doi.org/10.1007/978-3-642-29011-4_41

25. Mughees, M.H., Chen, H., Ren, L.: OnionPIR: response efficient single-server PIR. In: Vigna, G., Shi, E. (eds.) ACM CCS 2021, pp. 2292–2306. ACM Press, November 2021. https://doi.org/10.1145/3460120.3485381

26. Murphy, S., Player, R.: δ-subgaussian random variables in cryptography. In: Jang-Jaccard, J., Guo, F. (eds.) ACISP 2019. LNCS, vol. 11547, pp. 251–268. Springer, Cham (2019). https://doi.org/10.1007/978-3-030-21548-4_14

27. Park, J., Tibouchi, M.: SHECS-PIR: somewhat homomorphic encryption-based compact and scalable private information retrieval. In: Chen, L., Li, N., Liang, K., Schneider, S. (eds.) ESORICS 2020. LNCS, vol. 12309, pp. 86–106. Springer, Cham (2020). https://doi.org/10.1007/978-3-030-59013-0_5

28. Stromberg, K.: Probability For Analysts. Chapman & Hall/CRC Probability Series, Taylor & Francis (1994). https://books.google.co.kr/books?id=gQaz79fv6QUC

29. Zhang, S., Yu, Y.: Towards a simpler lattice gadget toolkit. In: Hanaoka, G., Shikata, J., Watanabe, Y. (eds.) Public-Key Cryptography - PKC 2022, pp. 498–520. Springer, Cham (2022). https://doi.org/10.1007/978-3-030-97121-2_18

Covercrypt: An Efficient Early-Abort
KEM for Hidden Access Policies
with Traceability from the DDH and LWE

Théophile Brézot[1], Paola de Perthuis[1,2](✉) ⓘ, and David Pointcheval[2] ⓘ

[1] Cosmian, Paris, France
[2] DIENS, École normale supérieure, université PSL, CNRS, Inria, Paris, France
paola.de.perthuis@ens.fr

Abstract. Attribute-Based Encryption (ABE) is a very attractive primitive to limit access according to specific rights. While very powerful
instantiations have been offered, under various computational assumptions, they rely on either classical or post-quantum problems, and are
quite intricate to implement, generally resulting in poor efficiency; the
construction we offer results in a powerful efficiency gap with respect to
existing solutions. With the threat of quantum computers, post-quantum
solutions are important, but not yet tested enough to rely on such problems only. We thus first study an hybrid approach to rely on the best of
the two worlds: the scheme is secure if at least one of the two underlying
assumptions is still valid (i.e. the DDH and LWE). Then, we address the
ABE problem, with a practical solution delivering encrypted contents
such that only authorized users can decrypt, without revealing the target sets, while also granting tracing capabilities. Our scheme is inspired
by the Subset Cover framework where the users' rights are organized as
subsets and a content is encrypted with respect to a subset covering of
the target set. Quite conveniently, we offer black-box modularity: one
can easily use any public-key encryption of their choice, such as Kyber,
with their favorite library, to combine it with a simple ElGamal variant
of key encapsulation mechanisms, providing strong security guarantees.

1 Introduction

Key Encapsulation Mechanisms (KEM) enable the transmission of symmetric
keys at the beginning of an interaction while retaining trust that only the
intended recipient will be able to get access to this encapsulated key. Once
this trusted transmission has been established, users can privately communicate
using this encapsulated secret key with the advantages of symmetric encryption, granting compact ciphertexts of similar size as corresponding cleartexts.
Namely, they can be used to build Public-Key Encryption (PKE) schemes in
the KEM-DEM (for Data Encapsulation Mechanism) paradigm [18].

In organizations with complex structures, one will want to have more functionalities, namely being able to share a key among all users verifying a policy on

G. Tsudik et al. (Eds.): ESORICS 2023, LNCS 14344, pp. 372–392, 2024.
https://doi.org/10.1007/978-3-031-50594-2_19

a set of attributes, all at once. To this aim, KEMs constructed out of Attribute-Based Encryption (ABE) have been designed, in which keys can be encapsulated by being encrypted with these schemes for which all users verifying the specified attributes policy will be able to decrypt and thus decapsulate the key. These ABE primitives (stemming from [12]) are very powerful as they can cover any possible logical combination of the attributes, however this comes at an efficiency cost, and for practical use-cases, one will only need to encrypt for some of these existing combinations, for a limited number of attributes; this work is in this setting's scope, in which one can actually replace ABE constructions with encryption with respect to a union of attribute subsets. In these use-cases, it can also be relevant to get anonymity, meaning that a user should never know for which policy a ciphertext was produced, except if it is the policy they are using to successfully decrypt. In the case of ABE, this is called *attribute hiding*. This can also be used to get anonymous authentication (for instance in mobile network contexts) to service providers sending encapsulations without users needing to send out requests that would identify them.

Additionally, with current preoccupations with respect to the threat of quantum computers on classical cryptography, granting resistance to these for data that needs to be kept private on the long term is becoming a necessity. However, post-quantum cryptographic schemes are newer and only beginning to be used, one should try to keep current schemes' security properties. In fact, several security agencies are handing out guidelines for pre- and post-quantum security hybridization, meaning that cryptographic schemes should retain all their security properties even if one of the two pre- or post-quantum schemes is broken.

Another area of interest in this context in which users share some common keys, is the ability to still identify them uniquely, in case they choose to send some of there decapsulation capabilities to another party. Thus, if someone leaks some secret information they were supposed to keep to themselves, we would like to trace these so-called traitors, with *traceability*.

Related Work. This work combines many desirable properties for the use of KEMs in practical contexts, that other previous works had not, and since it covers only the practical contexts in which one would wish for ABE-based constructions, it compares favorably in efficiency with respect to such post-quantum schemes built from ABE, in addition with providing traceability and post- and pre-quantum hybridization.

Anonymous Broadcast Encryption. Our simplified access structure with strong privacy has a similar flavor as previous works [10, 15, 16] on broadcast encryption with anonymity, with optimizations on the decryption time. However, they do not handle black-box post-quantum security nor traceability.

Post-Quantum Key-Policy ABE. Then, providing post-quantum resistance, the closest related works are Key-Policy ABEs (KP-ABE) based on LWE. Some theoretical works such as [19] provide results with good asymptotic bounds, but are unsuited for use with practical parameters, and others, like [8], provide implementable results, but even with their comparable lowest policy circuit depth, their encryption time is about a hundred times bigger than ours, their decryption time about ten times bigger, and their RLWE parameters lead to bigger ciphertext sizes than ours. Also, they do not provide anonymity nor traceability.

Hybridization for Pre and Post-Quantum Security. Our work, in the line of security agency and standardization organizations recommendations, enables the hybridization of both pre- and post-quantum schemes, so that its security holds if it does either one of the underlying schemes. The use of the post-quantum scheme is totally black-box, enabling combinations with other semantically secure public-key encryption schemes. This is in the line of previous work to combine KEMs to get the best security out of the individual ones combined, such as [11], and in [4], where the specific problem of combining pre- and post-quantum schemes against various types of classical or quantum adversaries was studied.

Our Contributions. Our final instantiation called Covercrypt provides an efficient KEM for hidden access policies with traceability, ensuring both pre- and post-quantum securities, along with a Rust implementation of the scheme[1].

An Efficient KEM with Hidden Access Policies. Our scheme provides efficiency with respect to the state-of-the-art in KP-ABE schemes by restricting its scope to depth-one policy circuits. The attributes for which a key is encapsulated are kept hidden, providing anonymity. Also, we gain time on the decryption with an early-abort paradigm, in which one can quickly test whether a ciphertext was encrypted for one of their attributes, using a tag, and retaining the anonymity properties of the scheme. Our ciphertexts are of size $96 + \#B \times 1088$ Bytes, where B is the list of attribute-subsets the key is encapsulated for. On the other hand, user's keys are of size $(\#A + 1) \times 64$ Bytes, where A is the list of attributes for the user. For $\#B$ ranging from 1 to 5, encapsulation takes from 350 to 950 microseconds, and decapsulation, from 230 to 480 microseconds, with an affine dependency in the user's attributes (see Sect. 7).

Traceability. As an optional feature, the pre-quantum ElGamal part of our scheme provides traceability under the Decisional Diffie-Hellman (DDH) assumption. It makes sense to consider traceability with pre-quantum security as this is a short-term security requirement, if users are currently misbehaving, whereas the post-quantum security preserves the privacy property, which is important on the long-term, as ciphertexts can be stored until their security is broken in the future. Our implementation covers the case were traitors do not collude; we also show how the scheme can be instantiated for arbitrarily t-large collusions, but the tracing time then grows exponentially in t. A KEM can be used to broadcast symmetric encryption keys, but also for authentication, and in such an interactive context, implementing tracing requests is easily done in practice.

---

[1] https://github.com/Cosmian/cover_crypt.

2   Definitions

Public-Key Encryption (PKE) allows the transmission of hidden information that only the intended recipient will be able to uncover. To make the scheme independent of the format of the cleartext message, the usual paradigm for encryption is the KEM-DEM [18], where one first encapsulates a session key that only the recipient can recover, and then encrypts the payload under that key. The former step uses a Key Encapsulation Mechanism (KEM) and the latter a Data Encapsulation Mechanism (DEM), that is usually instantiated with an Authenticated Encryption, such as AES256-GCM[2], providing both privacy and authenticity of plaintexts. We hereafter recall some formal definitions.

Notations. Henceforth, many security notions will be characterized by the computational indistinguishability between two distributions $\mathcal{D}_0$ and $\mathcal{D}_1$. It will be measured by the advantage an adversary $\mathcal{A}$ can have in distinguishing them:

$$\mathsf{Adv}(\mathcal{A}) = \Pr_{\mathcal{D}_1}[\mathcal{A}(x) = 1] - \Pr_{\mathcal{D}_0}[\mathcal{A}(x) = 1] = 2 \times \Pr_{\mathcal{D}_b}[\mathcal{A}(x) = b] - 1.$$

Then, we will denote $\mathsf{Adv}(\tau)$ the maximal advantage over all the adversaries with running-time bounded by τ. A first pair of distributions is used in the famous ElGamal encryption scheme, with Diffie-Hellman tuples in $\mathbb{G} = \langle g \rangle$, a group of prime order p, spanned by a generator g, and denoted multiplicatively:

Definition 1 (Decisional Diffie-Hellman Problem). *The DDH assumption in a group $\mathbb{G}$ (DDH$_\mathbb{G}$) of prime order p, with a generator g, states that the distributions $\mathcal{D}_0$ and $\mathcal{D}_1$ are computationally hard to distinguish, where*

$$\mathcal{D}_0 = \{(g^a, g^b, g^{ab}), a, b \xleftarrow{\$} \mathbb{Z}_p\} \qquad \mathcal{D}_1 = \{(g^a, g^b, g^c), a, b, c \xleftarrow{\$} \mathbb{Z}_p\}$$

and we will denote $\mathsf{Adv}_\mathbb{G}^{\mathsf{ddh}}(\mathcal{A})$ the advantage of an adversary $\mathcal{A}$.

When studying the Kyber post-quantum encryption scheme, we will also need another algebraic structure, with indistinguishable distributions. We will denote $\mathsf{R} = \mathbb{Z}[X]/(X^n + 1)$ (resp. $\mathsf{R}_q = \mathbb{Z}_q[X]/(X^n + 1)$) the ring of polynomials of degree at most $n - 1$ with integer coefficients (resp. with coefficients in $\mathbb{Z}_q$, for a small prime q). We take n as power of 2, where $X^n + 1$ is the $\frac{n}{2}$-th cyclotomic polynomial. We denote $\mathcal{B}_\eta$ the centered binomial distribution of parameter η. When a polynomial is sampled according to $\mathcal{B}_\eta$, it means each of its coefficient is sampled from that distribution. We will also use vectors $\mathbf{e} \in \mathsf{R}_q^k$ and matrices $\mathbf{A} \in \mathsf{R}_q^{m \times k}$ in R_q:

Definition 2 (Decisional Module Learning-with-Error Problem). *The DMLWE assumption in R_q (DMLWE$_{\mathsf{R}_q, m, k, \eta}$) states that the distributions $\mathcal{D}_0$ and $\mathcal{D}_1$ are computationally hard to distinguish, where*

$$\mathcal{D}_0 = \{(\mathbf{A}, \mathbf{b}), \mathbf{A} \xleftarrow{\$} \mathsf{R}_q^{m \times k}, (\mathbf{s}, \mathbf{e}) \xleftarrow{\$} \mathcal{B}_\eta^k \times \mathcal{B}_\eta^m, \mathbf{b} \leftarrow \mathbf{As} + \mathbf{e}\}$$
$$\mathcal{D}_1 = \{(\mathbf{A}, \mathbf{b}), \mathbf{A} \xleftarrow{\$} \mathsf{R}_q^{m \times k}, \mathbf{b} \xleftarrow{\$} \mathcal{B}_\eta^m\}$$

---

[2] https://docs.rs/aes-gcm/latest/aes_gcm/.

We will denote $\mathsf{Adv}^{\mathsf{dmlwe}}_{R_q,m,k,\eta}(\mathcal{A})$ the advantage of an adversary $\mathcal{A}$.

Pseudorandom Generators (PRG). A long line of cryptographic works consider PRGs [1,13], as one of the theoretical foundations of modern cryptography. A PRG $\mathsf{PRG} : \{0;1\}^\mu \to \{0;1\}^\nu$ is deterministic function which should have the property that uniformly distributed inputs on $\{0;1\}^\mu$ should have outputs through PRG indistinguishable from uniformly random samples of $\{0;1\}^\nu$ with respect to a PPT adversary. The bigger ν is with respect to μ, the more challenging constructing such a PRG becomes. We define a PRG's security as:

Definition 3 (IND-security of a PRG). *Let* $\mathsf{PRG} : \{0;1\}^\mu \to \{0;1\}^\nu$ *be a deterministic function. Then* PRG *is an IND-secure PRG if the distributions* $\mathcal{D}_0$ *and* $\mathcal{D}_1$ *are computationally hard to distinguish, where*

$$\mathcal{D}_0 = \{y, x \xleftarrow{\$} \{0;1\}^\mu, y \leftarrow \mathsf{PRG}(x)\} \qquad \mathcal{D}_1 = \{y, y \xleftarrow{\$} \{0;1\}^\nu\}$$

We will denote $\mathsf{Adv}^{\mathsf{ind}}_{\mathsf{PRG}_{\mu,\nu}}(\mathcal{A})$ the advantage of an adversary $\mathcal{A}$.

Key Encapsulation Mechanism. A Key Encapsulation Mechanism KEM is defined by three algorithms:

- $\mathsf{KEM.KeyGen}(1^\kappa)$: the *key generation algorithm* outputs a pair of public and secret keys $(\mathsf{pk},\mathsf{sk})$;
- $\mathsf{KEM.Enc}(\mathsf{pk})$: the *encapsulation algorithm* generates a session key K and an encapsulation C of it, and outputs the pair (C, K);
- $\mathsf{KEM.Dec}(\mathsf{sk}, C)$: the *decapsulation algorithm* outputs the key K encapsulated in C.

Correctness. A correct KEM satisfies $\mathsf{Adv}^{\mathsf{cor}}_{\mathsf{KEM}}(\kappa) = 1 - \Pr_{\mathcal{D}}[\mathsf{Ev}] = \mathsf{negl}(\kappa)$, for

$$\mathcal{D} = \{(\mathsf{pk},\mathsf{sk}) \leftarrow \mathsf{KEM.KeyGen}(1^\kappa), (C, K) \leftarrow \mathsf{KEM.Enc}(\mathsf{pk}) : (\mathsf{sk}, C, K)\}$$
$$\mathsf{Ev} = [\mathsf{KEM.Dec}(\mathsf{sk}, C) = K]$$

Session-Key Privacy. On the other hand, such a KEM is said to provide *session-key privacy* (denoted SK-IND) in the key space $\mathcal{K}$, if the encapsulated key is indistinguishable from a random key in $\mathcal{K}$. More formally, a KEM is SK-IND-secure if for any adversary $\mathcal{A}$, $\mathsf{Adv}^{\mathsf{sk\text{-}ind}}_{\mathsf{KEM}}(\mathcal{A}) = \mathsf{negl}(\kappa)$, in distinguishing $\mathcal{D}_0$ and $\mathcal{D}_1$, where

$$\mathcal{D}_b = \left\{ \begin{array}{l} (\mathsf{pk},\mathsf{sk}) \leftarrow \mathsf{KEM.KeyGen}(1^\kappa), \\ (C, K_0) \leftarrow \mathsf{KEM.Enc}(\mathsf{pk}), K_1 \xleftarrow{\$} \mathcal{K} \end{array} : (\mathsf{pk}, C, K_b) \right\}$$

Public-Key Privacy. One can additionally expect anonymity of the receiver, also known as *public-key privacy* (denoted PK-IND), if the encapsulation does not leak any information about the public key, first defined in [3]. More formally, a KEM is PK-IND-secure if for any adversary $\mathcal{A}$, $\mathsf{Adv}_{\mathsf{KEM}}^{\mathsf{pk\text{-}ind}}(\mathcal{A}) = \mathsf{negl}(\kappa)$, in distinguishing $\mathcal{D}_0$ and $\mathcal{D}_1$, where

$$\mathcal{D}_b = \left\{ \begin{array}{l} \text{For } i = 0, 1: \\ (\mathsf{pk}_i, \mathsf{sk}_i) \leftarrow \mathsf{KEM.KeyGen}(1^\kappa), \\ (C_i, K_i) \leftarrow \mathsf{KEM.Enc}(\mathsf{pk}_i) \end{array} : (\mathsf{pk}_0, \mathsf{pk}_1, C_b) \right\}$$

ElGamal-based KEM. In a group $\mathbb{G}$ of prime order p, with a generator g:

- EG.KeyGen(1^κ): sample random $\mathsf{sk} = x \xleftarrow{\$} \mathbb{Z}_p$ and set $\mathsf{pk} = h \leftarrow g^x$;
- EG.Enc(pk): sample a random $r \xleftarrow{\$} \mathbb{Z}_p$ and set $C \leftarrow g^r$ together with $K \leftarrow h^r$;
- EG.Dec(sk, C): output $K \leftarrow C^x$.

Under the DDH assumption in $\mathbb{G}$, this KEM is both SK-IND and PK-IND with $\mathcal{K} = \mathbb{G}$. The formal security proofs for an extended version of this scheme will be given later, we thus postpone the analysis of this scheme.

Key Encapsulation Mechanism with Access Control. A KEM with Access Control allows multiple users to access the encapsulated key K from C, according to a rule $\mathcal{R}$ applied on X in the user's key usk and Y in the encapsulation C. It is defined by four algorithms:

- KEMAC.Setup(1^κ) outputs the global public parameters PK and the master secret key MSK;
- KEMAC.KeyGen(MSK, Y) outputs the user's secret key usk according to Y;
- KEMAC.Enc(PK, X) generates a session key K and an encapsulation C of it according to X;
- KEMAC.Dec(usk, C) outputs the key K encapsulated in C.

Correctness. A KEMAC is correct if $\mathsf{Adv}_{\mathsf{KEMAC}}^{\mathsf{cor}}(\kappa) = 1 - \Pr_{\mathcal{D}}[\mathsf{Ev}] = \mathsf{negl}(\kappa)$, for

$$\mathcal{D} = \left\{ \begin{array}{l} \forall (X, Y) \text{ such that } \mathcal{R}(X, Y) = 1, \\ (\mathsf{PK}, \mathsf{MSK}) \leftarrow \mathsf{KEMAC.KeyGen}(1^\kappa), \\ \mathsf{usk} \leftarrow \mathsf{KEMAC.KeyGen}(\mathsf{MSK}, Y), \\ (C, K) \leftarrow \mathsf{KEMAC.Enc}(\mathsf{PK}, X) \end{array} : (\mathsf{usk}, C, K) \right\}$$

$$\mathsf{Ev} = [\mathsf{KEMAC.Dec}(\mathsf{usk}, C) = K].$$

Session-Key Privacy. As for the basic KEM, one may expect some privacy properties. Session-key privacy is modeled by indistinguishability of ciphertexts, even if the adversary has received some decryption keys, as soon as associated Y_i are incompatible with X ($\mathcal{R}(X, Y_i) = 0$). Such a KEMAC is said to be SK-IND-secure in the key space $\mathcal{K}$ if for any adversary $\mathcal{A}$, that can ask any key usk_i, using oracle $\mathcal{O}\mathsf{KeyGen}(Y_i)$ that stores Y_i in the set $\mathcal{Y}$ and outputs $\mathsf{KEMAC.KeyGen}(\mathsf{MSK}, Y_i)$,

$\mathsf{Adv}_{\mathsf{KEMAC}}^{\mathsf{sk\text{-}ind}}(\mathcal{A}) = \mathsf{negl}(\kappa)$, for $b \xleftarrow{\$} \{0;1\}$ and

$$\mathcal{D}_b = \left\{ \begin{array}{l} (\mathsf{PK}, \mathsf{MSK}) \leftarrow \mathsf{KEMAC.Setup}(1^\kappa), \\ (\mathsf{state}, X) \leftarrow \mathcal{A}^{\mathcal{O}\mathsf{KeyGen}(\cdot)}(\mathsf{PK}), \\ (C, K_0) \leftarrow \mathsf{KEMAC.Enc}(\mathsf{PK}, X), K_1 \xleftarrow{\$} \mathcal{K} \end{array} : (\mathsf{state}, C, K_b) \right\}$$

$$\mathsf{BadXY} = [\exists Y_i \in \mathcal{Y}, \mathcal{R}(X, Y_i) = 1]$$

$$\mathsf{Adv}_{\mathsf{KEMAC}}^{\mathsf{pk\text{-}ind}}(\mathcal{A}) = 2 \times \Pr_{\mathcal{D}_b}[\mathcal{A}^{\mathcal{O}\mathsf{KeyGen}(\cdot)}(\mathsf{state}, C, K_b) = b \mid \neg\mathsf{BadXY}] - 1.$$

We note the bad event BadXY (decided at the end of the game) should be avoided by the adversary, as it reduces its advantage: this indeed leads to a trivial guess, and this is considered as a non-legitimate attack.

Access-Control Privacy. In addition, one could want to hide the parameter X used in the encapsulation C even if the adversary $\mathcal{A}$ can ask any key usk_i for Y_i such that $\mathcal{R}(X_0, Y_i) = \mathcal{R}(X_1, Y_i) = 0$ for all i, using oracle $\mathcal{O}\mathsf{KeyGen}(Y_i)$ that stores Y_i in the set $\mathcal{Y}$ and outputs $\mathsf{KEMAC.KeyGen}(\mathsf{MSK}, Y_i)$. A KEMAC is said to be AC-IND-secure if for any adversary $\mathcal{A}$, that can ask any key usk_i, using oracle $\mathcal{O}\mathsf{KeyGen}(Y_i)$ that stores Y_i in the set $\mathcal{Y}$ and outputs $\mathsf{KEMAC.KeyGen}(\mathsf{MSK}, Y_i)$, $\mathsf{Adv}_{\mathsf{KEMAC}}^{\mathsf{ac\text{-}ind}}(\mathcal{A}) = \mathsf{negl}(\kappa)$, for $b \xleftarrow{\$} \{0;1\}$ and

$$\mathcal{D}_b = \left\{ \begin{array}{l} (\mathsf{PK}, \mathsf{MSK}) \leftarrow \mathsf{KEMAC.Setup}(1^\kappa), \\ (\mathsf{state}, X_0, X_1) \leftarrow \mathcal{A}^{\mathcal{O}\mathsf{KeyGen}(\cdot)}(\mathsf{PK}), \\ (C_i, K_i) \leftarrow \mathsf{KEMAC.Enc}(\mathsf{PK}, X_i), \text{ for } i = 0, 1 \end{array} : (\mathsf{state}, C_b) \right\}$$

$$\mathsf{BadXY} = [\exists Y_i \in \mathcal{Y}, \mathcal{R}(X_0, Y_i) = 1 \vee \mathcal{R}(X_1, Y_i) = 1]$$

$$\mathsf{Adv}_{\mathsf{KEMAC}}^{\mathsf{ac\text{-}ind}}(\mathcal{A}) = 2 \times \Pr_{\mathcal{D}_b}[\mathcal{A}^{\mathcal{O}\mathsf{KeyGen}(\cdot)}(\mathsf{state}, C_b) = b \mid \neg\mathsf{BadXY}] - 1,$$

where we again condition the advantage to legitimate attacks only.

Traceability. In any multi-user setting, to avoid abuse of the decryption keys, one may want to be able to trace a user (or their personal key) from the decryption mechanism, and more generally from any *useful* decoder, either given access to the key material in the device (white-box tracing) or just interacting with the device (black-box tracing). Without any keys, one expects session-key privacy, but as soon as one knows a key, one can distinguish the session-key. Then, we will call a *useful* pirate decoder $\mathcal{P}$ a good distinguisher against session-key privacy, that behaves differently with the real and a random key. But of course, this pirate decoder can be built from multiple user' keys, called traitors, and one would like to be able to trace at least one of them.

A weaker variant of traceability is just a confirmation of candidate traitors, and we will target this goal: if a pirate decoder $\mathcal{P}$ has been generated from a list $\mathcal{T} = \{Y_i\}$ of traitors' keys, a confirmer algorithm $\mathcal{C}$ can output, from a valid guess $\mathcal{G}$ for $\mathcal{T}$, at least one traitor in $\mathcal{T}$. More formally, let us consider any adversary $\mathcal{A}$ that can ask for key generation through oracle $\mathcal{O}\mathsf{KeyGen}(Y_i)$, that gets $\mathsf{usk}_i \leftarrow \mathsf{KEMAC.KeyGen}(\mathsf{MSK}, Y_i)$, outputs nothing but appends the new user Y_i in $\mathcal{U}$, and then corrupt some users through the corruption oracle $\mathcal{O}\text{Corrupt}(Y_i)$, that outputs usk_i and appends Y_i in $\mathcal{T}$, to build a *useful* pirate decoder $\mathcal{P}$, then there is a *correct* confirmer algorithm $\mathcal{C}$ that outputs a traitor T, with *negligible error*: for $b \xleftarrow{\$} \{0; 1\}$ and

$$\mathcal{D} = \left\{ \begin{array}{l} (\text{PK}, \text{MSK}) \leftarrow \text{KEMAC.Setup}(1^\kappa), \mathcal{P} \leftarrow \mathcal{A}^{\mathcal{O}\text{KeyGen}(\cdot), \mathcal{O}\text{Corrupt}(\cdot)}(\text{PK}), \\ X \text{ such that } \forall Y_i \in \mathcal{T}, \mathcal{R}(X, Y_i) = 1, \\ (C, K_0) \leftarrow \text{KEMAC.Enc}(\text{PK}, X), K_1 \xleftarrow{\$} \mathcal{K} : \\ \qquad\qquad (\text{MSK}, \mathcal{P}, \mathcal{U}, \mathcal{T}, C, K_0, K_1) \end{array} \right\},$$

we denote:

- $\mathcal{P}$ as useful, if $2 \times \Pr_{\mathcal{D},b}[\mathcal{P}(C, K_b) = b] - 1$ is non-negligible;
- $\mathcal{C}$ as correct, if $\Pr_{\mathcal{D}}[T \in \mathcal{T} \mid T \leftarrow \mathcal{C}^{\mathcal{P}(\cdot, \cdot)}(\text{MSK}, \mathcal{T})]$ is overwhelming;
- $\mathcal{C}$ as error-free if for any $\mathcal{G} \subset \mathcal{U}$, $\Pr_{\mathcal{D}}[T \notin \mathcal{T} \mid T \leftarrow \mathcal{C}^{\mathcal{P}(\cdot, \cdot)}(\text{MSK}, \mathcal{G}) \wedge T \neq \perp]$ is negligible.

More concretely, we say that the decoder $\mathcal{P}$ is *useful* if it can distinguish the real key from a random key with significant advantage. Then, from such a useful decoder, the confirmer $\mathcal{C}$ is *correct* if it outputs a traitor with overwhelming probability, when it starts from the correct set $\mathcal{T}$ of candidates. Eventually, it should be *error-free*: $\mathcal{T}$ does not output an honest user, but with negligible probability. The t-confirmation limits the number of corrupted users in $\mathcal{T}$ to t.

Hybrid KEM. While one can never exclude an attack against a cryptographic scheme, combining several independent approaches reduces the risks. This is the way one suggests to apply post-quantum schemes, in combination with classical schemes, in order to be sure to get the best security.

Hybrid KEM *Construction.* Let us first study the combination of two KEMs (KEM_1 and KEM_2), so that as soon as one of them achieves SK-IND security, the hybrid KEM achieves SK-IND security too.

We need both KEMs to generate keys in $\mathcal{K}$, with a group structure and internal law denoted $\oplus$:

- KEM.KeyGen(1^κ) calls $(\text{pk}_i, \text{sk}_i) \leftarrow \text{KEM}_i.\text{KeyGen}(1^\kappa)$, for $i \in \{1, 2\}$ and outputs $\text{pk} \leftarrow (\text{pk}_1, \text{pk}_2)$ and $\text{sk} \leftarrow (\text{sk}_1, \text{sk}_2)$;
- KEM.Enc(pk) parses pk as $(\text{pk}_1, \text{pk}_2)$, calls $(C_i, K_i) \leftarrow \text{KEM}_i.\text{Enc}(\text{pk}_i)$ for $i \in \{1, 2\}$, and outputs $(C = (C_1, C_2), K = K_1 \oplus K_2)$;
- KEM.Dec(sk, C) parses sk as $(\text{sk}_1, \text{sk}_2)$ and C as (C_1, C_2), then calls both $K_i \leftarrow \text{KEM}_i.\text{Dec}(\text{sk}_i, C_i)$, and outputs $K = K_1 \oplus K_2$.

Security Properties. As expected, we can prove that as soon as one of them achieves SK-IND security, the hybrid KEM achieves SK-IND security too. This also follows from [11]'s first lemma. However, for PK-IND security of KEM, we need both the underlying schemes to be PK-IND secure. This second property is not as crucial as the first one: none of the other security properties we show for the schemes depend on it, and here the only property at stake is the anonymity of the receiver of the encapsulated keys, not the keys themselves.

Theorem 1 (Session-Key Privacy). *If at least one of the underlying* KEM_1 *and* KEM_2 *is SK-IND-secure, the hybrid* KEM *is SK-IND-secure:*

$$\mathsf{Adv}_{KEM}^{sk\text{-}ind}(\tau) \leq \min\{\mathsf{Adv}_{KEM_1}^{sk\text{-}ind}(\tau), \mathsf{Adv}_{KEM_2}^{sk\text{-}ind}(\tau)\}.$$

Theorem 2 (Public-Key Privacy). *If both underlying* KEM_1 *and* KEM_2 *are PK-IND-secure, the hybrid* KEM *is PK-IND-secure:*

$$\mathsf{Adv}_{KEM}^{pk\text{-}ind}(\tau) \leq \mathsf{Adv}_{KEM_1}^{pk\text{-}ind}(\tau) + \mathsf{Adv}_{KEM_2}^{pk\text{-}ind}(\tau).$$

We will also use Public-Key Encryption (PKE), which is recalled in the Appendix A.

3   Authenticated Key Encapsulation Mechanism

With public-key privacy, one cannot know who is the actual receiver, and needs to check the decapsulated session key with an authenticated encryption scheme to know whether they were a recipient or not. The latter check can be time-consuming when applied on a large data content (or when there are multiple decryption keys to try). We can hope to have quick key confirmation, if the additional *Authentication* (AUTH) property is satisfied.

Authentication. A KEM provides *authentication* (denoted AUTH) if it satisfies $\mathsf{Adv}_{KEM}^{auth}(\kappa) = 1 - \Pr_{\mathcal{D}}[\mathsf{Ev}] = \mathsf{negl}(\kappa)$, for

$$\mathcal{D} = \left\{ \begin{array}{l} \forall i \in \{0;1\}, (\mathsf{pk}_i, \mathsf{sk}_i) \leftarrow \mathsf{KEM.KeyGen}(1^\kappa), \\ (C, K) \leftarrow \mathsf{KEM.Enc}(\mathsf{pk}_0) : (\mathsf{sk}_1, C) \end{array} \right\}$$

$$\mathsf{Ev} = [\mathsf{KEM.Dec}(\mathsf{sk}_1, C) = \perp].$$

We stress this is a weak authentication definition, but strong enough for our further early-abort technique. We indeed just want to exclude a ciphertext to be valid under two keys, at random. There is no malicious behavior.

We present a generic conversion to add the AUTH property to any KEM, while retaining previous properties (SK-IND and PK-IND). To this aim, we use a PRG.

Key Encapsulation Mechanisms with Authentication. We present below a KEM′ with authentication from a KEM that outputs κ-bit keys, with two security parameters: k, the length of the new encapsulated key, and ℓ, the length of the verification tag. We also use a PRG PRG : $\{0;1\}^\kappa \rightarrow \{0;1\}^{k+\ell}$. We require that in KEM.Enc's outputs (C, K), with K looking uniform in $\{0;1\}^\kappa$.

- KEM′.KeyGen(1^κ) runs $(\mathsf{pk}, \mathsf{sk}) \leftarrow \mathsf{KEM.KeyGen}(1^\kappa)$;
- KEM′.Enc(pk) runs $(c, s) \leftarrow \mathsf{KEM.Enc}(\mathsf{pk})$ and gets $U\|V \leftarrow \mathsf{PRG}(s)$. One then outputs $C \leftarrow (c, V)$ together with the encapsulated key $K \leftarrow U$;
- KEM′.Dec(sk, $C = (c, V)$) runs $s \leftarrow \mathsf{KEM.Dec}(\mathsf{sk}, c)$, gets $U'\|V' \leftarrow \mathsf{PRG}(s)$, and checks whether $V = V'$. In the positive case, one outputs $K' \leftarrow U'$, otherwise one outputs $\perp$.

Correctness. If the KEM KEM is correct, then the derived KEM' with authentication is also correct, has the decapsulation of c outputs the same s as during encapsulation, and then $\mathsf{PRG}(s)$ gives the same key and tag.

Security Properties. We will now show the previous security notions still hold, and we really provide authentication. We can claim that the above KEM' retains the initial security properties of the KEM scheme, but as the proofs essentially rely of the PRG properties, we defer the proofs to the full version [6].

Theorem 3 (Session-Key Privacy). *If the KEM KEM is SK-IND-secure, and outputs (C, K)'s of KEM.Enc have uniformly distributed K's in $\{0, 1\}^\kappa$, then its derived KEM' with authentication using the IND-secure PRG PRG : $\{0; 1\}^\kappa \to \{0; 1\}^{k+\ell}$ is SK-IND-secure:* $\mathsf{Adv}^{sk\text{-}ind}_{KEM'}(\tau) \le 2 \cdot \mathsf{Adv}^{sk\text{-}ind}_{KEM}(\tau) + 2 \cdot \mathsf{Adv}^{ind}_{\mathsf{PRG}_{\kappa,k+\ell}}(\tau)$, *for any running time τ.*

Theorem 4 (Public-Key Privacy). *If the KEM KEM is both SK-IND and PK-IND-secure, outputs (C, K)'s of KEM.Enc have uniformly distributed K's in $\{0, 1\}^\kappa$, and PRG : $\{0; 1\}^\kappa \to \{0; 1\}^{k+\ell}$ is an IND-secure PRG, then its derived KEM' using PRG is PK-IND-secure:* $\mathsf{Adv}^{pk\text{-}ind}_{KEM'}(\tau) \le \mathsf{Adv}^{pk\text{-}ind}_{KEM}(\tau) + 4 \cdot \mathsf{Adv}^{sk\text{-}ind}_{KEM}(\tau) + 4 \cdot \mathsf{Adv}^{ind}_{\mathsf{PRG}_{\kappa,k+\ell}}(\tau)$, *for any running time τ.*

We develop the authentication property, with the proof in the Appendix B:

Theorem 5 (Authentication). *If the KEM KEM is SK-IND, outputs (C, K)'s of KEM.Enc have uniformly distributed K's in $\{0, 1\}^\kappa$, and PRG : $\{0; 1\}^\kappa \to \{0; 1\}^{k+\ell}$ is an IND-secure PRG, then the corresponding authenticated KEM KEM' using PRG provides authentication:* $\mathsf{Adv}^{auth}_{KEM'}(\kappa) \le 2^{-\ell} + \mathsf{Adv}^{sk\text{-}ind}_{KEM}(\tau) + \mathsf{Adv}^{ind}_{\mathsf{PRG}_{\kappa,k+\ell}}(\tau')$, *for some small running times τ, τ'.*

4   Subset-Cover **KEMAC**

The above notion of access control is quite general and includes both key-policy ABE and ciphertext-policy ABE, where one can have policies $\mathcal{P}$ and attributes such that given a subset of attributes, this defines a list of Boolean B (according to the presence or not of the attribute), and $\mathcal{P}(B)$ is either true or false.

For efficiency considerations, we will focus on the subset-cover approach: during the Setup, one defines multiple sets S_i; when generating a user key usk_j, a list A_j of subsets if specified, which implicitly means user $U_j \in S_i$ for all $i \in A_j$; at encapsulation time, a target set T is given by B, such that $T = \cup_{i \in B} S_i$.

Intuitively, S_i's are subsets of the universe of users, and to specify the receivers, one encapsulates the key K for a covering of the target set T. A KEMAC, for a list Σ of sets S_i, can then be defined from any KEM in $\mathcal{K}$ that is a group with internal law denoted $\oplus$. We now describe a subset cover KEMAC with anonymity and early aborts, our main contribution.

Anonymous Subset-Cover KEMAC with Early Aborts. To avoid sending B together with the ciphertext, but still being able to quickly find the correct matching indices in the ciphertext and the user's key, one can use a KEM$'$ with authentication:

- KEMAC.Setup(Σ), for each $S_i \in \Sigma$, runs $(\mathsf{pk}_i, \mathsf{sk}_i) \leftarrow$ KEM$'$.KeyGen(1^κ): PK $\leftarrow (\mathsf{pk}_i)_i$ and MSK $\leftarrow (\mathsf{sk}_i)_i$;
- KEMAC.KeyGen(MSK, A_j) defines the user's secret key $\mathsf{usk}_j \leftarrow (\mathsf{sk}_i)_{i \in A_j}$;
- KEMAC.Enc(PK, B) generates à random session key $K \xleftarrow{\$} \{0;1\}^k$, and, for all $i \in B$, runs $(C_i, K_i) \leftarrow$ KEM$'$.Enc(pk_i) and outputs $C \leftarrow (C_i, E_i = K \oplus K_i)_{i \in B}$ together with the encapsulated key K;
- KEMAC.Dec(usk, C), for all sk_i in usk and all (C_j, E_j) in C, runs $K'_{i,j} \leftarrow$ KEM$'$.Dec(sk_i, C_j). It stops for the first valid $K'_{i,j}$, outputs $K \leftarrow K'_{i,j} \oplus E_j$.

For this above scheme, we can claim both the SK-IND security and the AC-IND security, for selective key queries. But first, let us check the correctness, thats fails if a wrong key, among the $S_A S_B$ possibilities, makes accepts:

Theorem 6 (Correctness). *If the underlying KEM$'$ is AUTH-secure, the above subset-cover KEMAC is correct:* $\mathsf{Adv}^{cor}_{KEMAC}(\kappa) \leq S_A S_B \times \mathsf{Adv}^{auth}_{KEM'}(\kappa)$, *where S_A and S_B are the sizes of the user' sets of attributes and the number of subsets in the ciphertext, respectively.*

About SK-IND and AC-IND security, the proofs follow the classical hybrid technique, they are thus deferred to the full version [6].

Theorem 7 (Session-Key Privacy). *If the underlying KEM$'$ is SK-IND-secure, the above subset-cover KEMAC is also SK-IND-secure, for selective key-queries:* $\mathsf{Adv}^{sk-ind}_{KEMAC}(\tau) \leq 2q_k \times \mathsf{Adv}^{sk-ind}_{KEM'}(\tau)$, *where q_k is the number of key-queries.*

Theorem 8 (Access-Control Privacy). *If the underlying KEM$'$ is AC-IND-secure, the above subset-cover KEMAC is AC-IND-secure, for selective key-queries and constant-size sets B:* $\mathsf{Adv}^{ac-ind}_{KEMAC}(\tau) \leq 2S_B \times \mathsf{Adv}^{pk-ind}_{KEM}(\tau)$, *where S_B is the constant-size of the sets B.*

We stress that B must have a constant size to achieve access-control privacy.

5   Traceable KEM

In a subset-cover-based KEMAC, a same decapsulation key sk_i is given to multiple users, for a public key pk_i. In case of abuse, one cannot trace the defrauder. We offer an ElGamal-based KEM with traceability, in the same vein as [5].

Traceable ElGamal-based TKEM. Let $\mathbb{G}$ be a group of prime order q, with a generator g, in which the Computational Diffie-Hellman problem is hard. We describe below a TKEM with n multiple decapsulation keys for a specific public key, allowing to deal with collusions of at most t users:

- TKEM.KeyGen($1^\kappa, n, t, g, \mathbb{G}, q$): returns a public key pk, n secret keys usk_j:

- it samples random $s, s_k \xleftarrow{\$} \mathbb{Z}_q^*$, for $k = 1 \ldots, t+1$ and sets $h \leftarrow g^s$ as well as $h_k \leftarrow g^{s_k}$ for each k;
- for users U_j, for $j = 1 \ldots, n$, one samples random $(v_{j,k})_k \xleftarrow{\$} \mathbb{Z}_q^{t+1}$, such that $\sum_k v_{j,k} s_k = s$, for $j = 1 \ldots, n$. Then, $\mathsf{pk} \leftarrow ((h_k)_k, h)$, while each $\mathsf{usk}_j \leftarrow (v_{j,k})_k$.
- TKEM.Enc($\mathsf{pk} = ((h_k)_k, h)$): it samples a random $r \xleftarrow{\$} \mathbb{Z}_q$, and sets $C = (C_k \leftarrow h_k^r)_k$, as well as $K \leftarrow h^r$.
- TKEM.Dec($\mathsf{usk}_j = (v_{j,k})_k, C = (C_k)_k$): it outputs $K \leftarrow \prod_k C_k^{v_{j,k}}$.

One notes: $\prod_k C_k^{v_{j,k}} = \prod_k h_k^{r v_{j,k}} = \prod_k (g^r)^{s_k v_{j,k}} = g^{r \sum_k s_k v_{j,k}} = g^{sr} = h^r = K$.

Security Properties. First, we will show that the above TKEM construction achieves both SK-IND and PK-IND security. But it also allows to confirm traitors, from a stateless pirate decoder $\mathcal{P}$ (in particular, this means that $\mathcal{P}$ never blocks itself after several invalid ciphertexts). The proofs of Theorems 9 and 10 are deferred to the full version [6].

Theorem 9 (Session-Key Privacy). *The above TKEM achieves SK-IND security under the DDH assumption in $\mathbb{G}$:* $\mathsf{Adv}_{TKEM}^{sk-ind}(\tau) \leq \mathsf{Adv}_{\mathbb{G}}^{ddh}(\tau)$.

Theorem 10 (Public-Key Privacy). *The above TKEM achieves PK-IND security under the DDH assumption in $\mathbb{G}$:* $\mathsf{Adv}_{TKEM}^{pk-ind}(\tau) \leq \mathsf{Adv}_{\mathbb{G}}^{ddh}(\tau)$.

Theorem 11 (t-Confirmation). *A collusion of at most t keys can be confirmed from a useful stateless pirate decoder $\mathcal{P}$: starting from a correct guess for $\mathcal{T}$, the traitors' keys used for building the pirate decoder $\mathcal{P}$, by accessing the decoder, one can confirm a traitor in $\mathcal{T}$, with negligible error.*

Proof. To prove this theorem, we first give a description of the confirmer algorithm $\mathcal{C}$, then we provide the indistinguishability analysis, and eventually prove $\mathcal{C}$ will give a correct answer. This proof can be found in the Appendix C.

Corollary 1. *In the particular case of $t = 1$, one can efficiently trace one traitor, from a useful stateless pirate decoder: by trying $\mathcal{G} = \{J\}$ sequentially for each $J = 1, \ldots, n$, and evaluating $p_{\mathcal{G}}$, one should get either a significant advantage (for the traitor) or 0 (for honest keys).*

6 Our KEMAC Scheme

We have already presented a traceable KEM that is secure against classical adversaries. If we combine it with another scheme expected secure against quantum adversaries, we can thereafter combine them into an hybrid-KEM, that inherits security properties from both schemes, with still traceability against classical adversaries. But we will actually exploit the properties of a Public-Key Encryption (PKE) scheme in order to improve efficiency of the combination. Given a PKE, that is both indistinguishable and anonymous, we can trivially get a KEM that is both SK-IND and PK-IND secure:

- KEM.KeyGen(1^κ) gets (pk, sk) ← PKE.KeyGen(1^κ), and outputs (pk, sk);
- KEM.Enc(pk) gets $K \xleftarrow{\$} \mathcal{K}$, C ← PKE.Enc(pk, K), and outputs (K, C);
- KEM.Dec(sk, C) outputs PKE.Dec(sk, C).

CRYSTALS-Kyber PKE We recall the algorithms of the CRYSTALS-Kyber [2] public-key encryption whose both indistinguishability and anonymity rely on the hardness of Module-LWE [14]. We identify R_q with $\mathbb{Z}_q^n$ that contains the plaintext space $\mathcal{K} = \{0; 1\}^n$, and use two noise parameters $\eta_1 \geq \eta_2$, for the Gaussian distributions $\mathcal{B}_{\eta_1}$ and $\mathcal{B}_{\eta_2}$:

- Kyber.KeyGen(1^κ): sample random $\mathbf{A} \xleftarrow{\$} R_q^{k \times k}$ and $(\mathbf{s}, \mathbf{e}) \xleftarrow{\$} \mathcal{B}_{\eta_1}^k \times \mathcal{B}_{\eta_1}^k$, then set pk ← $(\mathbf{A}, \mathbf{b} = \mathbf{As} + \mathbf{e})$ and sk ← $\mathbf{s}$.
- Kyber.Enc(pk, K): $\mathbf{r} \xleftarrow{\$} \mathcal{B}_{\eta_1}^k$, and $(\mathbf{e}_1, e_2) \xleftarrow{\$} \mathcal{B}_{\eta_2}^k \times \mathcal{B}_{\eta_2}$, then set $\mathbf{u} = \mathbf{A}^T \mathbf{r} + \mathbf{e}_1$ and $v = \mathbf{b}^T \mathbf{r} + e_2 + \lfloor \frac{q}{2} \rfloor \cdot K$, and return $C = (\mathbf{u}, v)$.
- Kyber.Dec(sk, C): compute $w \leftarrow v - \mathbf{s}^T \mathbf{u}$ and output $K = \lceil \frac{2}{q} \cdot w \rfloor$.

Theorem 12 follows from [2], and Theorem 13 is also in the scope of [17]:

Theorem 12 (Indistinguishability of Kyber.) Kyber *is IND-secure under the decisional Module-LWE assumption:*

$$\mathsf{Adv}_{\mathsf{Kyber}}^{\mathsf{ind}}(\tau) \leq \mathsf{Adv}_{R_q,k,k,\eta_1}^{\mathsf{dmlwe}}(\tau) + \mathsf{Adv}_{R_q,k+1,k,\eta_2}^{\mathsf{dmlwe}}(\tau) \leq 2 \times \mathsf{Adv}_{R_q,k+1,k,\eta_2}^{\mathsf{dmlwe}}(\tau).$$

Theorem 13 (Anonymity of Kyber.) Kyber *is PK-IND-secure under the decisional Module-LWE assumption:*

$$\mathsf{Adv}_{\mathsf{Kyber}}^{\mathsf{pk\text{-}ind}}(\tau) \leq 2 \times \mathsf{Adv}_{R_q,k,k,\eta_1}^{\mathsf{dmlwe}}(\tau) + \mathsf{Adv}_{R_q,k+1,k,\eta_2}^{\mathsf{dmlwe}}(\tau) \leq 3 \times \mathsf{Adv}_{R_q,k+1,k,\eta_2}^{\mathsf{dmlwe}}(\tau).$$

Hybrid KEM, from KEM and PKE. Using the ElGamal KEM that is both SK-IND and PK-IND-secure under the DDH assumption, together with the Kyber PKE that is both SK-IND and PK-IND-secure under the DMLWE assumption, the hybrid KEM is:

- SK-IND-secure, as soon as either the DDH or the DMLWE assumptions hold;
- PK-IND-secure, under both the DDH and the DMLWE assumption.

according to Sect. 2. But with a PKE scheme, we can optimize a bit with:

- Hyb.KeyGen(1^κ): generate both pairs of keys $(\mathsf{pk}_1, \mathsf{sk}_1)$ ← KEM.KeyGen(1^κ) and $(\mathsf{pk}_2, \mathsf{sk}_2)$ ← PKE.KeyGen(1^κ), then output pk ← $(\mathsf{pk}_1, \mathsf{pk}_2)$ and sk ← $(\mathsf{sk}_1, \mathsf{sk}_2)$;
- Hyb.Enc(pk): parse pk as $(\mathsf{pk}_1, \mathsf{pk}_2)$, choose a random $K \xleftarrow{\$} \mathcal{K}$, call (C_1, K_1) ← KEM.Enc(pk_1) and C_2 ← PKE.Enc($\mathsf{pk}_2, K \oplus K_1$). Output $(C = (C_1, C_2), K)$;
- Hyb.Dec(sk, C): parse sk as $(\mathsf{sk}_1, \mathsf{sk}_2)$ and C as (C_1, C_2), then call both K_1 ← KEM.Dec(sk_1, C_1), K_2 ← PKE.Dec(sk_2, C_2), and output $K = K_1 \oplus K_2$.

Hybrid Traceable KEMAC. We can apply the above generic combination to build an anonymous subset-cover KEMAC with early abort, with the traceable ElGamal KEM and Kyber PKE to get a Key Encapsulation Mechanism with Access Control and Black-Box traceability (without collusions, so with $t = 1$ using notations from Sect. 5), where message-privacy hold as soon as at least the DDH or the DMLWE assumption holds, while the target-set privacy holds under both the DDH and DMLWE, and traceability works under the DDH assumption.

To have authentication properties, the ElGamal TKEM is slightly modified to fit Theorems 3, 4 and 5's requirements, in which the element K output by the encapsulation algorithm should be uniform in $\{0;1\}^\kappa$. This modification can be done either in the Random Oracle Model (ROM) with a hash function modelled as a random oracle, and outputting a hash of the original key into $\{0;1\}^\kappa$, or, without the ROM, using a twist augmented technique from [7]. The KEMs derived with these two techniques are deferred to the full version [6]. We describe here the one in the ROM. Proofs for SK-IND and PK-IND-securities follow immediately from the proofs that TKEM is SK-IND and PK-IND-secure.

Detailled Description. The straightforward construction of the hybrid traceable KEMAC with early abort is the simple instantiation of the KEMAC scheme from Sect. 4 from a KEM with authentication (from Sect. 3), itself based on our hybrid KEM from the previous subsection. A naïve instantiation would draw independent keys in the hybrid schemes and send their $\oplus$'s with the encapsulated key. But as K is chosen beforehand, the same K can be chosen for all the subsets. This optimized version is described with the following algorithms, where $\mathcal{H}$ is a hash function modeled as a random oracle with output length κ, PRG : $\{0;1\}^\kappa \rightarrow \{0;1\}^{k+\ell}$ a PRG, where k is the length of the encapsulated key, ℓ the length of the verification tag, and Σ the set of subsets $(S_i)_i$ (or attributes). We instantiate it with the Kyber PKE, but it would work with any PKE that is both indistinguishable and anonymous. We call this KEMAC Covercrypt:

- Covercrypt.Setup($\Sigma, 1^\kappa$):
  1. For a group $\mathbb{G}$ of prime order p, generated by g, one samples $s, s_1, s_2 \xleftarrow{\$} \mathbb{Z}_p$, then sets $h = g^s$, and $g_1 = g^{s_1}, g_2 = g^{s_2}$ (for tracing purposes).
  2. Then, for tracing, we set tsk $= (s, s_1, s_2, \mathcal{ID})$, where $\mathcal{ID}$ is the set of the users' identifiers uid, initialized as an empty set here, and tpk $= (g, h, g_1, g_2)$.
  3. For each $S_i \in \Sigma$, one samples a random scalar $x_i \xleftarrow{\$} \mathbb{Z}_p$, a $(\mathsf{pk}_i, \mathsf{sk}_i) \leftarrow$ Kyber.KeyGen(1^κ), then sets $\mathsf{pk}'_i \leftarrow (h_i = h^{x_i}, \mathsf{pk}_i)$, and $\mathsf{sk}'_i \leftarrow (x_i, \mathsf{sk}_i)$.
  4. Finally, the global public key is set to PK $\leftarrow$ (tpk, $\{\mathsf{pk}'_i\}_i$), and the master secret key to MSK $\leftarrow$ (tsk, $\{\mathsf{sk}'_i\}_i, \mathcal{UP}$), where $\mathcal{UP}$ is the set of user's secret keys, showing their permissions, but initialized as an empty set. One returns (MSK, PK).
- Covercrypt.KeyGen(MSK, U, A):
  1. For a user U, with attributes A (a list of subsets, or equivalently their indices), one samples $(\alpha, \beta) \in \mathbb{Z}_p^2$ such that $\alpha s_1 + \beta s_2 = s$, and sets the corresponding user secret identifier uid $\leftarrow (\alpha, \beta)$.

2. The tracing secret key tsk is updated as tsk$'$ by adding (U, uid) in $\mathcal{ID}$.
3. Finally, the user's secret key is defined as usk $\leftarrow (\mathsf{uid}, \{\mathsf{sk}'_j\}_{j \in A})$, and one outputs it along with MSK$'$, the master secret key MSK updated with usk added in $\mathcal{UP}$, and tsk$'$ instead of tsk.

- Covercrypt.Enc(PK, B):
  1. For a target set that covers all the users with an attribute in B (or equivalently the indices of attributes, such that $A \cap B \neq \emptyset$), one generates a random seed for the key to be encapsulated, $S \xleftarrow{\$} \{0;1\}^\kappa$, then draws $r \xleftarrow{\$} \mathbb{Z}_p^*$, sets $c = (C_1 = g_1^r, C_2 = g_2^r)$, and, for each $i \in B$, with $\mathsf{pk}'_i = (h_i = h^{x_i}, \mathsf{pk}_i)$, sets $K_i = \mathcal{H}(h_i^r)$, and then sets $E_i \leftarrow \mathsf{Kyber.Enc}(\mathsf{pk}_i, S \oplus K_i)^3$.
  2. One then computes $K \| V \leftarrow \mathsf{PRG}(S)$, in order to grant the early aborts paradigm, and sets the encapsulation as: $C \leftarrow (c, \{E_i\}_{i \in B}, V)$, the encapsulated key as K, and outputs: (K, C).
- Covercrypt.Dec(usk $= (\mathsf{uid} = (\alpha, \beta), \{\mathsf{sk}_j\}_{j \in A}), C = (c, \{E_i\}_{i \in B}, V))$: For $i \in B$, for each $\mathsf{sk}'_j = (x_j, \mathsf{sk}_j)$ in usk and (c, E_i, V) in C, one decapsulates the underlying hybrid KEM to get the potential seed S used for the key:
  - first, $K'_{i,j} \leftarrow \mathsf{Kyber.Dec}(\mathsf{sk}_j, E_i)$;
  - for ElGamal, from $c = (C_1, C_2)$, one computes $K_j \leftarrow \mathcal{H}((C_1^\alpha C_2^\beta)^{x_j})$;
  - $S_{i,j}$ is then computed as $S_{i,j} \leftarrow K'_{i,j} \oplus K_j$.

  In the early-abort check, one computes $U'_{i,j} \| V'_{i,j} \leftarrow \mathsf{PRG}(S_{i,j})$, and checks whether $V'_{i,j} = V$. In the positive case, one returns $K \leftarrow U'_{i,j}$, for this first valid (i,j), as the session key. Else, if $V'_{i,j} \neq V$, the ciphertext is rejected and the loop on the i, j indices goes on[4].

Security Analysis. Our Covercrypt scheme inherits its security properties from the underlying hybrid KEM scheme using both the Kyber PKE and the traceable ElGamal KEM, and as such, is SK-IND-secure as soon as either the DDH or the DMLWE assumptions hold, and PK-IND-secure under both the DDH and the DMLWE assumptions. Correctness also follows from the authentication property of the hybrid KEM, and thus under either the DDH or the DMLWE assumptions.

Traceability. The traceability is inherited from the underlying traceable ElGamal KEM scheme, with $t = 1$ in Sect. 5's notations; it relies on the DDH. To check whether a user U with $\mathsf{uid} = (\alpha, \beta)$ using the key sk – which is shared among her and other users – is corrupted, one encapsulates a key that only this user can decapsulate with sk, because the ElGamal encapsulations are group elements with exponent a random linear combination of a vector which is orthogonal to (α, β), following the confirmer construction from Sect. 5. We stress that our construction with $t = 1$ does not allow collusions. But it can be extended to confirm larger t-big collusions of traitors.

---

[3] Note that this is the optimized version of a generic one where one would have drawn $|B|$ extra session keys K'_i, E_i would actually have been a Kyber encryption of these K'_i's instead of the $S \oplus K_i$, and one would have had to send $|B|$ extra $F_i \leftarrow K_i \oplus K' \oplus S$.

[4] Again, this corresponds to our optimized version, taking advantage of the encrypting properties of Kyber. For a generic hybrid KEMAC, one would have output $U'_{i,j} \oplus F_i$ when $V'_{i,j} = V$ (cf. previous footnote for the definition of F_i).

7 Implementation

Parameters of Covercrypt. We have done an implementation in Rust of Covercrypt (a pre- and post-quantum hybridized Anonymous Subset-Cover KEMAC with Early-Aborts), with optimization for a security of 128 bits[5]. We use Kyber-768 (and its `pqd_kyber` library[6]) and ElGamal on the Curve25519, as group that is of prime order $p = 2^{255} - 19$. The hash algorithm used to generate the Early-Abort tags (256 bits) and the keys (256 bits) generated by the KEM is SHAKE-256. Then we present the sizes of the keys and ciphertexts, according to the sizes of A and B, in Table 1. We compare these with the sizes obtained for a KEM based on a pre-quantum [12] ABE scheme[7], way more efficient than post-quantum ones such as [9][8].

Table 1. Sizes of keys and encapsulations (in Bytes) according the sizes of A and B.

Size of A	1	2	3	4	5
Covercrypt Secret Key usk	1250	2435	3620	4805	5990
Coverc. Pre-Quant. S. K. (uid, $\{x_i\}_i$)	98	131	164	197	230
User Secret Key with GPSW	340	504	668	832	996
Size of B	1	2	3	4	5
Covercrypt Encapsulation C	1171	2260	3349	4438	5527
Covercrypt Pre-Quant. Encaps. (c, V)	115	148	181	214	247
GPSW KEM Encapsulation	400	452	504	556	608

---

[5] https://github.com/Cosmian/cover_crypt.

[6] https://docs.rs/pqc_kyber/latest/pqc_kyber/.

[7] Whose implementation can be found at: https://github.com/Cosmian/abe_gpsw.

[8] In this comparison, to translate the attribute setting into a subset-cover one, we consider a context in which users hold $|A| + 1$ attributes, corresponding to $|A|$ subsets in the subset-cover setting, the subsets being the intersection of one of these attributes with each of the other ones, and that encapsulations are made in the same way with respect to $|B| + 1$ attributes corresponding to $|B|$ subsets, and for the decapsulation timings, we suppose there is always exactly one subset in the intersection of the ones the user has access to and the ones in the encapsulation.

388   T. Brézot et al.

Table 2. Comparisons of Covercrypt and GPSW-based encapsulation/decapsulation times. For decapsulation, the GPSW-based KEM has a constant runtime of approximately 3880 μs.

Size of B	1	2	3	4	5
Covercrypt	191	272	329	401	487
GPSW KEM	4793	5431	6170	6607	7245

Encapsulation time (in μs)

$\|A\| \downarrow \ \backslash \|B\| \rightarrow$	1	2	3	4	5
1	214	247	288	345	454
2	311	386	466	543	562
3	334	400	505	608	702
4	471	613	781	908	1072
5	467	646	831	1058	1212

Covercrypt decapsulation time (in μs)

Benchmarks The benchmarks in Table 2 are performed on an Intel Core Processor (Haswell, no TSX) CPU @3MHz. The table shows the time required to generate Covercrypt encapsulations and decapsulations for a 32-Byte symmetric key, with the same definitions for the sizes $|A|$ and $|B|$ as in Table 1. These performances are, as before, compared with the [12]-based KEM's.

Acknowledgments. This work was supported in part by the France 2030 ANR Project ANR-22-PECY-003 SecureCompute.

Appendix

A   Public-Key Encryption

A Public-Key Encryption (PKE) scheme is defined by 3 algorithms:

- PKE.KeyGen(1^κ): the *key generation algorithm* outputs a pair of public and secret keys (pk, sk);
- PKE.Enc(pk, m): the *encryption algorithm* encrypts the input message m under the public key pk and outputs the ciphertext C;
- PKE.Dec(sk, C): the *decryption algorithm* outputs the message m encrypted in C.

We will use the classical notion of indistinguishability and of anonymity of such a PKE scheme, similarly to the same notions for KEMs:

- Indistinguishability. For an honestly generated pk, if the adversary chooses two messages m_0 and m_1, it cannot distinguish an encryption of m_0 from an encryption of m_1, both under pk.

– Anonymity. For two honestly generated pk_0 and pk_1, if the adversary chooses a message m, it cannot distinguish an encryption of m under pk_0 from the encryption of m under pk_1.

B   Proof of Theorem 5

We present a sequence of games, from the AUTH security game against KEM'.

Game G_0: In the initial game, one runs $(\mathsf{pk}_i, \mathsf{sk}_i) \leftarrow \mathsf{KEM}'.\mathsf{KeyGen}(1^\kappa)$, $(c, s) \leftarrow \mathsf{KEM}.\mathsf{Enc}(\mathsf{pk}_0)$ and $K_0 \| V \leftarrow \mathsf{PRG}(s)$. One then runs $s' \leftarrow \mathsf{KEM}.\mathsf{Dec}(\mathsf{sk}_1, c)$, followed by $U' \| V' \leftarrow \mathsf{PRG}(s')$. We denote P_0 the probability $V' = V$. This is $\mathsf{Adv}^{\mathsf{auth}}_{\mathsf{KEM}'}(1^\kappa)$.

Game G_1: In this game, we just replace $s \xleftarrow{\$} \{0; 1\}^\kappa$, that is drawn uniformly at random from the session-key space of KEM, $\{0; 1\}^\kappa$. The difference between this game and the previous one is the SK-IND-game on the underlying KEM, against a trivial adversary $\mathcal{A}_0$. Hence, $P_0 - P_1 \leq \mathsf{Adv}^{\mathsf{sk\text{-}ind}}_{\mathsf{KEM}}(\tau)$, τ the running time of the trivial adversary $\mathcal{A}_0$ that runs two key generations, one encapsulation, two PRG evaluations, and one decapsulation.

Game G_2: In this game, one takes $K_0 \| V \xleftarrow{\$} \{0; 1\}^{k+\ell}$. This is indistinguishable from the previous game except with probability $\mathsf{Adv}^{\mathsf{ind}}_{\mathsf{PRG}_{\kappa,k+\ell}}(\tau')$. Hence, $P_1 - P_2 \leq \mathsf{Adv}^{\mathsf{ind}}_{\mathsf{PRG}_{\kappa,k+\ell}}(\tau')$, where τ' is the running time of another trivial adversary $\mathcal{A}_1$ that runs two key generations, one encapsulation, one PRG evaluations, and one decapsulation.

In this game, as V is drawn uniformly at random from $\{0; 1\}^\ell$, the probability that it is equal to $V' \in \{0; 1\}^\ell$ is equal to $2^{-\ell}$: $P_2 = 2^{-\ell}$.

Finally, from the above, one deducts that:

$$\mathsf{Adv}^{\mathsf{auth}}_{\mathsf{KEM}'}(\kappa) \leq 2^{-\ell} + \mathsf{Adv}^{\mathsf{sk\text{-}ind}}_{\mathsf{KEM}}(\tau) + \mathsf{Adv}^{\mathsf{ind}}_{\mathsf{PRG}_{\kappa,k+\ell}}(\tau')$$

C   Proof of Theorem 11

To prove this theorem, we first give a description of the confirmer algorithm $\mathcal{C}$, then we provide the indistinguishability analysis, and eventually prove $\mathcal{C}$ will give a correct answer.

Description of the Confirmer $\mathcal{C}$: The confirmer algorithm $\mathcal{C}$ can proceed as follows, for a candidate subset $\mathcal{G}$: $\{\mathsf{usk}_j = (v_{j,k})_k\}_{j \in \mathcal{G}}$, for $\mathcal{G}$ of size at most t: it chooses $(u_k)_k$ orthogonal to the subvector-space spanned by $\{(v_{j,k})_k\}_{j \in \mathcal{G}}$, which means that: $\sum_k u_k v_{j,k} = 0, \forall j \in \mathcal{G}$. This is possible as $(v_{j,k})_{k \in [1,t+1], j \in \mathcal{G}}$ is of rank at most t in $\mathbb{Z}_q^{t+1}$. Then the kernel is of dimension at least 1. One generates a fake ciphertext $C = (C_k)_k$, with $C_k \leftarrow h_k^r \cdot g^{u_k s'}$, for random $r, s' \xleftarrow{\$} \mathbb{Z}_q$, and then $K \leftarrow h^r$:

– Any key usk_j in $\mathcal{G}$ will lead to:

$$\prod_k C_k^{v_{j,k}} = \prod_k g^{(rs_k + s' u_k) \cdot v_{j,k}} = g^{r \sum_k s_k v_{j,k} + s' \sum_k u_k v_{j,k}} = g^{rs + s' \times 0} = K;$$

– and any key usk_j outside $\mathcal{G}$ will lead to: $\prod_k C_k^{v_{j,k}} = K \times (g^{\sum_k u_k v_{j,k}})^{s'} \neq K$.

we will show this allows to confirm at least one traitor from a candidat subset of traitors.

Indistinguishability Analysis. The above remark about the output key from a pirate decoder $\mathcal{P}$ assumes an honest behavior, whereas it can stop answering if it detects the fake ciphertext. We first need to show that, with the public key $pk = ((h_k)_k, h)$ and only $\{usk_j = (v_{j,k})_k\}_{j \in \mathcal{G}}$, one cannot distinguish the fake ciphertext from a real ciphertext, generated as above: from a Diffie-Hellman tuple $(A = g^a, B = g^r, C)$, one can derive, from random scalars $s, s'_k, u_k \xleftarrow{\$} \mathbb{Z}_q$, such that $\sum_k v_{j,k} s'_k = s$ and $\sum_k v_{j,k} u_k = 0$, for $j = 1 \ldots, n$:

$$h_k \leftarrow A^{u_k} \cdot g^{s'_k} = g^{au_k + s'_k} \qquad h \leftarrow g^s \qquad usk_j = (v_{j,k})_k \text{ for } j \in \mathcal{G}$$

where we implicitly define $s_k \leftarrow au_k + s'_k$, that satisfy

$$\sum_k v_{j,k} s_k = \sum_k v_{j,k}(s'_k + au_k) = \sum_k v_{j,k} s'_k + a \sum_k v_{j,k} u_k = s + 0 = s.$$

Then, one defines $C_k \leftarrow C^{u_k} \cdot B^{s'_k}$ and $K \leftarrow B^s$.

Let us note $C = g^{r-c}$, where c is either 0 (a Diffie-Hellman tuple) or random:

$$C_k = A^{(r+c)u_k} \cdot g^{rs'_k} = (A^{u_k} \cdot g^{s'_k})^r \cdot A^{cu_k} = h_k^r \cdot (A^c)^{u_k}.$$

One can remark that: when $c = 0$ (Diffie-Hellman tuple), $C = (C_k)_k$ is a normal ciphertext; when $c = s'$ (random tuple), this is a fake ciphertext. Under the DDH assumption, they are thus indistinguishable for an adversary knowing the keys $(usk_i)_{i \in \mathcal{G}}$.

Confirmation of a Traitor. The above analysis shows that a pirate decoder $\mathcal{P}$ built from $(usk_i)_{i \in \mathcal{G}}$ cannot distinguish the fake ciphertext from a real ciphertext. A useful pirate decoder should necessarily distinguish real key from random key. Then, several situations may appear, according to the actual set $\mathcal{T}$ of traitors' keys used to build the pirate decoder $\mathcal{P}$ by the adversary $\mathcal{A}$:

– If $\mathcal{T} \subseteq \mathcal{G}$, a useful decoder $\mathcal{P}$ can distinguish keys;
– If $\mathcal{T} \cap \mathcal{G} = \emptyset$, $\mathcal{P}$ cannot distinguish keys, as it can get several candidates, independent from the real or random keys.

Let us now assume we started from $\mathcal{G} \supseteq \mathcal{T}$, then the advantage of $\mathcal{P}$ in distinguishing real and random keys, denoted $p_{\mathcal{G}}$, is non-negligible, from the usefulness of the decoder. The following steps would also work if one starts with $\mathcal{G} \cap \mathcal{T} \neq \emptyset$, so that the advantage $p_{\mathcal{G}}$ is significant.

One then removes a user J from $\mathcal{G}$ to generate $\mathcal{G}'$ and new ciphertexts to evaluate $p_{\mathcal{G}'}$: if $J \notin \mathcal{T}$, usk_J is not known to the adversary, and so there is no way to check whether $\sum_k v_{J,k} s'_k = s$ and $\sum_k v_{J,k} u_k = 0$, even for a powerful adversary. So necessarily, $p_{\mathcal{G}'} = p_{\mathcal{G}}$.

On the other hand, we know that $p_\emptyset = 0$. So, one can sequentially remove users until a significant gap appears: this is necessarily for a user in $\mathcal{T}$.   □

References

1. Applebaum, B.: Pseudorandom generators with long stretch and low locality from random local one-way functions. In: Karloff, H.J., Pitassi, T. (eds.) 44th ACM STOC, pp. 805–816. ACM Press, May 2012. https://doi.org/10.1145/2213977.2214050

2. Avanzi, R., et al.: Crystals-Kyber algorithm specifications and supporting documentation (2021). https://pq-crystals.org/kyber/resources.shtml

3. Bellare, M., Boldyreva, A., Desai, A., Pointcheval, D.: Key-privacy in public-key encryption. In: Boyd, C. (ed.) ASIACRYPT 2001. LNCS, vol. 2248, pp. 566–582. Springer, Heidelberg (2001). https://doi.org/10.1007/3-540-45682-1_33

4. Bindel, N., Brendel, J., Fischlin, M., Goncalves, B., Stebila, D.: Hybrid key encapsulation mechanisms and authenticated key exchange. In: Ding, J., Steinwandt, R. (eds.) PQCrypto 2019. LNCS, vol. 11505, pp. 206–226. Springer, Cham (2019). https://doi.org/10.1007/978-3-030-25510-7_12

5. Boneh, D., Franklin, M.: An efficient public key traitor tracing scheme. In: Wiener, M. (ed.) CRYPTO 1999. LNCS, vol. 1666, pp. 338–353. Springer, Heidelberg (1999). https://doi.org/10.1007/3-540-48405-1_22

6. Brézot, T., de Perthuis, P., Pointcheval, D.: Covercrypt: an efficient early-abort Kem for hidden access policies with traceability from the DDH and LWE. Cryptology ePrint Archive, Report 2023/836 (2023). https://eprint.iacr.org/2023/836

7. Chevassut, O., Fouque, P.-A., Gaudry, P., Pointcheval, D.: The twist-AUgmented technique for key exchange. In: Yung, M., Dodis, Y., Kiayias, A., Malkin, T. (eds.) PKC 2006. LNCS, vol. 3958, pp. 410–426. Springer, Heidelberg (2006). https://doi.org/10.1007/11745853_27

8. Dai, W., et al.: Implementation and evaluation of a lattice-based key-policy ABE scheme. Cryptology ePrint Archive, Report 2017/601 (2017). https://eprint.iacr.org/2017/601

9. Dai, W., et al.: Implementation and evaluation of a lattice-based key-policy ABE scheme. IEEE Trans. Inf. Forensics Secur. **13**(5), 1169–1184 (2018)

10. Fazio, N., Perera, I.M.: Outsider-anonymous broadcast encryption with sublinear ciphertexts. In: Fischlin, M., Buchmann, J., Manulis, M. (eds.) PKC 2012. LNCS, vol. 7293, pp. 225–242. Springer, Heidelberg (2012). https://doi.org/10.1007/978-3-642-30057-8_14

11. Giacon, F., Heuer, F., Poettering, B.: KEM combiners. In: Abdalla, M., Dahab, R. (eds.) PKC 2018. LNCS, vol. 10769, pp. 190–218. Springer, Cham (2018). https://doi.org/10.1007/978-3-319-76578-5_7

12. Goyal, V., Pandey, O., Sahai, A., Waters, B.: Attribute-based encryption for fine-grained access control of encrypted data. In: Juels, A., Wright, R.N., De Capitani di Vimercati, S. (eds.) ACM CCS 2006. pp. 89–98. ACM Press, October/November 2006. https://doi.org/10.1145/1180405.1180418. Cryptology ePrint Archive Report 2006/309

13. Håstad, J., Impagliazzo, R., Levin, L.A., Luby, M.: A pseudorandom generator from any one-way function. SIAM J. Comput. **28**(4), 1364–1396 (1999)

14. Langlois, A., Stehlé, D.: Worst-case to average-case reductions for module lattices. Des. Codes Cryptogr. **75**(3), 565–599 (2015)

15. Li, J., Gong, J.: Improved anonymous broadcast encryptions. In: Preneel, B., Vercauteren, F. (eds.) ACNS 2018. LNCS, vol. 10892, pp. 497–515. Springer, Cham (2018). https://doi.org/10.1007/978-3-319-93387-0_26

16. Libert, B., Paterson, K.G., Quaglia, E.A.: Anonymous broadcast encryption: adaptive security and efficient constructions in the standard model. In: Fischlin, M., Buchmann, J., Manulis, M. (eds.) PKC 2012. LNCS, vol. 7293, pp. 206–224. Springer, Heidelberg (2012). https://doi.org/10.1007/978-3-642-30057-8_13

17. Maram, V., Xagawa, K.: Post-quantum anonymity of kyber. Cryptology ePrint Archive, Report 2022/1696 (2022). https://eprint.iacr.org/2022/1696

18. Shoup, V.: A proposal for an ISO standard for public key encryption, December 2001. https://shoup.net/papers/iso-2_1.pdf

19. Wee, H.: ABE for DFA from LWE against bounded collusions, revisited. In: Nissim, K., Waters, B. (eds.) TCC 2021. LNCS, vol. 13043, pp. 288–309. Springer, Cham (2021). https://doi.org/10.1007/978-3-030-90453-1_10

Committed Private Information Retrieval

Quang Cao[1]([✉])[iD], Hong Yen Tran[2], Son Hoang Dau[1], Xun Yi[1],
Emanuele Viterbo[3], Chen Feng[4], Yu-Chih Huang[5], Jingge Zhu[6],
Stanislav Kruglik[7], and Han Mao Kiah[7]

[1] RMIT University, Melbourne, Australia
{nhat.quang.cao2,sonhoang.dau,xun.yi}@rmit.edu.au
[2] The University of New South Wales, Canberra, Australia
hongyen.tran@unsw.edu.au
[3] Monash University, Melbourne, Australia
emanuele.viterbo@monash.edu
[4] The University of British Columbia, Kelowna, Canada
chen.feng@ubc.ca
[5] NYCU University, Hsinchu, Taiwan
jerryhuang@nctu.edu.tw
[6] The University of Melbourne, Melbourne, Australia
jingge.zhu@unimelb.edu.au
[7] Nanyang Technological University, Singapore, Singapore
{stanislav.kruglik,hmkiah}@ntu.edu.sg

Abstract. A *private information retrieval* (PIR) scheme allows a client
to retrieve a data item x_i among n items $x_1, x_2, \ldots, x_n$ from k servers,
without revealing what i is even when $t < k$ servers collude and try
to learn i. Such a PIR scheme is said to be *t-private*. A PIR scheme
is *v-verifiable* if the client can verify the correctness of the retrieved x_i
even when $v \leq k$ servers collude and try to fool the client by sending
manipulated data. Most of the previous works in the literature on PIR
assumed that $v < k$, leaving the case of *all-colluding* servers open. We
propose a generic construction that combines a *linear map commitment*
(LMC) and an arbitrary linear PIR scheme to produce a k-verifiable PIR
scheme, termed a *committed PIR* scheme. Such a scheme guarantees that
even in the worst scenario, when all servers are under the control of an
attacker, although the privacy is unavoidably lost, the client won't be
fooled into accepting an incorrect x_i. We demonstrate the practicality of
our proposal by implementing the committed PIR schemes based on the
Lai-Malavolta LMC and three well-known PIR schemes using the GMP
library and blst, the current fastest C library for elliptic curve pairings.

Keywords: Private information retrieval · verifiability · malicious
server · commitment scheme · pairing · elliptic curve

Supported by the Australian Research Council through the Discovery Project under
Grant DP200100731. The work of Hong Yen Tran was partly done when she was with
RMIT University.

1 Introduction

In this work, we revisit private information retrieval (PIR), a classic tool in cryptography, and investigate the extent that PIR can be used in a *trustless* system in which participants can be corrupted. While the basic PIR only provides privacy, i.e., making sure that a client can privately retrieve a data item of interest without revealing it to any server that stores the collection of data, we are interested in three extra *security*[1] requirements, namely, *verifiability*, *accountability*, and *Byzantine-robustness*. These requirements are made under the assumption that a group of malicious servers are not only keen on learning the retrieved data but also on making the client recover *incorrect* data to achieve certain purposes. This type of security requirements are crucial to extend the usage of PIR beyond trusted systems, which make sense mostly in theory, to the more practical *trustless* systems, which are capable of governing both trusted and malicious parties. Note that 'trusted' is also a very shaky status: even a supposedly trusted party like a well-established bank or a government agency can still be attacked and temporarily become a malicious party, which may cause severe damage to the customers (see, e.g. devastating attacks on Australian universities, Medibank, Optus, and Fire Rescue Victoria in 2022 [1,2]).

A basic *private information retrieval* (PIR) scheme allows a client to download a data item x_i among a collection of n items $x_1, x_2, \ldots, x_n$ from $k \geq 1$ servers without revealing the index i to any curious server. The very first private information retrieval (PIR) scheme with two servers was introduced in the seminal work of Chor-Kushilevitz-Goldreich-Sudan [3], which works as follows. The two servers both store $x_1, x_2, \ldots, x_n$, which are elements from a finite field $\mathbb{F}$ of characteristic 2. To privately retrieve x_i, the client selects a random set $J \subseteq \{1, 2, \ldots, n\}$ and requests $\sum_{j \in J} x_j$ from Server 1 and $x_i + \left(\sum_{j \in J} x_j \right)$ from Server 2. As $\mathbb{F}$ has characteristic 2, the client can simply add the two answers to extract x_i. Moreover, as J is a random set, from the query, each server achieves no information (in Shannon's sense) about i. We refer to this as the CKGS scheme and use it as a toy example to demonstrate our approach below.

The CKGS scheme, while providing privacy against an *honest-but-curious* server, doesn't protect the client against a *malicious* one: if the malicious server sends an incorrect answer, the client will end up with an incorrect data item $\hat{x}_i \neq x_i$. To construct a secure PIR scheme that can deal with malicious servers, there are two approaches: the *joint-design approach* (a PIR scheme is designed with built-in security) and the *modular approach* (combining a PIR and another cryptographic primitive, both of which are separately designed). As far as we know, most related works in the literature [4–11] (except for [12]) followed the former. While the first approach requires more tailor-made designs, which are harder to develop but potentially achieve better performance, the second provides greater simplicity and flexibility: an arbitrary PIR scheme and an arbitrary

---

[1] In the PIR literature, 'security' was often used to refer to the concept of 'verifiability' defined in this work. However, in our opinion, 'security' is a rather broad term and should not be used as the name of a specific property. We make an effort to fix that terminology issue in this work, using 'security' as an umbrella term instead.

commitment scheme will work together to achieve a secure PIR scheme. More-over, any improvement in either PIR or commitment schemes will automatically translate to an improvement to this approach. In the cope of this work, we focus on the second approach, applying a *commitment scheme* on top of a PIR. The gist of this approach is to publish a digest of the data, referred to as the *commitment*, before the PIR session starts. Once the commitment has been produced and made public, the client can use the commitment to confirm the correctness of its desired data item, even when *all* servers are malicious.

An obvious commitment-based solution that allows the client to verify the correctness of its derived data is using (cryptographic) hashes of the data as the commitment: the hashes $h_j = h(x_j)$, $j = 1, 2, \ldots, n$ are made public before the PIR session starts, and then the client can download all the hashes[2] and perform a hash verification on the derived $\hat{x}_i$ and accepts it if $h(\hat{x}_i) = h_i$. This solution, however, increases the download cost for the client due to the extra sn hashes coming from s servers for some constant s. More importantly, this makes the PIR protocol cumbersome and unsuitable to systems requiring compact data-commitments such as the blockchains, where the commitment to the data (transactions, chain states) is often a single 256-bit hash (the Merkle proof) stored in a small block header of a rather limited size, e.g. 80 bytes in Bitcoin and around 500 bytes in Ethereum. Here, a potential application in this context is for a client to privately retrieve a transaction in a block.

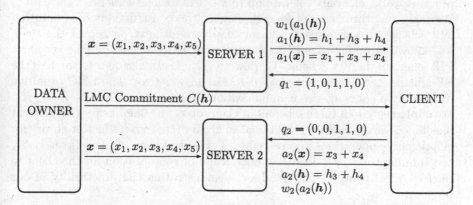

Fig. 1. An example of a 2-server committed PIR scheme based on an LMC and the CKGS PIR scheme [3] (see Example 1 for more details). The client privately requests both x_1 and $h_1 = h(x_1)$, where the correctness of the retrieved *hash* $\hat{h}_1$ can be verified thanks to the LMC. It can then verify the correctness of the retrieved *data* $\hat{x}_1$ by performing a hash verification $h(\hat{x}_1) \stackrel{?}{=} \hat{h}_1$. The size of the x_j's can be arbitrarily large. The commitment $C(\boldsymbol{h})$ and the witnesses $w_1(a_1(\boldsymbol{h})), w_2(a_2(\boldsymbol{h}))$ are of size only 384 bits (equivalent to 1.5× SHA3-256 hash) if the Lai-Malavolta LMC [13] is used.

---

[2] The client can gather the hashes by downloading them from the data owner, or from a few random servers in a decentralized system (e.g. a blockchain) and using a majority vote to determine the correct h_i.

We address the aforementioned drawback of the hash-based solution by using linear map commitments with a *constant-size* commitment on top of linear PIR schemes to provide verifiability. A linear map commitment (LMC) [13–16] allows the prover to generate a *commitment* $C(x)$ to a vector $x = (x_1, x_2, \ldots, x_n) \in \mathbb{F}^n$ and a *witness* $w_a(x)$ based on which the verifier can verify that a retrieved value $y \in \mathbb{F}$ is indeed the value of the linear combination $a \cdot x = \sum_{j=1}^{n} a_j x_j$. In a compact LMC, e.g. [13], the sizes of the commitment $C(x)$ and the witness $w_a(x)$ (in bits) are constant, i.e. together their sizes are equivalent to a couple of field elements only. To make the PIR scheme suitable to a database with large-size data items, we let $x_i \in \mathbb{F}^m$ where m can be arbitrarily large and the LMC can be applied instead to the hashes $h = (h_1, h_2, \ldots, h_n)$ of $x \in \mathbb{F}^{m \times n}$ (see Fig. 1 for a toy example). Our proposed scheme, referred to as the *committed PIR* scheme, provides k-verifiability: even in the extreme case where all servers are attacked and controlled by a malicious attacker, although the privacy is unavoidably lost, the scheme is still capable of protecting the client from accepting fault data.

Our main contributions are summarized below.

- We propose a novel modular approach that combines a *linear map commitment* scheme and a linear PIR scheme to construct a *committed PIR* scheme that provides verifiability on top of the traditional privacy. Our proposed scheme is capable of preventing the client from accepting an incorrect data item, even when *all* k servers are malicious and send manipulated data. Most previous works can only tolerate up to $k - 1$ malicious servers.
- We carry out three case studies discussing the constructions of committed PIR schemes using a specific linear map commitment on top of the three well-known representative PIR schemes: the CKGS scheme [3] (the very first PIR scheme), the WY scheme [17] (lowest *upload cost*, aka query size), and the BE scheme [18] (lowest *download cost*, aka answer size). The LMC primitive incurs only a constant-size communication overhead.
- We implemented all three schemes in C on top of the GMP library (for efficient handling of large numbers) and the blst library (the current fastest library for elliptic curve operations and pairings). Two out of three achieved reasonably fast running times, e.g. less than one second of computation for the client to retrieve 3 MB from a 3 GB-database, demonstrating the practicality of our proposal.

We want to highlight another advantage of LMCs as the primitive for the committed PIR: as more advanced LMCs are developed, new features will be automatically added to the proposed scheme with no modifications to the underlying PIR schemes. For example, the LMC introduced in [16] allows *updatability*, or the lattice-based LMC developed in [15] provides *post-quantum security*.

The remainder of the paper is organized as follows. We first define formally the PIR and committed PIR schemes as well as their performance metrics in Sect. 2. We then introduce a generic construction for a committed PIR in Sect. 3. In Sect. 4, we demonstrate the proposed method with three case studies in which a linear map commitment is applied to three well-known PIR schemes. Section 5 is devoted to implementations and evaluations.

2   Committed Private Information Retrieval

2.1   Basic Notations

We use $\mathbb{F}$ to denote a general finite field and $\mathbb{F}_p$ to denote a finite field of p elements, where p is a prime power. Within the scope of this work, we usually assume that p is a prime and hence, $\mathbb{F}_p \equiv Z_p$, the integers mod p. For implementation, we use a specific prime p of size about 256 bits (following the parameter of the BLS12-381 elliptic curve). We use $[n]$ to denote the set $\{1, 2, \ldots, n\}$. The data is represented by $x = (x_1, x_2, \ldots, x_n)$, where $x_j \in \mathbb{F}^m$, $j \in [m]$, and $m \geq 1$ represents the size of each data item x_j (in field elements). We call n the number of items or the size of the data. The data can also be regarded as an $m \times n$ matrix $x \in \mathbb{F}^{m \times n}$ and each data item x_j corresponds to the j-th column of the matrix.

Throughout this work we denote by $\lambda \in \mathbb{N}$ the security parameter, e.g. $\lambda = 128$, and $\mathsf{negl}(\lambda)$ the set of *negligible functions* in λ. A positive-valued function $\varepsilon(\lambda)$ belongs to $\mathsf{negl}(\lambda)$ if for every $c > 0$, there exists a $\lambda_0 \in \mathbb{N}$ such that $\varepsilon(\lambda) < 1/\lambda^c$ for all $\lambda > \lambda_0$. We use $\mathsf{poly}(\lambda)$ for the set of polynomials in λ.

Before introducing the notation of a committed PIR scheme, we discuss the basic PIR and its performance metrics below.

2.2   Private Information Retrieval

A (replicated) PIR scheme has k servers, each of which stores the data $x = (x_1, x_2, \ldots, x_n)$, and one client, who is interested in retrieving x_i for some $i \in [n]$.

Definition 1 (PIR). *A k-server n-dimensional PIR scheme Π_0 over a field $\mathbb{F}$ consists of three algorithms* (QueriesGen, AnswerGen, Extract) *defined as follows.*

- $(\{q_j\}_{j \in [k]}, \mathsf{aux}) \leftarrow \mathsf{QueriesGen}(n, k, i)$: *run by the client, this randomized algorithm takes as input $n > 1$, $k \geq 1$, an index $i \in [n]$, and outputs k queries to be sent to k servers and an auxiliary information* aux.
- $a_j \leftarrow \mathsf{AnswerGen}(x, q_j)$: *run by a server, this deterministic algorithm takes as input the data $x \in \mathbb{F}^n$, the query q_j, and outputs an answer a_j to be sent to the client.*
- $\{x_i\} \leftarrow \mathsf{Extract}(n, i, \{a_j\}_{j \in [k]}, \mathsf{aux})$: *run by the client, this deterministic algorithm takes as input n, i, the auxiliary information* aux, *the answers from all k servers, and outputs x_i.*

A PIR scheme is called *linear* if each answer a_j is a linear combination of x. We define below the correctness and privacy of a PIR scheme.

Definition 2 (Correctness of PIR).   *The k-server n-dimensional PIR scheme defined in Definition 1 is correct if for any $i \in [n]$, $x \in \mathbb{F}^n$, $(\{q_j\}_{j \in [k]}, \mathsf{aux}) \leftarrow \mathsf{QueriesGen}(n, i)$, and $a_j \leftarrow \mathsf{AnswersGen}(x, q_j)$, $j \in [k]$, it holds that*

$$\mathsf{Extract}(n, i, \{a_j\}_{j \in [k]}, \mathsf{aux}) = x_i.$$

Definition 3 (Privacy of PIR). *The k-server n-dimensional PIR scheme defined in Definition 1 is (unconditionally) t-private if no collusion of up to t servers can learn any information about i, or more formally, for any $i, i' \in [n]$, and any subset $T \subsetneq [k]$ of size $|T| \leq t$, the distributions of* QueriesGen$_T(n, k, i)$ *and* QueriesGen$_T(n, k, i')$ *are identical, where* QueriesGen$_T(n, k, i)$ *denotes the concatenation of the $|T|$ output queries $\{q_j\}_{j \in T}$ generated by* QueriesGen(n, k, i).

2.3 Communication and Computation Costs of PIR

The efficiency of a PIR scheme can be measured based on its *communication* and *computation* costs. We first discuss the communication cost, which can be formally defined as follows.

Definition 4 (Communication Cost of PIR). *The communication cost of a PIR scheme Π_0 over a field $\mathbb{F}$ given in Definition 1 is defined as*

$$\mathsf{comm}(\Pi_0) = \mathsf{up}(\Pi_0) + \mathsf{down}(\Pi_0) \triangleq \max_i \sum_{j \in [k]} |q_j| + \max_i \sum_{j \in [k]} |a_j|,$$

where $|q_j|$ and $|a_j|$ denote the sizes (in field elements) of q_j and a_j. The first term is the upload cost whereas the second is the download cost.

For instance, in the aforementioned CKGS scheme [3], to represent a random subset of $\{1, 2, \ldots, n\}$, the client must use a vector of n bits, which means that the upload cost is kn bits. Straightforward generalizations of this scheme to $k > 2$ servers (see, e.g. [19]) require an upload cost of kn $\mathbb{F}$-elements, which is already significant for large n. The main goal of the majority of early works on PIR was to optimize the communication cost. The lowest known communication cost, namely, $O(kn^{1/d})$, for any $d \geq 1$, was achieved in the work of Woodruff and Yekhanin [17]. Their idea is to transform the PIR problem into the secret sharing problem while representing an index $i \in \{1, 2, \ldots, n\}$ by a vector of length $O(n^{1/d})$ of Hamming weight d. We refer to this as the WY scheme.

Download Rate. Another approach to reduce the communication cost is to optimize the download cost, assuming that the data items are of large size and hence the upload cost will be overshadowed by the download cost (see, e.g. Sun and Jafar [20]). More precisely, one can aim for maximizing the *download rate*, defined as $\max_{i \in [n]} \frac{|x_i|}{\sum_{j \in [k]} |a_j|}$, which is the ratio of the size of the desirable data to the total amount of data downloaded by the client. Note that in the CKGS scheme, as the client downloads k field elements from k servers to recover one element, the download rate is $1/k$, which is quite small. PIR schemes such as BE [18] can achieve an asymptotically optimal rate of $(k-1)/k$.

Computation Cost. The computation cost of a PIR scheme typically consists of the computation time required by the client in generating the request and in recovering the desired data x_i, and the computation time required by the servers in producing the answers (taking the average or maximum among all servers). In general, as the client often has low computational capacity, its computation load, ideally, should be much less than that of the servers.

2.4   Committed Private Information Retrieval

Apart from the large amount of research aiming for optimizing the upload or the download costs of a PIR scheme, there have also been a number of proposals in the literature that seek to extend the basic setting of the PIR problem (see, e.g. [21] for a survey). In the scope of this work, we are interested in the *verifiablity, accountability,* and *Byzantine-robustness* of a PIR scheme.

A k-server PIR scheme is *v-verifiable* if the client can verify the correctness of the retrieved x_i even when $v \leq k$ servers are colluding and try to fool the client by sending manipulated data. A scheme is *a-accountable* if the client can identify all servers that sent incorrect data when at most $a \leq k$ servers did so. A scheme is *b-Byzantine-robust* if the client can recover the correct desired item x_i when at most $b < k$ servers sent incorrect data. It is clear that Byzantine-robustness implies accountability, which in turn implies verifiability. The converse is not true. However, it seems that a b-Byzantine-robust scheme can be obtained from a b-accountable scheme by increasing the number of servers communicated to obtain extra data for recovery (discarding the data received from identified malicious servers). Readers who are familiar with coding theory may notice that the concepts of verifiability, accountability, and Byzantine-robustness defined above correspond to the classical concepts of *error detection, error-location identification,* and *error correction,* respectively, in the study of channel coding.

Following the notations of [12], we consider three types of participants: a *data owner*[3], k *servers* $S_1, \ldots, S_k$, and a *client*. The data owner owns the data $\boldsymbol{x}$. Although treated as a single trusted entity in theory, the data owner may also consist of multiple decentralized entities, e.g. a blockchain, which is maintained by a large number of miners. Although each individual miner should not be trusted, the whole miner group are collectively trusted to produce valid commitments to the data, i.e., the block headers or the Merkle roots of transactions inside the block headers. The servers, on the other hand, are considered untrusted.

We formally define the Committed Private Information Retrieval (Com-PIR) scheme in Definition 5. Compared to the basic PIR (see Definition 1), we also include one more dimension, m, to explicitly include the size of each data item.

Definition 5 (Com-PIR).   *A k-server $m \times n$-dimensional committed PIR scheme Π over a field $\mathbb{F}$ consists of six algorithms defined as follows.*

- pp $\leftarrow$ Setup($1^\lambda, k, m, n$): *run by the data owner or a trusted setup*[4], *this randomized algorithm takes as input λ, k, m, n, where λ is the security parameter, k is the number of servers, m is the size of each data item, n is the number of data items, and outputs a public parameter* pp *known to everyone.*

---

[3] In PIR's original setting, the servers are (implicitly) identical to the data owner. With the ubiquity of cloud computing and the various benefits they offer, outsourcing storage/computing tasks to hired servers has become the trend. Thus, it is more practical to explicitly separate the data owner and the storage servers.

[4] In practice, a trusted setup can be run by a group of many participants (the power-of-τ ceremony [22]), and as long as one person discards their piece of data, the secret key used in the setup remains secret and unrecoverable).

- $C(\boldsymbol{x}) \leftarrow$ CommitmentGen($\mathsf{pp}, \boldsymbol{x}$): *run by the data owner, this deterministic algorithm takes as input the public parameter and the data $\boldsymbol{x} \in \mathbb{F}^{m \times n}$ and outputs the commitment $C(\boldsymbol{x})$.*
- $(\{q_j\}_{j \in [k]}, \mathsf{aux}) \leftarrow$ QueriesGen(pp, k, m, n, i): *run by the client, this randomized algorithm takes as input the public parameter, k, m, n, $i \in [n]$, and outputs k queries to be sent to k servers and an auxiliary information aux.*
- $a_j \leftarrow$ AnswerGen($\mathsf{pp}, \boldsymbol{x}, q_j$): *run by a server, this deterministic algorithm takes as input the public parameter, the data $\boldsymbol{x}$, the query q_j, and outputs an answer a_j to be sent to the client.*
- $w_j \leftarrow$ WitnessGen($\mathsf{pp}, \boldsymbol{x}, q_j$): *run by a server, this deterministic algorithm takes as input the public parameter, the data $\boldsymbol{x}$, and the query q_j, and outputs a witness w_j to be sent to the client.*
- $\{x_i, \perp\} \leftarrow$ Extract($\mathsf{pp}, C, m, n, i, \{a_j, w_j\}_{j \in [k]}, \mathsf{aux}$): *run by the client, this deterministic algorithm takes as input the public parameter, a commitment C, m, n, $i \in [n]$, the answers and witnesses from all servers, the auxiliary information aux, and outputs either x_i (successful) or $\perp$ (unsuccessful). Note that x_i denotes the ith column of the matrix $\boldsymbol{x}$.*

A Com-PIR works as follows. First, the data owner or a trusted setup generates the public parameter pp, which is available to everyone. Next, the data owner generates the commitment $C(\boldsymbol{x})$, which is made publicly available to everyone, e.g. by being embedded into a block header in a blockchain. The client, who wants to retrieve x_i privately, generates and sends queries to all servers. The servers generate and send the answers and the witnesses of the answers back to the client. Finally, the client recovers x_i and also performs the verification of the result using the commitment and the witnesses. The correctness, privacy, and verifiability of a Com-PIR scheme are formally defined below.

Definition 6 (Correctness of Com-PIR). *The k-server $m \times n$-dimensional Com-PIR scheme defined in Definition 5 is correct if the client can recover x_i when all servers are honest, or more formally, for any $i \in [n]$, $\boldsymbol{x} \in \mathbb{F}^{m \times n}$, and $\mathsf{pp} \leftarrow$ Setup($1^\lambda, k, m, n$), and $(\{q_j\}_{j \in [k]}, \mathsf{aux}) \leftarrow$ QueriesGen(pp, k, m, n, i), and $a_j \leftarrow$ AnswersGen($\mathsf{pp}, \boldsymbol{x}, q_j$), $w_j \leftarrow$ WitnessGen($\mathsf{pp}, \boldsymbol{x}, q_j$), $j \in [k]$, it holds that*

$$\mathsf{Extract}(C(\boldsymbol{x}), m, n, i, \{a_j, w_j\}_{j \in [k]}, \mathsf{aux}) = x_i.$$

Definition 7 (Privacy of Com-PIR). *The k-server $m \times n$-dimensional Com-PIR scheme defined in Definition 5 is (unconditionally) t-private if no collusion of up to t servers can learn any information about i, or more formally, for any $i, i' \in [n]$, and any subset $T \subsetneq [k]$ of size $|T| \leq t$, the distributions of $\mathsf{QueriesGen}_T(\mathsf{pp}, k, m, n, i)$ and $\mathsf{QueriesGen}_T(\mathsf{pp}, k, m, n, i')$ are identical, where $\mathsf{QueriesGen}_T(\mathsf{pp}, k, m, n, i)$ denotes the concatenation of the $|T|$ queries $\{q_j\}_{j \in T}$ output by $\mathsf{QueriesGen}(\mathsf{pp}, k, m, n, i)$.*

The *verifiability* property of a Com-PIR is defined through the notion of a security experiment, in which an adversary $\mathcal{A}$ controls a group of Byzantine servers $\{S_j\}_{j \in B}$, $B \subseteq [k]$, knows the data $\boldsymbol{x}$, the index i (which means the privacy can be lost), and crafts the answers $\{\hat{a}_j\}_{j \in B}$ after receiving the queries $\{q_j\}_{j \in B}$. The goal of the adversary is to make the client accept an output $\hat{x}_i \notin \{x_i, \perp\}$.

Definition 8 (Security Experiment for Verifiability). *The Com-PIR sche-me Π defined in Definition 5 is v-verifiable if for any probabilistic polynomial time (PPT) adversary $\mathcal{A}$, there exists a negligible function $\varepsilon(\lambda) \in \mathsf{negl}(\lambda)$ such that for any $i \in [n]$, any $\boldsymbol{x} \in \mathbb{F}_q^{m \times n}$, and any subset $B \subseteq [k]$, $|B| \leq v$, it holds that*

$$\Pr[\mathsf{EXP}_{\mathcal{A},\Pi}(k,m,n,\boldsymbol{x},i,B) = 1] \leq \varepsilon(\lambda),$$

where the security experiment $\mathsf{EXP}_{\mathcal{A},\Pi}(k,m,n,\boldsymbol{x},i,B)$ between an adversary and a challenger is described as follows.

- *The challenger picks $(\mathsf{sk},\mathsf{pp}) \leftarrow \mathsf{Setup}(1^\lambda, k, m, n)$ and gives pp to $\mathcal{A}$.*
- *The adversary picks an $\boldsymbol{x} \in \mathbb{F}_q^{m \times n}$, an $i \in [n]$, and a set $B \subseteq [k]$, $|B| \leq v$, and gives $\boldsymbol{x}$, i, and B to the challenger.*
- *The challenger generates $C(\boldsymbol{x}) \leftarrow \mathsf{CommitmentGen}(\mathsf{pp}, \boldsymbol{x})$ and $(\{q_j\}_{j \in [k]}, \mathsf{aux})$ $\leftarrow \mathsf{QueriesGen}(\mathsf{pp}, k, m, n, i)$ and gives $\{q_j\}_{j \in B}$ to $\mathcal{A}$.*
- *The adversary crafts and gives $|B|$ answers and witnesses to the challenger*

$$\{\hat{a}_j, \hat{w}_j\}_{j \in B} \leftarrow \mathcal{A}(\mathsf{pp}, k, \mathbf{x}, i, B, \{q_j\}_{j \in B}).$$

- *The challenger computes $\{a_j\}_{j \in [k] \setminus B} \leftarrow \mathsf{AnswerGen}(\mathsf{pp}, \boldsymbol{x}, \{q_j\}_{j \in [k] \setminus B})$ and $\{w_j\}_{j \in [k] \setminus B} \leftarrow \mathsf{WitnessGen}(\mathsf{pp}, \boldsymbol{x}, \{q_j\}_{j \in [k] \setminus B})$.*
- *The challenger runs the extraction algorithm*

$$\hat{x}_i \leftarrow \mathsf{Extract}(\mathsf{pp}, C(\boldsymbol{x}), m, n, i, \{\hat{a}_j, \hat{w}_j\}_{j \in B}, \{a_j, w_j\}_{j \in [k] \setminus B}, \mathsf{aux}).$$

- *If $\hat{x}_i \notin \{x_i, \bot\}$ then set $\mathsf{EXP}_{\mathcal{A},\Pi}(k,m,n,\boldsymbol{x},i,B) = 1$, and 0, for otherwise.*

Note that to allow accountability and Byzantine-robustness for Com-PIR, one can include a set $B \subseteq [k]$ in the output of the algorithm $\mathsf{Extract}(\cdot)$ to list identified Byzantine servers and then define corresponding security experiments. We omit the details and focus on verifiability only.

3   A Generic Construction of k-Verifiable Committed Private Information Retrieval Schemes

We propose a generic construction for k-verifiable committed PIR schemes based on linear map commitment schemes and linear PIR schemes. The key idea is for the client to privately retrieve both x_i and it hash h_i using the same PIR scheme, where the correctness of the hash can be guaranteed by the linear map commitment. The client then verifies if the hash matches the data in the verification step. We first discuss the linear map commitment.

3.1   Linear Map Commitments

An n-dimensional linear map commitment allows a prover to first commit to a vector $\boldsymbol{x} = (x_1, x_2, \ldots, x_n)$ and then prove to a verifier that a linear combination of x_i's is correct, i.e. consistent with the commitment. We formally define the linear map commitment schemes below, following [13,23].

Definition 9 (Linear Map Commitments). *An n-dimensional linear map commitment (LMC) scheme Λ over a field $\mathbb{F}$ consists of four algorithms defined as follows.*

- pp $\leftarrow$ Setup($1^\lambda, n; \omega$): *this randomized algorithm takes as input λ, n, and ω, where λ is the security parameter, n is the number of data items, ω is a random tape, and outputs a public parameter* pp *known to all parties.*
- $C \leftarrow$ CommitmentGen(pp, $\boldsymbol{x}$): *run by the prover, this deterministic algorithm takes as input the public parameter* pp *and the data $\boldsymbol{x} = (x_1, x_2, \ldots, x_n) \in \mathbb{F}^n$ and outputs the commitment $C = C(\boldsymbol{x})$.*
- $w_j \leftarrow$ WitnessGen(pp, $\boldsymbol{x}, \boldsymbol{c}, y$): *run by a prover, this deterministic algorithm takes as input the public parameter* pp, *the data $\boldsymbol{x} = (x_1, x_2, \ldots, x_n) \in \mathbb{F}^n$, the vector of coefficients $\boldsymbol{c} = (c_1, c_2, \ldots, c_n) \in \mathbb{F}^n$, a value $y \in \mathbb{F}$, and outputs a witness w that proves that $y = \boldsymbol{c} \cdot \boldsymbol{x} = \sum_{j \in [n]} c_j x_j$.*
- $\{0,1\} \leftarrow$ Verify(pp, $C, \boldsymbol{c}, y, w$): *run by the verifier, this deterministic algorithm takes as input the public parameter* pp, *a commitment C, a coefficient vector $\boldsymbol{c}$, an element y, a witness w, and outputs either 1 or 0 to accept or reject that $y = \boldsymbol{c} \cdot \boldsymbol{x}$, respectively.*

There have been a few different constructions of LMC and variants/extensions recently proposed in the literature [13–16,23]. The LMC in [14] is based on a ring and may not work immediately with a linear PIR scheme, which is often based on a finite field. We use in this work the version of LMC introduced in the work of Lai and Malavolta [13,23], which is the most straightforward to implement and sufficient for our purpose. We refer to it as the Lai-Malavolta (LM) linear map commitment. This LMC is based on an observation that the inner product of $\boldsymbol{c}$ and $\boldsymbol{x}$ is equal to the coefficient of z^{n+1} in the product of the polynomials $f_c(z) \triangleq \sum_{j \in [n]} c_j z^{n+1-j}$ and $f_x(z) \triangleq \sum_{j \in [n]} x_j z^j$.

Algorithm 1. The Lai-Malavolta linear map commitment scheme [13,23].

Setup($1^\lambda, n; \omega$)

BG $\leftarrow$ BGGen($1^\lambda; \omega$)

where BG $\triangleq (p, \mathbb{G}_1, \mathbb{G}_2, \mathbb{G}_T, G_1, G_2, e)$

$\alpha \leftarrow \mathbb{Z}_p$

pp $= \left(\text{BG}, \{G_1^{\alpha^j}\}_{j \in [n]}, \{G_2^{\alpha^j}\}_{j \in [2n]\setminus\{n+1\}}\right)$

return pp

CommitmentGen(pp, $\boldsymbol{x}$)

---

return $C \triangleq \prod_{j \in [n]} \left(G_1^{\alpha^j}\right)^{x_j}$

WitnessGen(pp, $\boldsymbol{x}, \boldsymbol{c}$)

$w \triangleq \prod_{j \in [n]} \prod_{j' \in [n]\setminus\{j\}} \left(G_2^{\alpha^{n+1+j-j'}}\right)^{c_j x_{j'}}$

return w

Verify(pp, $C, \boldsymbol{c}, y, w$)

$b_0 \triangleq \left(y \in \mathbb{Z}_p\right)$

$b_1 \triangleq \begin{pmatrix} e\left(C, \prod_{j \in [n]} \left(G_2^{\alpha^{n+1-j}}\right)^{c_j}\right) \\ = e\left(\left(G_1^\alpha\right)^y, G_2^{\alpha^n}\right) e(G_1, w) \end{pmatrix}$

return b_0 **AND** b_1

Lai-Malavolta Linear Map Commitment (Algorithm 1). Setup takes as input the security parameter λ, the vector length n, and a (private) random tape

ω and outputs the public parameter pp. First, BGGen generates a bilinear group BG, which includes a prime p, three cyclic groups $\mathbb{G}_1$, $\mathbb{G}_2$, $\mathbb{G}_T$ of order p (written multiplicatively), where G_1 and G_2 are generators of $\mathbb{G}_1$ and $\mathbb{G}_2$, respectively, and $e\colon \mathbb{G}_1 \times \mathbb{G}_2 \to \mathbb{G}_T$ is a pairing satisfying the following properties:

- e is efficiently computable,
- e is non-degenerate: $e(G_1, G_2) \neq 1_{\mathbb{G}_T}$,
- e is bilinear: $e(A^x, B^y) = e(A, B)^{xy}$, for every $A \in \mathbb{G}_1$, $B \in \mathbb{G}_2$, and $x, y \in \mathbb{Z}$.

Next, a random element α is sampled from $\mathbb{Z}_p$. The output pp consists of the bilinear group, $\{G_1^{\alpha^j}\}_{j \in [n]}$, and $\{G_2^{\alpha^j}\}_{j \in [2n] \setminus \{n+1\}}$. The commitment of x and the witness for a linear combination $y = c \cdot x$ are computed as illustrated in Algorithm 1 (note that y is not used in WitnessGen in this scheme). Finally, Verify checks if y is an element in $\mathbb{Z}_p$ and verify if the first pairing is equal to the product of the other two. It accepts that $y = c \cdot x$ if both checks pass.

Computational complexity of Lai-Malavolta LMC. The LMC scales linearly for the verifier and quadratically in n for the server. More specifically, in our implementation, the prover performs $O(n)$ elliptic curve operations and $O(n^2)$ field operations (cheaper) per linear combination. The verifier performs $O(n)$ elliptic curve operations and three pairings per linear combinations. Note that elliptic curve pairing $e(G, H)$ is more expensive than exponentiation G^x, which is more expensive than product GH, which in turn is more expensive than operations on finite fields. The Lai-Malavolta LMC requires a trusted setup and a linear-size public parameter, but provides a constant-size commitment and witness. Others constructions of LMC bring in different trade-offs, e.g. no trusted setup but log-size commitment/witness, and additional properties [14–16].

3.2   A Generic Construction of Com-PIR

We now introduce a generic construction that combines an n-dimensional LMC and a linear k-server $m \times n$-dimensional PIR to produce a k-verifiable Com-PIR (see Fig. 2 for an illustration). The construction first applies a cryptographic hash function $h^*(\cdot)$ followed by a modulo operation to each column of the database x to achieve $h_j = h^*(x_j) \pmod{p}$, where x_j denotes the jth column of $x \in \mathbb{F}^{m \times n} = \mathbb{Z}_p^{m \times n}$. It then applies an LMC to the vector $h = (h_1, h_2, \ldots, h_n) \in \mathbb{F}^n$. The client performs PIR requests for *both* x_i and h_i. As the correctness of the received h_i is guaranteed by the LMC, the verification $h_i \overset{?}{=} h(\hat{x}_i)$ is reliable.

A Generic Construction of Com-PIR. Let Π be the target Com-PIR scheme, which will be constructed based on an LMC and a linear PIR scheme. We use the '.' sign to refer to the algorithm of each scheme, e.g. PIR.QueriesGen().

- pp $\leftarrow$ Π.Setup($1^\lambda, k, m, n$): The algorithm invokes LMC.Setup($1^\lambda, n$), the setup algorithm of the LMC.
- $C \leftarrow$ Π.CommitmentGen(pp, x): The algorithm first computes $h_j = h^*(x_j)$ $\pmod{p}, j \in [n]$, where $h^*(\cdot)$ is a cryptographic hash function, e.g. SHA3-256, and p is the order of the cyclic groups as part of pp. It then computes $C = C(h) \leftarrow$ LMC.CommitmentGen(pp, h), where $h = (h_1, h_2, \ldots, h_n)$.

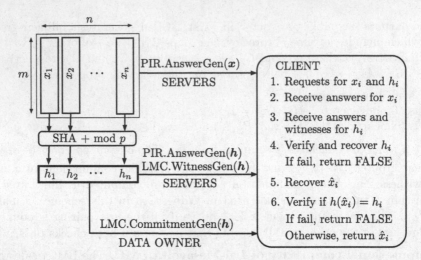

Fig. 2. Illustration of a generic construction of Com-PIR using an LMC and a linear PIR. When using SHA3-256 and the BLS12-381, each x_j is first hashed by SHA3-256 to generate a 256-bit digest $h^*(x_j)$, which in turn is taken modulo p, a 255-bit prime, to produce $h_j \in \mathbb{Z}_p$. This only reduces the security of SHA3-256 by at most one bit. The modulo operation is necessary to turn the hashes into valid input to the LMC. The LMC computation is carried out over the n hashes only, making it independent of the data item size m.

– $(\{q_j\}_{j\in[k]}, \mathsf{aux}) \leftarrow \Pi.\mathsf{QueriesGen}(\mathsf{pp}, k, m, n, i)$: The algorithm invokes the corresponding PIR algorithm, namely, $\mathsf{PIR.QueriesGen}(\mathsf{pp}, k, m, n, i)$.

– $a_j \leftarrow \Pi.\mathsf{AnswersGen}(\mathsf{pp}, \boldsymbol{x}, q_j)$: The algorithm invokes the corresponding PIR algorithm on both $\boldsymbol{x}$ and $\boldsymbol{h}$, i.e. $a_j(\boldsymbol{x}) \leftarrow \mathsf{PIR.AnswersGen}(\mathsf{pp}, \boldsymbol{x}, q_j)$ and $a_j(\boldsymbol{h}) \leftarrow \mathsf{PIR.AnswersGen}(\mathsf{pp}, \boldsymbol{h}, q_j)$, and outputs $a_j \triangleq (a_j(\boldsymbol{x}), a_j(\boldsymbol{h}))$. Note that each server can compute $\boldsymbol{h}$ from $\boldsymbol{x}$ on its own just once.

– $w_j \leftarrow \Pi.\mathsf{WitnessGen}(\mathsf{pp}, \boldsymbol{x}, q_j)$: The algorithm first converts q_j into a coefficient vector $\boldsymbol{c}(q_j) \in \mathbb{Z}_p^n$ such that $a_j(\boldsymbol{h}) = \boldsymbol{c}(q_j) \cdot \boldsymbol{h}$. Then, it invokes $w_j \leftarrow \mathsf{LMC.WitnessGen}(\mathsf{pp}, \boldsymbol{h}, \boldsymbol{c}, y)$, where $y \triangleq \boldsymbol{c} \cdot \boldsymbol{h}$.

– $\{x_i, \perp\} \leftarrow \Pi.\mathsf{Extract}(\mathsf{pp}, C, m, n, i, \{a_j, w_j\}_{j\in[k]}, \mathsf{aux})$: The algorithm first parses each answer a_j as $(a_j(\boldsymbol{x}), a_j(\boldsymbol{h}))$. Next, it converts q_j into a coefficient vector $\boldsymbol{c}(q_j) \in \mathbb{Z}_p^n$ such that $a_j(\boldsymbol{h}) = \boldsymbol{c}(q_j) \cdot \boldsymbol{h}$. Then, it verifies $a_j(\boldsymbol{h})$ by running $\mathsf{LMC.Verify}(\mathsf{pp}, C, \boldsymbol{c}(q_j), a_j(\boldsymbol{h}), w_j), j \in [k]$. If the verification fails for $j \in [k]$, it returns $\perp$. Otherwise, it calls $\mathsf{PIR.Extract}(n, i, \{a_j(\boldsymbol{h})\}_{j\in[k]}, \mathsf{aux})$ and $\mathsf{PIR.Extract}(n, i, \{a_j(\boldsymbol{x})\}_{j\in[k]}, \mathsf{aux})$ to obtain $\hat{h}_i$ and $\hat{x}_i$. It then performs the final hash verification $h(\hat{x}_i) \stackrel{?}{=} \hat{h}_i$ and returns $\hat{x}_i$ if passes and $\perp$ if fails.

Note that in the generic construction above, the PIR scheme is applied to $\boldsymbol{x} \in \mathbb{Z}_p^{m\times n}$ instead of $\mathbb{Z}_p^n$ as in Definition 1. This can be done in a straightforward manner in which the PIR scheme on $\mathbb{Z}_p^n$ is applied repeatedly m times to the m rows of $\boldsymbol{x} \in \mathbb{Z}_p^{m\times n}$ using the same set of queries. The communication and computation costs of a Com-PIR scheme based on the generic construction can be calculated easily based on the costs of the underlying PIR and LMC. Note that the LMC doesn't depend on m. Although the final hash check $h(\hat{x}_i) \stackrel{?}{=} \hat{h}_i$ depends on m because $|\hat{x}_i| = m$, $h(\cdot)$ is very efficient and its cost is negligible.

Lemma 1 (Correctness/Privacy). *The Com-PIR constructed by the generic construction is correct and t-private if the underlying LMC scheme is correct and the underlying PIR scheme is both correct and t-private.*

Proof. The correctness of the constructed Com-PIR scheme can be proved in a straightforward manner, implied directly from the correctness of the underlying LMC and PIR schemes. The privacy of the Com-PIR follows from the privacy of the underlying PIR scheme because the queries sent from the client are identical to those in the original PIR scheme.

Next, we prove (see Appendix A) that the generic construction generates a k-server $m \times n$-dimensional Com-PIR that is k-verifiable, assuming that the Lai-Malavolta LMC is used in conjunction with an arbitrary linear PIR scheme.

Lemma 2 (Verifiability). *Let $k, m, n \in \mathsf{poly}(\lambda)$ and $1/p \in \mathsf{negl}(\lambda)$. Then the k-server $m \times n$-dimensional Com-PIR using the Lai-Malavolta LMC is k-verifiable in the generic bilinear group model.*

4 Three Case Studies

We discuss in detail how the generic construction proposed in Sect. 3.2 performs for the Lai-Malavolta LMC and the three representative linear PIR schemes with respect to the communication and computation costs.

Chor-Kushilevitz-Goldreich-Sudan (CKGS) Scheme [3]. This is a linear 2-server n-dimensional PIR scheme working over an arbitrary finite field $\mathbb{F}$. We also use 2-CKGS to refer to this scheme, while using k-CKGS to refer to its straighforward generalization to the k-server setting (see [19, Section 3.2.1]).

- $(\{q_1, q_2\}, \mathsf{aux}) \leftarrow \mathsf{QueriesGen}(n, 2, i)$: the algorithm first picks a random subset $J \subseteq [n]$ and let $q_1 \in \mathbb{F}^n$ be the characteristic vector for J, i.e., q_1 has a '1' at the jth component if $j \in J$, and 0 otherwise. Next, q_2 is obtained from q_1 by flipping its ith component ($0 \to 1$ or $1 \to 0$). Then either $e_i = q_1 - q_2$ or $e_i = q_2 - q_1$, where $e_i \in \mathbb{F}^n$ is the unit vector with a '1' at the ith component. Set $\mathsf{aux} = 1$ or $\mathsf{aux} = 2$, respectively.
- $a_j \leftarrow \mathsf{AnswerGen}(\boldsymbol{x}, q_j)$: The algorithm returns $a_j = q_j \cdot \boldsymbol{x}$.
- $\{x_i\} \leftarrow \mathsf{Extract}(n, i, \{a_j\}_{j \in [k]}, \mathsf{aux})$: The algorithm returns $a_1 - a_2$ if $\mathsf{aux} = 1$ or $a_2 - a_1$ if $\mathsf{aux} = 2$.

The CKGS scheme and the Lai-Malavolta LMC scheme work together in a straightforward manner.

Example 1. We consider in Fig. 1 a toy example of a 2-server $m \times 5$-dimensional Com-PIR based on an LMC and CKGS PIR scheme [3] (see Fig. 1 for an illustration). The client, who wants x_1, picks a random subset $J = \{1, 3, 4\} \subseteq [5]$ and creates the corresponding queries $q_1 = (1, 0, 1, 1, 0)$ and $q_2 = (0, 0, 1, 1, 0)$.

Server 1, if acting honestly, sends back the answers $a_1(\boldsymbol{h}) = h_1 + h_3 + h_4$, $a_1(\boldsymbol{x}) = x_1 + x_3 + x_4$, and the witness $w_1(a_1(\boldsymbol{h}))$, which allows the client to verify the correctness of $a_1(\boldsymbol{h})$. Server 2, if acting honestly, sends back the answers $a_2(\boldsymbol{h}) = h_3 + h_4$, $a_2(\boldsymbol{x}) = x_3 + x_4$, and the witness $w_2(a_2(\boldsymbol{h}))$, which allows the client to verify the correctness of $a_2(\boldsymbol{h})$. The client, knowing the LMC commitment $C(\boldsymbol{h})$, can verify the correctness of both $a_1(\boldsymbol{h})$ and $a_2(\boldsymbol{h})$ and then extract the (verifiably correct) $\hat{h}_1 = a_1(\boldsymbol{h}) - a_2(\boldsymbol{h})$. It can also extract $\hat{x}_1 = a_1(\boldsymbol{x}) - a_2(\boldsymbol{x})$ and verify the correctness of the result by performing a hash verification $h(\hat{x}_1) \overset{?}{=} \hat{h}_1$.

Woodruff-Yekhanin (WY) Scheme [17]. This is a linear k-server n-dimensional PIR scheme working over an arbitrary finite field $\mathbb{F}$. See Appendix B for the detail. Note that each server generates $\ell \in O(n^{1/d})$ linear combinations of $\boldsymbol{x}$. Although in Algorithm 1, we let the LMC verify just one linear combination of $\boldsymbol{x}$ for simplicity, in its original form, Lai-Malavolta LMC can produce a single witness for and verify multiple linear combinations.

Bitar-El Rouayheb (BE) Scheme [18]. We present a simplified version of this scheme (dropping unnecessary properties like universality) in Appendix B (see, also Goldberg [11]). Note that the LMC is applied on $(k-t)n$ hashes instead of n like in other schemes.

Table 1. Comparisons of different Com-PIR schemes with k-verifiability. For the computation costs at each server and client, we count the number of field additions '+' and multiplications '×', elliptic curve additions '⊞' and multiplications '⊠', and pairings '⊡' in big-O notation (with $\ell \in O(n^{1/d})$ for the WY-based scheme). The top sub-row counts the operations on *data* while the bottom sub-row counts the operations related to *verification*. The verification time of the proposed Com-PIR schemes (mostly) doesn't depend on the size of the retrieved data m but on the size of the database n and the number of servers k.

	Upload Cost ($\#\mathbb{Z}_p$-elts)	Download Rate	Server (#operations)	Client (#operations)
Com-PIR (2-CKGS)	$2n$ bits	$1/2$	$mn+$	$m+$
			$n^2+,\ n^2\times,\ n\boxplus,\ n\boxtimes$	$2n\boxplus,\ 2n\boxtimes,\ 6\boxdot$
Com-PIR (k-CKGS)	kn	$1/k$	$mn+,\ mn\times$	$km+$
			$n^2+,\ n^2\times,\ n\boxplus,\ n\boxtimes$	$kn\boxplus,\ kn\boxtimes,\ 3k\boxdot$
Com-PIR (WY)	$k\ell$	$1/k$	$\ell mn+,\ \ell mnd\times$	$mt(k\ell + d^3t^2)+,\ mt(k\ell + d^3t^2)\times$
			$\ell n^2+,\ \ell n^2\times,\ \ell n\boxplus,\ \ell n\boxtimes$	$k\ell n\boxplus,\ k\ell n\boxtimes,\ 3k\boxdot$
Com-PIR (BE)	$k(k-t)n$	$(k-t)/k$	$(k-t)mn+,\ (k-t)mn\times$	$k((k-t)(kn+m)+km)+,$ $k^2((k-t)n+m)\times$
			$(k-t)^2n^2+,\ (k-t)^2n^2\times,$ $(k-t)n\boxplus,\ (k-t)n\boxtimes$	$k(k-t)n\boxplus,\ k(k-t)n\boxtimes,\ 3k\boxdot$

Comparison of the Three Com-PIR Schemes. We compare these schemes based on their communication and computation complexities (Table 1).

- **LM-CKGS:** this scheme has the *lowest computation time* among the three for both servers and client. The reason is that each server only performs cheap field additions for the data part and generates LMC witness for a single linear combination of hashes. The client performs one LMC verification per server.
- **LM-WY:** although having the *lowest upload cost*, the computation cost of this scheme is the highest among the three. The reason is that its running time also depends on $\ell \in O(n^{1/d})$. See Appendix C for more details.
- **LM-BE:** this scheme achieves the *optimal download rate* and has computation cost lying in between the other two. Computation-wise, the smaller the difference $k - t$, the lower the running time of both servers and client. The reason is that the LMC has to run not on n but on $(k - t)n$ hashes.

Comparisons with Related Works. The work of Zhang-Safavi Naini [12] is the closest to ours and provides k-accountability. Their idea is to apply a verifiable computing scheme [24] on top of WY [17], followed by several optimization steps to improve the performance. Originally designed for a $1 \times n$ database ($m = 1$), the verification time of their main scheme Γ_1 is in $O(kmn^{1/d})$, which becomes very slow for large m. Moreover, while our scheme has a constant witness size (from each server), their witness size is in $O(mn^{1/d})$. All other works in the literature, to our best knowledge, do not provide k-verifiability. For instance, Ke and Zhang [4] constructed a 2-server PIR scheme that can (information theoretically) verify the correctness of the result given at most one malicious server. Zhang and Wang [6] introduced k-server PIR schemes that are privately and publicly v-verifiable for $v < k$. These schemes were also designed for $m = 1$. Zhao *et al.* [5] proposed a construction of verifiable PIR scheme based on the Learning with Errors problem. The main issue in their construction is that the server can pass the client's verification if using the same *incorrect* database in generating the answer for the query and the response to the challenge (see [5, Def. 7]). PIR schemes with Byzantine-robustness were investigated in [7–9,11].

5 Experiments and Evaluations

Experiment Setup. We implemented three Com-PIR schemes in C using the libraries GMP 6.2.1, OpenSSL 2022, and blst v.0.3.10. We compiled the code with GCC 11.3.0 and ran our experiments on Ubuntu 22.04.1 environment (Intel Core i5-1035G1 CPU @1.00GHz×8, 15 GB System memory). The code is available on GitHub at https://github.com/PIR-PIXR/CPIR.

Evaluations. The LMC component in the Com-PIR schemes incurs an extra communication/computation overhead on top of the original PIR schemes [3,17, 18]. However, the LMC communication overhead is only $O(k)$ while the computation overhead doesn't grow with m, the size of each data item. Hence, as the size of each data item increases, the LMC overhead becomes smaller and smaller compared to the computation time of the PIR scheme (see Fig. 3). The computation time of LM-WY is significantly higher than the other two schemes (see Fig. 3, Fig. 4), hence consistent with the theoretical analysis presented earlier.

Figure 4 also demonstrates a trade-off between the download rate and the computation time for LM-BE: larger t leads to smaller download rate but cheaper computation. More evaluations of these Com-PIR schemes are in Appendix C.

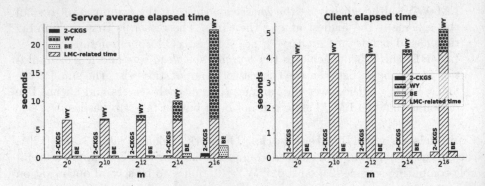

Fig. 3. The average server and client computation times of LM-CKGS, LM-WY, and LM-BE for $k = 2$, $t = 1$, $n = 2^{10}$, and $m \in \{2^0, 2^{10}, 2^{12}, 2^{14}, 2^{16}\}$.

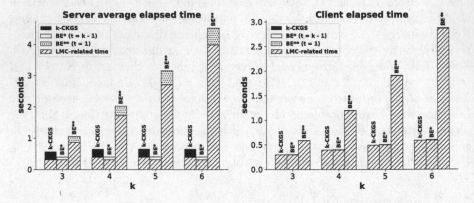

Fig. 4. The average server and client computation times of LM-CKGS and LM-BE for $n = 2^{10}$, $m = 2^{12}$, $k \in \{3, 4, 5, 6\}$, and $t = 1$ or $k - 1$.

6   Conclusions

We proposed a modular approach to combine a linear map commitment and a linear PIR scheme to achieve a k-verifiable PIR scheme, which guarantees that the client will never accept wrong data even in the extreme case when all servers are malicious. By applying the commitment scheme on hashes of data rather than on data themselves, the construction is reasonably practical, taking less than one second to privately retrieve 3MB of data from a database of size 3 GB. A drawback of our approach is that the commitment scheme may incur a significant computation overhead on top of the PIR scheme if the database consists of a large number of small-sized items.

Acknowledgement. We thank Russell W. F. Lai and Liangfeng Zhang for helpful discussions.

Appendix A: Verifiability Proof of Com-PIR

For simplicity, we consider one linear combination of x in the definition below.

Definition 10 (Function Binding for LMC). *[13] An LMC over $\mathbb{F}$ is function binding if for any PPT adversary $\mathcal{A}$, any positive integer $n \in \mathsf{poly}(\lambda)$, there exists a negligible function $\varepsilon(\lambda)$ such that*

$$\Pr\left[\begin{array}{c} y \in \mathbb{F} \\ \mathsf{Verify}(C, c, y, w) = 1 \\ \nexists x \in \mathbb{F}^n \text{ s.t. } \sum_{j \in [n]} c_j x_j = y \end{array} \middle| \begin{array}{c} \omega \leftarrow_{\$} \{0,1\}^\lambda \\ \mathsf{pp} \leftarrow \mathsf{Setup}(1^\lambda, n; \omega) \\ (C, c, y, w) \leftarrow \mathcal{A}(\mathsf{pp}) \end{array} \right] \leq \varepsilon(\lambda).$$

Lemma 3 ([13]). *Let $n \in \mathsf{poly}(\lambda)$ and $1/p \in \mathsf{negl}(\lambda)$. Then Lai-Malavolta LMC is function binding in the generic bilinear group model.*

Proof. [Proof of Lemma 2] According to the generic construction, the adversary wins the security experiment, i.e., $\mathsf{EXP}_{\mathcal{A},\Pi}(k, m, n, x, i, B) = 1$, if and only if the challenger extracts $\hat{x}_i \notin \{x_i, \bot\}$. This happens only when one of the following two independent events occur: either $\hat{h}_i = h_i$, i.e., the adversary finds a hash collision $h(\hat{x}_i) = h(x_i) = h_i$, or $\hat{h}_i \neq h_i$ but the adversary manages to fool LMC.Verify() with at least one wrong linear combination of h_i's. Therefore,

$$\Pr[\mathsf{EXP}_{\mathcal{A},\Pi}(k, m, n, x, i, B) = 1] = \Pr[\hat{x}_i \neq x_i \wedge h(\hat{x}_i) = h(x_i)]$$
$$+ \Pr[\text{At least one linear combination is wrong but still passes LMC.Verify()}]$$
$$\leq \varepsilon_1(\lambda) + \varepsilon_2(\lambda) \in \mathsf{negl}(\lambda),$$

as both events happen with probabilities negligible in λ assuming that $1/p$ is negligible in λ and that the security is considered under the generic bilinear group model (Lemma 3).

Appendix B: WY and BE PIR Schemes

Woodruff-Yekhanin (WY) Scheme [17]. This is a linear k-server n-dimensional PIR scheme working over an arbitrary finite field $\mathbb{F}$. Let $1 \leq t < k$ and $d = \lfloor (2k - 1)/t \rfloor$. Let $\ell \in O(n^{1/d})$ be the smallest integer satisfying $\binom{\ell}{d} \geq n$ and $E: [n] \to \mathbb{F}^\ell$ a 1-to-1 mapping that maps an index $j \in [n]$ to a vector in $\mathbb{F}^\ell$ of Hamming weight d. Each $x \in \mathbb{F}^n$ is encoded by a multivariate polynomial $F_x(z)$, where $z = (z_1, \ldots, z_\ell)$, defined as follows.

$$F_x(z) \triangleq \sum_{j \in [n]} x_j \prod_{u \in [\ell] : E(j)_u = 1} z_u.$$

Then, $\deg(F) = d$ and $x_i = F_x(E(i))$. Fix k distinct elements $\{\beta_j\}_{j \in [k]} \subseteq \mathbb{F}_p^*$.

- $(\{q_j\}_{j\in[k]}, \mathsf{aux}) \leftarrow \mathsf{QueriesGen}(n, k, i)$: The algorithm picks t random vectors $\{v^{(s)}\}_{s\in[t]} \subseteq \mathbb{F}^\ell$ and outputs $q_j \triangleq E(i) + \sum_{s\in[t]} \beta_j^s v_s$ and $\mathsf{aux} = \{v^{(s)}\}_{s\in[t]}$.
- $a_j \leftarrow \mathsf{AnswerGen}(x, q_j)$: The algorithm computes $a_j = (a_{j,0}, a_{j,1}, \ldots, a_{j,\ell})$, where $a_{j,0} \triangleq F_x(q_j)$ and $a_{j,u} \triangleq \frac{\partial F_x}{z_u}|_{q_j}$, $u \in [\ell]$.
- $\{x_i\} \leftarrow \mathsf{Extract}(n, i, \{a_j\}_{j\in[k]}, \mathsf{aux})$: The algorithm reconstructs the polynomial $f(y) \triangleq F_x\big(E(i) + \sum_{s\in[t]} y^s v^{(s)}\big)$ and outputs $f(0) = F_x(E(i)) = x_i$. The reconstruction of f is possible because $\deg(f) \leq dt \leq 2k - 1$ while $2k$ linear combinations of its coefficients, namely, $\{f(\beta_j), f'(\beta_j)\}_{j\in[k]}$, can be extracted from the answers $\{a_j\}_{j\in[k]}$ and $\mathsf{aux} = \{v^{(s)}\}_{s\in[t]}$ as follows. For $j \in [k]$, $f(\beta_j) = F_x(q_j) = a_{j,0}$, and

$$f'(\beta_j) = \sum_{u\in[\ell]} \frac{\partial F}{\partial z_u}\bigg|_{q_j} \frac{\partial}{\partial y}\bigg(E(i)_u + \sum_{s\in[t]} y^s v_u^{(s)}\bigg)\bigg|_{\beta_j} = \sum_{u\in[\ell]} a_{j,u} \frac{\partial}{\partial y}\bigg(E(i)_u + \sum_{s\in[t]} y^s v_u^{(s)}\bigg)\bigg|_{\beta_j}.$$

Note that each server generates $\ell \in O(n^{1/d})$ linear combinations of x. Although in Algorithm 1 we let the LMC verify just one linear combination of x for simplicity, in its original form, Lai-Malavolta LMC can verify multiple linear combinations using a single witness.

Bitar-El Rouayheb (BE) Scheme [18]. This scheme works slightly different from the previous ones in that the client retrieves a fixed block of $k - t$ components of x instead of a single component. All definitions of a PIR scheme can be generalized to this block form in a straightforward manner. Let $x = (x_1, \ldots, x_{(k-t)n}) \in \mathbb{F}^{(k-t)n}$ and assume the client wants to retrieve the ith block $\big(x_{(i-1)(k-t)+1}, \ldots, x_{i(k-t)}\big)$ for some $i \in [n]$.

- $(\{q_j\}_{j\in[k]}, \mathsf{aux}) \leftarrow \mathsf{QueriesGen}(n, k, i)$: The algorithm picks a $k \times k$ Vandermonde matrix $V = \big(\beta_a^{b-1}\big)_{a,b\in[k]}$, where $\{\beta_s\}_{s\in[t]}$ is a set of k distinct elements in $\mathbb{F}$. It also picks t random vectors $\{v^{(s)}\}_{s\in[t]} \subseteq \mathbb{F}^{(k-t)n}$ and set the queries to be the rows of the matrix $Q = VM$ given as follows.

$$Q = \begin{pmatrix} q_1 \\ q_2 \\ \vdots \\ q_k \end{pmatrix} \triangleq VM = V \left(\begin{array}{c} v^{(1)} \\ \vdots \\ v^{(t)} \\ \hline e_{(i-1)(k-t)+1} \\ \vdots \\ e_{i(k-t)} \end{array} \right).$$

- $a_j \leftarrow \mathsf{AnswerGen}(x, q_j)$: The algorithm outputs $a_j \triangleq q_j \cdot x$.
- $\{x_i\} \leftarrow \mathsf{Extract}(n, i, \{a_j\}_{j\in[k]}, \mathsf{aux})$: The algorithm calculates $V^{-1}Qx = Mx$, which gives $\big(x_{(i-1)(k-t)+1}, \ldots, x_{i(k-t)}\big)$.

The t-privacy is guaranteed because any set of t queries has t random vectors $\{v^{(s)}\}_{s\in[t]}$ well mixed (the submatrix of Q formed by any t rows and the first t columns is always invertible) and hence appears completely random.

Appendix C: Extra Performance Evaluations of Com-PIR

In Fig. 5, with a medium m and a growing n, the computation time of Com-PIR is dominated by the LMC. Note that LMC on its own scales linearly for the verifier and quadratically in n for the server. More specifically, in our implementation, $O(n)$ elliptic curve operations (expensive) and $O(n^2)$ field operations (cheaper) are required for the server. Applied on top of a PIR, the LMC-related running time also depends on k, t, and $\ell \in O(n^{1/d})$. Lai-Malavolta LMC runs reasonably fast on small and medium n (thousands) but slow on larger n. In Fig. 6, we plot the running times of LM-WY as d increases, which means that k increases (to satisfy $2k - 1 \geq td$ for a fixed t) and ℓ decreases. While the PIR time increases for both servers and clients, the LMC time for servers (depending on ℓ) decreases as d grows. For the client, the LMC time fluctuates as it depends on $k\ell$.

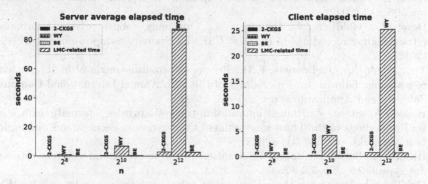

Fig. 5. The comparison of the average server and client computation times of LM-CKGS, LM-WY, and LM-BE for $k = 2$, $t = 1$, $m = 2^{10}$, and $n \in \{2^8, 2^{10}, 2^{12}\}$.

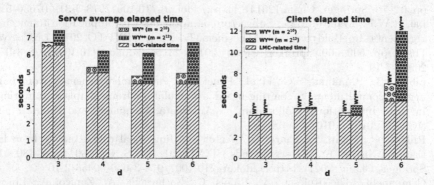

Fig. 6. The comparison of the average server and client computation times of LM-WY for $t = 1$, $n = 2^{10}$, $m \in \{2^{10}, 2^{12}\}$, and $(d, k) \in \{(3, 2), (4, 3), (5, 3), (6, 4)\}$.

References

1. Uribe, A.: Cyberattack on optus potentially exposes millions of customer accounts; Australian telecoms company says mass breach could have exposed birth dates, phone numbers and other personal data. Wall Street J. Eastern edn. (2022)
2. Biddle, N., Gray, M., McEachern, S.: Public exposure and responses to data breaches in Australia (2022)
3. Chor, B., Kushilevitz, E., Goldreich, O., Sudan, M.: Private information retrieval. J. ACM (JACM) **45**(6), 965–981 (1998)
4. Ke, P., Zhang, L.F.: Two-server private information retrieval with result verification. In: Proceedings of the IEEE International Symposium on Information Theory (ISIT), pp. 408–413 (2022)
5. Zhao, L., Wang, X., Huang, X.: Verifiable single-server private information retrieval from LWE with binary errors. Inf. Sci. **546**, 897–923 (2021)
6. Zhang, L.F., Wang, H.: Multi-server verifiable computation of low-degree polynomials. In: Proceedings of the IEEE Symposium on Security and Privacy (S&P), pp. 596–613 (2022)
7. Devet, C., Goldberg, I., Heninger, N.: Optimally robust private information retrieval. In: Proceedings of the 21st USENIX Security Symposium, pp. 269–283 (2012)
8. Yang, E.Y., Xu, J., Bennett, K.H.: Private information retrieval in the presence of malicious failures. In: Proceedings of the 26th Annual International Computer Software and Applications, pp. 805–810 (2002)
9. Beimel, A., Stahl, Y.: Robust information-theoretic private information retrieval. In: Proceedings of the Third International Conference on Security in Communication Networks, pp. 326–341 (2003)
10. Beimel, A., Stahl, Y.: Robust information-theoretic private information retrieval. J. Cryptol. **20**, 295–321 (2007)
11. Goldberg, I.: Improving the robustness of private information retrieval. In: IEEE Symposium on Security and Privacy (SP 2007), pp. 131–148. IEEE (2007)
12. Zhang, L.F., Safavi-Naini, R.: Verifiable multi-server private information retrieval. In: Boureanu, I., Owesarski, P., Vaudenay, S. (eds.) ACNS 2014. LNCS, vol. 8479, pp. 62–79. Springer, Cham (2014). https://doi.org/10.1007/978-3-319-07536-5_5
13. Lai, R.W.F., Malavolta, G.: Subvector commitments with application to succinct arguments. In: Boldyreva, A., Micciancio, D. (eds.) CRYPTO 2019. LNCS, vol. 11692, pp. 530–560. Springer, Cham (2019). https://doi.org/10.1007/978-3-030-26948-7_19
14. Libert, B., Ramanna, S.C., et al.: Functional commitment schemes: from polynomial commitments to pairing-based accumulators from simple assumptions. In: 43rd International Colloquium on Automata, Languages and Programming (ICALP 2016) (2016)
15. Peikert, C., Pepin, Z., Sharp, C.: Vector and functional commitments from lattices. In: Nissim, K., Waters, B. (eds.) TCC 2021. LNCS, vol. 13044, pp. 480–511. Springer, Cham (2021). https://doi.org/10.1007/978-3-030-90456-2_16
16. Campanelli, M., Nitulescu, A., Ràfols, C., Zacharakis, A., Zapico, A.: Linear-map vector commitments and their practical applications. In: Agrawal, S., Lin, D. (eds.) ASIACRYPT 2022. LNCS, vol. 13794, pp. 189–219. Springer, Cham (2022). https://doi.org/10.1007/978-3-031-22972-5_7
17. Woodruff, D., Yekhanin, S.: A geometric approach to information-theoretic private information retrieval. In: 20th Annual IEEE Conference on Computational Complexity (CCC 2005), pp. 275–284. IEEE (2005)

18. Bitar, R., El Rouayheb, S.: Staircase-PIR: universally robust private information retrieval. In: IEEE Information Theory Workshop (ITW), pp. 1–5. IEEE (2018)

19. Demmler, D., Herzberg, A., Schneider, T.: Raid-PIR: practical multi-server PIR. In: Proceedings of the 6th Edition of the ACM Workshop on Cloud Computing Security, pp. 45–56 (2014)

20. Sun, H., Jafar, S.A.: The capacity of robust private information retrieval with colluding databases. IEEE Trans. Inf. Theory **64**(4), 2361–2370 (2017)

21. Ulukus, S., Avestimehr, S., Gastpar, M., Jafar, S.A., Tandon, R., Tian, C.: Private retrieval, computing, and learning: recent progress and future challenges. IEEE J. Sel. Areas Commun. **40**(3), 729–748 (2022)

22. Nikolaenko, V., Ragsdale, S., Bonneau, J., Boneh, D.: Powers-of-tau to the people: decentralizing setup ceremonies. Cryptology ePrint Archive (2022)

23. Lai, R.W.: Succinct arguments: constructions and applications. Ph.D. dissertation, Friedrich-Alexander-Universitaet Erlangen-Nuernberg (Germany) (2022)

24. Papamanthou, C., Shi, E., Tamassia, R.: Signatures of correct computation. In: Sahai, A. (ed.) TCC 2013. LNCS, vol. 7785, pp. 222–242. Springer, Heidelberg (2013). https://doi.org/10.1007/978-3-642-36594-2_13

Two-Message Authenticated Key Exchange from Public-Key Encryption

You Lyu[1,2] and Shengli Liu[1,2(✉)]

[1] Department of Computer Science and Engineering, Shanghai Jiao Tong University, Shanghai 200240, China
{vergil,slliu}@sjtu.edu.cn
[2] State Key Laboratory of Cryptology, P.O. Box 5159, Beijing 100878, China

Abstract. In two-message authenticated key exchange (AKE), it is necessary for the initiator to keep a round state after sending the first round-message, because he/she has to derive his/her session key after receiving the second round-message. Up to now almost all two-message AKEs constructed from public-key encryption (PKE) only achieve weak security which does not allow the adversary obtaining the round state. How to support state reveal to obtain a better security called IND-AA security has been an open problem proposed by Hövelmann et al. (PKC 2020).

In this paper, we solve the open problem with a generic construction of two-message AKE from any CCA-secure Tagged Key Encapsulation Mechanism (TKEM). Our AKE supports state reveal and achieves IND-AA security. Given the fact that CCA-secure public-key encryption (PKE) implies CCA-secure TKEM, our AKE can be constructed from any CCA-secure PKE with proper message space. The abundant choices for CCA-secure PKE schemes lead to many IND-AA secure AKE schemes in the standard model. Moreover, following the online-extractability technique in recent work by Don et al. (Eurocrypt 2022), we can extend the Fujisaki-Okamoto transformation to transform any CPA-secure PKE into a CCA-secure Tagged KEM in QROM. Therefore, we obtain the first generic construction of IND-AA secure two-message AKE from CPA-secure PKE in QROM. This construction does not need any signature scheme, and this result is especially helpful in the post-quantum world, since the current quantum-secure PKE schemes are much more efficient than their signature counterparts.

Keywords: Authenticated key exchange · State reveal · PKE

1 Introduction

Authenticated Key Exchange (AKE) is an important technical tool of establishing a secure channel for two communication parties, and is widely deployed in a variety of information systems for security. Running with an AKE protocol, two parties can compute a shared session key which is used for the later communications. The security of AKE requires pseudo-randomness of the session key in

© The Author(s), under exclusive license to Springer Nature Switzerland AG 2024
G. Tsudik et al. (Eds.): ESORICS 2023, LNCS 14344, pp. 414–434, 2024.
https://doi.org/10.1007/978-3-031-50594-2_21

Party $P_i(pk_i, sk_i)$:   Party $P_j(pk_j, sk_j)$:

$(M_1, st) \leftarrow \mathsf{Init}(sk_i, pk_j)$ $\xrightarrow{\quad M_1 \quad}$

$\downarrow st$ $\xleftarrow{\quad M_2 \quad}$ $(M_2, K_j) \leftarrow \mathsf{Der_{resp}}(sk_j, pk_i, M_1)$

$K_i \leftarrow \mathsf{Der_{init}}(sk_i, pk_j, M_2, st)$

Fig. 1. Two-message AKE protocol.

case of passive attacks and (implicit or explicit) authentication in case of active
attacks. AKE is a well-studied topic and many generic AKE constructions are
available up to now [9,10,13,20]. Generally, AKE relies on public-key primitives
for security and its building blocks include public-key encryption (PKE), digital
signature (SIG) and key encapsulation mechanism (KEM).

SECURITY MODELS FOR AKE. Bellare and Rogaway [3] introduced the original
security model, which was later developed to several different models, like CK
model, eCK model, CK+ model, etc. Lately, Hövelmanns et al. [10] proposed
the so-called IND-AA/IND-StAA models for two-message AKEs. IND-AA model
captures not only the classical security requirement of pseudo-randomness for
session keys, but also security against key compromise (KCI) attack, reflection
attack, state reveal attack, and weak forward security. IND-StAA model is similar to but weaker than IND-AA model, since it does not consider state reveal
attack. As pointed by [5,10], IND-AA model is strictly stronger than the CK
model, but incomparable to eCK model.

AKE FROM PKE. There are two essential factors affecting the efficiency of
AKE. One is the number of rounds and the other is the efficiency of its building blocks. Clearly the optimal round number is 2 for AKE, so two-message
AKE has optimal round efficiency. Among the public key primitives, SIG is
often used to achieve authentication for AKE. However, generally SIG is not
as efficient as PKE, and this is especially true for PKE/SIG schemes with
security against quantum computers. For example, in the NIST post-quantum
competition, CRYSTALS-Dilithium (SIG) has key size two times larger than
CRYSTALS-Kyber (KEM), its signature size is three times larger than the
ciphertext size of CRYSTALS-Kyber (KEM), and its signing time is 10 times
slower than the encapsulation algorithm of CRYSTALS-Kyber. This motivates
the research [10,11,19] on designing AKE solely from PKE. The AKE schemes
proposed in [11,19] are constructed from KEM, but have at least three rounds.

The question of designing two-message AKE from PKE was partially solved
by Hövelmanns et al. [10]. Recall that a two-message AKE protocol for parties
P_i and P_j is captured by three PPT algorithms as shown in Fig. 1. Let (pk_i, sk_i)
(resp.(pk_j, sk_j)) be the public/secret key pairs for P_i (resp.P_j).

(1) $\mathsf{Init}(sk_i, pk_j)$. Initiator P_i invokes $\mathsf{Init}(sk_i, pk_j)$ to generate the first-round
    message M_1 and a round state st.
(2) $\mathsf{Der_{resp}}(sk_j, pk_i, M_1)$. After receiving M_1, responder P_j invokes $\mathsf{Der_{resp}}$
    (sk_j, pk_i, M_1) to generate the second-round message M_2 and the session
    key K_j.

(3) $\mathsf{Der}_{\mathsf{init}}(sk_i, pk_j, M_2, st)$. Upon receiving M_2, P_i invokes $\mathsf{Der}_{\mathsf{init}}(sk_i, pk_j, M_2, st)$ to generate its session key K_i.

Compared with IND-StAA security, IND-AA security allows the adversary to implement a so-called "state reveal attack", which is an active attack with initiator P_i's state st_i. So IND-AA security is strictly stronger than IND-StAA security. In [10], Hövelmanns et al. presented a generic construction of two-message AKE from passively (i.e., CPA) secure PKE in the quantum random oracle model (QROM). However, their AKE construction only achieves weak IND-StAA security, so they left an open problem (Sect. 1.1.5 in [10]):

> *How to design a generic and efficient two-message*
> *AKE protocol with IND-AA security?*

OUR CONTRIBUTION. We solve the open problem in this paper. Our contribution has two folds.

1. We propose a generic construction of IND-AA secure two-message AKE from CCA-secure Tagged-KEM [1], CPA-secure PKE, target collision resistant (TCR) hash function, and pseudo-random function (PRF). The IND-AA security of AKE is proven in the standard model.
   - The existence of one-way function implies PRF and TCR-Hash function, and CCA-secure Tagged-KEM can be constructed by CCA-secure PKE. So our AKE can essentially be constructed from CCA-secure PKE.
   - Given many choices for the standard-model instantiations of the building blocks, we obtain the first generic two-message AKE schemes from PKE with IND-AA security in the standard model.
2. Following the online-extractability technique in [6], we extend the Fujisaki-Okamoto transformation to transform any passively (i.e., CPA) secure PKE into a CCA-secure Tagged KEM in the QROM model. As a result, we obtain the first generic construction of two-message AKE from passively secure PKE with IND-AA security proven in the QROM model.

COMPARISON. We compare our two AKE constructions, AKE_1 in standard model and AKE_2 in the QROM model, with other AKEs constructed from PKE. Comparing the FSXY scheme [7] in the standard model, our AKE_1 has comparable efficiency as FSXY, but shorter secret key and better security of IND-AA. Comparing the $\mathsf{AKE}_{\mathsf{FO}}$ scheme [10] in the QROM model, our AKE_2 has comparable efficiency as $\mathsf{AKE}_{\mathsf{FO}}$, but enjoys shorter secret key and better security of IND-AA.

TECHNIQUE OVERVIEW. First we review some security requirements for AKE. Plain security means pseudo-randomness of session key but the adversary $\mathcal{A}$ is neither allowed to corrupt users' secret key nor reveal the initiator's round state. Weak forward security (wFS) asks pseudo-randomness of session key in case of passive attacks but $\mathcal{A}$ may corrupt secret keys of both initiator and responder (in this case $\mathcal{A}$ cannot reveal the initiator's round state to avoid trivial attack).

Table 1. Comparison of our AKE_1 (in the standard model) and AKE_2 (in QROM) with AKEs constructed from PKE/KEM. **Comm** denotes the communication overhead of the protocols, where "$|\mathsf{C}|$" and "$|\mathsf{pk}|$" denote the size of ciphertext and public key of IND-CCA secure KEM. "$|c|$" denotes the size of ciphertext of IND-CPA secure PKE/KEM. "λ" denotes the security parameter. $(|c| + |\mathsf{C}|)$ (w.r.t. $(|c| + |c|)$) in AKE_1 (w.r.t. AKE_2) denotes the size of ciphertext of IND-CPA secure PKE, because the ciphertext is an (KEM + DEM) encryption of the ciphertext of IND-CCA (w.r.t. IND-CPA) secure KEM. **CompI** and **CompR** denote the computational complexity of initiator and responder. "E" and "D" denote one encapsulation and one decapsulation of an IND-CCA secure KEM, and "e" and "d" denote one encapsulation and one decapsulation of IND-CPA secure KEM. **KeySize** denotes the size of long-term secret key per user. "$|\mathsf{sk}_{cca}|, |\mathsf{sk}_{cpa}|, |\mathsf{sk}_{prf}|, |\mathsf{sk}_{se}|$" denote the secret key sizes of IND-CCA secure KEM, IND-CPA secure PKE/KEM, PRF and symmetric encryption, respectively.

AKE schemes	Comm	CompI	CompR	KeySize	Security	Model
FSXY [7]	$|\mathsf{pk}| + 2|\mathsf{C}| + |c|$	$E + D + d$	$E + D + e$	$|\mathsf{sk}_{cca}| + |\mathsf{sk}_{prf}|$	IND-stAA	Standard
Our AKE_1	$|\mathsf{pk}| + |\mathsf{C}| + (|c| + |\mathsf{C}|) + \lambda$	$E + D + d$	$E + D + e$	$|\mathsf{sk}_{cca}|$	IND-AA	Standard
JKRS [13]	$|\mathsf{pk}| + 2|\mathsf{C}| + |c|$	$E + D + d$	$E + D + e$	$|\mathsf{sk}_{cca}| + |\mathsf{sk}_{se}|$	IND-AA	ROM
AKE_{FO} [10]	$|\mathsf{pk}| + 3|c|$	$2e + 2d$	$3e + d$	$|\mathsf{sk}_{cpa}| + |\mathsf{sk}_{prf}|$	IND-stAA	QROM
Our AKE_2	$|\mathsf{pk}| + |c| + (|c| + |c|) + \lambda$	$2e + 2d$	$3e + d$	$|\mathsf{sk}_{cpa}|$	IND-AA	QROM

Party $P_i(pk_i, sk_i)$:
$m_1 \leftarrow_\$ \mathcal{M}, c_1 \leftarrow \mathsf{Enc}(pk_j, m_1)$

$(\tilde{pk}, \tilde{sk}) \leftarrow \mathsf{Gen}$

$\quad\Big\downarrow st = (m_1, \tilde{sk})$

$m_2 \leftarrow \mathsf{Dec}(sk_i, c_2)$

$\tilde{m} \leftarrow \mathsf{Dec}(\tilde{sk}, \tilde{c})$

$K_i := H(m_1|m_2|M_1|M_2|\tilde{m})$

$\xrightarrow{\quad M_1 = (\tilde{pk}, c_1) \quad}$

$\xleftarrow{\quad M_2 = (\tilde{c}, c_2) \quad}$

Party $P_j(pk_j, sk_j)$:

$m_1 \leftarrow \mathsf{Dec}(sk_j, c_1)$

$m_2 \leftarrow_\$ \mathcal{M}, c_2 \leftarrow \mathsf{Enc}(pk_i, m_2)$

$\tilde{m} \leftarrow_\$ \mathcal{M}, \tilde{c} \leftarrow \mathsf{Enc}(\tilde{pk}, \tilde{c})$

$K_j := H(m_1|m_2|M_1|M_2|\tilde{m})$

Fig. 2. Plain AKE (without gray box) and AKE_{FO} [10] (with gray box).

State-reveal security requires that $\mathcal{A}$ is not able to implement successful active attack to learn party's session key even if it obtains the initiator's round state.

We start with a plain construction of AKE which has plain security but has neither forward security nor state-reveal security. Then we show why the AKE_{FO} scheme in [10] achieves wFS security but suffers from state-reveal attack. Lastly, we describe how to design our AKE to resist the state-reveal attack while keeping the wFS security, so that IND-AA security is achieved.

Plain AKE. Let $\mathsf{PKE} = (\mathsf{Gen}, \mathsf{Enc}, \mathsf{Dec})$ be a public key encryption scheme. There is a plain construction of AKE. P_i and P_j just use its peer's public key to encrypt a random message. Let $c_1 \leftarrow \mathsf{Enc}(pk_j, m_1)$ and $c_2 \leftarrow \mathsf{Enc}(pk_i, m_2)$. P_i has state $st_i := m_1$. After exchanging the ciphertexts c_1 and c_2, they can decrypt the ciphertexts to recover m_1 and m_2 respectively. The final session key is computed by $K_i = K_j = H(m_1|m_2|c_1|c_2)$. See Fig. 2.

$$
\begin{array}{ll}
\text{Party } P_i(pk_i, sk_i) & \text{Party } P_j(pk_j, sk_j) \\
\end{array}
$$

Party $P_i(pk_i, sk_i)$

$m_{11}, m_{12} \leftarrow_\$ \mathcal{M}, \ \sigma := \mathsf{H}(m_{12})$

$c_1 \leftarrow \mathsf{Enc}(pk_j, m_{11}|m_{12}|i)$

$(\tilde{pk}, \tilde{sk}) \leftarrow \mathsf{Gen}$

$\qquad \downarrow st = (m_{11}, \tilde{sk}, \sigma)$

$\qquad \qquad \qquad \xrightarrow{\quad M_1 = (\tilde{pk}, c_1) \quad}$

$c_2 \leftarrow \mathsf{Dec}(\tilde{sk}, \tilde{c})$

$m_{21}|m_{22} \leftarrow \mathsf{Dec}(sk_i, c_2)$

If $\mathsf{H}(m_{22} \oplus C) \neq \sigma$: abort

$\qquad \qquad \qquad \xleftarrow{\quad M_2 = (\tilde{c}, C) \quad}$

$K_i := \mathsf{PRF}(m_{11}, M_1|M_2)$

$\qquad \oplus \mathsf{PRF}(m_{21}, M_1|M_2)$

Party $P_j(pk_j, sk_j)$

$m_{11}|m_{12}|i \leftarrow \mathsf{Dec}(sk_j, c_1)$

$m_{21}, m_{22} \leftarrow_\$ \mathcal{M}$

$c_2 \leftarrow \mathsf{Enc}(pk_i, m_{21}|m_{22})$

$\tilde{c} \leftarrow \mathsf{Enc}(\tilde{pk}, c_2)$

$C = m_{12} \oplus m_{22}$

$K_j := \mathsf{PRF}(m_{11}, M_1|M_2)$

$\qquad \oplus \mathsf{PRF}(m_{21}, M_1|M_2)$

Fig. 3. Our generic construction of AKE.

- Without the knowledge of sk_i and sk_j, the session key $\mathsf{H}(m_1|m_2|c_1|c_2)$ is pseudo-random (assuming by now H is a random oracle). Therefore, this plain AKE has plain security if the underlying PKE has CCA security. The CCA security is required for PKE so that the security reduction algorithm is able to compute session keys for other session instance of the same user.
- If P_i and P_j are corrupted, adversary $\mathcal{A}$ obtains sk_i and sk_j, then $\mathcal{A}$ is also able to decrypt c_1, c_2 to obtain m_1, m_2. Obviously $\mathcal{A}$ also gets the session key $\mathsf{H}(m_1|m_2|c_1|c_2)$. Therefore, this plain AKE has no wFS security.
- If state $st_i = m_1$ is exposed to $\mathcal{A}$, then $\mathcal{A}$ can impersonate P_j to send $\hat{c}_2 \leftarrow \mathsf{Enc}(pk_i, \hat{m}_2)$ to P_i. Obviously $\mathcal{A}$ can compute P_i's session key $K_i := \mathsf{H}(m_1|\hat{m}_2|c_1|\hat{c}_2)$. Therefore, this plain AKE cannot resist state reveal attack.

$\mathsf{AKE_{FO}}$ [10] **with wFS Security.** To obtain wFS security, an ephemeral public/secret key pair $(\tilde{pk}, \tilde{sk})$ is augmented to the plain AKE, resulting in $\mathsf{AKE_{FO}}$ [10]. P_i also sends $\tilde{pk}$ to P_j and P_j provides P_i a ciphertext $\tilde{c}$ encrypting another random message $\tilde{m}$ under $\tilde{pk}$. The state of P_i is $st_i = (m_1, \tilde{sk})$. Then P_i and P_j can share the ephemeral random $\tilde{m}$, and embed it in the input of the hash function so that $K_i = K_j = \mathsf{H}(m_1|m_2|M_1|M_2|\tilde{m})$, where $M_1 = (\tilde{pk}, c_1)$ and $M_2 = (\tilde{c}, c_2)$. See also Fig. 2.

- Even if $\mathcal{A}$ obtains sk_i and sk_j by corruption, $\mathcal{A}$ cannot determine $\tilde{m}$ without the knowledge of $\tilde{sk}$. Therefore, $K_i = K_j = \mathsf{H}(m_1|m_2|M_1|M_2|\tilde{m})$ is still random to $\mathcal{A}$. So $\mathsf{AKE_{FO}}$ achieves wFS security.
- If state $st_i = (m_1, \tilde{sk})$ is exposed to $\mathcal{A}$, then $\mathcal{A}$ can impersonate P_j in the protocol and share a session key with P_i, since it knows m_1 and can choose $\tilde{m}$ and $\hat{m}_2$ so as to derive P_i's session key $K_i = \mathsf{H}(m_1|\hat{m}_2|M_1|M_2|\tilde{m})$. Therefore, $\mathsf{AKE_{FO}}$ cannot resist state reveal attack.

Our Approach to IND-AA Security. In plain AKE and $\mathsf{AKE_{FO}}$, m_1 has two roles. One is used to derive the session key, and the other is used as a token to authenticate P_j since only P_j is able to decrypt c_1 to obtain m_1 (when sk_j is not corrupted). However, with state reveal, $\mathcal{A}$ obtains token m_1 from st_i, so it can always impersonate P_j in plain AKE and $\mathsf{AKE_{FO}}$. That is why they suffer from the state-reveal attack and only achieve IND-StAA security.

To achieve IND-AA security, we have to deal with the above impersonation attack due to the leakage of m_1 from state reveal. Intuitively, we have to find a way of authenticating P_j even if st_i is leaked to $\mathcal{A}$.

Now we briefly show how to construct our AKE from the plain AKE step by step. Steps (1)–(5) show how to support state reveal to avoid the impersonation attack, and (6) shows how to achieve wFS security.

(1) **Partition m_1 by functionality.** In algorithm Init, m_1 is divided into two parts $m_{11}|m_{12}$, where m_{11} is used to derive the session key and m_{12} is used as P_j's authenticating token.

(2) **Limit information leakage of token m_{12} in state st_i.** We do not put token m_{12} in st_i. Instead, only the hash value $\sigma := \mathsf{H}(m_{12})$ (rather than m_{12}) is stored in state st_i (where m_{11} is stored as well). Now even if $\mathcal{A}$ obtains σ from st_i, $\mathcal{A}$ can hardly recover the token m_{12}.

(3) **Protect token m_{12} in the second round-message M_2.** For explicit authentication, P_j has to transmit the token m_{12} via M_2. Thus we have to protect m_{12} in M_2 to avoid leakage. To this end, in $\mathsf{Der_{resp}}$, m_2 is further divided into two parts $m_{21}|m_{22}$, where m_{21} is used to derive the session key and m_{22} is used to encrypt m_{22} via one-time pad. Now $M_2 = c_2$ (in the plain AKE) is changed to $M_2 = (c_2, C := m_{12} \oplus m_{22})$.

(4) **Authenticate P_j with $\sigma = \mathsf{H}(m_{12})$.** P_i can decrypt c_2 to obtain m_{22} and recover $m_{12} := C \oplus m_{22}$. By retrieving σ from st_i, P_i can authenticte P_j by checking whether m_{12} is the hash pre-image of σ.

(5) **Avoid leakage m_{12} from man-in-the-middle (MITM) attack.** Now that both $M_1 = c_1 = \mathsf{Enc}(pk_j, m_{11}|m_{12})$ and $M_2 = (c_2, m_{12} \oplus m_{22})$ contain the information of m_{12}. But P_j is not able to authenticate P_i by M_1. Then it is possible for $\mathcal{A}$ to implement a MITM attack: copy c_1 from M_1 as its own first round-message; P_j will output $M_2 = (\hat{c}_2 = \mathsf{Enc}(\hat{pk}, \hat{m}_{21}|\hat{m}_{22}), C = m_{12} \oplus \hat{m}_{22})$; $\mathcal{A}$ decrypts $\hat{m}_{21}|\hat{m}_{22} \leftarrow \mathsf{Dec}(\hat{sk}, \hat{c}_2)$ with its own secret key $\hat{sk}$. Then $\mathcal{A}$ can recover the token $m_{12} := C \oplus \hat{m}_{22}$ and then impersonate P_j with the token. This MITM attack can be easily avoided by attaching P_i's identity i to $m_{11}|m_{12}$[1]. So $c_1 \leftarrow \mathsf{Enc}(pk_j, m_{11}|m_{12}|i)$. The CCA security of PKE will guarantee that $\mathcal{A}$'s MITM attack either results decryption failure or a totally different decryption result.

(6) **Encryption of c_2 with ephemeral key for the wFS security.** P_i puts the ephemeral public key $\tilde{pk}$ in $M_1 = (\tilde{pk}, c_1)$ and the ephemeral secret key $\tilde{sk}$ in $st_i = (m_{11}, \tilde{sk}, \sigma)$. P_j uses $\tilde{pk}$ to encrypt c_2 to obtain $\tilde{c} \leftarrow \mathsf{Enc}(\tilde{pk}, c_2)$. So $M_2 = (\tilde{c}, C)$. Now we arrive at our final AKE construction.

With the protection of ephemeral key, even sk_i and sk_j are corrupted, c_2 is still well-protected from $\mathcal{A}$ as long as $\mathcal{A}$ does not reveal state to obtain $\tilde{sk}$. Consequently, $\mathcal{A}$ knows nothing about m_{21} and the final session key $K_i = K_j = \mathsf{H}(m_{11}|m_{21}|M_1|M_2)$ is still random to $\mathcal{A}$. In fact, as long as $\mathcal{A}$

---

[1] In our final generic construction of AKE, we use tagged KEM to generate c_1 with identity as the tag. Here PKE is only specific construction of tagged KEM.

does not obtain both the initiator's the long-term key and its round state (to avoid trivial attack), the session key from a non-tampered session is pseudo-random to the adversary. So our AKE achieves the wFS security.

In the session key generation, we can always change the hash function with PRF function so that $K_i = K_j = \mathsf{PRF}(m_{11}|M_1|M_2) \oplus \mathsf{PRF}(m_{21}|M_1|M_2)$. In this way, the IND-AA security is proven in the standard model. Our AKE construction is shown in Fig. 3.

Moreover, we can also change PKE to tagged TKEM and KEM for the generation of c_1 and c_2. Since PKE can be considered a specific instantiation of KEM (or TKEM), this change only makes our AKE construction more general.

Related Works. The FSXY scheme in [7] is a two-message AKE constructed from KEM in the standard model. As noted in [10], its security is essentially the IND-StAA security. As far as we know, the AKE$_{\mathsf{FO}}$ [10] is the only generic two-message AKE construction from PKE in QROM, achieving IND-StAA security. The performances of FSXY and AKE$_{\mathsf{FO}}$ are shown in Table 1.

There are also other AKE schemes [8,9,13] supporting state reveal (i.e., resisting state reveal attack). In [8,13], a symmetric encryption (SE) is employed to encrypt the round state to support state reveal. As a result, the secret key of SE has to be included into the long-term secret key. Besides, the AKE scheme in [13] is based on the random oracle (RO) model and those in [8,9] rely on SIG to provide authentication. We note that the SE approach to support state reveal may also apply to AKE$_{\mathsf{FO}}$ [10] but a rigorous proof in QROM is needed.

The HMQV protocol [14] also supports state reveal, but it is Diffie-Hellman type AKE scheme in the RO model, rather than a generic construction. Its solution to state reveal is specific to the Diffie-Hellman algebraic structure.

In ISO/IEC 11770-3 [12], there are standardized two-round PKE-based AKE schemes. However, these AKE schemes do not consider state-reveal attacks (in fact, they are susceptible to such attacks since the randomness used in the first round-message must be kept to derive the final session key by the initiator).

2 Preliminary

Let $\emptyset$ denote the empty set. If x is defined by y or the value of y is assigned to x, we write $x := y$. For $\mu \in \mathbb{N}$, define $[\mu] := \{1, 2, \ldots, \mu\}$. Denote by $x \leftarrow_\$ \mathcal{X}$ the procedure of sampling x from set $\mathcal{X}$ uniformly at random. Let $|\mathcal{X}|$ denote the number of elements in $\mathcal{X}$. All our algorithms are probabilistic unless states otherwise. PPT abbreviates probabilistic polynomial time. We use $y \leftarrow \mathcal{A}(x)$ to define the random variable y obtained by executing algorithm $\mathcal{A}$ on input x. We use $y \in \mathcal{A}(x)$ to indicate that y lies in the support of $\mathcal{A}(x)$. We also use $y \leftarrow \mathcal{A}(x; r)$ to make explicit the random coins r used in the probabilistic computation. Let λ denote the security parameter. We assume all algorithms take 1^λ as an implicit input.

The definitions of PRG and PRF and the one-wayness and TCR property of hash function are shown in Appendix A.

2.1   Public Key Encryption

A public key encryption scheme consists of three algorithms $\mathsf{PKE} = (\mathsf{Gen}, \mathsf{Enc}, \mathsf{Dec})$, where $(pk, sk) \leftarrow \mathsf{Gen}$ generates public/secret key pair, $c \leftarrow \mathsf{Enc}(pk, m)$ encrypts plaintext m to ciphertext c and $m/\bot \leftarrow \mathsf{Dec}(sk, c)$ decrypts ciphertext c to recover the plaintext m. The $(1 - \delta)$ correctness of PKE requires decryption error is bounded by δ, where the probability is over $(pk, sk) \leftarrow \mathsf{Gen}$ and $c \leftarrow \mathsf{Enc}(pk, m)$.

Definition 1 (γ-Spreadness of PKE). PKE *is γ-spread if for all key pairs* $(pk, sk) \in \mathsf{Gen}(\mathsf{pp}_{\mathsf{PKE}})$ *and all messages* $m \in \mathcal{M}$, *it holds that*

$$\max_{c \in \mathcal{C}} \Pr\left[r \leftarrow_\$ \mathcal{R} : \mathsf{Enc}(pk, m; r) = c\right] \leq 2^{-\gamma}.$$

Definition 2 (γ-Key Diversity of PKE). PKE *is γ-key diverse if*

$$\Pr\left[\begin{array}{c} r_1, r_2 \leftarrow_\$ \mathcal{R} \\ (pk_1, sk_1) \leftarrow \mathsf{Gen}(\mathsf{pp}_{\mathsf{PKE}}; r_1) \\ (pk_2, sk_2) \leftarrow \mathsf{Gen}(\mathsf{pp}_{\mathsf{PKE}}; r_2) \end{array} : pk_1 = pk_2 \right] \leq 2^{-\gamma}.$$

Definition 3 (IND-CPA Security for PKE). *For PKE, an adversary $\mathcal{A}$'s advantage is defined by* $\mathsf{Adv}_{\mathsf{PKE}}^{\mathsf{CPA}}(\mathcal{A}) := \left|\Pr\left[\mathsf{Exp}_{\mathsf{PKE},\mathcal{A}}^{\mathsf{CPA}\text{-}0} \Rightarrow 1\right] - \Pr\left[\mathsf{Exp}_{\mathsf{PKE},\mathcal{A}}^{\mathsf{CPA}\text{-}1} \Rightarrow 1\right]\right|,$ *where*

$$\Pr\left[\mathsf{Exp}_{\mathsf{PKE},\mathcal{A}}^{\mathsf{CPA}\text{-}b} \Rightarrow 1\right] := \Pr\left[\begin{array}{c} (pk, sk) \leftarrow \mathsf{Gen}(\mathsf{pp}_{\mathsf{PKE}}); (m_0, m_1, st) \leftarrow \mathcal{A}(pk) \\ c_b \leftarrow \mathsf{Enc}(sk, m_b); b' \leftarrow \mathcal{A}(st, pk, c_b) \end{array} : b' = 1\right].$$

The IND-CPA security of PKE requires $\mathsf{Adv}_{\mathsf{PKE}}^{\mathsf{CPA}}(\mathcal{A}) = \mathsf{negl}(\lambda)$ for all PPT $\mathcal{A}$.

2.2   Tagged Key Encapsulation Mechanism

Definition 4 (TKEM). *A tagged key encapsulation mechanism (TKEM) scheme* $\mathsf{TKEM} = (\mathsf{TKEM.Setup}, \mathsf{TKEM.Gen}, \mathsf{TKEM.Encap}, \mathsf{TKEM.Decap})$ *consists of four algorithms.*

- $\mathsf{TKEM.Setup}$. *The setup algorithm outputs public parameters* $\mathsf{pp}_{\mathsf{TKEM}}$, *which determine an encapsulation key space $\mathcal{K}$, public key space $\mathcal{PK}$, secret key space $\mathcal{SK}$, tag space $\mathcal{T}$ and a ciphertext space $\mathcal{CT}$.*
- $\mathsf{TKEM.Gen}(\mathsf{pp}_{\mathsf{TKEM}})$. *Taking $\mathsf{pp}_{\mathsf{TKEM}}$ as input, the key generation algorithm outputs a pair of public key and secret key $(pk, sk) \in \mathcal{PK} \times \mathcal{SK}$.*
- $\mathsf{TKEM.Encap}(pk, \tau)$. *Taking pk and a tag τ as input, the encapsulation algorithm outputs a pair of ciphertext $c \in \mathcal{CT}$ and encapsulated key $K \in \mathcal{K}$.*
- $\mathsf{TKEM.Decap}(sk, c, \tau)$. *Taking as input sk and c and a tag τ, the deterministic decapsulation algorithm outputs $K \in \mathcal{K} \cup \{\bot\}$.*

The $(1 - \delta)$-correctness of TKEM requires that for all tag $\tau \in \mathcal{T}$,

$$\Pr\left[\begin{array}{c} (pk, sk) \leftarrow \mathsf{TKEM.Gen}(\mathsf{pp}_{\mathsf{KEM}}) \\ (c, K) \leftarrow \mathsf{TKEM.Encap}(pk, \tau) \end{array} : \mathsf{TKEM.Decap}(sk, c, \tau) \neq K\right] \leq \delta.$$

We recall the IND-CCA security of TKEM.

$$
\begin{array}{|l|l|}
\hline
\begin{aligned}
&\mathsf{Exp}_{\mathsf{KEM},\mathcal{A}}^{\mathsf{CCA\text{-}b}}: \\
&(\tau^*, st) \leftarrow \mathcal{A};\ \mathsf{pp_{TKEM}} \leftarrow \mathsf{TKEM.Setup} \\
&(pk, sk) \leftarrow \mathsf{TKEM.Gen(pp_{TKEM})} \\
&(c^*, K_0^*) \leftarrow \mathsf{TKEM.Encap}(pk, \tau^*) \\
&K_1^* \leftarrow \mathcal{K};\ b' \leftarrow \mathcal{A}^{\mathcal{O}_{\mathrm{DEC}}(\cdot,\cdot)}(st, pk, c^*, K_b^*) \\
&\text{Return } b'
\end{aligned}
&
\begin{aligned}
&\mathcal{O}_{\mathrm{DEC}}(c, \tau): \\
&\quad \text{If } (c, \tau) = (c^*, \tau^*): \text{Return } \bot \\
&\quad K \leftarrow \mathsf{TKEM.Decap}(sk, c, \tau) \\
&\quad \text{Return } K
\end{aligned}
\\
\hline
\end{array}
$$

Fig. 4. The IND-CCA security experiment $\mathsf{Exp}_{\mathsf{KEM},\mathcal{A}}^{\mathsf{CCA\text{-}b}}$ of Tagged-KEM.

Definition 5 (IND-CCA Security for TKEM[1]). *To a tag key encapsulation mechanism* TKEM, *the advantage functions of an adversary $\mathcal{A}$ is defined by* $\mathsf{Adv}_{\mathsf{TKEM}}^{\mathsf{CCA}}(\mathcal{A}) := \left| \Pr\left[\mathsf{Exp}_{\mathsf{TKEM},\mathcal{A}}^{\mathsf{CCA\text{-}0}} \Rightarrow 1\right] - \Pr\left[\mathsf{Exp}_{\mathsf{TKEM},\mathcal{A}}^{\mathsf{CCA\text{-}1}} \Rightarrow 1\right] \right|$, *where the experiments* $\mathsf{Exp}_{\mathsf{TKEM},\mathcal{A}}^{\mathsf{CCA\text{-}b}}$ *for $b \in \{0,1\}$ are defined in Fig. 4. The IND-CCA security of tag KEM requires* $\mathsf{Adv}_{\mathsf{TKEM}}^{\mathsf{CCA}}(\mathcal{A}) = \mathsf{negl}(\lambda)$ *for all PPT algorithm $\mathcal{A}$.*

When τ is null, TKEM becomes canonical KEM, and IND-CCA security can be similarly defined for KEM. Now we define the output pseudo-randomness of KEM w.r.t. its input randomness. Roughly speaking, output pseudo-randomness requires the encapsulation key K is indistinguishable from a random key even if $\mathcal{A}$ gets both pk and sk but has no information about ciphertext c . ·

Definition 6 (Output Pseudo-Randomness of KEM). *A key encapsulation mechanism* KEM $=$ (KEM.Setup, KEM.Gen, KEM.Encap, KEM.Decap) *has output pseudo-randomness if for any PPT adversary $\mathcal{A}$,* $\mathsf{Adv}_{\mathsf{KEM}}^{\mathsf{ps}}(\mathcal{A}) := \left| \Pr\left[\mathsf{Exp}_{\mathsf{KEM}}^{\mathsf{ps\text{-}0}} \Rightarrow 1\right] - \Pr\left[\mathsf{Exp}_{\mathsf{KEM}}^{\mathsf{ps\text{-}1}} \Rightarrow 1\right] \right| = \mathsf{negl}(\lambda)$, *where*

$$
\Pr\left[\mathsf{Exp}_{\mathsf{KEM}}^{\mathsf{ps\text{-}b}} \Rightarrow 1\right] := \Pr\left[
\begin{array}{c}
\mathsf{pp_{KEM}} \leftarrow \mathsf{KEM.Setup} \\
(pk, sk) \leftarrow \mathsf{KEM.Gen(pp_{KEM})} \\
(c, K_0) \leftarrow \mathsf{KEM.Encap}(pk); K_1 \leftarrow_\$ \mathcal{K} \\
b' \leftarrow \mathcal{A}(pk, sk, K_b)
\end{array}
: b' = 1
\right].
$$

3 Two-Message AKE and Its IND-AA Security

A two-message AKE (see Fig. 1) is characterized by four algorithms. Each party, say P_i, will invoke the key generation algorithm $\mathsf{Gen}(i)$ to generate its own public/secret key pair (pk_i, sk_i). An initiator P_i then invokes the initialization algorithm $\mathsf{Init}(sk_i, pk_j)$ to generate the first round-message M_1 and its state st. P_i sends M_1 to its responder P_j and stores the state st locally. Upon receiving M_1, P_j invokes the responder-derivatation algorithm $\mathsf{Der_{resp}}(sk_j, pk_i, M_1)$ to generate the second round-message M_2 and its session key K_j. P_j sends M_2 to P_i. Upon receiving M_2, P_i invokes the initiator-derivatation algorithm $\mathsf{Der_{init}}(sk_i, pk_j, M_2, st)$ to derive its session key K_i. The formal definition for two-message AKE is given below.

Definition 7 (Two-Message AKE). *A two-message AKE scheme* AKE $=$ (Gen, Init, $\mathsf{Der_{init}}$, $\mathsf{Der_{resp}}$) *consists of the following four algorithms.*

- Gen(i). *Taking a party identity i as input, the key generation algorithm outputs a key pair (pk_i, sk_i).*
- Init(sk_i, pk_j). *Taking as input a secret key sk_i and a public key pk_j, the initialisation algorithm outputs a message M_1 and a state st.*
- Der$_{\mathsf{resp}}$(sk_j, pk_i, M_1). *Taking as input a secret key sk_j, a public key pk_i and a message M_1, the responder derivation algorithm outputs a message M_2 and a session key K_j.*
- Der$_{\mathsf{init}}$(sk_i, pk_j, M_2, st). *Taking as input a secret key sk_i, a public key pk_j, a message M_2 and a state st, the initiator derivation algorithm outputs a session key K_i.*

$(1 - \delta)$-*Correctness of AKE.* For any distinct and honest parties P_i and P_j with $(pk_i, sk_i) \leftarrow$ Gen(i) and $(pk_j, sk_j) \leftarrow$ Gen(j), after their protocol execution of $(M_1, st) \leftarrow$ Init(sk_i, pk_j), $(M_2, K_j) \leftarrow$ Der$_{\mathsf{resp}}$(sk_j, pk_i, M_1) and $K_i \leftarrow$ Der$_{\mathsf{init}}$(sk_i, pk_j, M_2, st), the probability that $K_i = K_j \neq \emptyset$ is at least $1 - \delta$.

Remark 1. Note that in a two-message AKE, the initiator P_i has to invoke two algorithms. Therefore, P_i has to transmit a round state st_i from Init to Der$_{\mathsf{init}}$. However, responder P_j does not have to store any (secret) state, since P_j only invokes one algorithm for session key.

We will use the IND-AA security model proposed in [10]. This model formalizes the adversary's passive attack, active attack, state reveals of session instances. Suppose there are at most μ users $P_1, P_2, \ldots, P_\mu$, and each user will involve at most ℓ sessions. The sessions run the protocol algorithms with access to the party's long-term key material, and also have their own local variables. The local variables of each session, indexed by the integer sID, are shown below.

holder[sID] : the party running the session sID; peer[sID] : the intended communication peer of holder[sID]; sent[sID] : the message sent by the session sID; recv[sID] : the message received by the session sID; role[sID] $\in$ {initiator, responder} : it indicates holder plays the role of initiator or responder; st[sID] : round state in sID. If role[sID] $=$ initiator, then st is output by Init, otherwise, $st = \perp$; sKey[sID] : the session key of sID.

Definition 8 (Matching Sessions). *We say two sessions* sID *and* sID$'$ *are matching if the following requirements hold: 1.* (holder[sID], peer[sID]) $=$ (peer[sID$'$], holder[sID$'$])*; 2.* (sent[sID], recv[sID]) $=$ (recv[sID$'$], sent[sID$'$])*; 3.* role[sID] $\neq$ role[sID$'$]*.*

Let $\mathfrak{M}$(sID) denote the set of session identities which match sID.

Definition 9 (Partner Sessions). *We say two sessions* sID *and* sID$'$ *are partner if the following requirements hold: 1.* (holder[sID], peer[sID]) $=$ (peer[sID$'$], holder[sID$'$])*; 2.* role[sID] $\neq$ role[sID$'$]*. Let* $\mathfrak{P}$(sID) *denote the set of session identities which are partnered to* sID*.*

Next, we formalize the oracles that deal with $\mathcal{A}$'s queries as follows.

EST(i,j): The query means that $\mathcal{A}$ wants to establish a new session sID for holder i and its peer j. Upon such a query, oracle EST assigns a new session identity sID $:= cnt$ and sets holder[sID] $:= i$ and peer[sID] $:= j$ for $\mathcal{A}$.

INIT(sID): The query means that $\mathcal{A}$ wants to initiate session sID. Then the oracle generates the first round message $M \leftarrow \mathsf{Init}(sk_i, pk_j)$ and replies M to $\mathcal{A}$. Here sk_i is the secret key of holder[sID] and pk_j is the public key of peer[sID].

DER$_{\mathsf{resp}}$(sID, M): This query means that $\mathcal{A}$ asks session sID to respond the first-round message M (so role[sID] = responder). The oracle will invoke $M' \leftarrow \mathsf{Der_{resp}}(sk_j, pk_i, M)$ and return M' as the second round message to $\mathcal{A}$. Here sk_j is the secret key of holder[sID] and pk_i is the public key of peer[sID].

DER$_{\mathsf{init}}$(sID, M'): This query means that $\mathcal{A}$ asks session sID to respond the second-round message M' (so role[sID] = initiator). The oracle will invoke $K_i \leftarrow \mathsf{Der_{init}}(sk_i, pk_j, M, st[\text{sID}])$ to generate the session key sKey[sID] $:= K_i$. Here sk_i is the secret key of holder[sID] and pk_j is the public key of peer[sID].

REVEAL(sID): It means that $\mathcal{A}$ reveals the session key of session sID. The oracle will return sKey[sID] to $\mathcal{A}$.

REV-STATE(sID): It means that $\mathcal{A}$ reveals the state of session sID. The oracle will return $st[\text{sID}]$ to $\mathcal{A}$

CORRUPT(i): It means that $\mathcal{A}$ reveals the long-term key of party P_i. The oracle will return sk_i to $\mathcal{A}$.

TEST(sID): It means that $\mathcal{A}$ chooses sID as the target session and the session key of sID for challenge (test). The oracle will set $K_0 :=$ sKey[sID], sample $K_1 \leftarrow_\$ \mathcal{K}$, and return K_b to $\mathcal{A}$.

Trivial(sID*): It identifies whether $\mathcal{A}$'s behavior leads to a trivial attack for the target (test) session sID*. The oracle will first create a list of all matching sessions for sID*. The list is denoted by $\mathfrak{M}(\text{sID}^*)$. Then the oracle outputs 1 in case of the following trivial attacks.
  - session sID* is tested but sKey[sID*] is revealed to $\mathcal{A}$.
  - session sID* is tested and both long-term key sk_i of holder[sID*] and secret state $st[\text{sID}^*]$ are revealed to $\mathcal{A}$.
  - session sID* is tested, there is only one matching session ptr (i.e., $\mathfrak{M}(\text{sID}^*) = \{ptr\}$), and the session key sKey[ptr] of matching session ptr is revealed.
  - session sID* is tested, there is only one matching session ptr (i.e., $\mathfrak{M}(\text{sID}^*) = \{ptr\}$), and both long-term key sk_j of peer[sID] = holder[ptr] and secret state $st[ptr]$ of session ptr are revealed to $\mathcal{A}$.
  - session sID* is tested, there is no matching session with sID* (i.e., $\mathfrak{M}(\text{sID}^*) = \emptyset$), and the long-term key sk_j of $j :=$ peer[sID*] is revealed to $\mathcal{A}$.

Recall that μ is the number of users and ℓ is the maximum number of sessions per user. The security experiment $\mathsf{Exp}_{\mathsf{AKE},\mu,\ell,\mathcal{A}}^{\mathsf{IND\text{-}AA\text{-}}b}$ with $b \in \{0,1\}$ is played between challenger $\mathcal{C}$ and adversary $\mathcal{A}$.

1. For each party P_i, $\mathcal{C}$ runs $\mathsf{Gen}(i)$ to get the long-term key pair (pk_i, sk_i). Then $\mathcal{C}$ provides $\mathcal{A}$ with the list of public keys $(pk_1, \ldots, pk_\mu)$.

2. $\mathcal{A}$ has access to oracles EST, INIT, $\mathrm{DER_{resp}}$, $\mathrm{DER_{init}}$, REVEAL, REV-STATE, CORRUPT, and TEST. Note that $\mathcal{A}$ can issue only one query to TEST. The oracles will reply the corresponding answers to $\mathcal{A}$.

3. At the end of the experiment, $\mathcal{A}$ terminates with an output b'.

4. If $\mathsf{Trivial}(\mathsf{sID}^*) = \mathbf{true}$, the experiment returns 0. Otherwise, return b'.

Details of experiment $\mathsf{Exp}_{\mathsf{AKE},\mu,\ell,\mathcal{A}}^{\mathsf{IND\text{-}AA}\text{-}b}$ are given in Fig. 9 in Appendix C.

Definition 10 (IND-AA Security of AKE). *In* $\mathsf{Exp}_{\mathsf{AKE},\mu,\ell,\mathcal{A}}^{\mathsf{IND\text{-}AA}\text{-}b}$ *with* $b \in \{0,1\}$, *the IND-AA advantage function of an adversary* $\mathcal{A}$ *against AKE is defined as*

$$\mathsf{Adv}_{\mathsf{AKE},\mu,\ell,\mathcal{A}}^{\mathsf{IND\text{-}AA}} := \left| \Pr\left[\mathsf{Exp}_{\mathsf{AKE},\mu,\ell,\mathcal{A}}^{\mathsf{IND\text{-}AA}\text{-}0} \Rightarrow 1\right] - \Pr\left[\mathsf{Exp}_{\mathsf{AKE},\mu,\ell,\mathcal{A}}^{\mathsf{IND\text{-}AA}\text{-}1} \Rightarrow 1\right] \right|.$$

The IND-AA Security of AKE asks $\mathsf{Adv}_{\mathsf{AKE},\mu,\ell,\mathcal{A}}^{\mathsf{IND\text{-}AA}} \leq \mathsf{negl}(\lambda)$ *for all PPT* $\mathcal{A}$.

4   Generic Construction of Two-Message AKE and Its Security Proof

$\mathsf{Init}(sk_i, pk_j)$:	$\mathsf{Der_{resp}}(sk_j, pk_i, M_1)$:	$\mathsf{Der_{init}}(sk_i, pk_j, M_2, st)$:
$(c_1, seed_i) \leftarrow \mathsf{TKEM.Encap}(pk_j, i)$	Parse $M_1 = (\hat{pk}, c_1)$	Parse $M_2 = (\bar{c}, C)$
$m_{11}\|m_{12} \leftarrow \mathsf{PRG}(seed_i)$	If $\mathsf{TKEM.Decap}(sk_j, c_1, i) = \bot$:	Parse $st = (m_{11}, \hat{sk}, \sigma, M_1 = (\hat{pk}, c_1))$
$\sigma := \mathsf{H}(m_{12})$	Return $\bot$	If $\mathsf{PKE.Dec}(\hat{sk}, \bar{c}) = \bot$:
$(\hat{pk}, \hat{sk}) \leftarrow \mathsf{PKE.Gen}$	$seed'_i \leftarrow \mathsf{TKEM.Decap}(sk_j, c_1, i)$	Return $\bot$
$M_1 := (\hat{pk}, c_1)$	$m'_{11}\|m'_{12} \leftarrow \mathsf{PRG}(seed'_i)$	$c'_2 \leftarrow \mathsf{PKE.Dec}(\hat{sk}, \bar{c})$
$st := (m_{11}, \hat{sk}, \sigma, M_1)$	$(c_2, seed_j) \leftarrow \mathsf{KEM.Encap}(pk_i)$	If $\mathsf{KEM.Decap}(sk_i, c'_2) = \bot$:
Return (M_1, st)	$m_{21}\|m_{22} \leftarrow \mathsf{PRG}(seed_j)$	Return $\bot$
	$\bar{c} \leftarrow \mathsf{PKE.Enc}(\hat{pk}, c_2)$	$seed'_j \leftarrow \mathsf{KEM.Decap}(sk_i, c'_2)$
	$C := m'_{12} \oplus m_{22}$	$m'_{21}\|m'_{22} \leftarrow \mathsf{PRG}(seed'_j)$
	$M_2 := (\bar{c}, C)$	If $\mathsf{H}(C \oplus m'_{22}) \neq \sigma$:
	$K := \mathsf{PRF}(m'_{11}, M_1\|M_2) \oplus \mathsf{PRF}(m_{21}, M_1\|M_2)$	Return $\bot$
	Return (M_2, K)	$K := \mathsf{PRF}(m_{11}, M_1\|M_2) \oplus \mathsf{PRF}(m'_{21}, M_1\|M_2)$
		Return K

Fig. 5. Generic construction of two-message AKE.

We propose a generic construction of $\mathsf{AKE} = (\mathsf{Gen}, \mathsf{Init}, \mathsf{Der_{init}}, \mathsf{Der_{resp}})$ with session key space $\mathcal{K}$ from the following building blocks.

- A tagged key encapsulation mechanism scheme $\mathsf{TKEM} = (\mathsf{TKEM.Gen}, \mathsf{TKEM.Encap}, \mathsf{TKEM.Decap})$, where the encapsulation key space is $\mathcal{K}$.
- A key encapsulation mechanism scheme $\mathsf{KEM} = (\mathsf{KEM.Gen}, \mathsf{KEM.Encap}, \mathsf{KEM.Decap})$ with encapsulation key space is $\mathcal{K}$ and ciphertext space $\mathcal{E}$.
- A public key encryption scheme $\mathsf{PKE} = (\mathsf{PKE.Gen}, \mathsf{PKE.Enc}, \mathsf{PKE.Dec})$ with message space $\mathcal{E}$.
- A pseudo-random generator $\mathsf{PRG} : \mathcal{K} \rightarrow \mathcal{K} \times \mathcal{K}$.
- A pseudo-random function $\mathsf{PRF} : \mathcal{K} \times \{0,1\}^* \rightarrow \mathcal{K}$.
- A target collision resistant hash function $\mathsf{H} : \mathcal{K} \rightarrow \Sigma$, which is randomly chosen from hash family $\mathcal{H}$. Suppose $\mathcal{K} = \Sigma \times \Sigma$.

Our generic construction is given in Fig. 5.

Correctness. Suppose the KEM, PKE, TKEM are all $(1-\delta)$-correct, then the AKE construction is $(1-3\delta)$-correct.

Next we consider the security of our generic AKE construction.

Theorem 1 (Key Indistinguishablity of AKE). *Suppose that* KEM, TKEM, PKE *are* $(1-\delta)$*-correct,* TKEM *is an IND-CCA tagged-KEM scheme,* KEM *is an IND-CCA secure KEM scheme with output pseudo-randomness,* PKE *is an IND-CPA secure PKE scheme satisfying* γ*-spreadness and* γ*-key diverse,* H *is a target collision·resistant hash function (and also a one way function),* PRG *is a pseudo-random generator, and* PRF *is a pseudo-random function. Then for any PPT adversary* $\mathcal{A}$ *against AKE that establishes sessions among at most* μ *users and at most* ℓ *sessions per user, we have*

$$
\begin{aligned}
\mathsf{Adv}^{\mathsf{IND\text{-}AA}}_{\mathsf{AKE},\mu,\ell,\mathcal{A}} = {} & 2\mu^2\ell \cdot \Big((\ell+2) \cdot \mathsf{Adv}^{\mathsf{CCA}}_{\mathsf{KEM}}(\mathcal{B}_{\mathsf{KEM}}) + (\ell+1) \cdot \mathsf{Adv}^{\mathsf{CCA}}_{\mathsf{TKEM}}(\mathcal{B}_{\mathsf{TKEM}}) + \mathsf{Adv}^{\mathsf{tcr}}_{\mathsf{H}}(\mathcal{B}_{\mathsf{H}}) \\
& + \ell \cdot \mathsf{Adv}^{\mathsf{ps}}_{\mathsf{KEM}}(\mathcal{B}_{\mathsf{KEM}}) + \mathsf{Adv}^{\mathsf{owf}}_{\mathsf{H}}(\mathcal{B}_{\mathsf{H}}) + (3\ell+2) \cdot \mathsf{Adv}^{\mathsf{ps}}_{\mathsf{PRF}}(\mathcal{B}_{\mathsf{PRF}}) \\
& + \ell \cdot \mathsf{Adv}^{\mathsf{CPA}}_{\mathsf{PKE}}(\mathcal{B}_{\mathsf{PKE}}) + (3\ell+3) \cdot \mathsf{Adv}^{\mathsf{ps}}_{\mathsf{PRG}}(\mathcal{B}_{\mathsf{PRG}}) + (4\ell^2+\ell+5) \cdot \delta + 2^{-\gamma+1} \Big).
\end{aligned}
$$

Proof. The formal proof of Theorem 1 is given in the full version [15]. Here we sketch the proof. We first guess sID^* will be the test session, which holds with probability $\frac{1}{\mu^2\ell}$. Let $\mathfrak{M}(\mathsf{sID}^*)$ be the set of all session identities matching with sID^* and $(i^*,j^*) := (\mathsf{holder}[\mathsf{sID}^*],\mathsf{peer}[\mathsf{sID}^*])$. Then we can divide the proof into the following cases:

Case 1: $\mathfrak{M}(\mathsf{sID}^*) = \emptyset \wedge \mathsf{role}[\mathsf{sID}^*] = \mathsf{initiator}$. Since the test session sID^* has no partner session in this case, user j^* cannot be corrupted due to the requirement of trivial attack. Besides, the adversary cannot both corrupt user i^* and reveal the secret state of test session sID^*. Therefore, Case 1 can be further divided into two subcases.

Case 1.1: $\neg crp[i^*] \wedge \neg crp[j^*]$. In Case 1.1, the long-term keys of both initiator and responder are not corrupted. Since user j^* is not corrupted, the ciphertext c_1 in the first message $M_1 = (\tilde{pk}, c_1)$ leaks no information of m_{11} and m_{12} to the adversary by CCA security of KEM and pseudo-randomness of PRG. Due to user i^* is not corrupted. the ciphertext c_2 contained in $\tilde{c}$ of the second message $M_2 = (\tilde{c}, C)$ leaks no information of m_{21} and m_{22} to the adversary by CCA security of TKEM and pseudo-randomness of PRG. Then by one-time pad encryption, C leaks no information of m_{12}. Only $\sigma = \mathsf{H}(m_{12})$ contained in the secret state will leak the information of m_{12}. However, the adversary cannot pass the verification of initiator sID^* using a different $m'_{12} \neq m_{12}$ because hash function H is collision resistant. Thanks to the one-wayness of hash function H, the adversary cannot recover m_{12} either. So if the adversary passes the verification of initiator sID^*, then there must exist some session sID' shares the same m_{21} and m_{22} with sID^*. Since the adversary has no information of m_{21} and m_{22}, by the pseudo-randomness of PRF, session key $\mathsf{sKey}[\mathsf{sID}^*]$ is uniform to the adversary.

Case 1.2: $\neg stRev[\mathsf{sID}^*] \wedge \neg crp[j^*]$. In Case 1.2, both the secret state of initiator and the long-term key of responder are not corrupted. Note that the second message M_2 is independent of m_{11} generated by sID^*. By CCA security of KEM and pseudo-randomness of PRG, c_1 leaks no information about m_{11}. Since the adversary cannot reveal the secret state of sID^*, m_{11} is uniformly random in the view of adversary. Due to the pseudo-randomness of PRF, the session key $sKey[sID^*]$ is uniform to the adversary.

Case 2: $\mathfrak{M}(sID^*) = \emptyset \wedge role[sID^*] = $ responder. Since the test session sID^* has no partner session in this case, user j^* (initiator) cannot be corrupted due to the requirement of trivial attack. By the CCA security of KEM and pseudo-randomness of PRG, the message m_{21} is uniform in the view of adversary and hence the session key $sKey[sID^*]$ is uniform to the adversary from the pseudo-randomness of PRF.

Case 3: $\mathfrak{M} \neq \emptyset$. Due to the γ-diversity and γ-spreadness, we can proof $|\mathfrak{M}| = 1$ with overwhelming probability. Let $\mathfrak{M} = \{sID'\}$ be the partner session with sID^*. We can guess sID' with security loss ℓ. Let (sID_I, sID_R) define the initiator session and responder session in sID^* and sID' respectively. Define $(I, R) = (holder[sID_I], peer[sID_R])$. To avoid trivial attacks, the long-term key of initiator party I and the secret state of I cannot be corrupted simultaneously. Therefore, Case 3 can be further divided into two subcases.

Case 3.1: $\neg crp[I]$. In Case 3.1, the initiator party I remains uncorrupted, and there are no active attacks on sID^*. As a result, the message m_{21} is uniformly distributed due to the CCA security of KEM and the pseudo-randomness of PRG. This uniform distribution of m_{21} and PRF further ensure the pseudo-randomness of the session key $sKey[sID^*]$.

Case 3.2: $\neg stRev[sID_I]$. In Case 3.2, the secret state of session sID^* is never corrupted, and there are no active attacks on sID^*. Therefore, the secret key $\tilde{sk}$ stored in the state of sID^* is not corrupted and hence the ciphertext $\tilde{c}$ hides the information of c_2 by the CPA security of PKE. Without the information of ciphertext c_2, the message m_{21} is still uniform even if the adversary has the long-term key of party I due to the output pseudo-randomness of KEM and pseudo-randomness of PRG. Finally, the uniform distribution of m_{21} and PRF further guarantees the pseudo-randomness of the session key $sKey[sID^*]$. $\square$

Note that if the building block PKE is replaced by an CCA-secure one, it is possible for us to achieve unidirectional explicit authentication, i.e., the initiator can authenticate the responder. The reason is as follows. For the second message $M_2 = (\tilde{c}, C)$), if $\tilde{c}$ is an invalid ciphertext, it either results in abort or leads to a different message m'_{22}, where $m'_{22} \leftarrow Dec(sk_i, Dec(\tilde{sk}, \tilde{c}))$. Consequently, $H(m'_{22} \oplus C) \neq \sigma$ unless the one-wayness or TCR property of H is broken.

5 Instantiations of Two-Message AKE

In this section, we will present instantiations of AKE in the standard model and the quantum random oracle model (QROM) respectively. To this end, we consider instantiations of the underlying building blocks of AKE.

In [1], Abe et al. presented a simple tranformation from any IND-CCA secure PKE with proper plaintext ciphertext to an IND-CCA secure TKEM. So we will seek IND-CCA secure PKE scheme instead of IND-CCA secure TKEM.

5.1   Instantiation of AKE in the Standard Model

Here we show the instantiation of AKE from the LWE assumption.

- We take Peikeit's LWE-based PKE [17] as the underlying CCA secure PKE.
- We take Regev's LWE-based PKE [18] as the underlying CPA secure PKE.
- We take the LWE-based BPR-PRF [2] as the underlying PRF (PRG as well).
- We take the LMPR-Hash [16] as the underlying TCR hash function. Then the TCR security is based on the Short-Interger-Solution (SIS) assumption.

Note that when PKE is used as KEM, the plaintext is uniformly chosen as the encapsulation key and independent of the secret key and the public key. Therefore, without the knowledge of ciphertext, the plaintext is uniform to the adversary even if the adversary obtains the public/secret key pair. Consequently, the output pseudo-randomness of KEM holds naturally in this case.

Since the LWE assumption implies the SIS assumption, we immediately obtain an LWE-based two-message AKE in the standard model.

In fact, there are many other choices for the building blocks, so our generic construction actually leads to many two-message AKE schemes from standard assumptions in the standard model.

5.2   AKE from CPA-Secure PKE in the QROM

5.2.1   PRF and TCR

We simply take hash function as PRF and TCR.

- We take a hash function $H_1 : \mathcal{K} \times \mathcal{X} \to \mathcal{K}$ as a PRF.
- We take a hash function $H_2 : \mathcal{K} \to \Sigma$, where $\mathcal{K} = \Sigma \times \Sigma$ as a TCR.

The securities of PRF and TCR have already proved in QROM, as shown in Lemma 1 and Lemma 2.

Lemma 1 (PRF from QROM, Corollary 1 from [4]). *Let $H : \mathcal{K} \times \mathcal{X} \to \mathcal{Y}$ be a quantum-accessible random oracle. This function $\mathsf{PRF}(k, x) := H(k, x)$ may be used as a quantum-accessible PRF with a key $k \leftarrow_\$ \mathcal{K}$. For any PRF-adversary $\mathcal{A}$ making at most q queries to H and any number of queries to F_k, its advantage satisfies $\mathsf{Adv}_{\mathsf{PRF}}^{\mathsf{ps}}(\mathcal{A}) \leq 2q/\sqrt{|\mathcal{K}|}$.*

Lemma 2 (TCR Hash from QROM, Theorem 3.1 from [21]). *There is a universal constant α such that the following holds. Let $H : \mathcal{K} \to \Sigma$ be a quantum-accessible random oracle. Then any algorithm making q quantum queries to H outputs a collision for H with probability at most $\alpha(q + 1)^3/|\Sigma|$.*

5.2.2   KEM and TKEM from FO Transformation in QROM

Lately, Don et al. [6] proved FO-transform with explicit rejection can be applied in QROM. Hence, an IND-CCA secure KEM can be constructed from IND-CPA secure PKE, via FO-transform. The constructed scheme $\mathsf{KEM_{FO}}$ is shown in Fig. 6 and its security is given in Lemma 3.

Encap(pk, τ)	Decap(sk, c, τ) :
$m \leftarrow_s \mathcal{M}$	$m' := \mathsf{Dec}(sk, c)$
$c := \mathsf{Enc}(pk, m; G(m \mid \tau))$	If $m' = \bot$ or $\mathsf{Enc}(pk, m'; G(m' \mid \tau)) \neq c$:
$K := H(m \mid \tau)$	Return $\bot$
Return (c, K)	Else return $K := H(m' \mid \tau)$

Fig. 6. KEM$_{\mathsf{FO}}$ from FO transformation (without gray box) and TKEM$_{\mathsf{FO}}$ from FO transformation (with gray box).

Lemma 3 (IND-CCA Security of KEM$_{\mathsf{FO}}$, Theorem 6.1 from [6]). *If* PKE *is a* $(1-\delta)$*-correct IND-CPA secure public key encryption scheme satisfying* γ*-spreadness and* G,H *are quantum-accessible random oracles, then the* KEM$_{\mathsf{FO}}$ *in Fig. 6 is IND-CCA secure.*

Lemma 1 implies output pseudo-randomness of KEM$_{\mathsf{FO}}$ as shown below.

Lemma 4 (Output Pseudo-Randomness of KEM$_{\mathsf{FO}}$). *For any adversary* $\mathcal{A}$ *against output pseudo-randomness of* KEM$_{\mathsf{FO}}$*, issuing at most* q *(quantum) queries to* H*, its advantage satisfies* $\mathsf{Adv}^{\mathsf{ps}}_{\mathsf{KEM}}(\mathcal{A}) \leq 2q/\sqrt{|\mathcal{M}|}$.

Proof. The output pseudo-randomness of KEM$_{\mathsf{FO}}$ requires the two distributions $\{ H(m) \mid m \leftarrow_s \mathcal{M} \}$ and $\{ K \mid K \leftarrow_s \mathcal{K} \}$ are computational indistinguishable even if $\mathcal{A}$ makes at most q (quantum) queries to H. Lemma 1 already shows that H can be used as a PRF. Consequently, $H(m)$ is pseudo-random to $\mathcal{A}$ since m is randomly chosen. $\qquad\square$

Now we extend FO-transform to Tagged KEM in QROM. The construction of Tagged KEM is almost the same as KEM$_{\mathsf{FO}}$. We just attach the tag τ to message m (m') as the input of G and H. Assume PKE is IND-CPA secure with γ-spreadness. The construction of TKEM$_{\mathsf{FO}}$ from PKE is shown in Fig. 6.

In Lemma 5, we show that the IND-CCA security of TKEM$_{\mathsf{FO}}$ can be reduced to IND-CPA security of PKE in QROM.

Lemma 5 (IND-CCA security of TKEM$_{\mathsf{FO}}$). *If* PKE *is a* $(1-\delta)$*-correct IND-CPA secure public key encryption scheme satisfying* γ*-spreadness and* G,H *are quantum-accessible random oracles, then* TKEM$_{\mathsf{FO}}$ *in Fig. 6 is IND-CCA secure.*

The intuition for the proof of Lemma 5 is as follows. Suppose that $G : \mathcal{M} \times \mathcal{T} \to \mathcal{K}$ is a quantum-accessible random oracle, then for each $\tau \in \mathcal{T}$, $G_\tau : \mathcal{M} \to \mathcal{K}$ defined by $G_\tau(m) := G(m, \tau)$ is also a quantum-accessible random oracle. Hence, the proof of Lemma 5 almost verbatim follows that of Lemma 3. The formal proof of Lemma 5 is given in the full version [15]. We omit it here.

5.2.3 The Final AKE in QROM

Given the above instantiations of PRG, PRF, TCR Hash, and KEM and TKEM constructed from CPA-secure PKE in QROM, we immediately obtain a generic construction of AKE from CPA-secure PKE in QROM. For further optimization, we replace the computation of session key $K := \mathsf{PRF}(m_{11}, M_1|M_2) \oplus \mathsf{PRF}(m_{21}, M_1|M_2)$ with hash function $K := H(m_{11}|m_{21}|M_1|M_2)$. With the following quantum-accessible random oracles, we obtain the final construction of our AKE protocol in Fig. 8 (See Appendix B).

Acknowledgements. We would like to thank the reviewers for their valuable comments. This work was partially supported by National Natural Science Foundation of China under Grant 61925207, Guangdong Major Project of Basic and Applied Basic Research (2019B030302008), and the National Key R&D Program of China under Grant 2022YFB2701500.

Appendix

A   PRG, PRF, One-Wayness and TCR of Hash Function

Definition 11 (PRG). *Pseudo-Random Generator (PRG) is a polynomially computable deterministic function* $\mathsf{PRG} : \mathcal{K} \to \mathcal{K}'$, *where* $\mathcal{K}$ *is seed space and* $\mathcal{K}'$ *is output space with* $|\mathcal{K}| < |\mathcal{K}'|$. *The pseudo-randomness of* PRG *requires* $\mathsf{Adv}^{ps}_{\mathsf{PRG}}(\mathcal{A}) = \mathsf{negl}(\lambda)$ *for all PPT* $\mathcal{A}$, *where* $\mathsf{Adv}^{ps}_{\mathsf{PRG}}(\mathcal{A}) := |\Pr[s \leftarrow_\$ \mathcal{K}; y \leftarrow \mathsf{PRG}(x) : \mathcal{A}(y) \Rightarrow 1] - \Pr[y \leftarrow_\$ \mathcal{K}' : \mathcal{A}(y) \Rightarrow 1]|$.

Definition 12 (PRF). *Pseudo-Random Function (PRF) is a polynomially computable deterministic function* $\mathsf{PRF} : \mathcal{K} \times \mathcal{X} \to \mathcal{Y}$, *with key space* $\mathcal{K}$, *input space* $\mathcal{K}$ *and output space* $\mathcal{Y}$. *the advantage function of an adversary* $\mathcal{A}$ *is defined by*

$$\mathsf{Adv}^{ps}_{\mathsf{PRF}}(\mathcal{A}) := \left| \Pr\left[k \leftarrow_\$ \mathcal{K}, x^* \leftarrow \mathcal{A}^{\mathcal{O}_{\mathsf{PRF}}(\cdot)}; y \leftarrow \mathsf{PRF}(k, x^*) : \mathcal{A}^{\mathcal{O}_{\mathsf{PRF}}(\cdot)}(x^*, y) \Rightarrow 1 \right] \right.$$
$$\left. - \Pr\left[k \leftarrow_\$ \mathcal{K}, x^* \leftarrow \mathcal{A}^{\mathcal{O}_{\mathsf{PRF}}(\cdot)}; y \leftarrow_\$ \mathcal{Y} : \mathcal{A}^{\mathcal{O}_{\mathsf{PRF}}(\cdot)}(x^*, y) \Rightarrow 1 \right] \right|,$$

where $\mathcal{O}_{\mathsf{PRF}}(x)$ *returns* $\mathsf{PRF}(k, x)$ *and* x^* *is never queried to* $\mathcal{O}_{\mathsf{PRF}}(\cdot)$. *The pseudorandomness of* PRF *requires* $\mathsf{Adv}^{ps}_{\mathsf{PRF}}(\mathcal{A}) = \mathsf{negl}(\lambda)$ *for all PPT* $\mathcal{A}$.

Definition 13 (One-Wayness of Hash). *A hash family* $\mathcal{H} = \{\mathsf{H} : \{0,1\}^n \to \{0,1\}^{\ell(n)}\}$ *has One-Wayness if the advantage functions of an adversary* $\mathcal{A}$ *defined by* $\mathsf{Adv}^{owf}_{\mathsf{H}}(\mathcal{A}) := \Pr\left[\mathsf{Exp}^{owf}_{\mathsf{H}} \Rightarrow 1\right]$ *is negligible for all PPT* $\mathcal{A}$, *where the experiments* $\mathsf{Exp}^{owf}_{\mathsf{H}}$ *are defined in Fig. 7 (left).*

Definition 14 (TCR of Hash). *A hash family* $\mathcal{H} = \{\mathsf{H} : \{0,1\}^n \to \{0,1\}^{\ell(n)}\}$ *is Target Collision Resistant (TCR), if the advantage function of adversary* $\mathcal{A}$ *defined by* $\mathsf{Adv}^{tcr}_{\mathsf{H}}(\mathcal{A}) := \Pr\left[\mathsf{Exp}^{tcr}_{\mathsf{H}} \Rightarrow 1\right]$ *is negligible for all PPT* $\mathcal{A}$, *where the experiments* $\mathsf{Exp}^{tcr}_{\mathsf{H}}$ *are defined in Fig. 7 (right).*

When $n - \ell(n) \geq \lambda$, TCR property of $\mathcal{H}$ implies one-wayness.

$\mathsf{Exp}_H^{\mathsf{owf}}$:	$\mathsf{Exp}_H^{\mathsf{tcr}}$:
$H \leftarrow_\$ \mathcal{H};\ m \leftarrow \{0,1\}^n$	$H \leftarrow_\$ \mathcal{H};\ m \leftarrow \{0,1\}^n$
$\sigma \leftarrow H(m);\ m' \leftarrow \mathcal{A}(H,\sigma)$	$m' \leftarrow \mathcal{A}(H,m)$
If $H(m') = \sigma$: Return 1	If $m \neq m' \wedge H(m) = H(m')$: Return 1
Else: Return 0	Else: Return 0

Fig. 7. $\mathsf{Exp}_H^{\mathsf{owf}}$ (left) and $\mathsf{Exp}_H^{\mathsf{tcr}}$ (right) for $\mathcal{H}$.

B The Final AKE in QROM

- $G : \mathcal{K} \times \mathcal{T} \rightarrow \mathcal{R}$, which is used to generate randomness in PKE.
- $H : \mathcal{K} \rightarrow \Sigma$, which is used as a target collision resistant hash function. Here $\mathcal{K} = \Sigma \times \Sigma$,
- $H_1 : \mathcal{K} \times \mathcal{T} \rightarrow \mathcal{K}$, which is used to generate encapsulation key.
- $H_2 : \mathcal{K} \times \{0,1\} \rightarrow \mathcal{K}$, which is used as a pseudo-random generator.
- $H : \{0,1\}^* \rightarrow \mathcal{K}$, which is used to generate session key.

$\mathsf{Init}(sk_i, pk_j)$:	$\mathsf{Der}_{\mathsf{resp}}(sk_j, pk_i, M_1)$:	$\mathsf{Der}_{\mathsf{init}}(sk_i, pk_j, M_2, st)$:
$m_1 \leftarrow_\$ \mathcal{K}$	Parse $M_1 = (\bar{pk}, c_1)$	Parse $M_2 = (\bar{c}, C)$
$c_1 \leftarrow \mathsf{Enc}(pk_j, m_1; G(m_1\|i))$	$m_1' \leftarrow \mathsf{Dec}(sk_j, c_1)$	Parse $st = (m_{11}, \bar{sk}, \sigma, M_1 = (\bar{pk}, c_1))$
$seed_i \leftarrow H_1(m_1\|i)$	If $m_1' = \bot \vee \mathsf{Enc}(pk_j, m_1'; G(m_1'\|i)) \neq c_1$:	If $\mathsf{Dec}(\bar{sk}, \bar{c}) = \bot$:
$m_{11} \leftarrow H_2(seed_i\|0)$	Return $\bot$	Return $\bot$
$m_{12} \leftarrow H_2(seed_i\|1)$	else:	$c_2' \leftarrow \mathsf{Dec}(\bar{sk}, \bar{c})$
$\sigma := H(m_{12})$	$seed_i' := H_1(m_1'\|i)$	$m_2' \leftarrow \mathsf{Dec}(sk_i, c_2')$
$(\bar{pk}, \bar{sk}) \leftarrow \mathsf{PKE.Gen}$	$m_{11}' \leftarrow H_2(seed_i'\|0); m_{12}' \leftarrow H_2(seed_i'\|1)$	If $\mathsf{Enc}(pk_i, m_2'; G(m_2')) \neq c_2'$:
$M_1 := (\bar{pk}, c_1)$	$m_2 \leftarrow_\$ \mathcal{K}$	Return $\bot$
$st := (m_{11}, \bar{sk}, \sigma, M_1)$	$c_2 \leftarrow \mathsf{Enc}(pk_i, m_2; G(m_2))$	else:
Return (M_1, st)	$seed_j \leftarrow H_1(m_2)$	$seed_j' := H_1(m_2')$
	$m_{21} \leftarrow H_2(seed_j\|0); m_{22} \leftarrow H_2(seed_j\|1)$	$m_{21}' \leftarrow H_2(seed_j'\|0), m_{22}' \leftarrow H_2(seed_j'\|1)$
	$\bar{c} \leftarrow \mathsf{Enc}(\bar{pk}, c_2)$	If $H(C \oplus m_{22}') \neq \sigma$:
	$C := m_{12}' \oplus m_{22}$	Return $\bot$
	$M_2 := (\bar{c}, C)$	$K := H(m_{11}\|m_{21}'\|M_1\|M_2)$
	$K := H(m_{11}'\|m_{21}\|M_1\|M_2)$	Return K
	Return (M_2, K)	

Fig. 8. Generic construction of AKE from CPA-secure PKE in QROM.

C The Security Experiment $\mathsf{Exp}_{\mathsf{AKE}, \mu, \ell, \mathcal{A}}^{\mathsf{IND\text{-}AA}\text{-}b}$

The security experiment $\mathsf{Exp}_{\mathsf{AKE}, \mu, \ell, \mathcal{A}}^{\mathsf{IND\text{-}AA}\text{-}b}$ is shown in Fig. 9.

```
Exp_{AKE,μ,ℓ,A}^{IND-AA-b}                    // b ∈ {0,1}
cnt := 0                                      //session counter
sID* := 0                                     //test session's id
for i ∈ [μ]:
    (pk_i, sk_i) ← Gen(i)
    crp[i] := false           corruption variables
b' ← A^{O_AKE}(pk_1, ..., pk_μ)
If Trivial(sID*):
    Return 0
Return b'

EST((i,j) ∈ [μ]²):
cnt := cnt + 1
sID := cnt
holder[sID] := i
peer[sID] := j
stRev[sID] := false     //state reveal variables
rev[sID] := false       //session key reveal variables
Return sID

INIT(sID):
If holder[sID] = ⊥:
    Return ⊥              //session not established
If sent[sID] ≠ ⊥: Return ⊥        //no re-use
role[sID] := initiator
(i,j) := (holder[sID], peer[sID])
(M, st) := Init(sk_i, pk_j)
(sent[sID], st[sID]) := (M, st)
Return M

DER_resp(sID, M):
If holder[sID] = ⊥:
    Return ⊥
If sent[sID] ≠ ⊥:
    Return ⊥                      //no re-use
If role[sID] = initiator: Return ⊥
role[sID] := responder
(j,i) := (holder[sID], peer[sID])
(M', K') ← Der_resp(sk_j, pk_i, M)
sKey[sID] := K'
(recv[sID], sent[sID]) := (M, M')
Return M'

DER_init(sID, M):
If holder[sID] = ⊥ ∨ st[sID] = ⊥:
    Return ⊥
If sKey[sID] ≠ ⊥: Return ⊥        //no re-use


(i,j) := (holder[sID], peer[sID])
sKey[sID] := Der_init(sk_i, pk_j, M, st[sID])
recv[sID] := M
Return ∅

REVEAL(sID):
If sKey[sID] = ⊥: Return ⊥
rev[sID] := true
Return sKey[sID]

REV-STATE(sID):
If st[sID] = ⊥: Return ⊥
stRev[sID] := true
Return st[sID]

CORRUPT(i ∈ [μ]):
crp[i] := true
Return sk_i

TEST(sID):                              //only one query
sID* := sID
If sKey[sID*] = ⊥:
    Return ⊥
K_0* := sKey[sID*]
K_1* ← K
Return K_b*

Trivial(sID*):
(i,j) := (holder[sID*], peer[sID*])
If rev[sID*] = true: Return true
If crp[i] = true ∧ stRev[sID*] = true:
    Return true
M(sID*) := ∅;
For 1 ≤ ptr ≤ cnt:
    If (sent[ptr], recv[ptr]) = (recv[sID*], sent[sID*])
        ∧(holder[ptr], peer[ptr]) = (j,i) ∧ role[sID*] ≠ role[ptr]:
        M(sID*) := M(sID*) ∪ {ptr}        //session matches
If |M(sID*)| = 0:                              // active attack
    If crp[j] = true: Return true
    Else: Return false
If |M(sID*)| > 1:                     //multiple matching sessions
    Return false            //This is not a trivial attack.
If |M(sID*)| = 1:
    Let M(sID*) = {ptr}
    If rev[ptr] = true: Return true
    If crp[j] = true ∧ stRev[ptr] = true: Return true
    Return false
```

Fig. 9. The security experiments $\mathsf{Exp}_{AKE,\mu,\ell,\mathcal{A}}^{IND\text{-}AA\text{-}b}$ where $b \in \{0,1\}$, where $\mathcal{O}_{AKE} :=$ {EST, INIT, DER$_{resp}$, DER$_{init}$, REVEAL, REV-STATE, CORRUPT, TEST}.

References

1. Abe, M., Gennaro, R., Kurosawa, K.: Tag-KEM/DEM: a new framework for hybrid encryption. J. Cryptol. **21**(1), 97–130 (2008). https://doi.org/10.1007/s00145-007-9010-x
2. Banerjee, A., Peikert, C., Rosen, A.: Pseudorandom functions and lattices. In: Pointcheval, D., Johansson, T. (eds.) EUROCRYPT 2012. LNCS, vol. 7237, pp. 719–737. Springer, Heidelberg (2012). https://doi.org/10.1007/978-3-642-29011-4_42

3. Bellare, M., Rogaway, P.: Entity authentication and key distribution. In: Stinson, D.R. (ed.) CRYPTO 1993. LNCS, vol. 773, pp. 232–249. Springer, Heidelberg (1994). https://doi.org/10.1007/3-540-48329-2_21
4. Bindel, N., Hamburg, M., Hövelmanns, K., Hülsing, A., Persichetti, E.: Tighter proofs of CCA security in the quantum random oracle model. In: Hofheinz, D., Rosen, A. (eds.) TCC 2019. LNCS, vol. 11892, pp. 61–90. Springer, Cham (2019). https://doi.org/10.1007/978-3-030-36033-7_3
5. Boyd, C., Cliff, Y., Gonzalez Nieto, J., Paterson, K.G.: Efficient one-round key exchange in the standard model. In: Mu, Y., Susilo, W., Seberry, J. (eds.) ACISP 2008. LNCS, vol. 5107, pp. 69–83. Springer, Heidelberg (2008). https://doi.org/10.1007/978-3-540-70500-0_6
6. Don, J., Fehr, S., Majenz, C., Schaffner, C.: Online-extractability in the quantum random-oracle model. In: Dunkelman, O., Dziembowski, S. (eds.) EUROCRYPT 2022. LNCS, vol. 13277, pp. 677–706. SPringer, Cham (2022). https://doi.org/10.1007/978-3-031-07082-2_24
7. Fujioka, A., Suzuki, K., Xagawa, K., Yoneyama, K.: Strongly secure authenticated key exchange from factoring, codes, and lattices. In: Fischlin, M., Buchmann, J., Manulis, M. (eds.) PKC 2012. LNCS, vol. 7293, pp. 467–484. Springer, Heidelberg (2012). https://doi.org/10.1007/978-3-642-30057-8_28
8. Han, S., et al.: Authenticated key exchange and signatures with tight security in the standard model. In: Malkin, T., Peikert, C. (eds.) CRYPTO 2021. LNCS, vol. 12828, pp. 670–700. Springer, Cham (2021). https://doi.org/10.1007/978-3-030-84259-8_23
9. Hashimoto, K., Katsumata, S., Kwiatkowski, K., Prest, T.: An efficient and generic construction for signal's handshake (X3DH): post-quantum, state leakage secure, and deniable. In: Garay, J.A. (ed.) PKC 2021. LNCS, vol. 12711, pp. 410–440. Springer, Cham (2021). https://doi.org/10.1007/978-3-030-75248-4_15
10. Hövelmanns, K., Kiltz, E., Schäge, S., Unruh, D.: Generic authenticated key exchange in the quantum random oracle model. In: Kiayias, A., Kohlweiss, M., Wallden, P., Zikas, V. (eds.) PKC 2020. LNCS, vol. 12111, pp. 389–422. Springer, Cham (2020). https://doi.org/10.1007/978-3-030-45388-6_14
11. Huguenin-Dumittan, L., Vaudenay, S.: On IND-qCCA security in the ROM and its applications - CPA security is sufficient for TLS 1.3. In: Dunkelman, O., Dziembowski, S. (eds.) EUROCRYPT 2022. LNCS, vol. 13277, pp. 613–642. Springer, Cham (2022)
12. Information security-Key management-Part 3: Mechanisms using asymmetric techniques. Standard, International Organization for Standardization (2021). https://www.iso.org/standard/82709.html
13. Jager, T., Kiltz, E., Riepel, D., Schäge, S.: Tightly-secure authenticated key exchange, revisited. In: Canteaut, A., Standaert, F.-X. (eds.) EUROCRYPT 2021. LNCS, vol. 12696, pp. 117–146. Springer, Cham (2021). https://doi.org/10.1007/978-3-030-77870-5_5
14. Krawczyk, H.: HMQV: a high-performance secure Diffie-Hellman protocol. In: Shoup, V. (ed.) CRYPTO 2005. LNCS, vol. 3621, pp. 546–566. Springer, Heidelberg (2005). https://doi.org/10.1007/11535218_33
15. Lyu, Y., Liu, S.: Two-message authenticated key exchange from public-key encryption. Cryptology ePrint Archive, Paper 2023/706 (2023). https://eprint.iacr.org/2023/706
16. Lyubashevsky, V., Micciancio, D., Peikert, C., Rosen, A.: SWIFFT: a modest proposal for FFT hashing. In: Nyberg, K. (ed.) FSE 2008. LNCS, vol. 5086, pp. 54–72. Springer, Heidelberg (2008). https://doi.org/10.1007/978-3-540-71039-4_4

17. Peikert, C.: Public-key cryptosystems from the worst-case shortest vector problem: extended abstract. In: STOC 2009 (2009). https://doi.org/10.1145/1536414.1536461
18. Regev, O.: On lattices, learning with errors, random linear codes, and cryptography. In: STOC 2005 (2005). https://doi.org/10.1145/1060590.1060603
19. Schwabe, P., Stebila, D., Wiggers, T.: Post-quantum TLS without handshake signatures. In: CCS 2020 (2020). https://doi.org/10.1145/3372297.3423350
20. Xue, H., Lu, X., Li, B., Liang, B., He, J.: Understanding and constructing AKE via double-key key encapsulation mechanism. In: Peyrin, T., Galbraith, S. (eds.) ASIACRYPT 2018. LNCS, vol. 11273, pp. 158–189. Springer, Cham (2018). https://doi.org/10.1007/978-3-030-03329-3_6
21. Zhandry, M.: A note on the quantum collision and set equality problems. Quantum Inf. Comput. **15**(7&8), 557–567 (2015). https://doi.org/10.26421/QIC15.7-8-2 https://doi.org/10.26421/QIC15.7-8-2 https://doi.org/10.26421/QIC15.7-8-2

Efficient Zero-Knowledge Arguments and Digital Signatures *via* Sharing Conversion *in the Head*

Jules Maire[✉] and Damien Vergnaud

Sorbonne Université, CNRS, LIP6, 75005 Paris, France
`Jules.maire@lip6.fr`

Abstract. We present a novel technique within the MPC-in-the-Head framework, aiming to design efficient zero-knowledge protocols and digital signature schemes. The technique allows for the simultaneous use of additive and multiplicative sharings of secret information, enabling efficient proofs of linear and multiplicative relations. The applications of our technique are manifold. It is first applied to construct zero-knowledge arguments of knowledge for Double Discrete Logarithms. The resulting protocol achieves improved communication complexity without compromising efficiency. We also propose a new zero-knowledge argument of knowledge for the Permuted Kernel Problem. Eventually, we propose a short (candidate) post-quantum digital signature scheme constructed from a new one-way function based on simple polynomials known as fewnomials. This scheme offers simplicity and ease of implementation.

1 Introduction

Zero-knowledge protocols have emerged as a pivotal tool in ensuring robust computer security and enhancing cryptographic protocols. They offer a powerful solution by allowing one party to prove knowledge of certain information to another party, without revealing any additional details. With the rapid advancements in quantum computing technology, the need for post-quantum security in cryptography and computer security has become of paramount importance. Post-quantum cryptography aims to develop communication protocols that can withstand attacks from both classical and quantum computers.

Secure multi-party computation (MPC) enables a group of $n \geq 2$ parties, who do not trust each other, to collaboratively compute a joint function using their private inputs. In 2007, Ishai, Kushilevitz, Ostrovsky, and Sahai [IKOS07] demonstrated that semi-honest multiparty computation (i.e. where adversaries follow the protocol description but may try to learn arbitrary information) is sufficient for constructing zero-knowledge protocols. This theoretical paradigm, deemed *MPC-in-the-Head*, has received considerable practical attention recently since it enables the construction of efficient and succinct protocols with good security properties. It has been used in particular to propose several innovative signature schemes with (alleged) post-quantum security. The goal of this article is

G. Tsudik et al. (Eds.): ESORICS 2023, LNCS 14344, pp. 435–454, 2024.
https://doi.org/10.1007/978-3-031-50594-2_22

to add another string to the *MPC-in-the-Head*'s bow by integrating secret sharing conversion, a technique that has already been used in general MPC [GPS12]. We show that this technique finds applications for (1) zero-knowledge arguments of knowledge of *Double Discrete Logarithms*, (2) zero-knowledge arguments of knowledge of *Permuted Kernel Problem* solutions, and (3) constructing a (candidate) post-quantum digital signature scheme from a new *somewhat minimalistic* one-way function in finite fields.

Related Works and Contributions of the Paper. The MPC-in-the-Head (MPCitH) framework [IKOS07] has gained considerable popularity in recent times. This framework leverages secure MPC techniques, where the prover mentally shares its secret information and emulates a semi-honest MPC protocol involving N parties and independently commits each party's view. The verifier then challenges the prover to reveal the views of a randomly selected subset of $N - 1$ parties. By design, no information about the original input is exposed, thereby achieving the zero-knowledge property. Besides, a malicious prover would need to deceive at least one party, which the verifier is likely to detect, ensuring the soundness property. In most practical applications, the secret is shared additively among the N parties, which makes proving linear relations easy but proofs of multiplicative relations more costly. Several techniques were introduced recently to improve the practical efficiency of the resulting schemes, for instance, the MPCitH with a *helper* as formalized in [Beu20], the MPCitH with *abort* introduced in [FMRV22] or the recent *hypercubing* optimization technique proposed in [MGH+23].

We present a new technique to expand this toolbox further by allowing a prover to use simultaneously in the MPC protocol additive sharings and multiplicative sharings of its secret information. The former are used for linear relations, while the latter are used to prove efficiently multiplicative relations. To ensure consistency, we propose a simple technique to transform a multiplicative share into an additive share of the same value. Converting shares from one type of secret sharing scheme into another is ubiquitous in MPC [GPS12] and the idea has already been used in the MPCitH realm [DGH+21] (but for different sharings). Our technique finds several applications in (post-quantum) zero-knowledge arguments and digital signature schemes.

Double Discrete Logarithm Problem (DDLP): A double discrete logarithm of an element $y \neq 1_{\mathbb{G}}$ in a cyclic group $\mathbb{G}$ of prime order q with respect to bases $g \in \mathbb{G}$ and $h \in \mathbb{F}_q^*$ (generators of $\mathbb{G}$ and $\mathbb{F}_q^*$ respectively) is an integer $x \in \{0, \ldots, q-1\}$ such that $y = g^{h^x}$. Initially introduced by Stadler [Sta96] for verifiable secret-sharing, this computational problem has found applications in various cryptographic protocols, including group signatures [CS97], blind signatures [ASM10], e-cash systems [CG07], credential systems [CGM16], and verifiable randomness generation [BTV20]. Stadler proposed a zero-knowledge protocol, which has a computational and communication complexity of $\Omega(\log q)$ (in terms of group elements). However, in the recent work [BTV20], Blazy, Towa, and Vergnaud presented a new protocol that outputs arguments with only $O(\log \log q)$ group elements. It relies on the *"Bulletproofs"* technique proposed by Bünz, Bootle,

Boneh, Poelstra, Wuille and Maxwell in 2018 [BBB+18]. This reduced communication complexity comes at a security price since the security analysis should rely on stronger idealized assumptions [GOP+22] or achieve only non-meaningful concrete security [DG23]. For a use-case considered in [BTV20], the length of Stadler arguments are 24.6 Kilobytes (KB) and those of Blazy *et al.* are 10.2 KB long. As a first simple application of our conversion *in the head* technique, we present (for similar prover and verifier efficiency) arguments of size about 16.6 KB (depending on the parameters). Even if this is longer than the previous approach, this still improves the communication complexity of Stadler's protocol by about 30%. By increasing the prover and verifier computational complexity, it is possible to decrease the communication complexity to 7.2 KB (with better security guarantees than [BTV20]). It is worth mentioning that even by increasing the prover/verifier running times, the arguments of [Sta96,BTV20] cannot be shortened.

Permuted Kernel Problem (PKP): The *Permuted Kernel Problem* (PKP) is a classical $\mathcal{NP}$-hard computational problem, where, given a matrix and a vector (of matching dimensions) defined over a finite field, one has to find a permutation of the vector coordinates that belongs to the matrix kernel. This problem was introduced in cryptography by Shamir [Sha90], who designed a zero-knowledge argument of knowledge of a solution of a PKP problem (and used it for a cryptographic (post-quantum) identification scheme). This protocol was improved subsequently in a long series of work [Ste94, BFK+19, Beu20, FJR23, Fen22, BG22]. We apply our technique to this problem and obtain a zero-knowledge argument of knowledge protocol which does not involve permutations that are not easy to implement securely, in particular in the presence of side-channel attacks.

One-Way Functions From "Fewnomials": A cryptographic one-way function $f : S \to S$ is a function that is computationally easy to compute but computationally difficult to invert. If S is a finite field (e.g. $S = \mathbb{F}_p$ for some prime number p), then it is well-known that f can be represented as a polynomial in $\mathbb{F}_p[X]$ (with degree upper-bounded by $(p-1)$). Ad hoc examples of such functions are cryptographic hash functions or functions derived from block ciphers (using for instance the Davies-Meyer construction [Win84]). Still, the polynomial representations of such functions are usually of very high complexity (which makes them not convenient for the MPCitH paradigm). Several works were devoted to designing efficient symmetric cryptographic primitives suitable for efficient implementation using MPCitH (e.g. the Picnic [CDG+20, KZ22] and the Rainier [DKR+22] signature schemes). As a third application of our technique, we propose a reverse approach to design a cryptographic system with simplicity and minimal complexity. The motivation is to remove potential points of failure and to obtain schemes easier to implement correctly. To do so, we consider the simplest polynomials defined over a finite field $\mathbb{F}_p$ that are good one-way function candidates. The simplest polynomials are certainly the monomials $f_1 : \mathbb{F}_p \to \mathbb{F}_p$, $x \mapsto f_1(x) = x^n \mod p$ but they are trivially not one-way. If n is coprime with $(p-1)$, this is a permutation on which one can apply the Davies-Meyer construction to obtain the binomials $f_2 : \mathbb{F}_p \to \mathbb{F}_p$, $x \mapsto f_2(x) = x^n + x \mod p$ which seem difficult to invert (the best-known algorithm for $n = \Omega(p)$ has arithmetic complexity $O(p^{1/2})$ [BCR13]). More generally, a *fewnomial* is a term used in algebraic geometry and computational algebra, to describe a polynomial with a few terms (i.e. with a relatively low number of monomials compared to its degree). If one considers a fewnomial of high degree with $t \geq 2$ monomials over $\mathbb{F}_p$, the best known algorithm has arithmetic complexity $O(p^{(t-1)/t})$ [BCR13]. These candidate one-way functions are not suitable for symmetric cryptography (since evaluating them is much more costly than popular hash functions and block ciphers) but they are particularly interesting for our new conversion technique. In particular, we propose (candidate) post-quantum signatures with lengths of about 10.5 KB. The produced signatures are thus not the shortest ones, but our goal with this application is to propose a new simpler, and cleaner one-way function suitable for the MPCitH paradigm with competitive performances and to motivate future research in this area.

Other Results: We present two additional results inspired by this work but using alternative approaches. We first describe a zero-knowledge argument of knowledge of an RSA plaintext for a small public exponent that significantly improves the state-of-the-art communication complexity [GQ90]. The scheme is very simple but seems to have been overlooked. Following a recent idea proposed by Joux [Jou23], we also propose a more efficient construction for the DDLP (without using our conversion in the head technique) achieving arguments about 6.6 KB long. This improves the communication complexity of Stadler's protocol by about 75% (for the same security guarantees and overall efficiency).

2   Preliminaries

We denote $\mathbb{F}_q$ the finite field with q elements (for q some prime power). Let $N \geq 2$ be some integer. We make use of N-out-of-N *additive* and *multiplicative sharing* of field elements $x \in \mathbb{F}_q$ and $x \in \mathbb{F}_q^\times$ (respectively); they are vectors in $\mathbb{F}_q{}^N$ and $\mathbb{F}_q^\times{}^N$ denoted $[\![x]\!] = ([\![x]\!]_1, \ldots, [\![x]\!]_N)$ and $\langle x \rangle = (\langle x \rangle_1, \ldots, \langle x \rangle_N)$ (respectively) such that

$$x = [\![x]\!]_1 + \cdots + [\![x]\!]_N \bmod q \text{ and } x = \langle x \rangle_1 \cdot \cdots \cdot \langle x \rangle_N \bmod q.$$

We use the same notations for the sharing of vectors. All logarithms are in base 2. We denote the security parameter by λ. The designation PPT stands for probabilistic polynomial-time in the security parameter. Random sampling from a finite set X according to the uniform distribution is denoted by $x \xleftarrow{\$} X$, whereas the symbol $\leftarrow$ is used for assignments from deterministic algorithms. We write $[0, n]$ to denote the set $\{0, \ldots, n\}$.

Two distributions $\{D_\lambda\}_\lambda$ and $\{\tilde{D}_\lambda\}_\lambda$ are called (t, ε)-indistinguishable if, for any algorithm $\mathcal{A}$ running in time at most $t(\lambda)$, we have

$$|\Pr[\mathcal{A}(1^\lambda, x) = 1 \mid x \xleftarrow{\$} D_\lambda] - \Pr[\mathcal{A}(1^\lambda, x) = 1 \mid x \xleftarrow{\$} \tilde{D}_\lambda]| \leq \varepsilon(\lambda).$$

A (ℓ, t, ε)-*pseudo-random generator* (PRG) is a deterministic algorithm G that, for all $\lambda \in \mathbb{N}$, on input a bit-string $x \in \{0,1\}^\lambda$ outputs $G(x) \in \{0,1\}^{\ell(\lambda)}$ with $\ell(\lambda) > \lambda$ such that the distributions $\{G(x) \mid x \xleftarrow{\$} \{0,1\}^\lambda\}_\lambda$ and $\{r \mid r \xleftarrow{\$} \{0,1\}^{\ell(\lambda)}\}_\lambda$ are (t, ε)-indistinguishable. From such a generator, with $\ell(\lambda) = 2\lambda$, it is possible to construct a *tree PRG* [KKW18], which takes a root $x \in \{0,1\}^\lambda$ as input and generates $N = 2^t$ pseudo-random λ-bit strings in a structured fashion as follows: x is the label of the root of a depth-t complete binary tree in which the right/left child of each node is labeled with the λ most/least significant bits of the output of the PRG applied to the root label. This structure allows revealing $N - 1$ pseudo-random values of the leaves by revealing only $\log(N)$ labels of the tree (by revealing the labels on the siblings of the paths from the root to the one remaining leaf).

2.1 Commitment Scheme

We define a commitment scheme as a pair of algorithms (Com, Verif) where:

- Com is a PPT taking as input a message m, that computes a commitment C of m and returns C and opening information ρ.
- Verif is a deterministic polynomial-time algorithm taking as input a message m, a commitment C and the opening information ρ, and returns a bit.

For all message m we have: $\forall (C, \rho) \xleftarrow{\$} \mathsf{Com}(m), \mathsf{Verif}(m, C, \rho) = 1$. A commitment scheme is said (t, ε)-computationally *hiding* if, for any two messages m_1, m_2, the distributions $\{c \mid c \xleftarrow{\$} \mathsf{Com}(m_1)\}$ and $\{c \mid c \xleftarrow{\$} \mathsf{Com}(m_2)\}$ are (t, ε)-indistinguishable. A commitment scheme is computationally *binding* if there exists a negligible function ν such that, for every PPT algorithm $\mathcal{A}$, the probability that the event

$$\left\{ \begin{array}{l} m_1 \neq m_2 \ \wedge \\ \mathsf{Verif}(, m_1, C, \rho_1) = \mathsf{Verif}(m_2, C, \rho_2) = 1 \end{array} \;\middle|\; (m_1, m_2, \rho_1, \rho_2, C) \xleftarrow{\$} \mathcal{A}(1^\lambda) \right\}$$

occurs is upper-bounded by $\nu(\lambda)$. In the following, we consider a commitment scheme that outputs a 2λ bit-long commitment.

2.2 Zero-Knowledge Arguments

A zero-knowledge protocol for a polynomial-time decidable binary relation $\mathcal{R}$ is defined by two interactive algorithms, a prover $\mathcal{P}$ and a verifier $\mathcal{V}$. Both algorithms are given a common input x, and $\mathcal{P}$ is given an additional *witness* w such that $(x, w) \in \mathcal{R}$. The two algorithms then exchange messages until $\mathcal{V}$ outputs a bit b ($b = 1$ to accept $\mathcal{P}$'s claim and $b = 0$ to reject). This sequence of messages and the answer b is referred to as a *transcript* and denoted $\mathsf{View}(\mathcal{P}(x, w), \tilde{\mathcal{V}}(x))$. In this paper, we consider *zero-knowledge argument of knowledge* which are protocols that allow a PPT prover to convince a PPT verifier that they *know* a witness w. There are three security notions underlying a zero-knowledge argument of knowledge.

Definition 1. *Let* $t : \mathbb{N} \to \mathbb{N}$, $\varepsilon, \alpha, \zeta : \mathbb{N} \to [0,1]$, *and* $\mathcal{R}$ *be a polynomial-time decidable binary relation. A zero-knowledge argument* $(\mathcal{P}, \mathcal{V})$ *for* $\mathcal{R}$ *achieves:*

- α-*completeness, if for all* $\lambda \in \mathbb{N}$ *and all* $(x,w) \in \mathcal{R}$, *with* $x \in \{0,1\}^\lambda$, $\Pr[\text{View}(\mathcal{P}(x,w), \mathcal{V}(x)) = 1] \geq 1 - \alpha(\lambda)$ *(i.e.* $\mathcal{P}$ *succeeds in convincing* $\mathcal{V}$, *except with probability* α).
- ε-*(special) soundness, if for all PPT algorithm* $\tilde{\mathcal{P}}$ *such that for all* $\lambda \in \mathbb{N}$ *and all* $x \in \{0,1\}^\lambda$, $\tilde{\varepsilon}(\lambda) := Pr[\text{View}(\tilde{\mathcal{P}}(x), \mathcal{V}(x)) = 1] > \varepsilon(\lambda)$, *there exists a PPT algorithm* $\mathcal{E}$ *(called the* extractor*) which, given rewindable black-box access to* $\tilde{\mathcal{P}}$ *outputs a witness* w *such that* $(x,w) \in \mathcal{R}$ *in time* $\text{poly}(\lambda, (\tilde{\varepsilon}-\varepsilon)^{-1})$ *with probability at least* $1/2$.
- (t, ζ)-*zero-knowledge, if for every PPT algorithm* $\tilde{\mathcal{V}}$, *there exists a PPT algorithm* $\mathcal{S}$ *(called the* simulator*) which, given the input statement* $x \in \{0,1\}^\lambda$ *and rewindable black-box access to* $\tilde{\mathcal{V}}$, *outputs a simulated transcript whose distribution is* (t, ζ)-*indistinguishable from* $\text{View}(\mathcal{P}(x,w), \tilde{\mathcal{V}}(x))$.

2.3 MPC in the Head

MPC in the Head. The concept of MPC-in-the-Head (MPCitH) [IKOS07] provides a method for constructing zero-knowledge protocols using secure MPC protocols. Let f be some (one-way) function and assume we have an MPC protocol where N parties securely compute f on a secret input x encoded as an N-out-of-N secret sharing. A prover $\mathcal{P}$ given a secret input x, generates a random sharing of x and mentally simulates all the parties of the MPC protocol. $\mathcal{P}$ sends commitments of each party's view in the protocol (including input share, secret random tape, and sent/received messages) and the output shares of $f(x)$ to the verifier $\mathcal{V}$. $\mathcal{V}$ selects $N-1$ parties randomly and requests $\mathcal{P}$ to reveal their views. Upon receiving them, $\mathcal{V}$ verifies their consistency with an honest execution of the MPC protocol and the commitments. Since the views of only $N-1$ parties are disclosed, this does not disclose any information about the secret x.

MPCitH with Helper. In this paper, we use the MPCitH with *Helper* paradigm introduced in [Beu20] by Beullens. This approach adds a trusted third party (called the helper) to the MPC protocol which runs a pre-processing phase. To then remove the helper, one uses a cut-and-choose strategy. This approach is typically useful when some correlated randomness has to be generated in the MPC protocol. This randomness structure is actually needed for our sharing conversion. Indeed, for each sharing conversion, $\mathcal{P}$ needs to produce a couple of sharing $(\llbracket r \rrbracket, \langle s \rangle)$ with $r = s$. To prove the validity of this couple (i.e. $r = s$), we follow a cut-and-choose approach. $\mathcal{P}$ produces M couples of sharing $(\llbracket r^{[\ell]} \rrbracket, \langle s^{[\ell]} \rangle)_{\ell \in [1,M]}$ and commits to them. Then $\mathcal{V}$ asks to open all the couples except one and checks that each couple encodes an identical value. Hence, $\mathcal{V}$ can trust the unopened sharing with a soundness error of $1/M$.

Hypercube Optimization. In [MGH+23], Melchor, Gama, Howe, Hülsing, Joseh, and Yue developed a geometrical approach for the MPC emulation phase. When dealing with additive and multiplicative secret sharing in finite fields, this optimization fits pretty well (due to the commutativity of the addition and multiplication laws). In the traditional approach of MPCitH, $\mathcal{P}$ simulates N parties during one emulation of one MPC protocol. By this hypercube approach, this number of parties can be reduced to $1 + \log_2 N$, with the same soundness error (see [MGH+23] for more details). This optimization makes the MPC emulation less costly and allows us to take a larger number of parties (and get smaller sizes). For example, for the same soundness error, when the traditional approach needs to simulate 2^8 parties, we only need to emulate 9 parties. The computational gain is attenuated by the number of repetitions since the total number of parties to emulate is $\tau(1 + \log_2 N) \approx \lambda(1 + 1/\log_2 N)$.

Sharing on the Integers. Finally, we also make use of a technique developed in [FMRV22] by Feneuil, Maire, Rivain, and Vergnaud, to encode a binary secret $x \in \mathbb{F}_q$ over the integers in the MPCitH paradigm, i.e. $x = \sum_{i=1}^{N} [\![x]\!]_i + \Delta x$ with $[\![x]\!]_i \xleftarrow{\$} [0, A-1]^n$ (with no modular reduction). To avoid information leakage, Feneuil *et al.* introduced the possibility for $\mathcal{P}$ to abort in the MPC protocol. This induces a rejection rate in the MPC protocol that can be decreased by increasing A (but this increases the communication complexity). Then they generalized this sharing to encode non-binary elements throughout the construction of a digital signature from Boneh-Halevi-Howgrave-Graham pseudo-random function. In this paper, we use this sharing to share on the integers some element in $\mathbb{F}_q$. We take $A > q$, and the rejection rate of the sharing becomes $1 - \left(1 - \frac{q-1}{A}\right)^n$. This approach is only used when constructing a PKP argument of knowledge.

3   Sharing Conversion and Design Principle

RSA-in-the-Head. In the MPCitH paradigm, when the secret is shared additively, multiplicative relations are costly to prove, and vice versa. Whence converting secret sharing *in-the-Head* naturally comes to mind. However, there exists a natural application where the conversion is not necessary, which seems to have been overlooked in the literature. Indeed, assume that we want to prove the knowledge of an RSA plaintext for a public exponent e, i.e. $x^e = y \bmod n$ where n is some RSA modulus. Then we could imagine sharing x multiplicatively as $x = \prod_{j=1}^{N} \langle x \rangle_j \bmod n$ and the corresponding MPC protocol consists simply in locally computing $\langle x \rangle^e$. Using straightforward techniques from MPCitH, this simple observation improves the communication complexity of the seminal protocol from Guillou and Quisquater [GQ90] for the public exponent $e = 3$ from around 20.4 KB to 6.6 KB for a 2048-bit modulus n and has similar efficiency. The communication complexity could be made even smaller by increasing N (but at the cost of an increased computational complexity). Interestingly, even if the hypercube technique [MGH+23] could be applied here, this would result in worse computation complexity. Details can be found in the full version of the paper.

Sharing Conversion. Let $\langle x \rangle$ be a multiplicative sharing of some field element $x \in \mathbb{F}_q$. The aim is to securely compute an additive sharing $[\![x]\!]$ of x. For the sharing conversion considered in the following, we need a uniformly random pre-computed couple of sharing $([\![r]\!], \langle s \rangle)$ such that $r = s \in \mathbb{F}_q^\times$. As explained in Sect. 2, we work in the MPCitH with Helper paradigm, and follow a cut-and-choose approach. The protocol is the following:

Input: The parties have $\langle x \rangle$.   Output: The parties get $[\![x]\!]$.
Preprocessing phase: A trusted dealer generates $t \xleftarrow{\$} \mathbb{F}_q^\times$, and random sharings $r = \sum_{i=1}^{N}[\![r]\!]_i$, $s = \prod_{i=1}^{N}\langle s \rangle_i$, such that $r = s = t$. They give $([\![r]\!]_i, \langle s \rangle_i)$ to party P_i for $i \in [1, N]$.   **Online phase:**   1. The parties compute $\langle \alpha \rangle = \langle x \rangle / \langle s \rangle$ and broadcast it.   2. The parties locally compute $\alpha [\![r]\!] := [\![x]\!]$.

Protocol 1: Sharing conversion protocol Π_{conv}

The pre-processing phase consists of generating $\{[\![r]\!]_i, \langle s \rangle_i\} \xleftarrow{\$} \mathbb{F}_q \times \mathbb{F}_q^\times$ for $i \in [1, N]$. Then define $r = \sum_{i=1}^{N}[\![r]\!]_i$, and compute Δs such that $r = \Delta s \prod_{i=1}^{N}\langle s \rangle_i := s$. If $r = s = 0$, i.e. $\Delta s = 0$, we start again. From the point of view of zero-knowledge proofs based on MPC, this offline step introduces one auxiliary value Δs to communicate. Since there is also the value α to communicate when running Π_{conv}, the sharing conversion protocol needs 2 field elements to communicate in total (we can not reuse the couple of sharing for another conversion).

General Protocol. We develop a 5-round protocol with helper. It is presented in a general manner, we explain later how to adapt it to each of the problems considered in this work. Let $x \in \mathbb{F}_q$ be a solution to an instance of some problem with f the underlying function, and let Π_f be the MPC protocol that securely computes f. Π_f takes as input a secret sharing of x which is either $[\![x]\!]$, $\langle x \rangle$, or a sharing on the integers as in [FMRV22]. It also takes as input a couple (or many couples) of secret sharing $([\![r]\!], \langle s \rangle)$ with $r = s \in \mathbb{F}_q^\times$ that is generated during a pre-processing phase. For the PKP application, Π_f takes as additional input, some prime number q' greater than q. Π_f outputs either $[\![f(x)]\!]$ or $\langle f(x) \rangle$.

Soundness Error. Let ε be the soundness of the protocol. We perform τ parallel repetitions of the protocol to get a soundness error $\varepsilon^\tau < (1/2)^\lambda$. As explained in the previous paragraph, each of these repetitions uses a cut-and-chose phase to prove the helper. Instead of performing $\tau \approx \lambda / \log_2(N)$ parallel cut-and-chose phases each resulting in trusting one couple of sharing $([\![r^{[\ell]}]\!], \langle s^{[\ell]} \rangle)$ among M, we follow the more efficient approach from [KKW18] and perform a global cut-and-choose phase resulting in τ trusted sharing among a larger M. The idea is that $\mathcal{V}$ asks to reveal $M - \tau$ out of M master seeds. The remaining τ executions of the pre-processing phase are used to emulate τ independent instances of the MPC protocol. When opening all but one seed, a wrong couple of sharing will not be detected with probability $\frac{1}{N} + \left(1 - \frac{1}{N}\right) \cdot \beta$, where β is a real between 0 and 1. This β will be zero when considering the DDLP and the fewnomial pre-image problem. If a cheating prover produces $M - k \leq \tau$ wrong couples of sharing, they will not be detected during the first phase (when revealing $M - \tau$ master seeds) with probability $\binom{k}{M-\tau} \cdot \binom{M}{M-\tau}^{-1}$. This leads to the soundness error

$$\varepsilon = \max_{M-\tau \leq k \leq M} \left\{ \frac{\binom{k}{M-\tau} \cdot \left(\frac{1}{N} + \left(1 - \frac{1}{N}\right) \cdot \beta\right)^{k-M+\tau}}{\binom{M}{M-\tau}} \right\}$$

(see [KKW18] for additional details).

We describe the zero-knowledge protocol that is used in the remaining of the paper. The protocol makes use of a pseudo-random generator PRG, a tree-based pseudo-random generator TreePRG, four collision-resistant hash functions $\mathcal{H}_i$ for $i \in [1, 4]$ and a commitment scheme (Com, Verif). The red part of the protocol has to be adapted depending on the problem considered, further details are provided in the following. We choose to use $[\![\cdot]\!]$ in the protocol for the sharing of x and $f(x)$, but it can be easily substituted by $\langle\cdot\rangle$.

Parameters Selection. Recall that we are dealing with a pre-processing phase, that is proved with a cut-and-choose strategy. The total number of parties to set up being $M \cdot N$, this impacts the prover/verifier computational complexity. We choose sets of parameters to keep a reasonable signing time. We start by fixing a number of parties N to be either 2^5 or 2^8. Then we look for the best trade-off between τ, M while keeping a soundness error below $2^{-\lambda}$. Decreasing τ leads to better sizes but to higher M and so slower signatures. The MPC emulation does not impact a lot the signing speed since the hypercube optimization is consistent with our scheme (see Sect. 2).

Prover's Computational Cost. Since we use the cut-and-choose approach, the tree expansion, randomness generation, share preparation, and commitments computation are affected by the factor M. However, the MPC protocol is run τ times and the hypercube approach is applied, so this emulation is quite efficient. In the following, for each application, we estimate the computation speed with the benchmark proposed in [Fen22], assuming a 4-core processor.

4 Proving Knowledge of a Double Discrete Logarithm

We present the Double Discrete Logarithm Problem (DDLP) which has found numerous applications in cryptography [CS97, ASM10, CG07, CGM16, BTV20].

Double Discrete Logarithm Problem (DDLP).

Let $\mathbb{G}$ be a cyclic group of prime order q with some generator $g \in \mathbb{G}$, and let $h \in \mathbb{F}_q^*$ of prime order p with $p|(q-1)$. Given $(y, g, h) \in \mathbb{G} \setminus \{1_{\mathbb{G}}\} \times \mathbb{G} \times \mathbb{F}_q^*$, the *DDLP* asks to find some $x \in \mathbb{F}_p^\times$ such that $y = g^{h^x}$.

Prover $\mathcal{P}$	Verifier $\mathcal{V}$
$x \in \mathbb{F}_q$	$y = f(x)$

$\mathsf{mseed}^{[0]} \xleftarrow{\$} \{0,1\}^\lambda$

$(\mathsf{mseed}^{[e]})_{e \in [1,M]} \leftarrow \mathsf{TreePRG}(\mathsf{mseed}^{[0]})$

For each $e \in [1, M]$:

   $(\mathsf{seed}_i^{[e]}, \rho_i^{[e]})_{i \in [1,N]} \leftarrow \mathsf{TreePRG}(\mathsf{mseed}^{[e]})$

   For each $i \in [1, N]$:

      $([\![x^{[e]}]\!]_i, [\![r^{[e]}]\!]_i, \langle s^{[e]} \rangle_i) \leftarrow \mathsf{PRG}(\mathsf{seed}_i^{[e]})$ $\triangleright\ [\![x^{[e]}]\!]_i, [\![r^{[e]}]\!]_i \in \mathbb{F}_q, \langle s^{[e]} \rangle_i \in \mathbb{F}_q^\times$

      $\mathsf{com}_i^{[e]} = \mathsf{Com}(\mathsf{seed}_i^{[e]}; \rho_i^{[e]})$

   $\Delta x^{[e]} = x - \sum_i [\![x]\!]_i^{[e]}$

   $r^{[e]} = \sum_i [\![r]\!]_i^{[e]}$

   $\Delta s^{[e]} = r^{[e]} / \prod_i \langle s \rangle_i^{[e]}$

   $s^{[e]} = \Delta s^{[e]} \prod_i \langle s \rangle_i^{[e]}$

   $h_e = \mathcal{H}_1(\Delta s^{[e]}, \mathsf{com}_1^{[e]}, \dots, \mathsf{com}_N^{[e]})$

$h = \mathcal{H}_2(h_1, \dots, h_M)$

$\xrightarrow{\hspace{3cm} h \hspace{3cm}}$

$\xleftarrow{\hspace{3cm} J \hspace{3cm}}$ $J \xleftarrow{\$} \{J \subset [1, M] \, ; \, |J| = \tau\}(\star)$

For each $e \in J$:

   The parties computes $\Pi_f([\![x^{[e]}]\!], \Delta x^{[e]})$

   $= [\![y^{[e]}]\!]$

   $h'_e = \mathcal{H}_3(\Delta x^{[e]}, [\![y^{[e]}]\!], \alpha^{[e]})$ $\triangleright\ \alpha^{[e]}$ is the broadcasted value in

$h' = \mathcal{H}_4((h'_e)_{e \in J})$ Π_{conv} called in Π_f

$\xrightarrow{\hspace{1cm} h', \, (\mathsf{mseed}^{[e]})_{e \in [1,M] \backslash J} \hspace{1cm}}$

$\xleftarrow{\hspace{3cm} L \hspace{3cm}}$ $L = \{\ell_e\}_{e \in J} \xleftarrow{\$} [1, n]^\tau$

$\xrightarrow{\left(\begin{array}{c} (\mathsf{seed}_i^{[e]}, \rho_i^{[e]})_{i \neq \ell_e} \\ \Delta x^{[e]}, \Delta s^{[e]}, \alpha^{[e]}, \mathsf{com}_{\ell_e}^{[e]} \end{array} \right)_{e \in J}}$

For each $e \notin J$:

   Compute h_e using $\mathsf{mseed}^{[e]}$

For each $e \in J$:

   For all $i \neq \ell_e$

      $\mathsf{com}_i^{[e]} = \mathsf{Com}(\mathsf{seed}_i^{[e]}; \rho_i^{[e]})$

      Rerun the party i

         as the prover to get $[\![y^{[e]}]\!]_i$

   $[\![y^{[e]}]\!]_{\ell_e} = y - \sum_{i \neq \ell_e} [\![y^{[e]}]\!]_i$

   $h_e = \mathcal{H}_1(\Delta s^{[e]}$

   $\mathsf{com}_1^{[e]}, \dots, \mathsf{com}_N^{[e]})$

   $h'_e = \mathcal{H}_3(\Delta x^{[e]}, [\![y^{[e]}]\!], \alpha^{[e]})$

Check $h = \mathcal{H}_2(h_1, \dots, h_M)$

Check $h' = \mathcal{H}_4((h'_e)_{e \in J})$

Return 1

Protocol 2: Zero knowledge protocol for proving the knowledge of a pre-image of a function f.

We first propose a direct application of our sharing conversion technique. However, even if it improves the state-of-the-art in terms of communication complexity (compared to schemes with the same assumptions), we present this scheme primarily for pedagogical purposes. Indeed, we then build another zero-knowledge argument of knowledge with a forward-backward technique that achieves more efficient performances.

First Construction. Consider the function $f : \mathbb{F}_p^\times \to \mathbb{G}, x \mapsto f(x) = g^{h^x}$ realizing the "double discrete exponentiation". We present the MPC protocol Π_{DDLP} to securely compute a multiplicative sharing of $f(x) \in \mathbb{G}$, given an additive secret sharing of $x \in \mathbb{F}_p^\times$.

Input: $y \neq 1_{\mathbb{G}}$ in a cyclic group $\mathbb{G}$ of prime order q, $h \in \mathbb{F}_q^*$ of prime order p with $p|(q-1)$. An additive sharing $[\![x]\!]$ of $x \in \mathbb{F}_p^\times$ such that $y = g^{h^x}$.
Output: $\langle g^{h^x} \rangle$

---

1. Parties locally compute a multiplicative sharing $\langle h^x \rangle$ via $h^x = \prod_{j=1}^N h^{[\![x]\!]_j} \bmod q$.
2. Parties convert it into an additive sharing $[\![h^x]\!]$ over $\mathbb{F}_q$ using Π_{conv} (protocol 1).
3. Parties locally compute $\langle g^{h^x} \rangle$ via $g^{h^x} = \prod_{j=1}^N g^{[\![h^x]\!]_j} \bmod q$.

Protocol 3: MPC protocol Π_{DDLP}

The correctness of Π_{DDLP} comes from the fact that $h^x = h^{\sum_{j=1}^N [\![x]\!]_j \bmod p} = \prod_{j=1}^N h^{[\![x]\!]_j}$ since h has order p. The same reasoning holds for Step 3 because g has order q. Plugging Π_{DDLP} into the red part of protocol 2, with $\alpha^{[e]} = h^{[e]}/s^{[e]}$, we readily get a zero-knowledge argument of knowledge of a solution to the given DDLP instance. Note that we should also slightly adapt protocol 2 since $x \in \mathbb{F}_p$ (with $p \leq q$), and $y^{[e]} := g^{h^x [e]}$ is shared multiplicatively, but this is straightforward.

The next theorems state the achieved security guarantees of the previous scheme. Proofs can be found in Appendix A.

Theorem 1 (perfect completeness). *A prover $\mathcal{P}$ who knows a solution to a DDLP instance and who follows the steps of protocol 3 convinces the verifier $\mathcal{V}$ with probability 1.*

Theorem 2 (special soundness). *Suppose that there is an efficient prover $\tilde{\mathcal{P}}$ that, on input (g, h, y), convinces the honest verifier $\mathcal{V}$ on input (g, h, y) to accept with probability $\tilde{\varepsilon} := \Pr[\text{View}(\tilde{\mathcal{P}}(g,h,y), \mathcal{V}(g,h,y)) = 1] > \varepsilon$ for a soundness error ε equal to*

$$\max_{M-\tau \leq k \leq M} \left\{ \frac{\binom{k}{M-\tau}}{\binom{M}{M-\tau} N^{k-M+\tau}} \right\}.$$

Then, there exists an efficient probabilistic extraction algorithm $\mathcal{E}$ that, given rewindable black-box access to $\tilde{\mathcal{P}}$, produces either a witness x such that $g^{h^x} = y$, or a commitment collision, by making an average number of calls to $\tilde{\mathcal{P}}$ which is upper bounded by

$$\frac{4}{\tilde{\varepsilon} - \varepsilon} \left(1 + \tilde{\varepsilon} \frac{8M}{\tilde{\varepsilon} - \varepsilon} \right).$$

Theorem 3 (honest verifier zero knowledge). *Let the PRG used in protocol 3 be (t, ε_{PRG})-secure and the commitment scheme Com be (t, ε_{Com})-hiding. There exists an efficient simulator $\mathcal{S}$ which, given random challenges J and L*

outputs a transcript which is $(t, \tau \varepsilon_{PRG} + \tau \varepsilon_{Com})$-*indistinguishable from a real transcript of protocol 3.*

To estimate the communication complexity, we remark that for each iteration of the protocol, three values have to be communicated: the auxiliary value $\Delta x \in \mathbb{F}_p$ to fix the secret, and $(\Delta s, \alpha) \in \mathbb{F}_q^2$ from the sharing conversion protocol 1 (there is a sole conversion). This leads to a total communication cost of at most:

$$4\lambda + \lambda\tau \log_2 \frac{M}{\tau} + \tau \left[2\log_2(q) + \log_2 p + \lambda \log_2 N + 2\lambda \right] \text{ bits.}$$

In [BTV20], the authors considered the case of a group $\mathbb{G}$ of prime order $q = (4p+18)p+1$ where p is the Sophie Germain prime $p = 2^{1535}+554415$ that divides $q - 1$. Their arguments involve $2\lceil \log_2(2(\lceil \log_2(\ell) \rceil + 1)) \rceil + 8$ elements in $\mathbb{G}$ and 5 elements in $\mathbb{F}_q$. Taking $\mathbb{G}$ as the subgroup of order q in $\mathbb{F}_\ell^*$ for $\ell = 1572q + 1$, one obtains an argument of size 10.2 KB for [BTV20] and of size 24.6 KB for [Sta96] (for a soundness error of 2^{-128}). Our arguments are always shorter than those from [Sta96] and provide better security guarantees than [BTV20] (as mentioned in the introduction). Contrary to [BTV20], we could compress our argument size and construct parameter sets with argument size below 10 KB (but at the cost of an increase in computational complexity for the prover and the verifier).

Second Construction. Actually, we could greatly improve the performance of our zero-knowledge argument of knowledge by considering another approach. This is based on an idea of Joux [Jou23], a forward-backward technique. Again, we start by sharing x additively. Then the prover $\mathcal{P}$ commits to the values

$$y_i := \left(\left(\left(g^{h^{[\![x]\!]_1}} \right)^{h^{[\![x]\!]_2}} \right)^{\cdots} \right)^{h^{[\![x]\!]_i}} \quad \text{mod } q \text{ for } i \in [1, N].$$

The correctness of this approach relies on the fact that $y_N = y \bmod q$. The verifier $\mathcal{V}$ sends a challenge $i^* \xleftarrow{\$} [1, N]$. The prover $\mathcal{P}$ answers by sending the seeds $\{\mathsf{seed}_i\}_{i \neq i^*}$ (i.e. opens all the shares of x except the i^*-th) and the value $\mathsf{Com}(y_{i^*})$ to $\mathcal{V}$. This last can check all the other committed values by a forward-backward technique: they iteratively compute y_i as

- $y_{i-1}^{h^{[\![x]\!]_i}} \bmod q$ if $2 \leq i \leq i^* - 1$;
- $y_{i+1}^{h^{-[\![x]\!]_{i+1}}} \bmod q$ if $i^* + 1 \leq i \leq N - 1$;

with $y_1 = g^{h^{[\![x]\!]_1}} \bmod q$ and $y_N = y \bmod q$. This leads to a $(\lceil N/2 \rceil - 1)$-rounds MPC protocol, where a party $\mathcal{P}_i$ uses the output of $\mathcal{P}_{i-1}$ or $\mathcal{P}_{i+1}$ to compute their own output (for $1 < i < N$). The security of this second construction is analyzed in the full version of the paper.

Performances. Since no more cut-and-choose has to be produced, the argument size is shortened compared to the sharing conversion approach (and only one element field has to be communicated). This leads to the following performances, where the communication complexity of the argument proof is reduced by 77% compared to [Sta96], and beats the bulletproof approach of [BTV20]. Indeed, protocol 3 achieves 17.2 KB for a 2048-bit prime with $N = 2^8, M = 1744, \tau = 17$, whereas this protocol achieves 6.6 KB for a 3072-bit prime for the same number of parties.

5   Proving Knowledge of a IPKP Solution

We denote $\mathcal{S}_n$ the symmetric group of degree n. For a permutation $\pi \in \mathcal{S}_n$ and a vector $v \in \mathbb{F}_q^n$, $\pi(v)$ is the action of the permutation on the coordinates of v.

Permuted Kernel Problem (PKP/IPKP).

Let (q, m, n) be positive integers, $H \in \mathbb{F}_q^{m \times n}$ a random matrix, and a vector $v \in \mathbb{F}_q^n$. The PKP is to find a permutation $\pi \in \mathcal{S}_n$, such that $H\pi(v) = 0$. The inhomogeneous version of the problem (IPKP) is, given a target vector $y \in \mathbb{F}_q^m$, to find a permutation $\pi \in \mathcal{S}_n$, such that $H\pi(v) = y$.

We want to prove the knowledge of a solution to a IPKP instance, i.e., some $x \in \mathbb{F}_q^n$ such that $Hx = y$ and $\pi(v) = x$. For this purpose, we adapt the protocol 2 as follows:

- the input $x \in \mathbb{F}_q^n$ is a vector, so we should consider one conversion by coordinate;
- the sharing of x is over the integers so $[\![x^{[e]}]\!]_j \in [0, A-1]^n$ for some $A > q$. Thus, we should add a rejection rule as explained in Sect. 2;
- $\mathcal{V}$ sends an additional challenge $g \xleftarrow{\$} \mathbb{F}_{q'}^\times$ at the same time as the challenge J, where q' is a prime greater than q whose choice is explained afterward.

Proving the Knowledge of a Permutation. Consider the polynomial $f_{x,v}(X) = \sum_{i=1}^n X^{x_i} - \sum_{i=1}^n X^{v_i}$ of degree at most $q-1$ (x_i, v_i are the components of the vectors x, v), and some uniformly random element $g \in \mathbb{F}_{q'}$. If $x = \pi(v)$ for some $\pi \in \mathcal{S}_n$, then $f_{x,v}$ is identically zero. If there is no permutation $\pi \in \mathcal{S}_n$ such that $\pi(v) = x$, then via the Schwartz-Zippel Lemma [Sch80, Zip79], the probability that $f_{x,v}(g) = 0 \bmod q'$ is bounded by $(q-1)/q'$. Indeed, the probability that a random polynomial in $\mathbb{F}_{q'}[X]$ of degree at most $q-1$ be vanished by a random element in $\mathbb{F}_{q'}$ is at most $(q-1)/q'$.

When computing $f_{x,v}(g)$ over $\mathbb{F}_{q'}$ in a distributed way, the challenge g may not satisfy $g^q = 1 \bmod q'$ and then the modular sharing would lead to a wrong computation. This is the motivation for using a sharing over the integers for x. However, for each coordinate of the vector x, the verifier knows that $[\![x_i]\!]_j \in [0, A-1]$ for each $j \in [1, N]$ (this is verified for open parties) and checks that $-A + q \le x_i - [\![x_i]\!]_{j*} \le 0$ (otherwise they aborts). This implies that they knows that $-A+q \leq x_i \leq A-1$. In particular, the degree of the polynomial is bounded by $A-1$, whence the slack. Indeed, the degree should be bounded by $q-1$, but a malicious prover may choose some x whose coordinates are upper bounded by $A-1$. But this is not a problem as long as the modulus is large enough compared to $A-1$ (for the Schwartz-Zippel Lemma). If a cheating prover shares some coordinate $q \leq x_i \leq A-1$, then x can not the image of v under the action of some permutation, and so the probability that $f_{x,v}(g) = 0$ is bounded by $(A-1)/q'$.

MPC Protocol. We describe the MPC protocol Π_{IPKP} to plug in the red part of protocol 2. As input, x is shared among the parties via a secret sharing over the integers, i.e., $[\![x]\!]_j \xleftarrow{\$} [0, A-1]^n$ for $j \in [1, N]$. The rejection rate of the sharing is $1 - \left(1 - \frac{q-1}{A}\right)^n$ (see Sect. 2). Parties also get some $g \in \mathbb{F}_{q'}^\times$ with q' a prime number greater than $\beta(A-1)$. Π_{IPKP} allows parties to securely compute an additive secret sharing of $(Hx, f_{x,v}(g))$.

Input: $x \in \mathbb{F}_q^n$ shared over the integers as $x = \sum_{j=1}^N [\![x]\!]_j$ such that $Hx = 0 \bmod q$, and $\pi(x) = v$ for some $\pi \in \mathcal{S}_n$.
$g \xleftarrow{\$} \mathbb{F}_{q'}^\times$ with q' the next prime after $\beta(A-1)$.
Output: $[\![f_{x,v}(g)]\!]$ and $[\![Hx]\!]$ secret sharing modulo q'.

1. From the sharing over the integers of each x_i, parties locally compute $\langle g^{x_i} \rangle$, a multiplicative sharing of $g^{x_i} = \prod_{j=1}^N g^{[\![x_i]\!]_j} \bmod q'$, for each $i \in [1, n]$.
2. Parties convert it into an additive sharing $[\![g^{x_i}]\!]$ using Π_{conv} 1, for each $i \in [1, n]$.
3. Parties locally compute their share of $[\![f_{x,v}(g)]\!] = \sum_{i=1}^n [\![g^{x_i}]\!] - \sum_{i=1}^n g^{v_i} \bmod q'$.
4. Parties locally compute their share of $[\![Hx]\!] = H[\![x]\!] \bmod q'$.

Protocol 4: MPC protocol Π_{IPKP} to prove the knowledge to a IPKP solution

Notice that the correctness of $g^{x_i} = g^{\sum_{j=1}^N [\![x_i]\!]} \bmod q'$ follows from the sharing on the integers. For each coordinate, there is one conversion (so two values over $\mathbb{F}_{q'}$) and one auxiliary value for the secret (over $[0, A-1]$). Hence, the obtained argument size is

$$4\lambda + \lambda\tau \log_2 \frac{M}{\tau} + \tau\left[n(2\log_2 q' + \log_2(A-1)) + \lambda \log_2 N + 2\lambda\right] \text{ bits,}$$

where τ is the number of parallel repetitions and M the number of parallel phases in the cut-and-choose.

Security Proofs. Because of the rejection rate, the completeness is no longer perfect. Indeed, a prover $\mathcal{P}$ who knows a solution to a IPKP instance and who follows the steps of the protocol 2 adapted to the IPKP convinces the verifier $\mathcal{V}$ with probability $\left(1 - \frac{q-1}{A}\right)^{\tau n}$. The proofs of the soundness and the zero-knowledge property can be found in the full version.

Performances. The security of the PKP/IPKP has been well-studied for many years (see Sect. 1). We consider the parameter sets proposed in [BFK+19] to achieve 128 bits of security, i.e. $n = 61, m = 28, q = 997$. The choice of the remaining parameters τ and M are chosen as a trade-off between argument size and signing speed. We fix $\beta = 2^8$, i.e., q' is the next prime after $2^8(A-1)$. Hence, the rate of false-positive when checking the existence of a permutation is smaller than $1/2^8$. With $A = 2^{13}, N = 2^8, M = 1289, \tau = 19$, we get an argument of size 16.8 KB.

6 Proving Knowledge of a Fewnomial Pre-image

In this section, we propose a new (candidate) post-quantum one-way function and a digital signature scheme constructed as an argument of knowledge of a pre-image of the public key using the MPCitH paradigm. Our goal is to design a simple and somewhat minimalistic scheme.

We consider a prime number p and the simplest one-way polynomials defined over the finite field $\mathbb{F}_p$. Those polynomials are called *fewnomials* and are simply polynomials with a relatively low number of monomials compared to their degree. If one considers a fewnomial with $t \geq 2$ monomials of large degrees over $\mathbb{F}_p$, the best known classical algorithm has arithmetic complexity $O(p^{(t-1)/t})$ [BCR13]. Combining this algorithm with Grover's algorithm [Gro96], leads to the best-known quantum algorithm with complexity $O(p^{(t-1)/2t})$.

Fewnomial Inversion Problem (FIP).

Let q be a Sophie Germain prime number where $p = 2q+1$ is also a prime number. Let $t \geq 2$ be an integer and $f : \mathbb{F}_p \to \mathbb{F}_p$ be a fewnomial with t monomials defined as $f(X) = \sum_{i \in S} X^i$ where S is a set of t integers in $[\lceil q/2 \rceil, q - 1]$. The Fewnomial Inversion Problem is given $y = f(x) \in \mathbb{F}_p$ to find $x' \in \mathbb{F}_p$ such that $y = f(x')$.

We construct a digital signature scheme based on the hardness of the FIP. Note that we consider the case of unitary monomials but adding non-zero (public) coefficients does not change the following analysis and performances. We discuss later the choice of t and p. It is worth mentioning that if one uses instead a monomial $X^n \bmod p$, it would be easy to invert except if we replace the prime p by a modulus with unknown factorization, and this would be essentially an RSA instance with a larger modulus (and we can use the construction outlined in Sect. 3)

MPC Protocol. The prover/signer shares x multiplicative (to adapt in protocol 2). Using the MPC protocol Π_{FIP} to plug in protocol 2, parties compute an additive secret sharing of $f(x)$.

Proofs of security of the zero-knowledge protocol 2 adapted with the MPC protocol 5 are similar to those in appendix A and can be found in the full version.

Input: $x \in \mathbb{F}_p^{\times}$ shared multiplicative, i.e. $x = \prod_{j=1}^{N} \langle x \rangle_j \bmod p$.
A fewnomial $f : X \to \sum_{i \in S} X^i$, with a finite subset $S \subset \mathbb{N}^t$.
Output: $[\![f(x)]\!]$.

---

1. Parties locally compute $\langle x^i \rangle$ via $x^i = \prod_{j=1}^{N} \langle x \rangle_j^i \bmod p$ for $i \in S^{\times}$.
2. For each $i \in S^{\times}$, parties convert $\langle x^i \rangle$ into an additive sharing $[\![x^i]\!]$ using Π_{conv} 1.
3. Parties locally compute $[\![f(x)]\!] = \sum_{i \in S}[\![x^i]\!]$.

Protocol 5: MPC protocol Π_{FIP}

Fiat-Shamir Heuristic. We apply the Fiat-Shamir transform [FS87] to get a non-interactive protocol, and so a signature scheme. Since our protocols have 5 rounds, we have to take into consideration the attack of [KZ20] for the security of the signature. The forgery cost of the signature scheme is then given by

$$\min_{M-\tau \leq k \leq M} \left\{ \frac{\binom{M}{M-\tau}}{\binom{k}{M-\tau}} + N^{k-M+\tau} \right\}.$$

Signature Scheme. To build a signature, we choose $x \in \mathbb{F}_p^{\times}$ as the private key and $y = f(x) \bmod p$ as the public key. To achieve a forgery cost of $1/\varepsilon$, we could increase τ, but this would not lead to an efficient scheme. Instead, we transform our 5-round protocol into a 3-round before applying the Fiat-Shamir transform, hence [KZ20] attack does not apply anymore. The 5-to-3-round convert's idea is to emulate M MPC protocols before the first round of communication, i.e. before getting the challenges. After values are committed, $\mathcal{V}$ sends both challenges during the same round. There is an overhead in terms of signing speed, i.e., there are $M(1+\log_2(N))$ parties to emulate instead of $\tau(1+\log_2 N)$, but the hypercube optimization attenuates it. Moreover, the communication cost is slightly greater for the 3-round version, the size of the signature scheme is then

$$4\lambda + 3\lambda\tau \log_2 \frac{M}{\tau} + \tau \left[(1 + 2\,s) \log_2 p + \lambda \log_2 N + 2\lambda\right],$$

with s is the size of $S^{\times}$. Indeed, parties apply the conversion protocol for each $i \in S^{\times}$ and each conversion requests to communicate 2 field elements. The resulting 3-round protocol is also an honest-verifier zero-knowledge protocol with the same soundness. It can be checked that the round reduction described here does not impact the proofs of theorems in Appendix A.

Performances. As said above, considering a fewnomial with $t \geq 2$ monomials over $\mathbb{F}_p$, the best known algorithm has arithmetic complexity $O(p^{(t-1)/t})$ [BCR13]. Hence, there is a trade-off between the size of the modulus p and the number of monomials t to consider achieving (classical) 128 bits of security. The optimal one to minimize the proof size is a trinomial over a prime of 170 bits. The achieved signature length is 12.2 KB for $\tau = 28, N = 2^5, M = 389$, and 10.6 KB for $\tau = 18, N = 2^8, M = 1251$.

A   Security Proofs

Proof (Theorem 1). For any sampling of the random coins of $\mathcal{P}$ and $\mathcal{V}$, if the computation described in the protocol 3 is honestly performed, all the checks of $\mathcal{V}$ pass. The completeness is hence perfect. $\qquad\square$

Proof (Theorem 2). To prove the special soundness, one has to build an efficient knowledge extractor that returns a solution of the DDLP instance. We first show how to extract a DDLP solution from 3 specific transcripts. Then we explain how to get such transcripts from rewindable black-box access to $\tilde{\mathcal{P}}$. First, assume that we can get three transcripts $T_i = (\mathrm{COM}^{(i)}, \mathrm{CH}_1^{(i)}, \mathrm{RSP}_1^{(i)}, \mathrm{CH}_2^{(i)}, \mathrm{RSP}_2^{(i)})$ for $i \in \{1,2,3\}$ from $\tilde{\mathcal{P}}$, with $\mathrm{CH}_1^{(i)} := J^{(i)}$, $\mathrm{CH}_2^{(i)} := \{\ell_j^{(i)}\}_{j \in J^{(i)}}$, which satisfy the conditions:

1. $\mathrm{COM}^{(1)} = \mathrm{COM}^{(2)} = \mathrm{COM}^{(3)} = h$,
2. there exists $j_0 \in (J^{(1)} \cap J^{(2)}) \setminus J^{(3)}$ s.t. $\ell_{j_0}^{(1)} \neq \ell_{j_0}^{(2)}$
3. T_1 and T_2 are success transcripts (*i.e.* which pass all the tests of $\mathcal{V}$),
4. $\mathrm{seed}^{[j_0]}$ from $\mathrm{RSP}_1^{(3)}$ is consistent with the $(x^{[j_0]}, r^{[j_0]}, s^{[j_0]})$ from T_1 and T_2.

We show how to extract a solution of the DDLP instance (g, h, y) from the three transcripts. First, we can assume that all the revealed shares are mutually consistent between the three transcripts. Otherwise, we find a hash collision via condition 1. Thus, we know all the shares for the iteration j_0 from T_1 and T_2 using condition 2. For the sake of clarity, we only consider the variables of the iteration j_0. Thus, this notation is omitted in the following. Consider $x' := \sum_{j=1}^{N} [\![x]\!]_j \bmod p$ as a natural candidate solution for x. Via the multi-party computation, we know

- $h^{x'} = h^{\sum_{j=1}^{N}[\![x]\!]_j} = \prod_{j=1}^{N} h^{[\![x]\!]_j} = \prod_{j=1}^{N} \langle h^x \rangle_j \bmod q$
- the broadcasting of $\langle \alpha \rangle = \frac{\langle h^x \rangle}{\langle s \rangle}$ i.e. $\alpha = \frac{h^x}{s} \bmod q$
- an additive sharing of h^x via $\alpha [\![r]\!] = \frac{h^x}{s}[\![r]\!] = [\![h^x]\!]$, since from the checked equations at the end of T_3 we get that $r = s$.
- $y = \prod_{j=1}^{N} \langle y \rangle_j \bmod q$ with $\langle y \rangle_j = g^{[\![h^x]\!]_j} \bmod q$.

Hence, $g^{h^{x'}} = g^{\prod_{j=1}^{N}\langle h^x \rangle_j} = g^{\sum_{j=1}^{N}[\![h^x]\!]_j} = \prod_{j=1}^{N} g^{[\![h^x]\!]_j} = \prod_{j=1}^{N} \langle y \rangle_j = y \bmod q$. Therefore, x' is a solution of the considered DDLP. Now, the extractor for the three transcripts can be the one described in appendix E of [FJR23]. $\qquad\square$

Proof (Theorem 3). We build a simulator that outputs transcripts indistinguishable from real transcripts without knowing the secret. It has oracle access to some probabilistic polynomial time $\tilde{\mathcal{V}}$.

1. Sample $J \xleftarrow{\$} \{J \subset [1, M]; |J| = \tau\}$ and $L = \{\ell_e\}_{e \in J} \xleftarrow{\$} [1, N]^\tau$
2. Sample $\mathsf{mseed}^{[0]} \xleftarrow{\$} \{0,1\}^\lambda$
3. $(\mathsf{mseed}^{[e]})_{e \in [1,M]} \leftarrow \mathrm{TreePRG}(\mathsf{mseed}^{[0]})$

4. For $e \in [1, M] \backslash J$, follow honestly the protocol and deduce h_e
5. For $e \in J$,
   - Compute $(\text{seed}_1^{[e]}, \rho_1^{[e]}), \ldots, (\text{seed}_N^{[e]}, \rho_N^{[e]})$ with $\text{TreePRG}(\text{mseed}^{[e]})$
   - For each party $j \in [1, N] \backslash \{\ell_e\}$: $(\llbracket x^{[e]} \rrbracket_j, \llbracket r^{[e]} \rrbracket_j, \langle s^{[e]} \rangle_j) \leftarrow$ $\text{PRG}(\text{seed}_j^{[e]}), \text{com}_j^{[e]} = \text{Com}(\text{seed}_j^{[e]}; \rho_j^{[e]})$
   - Sample $\Delta x^{[e]} \xleftarrow{\$} \mathbb{F}_p, \llbracket r^{[e]} \rrbracket_{\ell_e} \xleftarrow{\$} \mathbb{F}_q, \langle s^{[e]} \rangle_{\ell_e} \xleftarrow{\$} \mathbb{F}_q^\times$
   - $\Delta s^{[e]} = \sum_{j=1}^N \llbracket r^{[e]} \rrbracket_j / \prod_j \langle s \rangle_j^{[e]} \bmod q$
   - $\alpha^{[e]} = h^{\sum_{j=1}^N \llbracket x^{[e]} \rrbracket_j + \Delta x^{[e]}} / (\Delta s^{[e]} \prod_{j=1}^N \langle s^{[e]} \rangle_j) \bmod q$
   - $\langle g^{h^{x^{[e]}}} \rangle_j = g^{\alpha^{[e]} \llbracket r^{[e]} \rrbracket_j} \bmod q$
   - Adapt the output of the party ℓ_e: $\langle g^{h^{x^{[e]}}} \rangle_{\ell_e} = y / \prod_{j \neq \ell_e} \langle g^{h^{x^{[e]}}} \rangle_j \bmod q$
   - Sample a random commitment $\text{com}_{\ell_e}^{[e]}$.
   - Compute $h_e = \mathcal{H}_1(\Delta s^{[e]}, \text{com}_1^{[e]}, \ldots, \text{com}_n^{[e]}), h'_e = \mathcal{H}_3(\Delta x^{[e]}, \langle g^{h^{x^{[e]}}} \rangle, \alpha^{[e]})$
6. Compute $h = \mathcal{H}_2(h_1, \ldots, h_M), h' = \mathcal{H}_4((h'_e)_{e \in J})$
7. Outputs the transcript

$$\left(h, h', (\text{mseed}^{[e]})_{e \in [1, M] \backslash J}, ((\text{seed}_i^{[e]}, \rho_i^{[e]})_{i \neq \ell_e}, \text{com}_{\ell_e}^{[e]}, \Delta x^{[e]}, \Delta s^{[e]}, \alpha^{[e]})_{e \in J} \right) .$$

The distribution of the output transcript is identical to a real one, except for the commitment of the party ℓ_e in each execution $e \in J$. Distinguishing them means breaking the commitment hiding property or the PRG security. $\qquad \square$

References

ASM10. Au, M.H., Susilo, W., Mu, Y.: Proof-of-knowledge of representation of committed value and its applications. In: Steinfeld, R., Hawkes, P. (eds.) ACISP 2010. LNCS, vol. 6168, pp. 352–369. Springer, Heidelberg (2010). https://doi.org/10.1007/978-3-642-14081-5_22

BBB+18. Bünz, B., Bootle, J., Boneh, D., Poelstra, A., Wuille, P., Maxwell, G.: Bulletproofs: short proofs for confidential transactions and more. In: 2018 IEEE Symposium on Security and Privacy, pp. 315–334. IEEE Computer Society Press, San Francisco, CA, USA (2018)

BCR13. Bi, J., Cheng, Q., Rojas, J.M.: Sub-linear root detection, and new hardness results, for sparse polynomials over finite fields. In: Kauers, M. (ed.) International Symposium on Symbolic and Algebraic Computation, ISSAC'13, Boston, MA, USA, 26–29 June 2013, pp. 61–68. ACM (2013)

Beu20. Beullens, W.: Sigma protocols for MQ, PKP and SIS, and fishy signature schemes. In: Canteaut, A., Ishai, Y. (eds.) EUROCRYPT 2020. LNCS, vol. 12107, pp. 183–211. Springer, Cham (2020). https://doi.org/10.1007/978-3-030-45727-3_7

BFK+19. Beullens, W., Faugère, J.-C., Koussa, E., Macario-Rat, G., Patarin, J., Perret, L.: PKP-based signature scheme. In: Hao, F., Ruj, S., Sen Gupta, S. (eds.) INDOCRYPT 2019. LNCS, vol. 11898, pp. 3–22. Springer, Cham (2019). https://doi.org/10.1007/978-3-030-35423-7_1

BG22. Bidoux, L., Gaborit, P.: Compact post-quantum signatures from proofs of knowledge leveraging structure for the PKP, SD and RSD problems. CoRR, abs/2204.02915 (2022)

BTV20. Blazy, O., Towa, P., Vergnaud, D.: Public-key generation with verifiable randomness. In: Moriai, S., Wang, H. (eds.) ASIACRYPT 2020. LNCS, vol. 12491, pp. 97–127. Springer, Cham (2020). https://doi.org/10.1007/978-3-030-64837-4_4

CDG+20. Chase, M., et al.: The Picnic Signature Scheme - Design Document. Version 2.2 - 14 April 2020 (2020)

CG07. Canard, S., Gouget, A.: Divisible E-cash systems can be truly anonymous. In: Naor, M. (ed.) EUROCRYPT 2007. LNCS, vol. 4515, pp. 482–497. Springer, Heidelberg (2007). https://doi.org/10.1007/978-3-540-72540-4_28

CGM16. Chase, M., Ganesh, C., Mohassel, P.: Efficient zero-knowledge proof of algebraic and non-algebraic statements with applications to privacy preserving credentials. In: Robshaw, M., Katz, J. (eds.) CRYPTO 2016. LNCS, vol. 9816, pp. 499–530. Springer, Heidelberg (2016). https://doi.org/10.1007/978-3-662-53015-3_18

CS97. Camenisch, J., Stadler, M.: Efficient group signature schemes for large groups. In: Kaliski, B.S. (ed.) CRYPTO 1997. LNCS, vol. 1294, pp. 410–424. Springer, Heidelberg (1997). https://doi.org/10.1007/BFb0052252

DG23. Dao, Q., Grubbs, P.: Spartan and bulletproofs are simulation-extractable (for free!). In: Hazay, C., Stam, M. (eds.) EUROCRYPT 2023. LNCS, vol. 14005, pp. 531–562. Springer, Cham (2023). https://doi.org/10.1007/978-3-031-30617-4_18

DGH+21. Dinur, I., et al.: MPC-friendly symmetric cryptography from alternating moduli: candidates, protocols, and applications. In: Malkin, T., Peikert, C. (eds.) CRYPTO 2021. LNCS, vol. 12828, pp. 517–547. Springer, Cham (2021). https://doi.org/10.1007/978-3-030-84259-8_18

DKR+22. Dobraunig, C., Kales, D., Rechberger, C., Schofnegger, M., Zaverucha, G.: Shorter signatures based on tailor-made minimalist symmetric-key crypto. In: Yin, H., Stavrou, A., Cremers, C., Shi, E. (eds.) ACM CCS 2022, pp. 843–857. ACM Press, Los Angeles, CA, USA (2022)

Fen22. Feneuil, T.: Building MPCitH-based signatures from MQ, MinRank, rank SD and PKP. Cryptology ePrint Archive, Report 2022/1512 (2022)

FJR23. Feneuil, T., Joux, A., Rivain, M.: Shared permutation for syndrome decoding: new zero-knowledge protocol and code-based signature. Des. Codes Cryptogr. **91**(2), 563–608 (2023)

FMRV22. Feneuil, T., Maire, J., Rivain, M., Vergnaud, D.: Zero-knowledge protocols for the subset sum problem from MPC-in-the-head with rejection. In: Agrawal, S., Lin, D. (eds.) ASIACRYPT 2022. LNCS, vol. 13792, pp. 371–402. Springer, Heidelberg (2022). https://doi.org/10.1007/978-3-031-22966-4_13

FS87. Fiat, A., Shamir, A.: How to prove yourself: practical solutions to identification and signature problems. In: Odlyzko, A.M. (ed.) CRYPTO 1986. LNCS, vol. 263, pp. 186–194. Springer, Heidelberg (1987). https://doi.org/10.1007/3-540-47721-7_12

GOP+22. Ganesh, C., Orlandi, C., Pancholi, M., Takahashi, A., Tschudi, D.: Fiat-Shamir bulletproofs are non-malleable (in the algebraic group model). In: Dunkelman, O., Dziembowski, S. (eds.) EUROCRYPT 2022. LNCS, vol. 13276, pp. 397–426. Springer, Heidelberg (2022). https://doi.org/10.1007/978-3-031-07085-3_14

GPS12. Ghodosi, H., Pieprzyk, J., Steinfeld, R.: Multi-party computation with conversion of secret sharing. Des. Codes Cryptogr. **62**(3), 259–272 (2012)

GQ90. Guillou, L.C., Quisquater, J.-J.: A "paradoxical" indentity-based signature scheme resulting from zero-knowledge. In: Goldwasser, S. (ed.) CRYPTO 1988. LNCS, vol. 403, pp. 216–231. Springer, New York (1990). https://doi.org/10.1007/0-387-34799-2_16

Gro96. Grover, L.K.: A fast quantum mechanical algorithm for database search. In: 28th ACM STOC, pp. 212–219. ACM Press, Philadephia, PA, USA (1996)

IKOS07. Ishai, Y., Kushilevitz, E., Ostrovsky, R., Sahai, A.: Zero-knowledge from secure multiparty computation. In: Johnson, D.S., Feige, U. (eds.) 39th ACM STOC, pp. 21–30. ACM Press, San Diego, CA, USA (2007)

Jou23. Joux, A.: MPC in the head for isomorphisms and group actions. IACR Cryptol. ePrint Arch., p. 664 (2023)

KKW18. Katz, J., Kolesnikov, V., Wang, X.: Improved non-interactive zero knowledge with applications to post-quantum signatures. In: Lie, D., Mannan, M., Backes, M., Wang, X. (eds.) ACM CCS 2018, pp. 525–537. ACM Press, Toronto, ON, Canada (2018)

KZ20. Kales, D., Zaverucha, G.: An attack on some signature schemes constructed from five-pass identification schemes. In: Krenn, S., Shulman, H., Vaudenay, S. (eds.) CANS 2020. LNCS, vol. 12579, pp. 3–22. Springer, Cham (2020). https://doi.org/10.1007/978-3-030-65411-5_1

KZ22. Kales, D., Zaverucha, G.: Efficient lifting for shorter zero-knowledge proofs and post-quantum signatures. Cryptology ePrint Archive, Paper 2022/588 (2022)

MGH+23. Aguilar-Melchor, C., Gama, N., Howe, J., Hülsing, A., Joseph, D., Yue, D.: The return of the SDitH. In: Hazay, C., Stam, M. (eds.) EUROCRYPT 2023. LNCS, vol. 14008, pp. 564–596. Springer, Cham (2023). https://doi.org/10.1007/978-3-031-30589-4_20

Sch80. Schwartz, J.T.: Fast probabilistic algorithms for verification of polynomial identities. J. ACM **27**(4), 701–717 (1980)

Sha90. Shamir, A.: An efficient identification scheme based on permuted kernels (extended abstract). In: Brassard, G. (ed.) CRYPTO 1989. LNCS, vol. 435, pp. 606–609. Springer, New York (1990). https://doi.org/10.1007/0-387-34805-0_54

Sta96. Stadler, M.: Publicly verifiable secret sharing. In: Maurer, U. (ed.) EUROCRYPT 1996. LNCS, vol. 1070, pp. 190–199. Springer, Heidelberg (1996). https://doi.org/10.1007/3-540-68339-9_17

Ste94. Stern, J.: Designing identification schemes with keys of short size. In: Desmedt, Y.G. (ed.) CRYPTO 1994. LNCS, vol. 839, pp. 164–173. Springer, Heidelberg (1994). https://doi.org/10.1007/3-540-48658-5_18

Win84. Winternitz, R.S.: A secure one-way hash function built from DES. In: Proceedings of the 1984 IEEE Symposium on Security and Privacy, Oakland, California, USA, April 29 - May 2, 1984, pp. 88–90. IEEE Computer Society (1984)

Zip79. Zippel, R.: Probabilistic algorithms for sparse polynomials. In: Ng, E.W. (ed.) Symbolic and Algebraic Computation. LNCS, vol. 72, pp. 216–226. Springer, Heidelberg (1979). https://doi.org/10.1007/3-540-09519-5_73

Scaling Mobile Private Contact Discovery to Billions of Users

Laura Hetz[1]([envelope]), Thomas Schneider[1], and Christian Weinert[2]

[1] ENCRYPTO, Technical University of Darmstadt, Darmstadt, Germany
{laura.hetz,schneider}@encrypto.cs.tu-darmstadt.de
[2] Royal Holloway, University of London, London, UK
christian.weinert@rhul.ac.uk

Abstract. Mobile contact discovery is a convenience feature of messengers such as WhatsApp or Telegram that helps users to identify which of their existing contacts are registered with the service. Unfortunately, the contact discovery implementation of many popular messengers massively violates the users' privacy as demonstrated by Hagen et al. (NDSS '21, ACM TOPS '23). Unbalanced private set intersection (PSI) protocols are a promising cryptographic solution to realize mobile *private* contact discovery, however, state-of-the-art protocols do not scale to real-world database sizes with billions of registered users in terms of communication and/or computation overhead.

In our work, we make significant steps towards truly practical large-scale mobile private contact discovery. For this, we combine and substantially optimize the unbalanced PSI protocol of Kales et al. (USENIX Security '19) and the private information retrieval (PIR) protocol of Kogan and Corrigan-Gibbs (USENIX Security '21). Our resulting protocol has a total communication overhead that is sublinear in the size of the server's user database and also has sublinear online runtimes. We optimize our protocol by introducing database partitioning and efficient scheduling of user queries. To handle realistic change rates of databases and contact lists, we propose and evaluate different possibilities for efficient updates. We implement our protocol on smartphones and measure online runtimes of less than 2 s to query up to 1 024 contacts from a database with more than two billion entries. Furthermore, we achieve a reduction in setup communication up to factor 32× compared to state-of-the-art mobile private contact discovery protocols.

Keywords: mobile contact discovery · PSI · PIR

1 Introduction

The number of users of mobile messengers such as WhatsApp, Telegram, and Signal has been rising for over a decade. In 2020, WhatsApp reached two billion monthly active users [25]. Messengers connect these users by presenting them a selection of their existing address book contacts who are registered with the same service. This convenient feature is called *mobile contact discovery* and requires matching users' contact lists with the service's database. The address book of users is also checked regularly to ensure an up-to-date list of possible contacts.

© The Author(s), under exclusive license to Springer Nature Switzerland AG 2024
G. Tsudik et al. (Eds.): ESORICS 2023, LNCS 14344, pp. 455–476, 2024.
https://doi.org/10.1007/978-3-031-50594-2_23

However, a recent survey [33] showed that five out of eleven studied messengers, including WhatsApp and Telegram, implement contact discovery by obtaining their users' contact lists in plaintext. Thus, service providers not only learn about mutual contacts, but also information of unregistered contacts. Based on this, the entire social graph of users, possibly containing sensitive information, can be inferred. Even if a user has never signed up with a messenger or social media platform, contact discovery services might have already stored their personal data. Meta, WhatsApp's and Facebook's parent company, which acquired WhatsApp in 2014 for 16 billion USD [58], has acknowledged this with a tool that lets non-users check, delete, and block their data from several of their services' contact discovery databases, however, excluding WhatsApp [29]. It is currently unclear how these block lists are implemented and which privacy implications they entail. Due to the availability of information, access to it might be enforced legally (by governments) or illegally (by hackers).

A naive approach used by some messengers to protect privacy is to apply a cryptographic hash function before uploading phone numbers. However, due to the clearly defined structure and low entropy of phone numbers, the reversal of a single hash is possible in less than 0.1 ms on commodity hardware [33]. The privacy-preserving messenger Signal thus uses hardware enclaves, specifically Intel SGX, to securely realize mobile contact discovery. However, the security of enclaves is not trivial as even code without vulnerabilities can be subject to various types of attacks [9,21,64,72].

The cryptographic approach for mobile *private* contact discovery is to apply protocols for unbalanced *private set intersection (PSI)*. In our setting, the server's user database DB and the client's phone contacts X each represent one set ($|X| \ll |DB|$) while only the client learns about the mutual elements.

Recent works [15,28,57,65] show promising results for fast and communication-efficient PSI in different use cases, but are still impractical for mobile private contact discovery at large scale due to the required online computation performed by the server. With over two billion WhatsApp users [25], the unbalanced PSI protocol by Cong et al. [15] requires less than 80 MiB of total communication, but more than 35 s online time with multi-threading (T=24 threads) to query $|X| = 2^{10}$ client contacts. Hence, the protocol by Kales et al. [43] based on oblivious pseudorandom functions (OPRFs) is still state of the art for private contact discovery due to its fast online runtimes (linear in $|X|$ and less than 3 s for $|DB| = 2^{28}$, $|X| = 2^{10}$ [43]) and optimization for mobile devices. However, this protocol has setup communication and client storage costs linear in the database size – 8 GiB for $|DB| = 2^{31}$ – which also makes it impractical for large-scale messengers. To make such protocols viable, communication sublinear in the database size is necessary. The authors of [23,43] thus recommend using a protocol for multi-server private information retrieval (PIR) in PSI to achieve sublinear communication.

Our Contributions. In this work, we make big steps towards truly practical mobile private contact discovery by reducing the setup communication to be sublinear in the size of the server's database. The authors of [23] already achieved this, however, their protocol requires online computation linear in the database size. We achieve both, total communication and online computation sublinear in the database size. For this, we survey the current literature and select the offline online PIR (OO-PIR) protocol by Kogan and Corrigan-Gibbs [46] as a building block for its sublinear complexities. By combining the state-of-the-art protocol for unbalanced PSI on mobile devices [43] with OO-PIR [46], we obtain an asymptotically and concretely efficient mobile private contact discovery protocol.

We further extend our protocol to handle large sets, i.e., databases with up to $|DB| = 2^{31}$ items, to meet the requirements of real-world messengers. To our knowledge, we are the first to consider a database with more than a billion records in unbalanced PSI (8× more than related works [23,43,45,66,70]). For this setting, we reduce the setup communication by up to factor 32× over the state-of-the-art protocol of [43]. To prevent the inefficient processing of a large database as a whole, we let multiple instances of the PIR protocol operate on smaller database partitions. Queries to these partitions should not reveal to the server which database partitions are of interest to the client. Therefore, we schedule these queries based on a balls-to-bin analysis similar to [23,60,62]. This reduces communication by a factor up to 24× compared to the naive approach of sending the maximum possible number of queries to all partitions to hide the information which partitions are of interest.

We also study ways to efficiently handle updates to client contact lists and server databases. For this, we evaluate solutions for dynamic databases proposed by recent literature [23,43,46,51] and improve on their ideas for our protocol design. With less than 3 MiB/day for processing a realistic number of 2^{21} daily updates [32,33], our resulting protocol has the lowest communication cost.

Finally, we implement our protocol on smartphones to demonstrate feasibility and obtain concrete runtime measurements in realistic WiFi and LTE network settings. Over WiFi, we achieve an online runtime of less than 2 s for $|DB| = 2^{31}$ database records and $|X| = 2^{10}$ phone contacts. Further highlights of our implementation include containerized builds for improved reproducibility, multi-threading for additional runtime improvements, and significant optimizations of the original PIR implementation of [46]. Our implementation "DISCO" (short for "DIScover COntacts") is available at https://encrypto.de/code/disco.

To summarize, our main contributions are as follows:

- New mobile private contact discovery protocol based on unbalanced PSI [43] and private information retrieval (PIR) [46] with sublinear total communication and online runtime.
- Reproducible, multi-threading-capable implementation on mobile clients.
- Large-scale evaluation for databases with more than two billion records and online runtime of less than 2 seconds over WiFi.
- Efficient update strategy with less than 3 MiB / day of additional communication costs.

2   Preliminaries

In this section, we describe the basic concepts used in our work, specifically protocols for oblivious pseudorandom function (OPRF), private set intersection

(PSI), and private information retrieval (PIR). We also explain Cuckoo filters (CFs), a probabilistic data structure used in our protocol.

Oblivious Pseudorandom Function. An oblivious pseudorandom function (OPRF) is a secure two-party computation (STPC) protocol where the computed public function f is a keyed pseudorandom function (PRF). Party P_2 inputs key k and P_1 inputs a value x for which P_1 obtains the PRF output $f_k(x)$. Both parties stay oblivious about the other party's input and only P_1 obtains the OPRF output. OPRF constructions can be used to realize PSI protocols, as shown in a variety of works, including [27,34,43,45,61]. We focus on the Naor-Reingold PRF (NR-PRF) [56] and PRFs that evaluate block ciphers such as AES and the STPC-friendly cipher LowMC [1] using Yao's garbled circuit (GC) [73], a generic protocol for STPC. These OPRFs offer malicious client security [45, 61] and their implementations were already optimized for mobile devices [43]. While recent works [12,65,67] improve over our selected OPRFs, we leave their evaluation as future work and focus on reducing the setup communication and client storage of the state-of-the-art protocol for mobile private contact discovery.

Cuckoo Filter. A Cuckoo filter (CF) is a probabilistic data structure for fast membership testing. A CF stores tags (i.e., short representations of items), where each tag is located in one of h possible buckets and each bucket contains up to b tags. The tag of x with length v is computed using hash function H_t: $t_x = H_t(x) \in \{0,1\}^v$ and its possible positions are determined by h hash functions [26]. CFs are similar to Bloom filters (BFs) [7], but have better performance, reduced storage, and allow item deletion. Hash collisions for tags can result in false positives. We follow the parameter recommendations in [43] with bucket size $b = 3$ and tag size $v = 32$ for a false positive probability (FPP) of $\epsilon \leq 2b/2^v \approx 2^{-29}$.

Private Set Intersection. In protocols for private set intersection (PSI), two parties P_1 and P_2 hold sets X_1 and X_2, respectively. They want to know their mutual items (i.e., $X_1 \cap X_2$) without revealing anything else about their sets. State-of-the-art PSI protocols for large sets build on the oblivious key-value store (OKVS) data structure [28,57,65]. However, they require online communication linear in the size of the larger set. Another line of work on *unbalanced* PSI based on fully homomorphic encryption (FHE) [13–15] has a small communication footprint, but is not well suited for large-scale contact discovery as the server online computation is linear in the database size for each client.

In this work, we thus focus on unbalanced OPRF-based PSI protocols [20, 34,43,45,61] for mobile private contact discovery. The high-level idea requires server S, holding the larger set DB, to sample a secret key k and to encrypt its input using a PRF and k to obtain $PRF_k(DB[i])$ for $i \in \{1,\ldots,|DB|\}$. This encrypted set is sent to the client C who stores it. Both parties then run the corresponding OPRF protocol on C's input $X[i]$ for $i \in \{1,\ldots,|X|\}$ and S's key k such that C obtains the encrypted values $PRF_k(X[i])$ and locally checks which of them are contained in the server's encrypted set. The performance of such PSI protocols is great in the online phase (independent of $|DB|$), but suffers from high setup communication and client storage requirements (linear in $|DB|$), which prohibits applicability for mobile private contact discovery at large scale. In this work, we make significant steps towards practicality by replacing the download in the setup phase with a protocol for PIR for reduced communication and storage requirements.

Private Information Retrieval. Protocols for PIR enable a client C to privately obtain a record from a public database with N_{PIR} records while the server stays oblivious about the requested item. The server's computational cost must be inherently linear in the database size, as the server would otherwise learn which elements the client is not interested in [6]. PIR with preprocessing is thus critical to achieve online complexities sublinear in the database size N_{PIR} by shifting the linear costs to an offline phase. We comprehensively surveyed single- and multi-server PIR protocols with preprocessing for our use case (cf. Sect. A). The state-of-the-art single-server PIR protocols [22,37,53,55] are based on FHE: The client uses FHE to hide their query from the server while also enabling the server to answer their query under encryption. In a large-scale deployment scenario, the client-independent preprocessing in [22,37] offers a significant advantage as server costs otherwise depend on the high number of clients. While these protocols are most promising in the single-server setting, the parties still perform online computation linear in N_{PIR}. Also, online communication costs with query batching are impractically high at large scale. Moreover, FHE-based protocols have yet to be implemented and evaluated for this use case on mobile devices.

In the setting with multiple non-colluding servers (see Sect. 4.2 for a detailed discussion), different strategies have been proposed [10,18,31,46,51,68]. We select the two-server OO-PIR protocol in [46] for its sublinear online complexities (communication in $O(\log N_{PIR})$ and computation in $O(\sqrt{N_{PIR}})$), existing mobile implementation, and database update strategies [46,51]. We refer to the required servers as offline server S_{off} and online server S_{on}, and give an informal protocol description of the protocol in [46]: In the *offline phase*, S_{off} randomly samples N_{Sets} sets, each containing $\sqrt{N_{PIR}}$ database indices, calculates the parity of each set, and sends sets and parities as hints to client C. The parameter $N_{Sets} = \lambda\sqrt{N_{PIR}}\log 2$ is chosen to ensure that any database index appears in at least one set with overwhelming probability [46] based on the statistical security parameter λ. In the *online phase*, the client finds a set that contains the index idx they want to query, and they remove it from the set in a process called *puncturing*, i.e., $Set_i' = Set_i \setminus \{idx\}$. The client sends the punctured set Set_i' to the online server S_{on}, which returns the parity of the received set. The requested database record $DB[idx]$ is reconstructed from the punctured and the unpunctured sets' parities, i.e., $y_{idx} = p_{Set_i} \oplus p_{Set_i'}$. Reusing the set Set_i leaks information about the queries to the server. Thus, the client generates a new set containing the requested index to ensure that the set remains random while at least one set still contains index idx. The client obtains the parity for the new set by puncturing it, requesting the punctured set's parity from the offline server, and adding the database record they just retrieved for idx to the parity. The sublinear communication cost of [46] is achieved by transmitting the sets in compressed form as set keys, which are puncturable PRF keys.

3   Related Work

We focus our discussion of related works on *unbalanced* PSI for mobile private contact discovery. Nevertheless, we acknowledge the existence of further unbalanced PSI protocols based on FHE [13–15], which are not suitable for large-scale contact discovery because the server performs computation linear in the large database for each client in the online phase (cf. Sect. 2).

Our protocol is based on the mobile private contact discovery protocols in [23, 43,45]. In [45], the authors improve PSI for the unbalanced setting and mobile clients by shifting the required setup computation and communication costs that depend linearly on the database size $|DB|$ to a novel precomputation phase. They further reduce the communication and storage costs by storing the larger set in a Bloom filter, a probabilistic data structure similar to Cuckoo filters (CFs). The authors of the state-of-the-art unbalanced PSI protocol for mobile private contact discovery [43] build on the promising results of [45] and optimize the performance as well as communication cost of two OPRF-based PSI protocols with malicious client security. By integrating and optimizing a two-server PIR protocol [46] in the protocol design of [43], we achieve a reduction in setup communication by 32× at only marginally higher online costs (cf. Sect. 5).

A combination of two-server PIR and PSI for private contact discovery was first proposed in [23] with PIR-PSI. Their protocol also achieves sublinear communication complexity in the database size. However, due to a lack of PIR-preprocessing, the servers in PIR-PSI perform online computation linear in the database size for each query, which prohibits large-scale deployments. Furthermore, the constructions and base protocols differ: The authors of [23] improve the performance of the balanced PSI protocol of [47] by running PIR based on distributed point functions (DPFs) [10,11] to reduce the input set sizes. Instead, we use OO-PIR by [46] to reduce the communication of unbalanced OPRF-based PSI [43] for mobile devices. PIR-PSI, similar to our work, models query scheduling as a ball-to-bins problem (cf. Sect. 4.3). In contrast to our protocol, PIR-PSI requires inter-server online communication (32 kiB for $|X| = 2^{10}$ for each client), which incurs 8× higher financial costs compared to computation [41].

In addition to mobile contact discovery, contact tracing and compromised credential checking (C3) are two other use cases for our protocol. Epione [70] combines public key (PK)-based PSI with keyword-PIR for efficient privacy-preserving contact tracing. Epione also achieves sublinear online communication but requires online computation linear in $|DB|$ and has a high online inter-server communication cost. Protocols for C3 are deployed in web browsers to check if *one* credential is in a database of leaked credentials ($|DB| \approx 12.5$ billion [31, 46,71]). For this, PK-based PSI protocols are used in practice; however, to reduce communication overhead, a hash prefix is leaked to the server to indicate which partition of the encrypted database must be downloaded [49,69]. PIR protocols such as [31,46], as well as our work, could be used to mitigate attacks that leverage this leakage.

4   Our Protocol

Our protocol (Fig. 1) provides computational security and assumes a semi-honest setting with two non-colluding servers, S_{off} and S_{on} (we discuss malicious client security in Sect. 4.2). Client C inputs their set of phone contacts X of size $|X|$, and the messaging service inputs their user database DB of size $|DB|$, which is encrypted and encoded in a Cuckoo filter CF. We divide the database of the PIR protocol into N_{Part} partitions, where $CF_p \in \{CF_1, \ldots, CF_{N_{Part}}\}$, to allow for large databases. This requires a scheduling of queries to reduce communication while preventing leakage (cf. Sect. 4.1).

Our protocol is divided into *base*, *setup*, and *online* phase, as introduced by [45]. The client-input-independent parts of the protocol, i.e., base and setup phase, are considered to be *offline*. The base phase of our protocol is input-independent and contains the OPRF precomputation between C and S_{off} as well as the server's generation of the secret key k. This phase is identical to the base phase in [43]; it has a communication complexity of $O(|X|^{pre})$ and allows the client to check up to $|X|^{pre}$ contacts in the online phase. We split the server-input-dependent setup phase into client-independent setup and per-client setup. The server setup is run only once and includes the encoding of the database and CF creation by S_{off}. S_{on} receives no cleartext data, only the CF containing the encrypted and hashed values. The per-client setup has to be executed once for each client and consists of the offline phase of our extended PIR protocol [46].

Our protocol's online phase combines those of [43] and [46]. C and S_{off} run the OPRF protocol on their respective inputs $x_i \in X$ and k, and C obliviously obtains $e_i = PRF_k(x_i)$ for $i \in \{1, \ldots, |X|\}$. C simulates the offline server's data placement in the CF for their encrypted inputs to learn which CF buckets to retrieve via PIR. The encrypted value e_i is in one of two possible CF buckets if $x_i \in DB$, and C retrieves both to locally check if $e_i \in CF$, i.e., $x_i \in DB$. PIR queries to S_{off} and S_{on} are generated for each index based on the stored hints for CF_{Part}. Sending only those actual queries reveals to the server which partitions interest the client. We show in Sect. 4.1 how to avoid this by sending dummy queries in a communication-efficient manner.

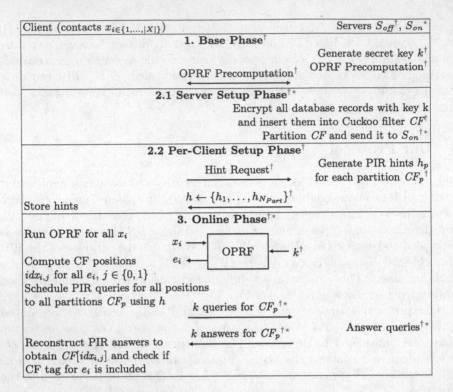

Fig. 1. Protocol phases for communication-efficient OPRF-based unbalanced PSI with two-server PIR. Offline server S_{off} marked with †, online server S_{on} with *.

4.1 Database Partitioning and Querying

We assume messenger services with up to $|DB| = 2^{31}$ users and CFs with up to $N_{CF} = 2^{\lceil \log_2(|DB|/b) \rceil} = 2^{30}$ buckets. To our knowledge, this work is the first to consider a database of this size in the context of mobile private contact discovery. Our selected PIR protocol [46] requires offline computational cost linear in the database size and parties have to process sets with $\sqrt{N_{PIR}}$ items. Using the CF as PIR database (i.e., $N_{PIR} = N_{CF}$) thus leads to poor performance and high memory requirements. Additionally, sets of this size are not supported by the existing OO-PIR implementation [46].

We avert these limitations by partitioning the database and running the protocol on smaller database partitions at a time. The PIR database size now depends on the number of partitions N_{Part} where $N_{PIR} = N_{CF}/N_{Part}$. A smaller number of partitions generally requires less communication since less PIR executions are needed, but higher computational cost due to the increased database size N_{PIR}. We consider this trade-off in the parameter selection for our partitioning. Database partitioning further allows us to distribute the workload between multiple servers to improve the performance and scalability of our protocol.

With database partitioning, if the client would only query the desired indices, the server would learn which partitions are of interest to the client. This leakage could easily be prevented with dummy queries to all other partitions to conceal the actual queries. However, this naive approach requires in the worst case $2|X|N_{Part}$ queries – more than 73 MiB of online communication for $|DB| = 2^{31}$, $|X| = 2^{10}$.

The literature presents various approaches for scheduling queries [3,36,42], also called batching, to reduce communication or computational cost. In [74], the feasibility of using batching techniques in OO-PIR protocols is studied, and a lower bound for communication and time in the preprocessing phase of $t \cdot r = \Omega(N_{PIR}k)$ is proven for batch size k, hint size r, and online time t. The authors show that server performance improves at the cost of higher client runtime, and communication. They conclude that the benefits of PIR protocols in the offline-online model and batching are not compatible. Probabilistic batch codes [3] in OO-PIR achieve this lower bound, but due to the high storage requirements and client costs of this technique, we conclude that (probabilistic) batch codes are not practical for our use case.

Instead of optimizing the query scheduling with batch codes, we focus on leveraging our protocol's underlying data structure: Cuckoo filters. Items in a CF are distributed uniformly under the assumption of uniformly random hash functions, and that the items are chosen independently from the hash functions and from each other (note that our items are encrypted set elements) [24]. This allows us to represent the query scheduling as a balls-to-bin problem, where we ask for the maximum number of balls in any bin when placing n balls independently into β bins chosen uniformly at random. We assume $\beta = N_{Part}$ bins (i.e., DB partitions) and $n = 2|X|$ balls (i.e., queries), and use Eq. (1) based on [62,63] to calculate the probability p of any bin containing more than k balls after inserting n balls into β bins.

$$p = 1 - \left(\sum_{i=0}^{k-1} \binom{n}{i} \cdot \left(\frac{1}{\beta}\right)^i \cdot \left(1 - \frac{1}{\beta}\right)^{n-i} \right)^{\beta}. \qquad (1)$$

We require this probability to be negligible, i.e., $p < 2^{-40}$. Based on this formula, we determine k via a Mathematica script as the maximum number of queries made to each of N_{Part} partitions for $2|X|$ actual queries, and achieve a reduction in communication in the worst case by up to factor 24×, and only require 3 MiB instead of 73 MiB for $|DB| = 2^{31}$, $|X| = 2^{10}$. We note that [63] provide a closed-form solution for the balls-to-bin problem (but with an unspecified constant γ), which we leverage for our asymptotic analysis in Sect. 4.2.

4.2 Complexity and Security Analysis

We now discuss our protocol's communication complexity and analyze its security.

Complexity. Our protocol consists of OPRF and PIR invocations. The considered parameters are the client contact list with size $|X|$ and at most $|X|^{pre}$ precomputed entries; the server database has $|DB|$ entries, which are processed in our protocol in N_{Part} database partitions of size N_{PIR}. The asymptotic communication complexity for OPRF is the same as in [43], namely $O(|X|^{pre})$ in

Table 1. Comparison of asymptotic communication complexities considering database size $|DB|$, client set size $|X|$ with at most $|X|^{pre}$ elements, and the number of database partitions $N_{Part} = N_{CF}/N_{PIR}$ for partition size N_{PIR}.

Phase	[43]	Ours
Base	$O(|X|^{pre})$	$O(|X|^{pre})$
Setup	$O(|DB|)$	$O(N_{Part}\sqrt{N_{PIR}})$
Online	$O(|X|)$	$O((|X| + \sqrt{|X|N_{Part}\log N_{Part}})\log N_{PIR})$

the base and $O(|X|)$ in the online phase. In our PIR protocol, each CF bucket with $b = 3$ tags of size $v = 32$ bit is one record of length $\ell = v \cdot b = 96$ bit. The concrete communication cost for running PIR on N_{Part} partitions of size $N_{PIR} = |DB|/N_{Part}$, $|X|$ client inputs, record length ℓ, and a constant factor γ is as follows:

- offline communication: $N_{Part} \cdot \lambda(\ell\sqrt{N_{PIR}} + 1)$ bits.
- online communication:

$$N_{Part} \cdot \underbrace{\left(\frac{2|X|}{N_{Part}} + \gamma\sqrt{\frac{2|X|}{N_{Part}}} \cdot \log_2 N_{Part} \right)}_{\text{num. queries to each partition } [60,62,63]} \cdot \underbrace{(2(\lambda + 1)\log_2 N_{PIR} + 4\ell)}_{\text{bits per PIR query } [46]} \text{ bits.}$$

Based on this, we can compare the asymptotic communication complexities of our full protocol with the state-of-the-art protocol in [43] in Table 1. Our protocol achieves sublinear communication cost in the setup phase, improving significantly over the linear costs in [43]. The online phase of our protocol includes the communication cost of [43] in addition to the PIR protocol being executed for $|X|$ client items on N_{Part} partitions. The amortized total communication cost per client item is still significantly smaller in our protocol compared to [43] (cf. Sect. 5.3).

Security. We now discuss the security of our protocol provided by the underlying OPRF and PIR building blocks. We first discuss malicious client behavior and then assumptions required for the server side.

The OPRF protocols used in this work, NR-ECC-OPRF [27,34,43,56] and GC-LowMC-OPRF [1,20,43,61], guarantee malicious client security when using maliciously secure oblivious transfer (OT) [59] and OT extension [5,44] protocols. PIR protocols generally assume a public database with possible leakage to the client, hence there are no concerns regarding privacy leakage caused by malicious behavior of clients. Furthermore, our protocol's underlying structure prevents clients (and additional servers) from obtaining cleartext database records as they only ever receive encrypted and hashed values as part of the CF. However, in [51], the authors describe an attack on updated databases that enables a malicious client to obtain deleted database records. Therefore, no formal malicious client security is possible for our protocol with updates via in-place edits (cf. Sect. 4.3). We note that clients can generally monitor the database to learn about added and deleted items, so we consider the attack by [51] as irrelevant in our setting and leave the task of formally establishing malicious client security for OO-PIR without updates as future work. Malicious clients can also easily test if the database includes a certain number by running the PSI protocol. Due to the limited entropy of phone numbers, rate limiting of client queries is recommended to restrict the possibility of misuse via large-scale crawling attacks [32,33,43].

A malicious server could sabotage the OPRF and PIR sub-protocols by sending incorrect information or by using another input set. As only the client obtains the intersection, this only affects correctness. However, the authors of [43] observe that messengers will afterwards most likely receive the outcome of the intersection and could thus learn about non-registered users in the client's contact list in case they include additional entries in their database. Therefore, service providers must be semi-honest, which is reasonable to assume as they are bound by legal requirements and would face significant financial and reputational risk when detected cheating. As we operate in a multi-server PIR setting, we furthermore have to assume two non-colluding servers. This is a prominent assumption in multi-server protocols for reducing computation and communication costs. We see several successful real-world deployments of protocols utilizing this assumption, e.g., the Internet Security Research Group (ISRG) is providing a non-colluding server for data aggregation and analysis with their "Divvi Up" system [40] based on "Prio" [16] and "Poplar" [8]. The ISRG further runs non-colluding servers for privacy-preserving COVID-19 analysis in North America [4,39]. The use of financial incentives [30] and the execution of secure cryptographic protocols inside of trusted execution environments (TEEs) that provide remote attestation (e.g., Intel SGX) could further strengthen the non-collusion assumption between servers.

4.3 Updates

To design our protocol for real-world messaging applications, considering the ever-changing user base and client contacts is essential. The authors of [32,33] based on publicly available data assume daily change rates of $CR \approx 0.1\%$ for Signal, 0.5% for Telegram, and only 0.05% for WhatsApp. We therefore assume a slowly growing messenger user base with daily updates of at most 1%, which is already very high given the real-world data of messengers [32,33].

Updates to the client's phone contacts can include adding or deleting a phone number, and updating a contact's details. Since the client's input is only relevant in the online phase, the handling of updates is trivial: The client can simply run the online phase of the contact discovery protocol for newly added or updated phone numbers to obtain the information if these numbers are registered with a service. Deleted phone numbers are no longer included in the client's set.

Database updates in our protocol could be handled by rerunning the PIR setup and online phase. While this strategy would be simple, the costs would significantly increase with realistic database growth rates, thus making this approach impractical. We therefore propose and evaluate different update strategies for offline-online PIR [46,51] and PSI for mobile contact discovery [23,32].

Waterfall Updates. The authors of our selected PIR protocol [46] propose waterfall updates, an update strategy with tiered sub-databases (called buckets) of increasing size. The database is initially stored in one bucket for which the client obtains hints. Updates are inserted into the smallest bucket until this bucket reaches its maximum capacity and overflows into the next larger bucket. The client obtains new hints for all buckets that changed. With this strategy, hints for smaller buckets must be computed and communicated frequently, while larger buckets change less often. With frequent updates, the performance decreases and the client-dependent computational and communication costs increase significantly, which makes this strategy impractical for large-scale messengers and is thus excluded from further evaluations.

Updates via In-place Edits. The authors of [51] propose a different update strategy for OO-PIR [46,68] that avoids additional databases by updating the client hints to include the updated records. Within our protocol, PIR takes the static-sized CF as a database such that each bucket is a database record in PIR. Updates to the CF do not increase the number of buckets N_{CF}, only their contents and the CF's load factor, which indicates the occupancy level of the filter. Thanks to our protocol's underlying data structure, CFs, we can simplify the approach in [51] by only considering bucket changes, i.e., *in-place edits*. With this strategy, the server applies updates to the CF and sends the corresponding bucket index idx and content change Δ to the client. The client updates all set parities that contain idx by adding the received change, i.e., $p \leftarrow p \oplus \Delta$. While this approach seems straightforward, there is one caveat with the use of CFs: an insertion to the CF can cause a chain of reinsertions where every affected bucket changes and is thus another in-place edit, which potentially increases this strategy's communication cost a lot.

To better understand the impact of reinsertions to the CF, we simulate the growing user base of messengers by inserting a certain percentage CR of the initial database size $|DB|$ to the CF over multiple days. Our simulation shows that more than 80% of CF insertions are immediately successful during the first days. This number decreases with an increasing load factor α, and at $\alpha \approx 0.92$ insertions start to fail – independent of the change rate CR. Thus, in the following, we focus on the finer-grained change rate of 0.1% for a detailed analysis of how many positions in the CF must be changed over time.

In Fig. 2a, we give the daily percentage of insertions that initially failed and thus caused reinsertions. We see polynomial growth in the number of reinsertions with increasing load factor in Fig. 2b. With a decreasing number of empty slots,

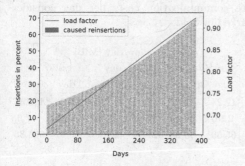 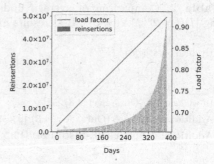

(a) Daily percentage of CF insertions that caused reinsertions displayed in blue.

(b) Daily number of CF reinsertions for the given updates.

Fig. 2. Simulation of updates to a CF for database size $|DB| = 2^{31}$, $N_{CF} = 2^{30}$ CF buckets, and a change rate of $CR = 0.1\%$/day.

more reinsertions are necessary to insert an item, decreasing the filter's performance. Our simulation shows that most insertions require only few reinsertions to be successful, even when the CF is almost full, however, the number of long reinsertion chains is significantly increasing. We calculate the communication cost of updates based on our simulation (cf. Table 2). Transmitting the in-place edits of a single bucket requires *bucket size + index length* bit, here 128 bit, with an average of 13.52 MiB/day for $|DB| = 2^{31}$, $CR = 0.1$, and 30 d.

Updates via in-place edits allow the client to update their already stored hints and to run the PIR protocol on the original CF. The daily download cost of CF updates is thus the only additional cost to our PSI protocol. The server-side computation of CF updates is client-independent and requires only *XOR* operations. In comparison, the client-side hint updates require higher computational costs as all set keys must be evaluated to identify sets with updated indices. Thus, the update procedure can either be applied at once or during the regular online phase (which requires more client storage).

Additional Update Database. Next to updates to the PIR database, we evaluate the strategy of incremental contact discovery [23,32], where updates are stored in an additional smaller database on which another PSI instance is run. The client then has to query each of their contacts on the original and the update database. With our PSI protocol, communication and client storage of updates require less than 3 MiB per day for $|X| = 2^{10}$ contacts with a change rate of $CR = 0.1\%$ / day for $|DB| = 2^{31}$.

We also evaluate the cost of running a simple public key (PK)-based PSI protocol [19,52] due to its trivial implementation and reasonable communication cost as well as computational efficiency for smaller set sizes [35]. However, this turns out to be significantly less efficient for the considered growth rates (cf. Table 2). With less updates and smaller set sizes, PK-based PSI and the state-of-the-art balanced PSI protocols could be more efficient though.

Table 2. Comparison of average update communication costs per day considering $|DB| = 2^{31}$, $|X| = 2^{10}$. Best results marked in bold.

Update Strategies	∅ Comm./day [MiB]					
	0.1%/day		0.5%/day		1.0%/day	
	1 day	30 days	1 day	30 days	1 day	30 days
In-place edits (Ours, Sect. 4.3) [51]	12.24	13.52	62.05	107.77	126.23	486.37
Additional database (Ours, Sect. 4.3) [23,32]	**2.90**	**2.90**	**5.63**	**5.63**	**7.65**	7.65
Additional database (PK-based PSI) [19,52]	65.60	65.54	327.74	327.68	655.42	655.36

Comparison and Privacy Considerations. We compare the proposed update methods in Table 2. Clearly, combining our PIR-based PSI protocol with the incremental contact discovery strategy of [23,32] is the most efficient solution. We note that updates via in-place edits leak some information to the client about the server's change rate. Likewise, the size of additional update databases clearly indicates this value. Also, when the client repeats the online phase of the protocol for new contacts, this leaks information to the server about the number of changes experienced by the client. Such information leakage can be prevented using dummy insertions and dummy queries.

5   Evaluation

We implemented our protocol in C++ and Go (based on the implementations of [43] and [46]) and describe our evaluation for large-scale set parameters next. Our implementation supports multi-threading on partition level for clients and servers, and introduces optimizations that reduce the client setup time by factor 2.8× over [46] (cf. Sect. 5.2). As described in Sect. 4.1, database partitioning is implemented to circumvent hardware and computational limitations of the underlying PIR protocol for large database sizes. For enhanced reproducability, the server-side implementation is containerized. Our implementation called "DISCO" (short for "DIScover COntacts") is available at https://encrypto.de/code/disco.

5.1   Experimental Setup

To meet the requirements of large-scale messengers, we evaluate server database sizes $|DB| \in \{2^{28}, 2^{31}\}$ and client contact list sizes $|X| \in \{1, 2^{10}\}$. The client is a OnePlus 8T smartphone with Snapdragon 865 octa-core CPU (1×2.84 GHz Cortex-A77, 3×2.42 GHz Cortex-A77, 4×1.80 GHz Cortex-A55) and 12 GiB RAM. Our protocol requires two servers that we set up as Linux VMs on a KVM host with two Intel Xeon Gold 6144 CPUs @ 3.50 GHz. Each VM has 8 logical cores (mapped to 4 physical ones) and 128 GiB RAM. In the multi-threaded benchmarks, denoted with T=4/8, the server uses 4 and the mobile client 8 threads. The number of threads is based on the number of available physical cores as we did not see sufficient performance increase on the server side when putting all logical cores under maximum load.

We consider two network settings: *WiFi* with 566 MBit/s down-/upload speed and 12.4 ms RTT, and *LTE* with 30 MBit/s down-/upload speed and 49.3 ms RTT. The settings are simulated in a real WiFi network by limiting bandwidth and introducing delay using tcconfig [38]. We evaluate the performance of our PSI protocol for the *NR-ECC*- and *GC-LowMC*-OPRF. The OPRF performance was measured on a single thread, the PIR costs on a single and multiple threads.

We benchmarked the impact of different partition sizes and select the best-performing size for each database size considering the trade-off between offline communication and online time.

5.2 Profiling and Optimizations

Via profiling we observed that a bottleneck in the online phase is the client's search for a hint/set that contains the desired index, which requires them to expand each set key until the index is found. The implementation of [46] therefore adds a precomputation step that accelerates this search significantly by generating a mapping between database indices and sets. We optimize the runtime of this client setup by covering not all but only a certain percentage of indices. This significantly reduces offline costs while the online computational costs increase only marginally in the rare case that an index is not found in the mapping table. Considering this trade-off and the requirement of a fast online phase, we use a threshold of 99.99% for the client preprocessing, reducing the one-time client setup time by $2.8\times$ compared to [46] ($286.78\,$s for $|DB| = 2^{31}$).

Another bottleneck in the protocol is the required one-time computation in the setup phase, including the server's CF creation and client-dependent preprocessing. With parallelization, we reduce the client-dependent setup costs significantly by up to $3.8\times$ with T=4/8 over our protocol's single-threaded setting.

Overall, we achieve a PIR online runtime of less than 1 s for $|X| \leq 2^{10}$ client contacts in the WiFi setting and an improvement of up to factor $8.3\times$ with multiple threads compared to the original single-threaded implementation.

5.3 Comparison to Related Work

We compare our protocol with the state-of-the-art mobile private contact discovery protocol in [43] and PIR-PSI [23] (cf. Sect. 3).

Mobile Private Contact Discovery [43] **(Table 3).** Our protocol replaces the costly CF download in [43] – including its communication cost linear in the database size – with a more communication-efficient PIR protocol. We give the benchmark results of these protocols for NR-ECC-OPRF and GC-LowMC-OPRF in Table 3. Since both protocols have the same OPRF and CF setup costs, we report these based on our Go implementation and calculate the CF transmission time in the setup phase of [43] based on our connection speeds. With

Table 3. Comparison of runtime and communication costs. Runtimes for [43] based on our Go implementation's CF setup and OPRF results. We set $|X|^{pre} = |X|$. Best results marked in bold.

					Base			Setup					Online		
		Protocols			Time [s]		Comm. [MiB]	Time				Comm. [MiB]	Time [s]		Comm. [kiB]
$|DB|$	$|X|$	PRF	PSI	Parameters	WiFi	LTE		Server [min]	Server [s] (Per-Client)	Client [s] WiFi	LTE		WiFi	LTE	
2^{28}	1	NR-ECC	[44]	$T=1$	**0.07**	**0.29**	**0.04**	590.46	–	15.17	285.95	1072.14	0.06	0.12	4.05
			Ours	$N_{Part}=32, T=1$	**0.07**	**0.29**	**0.04**	590.46	216.47	109.63	129.57	**66.00**	0.83	5.23	38.79
			Ours	$N_{Part}=32$, T=4/8	**0.07**	**0.29**	**0.04**	590.46	63.71	35.26	**57.76**	**66.00**	0.39	0.76	38.79
		GC-LowMC	[44]	$T=1$	0.09	0.36	0.06	33.26	–	15.17	285.95	1072.14	**0.04**	**0.07**	**2.02**
			Ours	$N_{Part}=32, T=1$	0.09	0.36	0.06	33.26	216.47	109.63	129.57	**66.00**	0.81	5.18	36.76
			Ours	$N_{Part}=32$, T=4/8	0.09	0.36	0.06	33.26	63.71	35.26	**57.76**	**66.00**	0.37	0.71	36.76
	2^{10}	NR-ECC	[44]	$T=1$	**0.15**	**0.52**	2.04	590.46	–	15.17	285.95	1072.14	2.20	2.29	4145.00
			Ours	$N_{Part}=32, T=1$	**0.15**	**0.52**	2.04	590.46	216.47	109.63	129.57	**66.00**	5.59	12.17	6097.25
			Ours	$N_{Part}=32$, T=4/8	**0.15**	**0.52**	2.04	590.46	63.71	35.26	**57.76**	**66.00**	2.65	3.47	6097.25
		GC-LowMC	[44]	$T=1$	1.26	5.39	21.56	33.26	–	15.17	285.95	1072.14	**0.63**	**1.22**	**2064.00**
			Ours	$N_{Part}=32, T=1$	1.26	5.39	21.56	33.26	216.47	109.63	129.57	**66.00**	4.02	11.10	4016.25
			Ours	$N_{Part}=32$, T=4/8	1.26	5.39	21.56	33.26	63.71	35.26	**57.76**	**66.00**	1.08	2.40	4016.25
2^{31}	1	NR-ECC	[44]	$T=1$	**0.07**	**0.29**	**0.04**	4752.34	–	121.23	2286.98	8576.00	0.06	0.12	4.05
			Ours	$N_{Part}=64, T=1$	**0.07**	**0.29**	**0.04**	4752.34	1988.81	961.48	1035.53	**264.00**	1.93	10.78	77.54
			Ours	$N_{Part}=64$, T=4/8	**0.07**	**0.29**	**0.04**	4752.34	525.09	286.78	**392.35**	**264.00**	0.49	1.43	77.54
		GC-LowMC	[44]	$T=1$	0.09	0.36	0.06	269.82	–	121.23	2286.98	8576.00	**0.04**	**0.07**	**2.02**
			Ours	$N_{Part}=64, T=1$	0.09	0.36	0.06	269.82	1988.81	961.48	1035.53	**264.00**	1.91	10.73	75.51
			Ours	$N_{Part}=64$, T=4/8	0.09	0.36	0.06	269.82	525.09	286.78	**392.35**	**264.00**	0.47	1.38	75.51
	2^{10}	NR-ECC	[44]	$T=1$	**0.15**	**0.52**	2.04	4752.34	–	121.23	2286.98	8576.00	2.20	2.29	4145.00
			Ours	$N_{Part}=64, T=1$	**0.15**	**0.52**	2.04	4752.34	1988.81	961.48	1035.53	**264.00**	8.31	21.50	6801.49
			Ours	$N_{Part}=64$, T=4/8	**0.15**	**0.52**	2.04	4752.34	525.09	286.78	**392.35**	**264.00**	2.94	4.68	6801.49
		GC-LowMC	[44]	$T=1$	1.26	5.39	21.56	269.82	–	121.23	2286.98	8576.00	**0.63**	**1.22**	**2064.00**
			Ours	$N_{Part}=64, T=1$	1.26	5.39	21.56	269.82	1988.81	961.48	1035.53	**264.00**	6.75	20.43	4720.49
			Ours	$N_{Part}=64$, T=4/8	1.26	5.39	21.56	269.82	525.09	286.78	**392.35**	**264.00**	1.37	3.61	4720.49

our PIR-based protocol, we achieve total communication costs of 272.68 MiB for $|DB| = 2^{31}$, $N_{Part} = 64$, and $|X| = 2^{10}$ (cf. Table 3). This is an improvement by factor $32\times$ compared to ≈ 8 GiB in [43] at only marginally higher runtimes.

PIR-PSI [23] **(Table 4).** We further compare our protocol implementation with PIR-PSI based on the results in [23, Table 2]. The authors of [23] evaluate their performance on a single server with two 18-core Intel Xeon E5-2699 CPUs at 2.30 GHz, 156 GiB RAM, and simulated LAN setting with 10 GB/s bandwidth and 0.02 ms RTT. In comparison, our results are obtained in our WiFi setting using a mobile client and two virtual servers with fewer cores, i.e., 8 vs 18 per machine, and less RAM. Our comparison in Table 4 excludes the OPRF costs of our protocol as these would also have to be applied to [23] to strengthen their protocol's non-collusion assumption. As server setup costs are not reported in [23], we exclude them from this comparison.

We compare the runtimes for both protocols using a single (T=1) and multiple threads (T=4/8) in Table 4. While PIR-PSI does not require an offline phase, marked with "–", our protocol has client-dependent one-time costs, which can be amortized over all online queries. The DPF-PIR protocol [10,11] used in PIR-PSI requires online computation linear in the database size, whereas OO-PIR [46] in our protocol has sublinear complexity. For $|DB| = 2^{28}$, our implementation's

Table 4. Comparison to PIR-PSI [23]. Results for PIR-PSI are from [23, Table 2] with parameters block size b and $\beta = c \cdot |DB| / \log_2(|DB|)$ bins, where c is a scaling factor. The protocols are compared in a single- (T=1) and multi-threading (T=4/8) setting. Best results in the online phase are marked in bold.

|DB|	|X|	Parameters		Offline			Online		
		Protocols PSI	Param.	Time [s] T=1	T=4/8	Comm. [MiB]	Time [s] T=1	T=4/8	Comm. [kiB]
2^{28}	1	[23]	$c = 1, b = 32$	–	–	–	1.21	–	**30.72**
		Ours	$N_{Part} = 32$	326.10	98.97	66.00	**0.77**	**0.33**	34.74
	2^{10}	[23]	$c = 0.25, b = 1$	–	–	–	33.02	13.22	5048.32
		[23]	$c = 4, b = 16$	–	–	–	4.07	1.60	28979.20
		Ours	$N_{Part} = 32$	326.10	98.97	66.00	**3.39**	**0.45**	1952.25

online runtime is significantly faster for single- and multi-threading, especially considering the hardware and network limitations in our setting. We expect the benefit of our protocol's low online costs to become even more visible for larger database sizes ($|DB| = 2^{31}$), for which PIR-PSI does not report results.

FHE-based PSI [15]. The authors of [15] consider their protocol for the use case of mobile private contact discovery and acknowledge increasing hardware requirements for large-scale database sizes. Based on their recommendation to partition the database, as done in our work, their protocol has 76.2 MiB online communication for $|DB| = 2^{31}$, $|X| = 2^{10}$. Our protocol requires 16.5× less online communication – only 4.61 MiB per online phase – but has additional one-time offline costs, which amortize over many queries. Based on [15, Tab. 2], the runtimes for a single partition of size 2^{28} with T=24 threads are 2487 s offline and 4.54 s online, which is significantly higher than those of our work. These additional costs, and the lack of a mobile implementation, currently hinder the use of FHE-based protocols for mobile private contact discovery.

6 Conclusion

In this work, we proposed a new communication-efficient unbalanced PSI protocol by combining and further optimizing OPRF-based unbalanced PSI [43] with two-server PIR [46]. With this, we take big steps towards practicality of large-scale mobile private contact discovery. While our protocol achieves a significant reduction in communication and thus outperforms the state-of-the-art protocol mobile private contact discovery [43] in this regard, the client-dependent setup and update costs are still limiting factors for real-world practicality with large-scale messengers. Continuing research on PIR protocols with client-independent preprocessing is thus a crucial area of future work.

Acknowledgements. This project received funding from the European Research Council (ERC) under the European Union's Horizon 2020 research and innovation program (grant agreement No. 850990 PSOTI). It was co-funded by the Deutsche Forschungsgemeinschaft (DFG) within SFB 1119 CROSSING/236615297 and GRK 2050 Privacy & Trust/251805230.

Appendix

A   PIR Survey

In Table 5, we summarize our survey of recent PIR protocols for their use in OPRF-based PSI based on which we selected the OO-PIR by Kogan and Corrigan-Gibbs [46].

Table 5. Surveyed PIR protocols for OPRF-based PSI. Complexities are simplified. We distinguish between client C's and server(s) S's computational costs where possible. Table entries are left empty when complexities are not clear from the original paper or related work.

n	Protocol	Assumption	Preprocessing	Updatability	Batching	Implementation	Offline Comp. C	Offline Comp. S	Offline Comm.	Online Comp. C	Online Comp. S	Online Comm.
1	SealPIR [3]	RLWE	✓	✗	✓	✓	–	N	–	N		$dN^{1/d}$
	MulPIR [2]	RLWE	✓	✗	✓	✓	–	N	–			$dN^{1/d}$
	[55]	RLWE	✓‡	✗	✓	✓	–	N	–	$B/pN_B^{2/d}$		$BN_B^{1/d}/p$
	Spiral (family) [53]	RLWE	✓	✗	✓	✓	–	N				$\log N$
	PIRANA [50]	RLWE	✓	✗	✓	✓	–	N		N/M	N/M	N/M
	[18]	LWE	✓†	✗	✗	✗	$\sqrt{N}$	N	$\sqrt{N}$	$\sqrt{N}$		$\sqrt{N}$
	OnionPIR [54]	RLWE	✓†	✗	✓	✓	N	N	N	N		N
	[48]	LWE	✓†	✗	✗	✗	N	N	N	$\sqrt{N}$	$\sqrt{N}$	$\sqrt{N}$
	[75]	LWE	✓†	✗	✓	✗		N	$\sqrt{N}$	$\sqrt{N}$	$\sqrt{N}$	1
	[17]	RLWE	✓†	✗	✓	✗	N	N	N	N	N	N
	SimplePIR [37]	LWE	✓†‡	✓	✓	✓	N/M	N	$\sqrt{N}$		N	$\sqrt{N}$
	DoublePIR [37]	LWE	✓†‡	✓	✓	✓	N	d_l^2				$\sqrt{N}$
	FrodoPIR [22]	LWE	✓†‡	✓	✓	✓	N	N	1	N	1	N
2+	DPF-PIR [10]	OWF	✗	–	✓	✓	–	–	–	$\log N$	N	$n \log N$
	CIP-PIR [31]	OWF	✓‡	✓‡	✓	✓	–	N	–	$\sqrt{N/n}$	N/n	$n\sqrt{N/n}$
	[18]	OWF	✓†	✗	✗	✗	$\sqrt{N}$	N	$\sqrt{N}$	$\sqrt{N}$	$\sqrt{N}$	$n \log N$
	[46]	OWF	✓†	✓¶	✓	✓*	$\sqrt{N}$	N	$\sqrt{N}$	$\sqrt{N}$	$\sqrt{N}$	$n \log N$
	[68]	LWE	✓†	✗	✓	✗	$\sqrt{N}$	N	$\sqrt{N}$	$\sqrt{N}$	$\sqrt{N}$	$n \log N$
	iCK [51]	OWF	✓†	✓‖	✓	✓	$\sqrt{N}$	N	$\sqrt{N}$	$\sqrt{N}$	$\sqrt{N}$	$n\sqrt{N}$
	iSACM [51]	LWE	✓†	✓‖	✓	✓	$\sqrt{N}$	N	$\sqrt{N}$	$\sqrt{N}$	$\sqrt{N}$	$n\sqrt{N}$

Database size N, number of servers n, plaintext size p, lattice dimension d_l, database hypercube dimension d, encryption parameter M, number of buckets B and bucket size N_B, † Stateful / offline-online, ‡ client-independent, ¶ waterfall updates, ‖ in-place edits, * includes mobile implementation.

References

1. Albrecht, M.R., Rechberger, C., Schneider, T., Tiessen, T., Zohner, M.: Ciphers for MPC and FHE. In: EUROCRYPT (2015)
2. Ali, A., et al.: Communication-computation trade-offs in PIR. In: USENIX Security (2021)
3. Angel, S., Chen, H., Laine, K., Setty, S.T.V.: PIR with compressed queries and amortized query processing. In: S&P (2018)
4. Apple, Google: Exposure Notification Privacy-preserving Analytics (ENPA) White Paper (2021). https://covid19-static.cdn-apple.com/applications/covid19/current/static/contact-tracing/pdf/ENPA_White_Paper.pdf
5. Asharov, G., Lindell, Y., Schneider, T., Zohner, M.: More efficient oblivious transfer extensions with security for malicious adversaries. In: EUROCRYPT (2015)
6. Beimel, A., Ishai, Y., Malkin, T.: Reducing the servers computation in private information retrieval: PIR with preprocessing. In: CRYPTO (2000)
7. Bloom, B.H.: Space/Time trade-offs in hash coding with allowable errors. Commun. ACM **13**(7), 422–426 (1970)
8. Boneh, D., Boyle, E., Corrigan-Gibbs, H., Gilboa, N., Ishai, Y.: Lightweight techniques for private heavy hitters. In: S&P (2021)
9. Borrello, P., Kogler, A., Schwarzl, M., Lipp, M., Gruss, D., Schwarz, M.: ÆPIC leak: Architecturally leaking uninitialized data from the microarchitecture. In: USENIX Security (2022)
10. Boyle, E., Gilboa, N., Ishai, Y.: Function secret sharing. In: EUROCRYPT (2015)
11. Boyle, E., Gilboa, N., Ishai, Y.: Function secret sharing: Improvements and extensions. In: CCS (2016)
12. Bui, D., Couteau, G.: Improved private set intersection for sets with small entries. In: PKC (2023)
13. Chen, H., Huang, Z., Laine, K., Rindal, P.: Labeled PSI from fully homomorphic encryption with malicious security. In: CCS (2018)
14. Chen, H., Laine, K., Rindal, P.: Fast private set intersection from homomorphic encryption. In: CCS (2017)
15. Cong, K., et al.: Labeled PSI from homomorphic encryption with reduced computation and communication. In: CCS (2021)
16. Corrigan-Gibbs, H., Boneh, D.: Prio: private, robust, and scalable computation of aggregate statistics. In: NSDI (2017)
17. Corrigan-Gibbs, H., Henzinger, A., Kogan, D.: Single-server private information retrieval with sublinear amortized time. In: EUROCRYPT (2022)
18. Corrigan-Gibbs, H., Kogan, D.: Private information retrieval with sublinear online time. In: EUROCRYPT (2020)
19. Cristofaro, E.D., Gasti, P., Tsudik, G.: Fast and private computation of cardinality of set intersection and union. In: CANS (2012)
20. Cristofaro, E.D., Tsudik, G.: Practical private set intersection protocols with linear complexity. In: FC (2010)
21. Cui, J., Yu, J.Z., Shinde, S., Saxena, P., Cai, Z.: SmashEx: smashing SGX enclaves using exceptions. In: CCS (2021)
22. Davidson, A., Pestana, G., Celi, S.: FrodoPIR: simple, scalable, single-server private information retrieval. PETS (2023)
23. Demmler, D., Rindal, P., Rosulek, M., Trieu, N.: PIR-PSI: scaling private contact discovery. PETS (2018)
24. Eppstein, D.: Cuckoo filter: simplification and analysis. In: SWAT (2016)

25. Facebook, Inc. (FB): First Quarter 2020 Results Conference Call (2020). https://s21.q4cdn.com/399680738/files/doc_financials/2020/q1/Q1'20-FB-Earnings-Call-Transcript.pdf

26. Fan, B., Andersen, D.G., Kaminsky, M., Mitzenmacher, M.: Cuckoo filter: practically better than bloom. In: CoNEXT (2014)

27. Freedman, M.J., Ishai, Y., Pinkas, B., Reingold, O.: Keyword search and oblivious pseudorandom functions. In: TCC (2005)

28. Garimella, G., Pinkas, B., Rosulek, M., Trieu, N., Yanai, A.: Oblivious key-value stores and amplification for private set intersection. In: CRYPTO (2021)

29. Ghosh, S.: Facebook probably has your phone number, even if you never shared it. Now it has a secret tool to let you delete it (2022). https://www.businessinsider.com/facebook-has-hidden-tool-to-delete-your-phone-number-email-2022-10

30. Gong, T., Henry, R., Psomas, A., Kate, A.: More is merrier in collusion mitigation (2022). CoRR arXiv:2305.08846

31. Günther, D., Heymann, M., Pinkas, B., Schneider, T.: GPU-accelerated PIR with client-independent preprocessing for large-scale applications. In: USENIX Security (2022)

32. Hagen, C., Weinert, C., Sendner, C., Dmitrienko, A., Schneider, T.: All the numbers are US: large-scale abuse of contact discovery in mobile messengers. In: NDSS (2021)

33. Hagen, C., Weinert, C., Sendner, C., Dmitrienko, A., Schneider, T.: Contact discovery in mobile messengers: Low-cost attacks, quantitative analyses, and efficient mitigations. TOPS (2023)

34. Hazay, C., Lindell, Y.: Efficient protocols for set intersection and pattern matching with security against malicious and covert adversaries. J. Cryptol. 23, 422–456 (2010)

35. Heinrich, A., Hollick, M., Schneider, T., Stute, M., Weinert, C.: PrivateDrop: Practical privacy-preserving authentication for Apple AirDrop. In: USENIX Security (2021)

36. Henry, R.: Polynomial batch codes for efficient IT-PIR. PETS (2016)

37. Henzinger, A., Hong, M.M., Corrigan-Gibbs, H., Meiklejohn, S., Vaikuntanathan, V.: One server for the price of two: Simple and fast single-server private information retrieval. In: USENIX Security (2023)

38. Hombashi, T.: Tcconfig (2022). https://github.com/thombashi/tcconfig

39. Internet Security Research Group: ISRG Prio Services for Preserving Privacy in COVID-19 EN Apps (2021). https://divviup.org/blog/prio-services-for-covid-en/

40. Internet Security Research Group: Divvi Up (2023). https://divviup.org/

41. Ion, M., et al.: On deploying secure computing: Private intersection-sum-with-cardinality. In: EuroS&P (2020)

42. Ishai, Y., Kushilevitz, E., Ostrovsky, R., Sahai, A.: Batch codes and their applications. In: STOC (2004)

43. Kales, D., Rechberger, C., Schneider, T., Senker, M., Weinert, C.: Mobile private contact discovery at scale. In: USENIX Security (2019)

44. Keller, M., Orsini, E., Scholl, P.: Actively secure OT extension with optimal overhead. In: CRYPTO (2015)

45. Kiss, Á., Liu, J., Schneider, T., Asokan, N., Pinkas, B.: Private set intersection for unequal set sizes with mobile applications. PETS (2017)

46. Kogan, D., Corrigan-Gibbs, H.: Private blocklist lookups with checklist. In: USENIX Security (2021)

47. Kolesnikov, V., Kumaresan, R., Rosulek, M., Trieu, N.: Efficient batched oblivious PRF with applications to private set intersection. In: CCS (2016)

48. Lazzaretti, A., Papamanthou, C.: Single server PIR with sublinear amortized time and polylogarithmic bandwidth. ePrint 2022/081 (2022)
49. Li, L., Pal, B., Ali, J., Sullivan, N., Chatterjee, R., Ristenpart, T.: Protocols for checking compromised credentials. In: SIGSAC (2019)
50. Liu, J., Li, J., Wu, D., Ren, K.: PIRANA: Faster multi-query PIR via constant-weight codes (2022). ePrint 2022/1401
51. Ma, Y., Zhong, K., Rabin, T., Angel, S.: Incremental Offline/Online PIR. In: USENIX Security (2022)
52. Meadows, C.A.: A more efficient cryptographic matchmaking protocol for use in the absence of a continuously available third party. In: S&P (1986)
53. Menon, S.J., Wu, D.J.: SPIRAL: fast, high-rate single-server PIR via FHE composition. In: S&P (2022)
54. Mughees, M.H., Chen, H., Ren, L.: OnionPIR: response efficient single-server PIR. In: CCS (2021)
55. Mughees, M.H., Ren, L.: Vectorized batch private information retrieval. S&P (2023)
56. Naor, M., Reingold, O.: Number-theoretic constructions of efficient pseudo-random functions. Journal of ACM **51**(2), 231–262 (2004)
57. Nevo, O., Trieu, N., Yanai, A.: Simple, fast malicious multiparty private set intersection. In: CCS (2021)
58. Olson, P.: Facebook Closes $19 Billion WhatsApp Deal (2014). https://www.forbes.com/sites/parmyolson/2014/10/06/facebook-closes-19-billion-whatsapp-deal/
59. Peikert, C., Vaikuntanathan, V., Waters, B.: A framework for efficient and composable oblivious transfer. In: CRYPTO (2008)
60. Pinkas, B., Schneider, T., Segev, G., Zohner, M.: Phasing: Private set intersection using permutation-based hashing. In: USENIX Security (2015)
61. Pinkas, B., Schneider, T., Smart, N.P., Williams, S.C.: Secure two-party computation is practical. In: AC (2009)
62. Pinkas, B., Schneider, T., Zohner, M.: Scalable private set intersection based on OT extension. TOPS (2018)
63. Raab, M., Steger, A.: "Balls into Bins" - A simple and tight analysis. In: RANDOM (1998)
64. Ragab, H., Milburn, A., Razavi, K., Bos, H., Giuffrida, C.: CrossTalk: Speculative data leaks across cores are real. In: S&P (2021)
65. Raghuraman, S., Rindal, P.: Blazing fast PSI from improved OKVS and subfield VOLE. In: CCS (2022)
66. Resende, A.C.D., Aranha, D.F.: Faster unbalanced private set intersection. In: FC (2018)
67. Rindal, P., Schoppmann, P.: VOLE-PSI: Fast OPRF and circuit-PSI from vector-OLE. In: EUROCRYPT (2021)
68. Shi, E., Aqeel, W., Chandrasekaran, B., Maggs, B.M.: Puncturable pseudorandom sets and private information retrieval with near-optimal online bandwidth and time. In: CRYPTO (2021)
69. Thomas, K., et al.: Protecting accounts from credential stuffing with password breach alerting. In: USENIX Security (2019)
70. Trieu, N., Shehata, K., Saxena, P., Shokri, R., Song, D.: Epione: lightweight contact tracing with strong privacy. IEEE Data Eng. Bull. **43**(2), 95–107 (2020)
71. Troy Hunt: Have I Been Pwned: Check if your email has been compromised in a data breach (2023). https://haveibeenpwned.com/

72. van Schaik, S., Minkin, M., Kwong, A., Genkin, D., Yarom, Y.: CacheOut: leaking data on intel CPUs via cache evictions. In: S&P (2021)
73. Yao, A.C.C.: How to generate and exchange secrets (extended abstract). In: FOCS (1986)
74. Yeo, K.: Lower bounds for (batch) PIR with private preprocessing. In: EUROCRYPT (2023)
75. Zhou, M., Lin, W.K., Tselekounis, Y., Shi, E.: Optimal single-server private information retrieval. In: EUROCRYPT (2023)

Author Index

G. Tsudik et al. (Eds.): ESORICS 2023, LNCS 14344, pp. 477–478, 2024.
https://doi.org/10.1007/978-3-031-50594-2

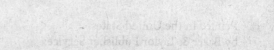

Printed in the United States
by Baker & Taylor Publisher Services